# Peterson's

# MASTER THE

# GRE®

# 2009

### Mark Alan Stewart

## PETERSON'S

A **nelnet** COMPANY

# PETERSON'S
A nelnet COMPANY

An ARCO Book

ARCO is a registered trademark of Peterson's, and is used herein under license by Peterson's.

## About Peterson's, a Nelnet company

Peterson's (www.petersons.com) is a leading provider of education information and advice, with books and online resources focusing on education search, test preparation, and financial aid. Its Web site offers searchable databases and interactive tools for contacting educational institutions, online practice tests and instruction, and planning tools for securing financial aid. Peterson's serves 110 million education consumers annually.

For more information, contact Peterson's, 2000 Lenox Drive, Lawrenceville, NJ 08648; 800-338-3282; or find us on the World Wide Web at www.petersons.com/about.

GRE® is a registered trademark of Educational Testing Service (ETS). This book is not endorsed or approved by ETS.

Previous editions © 1990, 1991, 1994, 1995, 1997, 1998, 1999, 2000, 2001, 2002, 2003, 2004, 2005, 2006, 2007

Editor: Therese DeAngelis; Production Editor: Mark D. Snider; Manufacturing Manager: Raymond Golaszewski; Composition Manager: Linda M. Williams; CD Producer: James Holsinger

ISBN-13: 978-0-7689-2605-7
ISBN-10: 0-7689-2605-X

Printed in the United States of America

10  9  8  7  6  5  4  3  2  1    10  09  08

Sixteenth Edition

## OTHER RECOMMENDED TITLES

*Peterson's 30 Days to the GRE®*
*Peterson's GRE® / GMAT® Math Review*

# Contents

## PART III: ANALYTICAL WRITING

## PART IV: QUANTITATIVE REASONING

## PART VI: FIVE PRACTICE TESTS

## APPENDIX

# Before You Begin

## HOW THIS BOOK IS ORGANIZED

Taking the GRE is a skill. It shares some aspects with other endeavors, such as competing in athletics. It requires discipline and practice to succeed.

These are skills that can be improved through coaching, but ultimately, improvement also requires practice. This book gives you both.

- **Top 10 Strategies to Raise Your Score** lists the 10 most important test-taking tips to help you score high on the GRE.

- **Part I** is essential reading if you're preparing to take the GRE. You'll find out about the overall structure of the GRE and what each section of the test covers. You'll also learn general test-taking strategies and specific tactics for GRE preparation. This part of the book also shows you each test section and each basic type of question up close; we've provided examples of each type of question (along with explanations), so you can get a good initial "feel" for the overall test.

- **Part II** will allow you to dip your toes into the GRE waters by taking one 45-minute Analytical Writing Issue task, one 30-minute Analytical Writing Argument task, one 45-minute Quantitative Reasoning test, and one 30-minute Verbal Reasoning test. Use the results of this Diagnostic Test to determine where you need to focus your GRE preparation.

- **Parts III–V** make up the coaching program. This part of the book analyzes each section of the GRE—Analytical Writing, Quantitative Reasoning, and Verbal Reasoning—and gives you powerful strategies for attacking every question type you'll encounter in the actual exam.

- **Part VI** consists of five full-length Practice Tests. Each test contains the same number and mix of question types you'll encounter on the actual exam. To accurately measure your performance on these Practice Tests, be sure to adhere strictly to the stated time limits for each section.

- **The Appendix** provides you with a handy vocabulary list to help you prepare for the Verbal Reasoning section of the GRE.

## SPECIAL STUDY FEATURES

*Peterson's Master the GRE* is designed to be as user friendly as it is complete. To this end, it includes several features to make your preparation more efficient.

## Overview

Each chapter begins with a bulleted overview listing the topics covered in the chapter. This will allow you to quickly target the areas in which you are most interested.

## Summing It Up

Each chapter ends with a point-by-point summary that reviews the most important items in the chapter. The summaries offer a convenient way to review key points.

## Bonus Information

As you work your way through the book, keep your eyes on the margins to find bonus information and advice. Information can be found in the following forms:

### NOTE

Notes highlight need-to-know information about the GRE, whether it's details about registration and scoring or the structure of a question type.

### TIP

Tips provide valuable strategies and insider information to help you score your best on the GRE.

### ALERT!

Alerts do just what they say—alert you to common pitfalls and misconceptions you might face or hear regarding the GRE.

# ABOUT THIS BOOK'S FORMAT

Here's something to keep in mind as you work with this book: Because the actual GRE exam is computerized, you'll be entering answers by typing on a keyboard or using a mouse. Some parts of the exam, such as the Analytical Writing section, require you to type sentences and paragraphs. Other sections require that you fill in the answer by typing a whole number in a box, checking off boxes in a grid using the computer mouse, or filling in blanks in a sentence with your mouse by "dragging and dropping" your chosen answer choices to the blanks. Obviously, answering in this fashion isn't possible in a printed book—you'll have to fill in your answers by hand when taking the tests we've provided. To remain consistent with the actual exam, however, we've retained references to "clicking," "typing," or "dragging and dropping" the answers.

# ABOUT THE CD

The CD accompanying this book puts at your disposal the latest computerized testing software, which closely replicates the testing experience you will experience on the actual test. The software was developed by Peterson's, and the Practice Test content was created by the test prep experts at Peterson's.

## YOU'RE WELL ON YOUR WAY TO SUCCESS

You've made the decision to apply to graduate school and have taken a very important step in that process. *Peterson's Master the GRE* will help you score high on the exam and prepare you for everything you'll need to know on the day of your exam. Good luck!

## GIVE US YOUR FEEDBACK

Peterson's publishes a full line of resources to help guide you through the graduate school admission process. Peterson's publications can be found at your local bookstore, library, and college guidance office, and you can access us online at www.petersons.com.

We welcome any comments or suggestions you may have about this publication and invite you to complete our online survey at www.petersons.com/booksurvey. Or you can fill out the survey at the back of this book, tear it out, and mail it to us at:

Publishing Department
Peterson's, a Nelnet Company
2000 Lenox Drive
Lawrenceville, NJ 08648

Your feedback will help us make your educational dreams possible.

# TOP 10 STRATEGIES TO RAISE YOUR SCORE

Regardless of the books, software, or other GRE-prep resources you're using, certain time-tested strategies for GRE preparation never go out of style. To attain your optimal GRE scores and to maximize your chances of getting into your first-choice graduate program, keep the following strategies in mind:

1. **Don't neglect your weaknesses.** When preparing for the GRE, some test-takers make the mistake of focusing on their strengths, and they neglect to work on eliminating their weaknesses. They tell themselves, "I can't handle these tough sections right now," and they decide either to face them later or skip them completely and take their chances on the actual exam. However, you can't "hide" your individual GRE scores from the admissions committees, and you don't want to be unprepared in any way. The best strategy here is to avoid spending more time than you need on any one area of the GRE. Don't waste time reviewing what you already know. Instead, devote as much time as possible to improving areas where you know you need extra practice.

2. **Don't neglect the two GRE essays.** Among GRE test-takers, it's especially common to neglect preparing for the essay sections of the exam. Don't make this mistake! This is one area where it's impossible to "guess" your way through the test. What's more, graduate schools are more frequently focusing on the GRE essays to help them make tough decisions among applicants—many of whom appear equally qualified otherwise. This means that your Analytical Writing score could very well make the difference between your being accepted to your preferred program and being rejected—especially at a school where you may be a "borderline" candidate.

3. **Practice under exam conditions.** When it comes to GRE preparation, there's simply no substitute for putting yourself to the test by taking the Practice Tests in this book under simulated testing conditions. Here are some suggestions:

    Adhere to the time limits that each exam section imposes. If possible, use a word processor to compose your practice essays (rather than writing them out), and use only the features that will be available on the stripped-down GRE word processor. If possible, take at least one computer-based Practice Test.

    Don't underestimate the role that endurance plays in taking the GRE exam. Half the battle is making it through the half-day ordeal with your wits intact. You can prepare for the long day of taking the exam by taking at least one full-length Practice Test straight through, with only a few short breaks.

4. **Take the real GRE once—just for practice.** If you have time and can afford to, register for and take the real GRE once as a "dress rehearsal." This can help you become comfortable with the testing environment, and you may be able to

rid yourself of a lot of anxiety and nervousness. If you're like most test-takers, you'll be far more relaxed and focused the second time around. In fact, ETS statistics show that among repeat test-takers, more than 90 percent improve their score the second time around. Those are great odds!

5. **Keep practice scores in perspective.** Most GRE test-takers have their sights on two or three specific academic programs as their top graduate school choices, so they have a good idea what GRE scores they'll need to have a strong chance of gaining admission to those programs. If this describes you, you may also have set a goal for your GRE scores. That's understandable, but don't obsess over your Practice Test scores. This can lead to complacency and overconfidence (if the scores are high) or anxiety and discouragement (if the scores are low). Either way, you risk sabotaging yourself for the real exam. The best strategy here is to focus not on the Practice Test scores themselves, but on what you can constructively accomplish between now and exam day to improve the scores.

6. **Maintain a positive attitude.** Of course, it's important to maintain a positive attitude about the GRE. But it's also important to avoid becoming complacent and overconfident. If you have the idea that you can just "wing it" on the GRE and still manage to score high, you'll want to think again. Remember that thousands of other students like you are taking the GRE—and they're also taking their scores very, very seriously.

7. **Be realistic in your expectations.** You'd love perfect GRE scores, wouldn't you? In theory, you can attain them. But in reality, you may not score as high as you'd like. Accept your limitations. With regular study and practice, you'll perform as well as you can reasonably expect to perform. Be realistic, too, about the benefits you can expect from this or any other GRE preparation book or program. There's only so much that you can do to boost your GRE score.

8. **Take steps to minimize GRE anxiety.** Test anxiety, whether it happens before or during a test, can hurt your performance. Although it's probably impossible to eliminate anxiety completely, you can take some steps to reduce it. Here are a few suggestions:

Practice testing under exam conditions. This is the single best method of reducing test anxiety. The more comfortable you can be in a simulated testing environment, the more likely you can remain calm during the real test.

Join or form a GRE study group. After you and your fellow test-takers take time to openly discuss your anxieties and review Practice Test questions, your apprehensions will begin to lessen.

Before taking practice tests, try simple relaxation techniques. Do some stretching, deep breathing, meditating, or whatever else works for you. Some people find that a quick burst of vigorous exercise is highly effective.

Stay busy with other activities and occupations. It's likely that the more you think about taking the GRE, the more anxious you'll become. So during the weeks that you're preparing for the test, try to keep yourself busy with your regular activities. Avoid discussing the GRE with others except during planned study sessions or classes.

9. **Know when you've peaked.** Preparing for the GRE is a bit like training for an athletic event. You need to familiarize yourself with the event, learn to be comfortable with it, and build up your skill and endurance. At some point, though—hopefully around exam day—your motivation, interest, and performance will peak. Of course, it takes time and effort to get comfortable with the exam, to correct poor test-taking habits, to review whatever math and grammar you might have forgotten, to develop an instinct for recognizing wrong-answer choices, and to find your optimal pace. But there's a point beyond which additional study and practice will give you little or no additional benefit. Don't drag out the process by starting to prepare too early or by postponing your test day to give yourself more time than you really need.

10. **Take the GRE early to allow yourself the option of retaking it.** Many graduate schools admit new students for the fall term only. Application deadlines vary widely among the schools, but if you take the GRE no later than the November before matriculation, you'll meet almost any program's deadline. Ideally, you'll want to take the exam early enough so that you can take it a second time if necessary and still meet application deadlines. In any event, schedule the exam at a time when you're sure you'll have adequate time to prepare.

# PART I
## GRE BASICS

# All About the General GRE

## OVERVIEW

- The GRE structure and testing format
- Your GRE scores
- Scoring Your Practice Tests—Quantitative Reasoning and Verbal Reasoning
- Taking the GRE computer-based test
- GRE availability and registration
- General test-taking tips
- Summing it up

The General Graduate Record Exam (GRE), or GRE General Test, is the primary standardized test for admission to graduate-level academic programs in the United States. The exam is designed and administered by the Educational Testing Service (ETS), the same company that produces the SAT. Since 2002, the GRE has been administered by computer only (except in certain remote locations outside the United States, where a paper-based version is offered instead).

Your GRE prep begins with an overview of the test. In this chapter, you'll look at the overall structure of the GRE and find out how the exam is scored and evaluated. This chapter concludes with GRE registration information and a need-to-know list of GRE test-taking tips.

## THE GRE STRUCTURE AND TESTING FORMAT

The computer-based GRE contains three scored sections:

1. One 75-minute Analytical Writing section (with two discrete timed parts)
2. One 45-minute Quantitative Reasoning section
3. One 30-minute Verbal Reasoning section

The exam also contains one additional, unscored section, either Quantitative Reasoning or Verbal Reasoning. The unscored section allows test-makers to try out new questions, mainly to assess their difficulty level based on test-takers' responses. You may not be able to tell which section is unscored—and in any event, you should approach each and every exam section with the assumption that it counts toward your GRE score.

## chapter 1

For some (but not all) test-takers, the exam will end with an identified, untimed research section, which is not scored and contains question types that are different than the ones in the other sections. (The research section contains experimental question types that are unlikely to appear on the GRE as scored questions any time soon.)

Excluding brief breaks between sections and the research section, total testing time runs from 3 hours to 3 hours, 15 minutes, depending on whether your unscored section is Quantitative Reasoning or Verbal Reasoning. In the following table, the number of Verbal and Quantitative Reasoning questions are approximate; your exam may contain a different number of any question type on these two sections.

| TEST SECTION | DESCRIPTION |
| --- | --- |
| **Analytical Writing** | 75 mins. (2 writing tasks):<br>• Present Your Perspective on an Issue (Issue task), 1 essay (45 mins.)<br>• Argument Analysis (Argument task), 1 essay (30 mins.) |
| **Quantitative Reasoning** | 45 mins. (28 multiple-choice questions)*:<br>• Quantitative Comparison (14 questions)<br>• Problem Solving (14 questions) |
| **Verbal Reasoning** | 30 mins. (30 multiple-choice questions):<br>• Analogies (9 questions)<br>• Sentence Completion (6 questions)<br>• Reading Comprehension (8 questions, divided among 2–4 sets)<br>• Antonyms (7 questions) |
| **Unscored Section** | 30 or 45 mins.:<br>• Verbal Reasoning (30 questions, 30 mins.)<br>OR<br>• Quantitative Reasoning (28 questions, 45 mins.) |
| **Research Section** | Untimed (number of questions varies) |
| *One of your Quantitative Reasoning questions may require you to enter (type in) your own numerical answer instead of selecting among multiple choices. | |

## Sequence of Exam Sections and Questions

The Analytical Writing section will be the *first* one on your exam. This section may start with either the Issue writing task or the Argument writing task.

The Quantitative Reasoning and Verbal Reasoning sections (including the unscored section) may appear in any order. For example, you might encounter two consecutive Quantitative Reasoning sections or two consecutive Verbal Reasoning sections. In these exam sections, question types are interspersed and there's no set order. (Take a quick peek at any of the Practice Tests in this book and you'll get the idea.)

The research section will be the *last* one on your exam. (Remember: It won't be scored, and it probably won't be timed.)

## Basic Ground Rules During the Exam

Here are some basic procedural rules for the GRE that will be explained in more detail later in this chapter:

- Once the timed test begins, you cannot stop the testing clock.
- If you finish any section before the time limit expires, you can proceed immediately to the next section, at your option.
- Once you exit a section, you can't return to it.
- The test provides an optional 10-minute break after the Analytical Writing section and an optional one-minute break after each subsequent section. Immediately after each break, the next timed section automatically commences.
- Pencils and "scratch" paper are provided for all exam sections.
- You compose both Analytical Writing essays using the word processor built into the GRE computerized testing system. Handwritten essays are not permitted. (Later in this chapter we'll review details about the GRE word processor.)

Here are some additional ground rules that apply specifically to the Quantitative and Verbal Reasoning sections. We'll go into these in more detail later in this chapter:

- The computerized test won't let you skip questions. Also, once you confirm your answer to a question, you can't return to it.
- An on-screen calculator is NOT provided, and calculators are prohibited in the testing room. So during the Quantitative Reasoning section(s), you'll need to use your scratch paper to perform calculations.
- During the Quantitative Reasoning and Verbal Reasoning sections, you'll be required to select among multiple choices by clicking on the ovals next to them. For one Quantitative Reasoning question, you might be required to enter (type in) your own numerical answer, instead of selecting among answer choices.

## YOUR GRE SCORES

You'll receive four different scores for the GRE:

1. A scaled Quantitative Reasoning score on a 200–800 scale (in 10-point increments)

2. A scaled Verbal Reasoning score on a 200–800 scale (in 10-point increments)

3. A *total* score on a 200–800 scale (in 10-point increments), based on both your Quantitative Reasoning and Verbal Reasoning scores

4. An Analytical Writing score, on a 0–6 scale, which averages the scores for each of your two GRE writing tasks

For each of these four scores, you'll also receive a percentile rank (0–99 percent). A percentile rank of 60 percent, for example, indicates that you scored higher than 59 percent (and lower than 40 percent) of all other test-takers. Percentile ranks reflect your performance relative to the entire GRE test-taking population during the most recent multi-year period.

**NOTE**

On the actual test, the ovals next to multiple choices are not lettered as they are throughout this book.

## The Scoring System for Quantitative and Verbal Reasoning

Scores for the Quantitative Reasoning and Verbal Reasoning sections are *not* based strictly on the number of correct answers. Instead, each of these two scores is based on three factors:

**1** The *number* of questions you attempt

**2** The *difficulty level* of the questions you answer correctly

**3** The *range* of question types and topics among the questions you answer correctly

Each multiple-choice section is "computer adaptive," which means that it continually adapts to your ability level. A computerized algorithm determines which questions are presented. Generally speaking, the more questions you answer correctly, the greater the difficulty level of subsequent questions and the greater credit you'll receive for answering them correctly as well. So even if you don't respond to all 28 Quantitative Reasoning or all 30 Verbal Reasoning questions, you can still attain a high score for that section if a high percentage of your responses are correct—especially if you respond correctly to a wide variety of question types.

**NOTE**

The computerized system's GRE scoring algorithms are well-guarded secrets, but knowing exactly how the system works wouldn't affect your exam preparation or test-taking strategy anyway.

## SCORING YOUR PRACTICE TESTS—QUANTITATIVE REASONING AND VERBAL REASONING

Because the Quantitative Reasoning and Verbal Reasoning sections are computer-adaptive, it's very difficult to gauge precisely how you'd score on the actual GRE based on your performance on the practice tests in this book. Nevertheless, the following GRE Score Conversion Table should give you a rough idea. The table provides average scaled scores and corresponding percentile ranks based on previously administered paper-based GRE exams, adjusted to reflect the fact that the practice tests in this book include a greater proportion of difficult questions than paper-based GRE tests.

For each practice test, determine your *raw score* (total number of correct responses) for the Verbal Reasoning section and for the Quantitative Reasoning section. Then, consult the table below to determine your approximate *scaled score* and corresponding *percentile rank* for each of these two sections.

## GRE SCORE CONVERSION TABLE FOR PRACTICE TESTS

| Raw Score | Scaled Score (Percentile Rank) Verbal Reasoning | Scaled Score (Percentile Rank) Quantitative Reasoning |
|---|---|---|
| 30 | 800 (99) | —— |
| 29 | 800 (99) | —— |
| 28 | 780–790 (99) | 800 (99) |
| 27 | 740–770 (98–99) | 780–800 (98–99) |
| 26 | 700–730 (94–97) | 760–770 (94–97) |
| 25 | 660–690 (90–93) | 730–750 (88–93) |
| 24 | 640–650 (87–89) | 700–720 (85–87) |
| 23 | 620–630 (83–86) | 680–690 (78–84) |
| 22 | 590–610 (77–82) | 660–670 (74–77) |
| 21 | 560–580 (71–76) | 640–650 (68–73) |
| 20 | 540–550 (65–70) | 620–630 (62–67) |
| 19 | 510–530 (57–64) | 600–610 (56–61) |
| 18 | 480–500 (49–56) | 580–590 (52–55) |
| 17 | 450–470 (40–48) | 550–570 (47–51) |
| 16 | 430–440 (35–39) | 530–540 (41–46) |
| 15 | 410–420 (27–34) | 510–520 (35–40) |
| 14 | 390–400 (22–26) | 490–500 (31–34) |
| 13 | 360–380 (15–21) | 460–480 (25–30) |
| 12 | 340–350 (12–14) | 440–450 (20–24) |
| 11 | 320–330 (8–11) | 420–430 (16–19) |
| 10 | 300–310 (6–7) | 390–410 (13–15) |
| 9 | 280–290 (3–5) | 360–380 (9–12) |
| 8 | 260–270 (2) | 330–350 (5–8) |
| 7 | 240–250 (1) | 300–320 (3–4) |
| 6 | 220–230 (1) | 260–290 (2) |
| 5 | 210 (1) | 210–250 (1) |
| 4–0 | 200 (1) | 200 (1) |

## How the GRE Essays Are Scored

Your GRE Analytical Writing score is based on your two GRE essays, so someone obviously must read and evaluate them. For this purpose, ETS enlists college and university faculty, mostly in the English and Communications fields.

Two GRE readers will read and evaluate your Issue essay, and two other readers will read and evaluate your Argument essay. Each reader will award a single score on a scale of 0–6 in whole-point intervals (6 is highest). If scores assigned by the two readers differ by more than one point, a third, very experienced reader will read the essay and adjust the discrepancy. Your final Analytical Writing score is the average of your final scores for each essay. The average is rounded up to the nearest half-point. Here's an example showing how the GRE essay-scoring system works:

> 5 Reader A's evaluation of your Issue essay
>
> 4 Reader B's evaluation of your Issue essay
>
> **4.5 Final score for your Issue essay**
>
> 3 Reader C's evaluation of your Argument essay
>
> 5 Reader D's evaluation of your Argument essay
>
> 4 Reader E's adjudicated score
>
> **4 Final score for your Argument essay**
>
> **4.5 Final Analytical Writing score (an average of 4.5 and 4, rounded up)**

GRE readers apply a *holistic* scoring approach. In other words, instead of awarding separate sub-scores for content, organization, writing style, and mechanics, the reader will consider how effective your essay is *as a whole*—accounting for all these factors. Nevertheless, GRE readers are instructed to focus primarily on your ideas, your analytic logic, and how well you've organized your thoughts. To ensure fairness toward ESL (English as a second language) test-takers, the readers will take into account your use of language and your writing mechanics only to the extent that these factors interfere with your ability to communicate your ideas.

All GRE readers are trained by ETS in applying the same scoring criteria. Here are the five essential requirements for a top-scoring ("6") Issue essay (notice that you can attain a top score of 6 even if your essays contain minor errors in grammar, word usage, spelling, and punctuation):

**❶** The essay develops a position on the issue through the use of incisive reasons and persuasive examples.

**❷** The essay's ideas are conveyed clearly and articulately.

**❸** The essay maintains proper focus on the issue and is well organized.

**❹** The essay demonstrates proficiency, fluency, and maturity in its use of sentence structure, vocabulary, and idiom.

**❺** The essay demonstrates an excellent command of the elements of Standard Written English, including grammar, word usage, spelling, and punctuation (but it may contain minor flaws in these areas).

NOTE

The two GRE readers who read each essay evaluate it independently of one another, and neither reader is informed of the other's evaluation.

Here are the five essential requirements for a top-scoring ("6") Argument essay (notice that the last two requirements are the same as for a top-scoring Issue essay):

**1** The essay identifies the key features of the argument and analyzes each one in a thoughtful manner.

**2** The essay supports each point of critique with insightful reasons and examples.

**3** The essay develops its ideas in a clear, organized manner, with appropriate transitions to help connect ideas.

**4** The essay demonstrates proficiency, fluency, and maturity in its use of sentence structure, vocabulary, and idiom.

**5** The essay demonstrates an excellent command of the elements of Standard Written English, including grammar, word usage, spelling, and punctuation (but it may contain minor flaws in these areas).

The criteria for lower scores are the same as the ones above; the only difference is that the standard for quality decreases for successively lower scores.

## TAKING THE GRE COMPUTER-BASED TEST

### The GRE Computer Interface

The three simulated screen shots on pages 10 and 12 show the GRE Computer-Based Test interface for the Analytical Writing section, the Quantitative Reasoning section, and the Verbal Reasoning section. Let's first examine the features of the interface that are common to all exam sections.

### The Title Bar

A dark title bar will appear across the top of the computer screen at all times during all test sections. (You cannot hide this bar.) The title bar displays three items:

**1** **Left corner:** The time remaining for the current section (hours and minutes)

**2** **Middle:** The name of the test (GRE) and current section number

**3** **Right corner:** The current question number and total number of questions in the current section

**NOTE**

The scoring criteria for all six score levels are published in the official *GRE Information and Registration Bulletin* as well as on the official GRE Web site (www.gre.org).

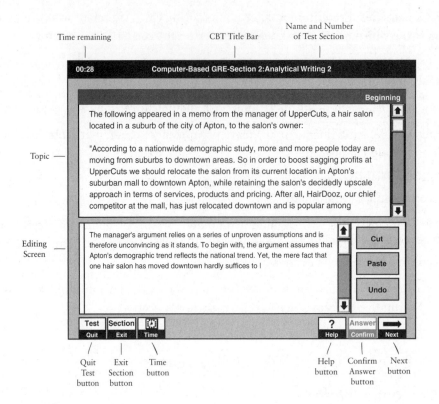

The Toolbar

A series of six buttons appears in a toolbar across the bottom of the computer screen at all times during all test sections. (You cannot hide the toolbar.) Here's a description of each button's function:

**Quit Test**
Click on this button to stop the test and cancel your scores for the *entire* test. (Partial score cancelation is not allowed in any event.) If you click here, a dialog box will appear on the screen, asking you to confirm this operation. Stay away from this button unless you're absolutely sure you wish your GRE score for the day to be deleted and you're willing to throw away your GRE registration fee.

**Exit Section**
Click on this button if you finish the section before the allotted time expires and wish to proceed immediately to the next section. A dialog box will appear on the screen asking you to confirm this operation. Stay away from this button unless you've already answered every question in the current section and don't feel you need a breather before starting the next one.

**Time**
Click on this button to display the time remaining to the nearest *second*. By default, the time remaining is displayed (in the upper left corner) in hours and minutes, but not to the nearest second.

**Help**
Click on this button to access the directions for the current question type, as well as the general test directions and the instructions for using the toolbar items.

**Next and Confirm Answer**
Click on the NEXT button when you're finished with the current question. When you click on NEXT, the current question will remain on the screen until you click on CONFIRM ANSWER. Until you confirm, you can change your answer as often as you wish (by clicking on a different oval). But once you confirm, the question disappears forever and the next one appears in its place. Whenever the NEXT button is enabled (appearing dark gray), the CONFIRM ANSWER button is disabled (appearing light gray), and vice versa.

## The Analytical Writing Screen

As illustrated in the screen shot on page 10, the Analytical Writing prompt appears at the top of your screen, and your essay response appears below it as you type your response. (The screen in the figure includes the first several lines of a response.) Notice that you have to scroll down to read the entire topic and question. You compose your essays using the GRE word processor. (Just ahead, you'll look closely at its features and limitations.)

## The Quantitative and Verbal Screens

To respond to multiple-choice questions, click on one of the ovals to the left of the answer choices. (You might need to use the keyboard to type a number answer to one Quantitative Reasoning question.) Notice that the answer choices are *not* lettered; you'll click on blank ovals.

**Split screens:** For some questions, the screen splits either horizontally or vertically.

*Reading Comprehension:* The screen splits vertically. The left side displays the passage; the right side displays the question and answer choices.

*Quantitative questions that include figures:* The screen splits horizontally. The figure appears at the top; the question and answer choices appear at the bottom.

**Vertical scrolling:** For some questions, you'll have to scroll up and down (using the vertical scroll bar) to view all the material that pertains to the current question.

*Reading Comprehension:* Passages are too long for you to see on the screen in their entirety; you'll need to scroll.

*Quantitative questions that include figures:* Some figures—especially charts and graphs—won't fit on the screen in their entirety; you might need to scroll.

NOTE

In the sample questions throughout this book, the answer choices are lettered for easy reference to corresponding explanations. You will not see this lettering on the actual GRE.

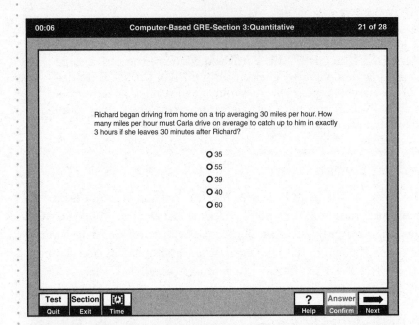

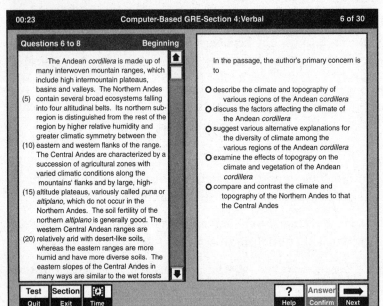

## The GRE's Word Processor

During the GRE Analytical Writing section, you'll use the simple word processor built into the computer system. While the word processor includes some features standard in programs like Word and WordPerfect, it also lacks many of these programs' features.

### KEYBOARD COMMANDS FOR NAVIGATION AND EDITING

Here are the navigational and editing keys available in the word processor:

- **Backspace** removes the character to the left of the cursor.
- **Delete** removes the character to the right of the cursor.

- **Home** moves the cursor to the beginning of the line.
- **End** moves the cursor to the end of the line.
- **Arrow Keys** move the cursor up, down, left, or right.
- **Enter** inserts a paragraph break (starts a new line).
- **Page Up** moves the cursor up one page (screen).
- **Page Down** moves the cursor down one page (screen).

Certain often-used features of standard word-processing programs are not available in the word processor. For example, no keyboard commands are available for the following:

- TAB—disabled (does not function)
- Beginning/end of paragraph (not available)
- Beginning/end of document (not available)
- No key combinations (using the CTRL, ALT, or SHIFT key) or other macros are available for editing functions. (You'll use your mouse for cutting and pasting text.)

## MOUSE-DRIVEN NAVIGATION AND EDITING FUNCTIONS

Just as with other word processors, to navigate the editing screen you can simply point the cursor to the position at which you wish to begin typing, and then click. The CBT word processor also includes mouse-driven CUT, PASTE, and UNDO.

**Selecting text you wish to cut:** You select text the same way as with standard word-processing programs: either (1) hold down your mouse button while sweeping the I-beam on the screen over the desired text, or (2) hold down the SHIFT key and use the navigation keys to select text.

**The CUT button:** If you wish to delete text but want to save it to a temporary clipboard for pasting elsewhere, select that text (see above), and then click on the CUT button. Cutting text is not the same as deleting it. When you delete text (using the DELETE key), you cannot paste it elsewhere in your document (but see UNDO below).

**The PASTE button:** If you wish to move text from one position to another, select and cut the text, then reposition your cursor where you want the text to go and click on the PASTE button.

**The UNDO button:** Click on this button to undo the most recent delete, cut, or paste that you performed.

**Limitations of CUT and UNDO:** The following mouse-driven features are not available:

- DRAG-AND-DROP cut-and-paste (not available)
- COPY (not available; to copy you need to cut, then paste, in the same spot)
- MULTIPLE UNDO (the word processor stores *only your most recent* delete, cut, paste, or keyboard entry)

**The vertical scroll bar:** Once you key in ten lines or so, you'll have to scroll to view your entire response. A vertical scroll bar also appears to the right of the prompt. Be sure to scroll all the way down to make sure you've read the entire prompt.

**Spell-checking, grammar-checking, fonts, attributes, hyphenation:** The word processor does not include a spell checker or grammar checker, nor does it allow you to choose typeface or point size. Neither manual nor automatic hyphenation is available. Attributes such as bold, italics, and underlining are not available.

## The GRE Computerized Test-Taking Experience

When you take a test as important as the GRE, it's a good idea to minimize test anxiety by knowing exactly what to expect on exam day—aside from the timed test itself. Let's walk you through the various pre-test and post-test procedures and describe the physical testing environment. Keep in mind: All of the procedures described here are subject to change. Consult the official GRE Web site for current procedures and policies.

### WHEN YOU ARRIVE AT THE TEST CENTER

Here's what you can expect when you arrive at the test center:

- The supervisor will show you a roster, which includes the names of test-takers scheduled for that day, and will ask you to initial the roster next to your name, and indicate on the roster your arrival time.

- The supervisor will ask you to read a list of testing procedures and rules. (These rules will be covered in the pages immediately ahead.)

- The supervisor will give you a "Nondisclosure Statement." You're to read the printed statement, then *write* the statement (in the space provided on the form) and sign it. In the statement, you agree to the testing policies and rules, and you agree not to reproduce or disclose any of the actual test questions. The supervisor will not permit you to enter the exam room until you've written and signed the statement.

- You might have to sit in a waiting room until the supervisor calls your name. A 5- to 10-minute wait beyond your scheduled testing time is not uncommon. (Taking the GRE is like going to the dentist—in more than one respect!)

- The supervisor will check your photo identification. (You won't be permitted to take the test unless you have one acceptable form of photo identification with you.)

- The test center will provide a secure locker (free of charge) for stowing your personal belongings during the test.

- To help ensure that nobody else takes any part of the exam in your place, the supervisor will take a photograph of you. A thumbprint may also be required.

- The supervisor might give you some rudimentary tips about managing your time during the exam.

- Before you enter the testing room, you must remove everything from your pockets except your photo I.D. and locker key.

- The supervisor will provide you with several pieces of scratch paper (stapled together), along with two pencils. These are the only items you'll have in hand as you enter the testing room.

## TESTING PROCEDURES AND RULES

- If you want to exit the testing room for any reason, you must raise your hand and wait for the supervisor to escort you from the room. (You won't be able to pause the testing clock for any reason.)
- No guests are allowed in the waiting room during your test.
- No food or drink is allowed in the testing room.
- You must sign out whenever you exit the testing room.
- You must sign in whenever you re-enter the testing room (the supervisor will ask to see your photo I.D. each time).
- If you need more scratch paper during the exam, raise your hand and ask for it. The supervisor will happily replace your bundle with a fresh one.
- The supervisor will replace your tired pencils with fresh, sharp ones upon your request anytime during the exam (just raise your hand).

## WHAT YOU SHOULD KNOW ABOUT THE COMPUTERIZED TESTING ENVIRONMENT

- Individual testing stations are like library carrels; they're separated by half-walls.
- The height of your chair's seat will be adjustable and the chair will swivel. Chairs at most testing centers have arms.
- You can adjust the contrast on your computer monitor. If you notice any flickering, ask the supervisor to move you to another station.
- If your mouse has two buttons, you can use either button to click your way through the exam (both buttons serve the same function). Don't expect to have a mouse with a wheel for easy scrolling. Trackballs are available, but only if you request one before you begin the test.
- Testing rooms are not soundproof. During your test, you might hear talking and other noise from outside the room.
- Expect the supervisor to escort other test-takers in and out of the room during your test. Do your best to ignore this potential distraction.
- If the testing room is busy, expect to hear lots of mouse-clicking during your test.
- Earplugs are available upon request.
- Expect anything in terms of room temperature, so dress in layers.
- You'll be under continual audio and video surveillance. To guard against cheating, and to record any irregularities or problems in the testing room as they occur, the room is continually audiotaped and videotaped.

**ALERT!**

You can't change the size of the font on the screen, unless you specifically request before the exam begins that a special ZOOMTEXT function be made available to you.

## BEFORE YOU BEGIN THE TEST—THE COMPUTER TUTORIAL

Okay, the supervisor has just escorted you to your station, and has wished you luck. Before you begin the test, the computerized system will lead you through a tutorial that includes five sections (each section steps you through a series of "screens"):

**1** How to use the mouse (six screens)

**2** How to select and change an answer (six screens)

**3** How to scroll the screen display up and down (six screens)

**4** How to use the toolbars (twenty-one screens); here you'll learn how to do the following:

- Quit the test

- Exit the current section

- Access the directions

- Confirm your response and move to the next question

**5** How to use the word processor features (fourteen screens)

Here's what you need to know about the GRE computer tutorial:

- You won't be able to skip any section or any screen during the tutorial.

- As you progress, the system requires that you demonstrate competency in using the mouse, selecting and confirming answer choices, and accessing the directions. So you can't begin taking the actual test unless you've shown that you know how to use the system.

- At the end of each tutorial section (series of screens), you can repeat that section at your option. But once you leave a section, you can't return to it.

- The Analytical Writing section of the tutorial allows you to practice using the word processor.

- If you carefully read all the information presented to you, expect to spend about 20 minutes on the tutorial.

## POST-TEST GRE PROCEDURES

It's been about 4 hours since you first entered the testing center, and you've just completed your final exam section. You may think you've finished the GRE, but you haven't. There are four more hoops to jump through before you're done:

**1** **Respond to a brief questionnaire.** The computer program will impose on you a brief questionnaire (presented in a series of screens) about your test-taking experience (these questions are multiple-choice, just like the exam itself). The questionnaire might ask you, for example:

- Whether your supervisor was knowledgeable and helpful

- Whether the testing environment was comfortable

- How long you waited after you arrived at the testing site to begin the test

- Whether you were distracted by noise during your exam

**2** **Cancel your test, at your option.** The most important question you'll answer while seated at your testing station is this next one. The computer program will ask you to choose whether to cancel your scores (no scores are recorded; partial cancelation is not provided for) *or* see your scores immediately.

Once you elect to see your scores, you can no longer cancel them. So you should take a few minutes to think it over. The program gives you 5 minutes to choose. If you haven't decided within 5 minutes, it will automatically show you your scores (and you forfeit your option to cancel).

**3** **View and record your scores.** If you elect to see your scores, write them down on your scratch paper. When you leave the testing room, the supervisor will allow you to transcribe them onto another sheet of paper (one that you can take home with you), so that you don't have to memorize them.

**4** **Direct your scores to the schools of your choice.** Once you've elected to see your scores, the program will ask you to select the schools you wish to receive your score report (you will be shown a complete list of schools).

### BEFORE YOU LEAVE THE TESTING CENTER

When you exit the testing room for the final time, the following three things will happen:

**1** The supervisor will collect your pencils and scratch paper and will count the number of sheets of paper to make sure you aren't trying to sneak out with any.

**2** The supervisor will remind you to collect your belongings from your locker (if you used one) and turn in your locker key.

**3** The supervisor will provide you with an ETS pamphlet that explains how to interpret your test scores. (You can take this home with you.)

## GRE AVAILABILITY AND REGISTRATION

The computer-based GRE is administered year-round at more than 500 locations, most of which are in North America. Testing centers are located at Prometric Testing Centers, Sylvan Learning Centers, certain colleges and universities, and ETS (Educational Testing Service) field offices. The official *GRE Information and Registration Bulletin* contains a complete list of GRE computer-based test centers; an updated list is available at the official GRE Web site (www.gre.org).

### Registering for the GRE

To take the GRE, you must schedule an appointment using any of the following three methods:

**1** Make an appointment online via the official GRE Web site (www.gre.org).

**ALERT!**

If you click on the CANCEL SCORES button, the program will then give you another 5 minutes to think over your decision. So you really have 10 minutes to make up your mind.

**TIP**

You can select as many as five schools at this time without incurring an additional fee. This is your last chance for a free report, so take full advantage of it. Be sure to compile your list of five schools before exam day.

**2** Call one of two central registration numbers: 1-800-GRE-CALL (1-800-473-2255) or the Prometric Candidate Services Call Center (1-443-751-4820).

**3** Make an appointment by mail. You'll need to complete and mail to ETS an Authorization Voucher Request Form. You can download the form from the official GRE Web site, or you can call ETS and request the form be sent to you by mail.

Keep in mind that popular test centers may experience backlogs of up to several weeks. Also, you might find it more difficult to schedule a weekend test date than a weekday test date. Be sure to plan ahead and schedule your GRE early enough to meet your grad-school application deadlines.

## Obtaining Up-to-Date GRE Information

For detailed information about GRE registration procedures, consult the official GRE Web site (www.gre.org) or refer to the printed *GRE Information and Registration Bulletin*, published annually by ETS. This free bulletin is available directly from ETS as well as through career-planning offices at most four-year colleges and universities. You can also download the *Bulletin* from the ETS Web site. The *Bulletin* provides detailed and current information about the following:

- Test format and testing procedures
- Test center locations, telephone numbers, and hours of operation
- Registration procedures
- Accommodations for disabled test-takers
- Requirements for admission to the GRE
- Registration and reporting fees, and refund policies
- What to do if you want to repeat the test
- The paper-based GRE (availability, registration procedures, etc.)
- Official scoring criteria for the essays
- How GRE scores are used by institutions

## Contacting the Testing Service

To obtain the *Bulletin,* or for other information about the GRE, you can contact ETS by several methods.

### Telephone
1-609-771-7670
Monday–Friday 8:00 a.m. to 7:45 p.m. Eastern Time (except for U.S. holidays)

1-866-473-4373
Monday–Friday 8:00 a.m. to 7:45 p.m. Eastern Time (toll-free for test-takers within the United States, U.S. Territories, and Canada)

1-609-771-7714 (TTY)
24 hours a day, 7 days a week for test-takers who are deaf or hearing-impaired

Recorded information is available 24 hours a day if you use a touch-tone phone. Phones are busiest between 11:00 a.m. and 2:00 p.m. every day and all day on Mondays.

**E-mail**

gre@ets.org

**World Wide Web**

www.gre.org

www.ets.org (ETS home page)

**Mail**

GRE-ETS

P.O. Box 6000

Princeton, NJ 08541-6000

There are several available methods for obtaining information about ETS disability services.

**Telephone**

1-866-387-8602 (toll-free for test-takers within the United States, U.S. Territories, and Canada)

1-609-771-7780 (all other locations)

Monday-Friday 8:00 a.m. to 5:00 p.m. Eastern Time

**E-mail**

stassd@ets.org

**TTY**

1-609-771-7714

**Mail**

ETS Disability Services

Educational Testing Service

P.O. Box 6054

Princeton, NJ 08541-6054

## GENERAL TEST-TAKING TIPS

In Parts III–V of this book, you'll learn strategies and tips for specific test sections and question types. Right now, however, let's review some general strategies for the GRE. Even if you've read about these eight strategies elsewhere or they seem like common sense to you, it's a good idea to reinforce them in your mind.

1. **Know your optimal pace and stay at it.** Time is definitely a factor on every section of the GRE. On the Quantitative Reasoning and Verbal Reasoning sections, expect to work at a quicker pace than is comfortable for you. Similarly, the 30-minute time limit for each GRE Analytical Writing essay requires a lively writing pace and allows little time for editing, revising, and fine-tuning.

   During the Quantitative and Verbal sections, check your pace after every ten questions or so (about twice during each section) and adjust it accordingly so that you have time at least to consider every question in the section. During each 30-minute writing task, be sure to leave enough time to cover all your main points and to wrap up your essay, so it looks and reads as though you finished in time. The best way to avoid the time squeeze is to practice under timed conditions before you take the actual exam. This will give you a sense of what your optimal pace should be.

**2** **If you're not sure about an answer, don't dwell on it—move on.** This tip follows logically from the first one. You might find yourself reluctant to leave a question until you're sure your answer is correct. While this is admirable, doing this under the strict time conditions of the test will only defeat you. Remember: You can miss *some* questions and still earn high scores. After you develop a sense of your best pace for the exam, you'll have a better idea of how much time you can safely spend on each question.

**3** **Avoid random guesswork if possible.** If you must guess, always try to eliminate obvious wrong-answer choices first; then go with your hunch. On multiple-choice questions, eliminating even one possible answer improves your odds. If you're out of time during a section and you haven't answered every available question, there's no advantage to making random guesses at the remaining questions.

**4** **Read each question in its entirety.** Beware: Some GRE questions offer wrong-answer choices that may seem correct if you haven't read the entire question and all the answer choices thoroughly. This is especially true in the Verbal Reasoning section. Unless you're running out of time, make sure you read every question from start to finish, and never confirm an answer unless you've first compared it with all the others for that question.

**5** **Maintain an active mind set.** When taking an exam such as the GRE, it's easy to fall into a passive mode in which you scan the answer choices and hope that the correct answer "jumps out" at you as you do so. Fight this tendency by keeping your mind engaged while reading each question. Remember that each question on the GRE is designed to measure a specific ability or skill. Try to adopt an active, investigative approach to answering the questions. Ask yourself: What skill is the question measuring? What is the most direct thought process for determining the correct response? How might I be tripped up on this type of question if I'm not careful?

**6** **Use your pencil and scratch paper, as well as the on-screen calculator.** Scratch work helps keep your mind in active mode. Make brief notes, draw simple diagrams and flow charts, and scribble equations and geometry figures. All of this will help you think clearly. Also, make sure that you confirm all but the most simple calculations by using the on-screen GRE calculator.

**ALERT!**

Take heed: Careless calculations are the leading cause of wrong answers on the GRE Quantitative Reasoning section.

**7** **Know the test directions inside and out—*before* you take the test.** Just before the first question of each type (e.g., Quantitative Comparison or Reading Comprehension), the directions for that question type will appear on the screen. Of course, the clock is running even while you're reading the directions. You can save time by clicking on the appropriate button to dismiss the directions as quickly as possible—if you've reviewed them thoroughly before the exam.

**8** **Take advantage of exam breaks, but keep an eye on the time.** You'll be allowed brief breaks between exam sections—10 minutes after the Analytical Writing section and 1 minute after each subsequent section. Keep in mind that the GRE clock is always running, even during these breaks. By all means, take full advantage of that first, 10-minute break to grab a quick snack from your locker or use a restroom. And use the 1-minute breaks to do some stretching or standing. But remember: These breaks go by very quickly, and the test will resume after break time has elapsed—with or without you.

# SUMMING IT UP

- The Quantitative Reasoning and Verbal Reasoning sections of the computerized GRE are "computer adaptive," which means that the test continually adjusts to your ability level as you answer each question in turn.

- The computer-based GRE contains three scored sections: a 75-minute Analytical Writing section, a 45-minute Quantitative Reasoning section, and a 30-minute Verbal Reasoning section. The exam also contains one additional, unscored section, either Quantitative Reasoning or Verbal Reasoning. Some test-takers may also see an identified, untimed, and unscored research section at the end of the exam; it will contain question types different from those in the other sections.

- The Analytical Writing section is always the first section. The Quantitative Reasoning and Verbal Reasoning sections (including the unscored section) may appear in any order.

- You'll receive four different scores for the GRE: a scaled Quantitative Reasoning score, a scaled Verbal Reasoning score, a total score based on both your Quantitative Reasoning and Verbal Reasoning scores, and an Analytical Writing score.

# GRE Questions—A First Look

## OVERVIEW

- A review of the GRE
- The Analytical Writing section
- The Quantitative Reasoning section
- The Verbal Reasoning section
- Summing it up

## A REVIEW OF THE GRE

The GRE contains three different sections, each of which contains various question types. All together, the exam contains seven basic question types, grouped as follows:

| Analytical Writing | Issue task |
|---|---|
| | Argument task |
| Quantitative Reasoning | Quantitative Comparison |
| | Problem Solving |
| Verbal Reasoning | Sentence Completion |
| | Reading Comprehension |
| | Analogies |
| | Antonyms |

In this chapter, you'll examine each of these eight question types in turn. For each type, you'll find out what skills and topics are covered, learn about its key features, read the directions, and examine at least one example and a detailed explanation.

## THE ANALYTICAL WRITING SECTION

The 75-minute Analytical Writing section consists of two separate timed writing tasks: an Issue task (Present Your Perspective on an Issue) and an Argument task (Argument Analysis). These two writing tasks have a lot in common. For each one:

- You compose an essay response using the built-in word processor.

- Your time limit is 30 minutes for the Argument task and 45 minutes for the Issue task.

- You respond to an essay topic, or "prompt," that the computerized test presents to you. (For the Issue task, you choose between two prompts.)
- Your essay will be evaluated based on four broad areas: content, organization, writing style, and mechanics (grammar, syntax, word usage, and so on).

## The Issue Task (45 Minutes)

This 45-minute writing task tests your ability to present a position on an issue effectively and persuasively. Your task is to compose an essay in which you respond to a brief (one- or two-sentence) opinion about an issue of general intellectual interest. Your job is to consider various perspectives, take a position on the issue, and argue for that position. Your essay will be evaluated based on how effectively you perform the following:

- Recognize and deal with the complexities and implications of the issue
- Organize, develop, and express your ideas
- Support your ideas (with reasons and examples)
- Control the elements of Standard Written English

Your Issue topic will consist of a statement of opinion, which appears in quotes, followed by a brief *directive* (statement of your task). Here's an example:

> "People often complain that the introduction of new labor-saving machines costs workers their jobs. However, most new technologies create more jobs than they destroy."

> In your view, how accurate is the foregoing statement? Develop and support your viewpoint with relevant reasons and examples and by considering ways in which the statement may or may not be true.

The test will present two Issue topics, and you select either one for your writing task. Your Issue topic might involve virtually any area of mainstream intellectual inquiry. Here are some of the possible themes for an Issue topic:

- Conformity and tradition vs. individuality and innovation
- Practicality and utility vs. creativity and personal enrichment
- The importance of cultural identity (customs, rituals, and ideals)
- Keys to individual success and progress
- Keys to societal progress and how we define it
- How we obtain or advance knowledge and what constitutes knowledge or advancement of knowledge
- The objectives and methods of formal education
- The value of studying history
- The impact of technology on society and on individuals
- The type of people society considers heroes or great leaders
- The function and value of art and science (for individuals and for society)
- The proper role of government, business, and individuals in ensuring the well-being of society

**KEY FACTS ABOUT GRE ISSUE ESSAYS**

- There is no "correct" answer for the Issue essay. What's important is not what your specific position is, but how effectively you present and support that position.

- The Issue task is not intended to test your knowledge of any topic. Of course, you'll need to be somewhat familiar with the topic at hand, but don't worry if you're not an expert on the subject. The test question is designed mainly to determine your ability to assemble a well-organized and cohesive essay.

- GRE readers appreciate your time constraint, and they'll focus mainly on the substance and organization of your essay. Writing style and mechanics (grammar, syntax, word usage, and so on) come into play only if problems in these areas interfere with the essay reader's understanding of the ideas you're intending to convey in your essay. You won't be penalized for errors in spelling and punctuation unless the errors are frequent and egregious.

## The Argument Task (30 Minutes)

The Argument writing task is designed to test your critical reasoning and analytical writing skills. Your job is to compose an essay in which you critique a paragraph-length argument containing a series of premises and a conclusion. You are to critique the argument's unstated assumptions, its logic (line of reasoning), or both. You might also indicate how the argument could be improved or what additional information might help you to evaluate it. Your Argument essay will be evaluated based on how effectively you perform the following:

- Identify and analyze the key elements of the argument

- Organize, develop, and express your critique

- Support your ideas (with reasons and examples)

- Control the elements of Standard Written English

Your essay prompt will consist of a brief *argument*, presented as a fictitious quotation, followed by a *directive* (statement of your task). The prompt might also indicate the source of a fictitious quote. Here's an example:

> The following recommendation appeared in a memo from the Hillsville City Council to the city's mayor:

> "The private firm Trashco provides refuse pickup and disposal as well as recycling services for the town of Plattsburg. Trashco's total fees for these services are about two-thirds what Hillsville pays Ridco for the same services. In order to save enough money to construct a refuse transfer station within our city limits, Hillsville should discontinue using Ridco's services and use Trashco's services instead."

> Discuss how well-reasoned you find the above argument.

**KEY FACTS ABOUT GRE ARGUMENT WRITING TASKS**

- Regardless of the Argument at hand, the directive is always the same: Discuss how well-reasoned you find the Argument.

**NOTE**

The GRE word processor does not include a grammar checker or spell checker. For more details about the exam's word processing features, see Chapter 1.

- Unlike the Issue task, you won't be able to choose between two Argument topics. The test will present only one argument to you.

- The Argument task is much different from the Issue task. There's no "correct" answer to any Issue prompt—but with this essay, the argument that you critique will contain *at least three* major problems in the use of evidence, reasoning, and/or logic. To score high on this essay, you must identify and discuss each major problem according to the specific directive.

- You don't need technical knowledge or special training in logic to score high on this essay. GRE Arguments are designed so that you can analyze them by applying general reasoning skills and common sense.

- Just as with the Issue task, GRE readers understand that you're under a time constraint, so they will focus less on the larger picture. You won't be penalized for occasional grammatical, spelling, or punctuation gaffes.

## THE QUANTITATIVE REASONING SECTION

The 45-minute Quantitative Reasoning section consists of 28 questions designed to measure the following:

- Your proficiency in arithmetical operations

- Your proficiency at solving algebraic equations

- Your ability to convert verbal information into mathematical terms

- Your ability to visualize geometric shapes and numerical relationships

- Your ability to devise intuitive and unconventional solutions to conventional mathematical problems

**NOTE**

The GRE does NOT provide an on-screen calculator, and you are NOT permitted to bring any type of calculator into the testing room.

You will need to perform simple calculations to answer many of the questions. But you won't need to do a lot of number crunching—that's not what you're being tested on.

Here's a breakdown of the specific areas covered on the Quantitative Reasoning section (the number of questions indicated for each area is approximate):

**Properties of Numbers and Arithmetical Operations (7–10 Questions):**

- Linear ordering (positive and negative numbers, absolute value)

- Properties of integers (factors, multiples, prime numbers)

- Arithmetical operations

- Laws of arithmetic

- Fractions, decimals, and percentages

- Ratio and proportion

- Exponents (powers) and roots

- Descriptive statistics (mean, median, mode, range, standard deviation)

- Basic probability, permutations, and combinations

**Algebraic Equations and Inequalities (8–9 Questions):**

- Simplifying linear and quadratic algebraic expressions

- Solving equations with one variable (unknown)
- Solving equations with two variables (unknowns)
- Solving factorable quadratic equations
- Inequalities

**Geometry, Including Coordinate Geometry (5–6 Questions):**

- Intersecting lines and angles
- Perpendicular and parallel lines
- Triangles
- Quadrilaterals (four-sided polygons)
- Circles
- Rectangular solids (three-dimensional figures)
- Cylinders
- Coordinate geometry

**Interpretation of Statistical Data Presented in Graphic Form (4–5 Questions):**

- Pie charts
- Tables
- Bar graphs
- Line charts
- Other types of graphical displays

You can assume the following about all Quantitative Reasoning questions you'll see on the GRE:

- All numbers are real numbers.
- All figures lie on a plane unless otherwise indicated.
- All lines shown as straight are straight. (Some may look a bit "jagged" on the computer screen, but they are straight.)

Some questions will be so-called story problems, meaning that the problem is presented in a real-world setting. Some questions will also be accompanied by geometry figures, which may or may not be drawn to scale (proportionately). GRE geometry figures are intended to be used only for the numerical information they provide, not for making actual measurements.

Each question in the Quantitative Reasoning sections is in one of two basic formats: Quantitative Comparison or Problem Solving. Any of the topics listed above may be presented in either format.

**NOTE**

The algebraic concepts you'll see on the GRE are normally covered in a first-year high school algebra course. The GRE does not cover more advanced areas, such as trigonometry and calculus.

## Quantitative Comparison (14 Questions)

Quantitative Comparisons each consist of two quantitative expressions labeled (A) and (B). You might also be provided with additional information that applies to both expressions. Your task is to analyze each of the two expressions and determine which quantity is greater, if either. Every Quantitative Comparison item includes the same *four* answer choices:

**(A)** The quantity in Column A is greater;
**(B)** The quantity in Column B is greater;
**(C)** The quantities are equal;
**(D)** The relationship cannot be determined from the information given.

Quantitative Comparison directions are similar to the following. Most of these directions are actually assumptions for interpreting figures (pay special attention to the last one).

**Directions:** Each of the following questions consists of two quantities, one in Column A and one in Column B. You are to compare the two quantities and choose whether
**(A)**   the quantity in Column A is greater;
**(B)**   the quantity in Column B is greater;
**(C)**   the quantities are equal;
**(D)**   the relationship cannot be determined from the information given.

**Common Information:** In a question, information concerning one or both of the quantities to be compared is centered above the two columns. A symbol that appears in both columns represents the same thing in Column A as it does in Column B.

**Notes:**
- All numbers used are real numbers.
- All figures lie on a plane unless otherwise indicated.
- All angle measures are positive.
- All lines shown as straight are straight. Lines that appear jagged can also be assumed to be straight (lines can look somewhat jagged on the computer screen).
- Figures are intended to provide useful information for answering the questions. However, except where a figure is accompanied by a "Note" stating that the figure is drawn to scale, solve the problem using your knowledge of mathematics, *not* by visual measurement or estimation.

Here's a moderately difficult example in which one quantity is greater than the other—in other words, the correct answer is either choice (A) or (B). Notice that, in this case, you're given additional information that applies to both quantities; this information is centered above the two quantities.

|      | **Column A** | **Column B** |
|------|--------------|--------------|

1.

A circle whose diameter is $d$ and a square
whose side is $s$ are equal in area.

$$s \hspace{6cm} d$$

**(A)** The quantity in Column A is greater;

**(B)** The quantity in Column B is greater;

**(C)** The quantities are equal;

**(D)** The relationship cannot be determined from the information given.

**The correct answer is (B).** To make the comparison, express the area of the circle in terms of $d$, and set it equal to the square's area:

$$\pi r^2 = \pi \left(\frac{d}{2}\right)^2 = \frac{\pi d^2}{4} = s^2$$

The value of $\pi$ is approximately 3.1, so it's certainly less than 4. Using 3 as the approximate value of $\pi$ yields the equation $\frac{3}{4}d^2 = s^2$. From this equation, you can see that $d^2 > s^2$. Therefore, $d > s$.

Next, take a look at a question in which the two quantities are equal, making the correct answer choice (C). This one also contains additional information that applies to both quantities but would be considered slightly easier than average.

|      | **Column A** | **Column B** |
|------|--------------|--------------|

2.

Set A: $\{-2, 0, 1, 3\}$

| The arithmetic mean (average) of the terms in Set A | The median of the terms in Set A |
|---|---|

**(A)** The quantity in Column A is greater;

**(B)** The quantity in Column B is greater;

**(C)** The quantities are equal;

**(D)** The relationship cannot be determined from the information given.

**The correct answer is (C).** To make the comparison, first find Quantity A: $\frac{-2+0+1+3}{4} = \frac{2}{4} = \frac{1}{2}$. Next, determine Quantity B. The median of a set of terms is the middle term in value, or, if the set includes an even number of terms, the average of the two middle terms in values, which in this case are 0 and 1. Hence, the median here is $\frac{0+1}{2} = \frac{1}{2}$. As you can see, the two quantities are equal.

Finally, here's a question for which you can't make the comparison without additional information. Most test-takers find this question moderately difficult.

|  | Column A |  | Column B |
|---|---|---|---|

**3.**
$$b < -1$$
$$a > 1$$

$a^3$ $\qquad\qquad\qquad\qquad\qquad\qquad\qquad\qquad a^2 - b^3$

**(A)** The quantity in Column A is greater;

**(B)** The quantity in Column B is greater;

**(C)** The quantities are equal;

**(D)** The relationship cannot be determined from the information given.

**The correct answer is (D).** This question focuses on *exponents* and *signs* (positive vs. negative). Since $a$ is a positive number greater than 1, $a^3 > a^2$. Since the value of $b$ is less than $-1$, the value of $b^3$ must also be less than $-1$ (with an even greater absolute value). Accordingly, subtracting $b^3$ (a negative number) from $a^2$ (a positive number) will yield a number greater than $a^2$. Whether $a^2 - b^3$ is greater than $a^3$, however, depends on the absolute value of $b$ compared to the value of $a$. For example, if $a = 100$ and $b = -2$, then Quantity A would clearly be greater than Quantity B. Conversely, if $a = 2$ and $b = -100$, then Quantity B would clearly be less than Quantity A. As you can see, the relationship between Quantity A and Quantity B cannot be determined from the information given.

### KEY FACTS ABOUT GRE QUANTITATIVE COMPARISON QUESTIONS

- Quantitative Comparisons are mixed with Problem Solving questions, so there's no set sequence.

- Quantitative Comparisons focus less on finding numerical solutions and more on concepts.

- For each question in the Quantitative Comparison section, the four answer choices are always the same.

- If determining which quantity (if either) is greater depends on any information you don't see in the question, then the correct answer is choice (D).

- Some Quantitative Comparison questions will provide additional, centered information; others won't.

- Some questions will involve simplified, real-world scenarios, but don't be fooled: These aren't necessarily more or less difficult than other Quantitative Comparison questions.

- Geometry figures are not necessarily drawn to scale.

## Problem Solving (14 Questions)

Problem Solving questions require you to work from a mathematical problem to determine a solution. They are conventional multiple-choice questions with five choices each.

Problem Solving directions are similar to the following. "Notes" are the same as for Quantitative Comparisons (pay special attention to the last one).

> **Directions:** Solve the problem and select the best answer choice.
>
> **Notes:**
> - All numbers used are real numbers.
> - All figures lie on a plane unless otherwise indicated.
> - All angle measures are positive.
> - All lines shown as straight are straight. Lines that appear jagged can also be assumed to be straight (lines can look somewhat jagged on the computer screen).
> - Figures are intended to provide useful information for answering the questions. However, except where a figure is accompanied by a "Note" stating that the figure is drawn to scale, solve the problem using your knowledge of mathematics, *not* by visual measurement or estimation.

Here's an example that would be considered slightly more difficult than average.

4. If $-27 = \left(-\frac{1}{3}\right)^k$, what is the value of $k$?

   **(A)** $-9$

   **(B)** $-3$

   **(C)** $-\frac{1}{3}$

   **(D)** $\frac{1}{3}$

   **(E)** $3$

   **The correct answer is (B).** This question is asking you to determine the power to which you must raise $-\frac{1}{3}$ to obtain $-27$. First, look at the numbers in the question. Note that $-27 = (-3)^3$ That's a good clue that the answer to the question involves the number $-3$. If the number we were raising to the power of $k$ were $-3$, then the value of $k$ would be 3. But the number we're raising to the power of $k$ is $-\frac{1}{3}$, which is the *reciprocal* of $-3$. (By definition, the product of a number and its reciprocal is 1.) This means that you need to apply the rule that a negative exponent reciprocates its base. In other words, raising a base number to a negative power is the same as raising the base number's reciprocal to the power's absolute value. Therefore, $\left(-\frac{1}{3}\right)^{-3} = (-3)^3$. As you can see, that value of $k$ is $-3$.

As of November 2007, one of your Problem Solving questions might be what the test designers call a "numeric entry" problem. In this question type, you'll be instructed to enter (type in) the correct numerical answer to get credit for completing the question. You can't improve your odds of guessing correctly by narrowing down answer choices. Here's an example:

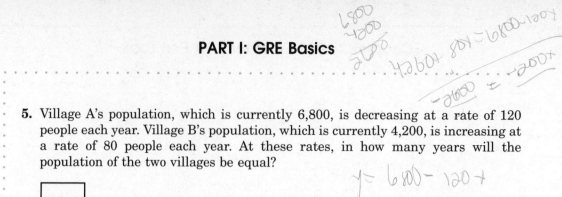

**5.** Village A's population, which is currently 6,800, is decreasing at a rate of 120 people each year. Village B's population, which is currently 4,200, is increasing at a rate of 80 people each year. At these rates, in how many years will the population of the two villages be equal?

*Click on the answer box, then type in a number. Backspace to erase.*

**The correct answer is 13.** One way to solve this problem is to subtract 120 from A's population and add 80 to B's population again and again until the two are equal, keeping track of the number of times you perform these simultaneous operations. But there's a faster way to solve this problem that will also help you avoid computation errors. The difference between the two populations is currently 2,600 (6,800 − 4,200). Each year, that gap closes by 200 (120 + 80). So you can simply divide 2,600 by 200 to determine the number of years for the gap to close completely. That's easy math: 2,600 ÷ 200 = 13. This is the number you'll type into the answer box.

Keep in mind: The correct answer to a numeric-entry question might be a positive or negative integer, a decimal number (which includes digits to the right of a decimal point), or a fraction. To enter a negative number, you use the dash (hyphen) key. If the question calls for an answer in the form of a fraction, you will enter two integers in two separate boxes—one above the other.

## KEY FACTS ABOUT GRE PROBLEM SOLVING QUESTIONS

- Numerical answer choices are listed in order, either from lowest to highest in value or vice-versa.

- Data analysis questions (which involve charts, tables, or other data presented in graphical form) often come in sets of two to four consecutive questions. In such cases, all the questions in the set will pertain to the same graphical data.

- Geometry figures are not necessarily drawn to scale.

- Expect that nearly half of the questions will involve story problems in a real-world setting.

# THE VERBAL REASONING SECTION

The 30-minute Verbal Reasoning section consists of 30 questions in four basic formats: Sentence Completion, Reading Comprehension, Analogies, and Antonyms. Each format covers a distinct set of verbal and verbal-reasoning skills.

## Sentence Completion

Sentence Completions are designed to measure the following four verbal skills (the first one is the primary skill being tested):

❶ Your ability to understand the relationships among ideas in a sentence, and your ability to choose how best to convey those ideas and relationships

❷ Your grasp of vocabulary

❸ Your facility with English-language idioms

❹ Your diction (using appropriate words in appropriate contexts)

For each test item, your task is to fill in either one or two blanks in a sentence in a way that makes sense and effectively conveys the intended meaning of the sentence. Most GRE Sentence Completions involve two blanks. Directions for these questions are similar to the following:

> **Directions:** This sentence has one or two blanks, each blank indicating that something has been omitted. Beneath the sentence are five lettered words or sets of words. Choose the word or set of words for each blank that best fits the meaning of the sentence as a whole.

Here's a Sentence Completion example that contains one blank.

1. Because frogs have no hair, skin, or feathers to protect their paper-thin skin, they are _____ changes in the quality of the air and water in their immediate environment.

   **(A)** impervious to
   **(B)** vulnerable to
   **(C)** benumbed by
   **(D)** responsive to
   **(E)** invigorated by

   **The correct answer is (B).** The sentence's overall grammatical structure suggests a cause-and-effect relationship between the unprotected nature of a frog's skin and whatever phrase should replace the blank. The fact that something is "unprotected" makes it *vulnerable*—by the very definitions of the two words.

**NOTE**

In addition to several Sentence Completions, your Verbal Reasoning section might contain one "Complex Text Completion" item involving one to five sentences and two to three blanks that you complete independently of one another. You'll examine this question type, which is new on the GRE as of November 2008, in Part V of this book.

Now here's a Sentence Completion containing two blanks. Notice that each choice provides completions for *both* blanks. This is how all two-blank Sentence Completions are designed.

2. Many avid hikers thrive on the _____ of peril and natural beauty, both of which are part and parcel of a trek over treacherous yet _____ terrain.

   (A) dual prospect . . navigable
   (B) promise . . hazardous
   (C) dichotomy . . alluring
   (D) juxtaposition . . unspoiled
   (E) excitement . . beautiful

   **The correct answer is (D).** To complete this sentence, it's easier to start with the second blank. The sentence's grammatical structure sets up a parallel between the phrase "peril and natural beauty" and the phrase "treacherous yet _____." So it would make sense to fill in the second blank with a word whose meaning is similar to *natural beauty*. You can easily eliminate choices (A) and (B). You can probably eliminate choice (E) as well. Comparing *natural beauty* to *beautiful* is redundant; so although *beautiful* makes some sense in the blank, the result is less than artful. That leaves choices (C) and (D), *alluring* and *unspoiled*.

   As for the first blank, since we've already eliminated choices (A), (B), and (E), the only viable choices for that blank are *dichotomy* and *juxtaposition,* provided in choices (C) and (D). Both words make sense in context, but *juxtaposition* is better. Moreover, the phrase *juxtaposition of* is idiomatic, while the phrase *dichotomy of* is not. (The proper idiom is *dichotomy between.*)

## KEY FACTS ABOUT GRE SENTENCE COMPLETIONS

- At least one Sentence Completion item will contain *one* blank, but most will contain two blanks.

- Dual-blank completions come in pairs, so you won't complete one blank independently of the other.

- For dual-blank Sentence Completions, the completion for one blank must make sense together with the accompanying completion for the other blank.

- The best completion (the correct answer) will give the sentence an overall meaning that makes perfect sense and that will be grammatically and idiomatically proper.

- Difficult Sentence Completions are more likely to incorporate challenging vocabulary either into the sentence itself or in the answer choices.

## Reading Comprehension

Reading Comprehension questions measure your ability to read carefully and accurately, to determine the relationships among the various parts of the passage, and to draw reasonable inferences from the material in the passage. The passages cover a variety of subjects, including the humanities, the social sciences, the physical sciences, ethics, philosophy, law, popular culture, and current events. Specific sources include professional journals, dissertations, and periodicals of intellectual interest. The test-makers edit the source material so it's appropriate for GRE purposes.

The directions for Reading Comprehension are very straightforward and are similar to the following:

> **Directions:** This passage is accompanied by questions based on its content. After reading the passage, choose the best answer to each question. Answer all the questions on the basis of what is stated or implied in the passage.

Reading Comprehension passages can range from 150 words (about fifteen lines on your computer screen) to 500 words (forty-five to fifty lines) long. Regardless of a passage's length, however, the emphasis is not on how quickly you can read but on how well you understand what you read. Expect to encounter two to four sets of questions (three sets is most common) and two to three questions per set. All questions in a set pertain to the same passage.

All Reading Comprehension questions are multiple choice (five choices), and most questions focus on the following six specific tasks:

1 Recognizing the central idea or primary purpose of the passage

2 Recalling information explicitly stated in the passage

3 Making inferences from specific information stated in the passage

4 Recognizing the purpose of specific passage information

5 Applying and extrapolating from the ideas presented in the passage

6 Understanding what specific words or phrases mean in the context of the passage

For practice, take a look at the following 200-word passage, along with two questions based on it. (Both questions are moderately difficult.)

*Line*   The post-WWI reinvigoration, or Renaissance, of Southern American literature, which culminated during the 1940s with certain works of William Faulkner and Tennessee Williams, shifted the focus of the region's literature away from the nobility of the Civil War's lost cause to
(5)   the war's enduring social and cultural consequences and the struggle for individualism in the South's culture of conformity. By the 1960s, however, contemporary literature of the American South and its academic study had become little more than a celebration of regional patriotism and local color. The sort of literary imagination that had
(10)   distinguished the Southern Renaissance writers had waned, and no new writers were emerging to take their place. Instead, a new genre, the nonfiction novel—in which fiction-writing techniques are employed in the representation of real events—seemed poised to supplant the nearly defunct novel. However, despite the wide acclaim of Capote's nonfiction
(15)   novel *In Cold Blood*, and to the surprise of all, this genre—and not the novel—soon withered away. The next two decades saw a veritable

explosion of talented young Southern novelists whose imaginative works captured the attention of readers and literary critics around the world.

3. It can be inferred from the information in the passage that

   (A) literature of the American South reached its peak in popularity during the 1960s
   (B) the writers of the Southern Renaissance primarily wrote novels
   (C) no writer of any significance took the place of the Southern Renaissance writers
   (D) very few famous American authors have emerged from the South
   (E) literary scholars tend to underestimate the potential influence of fiction writers

   **The correct answer is (B).** Choice (A) runs contrary to the fact that the new breed of Southern writers were "read and reviewed worldwide," which suggests that their novels were at least as popular as those of the 1960s Renaissance. In contrast, choice (B) is well-supported by the passage's information. Though the passage's author does not explicitly state that the Southern Renaissance writers were novel writers, the inference is reasonable based on the passage as a whole. Choice (C) runs contrary to the author's reference to the "explosion of important and interesting writers" who supplanted their predecessors. Choices (D) and (E) call for unwarranted speculation; neither is well supported by the information in the passage.

4. Which of the following best explains the "surprise" to which the author refers in line 15 of the passage?

   (A) The new breed of Southern writers were relatively young.
   (B) Literary critics had not thought highly of Southern literature.
   (C) Readers outside the United Sates had shown little interest in Southern literature.
   (D) Few significant writers of nonfiction novels were Southerners.
   (E) The Southern novel had previously appeared to be a dying art form.

   **The correct answer is (E).** In the two previous sentences, the author tells us that the literary imagination that characterized Southern writers "had waned" and that their genre was "nearly defunct." These facts explain why it was a "surprise" when another, emerging genre (the nonfiction novel) faded into obscurity, while the former genre enjoyed a resurgence.

## KEY FACTS ABOUT GRE READING COMPREHENSION

- Expect two to four passages (probably three) with two to four questions per passage—about eight questions altogether.

- Passages appear on the left side of the computer screen, and questions appear (one at a time) on the right side.

- A very short passage *might* completely fit on your screen. But most passages won't—you'll need to scroll vertically with your mouse to read the entire passage.

- Line numbers are usually provided to the left of a passage. Some questions may refer to specific portions of the passage by referring to line numbers.

- All but the easiest questions gauge your ability to assimilate, interpret, and apply the ideas presented in the passage, not just to recall them.

- Some questions require you to focus on an isolated sentence or two; others require that you assimilate information from various parts of the passage.

- Questions pertaining to information appearing early in the passage *usually* come before other questions; however, this isn't always the case.

- Tougher questions include not only a "best" answer choice but also a tempting second-best one. Recognizing the difference in quality between the two most viable responses is the key to answering these questions correctly.

- It's not important to have prior knowledge of a passage's subject matter. All questions are answerable by every test-taker based solely on the information provide in the passage.

NOTE

On the GRE Verbal Reasoning section, most test-takers will encounter three reading passages: two short passages and one lengthier one.

## Analogies

Analogies are designed to test your vocabulary and your ability to understand relationships between words in a pair. Each question starts with a word pair in capital letters. Your job is to determine which word pair among five others (the five answer choices) best expresses a relationship similar to the one the original pair expresses.

The directions for Analogies are similar to the following:

> **Directions:** In each of the following questions, a related pair of words or phrases is followed by five lettered pairs of words or phrases. Select the lettered pair that best expresses a relationship similar to that expressed in the original pair.

Now look at two examples, along with explanations. This first one is relatively easy; it contains no advanced vocabulary and the word-pair relationships are easy to figure out.

5. LIZARD : DRAGON ::
   - **(A)** sheep : lamb
   - **(B)** ram : stallion
   - **(C)** horse : unicorn
   - **(D)** reptile : scale
   - **(E)** mare : mermaid

**The correct answer is (C).** A *horse* is a real animal and a *unicorn* is an imaginary, horse-like animal, just as a LIZARD is a real animal and a DRAGON is an imaginary, lizard-like animal. Choice (A) is wrong because a *sheep* is an adult *lamb,* so the relationship is parent-child, not real-imaginary. Choice (B) is wrong because the only relationship between *ram* and *stallion* is that they are both male animals. In choice (D), the relationship is that a *reptile* is covered with *scales.* Choice (E) is close. A *mare* is real and a *mermaid* is imaginary, but a mermaid bears no resemblance to a female horse. So, choice (E) is not the best answer.

Now here's a more difficult GRE-style Analogy. It contains several advanced vocabulary, and the word-pair relationships are not easy to figure out.

**6.** DASTARD : COWARDICE ::

(A) cipher : importance

(B) pedant : intelligence

(C) native : intimacy

(D) refugee : nationality

(E) client : dependence

**The correct answer is (E).** By its very definition, a DASTARD is characterized by COWARDICE, just as a *client,* a person who relies on the professional services of another, by definition *depends* on the other for those services. Choice (E) is the only answer in which the second word defines the first, as in the original pair. Choice (A) is wrong because a *cipher* is something of no significance whatsoever, which is just the opposite of *importance.* Choice (B) is wrong because a *pedant* (a person who makes a display of his or her learning) might be learned but is not necessarily *intelligent.* Choice (C) is wrong because the definition of a *native* (born or belonging to a particular place) has nothing to do with *intimacy.* Choice (D) is wrong because a *refugee* (a person who flees from a place, especially from a particular country, for safety) is not defined by having a *nationality.*

## KEY FACTS ABOUT GRE ANALOGIES

- Analogy test items consist of words only (no phrases).

- The two headwords (the first word pair) will be in upper-case letters.

- The first words in the six pairs all match in their part of speech (noun, verb, or adjective); the same is true of the second words.

- Tougher vocabulary words make for a more difficult question. As you move up the difficulty ladder by answering previous Analogy questions correctly, expect to see advanced vocabulary—which in turn makes for tougher questions, of course, since you can't tell what the relationship is between two words if you don't know what they mean.

- Distinctions in quality between answer choices can be subtle, regardless of the vocabulary involved. So even if all the words in an Analogy are common everyday ones, don't assume the Analogy is easy to solve.

## Antonyms

Antonyms are designed to test your vocabulary directly. Each question starts with a word in capital letters. Your job is to determine which word or brief phrase among five choices provides the best antonym (a word opposite in meaning) of the capitalized word.

The directions for Antonyms are similar to the following:

**Directions:** Each question below consists of a word printed in capital letters followed by five lettered words or phrases. Choose the lettered word or phrase that is most nearly opposite in meaning to the word in capital letters. Since some of the questions require you to distinguish fine shades of meaning, be sure to consider all the choices before deciding which one is best.

Here's an example of a GRE-style Antonym in which the answer choices are all single words (not phrases). This example would be considered slightly more difficult than average.

7. ESTRANGE:

   **(A)** endear
   **(B)** familiarize
   **(C)** reassure
   **(D)** entomb
   **(E)** reciprocate

   **The correct answer is (A).** To ESTRANGE is to "alienate another, to cause another to turn away in fondness." To *endear* is to make oneself beloved by another, just the opposite of ESTRANGE. Choice (B) is tempting because the adjective *familiar* is the opposite of the adjective *strange*. Yet the verb forms given in the question are not good antonyms.

Now look at a GRE-style Antonym in which some of the answer choices are brief phrases. This Antonym would be considered moderately difficult.

8. FLAGRANT:

   **(A)** difficult to understand
   **(B)** even-tempered
   **(C)** modest in demeanor
   **(D)** tending to wither
   **(E)** barely perceptible

   **The correct answer is (E).** The word FLAGRANT means "obvious or conspicuous" and is generally used to characterize certain behavior or a certain act (as in a FLAGRANT disregard for the law). The word *imperceptible* means "incapable of being seen"; hence choice (E) provides a near opposite, or antonym, of the headword. Notice that choices (B), (C), and (D) also run contrary to the meaning of FLAGRANT. Yet none expresses the opposite of what FLAGRANT means as closely as the phrase *barely perceptible*.

## KEY FACTS ABOUT GRE ANTONYMS

- Each answer choice is of the same part of speech (noun, verb, or adjective) as the original. If a particular word could be considered as one of two or more parts of speech, then the other words in the question will reveal which part of speech you should assume it is.

- Headwords are always single words (no phrases), although answer choices can be either single words or short phrases.

- All words are part of the modern English language—no slang, archaic words, or non-English words that have not been adopted as part of the English language.

- The best choice isn't always a perfect opposite. Your task is to figure out which word or phrase is *most nearly* opposite in meaning to the word in capital letters. Some best answers will be near-perfect opposites; others won't.

- The second-best answer can come very close indeed to being the correct one. The official directions warn you that some questions may require you to "distinguish fine shades of meaning."

## SUMMING IT UP

- The GRE contains three different sections: Analytical Writing, Quantitative Reasoning, and Verbal Reasoning. In these sections, you'll encounter seven basic question types: Issue task and Argument task (Analytical Writing), Quantitative Comparison and Problem Solving (Quantitative Reasoning), and Sentence Completion, Reading Comprehension, Analogies, and Antonyms (Verbal Reasoning).

- There is no "correct" answer for the Issue or Argument essays. These are scored based on how effectively you present and support your position, or discuss the major problems in use of evidence, reasoning, or logic in the material presented to you.

- Quantitative Comparison questions focus on concepts more than on finding numerical solutions to the problems presented.

- Problem Solving questions require that you work from a mathematical problem to determine a solution.

- In the Sentence Completion section, some questions require more than one correct answer. You will not receive partial credit for one correct choice. Multiple-blank questions require that all parts of the text make sense in relation to all other parts.

- Reading Comprehension questions test your ability to assimilate, interpret, and apply the ideas presented in a passage.

- Analogy questions are designed to test your vocabulary and your ability to understand relationships between words in a pair.

- Antonyms are designed to test your vocabulary directly.

# PART II

## DIAGNOSING STRENGTHS AND WEAKNESSES

# Practice Test 1: Diagnostic

Now that you have an overview of the GRE and all its basic question types, it's time to try a full-length Practice Test, including an Analytical Writing section (one Issue essay and one Argument essay), a 45-minute Quantitative Reasoning section, and a 30-minute Verbal Reasoning section. This full-length Diagnostic Test should convey two benefits:

**1** It will give you an idea of how you might do if you were to take the real GRE today.

**2** It will allow you to pinpoint the areas in which you're strongest and target those in which you may need improvement, so you can fine-tune your GRE study plan accordingly.

All sections of this Diagnostic Test are just like the real GRE. Each contains the same number of questions as a real GRE section. Each provides the same mix of question types at the same levels of difficulty as the real exam.

However, in this Diagnostic Test, questions are grouped by format. In each group, easier questions come before more challenging ones. On the actual GRE, and in the Practice Tests in Part VI of this book, questions of all types and difficulty levels are interspersed.

Be sure to take all sections under simulated exam conditions—meaning straight through without a break in a quiet, test-like environment. The actual GRE is computerized; for the purposes of taking the Diagnostic Test in this book, you'll need a pencil and some scratch paper.

practice test 1

**TIP**

Answers and detailed
explanations follow the
diagnostic test. Be sure to read
the explanations—you may be
surprised by how much you
can learn.

## ANALYTICAL WRITING

### Issue Task

### *Time: 45 Minutes*

Using a word processor, compose a response to ONE of the two writing tasks presented below. Choose either task—there is no "correct" or "incorrect" choice. Do not use any spell-checking or grammar-checking functions (they are not available on the actual GRE).

### Issue Statement 1

"Government should play no role in subsidizing or otherwise supporting the arts; it should be left entirely up to individuals and private entities to do so."

Write an essay in which you present your perspective on the statement above. Develop and support your viewpoint with relevant reasons and examples.

### Issue Statement 2

"Look at any person today who has achieved great success in his or her career or profession, and you'll see either someone without a significant personal life or someone with significant personal failings."

In your view, how accurate is the statement above? Develop and support your viewpoint with relevant reasons and examples and by considering ways in which the statement may or may not be true.

## Argument Task

### *Time: 30 Minutes*

Using a word processor, compose a response to the writing task presented below. Do not use any spell-checking or grammar-checking functions (they are not available on the actual GRE).

> "People working as computer scientists and engineers must work more than sixty hours per week to further their careers. Accordingly, it is important that these workers have ready access to high-quality and affordable all-day child care. Also, the requirements for career advancement in these fields must be made more flexible so that children of pre-school age can spend a significant portion of each day with at least one parent."

Discuss how well-reasoned you find the argument above.

*diagnostic test*

## QUANTITATIVE REASONING

### 28 Questions • 45 Minutes

**Directions:** For Questions 1–14, each question involves two quantities: one in Column A and one in Column B. You are to compare the two quantities and choose whether

**(A)** the quantity in Column A is greater;

**(B)** the quantity in Column B is greater;

**(C)** the quantities are equal;

**(D)** the relationship between the two quantities cannot be determined from the information in the problem.

**Common Information:** In a question, information concerning one or both of the quantities to be compared is centered above the two columns. A symbol that appears in both columns represents the same thing in Column A as it does in Column B.

**Notes:**
- All number used are real numbers.
- All figures lie on a plane unless otherwise indicated.
- All angle measures are positive.
- All lines shown as straight are straight. Lines that appear jagged can also be assumed to be straight (lines can look somewhat jagged on the computer screen).
- Figures are intended to provide useful information for answering the questions. However, except where a figure is accompanied by a "Note" stating that the figure is drawn to scale, solve the problem using your knowledge of mathematics, *not* by visual measurement or estimation.

|  | **Column A** | **Column B** |
|---|---|---|
| **1.** | $\lvert n \rvert$ | $\lvert -n \rvert$ |

**2.** Of 40 pairs of socks in a drawer, $w$ pairs are solid white, $g$ pairs are solid gray, and at least 20 pairs are striped.

| | |
|---|---|
| $w - g$ | The number of striped pairs of socks in the drawer |

| | | |
|---|---|---|
| **3.** | 333% of 3 | 33% of 33 |

**4.** The integer $(k - 1)$ is a prime number between 40 and 50.

| | |
|---|---|
| The median among all possible values of $k$ | The arithmetic mean (simple average) of all possible values of $k$ |

| | | |
|---|---|---|
| **5.** | $\dfrac{3}{2}p + q = 3$ | $\dfrac{2}{3}q + p = 2$ |

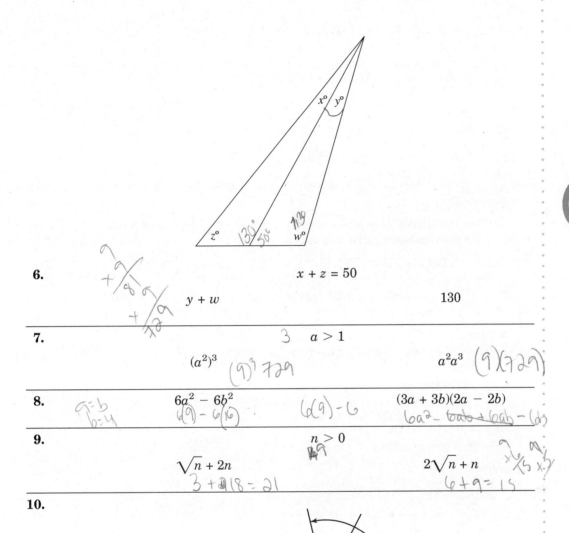

**6.**

$$x + z = 50$$

$y + w$ | | 130

**7.** | | $a > 1$

$(a^2)^3$ | | $a^2 a^3$

**8.** | $6a^2 - 6b^2$ | | $(3a + 3b)(2a - 2b)$

**9.** | | $n > 0$

$\sqrt{n} + 2n$ | | $2\sqrt{n} + n$

**10.**

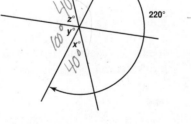

$x$ | | $\dfrac{y+z}{3}$

**11.** On a certain map, each centimeter represents 9 kilometers in actual distance.

The number of centimeters
on the map from City A to
City B | | 9% of the number of
kilometers from City A to
City B

**12.** At a garage sale, Jeff sold 80 percent of his books, which include only hardbacks and paperbacks. He sold an equal number of each of the two types of books, selling all paperbacks for $1 each and all hardbacks for $3 each. Jeff's total revenue from the sale of his books was $32.

| The number of books Jeff owned before the garage sale | Five times the number of books remaining unsold after the garage sale |

**13.** Cubes measuring 1 inch × 1 inch × 1 inch must be packed into a rectangular packing box.

| The number of complete cubes that fit into a box with dimensions 12 inches × 10 inches × 12.5 inches | The number of complete cubes that fit into a box with dimensions 10 inches × 15 inches × 10 inches |

**14.**

$$abc \neq 0$$
$$a > b$$

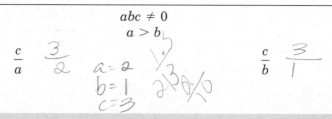

$\dfrac{c}{a}$        $\dfrac{c}{b}$

---

**Directions:** For Questions 15–28, solve the problem and select the best answer choice.

**Notes:**
- All numbers used are real numbers.
- All figures lie on a plane unless otherwise indicated.
- All angle measures are positive.
- All lines shown as straight are straight. Lines that appear jagged can also be assumed to be straight (lines can look somewhat jagged on the computer screen).
- Figures are intended to provide useful information for answering the questions. However, except where a figure is accompanied by a "Note" stating that the figure is drawn to scale, solve the problem using your knowledge of mathematics, *not* by visual measurement or estimation.

**15.** If $|x| > |y| > |z|$, which of the following equations CANNOT hold true?

(A) $x + y = 0$

(B) $y - z = 0$

(C) $xyz = 0$

(D) $x - y = z$

(E) $xyz = 1$

**16.** A compact disc player priced originally at $80 is sold at a discount for $68. What is the rate of the discount?

| 15 | percent

*Round a non-integer answer either up or down to the nearest integer.*

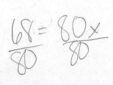

**17.** If $x \square y = x(x - y)$, then $(-1 \square -2) \square$
$(1 \square 2) =$

**(A)** 2

**(B)** 1

**(C)** 0

**(D)** −1

**(E)** −2

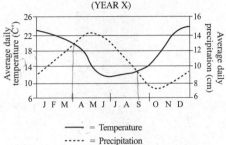

RAINFOREST TEMPERATURE
AND PRECIPITATION LEVELS
(YEAR X)

= Temperature
----- = Precipitation

AREA OF WAREHOUSE UNITS A, B, C, AND D
(AS PORTIONS OF TOTAL WAREHOUSE AREA)

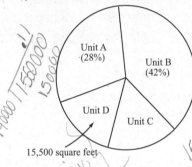

Unit A (28%)
Unit B (42%)
Unit D
Unit C

15,500 square feet

Total: 140,000 square feet

**20.** During year X, average daily temperature (in C°) and average daily precipitation (in centimeters) were measured at approximately the same *number* level sometime in

**(A)** late November

**(B)** early April

**(C)** mid-February

**(D)** early September

**(E)** late July

**18.** The graph shows the proportionate areas of 4 warehouse units: A, B, C, and D. Which of the following most closely approximates the square-foot area of Unit C?

**(A)** 19,500

**(B)** 23,000

**(C)** 26,500

**(D)** 37,500

**(E)** 42,000

**21.** If $m = 121 - 5k$, and if $m$ is divisible by 3, which of the following, each considered individually, COULD be true?

  I. $m$ is odd

  II. $m$ is even

 III. $k$ is odd

**(A)** II only

**(B)** I and II only

**(C)** I and III only

**(D)** II and III only

**(E)** I, II, and III

**19.** A certain clock runs 48 minutes slow every 12 hours. 4 hours after the clock is set correctly, the correct time is 4:00. In how many minutes, to the nearest minute, will the clock show 4:00?

**(A)** 16

**(B)** 17

**(C)** 18

**(D)** 19

**(E)** 20

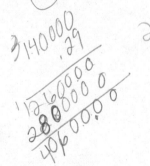

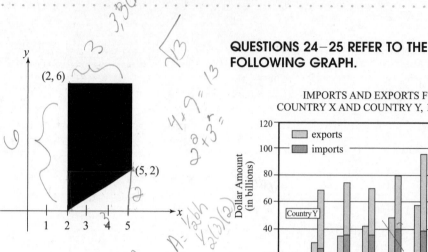

(2, 6)

(5, 2)

**22.** The shaded figure shown above is a trapezoid. What is its square unit area?

(A) 15

(D) 16

(C) 17

(D) 18

(E) 19

**23.** Machine X, Machine Y, and Machine Z each produce widgets. Machine Y's rate of production is one-third that of Machine X, and Machine Z's production rate is twice that of Machine Y. If Machine Y can produce 35 widgets per day, how many widgets can the three machines produce per day working simultaneously?

(A) 315

(B) 280

(C) 245

(D) 235

(E) 210

**QUESTIONS 24–25 REFER TO THE FOLLOWING GRAPH.**

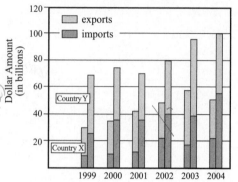

IMPORTS AND EXPORTS FOR
COUNTRY X AND COUNTRY Y, 1999–2004

**NOTE**: For each year, the combined height of two bar segments shows total imports and exports of a country.

**24.** In which of the following years did Country Y's imports exceed Country X's imports by the smallest percentage?

(A) 1999

(B) 2000

(C) 2001

(D) 2003

(E) 2004

**25.** Which of the following best describes Country X's overall import and export trend over the six-year period shown?

(A) The value of imports generally increased in value, but there was no clear export trend.

(B) The value of imports generally increased, while that of exports generally declined.

(C) Neither the value of imports nor that of exports exhibited a clear trend over the period.

(D) The value of imports and exports both increased steadily in dollar value.

(E) The value of imports increased but then declined, while the value of exports increased steadily.

**26.** If a portion of $10,000 is invested at 6% and the remaining portion is invested at 5%, and if $x$ represents the amount invested at 6%, what is the annual income in dollars from the 5% investment?

**(A)** $.05(x + 10,000)$

**(B)** $5(x - 10,000)$

**(C)** $.05(10,000 - x)$

**(D)** $5(10,000 - x)$

**(E)** $.05(x - 10,000)$

**27.** In the figure below, points X and Z lie along the circumference of the circle whose center is Y.

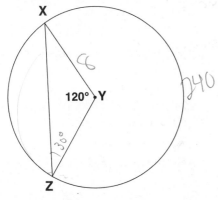

If the length of $\overline{XY}$ is 8, what is the length of minor arc $\overparen{XZ}$?

**(A)** $8\sqrt{3}$

**(B)** $4\pi$

**(C)** $16$

**(D)** $\dfrac{16\pi}{3}$

**(E)** $8\pi$

**28.** Patrons at a certain restaurant can select two of three appetizers—fruit, soup and salad—along with two of three vegetables—carrots, squash and peas. What is the statistical probability that a patron will select fruit, salad, squash and peas?

**(A)** $\dfrac{1}{12}$

**(B)** $\dfrac{1}{9}$

**(C)** $\dfrac{1}{6}$

**(D)** $\dfrac{1}{3}$

**(E)** $\dfrac{1}{2}$

# VERBAL REASONING

## 30 Questions • 30 Minutes

## Questions 1-9 (Analogies)

> **Directions:** In each of the following questions, a related pair of words or phrases is followed by five lettered pairs of words or phrases. Select the lettered pair that best expresses a relationship similar to that expressed in the original pair.

1. SCALE : TONE ::

   (A) spectrum : color
   (B) texture : sensation
   (C) wave : frequency
   (D) prism : hue
   (E) form : shape

2. SANDAL : FOOTPRINT ::

   (A) sock : carpet
   (B) river : gorge
   (C) galosh : puddle
   (D) cleat : turf
   (E) boat : wake

3. DAM : DELUGE ::

   (A) treat : disease
   (B) settle : dispute
   (C) lock : theft
   (D) harvest : crop
   (E) assemble : pieces

4. WAR : OFFENSIVE ::

   (A) school : student
   (B) waterfall : river
   (C) slumber : dream
   (D) stadium : soccer
   (E) game : poker

5. SONG : SERENADE ::

   (A) appointment : tryst
   (B) play : vignette
   (C) memorandum: letter
   (D) arrangement : commitment
   (E) book : novel

6. HAND : GNARLED ::

   (A) tree : tall
   (B) foot : cramped
   (C) flower : crushed
   (D) brow : creased
   (E) tire : flat

7. OSCILLATE : PENDULUM ::

   (A) obligate : promise
   (B) swim : pool
   (C) purchase : product
   (D) shake : earthquake
   (E) travel : automobile

8. ARCHITECT : CREATIVE ::

   (A) partisan : impartial
   (B) traitor : disloyal
   (C) soldier : obedient
   (D) consumer : prosperous
   (E) prisoner : rebellious

9. DESIGNATION : STIGMA ::

   (A) odor : fragrance
   (B) circumstance : predicament
   (C) legislation : statute
   (D) advice : command
   (E) falsehood : lie

## Questions 10-14 (Sentence Completions)

**Directions:** Each sentence below has one or two blanks, each blank indicating that something has been omitted. Beneath the sentence are five lettered words or sets of words. Choose the word or set of words for each blank that best fits the meaning of the sentence as a whole.

10. To marine biologists, the giant squid is especially _____, as it has never been seen alive, making it virtually impossible to study in its natural habitat.

    (A) dangerous
    (B) fascinating
    (C) mysterious
    (D) notorious
    (E) endangered

11. The main advantage of inertial guidance systems in modern aircraft, spacecraft, and submarines is that they are _____ and are able to function without _____ data.

    (A) reliable . . further
    (B) automatic . . external
    (C) scientific . . losing
    (D) computerized . . processing
    (E) internal . . vital

12. The _____ that computers are _____ educational tools has led many parents to believe that children don't need to be monitored when using the computer, as they do when watching television.

    (A) belief . . sophisticated
    (B) misconception . . benign
    (C) hypothesis . . powerful
    (D) argument . . effective
    (E) myth . . inimical

13. In the United States, the development of sociology was not _____ controversies; rather, it emerged from social experience, hence the relatively _____ approach among American sociologists to identifying and solving social problems.

    (A) impeded by political . . academic
    (B) challenged by academic . . theoretical
    (C) hindered by petty . . controversial
    (D) stimulated by ideological . . empirical
    (E) sparked by social . . experimental

**14.** The biography depicts the well-known actress as _____ but ruthless, _____ the popular notion that she attained stardom through a series of guileful maneuvers.

(A) scheming . . fostering

(B) talented . . undermining

(C) ambitious . . contravening

(D) vindictive . . verifying

(E) intelligent . . corroborating

## Question 15 (Complex Text Completion)

**Directions:** Select one entry from each column to fill in the corresponding blanks in the following text. Fill in the blanks in a way that provides the best completion for the text.

**15.** Quantitative data such as blood pressure, cholesterol level, and body weight are useful objective indicators of physical health. Yet, quantitative measurement and logic (i)_____ when it comes to determining the extent of a person's physical well-being. Levels of physical discomfort and pain, the most reliable indicators of physical well-being, cannot be quantified; (ii)_____, our emotional state and psychological well-being, which can have a profound impact on our physical health, defy objective measurement altogether.

| **(i)** |
| --- |
| can prove misleading |
| hardly suffice |
| are of little use |

| **(ii)** |
| --- |
| perhaps equally significant |
| not surprisingly |
| on the other hand |

## Questions 16–23 (Reading Comprehension)

**Directions:** Each passage in this group is followed by questions based on its content. After reading the passage, choose the best answer to each question. Answer all the questions following the passage on the basis of what is stated or implied in the passage.

**QUESTIONS 16 AND 17 ARE BASED ON THE FOLLOWING PASSAGE.**

*Line* The 35-millimeter (mm) format became the standard for movie production around 1913. The mid-1920s through the mid-1930s, however, saw
(5) a resurgence of wide-film (55-mm to 70-mm) formats. Development then slackened until the 1950s, when widescreen film-making came back in direct response to the erosion of box
(10) office receipts resulting from the rising popularity of television. This new era saw another flurry of specialized formats, including Cinema-Scope and, in 1956, Camera 65, which
(15) Panavision developed for MGM Studios and which was first used to film *Raintree Country*. Panavision soon contributed another key technical advance, spherical 65mm lenses,
(20) which eliminated the "fat faces" syndrome that had plagued CinemaScope films.

Though many films were made in widescreen formats during this
(25) period, these formats floundered because of expense, unwieldy cameras, and slow film stocks and lenses. After the invention of a set of 35-mm anamorphic lenses, which
(30) could be used to squeeze a widescreen image onto theatrical screens, film technology improved to the point where quality 70-mm prints could be enlarged from 35-mm negatives.

16. It can be inferred from the passage that wide-film formats were

   (A) in use before 1913
   (B) not used during the 1940s
   (C) more widely used during the 1920s than during the 1930s
   (D) not used after 1956
   (E) more widely used for some types of movies than for others

17. According to the passage, which of the following did NOT contribute to the increased use of wide-film formats for moviemaking?

   (A) Spherical camera lenses
   (B) Panavision's Camera 65
   (C) The advent of television
   (D) Anamorphic camera lenses
   (E) Movie theater revenues

**QUESTIONS 18 AND 19 ARE BASED ON THE FOLLOWING PASSAGE.**

*Line* Human cells are programmed to self-destruct at the same rate at which they are generated. However, the programs can malfunction, resulting
(5) either in excessive cell growth, which can lead to cancer, or excessive cell destruction, which can lead to degenerative diseases. As for the latter, using a tool called RNA interference,
(10) researchers can turn off the functions of genes individually and, by observing the results, determine which genes influence the process of cell death.
(15) Geneticists have isolated more than one hundred different human genes

that prevent cells from self-destructing. However, these genes operate interdependently toward this (20) end; moreover, most such genes serve other functions as well, including cell differentiation and proliferation. Scientists are just beginning to identify the gene groups that play key roles in (25) the prevention of cell death and to understand the intricacies of how these groups function, not just as units but also together, in what appears to be a vast network. Building (30) on this knowledge, researchers hope to learn how to precisely manipulate the process of cell death in humans—a crucial step toward the development of diagnostics and treatments that (35) target the specific diseases associated with out-of-control cell destruction.

**18.** It can be inferred from the passage that the author mentions "cell differentiation and proliferation" (lines 21–22) probably in order to

**(A)** point out that different genes generally perform different functions

**(B)** distinguish internal inputs that trigger cell self-destruction from external sources

**(C)** identify the mechanism by which human cells can multiply out of control

**(D)** differentiate the various types of genes that prevent cell death

**(E)** emphasize the complexity of the interplay among gene functions

**19.** The author's primary concern in the passage is to

**(A)** describe the process of cell death and regeneration in the human body

**(B)** explain the methodology by which researchers are learning how to control cell death

**(C)** summarize the findings of recent scientific research on degenerative diseases

**(D)** propose a theory to account for the increasing variety of degenerative diseases in humans

**(E)** provide hope that scientists will soon discover a cure for many degenerative diseases

## QUESTIONS 20–23 ARE BASED ON THE FOLLOWING PASSAGE, WHICH WAS WRITTEN IN 1994.

Line There are two cornerstones of economic reform in the former Communist states: liberalization of prices (including exchange rates) and priva-(5) tization. Radical economists call for immediate liberalization, with the only remaining wage regulation in the state sector, accompanied by a restrictive fiscal and monetary policy (10) to harness inflation. Conservative economists, who favor gradual deregulation, would have the government prepare enterprises for market shocks—for example, by breaking (15) monopolies before prices and foreign trade are liberalized or by limiting production of heavy industry products such as coal and steel. If the gradualists have their way, however, eco-(20) nomic reform could dissolve in the hands of bureaucrats unwilling to face the problems inherent in a real transition to a market economy.

Privatization also can be accom-(25) plished either gradually or rapidly. Under the former approach, a state bureau would decide if and when an enterprise was prepared for privatization and which form was most *(30)* suitable for it. Slow privatization, some claim, is the only way to establish true private ownership, because only those who must pay for enterprise-ownership rights will be *(35)* engaged in its management. But this method would only prolong the core problems of inefficiency and misallocation of labor and capital, and hence either of two approaches to rapid *(40)* privatization is preferable.

Under one such approach, shares of an enterprise would be distributed among its employees, who would become its owners. This socialist *(45)* reform method is deeply flawed; it discriminates in favor of workers who happen to be employed by modern, efficient enterprises, and it jeopardizes workers' property by requiring *(50)* them to invest in the same enterprise in which they are employed, rather than diversifying their investments. The better approach involves distribution of enterprise shares, free of *(55)* charge, among all the people by means of vouchers—a kind of investment money.

Some critics charge that voucher holders would not be interested in how *(60)* their enterprises are managed—as may be true of small corporate shareholders in capitalist countries who pay little attention to their investments until the corporation's profits wane, at *(65)* which time they rush to sell their securities. But while the resulting fall in stock prices can be perilous for the corporation, this very pressure is what drives private firms toward efficiency *(70)* and profitability. Other detractors predict that most people will sell their vouchers to foreign capitalists. However, these skeptics ignore the capacity of individuals to compare the *(75)* future flow of income secured by a voucher to the benefits of immediate consumption. Moreover, even if an individual should decide to sell, the aim of voucher privatization is to *(80)* secure equality not of property but of opportunity.

**20.** The author closely associates gradual market deregulation with

  **(A)** a restrictive monetary policy
  **(B)** government subsidization of steel producers
  **(C)** a policy requiring a monopoly to split into two or more enterprises
  **(D)** a fall in stock prices
  **(E)** state agency determinations as to when enterprises should be privatize

**21.** In responding to "skeptics" who claim that people will sell their vouchers to foreign capitalists (lines 70–77), the author implies that

  **(A)** foreign capitalists will not be willing to pay a fair price for the vouchers
  **(B)** the future flow of income may often exceed the present exchange value of a voucher
  **(C)** foreign investment in a nation's enterprises may adversely affect currency exchange rates
  **(D)** skeptics of privatization do not understand how capitalism works
  **(E)** foreign capitalists are less interested in the success of voucher privatization than in making a profit

**22.** The passage mentions all of the following as possible adverse consequences of rapid privatization EXCEPT

(A) instability in stock prices

(B) loss of ownership in domestic private enterprises to foreign concerns

(C) financial devastation for employees of private enterprises

(D) inequitable distribution of wealth among employees of various enterprises

(E) undue prolongation of inefficiency and misallocation

**23.** Which of the following would the author probably agree is the LEAST desirable outcome of economic reform in formerly Communist countries?

(A) Financial security of private enterprises

(B) Equitable distribution of property among citizens

(C) Financial security of citizens

(D) Equal opportunity for financial success among citizens

(E) Effective allocation of labor

## Questions 24–30 (Antonyms)

**Directions:** Each question below consists of a word printed in capital letters followed by five lettered words or phrases. Choose the lettered word or phrase that is most nearly opposite in meaning to the word in capital letters. Since some of the questions require you to distinguish fine shades of meaning, be sure to consider all the choices before deciding which one is best.

**24.** EXPLICIT:

(A) implied

(B) quiet

(C) modest

(D) omitted

(E) exclusive

**25.** PASSIVITY:

(A) confidence

(B) lack of restraint

(C) aggression

(D) vitality

(E) disrespect

**26.** PROXIMAL:

(A) mobile

(B) wavering

(C) vague

(D) peripheral

(E) adjoining

**27.** INSULATE:

(A) reflect

(B) dampen

(C) combine

(D) expose

(E) restrict

**28.** CURSIVE:

(A) spoken
(B) clumsy
(C) disjointed
(D) straight
(E) unadorned

**29.** PERTURB:

(A) stagnate
(B) sedate
(C) postpone
(D) halt
(E) deactivate

**30.** RAIL:

(A) conspire
(B) compromise
(C) tout
(D) esteem
(E) acquiesce

diagnostic test

# ANSWER KEY AND EXPLANATIONS

## Analytical Writing

### ISSUE TASK—EVALUATION AND SCORING

Evaluate your Issue task essay on a scale of 0 to 6 (6 being the highest score) according to the following five criteria (the same criteria apply to any GRE Issue essay):

1. Does your essay develop a position on the issue through the use of incisive reasons and persuasive examples?

2. Are your essay's ideas conveyed clearly and articulately?

3. Does your essay maintain proper focus on the issue, and is it well organized?

4. Does your essay demonstrate proficiency, fluency, and maturity in its use of sentence structure, vocabulary, and idiom?

5. Does your essay demonstrate command of the elements of Standard Written English, including grammar, word usage, spelling, and punctuation?

To evaluate and score your Issue essay, here are two full-length essays—one on each Issue task. Both essays meet all the criteria for a solid score of at least 5 on the 0–6 scale. Notice the following features of these essays:

- Each is brief enough for almost any test-taker to organize and compose on a word processor in 45 minutes.

- The introductory and concluding paragraphs show that the test-taker recognizes that the issue is complex, and both paragraphs express his viewpoint on the issue clearly and effectively.

- Each body paragraph presents a distinct reason for (or defense of) the test-taker's viewpoint.

Don't worry if your essay isn't as polished as the samples here, or if you adopted a different viewpoint and/or used entirely different reasons and examples to support your viewpoint. These essays are merely two samples of how a test-taker might have responded effectively to these two Issue statements.

### Sample Essay for Issue Statement 1 (350 words)

I strongly agree that government should not use its resources to support the arts in any way. The conventional justification for government subsidies and other support is that, without them, cultural decline and erosion of our social fabric will result. However, I find this argument unconvincing in light of three persuasive arguments that government has no business intervening in the arts.

First, subsidizing the arts is neither a proper nor necessary job for government. Although public health is critical to a society's very survival and therefore an appropriate concern of government, this concern should not extend tenuously to our cultural "health" or well-being. A lack of private funding might justify an exception; in my observation, however, ample funding from corporate and other private sources is readily available today.

As proof, we need look no further than PBS (public television), whose arts programming is entirely funded from such sources.

Second, government cannot possibly play an evenhanded role as arts patron. Inadequate resources call for restrictions, priorities, and choices. It seems unwise to leave decisions as to which art has "value" to a few legislators and jurists, who may be unenlightened in their notions about art. What's more, legislators are, unfortunately, all too likely to make choices in favor of the cultural agendas of whichever lobbyists have the most money and influence.

Third, when government sponsors arts projects, it often imposes constraints on what kind of artistic expression is suitable or acceptable for the project. A recent federally funded public mural project in Southern California comes to mind. To obtain funding, artists were required to create images that reflected a patriotic, nationalistic spirit. The result of artistic constraints such as that one is to stifle not only artistic creativity, thereby defeating the very purpose of subsidizing the arts, but also freedom of expression.

In the final analysis, government can neither philosophically nor economically justify its involvement in the arts, either by subsidy or sanction; nor do the arts need government's help. Therefore, I agree that sole responsibility to determine what art has value and to support that art should lie with individuals.

**Sample Essay for Issue Statement 2 (336 words)**

I agree with the statement insofar as great professional success often comes at the expense of one's personal life and can even be inextricably related to one's personal failings. However, the statement is problematic in that it unfairly suggests that personal and professional success are mutually exclusive in every case.

Undeniably, today's professionals must work long hours to keep their heads above water, let alone to get ahead in life financially. In fact, the two-income family is now the norm, not by choice but by necessity. However, our society's professionals are taking steps to remedy the problem. They're inventing ways—such as job sharing and telecommuting—to ensure that personal life is not sacrificed for career. Also, more professionals are changing careers to ones which allow for some degree of personal fulfillment and self-actualization. Besides, many professionals truly love their work and would do it without compensation, as a hobby. For them, professional and personal fulfillment are one and the same.

Admittedly, personal failings often accompany professional achievement. In fact, the two are often symbiotically related. The former test the would-be achiever's mettle; they pose challenges—necessary resistance that drives one to professional achievement despite personal shortcomings. In the arts, a personal failing may be a necessary ingredient or integral part of the process of achieving. Artists and musicians often produce their most creative works during periods of distress, while in business a certain amount of insensitivity to people can breed grand achievements. However, for every individual whose professional success is bound up in his or her personal failings, there is another individual who has achieved success in both realms.

In sum, I agree that as a general rule, people find it difficult to achieve great success both personally and professionally, and in fact history informs us that personal failings are often part and parcel of great achievements.

However, despite the growing demands of career on today's professionals, a fulfilling personal life remains possible—by working smarter, by setting priorities, and by making suitable career choices.

## ARGUMENT TASK—EVALUATION AND SCORING

Evaluate your Argument task essay on a scale of 1 to 6 (6 being the highest score) according to the following five criteria:

1. Does your essay identify and articulate the argument's key unstated assumptions?

2. Does your essay explain how the argument relies on these unstated assumptions and what the implications are if these assumptions are unwarranted?

3. Does your essay develop its ideas in a clear, organized manner, with appropriate transitions to help connect ideas together?

4. Does your essay demonstrate proficiency, fluency, and maturity in its use of sentence structure, vocabulary, and idiom?

5. Does your essay demonstrate command of the elements of Standard Written English, including grammar, word usage, spelling, and punctuation?

To help you further with your evaluation and scoring, here's a checklist of the kinds of problems you should have found with the Argument (paragraph numbers refer to the sample essays that follow):

- Drawing an overly broad recommendation (paragraph 1)

- Assuming that a course of action is necessary to achieve a certain objective (paragraph 2)

- Failing to defend a "threshold" but dubious assumption (paragraph 3)

- Arguing simultaneously for two competing objectives (paragraph 4)

Now here's a full-length essay on the Argument. This essay meets all the criteria for a solid score of at least 5 on the 0–6 scale. Notice the following additional features of this essay:

- It's brief enough for almost any test-taker to organize and compose in 30 minutes.

- Each body paragraph presents a distinct point of critique.

Don't worry if your essay isn't as polished as the sample here, or if yours doesn't include each and every one of the points of critique in this sample essay. Also, don't worry if your essay is organized differently, or if you expressed your points and supported them in a different way. This sample essay merely illustrate how a test-taker might respond effectively to this Argument.

### Sample Essay on the Argument Task (330 Words)

In a nutshell, this argument is not only poorly supported but also illogical on its face. A threshold problem with the argument is that it fails to distinguish between scientists and engineers with children and those without children. A worker with no young children obviously has no need for daycare services or for career advancement requirements that accommodate the special interests of parents. Thus, the author must narrow both conclusions so that they apply only to computer scientists and engineers with children.

Considering the author's first assertion apart from the second one, the author fails to consider and rule out other options for ensuring proper care for the workers' children during the workday. For instance, a computer scientist whose spouse (or partner) has time during each day to spend with their child might very well require no professional daycare. Besides, many working parents, including single-parent workers, might have friends or relatives who can provide child care. Thus, to the extent that computer scientists and engineers have other options to ensure daycare for their children, the author's first conclusion is unwarranted.

As for the author's second assertion, considered separately from the first one, the author fails to explain why it is important for children generally—let alone children of computer scientists and engineers in particular—to spend a significant portion of each day with a parent. Lacking a convincing explanation, I cannot accept the author's assertion that career-advancement requirements must be made more flexible merely for the sake of allowing significant parent-child contact each workday.

Considering the two assertions together, however, the argument becomes even less convincing. In essence, the second assertion undermines the first one. If the children of these workers spend significant time each day with a parent, without compromise to the parent's career, then all-day child care would seem unnecessary—in direct contradiction to the author's first assertion. Thus, the author must either reconcile the two assertions or choose one assertion over the other.

## Quantitative Reasoning

| | | |
|---|---|---|
| 1. C | 11. A | 20. E |
| 2. D | 12. C | 21. E |
| 3. B | 13. B | 22. A |
| 4. B | 14. D | 23. E |
| 5. D | 15. B | 24. D |
| 6. C | 16. 15 | 25. A |
| 7. A | 17. C | 26. C |
| 8. C | 18. C | 27. D |
| 9. D | 19. B | 28. B |
| 10. B | | |

1. **The correct answer is (C).** The absolute value (distance from the origin on the number line) of $n$ and $-n$ is the same.

2. **The correct answer is (D).** The drawer must include at least 20 pairs of striped socks. That leaves a total of 20 pairs of solid socks. If the drawer contains exactly 20 solid white pairs, then $w = 20$, the drawer contains no solid gray pairs ($g = 0$), and $w - g = 20$. Accordingly, Quantity A equals Quantity B in this case. However, if the drawer contains fewer than 20 solid white pairs, then $w < 20$ and $w - g < 20$, and Quantity A is less than Quantity B.

3. **The correct answer is (B).** You don't need to perform precise calculations to make the comparison. First, consider Quantity A. $333\% = 3.33$, and $(3.33)(3) < 10$. Now consider Quantity B. Since 10 (which we know exceeds Quantity A) is less than 33% of 33, Quantity B must be greater than Quantity A. (Quantity B is a fraction just under 11 but clearly greater than 10.)

4. **The correct answer is (B).** The centered information alone establishes that the integer $(k - 1)$ could

be 41, 43, or 47. Accordingly, the integer $k$ could be 42, 44, or 48. Their median (the middle value) is 44, while their average is

$$\frac{42 + 44 + 48}{3} = \frac{134}{3} > 44.$$

5. **The correct answer is (D).** The two equations are actually the same. (One way to confirm this is to multiply each term in the second equation by $\frac{3}{2}$.) Given one linear equation in two variables, it is impossible to determine the relative values of $p$ and $q$.

6. **The correct answer is (C).** $x + y$ is the measure of the top angle in the large triangle. Hence, $x + y + w + z = 180$. Since $x + z = 50$, $y + w = 130$.

7. **The correct answer is (A).** $(a^2)^3 = a^6$, while $a^2a^3 = a^5$. Since $a > 1$, $a^6 > a^5$, Quantity A is greater than Quantity B.

8. **The correct answer is (C).** Quantity A can be expressed as $6(a^2 - b^2)$. Factor out the constants (numbers) in Quantity B: $(3a + 3b)(2a - 2b) = (3)(a + b)(2)(a - b) = 6(a + b)(a - b) = 6(a^2 - b^2)$. As you can see, the two quantities are the same: $6(a^2 - b^2)$.

9. **The correct answer is (D).** Subtracting $\sqrt{n}$ and $n$ from both sides yields $n$ in Column A and $\sqrt{n}$ in Column B. If $n > 1$, then $n > \sqrt{n}$. But if $n < 1$, then $n < \sqrt{n}$. Thus, you do not have enough information to make the comparison.

10. **The correct answer is (B).** The sum of all six angles formed by the intersecting lines in the figure is 360°. Given that the sum of all angles other than $y°$ and $z°$ is 220°, $y + z$ must equal 140 $(360 - 220)$. Since angles $x°$, $y°$, and $z°$ form a straight line (180°), $x$ must equal 40. Since $x = 40$ and $y + z = 140$, $\frac{y+z}{3} > x$, Quantity B is greater than Quantity A.

11. **The correct answer is (A).** 1 centimeter = 9 kilometers, so the number of kilometers is 9 times greater than the number of centimeters. Conversely, the number of centimeters is $\frac{1}{9}$, or approximately 11%, of the number of kilometers.

12. **The correct answer is (C).** Given total revenue of $32, you can find the number of each type of book sold by setting up and solving a simple algebraic equation. Letting $x$ equal the number of each type of book sold: $3x + x = 32$. Thus, $x = 8$, and Jeff must have sold exactly eight $3 books and eight $1 books: 16 books altogether. Given that Jeff sold 80% of his books at the sale, he must have owned exactly 20 books before the sale (16 is 80% of 20), which is 5 times the number of books remaining after the sale (4).

13. **The correct answer is (B).** Both boxes have the same volume: 1,500 cubic inches. However, in the box described in Column A, 60 cubic inches of space must be left empty along the $12 \times 10$ face. On the other hand, the box described in Column B can be packed full of one-inch cubes without leaving any empty space. Hence, Quantity B is greater.

14. **The correct answer is (D).** Which quantity is greater depends on whether $a$, $b$, and $c$ are positive or negative. If you're the least bit unsure about this, it's a good idea to plug in a few simple numbers. For example, let $a = 2$ and $b = 1$. If $c = 1$ (a positive value), then $\frac{c}{a} < \frac{c}{b}$ $\left(\frac{1}{2} < \frac{1}{1}\right)$. But if $c = -1$ (a negative number), then $\frac{c}{a} > \frac{c}{b}$ $\left(-\frac{1}{2} > -\frac{1}{1}\right)$.

15. **The correct answer is (B).** For equation (B) to hold true, $y$ must equal $z$, which is impossible given that $|y| > |z|$. Equation (A) could be true because it is possible that $x = -y$. Equation (C) could hold true because it is possible that any one of the three variables could equal 0 (zero). Equation (D) could hold true—for example, if $x = 3$, $y = 2$, and $z = 1$. Equation (E) could hold true—for example if $x = 2$, $y = 1$, and $z = \frac{1}{2}$.

16. **The correct answer is 15.** Calculate the discount rate using the original price: $\frac{12}{80} = \frac{3}{20} = \frac{15}{100}$, or 15%. (There's no need to round the answer to the nearest integer.)

17. **The correct answer is (C).** First, apply the defined operation to each parenthesized pair:

$(-1 \,\square\, -2) = -1(-1 - -2) = -1(1) = -1$
$(1 \,\square\, 2) = 1(1 - 2) = 1(-1) = -1$

Then apply the defined operation again, substituting $-1$ for both $x$ and $y$:

$(-1 \; \square \; -1) = -1(-1 - -1]) =$

$-1(0) = 0$

18. **The correct answer is (C).** First, find the size of Unit D as a percentage of the total warehouse size. Unit D occupies 15,500 square feet—approximately 11%—of the 140,000 total square feet in the warehouse. Thus, Unit C occupies about 19% of that total $(100\% - 28\% - 42\% - 11\% = 19\%)$. In terms of square feet, then, the size of Unit C is approximately $(.19)(140,000) = 26,600$ square feet. Of the five answer choices, choice (C) most closely approximates this figure.

19. **The correct answer is (B).** After 4 hours, the clock will run behind the actual time by 16 minutes. Accordingly, at 4:00 the clock will show 3:44. It will take 16 minutes *plus* about one additional minute (because the clock runs 1 minute slow every quarter-hour) for the clock to advance to 4:00.

20. **The correct answer is (E).** Sometime in late July, when daily temperatures (measured by the scale on the left) averaged about 12 degrees, daily precipitation (measured by the scale on the right) averaged about 12 centimeters.

21. **The correct answer is (E).** A number divisible by 3 could either be odd or even. For example, $m$ could be 18 (even) or 21 (odd). Therefore, either I or II could be true. Also, $k$ could be odd. If $k$ were odd, the $5k$ would be an odd multiple of 5—for example, 5, 15, 25, 35, . . . ., and 121

$- 5k$ would result in a number ending in 6 (116, 106, 96, 86, . . .). The numbers 96, 66, and 36, and 6 are all possible results, and all are divisible by 3. Therefore, III could also be true.

22. **The correct answer is (A).** Divide the shaded figure into a rectangle with vertices at (2,6), (5,6), (2,2), and (5,2) and a right triangle with vertices at (5,2), (2,2), and (2,0). The rectangle's height and width are 4 and 3, respectively, and so its area is $4 \times 3 = 12$. The triangle has legs of lengths 3 and 2, so its area is $\frac{1}{2} \times 3 \times 2 = 3$. The sum of the two areas is $12 + 3 = 15$.

23. **The correct answer is (E).** The key to handling this question is to convert ratios to fractional parts that add up to 1. The ratio of X's rate to Y's rate is 3:1, and the ratio of Y's rate to Z's rate is 1:2. You can express the ratio among all three as 3:1:2 (X:Y:Z). Accordingly, Y's production accounts for $\frac{1}{6}$ of the total widgets that all three machines can produce per day. Given that Y can produce 35 widgets per day, all three machines can produce $(35)(6) = 210$ widgets per day.

24. **The correct answer is (D).** For each year, compare the heights of the two dark bars. The year 2003 was the only one among the five choices for which Country Y's imports (about $39B) were less than twice Country X's imports (about $21B).

25. **The correct answer is (A).** This question involves the left bar for the six years shown. The dark portion (imports) increases up to 2003 and

then remains steady from 2003 through 2004. The light portion (exports) appears to increase through 2001, then decrease in 2002, then increase again in 2003, and then decrease in 2004—in other words, there's no clear trend for the value of Country X's exports over the period in question.

26. **The correct answer is (C).** The amount invested at 5% is (10,000 − x) dollars. Thus, the income from that amount is .05(10,000 − x) dollars.

27. **The correct answer is (D).** $\overline{XY}$ is also the circle's radius. Since XY = 8, the circle's circumference = 2π(8), or 16π. ∠XYZ, given as 120°, accounts

for $\frac{120}{360}$, or $\frac{1}{3}$, of the entire 360° contained in the circle. Since minor arc $\overset{\frown}{XZ}$ is formed by that central angle, $\overset{\frown}{XZ}$ accounts for $\frac{1}{3}$ of the circle's circumference:

$$\frac{1}{3}(16\pi) = \frac{16\pi}{3}.$$

28. **The correct answer is (B).** In each set are three distinct member pairs. The probability of selecting any pair is one in three, or $\frac{1}{3}$. Accordingly, the probability of selecting fruit and salad from the appetizer menu along with squash and peas from the vegetable menu is $\frac{1}{3} \times \frac{1}{3} = \frac{1}{9}$.

## Verbal Reasoning

| | | |
|---|---|---|
| 1. A | 12. B | 21. B |
| 2. E | 13. D | 22. E |
| 3. C | 14. E | 23. A |
| 4. C | 15. (i) hardly suffice | 24. A |
| 5. A | (ii) perhaps equally | 25. C |
| 6. D | significant | 26. D |
| 7. E | 16. A | 27. D |
| 8. B | 17. D | 28. C |
| 9. B | 18. E | 29. B |
| 10. C | 19. B | 30. E |
| 11. B | 20. C | |

### Questions 1–9 (Analogies)

1. **The correct answer is (A).** This is a "part-to-whole" analogy. A musical SCALE is comprised of a series of TONES that are arranged in a fixed sequence; similarly, the *spectrum* is comprised of a series of *colors* arranged in a particular sequence.

2. **The correct answer is (E).** This is a "symptom or sign" analogy. A SANDAL leaves behind it a FOOT-PRINT that traces the sandal's path; similarly, a *boat* leaves behind it a *wake* that traces the boat's path.

3. **The correct answer is (C).** This is an "operates against" (prevention) analogy. You DAM (a body of water) to prevent a DELUGE (sudden, enormous flow); similarly, you *lock* something like a door or a safe in order to prevent a *theft*.

4. **The correct answer is (C).** This is an "environment for" analogy. An OFFENSIVE (a noun here) is an event—a planned attack—that typically occurs during a WAR. Similarly, a *dream* is an event that typically occurs during *slumber* (deep sleep). As for choice (D), soccer is an event that *might* take place in a

stadium. But to say that soccer usually occurs in a stadium would be an overstatement. Also, a stadium is a physical place, whereas WAR and *slumber* are events.

5. **The correct answer is (A).** This is a "type of" (special category) analogy. A SERENADE is a special kind of SONG, one sung by a lover to his beloved, sometimes in secret; similarly, a *tryst* is a special kind of *appointment*, one made by lovers, often in secret.

6. **The correct answer is (D).** This is a type of "symptom or manifestation" analogy. A HAND may become GNARLED (knotted and twisted) with age, just as a *brow* may become *creased* (wrinkled or ridged) with age. Gnarls and creases are each a manifestation of gradual deterioration. Since a *tire* goes *flat* abruptly and for one of many possible reasons, choice (E) is not as strong an analogy as choice (D).

7. **The correct answer is (E).** This is an "inherent function" analogy. A PENDULUM is designed to OSCILLATE (move back and forth);

similarly, an *automobile* is designed to *travel*.

8. **The correct answer is (B).** This is as "ideal characteristic" analogy. Ideally, an ARCHITECT is CREATIVE; similarly, an ideal *soldier* is one who is *obedient*; that is, one who obeys the orders of a superior officer. Choice (B) is incorrect because *disloyalty* is not just an ideal character-

istic of a *traitor*; it is the defining characteristic.

9. **The correct answer is (B).** This is a "negative form of" analogy. A STIGMA (mark or sign of disgrace) is an unwanted DESIGNATION. Similarly, a *predicament* (difficult situation) is an unwanted *circumstance*.

## Questions 10–14 (Sentence Completions)

10. **The correct answer is (C).** In the context of the sentence, the word *as* means "because." The second part of the sentence provides an explanation for the first part. The fact that the giant squid has "never been seen alive" would clearly explain why the squid would be *mysterious* to marine biologists.

11. **The correct answer is (B).** Notice that the word "advantage" is singular (not plural). This suggests that the two phrases "they are _____" and "they are able to . . ." must express nearly the same idea. Choice (B) helps convey the idea nicely: An *automatic* system is by definition one that functions without *external* help. (In the digital realm, the words "data" and "help" can carry essentially the same meaning.) None of the other answer choices establishes as close a relationship between these two phrases.

12. **The correct answer is (B).** The missing words should suggest a belief about computers that would lead parents to let their children use the devices without being watched. Only choice (B) works, because only

*benign* (harmless) is sufficiently positive to suggest that idea.

13. **The correct answer is (D).** The first operative word in the sentence is *rather*, which sets up a contrast between what precedes it and what follows it. So, the first clause must run contrary to the phrase "it emerged from social experience." Only choices (A), (C), and (D) serve this purpose. Of these three choices, choice (D) establishes the clearest contrast—between ideology and experience. A second operative word in the sentence is *hence*. What follows this phrase must be consistent with what precedes it. Choice (D) accomplishes just that. The word *empirical* means "based on observation or experience (as opposed to theory)."

14. **The correct answer is (E).** *Guileful* means "cunning or wily." It makes sense that someone who is "intelligent but ruthless" would engage in "guileful maneuvers" in order to succeed, and the word *corroborating* (which means "helping to

confirm or verify") sets up the appropriate match between the biography's account and the popular notion.

## Question 15 (Complex Text Completion)

15. **The correct answers are hardly suffice for blank (i) and perhaps equally significant for blank (ii).** The idea of the passage is that quantitative data are useful but insufficient (that is, they *hardly suffice*) to determine the extent of a person's well-being because they do not account for pain and discomfort, nor do they account for emotional or psychological states, which can have a profound effect on (that is, they are *perhaps equally significant* in determining) physical well-being.

## Questions 16–23 (Reading Comprehension)

16. **The correct answer is (A).** The passage refers to the establishment of a 35-mm standard around 1913, followed by a "resurgence" of wide-film formats (in the mid-1920s to the mid-1930s). This resurgence suggests that wide-film formats were not new because they had been used before the 35-mm standard was established; that is, before 1913.

17. **The correct answer is (D).** According to the passage's last sentence, anamorphic lenses made it possible to create quality 70-mm prints from 35-mm negatives. In this respect, the invention of the anamorphic camera lens contributed to the demise (not the increased use) of wide-film moviemaking.

18. **The correct answer is (E).** The author explains that many of the genes that prevent cell death operate individually and in groups to perform other functions as well, and so determining exactly what genes and groups of genes function to prevent various types of cells from self-destructing is an exceedingly complex undertaking.

19. **The correct answer is (B).** The author's overall concern is with describing the process researchers are following to identify the genes responsible for preventing cell death and with the direction (and goals) of current research based on their findings. Of the five choices, choice (B) best expresses the gist of the discussion.

20. **The correct answer is (C).** One of the possible features of gradual deregulation mentioned in the first paragraph is the breaking of monopolies by the government. Choice (C) restates this possible feature.

21. **The correct answer is (B).** The author responds to the skeptics' claim by pointing out that people are likely to weigh the future flow of income from a voucher against the benefits of selling their vouchers now and using the proceeds for consumption. Were people not likely (at least in many cases) to hold their vouchers after weighing these two alternatives, the author would not have made this argument. Thus, the author is implying that, indeed, in

many cases the future flow of income from a voucher will exceed the present value of the voucher.

**22. The correct answer is (E).** The author foresees prolonged inefficiency and misallocation as a consequence of gradual, not rapid, privatization (lines 30–40).

**23. The correct answer is (A).** The author's willingness to place a private enterprise at risk for the broader purpose of achieving a free-market system is suggested by at least two areas of discussion in the passage. In the first paragraph, the author tacitly disagrees with the gradualists who favor bracing enterprises for the shock of deregulation to help them survive the transition. In the final paragraph, while advocating voucher privatization, the author admits that this approach may very well result in the instability of stock prices; yet the author seems to view the insecurity caused by market pressures as good for private enterprises in that it will drive them to efficiency—a sort of sink-or-swim approach.

## Questions 24–30 (Antonyms)

**24. The correct answer is (A).** One meaning of EXPLICIT is "fully and clearly expressed, leaving nothing implied. *Implied* means "expressed indirectly."

**25. The correct answer is (C).** One meaning of PASSIVITY is *submission* (the condition of being submissive)—the opposite of *aggression*.

**26. The correct answer is (D).** PROXIMAL means "situated toward the center or point of attachment"; *peripheral* means "located away from the center, at the fringe, or near a boundary."

**27. The correct answer is (D).** To INSULATE is to "cause to become isolated or detached." To *expose* is to do quite the opposite, of course.

**28. The correct answer is (C).** CURSIVE refers to a flowing, continuous style of printing or writing. *Disjointed* means "disconnected or separated."

**29. The correct answer is (B).** To PERTURB is to "disturb or agitate," whereas *sedate* means "calm or quiet."

**30. The correct answer is (E).** To RAIL is to "complain or denounce vehemently" (as in "rail against injustice"), contrary to *acquiesce* (agree, comply, or consent, usually by silence or inaction).

# PART III

## ANALYTICAL WRITING

# The Issue Task

## OVERVIEW

- **Key facts about the GRE Issue task**
- **The 7-step plan**
- **5 tips for scoring high**
- **Issue task strategies**
- **Summing it up**

In this chapter, you'll find out how to write an effective GRE Issue essay. First, you'll learn a step-by-step approach to brainstorming, organizing, composing, and revising your Issue essay, all within the exam's 45-minute time limit. By adhering to this step-by-step plan, you'll attain a better-than-average Issue task score of at least 4 on the 0–6 scale.

But you won't stop there. Later in the chapter, you'll learn the finer points of writing GRE Issue essays: how to qualify an Issue statement, debate its pros and cons, and use rhetorical techniques for maximum persuasive impact in presenting your viewpoints. These are the skills that separate the cream-of-the-crop test-takers who attain the two highest scores of 5 and 6 from all the rest.

At the end of the chapter, you'll review the keys to writing a high-scoring GRE Issue essay.

## KEY FACTS ABOUT THE GRE ISSUE TASK

You first looked at the Issue writing task in Chapter 2 and in this book's Diagnostic Test. Here's a quick review of key facts about the Issue task component of GRE Analytical Writing.

**Where:** Either immediately before or after the Argument writing task (the two Analytical Writing tasks come at the beginning of the exam, before all Quantitative and Verbal Reasoning sections)

**How Many:** One essay

**Time Allowed:** 45 minutes

**General Directive:** You adopt, present, and develop your own viewpoint on a given Issue statement, considering various perspectives on the issue at hand.

**Abilities Tested:**

- Your ability to communicate a perspective on an issue effectively and persuasively

- Your ability to present your ideas in a cohesive, well-organized manner

- Your ability to communicate your ideas adequately, using the conventions of Standard Written English (but language, syntax, grammar, and writing mechanics are not nearly as important as content and organization).

**Other Key Facts:**

- The specific directive may vary slightly, depending on the Issue statement, but your basic task is always the same: Present and develop a viewpoint on the issue.

- There is no "correct" response to any Issue prompt.

- There is no prescribed or "correct" word length for an Issue essay.

- Scratch paper and pencils are provided (just as in the other exam sections).

- The system's basic word processor has a simple cut-and-paste function but no spell-checking or grammar-checking functions.

## THE 7-STEP PLAN

For a high-scoring Issue essay, you need to accomplish the following basic tasks:

- Recognize and handle the complexities and implications of the issue.

- Organize, develop, and express your ideas coherently and persuasively.

- Support your ideas with sound reasons and relevant examples.

- Demonstrate an adequate grasp of the elements of Standard Written English (including grammar, syntax, and usage).

Forty-five minutes isn't much time to accomplish these tasks, so you need to use that time wisely. This does not mean using every one of your 45 minutes to peck madly at the keyboard, however. The smart approach is to spend some time thinking about what you want to write and organize your thoughts, and to save some time after you've finished writing to proofread and fine-tune your essay.

Here's a 7-step plan (with suggested time for each step) to help you budget your time so that you can accomplish all the tasks listed above within the 45-minute time limit:

1. Choose a task, then brainstorm and make notes (3 minutes).

2. Review your notes and decide on a viewpoint (1 minute).

3. Organize your ideas into a logical sequence (1 minute).

4. Compose a brief introductory paragraph (2 minutes).

5. Compose the body of your essay (30 minutes).

6. Compose a brief concluding or summary paragraph (3 minutes).

7. Proofread for significant mechanical problems (5 minutes).

Notice that if you follow these suggested times, you'll spend about 5 minutes planning your essay, 35 minutes writing it, and 5 minutes proofreading and fine-tuning it.

In the following pages, we'll apply each of these steps to the following GRE-style Issue task (remember, the directive is essentially the same regardless of the specific task):

**Issue Statement 1 (preceded by the directive)**

"Schools should be responsible not only for teaching academic skills but also for teaching ethical and social values."

Present your perspective on the issue above. Use relevant reasons and/or examples to support your viewpoint.

## Step 1: Choose a Task, Then Brainstorm and Make Notes (3 minutes)

Your very first step is to choose one of the two tasks that the test presents. Don't waste time mulling over the choice. Neither is necessarily "easier" than the other. Commit right away to whichever task strikes you as the one you would probably have more to say about. Then, begin to develop your essay by brainstorming ideas.

Try to think of some reasons and examples that support *both* sides of the issue. At this stage, don't commit to a position on the issue, and don't try to filter out what you think might be unconvincing reasons or weak examples. Just let all your ideas flow onto your scratch paper, in no particular order. (You can sort through them during steps 2 and 3.) Here's what a test-taker's notes for Issue Statement 1 might look like after a few minutes of brainstorming:

> *Whose values?*
>     *Amish*
>     *suburbanites*
>     *yuppies*
>     *Southern Baptists*
> *pluralism*
> *schools need focus*
> *sex education*
> *classroom cooperation vs. competition*
> *teachers set examples—indirectly*
> *drugs & violence*

Notice that the first several lines reflect one train of thought (If schools are to teach ethical values, whose values should they teach?), while the rest of the notes reflect other random ideas. The notes are somewhat of a hodgepodge, but that's okay. The point of brainstorming is to generate as many ideas as possible. These make up the raw material for your Issue essay. Let your ideas flow freely, and you'll have plenty of fodder for this essay.

**NOTE**

The suggested time limits for each step are guidelines, not hard-and-fast rules. As you practice composing Issue essays under timed conditions, start with these guidelines and then adjust to a pace that works best for you.

**ALERT!**

Remember that there is no correct viewpoint or position on any GRE issue, so don't take too much time deciding which viewpoint you should defend. Choose whatever viewpoint seems easier or more natural for you.

## Step 2: Review Your Notes and Decide on a Viewpoint (1 minute)

Decide on the basic point of view (either "pro" or "con") that you want to take up in your essay—in other words, decide whether you are going to agree or disagree with the statement. Your notes from step 1 should help you decide which stand to take. Review the ideas you've jotted down, and then ask yourself whether you can make a stronger case for or against the statement presented to you.

Once you've decided, pick the three or four ideas from your notes that best support your chosen viewpoint. These should be ideas that you believe make sense and support your viewpoint reasonably well. You should also know enough about them to be able to write at least a few sentences. Put a checkmark next to those ideas to mark what you're sure you want to use in the essay. If you don't think you have enough, take one or two of the ideas you like best and elaborate on them. Think of related ideas, add details or examples, and then use these to fill out your list.

## Step 3: Organize Your Ideas into a Logical Sequence (1 minute)

Next, decide on a logical sequence for presenting your ideas. The best sequence might be the most obvious: One idea may lead logically to another. Or your ideas might involve historical examples, which lead chronologically from one to another. They might also range from the personal level to the family or community level, then to the societal or global level. Any of these "patterns" suggests a natural sequence for your Issue essay.

If you don't detect an obvious sequence, a good approach is to decide which two ideas you like best—the two you consider most convincing or happen to know the most about and can develop most fully. Earmark these ideas to discuss *first* and *last* in the body of your essay. Then arrange the remaining ideas in any order between your two best ideas. Why arrange ideas this way? The most emphatic and memorable parts of any essay are the beginning and the end. It makes sense, then, that you place your best material where it will have the greatest impact on the reader.

Now that you've settled on a sequence, number your ideas accordingly in your notes. Here's an example of how a test-taker might turn notes on Issue Statement 1 into a simple outline:

**NOTE**

It's perfectly acceptable to agree or disagree strongly with the Issue statement. But your agreement (or disagreement) should not keep you from fulfilling the directive for this writing assignment, which requires that you consider ways in which the statement *may or may not* be true.

---

2. ✔ <u>Whose values?</u>
   Amish
   suburbanites
   yuppies
   Southern Baptists

1. ✔ pluralism

3. ✔ schools need focus
   sex education
   classroom cooperation vs. competition
   teachers set examples-indirectly
   drugs & violence

4. ✔ U.S. Schools lag

---

Notice that this test-taker has decided to disagree with the statement—that is, to take the position that schools should teach academics only, and not ethical values. The first three points in his notes all fit nicely into an argument for this viewpoint. He also came up with a fourth idea that he thought might make a good ending—the point that U.S. schools lag behind most other countries in academic standards, so time shouldn't be taken away from teaching academic subjects to teach ethics. The test-taker made a note of that idea and checked it off as well.

This writer decided to start with the idea that America is pluralistic. From this point, it makes sense to ask, "Whose values would be taught in schools?" and use the examples listed. This leads nicely to the point about focusing on academics and, finally, the argument about how U.S. students lag behind others.

## Step 4: Compose a Brief Introductory Paragraph (2 minutes)

Now it's time to compose your essay. You begin with a brief introductory paragraph in which you need to accomplish the following:

- Demonstrate that you understand the issue the statement raises
- Let the reader know that you have a clear viewpoint on the issue
- Anticipate the ideas you intend to present in the body of your essay

You can probably accomplish all three tasks in two or three sentences. In your introductory paragraph, avoid going into detail about your reasoning, and don't provide specific examples. These are best left to the body of your essay. Don't begin your introductory paragraph by repeating the statement verbatim; this amounts to wasted time, since the reader is already familiar with the topic. Instead, show the reader from your very first sentence that you're thinking for yourself.

Here's an introductory paragraph for Issue Statement 1 based on the test-taker's original outline (above):

**Introductory Paragraph (Issue Statement 1)**

Schools, especially in a pluralistic nation such as the United States, should limit what they teach to academic subjects—leaving it to parents and clergy to teach ethics. To do otherwise, as the statement suggests, is to invite trouble, as this essay will show.

## Step 5: Compose the Body of Your Essay (30 minutes)

In this step, your chief ambition is to get your main points—as well as any supporting reasons and examples—from your brain and scratch paper onto the computer screen. Keep these points in mind as you compose the body of the essay:

- Be sure that the first sentence of each paragraph begins a distinct train of thought and clearly conveys the essence of the paragraph.

- Arrange your paragraphs so your essay flows logically and persuasively from one point to the next. Stick to your outline, but be flexible.

- Try to devote at least two, but no more than three or four, sentences to each main point in your outline.

- Don't worry if you don't have time to include every point from your outline. The GRE readers understand that the time constraint of the exam prevents most test-takers from covering every point they want to make.

- Don't stray from the issue at hand, or even from the points you seek to make. You don't have time. Stay focused on the issue and your points.

Now here are the body paragraphs of a response to Issue Statement 1—based on the outline on page 85:

**Four-Paragraph Body (Issue Statement 1)**

If our schools are to teach values, the most important question to answer is: Whose values would they teach? After all, not all ethical values are the same. The Amish have a way of life that stresses simplicity and austerity; they shun modern conveniences and even such activities as dancing. By contrast, the typical young, urban family enjoys buying the latest electronic gadgets and going on expensive vacations. Either group might be offended by the values of the other.

True, Amish and urban children aren't likely to attend the same schools; but what about children from Jewish and fundamentalist Christian households? These two religious groups may live in the same town or neighborhood, and either one might very well be incensed if the other group's moral teachings were imposed on them.

The only way to avoid the inevitable conflicts that teaching ethics would bring to our schools is by allowing teachers to focus on what they're paid to do: teach academics. We send children to school to learn math, English, history, and science. How would we feel if our kids came home ignorant about geometry but indoctrinated with someone else's religious or ethical ideas? Justly annoyed, I think.

Moreover, consider that schoolchildren in the United States lag behind those in most other nations in academic achievement. In light of this fact, it would seem foolish for us to divert classroom time from teaching academics to teaching "morality."

Let's take a look at some of the features of the body paragraphs, which show that the test-taker tried to stick to his outline while remaining flexible as new ideas for content or organization occurred to him:

- Point 2 in the outline ("Whose values?") became the basis for two paragraphs (the second and third ones), not just one.

- After writing about the Amish and urban families, the test-taker seemed to realize that the contrast between them, while illustrating the point, was a bit exaggerated. Rather than replacing the entire paragraph with a more realistic pairing, which would have cost a substantial amount of time, the test-taker added the second paragraph to provide a more down-to-earth pairing (Jewish and fundamentalist Christian families).

- The suburbanites got left out of the essay altogether, either because the test-taker realized they were unnecessary or because he was running short on time.

## Step 6: Compose a Brief Concluding or Summary Paragraph (3 minutes)

Unless your essay has a clear ending, the reader might think you didn't finish in time, and that's not the impression you want to give. Be sure to leave time to wrap up your discussion. Convey the main thrust of your essay in a clear, concise, and forceful way. Two or three sentences should suffice. If an especially insightful concluding point occurs to you, the final sentence of your essay is a good place for it.

In your final paragraph, be sure that you don't simply repeat your introductory paragraph. These two "bookend" paragraphs should complement one another—each providing its own distinct slant on your thesis. If you need to fine-tune your first paragraph, step 6 is the best time to do so.

Here's a brief but effective concluding paragraph for the essay on Issue Statement 1. Notice that it assures the reader that the test-taker has organized his time well and finished the writing task. Also, notice that this brief summary does not introduce any new reasons or examples; it's just a quick recapitulation that complements the introductory paragraph:

**Final Paragraph (Issue Statement 1)**

> Ironically, what is most ethical for our schools to do in the interest of educating our children is to avoid becoming entangled in ethical issues. Stick to academics, and let families and clergy teach morality in their own way and on their own time.

## Step 7: Proofread for Mechanical Problems (5 minutes)

To score high with your Issue essay, you don't need to compose a flawless work of art. The readers won't reduce your score because of an occasional awkward sentence or minor error in punctuation, spelling, grammar, or diction (word choice and usage). Don't get hung up on whether each sentence is something your English composition professor would be proud of. Instead, use whatever time remains to read your essay from start to finish and fix the most glaring mechanical problems. Here are some suggestions for

**TIP**

Your concluding remarks should complement, not simply repeat, your opening paragraph. Providing complementary "bookends" for the body of your Issue essay shows the reader you can compose a cohesive, well-planned essay under time pressure.

what you should and—just as importantly, should *not*—try to accomplish during this final step.

- Find and rework awkward sentences, especially ones in which the point you're trying to make is unclear.

- Find and correct accidental omissions of words, garbled phrases, grammatical errors, and typographical errors. It doesn't take much time to fix these kinds of mistakes, and doing so will go a long way toward making a positive impression on the reader.

- Correct spelling errors only when they might prevent the reader from understanding the point at hand.

- Don't spend valuable time correcting punctuation, removing extra character spaces between words, or correcting minor spelling errors.

- Don't get drawn into drastic rewriting. Accept that your essay is what it is and that you don't have time to reshape it substantially.

From beginning to end (including the introduction, the body, and the concluding paragraph), the sample essay we've used is a little more than 300 words long. It's not lengthy, nor is it a literary masterpiece. But it expresses a clear viewpoint, it's smartly organized, it employs relevant reasons and examples, and it's stylistically crisp and effective. In short, it contains all the elements of a successful GRE Issue essay.

## 5 TIPS FOR SCORING HIGH

As long as you provide sound reasons and relevant examples supporting a position on the issue at hand in your Issue essay, you can earn a decent score of 3 or more. But if your aim is to earn a top score of 5 or 6, here are five tips to help you reach that goal:

1. Qualify the statement

2. Debate the statement's pros and cons

3. Develop rhetorical techniques

4. Organize your essay carefully

5. Structure your essay for rhetorical effectiveness

### "Qualifying" an Issue Statement

To earn a top score you need to consider ways that the statement *may or may not be true*. This means that you should neither completely agree nor completely disagree with the statement; it shows that you're capable of considering all viewpoints on a specific issue. Here are two GRE-style Issue statements, each followed by a viewpoint that expresses how the test-taker might qualify it:

**Issue Statement 2**

> "To truly succeed in life, a person must assert his or her individuality rather than conforming to the expectations of others."

**Viewpoint:** Asserting individuality is important only to an extent. The key is to strike the optimal balance between individuality and conformity—a balance that varies depending on the particular activity or goal involved.

**Issue Statement 3**

"The greatest responsibility of a leader—whether in politics, business, or the military—is to serve the interests of his or her followers."

**Viewpoint:** The statement's accuracy depends on the category. Legitimate political leadership must, by definition, serve the citizenry, but the same can't be said for business or military leadership.

Perhaps you're wondering whether you'll appear "wishy-washy" or indecisive by qualifying the statement. In reality, however, you'll likely impress the reader as being thoughtful and insightful. Just be sure to persuade the reader, using sound reasoning and relevant examples, that your qualified agreement or disagreement is justifiable.

How do you find these qualifications? Look for any of these types of qualifiable Issue statements:

- A statement whose accuracy depends on varying factors.

- A statement that might be true or untrue generally, but that fails to account for significant exceptional cases.

- A statement that is unclear or vague: In other words, its accuracy depends on the meaning of key terms or how you interpret the statement as a whole.

- A statement that raises two distinct but related issues: One might be a so-called threshold issue that should be addressed before the main issue can be thoroughly analyzed.

- A statement that has merit but overlooks legitimate competing interests or contributing factors. Issue Statement 2, above, is a good example.

- A statement that lists or otherwise embraces two or more distinct categories. For example, in Issue Statement 3, above, different categories lend differing degrees of support to the statement.

## Debating a Statement's Pros and Cons

When we reviewed the basics of writing an Issue essay, we suggested that you take a few minutes before writing to brainstorm and jot down ideas, listing points for and against the statement as they occur to you. If you take that idea a step further, you can train yourself to think more consciously about the pros and cons of the statement while you're taking notes. A good way to do this is to think of the note-taking process as a debate, in which you formulate points and supporting examples to bolster one side of the issue, and then respond with counterpoints and counterexamples.

To organize the points of your debate, try creating two columns, one for points that support the statement and the other for opposing points. Here's what a test-taker's notes might look like after a few minutes of brainstorming the pros and cons of Issue Statement 4:

**Issue Statement 4**

"The best way to ensure protection and preservation of our natural environment is through governmental regulatory measures. We cannot rely on the voluntary efforts of individuals and private businesses to achieve these objectives."

| *PRO* | *CON* |
|---|---|
| • *self-interest rules ind. & bus.*<br>  • *e.g. auto emissions*<br>  • *but nations too*<br>• *environ. problems too widespread for ind. & bus.*<br>  • *but nations must cooperate* | • *lawmakers pander*<br>  • *but accountable to voters*<br>• *enforcement problems*<br>  • *e.g. bus. relocate*<br>• *bureaucratic problems*<br>  • *e.g. delays*<br>  • *e.g. compromises*<br>  • *e.g. admin. expense*<br>  • *but must put up with problems to save environ.* |

Notice that the test-taker supports each main point (indicated by a bullet) with one or more examples ("e.g.") and/or a counterpoint ("but").

## Developing Rhetorical Techniques

The word "rhetoric" describes the art of persuasive argument. A rhetorically effective Issue essay does more than simply itemize reasons and examples for supporting one viewpoint. It acknowledges possible problems with the viewpoint, then defends that viewpoint by responding to those problems directly. It also acknowledges at least one other position or viewpoint, then challenges that viewpoint directly as well.

As you take notes on your Issue statement, you'll naturally come up with ideas for responding to other viewpoints and you'll realize that your own viewpoint may have possible problems. But if you find yourself at a loss for ideas, draw upon the five tried-and-true techniques discussed in the next few pages to get your rhetorical juices flowing. To illustrate each technique, we'll use examples based on these two Issue statements, the first of which you've already encountered in this lesson:

**Issue Statement 4**

"The best way to ensure protection and preservation of our natural environment is through governmental regulatory measures. We cannot rely on the voluntary efforts of individuals and private businesses to achieve these objectives."

**Issue Statement 5**

> "Large businesses should focus on teamwork as the primary means of achieving success."

## TURN AROUND A WEAKNESS (OR A STRENGTH)

One of the strategies you can adopt in your Issue essay is to argue that an apparent weakness is actually not one—or an apparent strength isn't a strength—if you view it from a different perspective. The notes and outline for Issue Statement 3 provide a good example. The writer might first cite evidence that lends apparent support to the opposing position:

> Admittedly, businesses often attempt to avoid compliance by concealing their activities, or calculate the cost of polluting, in terms of punishment, then budget in advance for anticipated penalties and openly violate the law.

Then the writer might indicate how this point actually undermines that position:

> However, this behavior only serves to underscore the need for government intervention, because left unfettered, this type of behavior would only exacerbate environmental problems.

## TRIVIALIZE A WEAKNESS (OR A STRENGTH)

You can also argue that an apparent weakness in your position (or a strength in a different position) is trivial, minor, or insignificant. Issue Statement 4 provides a good opportunity to use this technique. The writer might first cite two examples that lend apparent support to those who might disagree with the statement:

> Detractors might cite the heavy manufacturing and natural resource industries, where the value of tangible assets—raw materials and capital equipment—are often the most significant determinant of business success.

Then the writer might explain away these examples:

> However, such industries are diminishing in significance as we move from an industrial society to an information age.

## APPEAL TO BROADER CONSIDERATIONS

Argue that any minor problems with your position seem trivial in light of the broad and serious implications that the Issue raises. The notes and outline for Issue Statement 3 are a good example. The writer might first acknowledge a certain problem with her position:

> Delays typically associated with bureaucratic regulation can thwart the purpose of the regulations, because environmental problems can quickly become grave indeed.

Then the writer might point out the broad societal consideration that puts this minor drawback in its proper perspective:

> But such delays seem trivial when we consider that many environmental problems carry not only a real threat to public health but also a potential threat to the very survival of the human species.

### ADOPT A "LESSER OF TWO EVILS" ARGUMENT

This technique is similar to the previous one; the difference is that you will argue that an opposing position is no stronger than yours, or is perhaps even weaker in a certain respect. As with the "broader considerations" technique, the writer might first acknowledge a certain weakness in her position:

> Delays typically associated with bureaucratic regulation can thwart the purpose of the regulations, because environmental problems can quickly become grave indeed.

But then the writer can point out an even greater weakness in the opposing position:

> However, given that unjustifiable reliance on volunteerism is the only alternative, government regulation seems necessary.

### TRY A "GREATER OF TWO VIRTUES" METHOD

Another avenue of attack is to argue that a particular strength of the opposing position is overshadowed by one or more virtues of your position. Issue Statement 5 provides a good opportunity to employ this rhetorical device. The writer might first admit that the opposing position has merit:

> No reasonable observer of the corporate business world could disagree that the leadership and vision of a company's key executives is of great importance to the organization's success.

Next, though, the writer would assert that the contrary position has even greater merit:

> Yet chief executives of our most successful corporations would no doubt admit that without the cooperative efforts of their subordinates, their personal vision would never become reality.

## Put It All Together

Here again are the notes on Issue Statement 4. The test-taker has now numbered his notes to indicate how he plans to organize his essay:

| *PRO* | *CON* |
|---|---|
| ① • self-interest rules ind. & bus.<br>　• *e.g.* auto emissions<br>　• *but* nations too<br>④ • environ. problems too widespread for ind. & bus.<br>　• *but* nations must cooperate | ② • lawmakers pander<br>　• *but* accountable to voters<br>• enforcement problems<br>　• *e.g.* bus. relocate<br>③ • bureaucratic problems<br>　• *e.g.* delays<br>　• *e.g.* compromises<br>　• *e.g.* admin. expense<br>　• *but* must put up with problems to save environ. |

Notice that he has decided to begin and end the body of the essay with "pro" points, possibly because he has weighed the pros and cons and thinks that these are the strongest arguments. He probably intends to agree, at least on balance, with the statement. Also notice that he plans to discuss two distinct "cons" in the same paragraph (2), possibly because he doesn't have enough to say about them to justify devoting an entire paragraph to either one alone.

Now here's a full length essay on Issue Statement 4, which pulls together the techniques you learned up to this point. It is about 430 words long—a bit longer than average, but still realistic for a 45-minute limit. Certain words and phrases that you might use in almost any Issue essay are underlined to help you see how the ideas flow naturally and persuasively from one to the next. (Remember, though, that the GRE's built-in word processor does not provide for underlining.) Notice the following features of the essay, which together boost the essay to the highest score level:

- The essay expresses overall but *qualified* agreement with the statement, a thoughtful viewpoint that shows that the writer recognizes the issue's complexity.

- The body of the essay begins and ends with pro arguments for rhetorical impact. The con arguments are positioned between them.

- For each of the con arguments (third and fourth paragraphs), the writer immediately responds with persuasive counterpoints.

Notice also that the writer tried to stick to his outline but also remained flexible as new ideas for content or organization occurred to him. For example, he repositioned certain points from the original outline. Additionally, the writer didn't incorporate every point from his outline, perhaps because he simply didn't have time in 30 minutes to cover all of them.

### Essay (Issue Statement 4)

In asserting that government regulation is the "best" way to ensure environmental protection, the speaker fails to acknowledge certain problems inherent with government regulation. Nevertheless, I agree with the statement to the extent that exclusive reliance on individual or business volunteerism would be naive and imprudent, especially considering the stakes involved.

Experience tells us that individuals and private corporations tend to act in their own short-term economic and political interest, not on behalf of the environment or the public at large. For example, current technology makes possible the complete elimination of polluting emissions from automobiles. Nevertheless, neither automobile manufacturers nor consumers are willing or able to voluntarily make the short-term sacrifices necessary to accomplish this goal. Only the government holds the regulatory and enforcement power to impose the necessary standards and to ensure that we achieve these goals.

Admittedly, government penalties do not guarantee compliance with environmental regulations. Businesses often attempt to avoid compliance by concealing their activities, lobbying legislators to modify regulations, or moving operations to jurisdictions that allow their environmentally harmful activities. Others calculate the cost of polluting, in terms of punishment, then budget in advance for anticipated penalties and openly violate the law. However, this behavior only serves to underscore the need for government intervention, because left unfettered this type of behavior would only exacerbate environmental problems.

One must admit as well that government regulation, environmental or otherwise, is fraught with bureaucratic and enforcement problems. Regulatory systems inherently call for legislative committees, investigations, and enforcement agencies, all of which add to the tax burden on the citizens whom these regulations are designed to protect. Also, delays typically associated with bureaucratic regulation can thwart the purpose of the regulations, because environmental problems can quickly become grave indeed. However, given that unjustifiable reliance on volunteerism is the only alternative, government regulation seems necessary. Moreover, such delays seem trivial when we consider that many environmental problems carry not only a real threat to public health but also a potential threat to the very survival of the human species.

Finally, environmental issues inherently involve public health and are far too pandemic in nature for individuals or even businesses to solve on their own. Many of the most egregious environmental violations traverse state and sometimes national borders. Individuals and businesses have neither the power nor the resources to address these widespread hazards.

In the final analysis, only the authority and scope of power that a government possesses can ensure the attainment of agreed-upon environmental goals. Since individuals are unable and businesses are by nature unwilling to assume this responsibility, government must do so.

## Structuring Your Essay for Rhetorical Effectiveness

So far, we've covered the basic strategy of starting the body of your essay with your best argument and finishing with your second-best argument, sandwiching your other arguments in between the two. We also saw, in the preceding essay, how you can adapt this strategy to a two-column list of pros and cons, alternating the two types of arguments.

Clearly, the way in which you arrange your ideas into paragraphs can make a big difference in how persuasive your final essay is. To score as high as possible on your GRE Issue task, you may want to consider alternative structures as well. The ways in which you can organize an Issue essay are limitless—but for our purposes, let's look at four fundamental structures that cover most situations. Take a look at the following templates (brackets indicate optional elements).

### ESSAY STRUCTURE 1

In a case where you have more reasons or examples supporting your position than against it, try the following structure to acknowledge one strong argument against your position:

**1st paragraph:** One reason and/or example supporting your position

**2nd paragraph:** A second reason and/or example supporting your position

**[3rd paragraph:** A third reason and/or example supporting your position]

**Final paragraph:** Chief counterargument » rebuttal

### ESSAY STRUCTURE 2

If you have better reasons and/or examples supporting your position than against it, try this structure to acknowledge one or more strong arguments against your position:

**1st paragraph:** Chief counterargument

**[Next paragraph:** A second counterargument]

**Next paragraph:** One reason and/or example supporting your position

**[Next paragraph:** A second reason and/or example supporting your position]

### ESSAY STRUCTURE 3

If the arguments for and against the statement's position are equally strong—that is, if it all depends on the area under consideration—try the following structure to balance the essay:

**1st paragraph (or 1st and 2nd paragraphs):** Area(s) or examples supporting one position

**2nd paragraph (or 3rd and 4th paragraphs):** Area(s) or examples supporting the contrary position

**NOTE**

You don't have to adhere strictly to one of these structures to write an effective Issue essay. Remember to stay flexible. The ideas you've jotted down might come together best in some other less conventional format—and that's just fine if it works well. In short, let your ideas drive your essay's structure, not vice versa.

**ESSAY STRUCTURE 4**

Finally, try this structure if you need to address two or more reasons supporting an opposing position, each one in turn:

**1st paragraph (or 1st and 2nd paragraphs):** Counterargument » rebuttal

**2nd paragraph (or 3rd and 4th paragraphs):** Counterargument » rebuttal

**[Next paragraph:** Counterargument » rebuttal]

# ISSUE TASK STRATEGIES

Here's a quick rundown of our very best advice for composing a GRE Issue essay. Some of these tips reiterate suggestions we've already made in this chapter, but they're well worth reviewing. Apply these points of advice to the practice tests in this book and then review them again, just before exam day.

## Adopt a Viewpoint . . . *Any* Viewpoint

It's perfectly acceptable to agree or disagree strongly with an Issue statement. Don't worry that your position may appear somewhat radical or even completely out of the mainstream. As long as you provide sound reasons and relevant examples to justify your strong viewpoint, you're following the directives for this section of the GRE. However, always try to qualify the statement by considering ways in which the statement may or may not be true.

## Explain How Your Examples Support Your Viewpoint

Anyone can list a string of examples and claim that they illustrate a point. But GRE readers are looking for incisive analysis, not fast typing. For each example you cite, make sure you tell the reader how that example supports the point you're trying to make. Otherwise, your argument will be unconvincing and your score might suffer as a result.

## Appeal to Reason, Not Emotion

Avoid inflammatory statements and don't preach or proselytize. Approach the Issue writing task as an intellectual exercise in which you dispassionately argue for a certain viewpoint. Although it's fine to take a strong stand, don't use the exam as a forum for explaining your personal belief system. It's perfectly appropriate to criticize particular behavior, policies, or viewpoints as operating against the best interest of an individual, a community, or a society, but refrain from condemning or extolling based on personal moral grounds. Also avoid demagoguery (an appeal to prejudice or emotion) and jingoism (excessive patriotism).

## Spare the Reader Rote Facts and Technical Details

The Issue essay is not like the TV show *Jeopardy!* or the board game *Trivial Pursuit*. You don't score points simply by recounting statistics, compiling long lists, or conjuring up little-known facts. Don't try to impress the reader with your technical knowledge of a particular subject, and resist the temptation to use the Issue essay as a forum to recapitulate your senior-year thesis. This is not the place to convince the reader of your firm grasp of the finest points of foreign policy, macroeconomic theory, or developmental psychology. That's what your GPA and undergraduate transcripts are for.

## Avoid Obvious and Hackneyed Examples

Many GRE test-takers will rely heavily on today's headlines and on history's most illustrious and notorious figures. If you can, avoid relying on these obvious examples. Try to dig a bit deeper and show the reader that you have a broader, more literate perspective.

## Don't Dwell on One Point; but Don't Try to Cover Everything, Either

Avoid harping on one particular point of argument that you believe is the most convincing, the one that you know most about, or the one that best illustrates your point. Try to cover as many points in your outline as possible in the time allotted, devoting no more than one paragraph to each. On the other hand, don't attempt to cover every single point you come up with about the issue; if you try, you're likely to become frustrated or even panic as the testing clock ticks away. Remember: The GRE essay readers understand your time constraints, so don't worry if you're forced to leave the secondary and more tangential points on your scratch paper. Stick to your outline, ration your time, and you'll do fine.

## Keep It Simple; the Reader Will Reward You for It

Don't make the Issue writing task more onerous than it needs to be for you to attain a solid score. Keep your sentences clear and simple. Use a straightforward structure for your essay. Avoid using "fancy" words just to impress the reader. Don't waste time figuring out ways to come across as exceedingly brilliant or eloquent. And by all means, don't waste brainpower or keystrokes trying to be clever or humorous. Trying to dazzle the essay reader with your amazing wit and wisdom is not the way to score high.

## Appear Organized and in Control of the Task

Use every tool at your disposal to show the reader that you can write well under pressure. Use logical paragraph breaks—one after your introduction, one after each of your main points, and one before your concluding paragraph. Present your main points in a logical, easy-to-follow sequence. (If you don't get it right the first time, you can use the word processor's cut-and-paste feature to rearrange your ideas.) If done right, your essay's "bookends"—the introductory and concluding sentences—can help you appear organized and in control. Make sure they're consistent with each other and that they reveal your viewpoint and recap the reasons for your viewpoint.

## Quality Counts, Not Quantity

The only restriction on your essay's length is the practical one that a 45-minute time limit imposes. But you may wonder: Do readers prefer brief or longer Issue essays? The answer: It all depends on the essay's quality. A lengthy essay that's articulate and includes many insightful ideas that are well supported by examples will score higher than a briefer essay that lacks substance. On the other hand, an essay that's concise and to the point can be more effective than a long-winded or rambling one. Don't worry about

**TIP**

Most GRE readers reside in the United States. If you're from elsewhere, cite examples from that region of the world. You're more likely to pique the reader's interest, which can only work in your favor.

the word length of your essay. GRE readers don't count words. As long as you incorporate all the suggested elements you learned about in this chapter, you don't need to worry about length. It's quality, not quantity, that counts.

## Remember Your Primary Objectives

The official scoring criteria for the Issue essay boils down to five questions that you should keep in mind during the 45 minutes of formulating and writing your essay:

**1** Do I have a clear point of view on the issue?

**2** Am I supporting my point of view with sound reasons and relevant examples?

**3** Have I considered ways in which the statement may or may not be true?

**4** Do I have in mind a clear, logical structure for presenting my ideas?
Once you can confidently answer "Yes" to each of these questions, start composing your essay. When you've finished your draft, ask yourself the same four questions, along with this fifth one:

**5** Have I demonstrated good grammar, diction, and syntax?

If you can answer "Yes" to all five questions, be assured that you've produced a solid, high-scoring Issue essay.

## SUMMING IT UP

- The Issue writing task comes either immediately before or after the Argument writing task on the GRE. It consists of one essay, for which you have 45 minutes. Your job is to adopt, present, and develop your own viewpoint on a given Issue statement, considering various perspectives on the issue at hand.

- Follow the 7-step plan in this chapter to score high on this essay. Give yourself time before you begin writing to organize your thoughts, and time after you're finished writing to fine-tune your essay.

- To score high on the Issue writing task, practice writing essays in which you work on these techniques: present ways in which the statement presented may or may not be true, think about the "pros" and "cons" of the statement, develop rhetorical techniques, and structure your essay for highest effectiveness.

- Follow and review the Issue task strategies in this chapter and apply them to this book's Practice Tests. Then review them again just before exam day.

# The Argument Task

## OVERVIEW

- **Key facts about the GRE Argument task**
- **The 7-step plan**
- **Tips for spotting common reasoning flaws**
- **Argument task strategies**
- **Summing it up**

In this chapter, you'll find out how to write an effective GRE Argument essay. First, you'll learn a step-by-step approach to brainstorming, organizing, composing, and fine-tuning your Argument essay, all within the exam's 30-minute time limit. By following this step-by-step plan, you'll attain a better-than-average Argument task score of at least 4 on the 0–6 scale.

Then, later in the chapter, you'll focus on the most common types of reasoning flaws in GRE Arguments. You'll learn how to recognize and handle each type, since this is the skill that separates the best Argument essays—those earning a score of 5 or 6—from all the others.

At the end of the chapter, you'll review the keys to writing a high-scoring GRE Argument essay.

## KEY FACTS ABOUT THE GRE ARGUMENT TASK

You first looked at the Argument writing task in Chapter 2 and in this book's Diagnostic Test. Here's a quick review of key facts about this component of GRE Analytical Writing.

**Where:** Either immediately before or after the Issue writing task (the two Analytical Writing tasks come at the beginning of the exam, before all Quantitative and Verbal Reasoning sections)

**How Many:** One essay

**Time Allowed:** 30 minutes

**General Directive:** You write an essay in which you discuss how well-reasoned you find a particular Argument—specifically, the following four aspects (1 and 2 are primary tasks):

1 The Argument's unsubstantiated or unreasonable assumptions

2 Problems with the Argument's internal logic or line of reasoning

**3** How the Argument can be strengthened (optional)

**4** What additional information is needed to better evaluate the Argument (optional)

**Abilities Tested:**

- Your ability to recognize unstated assumptions and other reasoning flaws in arguments

- Your ability to communicate your critique of an argument cogently and effectively, using relevant reasons and/or counter-examples

- Your ability to present your ideas in a cohesive, well-organized manner

- You ability to communicate your ideas adequately, using the conventions of Standard Written English (but language, syntax, grammar, and writing mechanics are not nearly as important as content and organization)

**Other Key Facts:**

- The Argument is presented in the form of a brief, paragraph-length quoted statement from a fictitious source.

- Regardless of the specific Argument that the test presents, the directive (your task) is always the same: Discuss how well-reasoned you find the argument.

- There is no prescribed or "correct" word length for an Argument essay.

- Scratch paper and pencils are provided (just as in the other exam sections).

- The system's basic word processor has a simple cut-and-paste function but no spell-checking or grammar-checking functions.

**TIP**

The Argument task prompt will direct you to discuss "how well-reasoned" you find the Argument; but in reality, your job will be to discuss how poorly reasoned it is—as you'll learn in this chapter.

## THE 7-STEP PLAN

For a high-scoring Argument essay, you need to accomplish the following basic objectives:

- Identify and analyze the Argument's key elements.

- Organize, develop, and express your critique in a coherent and logically convincing manner.

- Support your ideas with sound reasons and examples.

- Demonstrate adequate control of the elements of Standard Written English (grammar, syntax, and usage).

Thirty minutes isn't much time to accomplish these tasks, so you need to use that time wisely. This does *not* mean using every one of your 30 minutes to peck madly at the keyboard, however. You should spend some time first thinking about what you want to write and how to organize your ideas. You should also allocate at least the final few of your 30 minutes to proofread and fine-tune your essay.

Here's the 7-step plan (with suggested time for each step) to help you budget your time so you can accomplish all four objectives listed above within 30 minutes:

**1** Read the Argument and identify its conclusion(s) (1 minute).

**2** Examine the Argument's evidence and determine how strongly it supports the conclusion(s) (3 minutes).

**3** Organize and prioritize your points of critique (1 minute).

**4** Compose a brief introductory paragraph (2 minutes).

**5** Compose the body of your essay (16 minutes).

**6** Compose a final paragraph (2 minutes).

**7** Proofread for mechanical problems (5 minutes).

By following the suggested times for each step, you'll spend about 5 minutes planning your essay, 20 minutes writing, and 5 minutes proofreading it.

In the following pages, we'll go through each of these steps using the following GRE-style Argument prompt (remember, the directive is the same regardless of the Argument statement).

## Step 1: Read the Argument and Identify Its Conclusion(s) (1 minute)

**Argument Statement 1 (followed by the directive)**

The following appeared in a memo from the manager of UpperCuts hair salon:

"According to a nationwide demographic study, more and more people today are moving from suburbs to downtown areas. In order to boost sagging profits at UpperCuts, we should take advantage of this trend by relocating the salon from its current location in Apton's suburban mall to downtown Apton, while retaining the salon's decidedly upscale ambiance. Besides, Hair-Dooz, our chief competitor at the mall, has just relocated downtown and is thriving at its new location, and the most prosperous hair salon in nearby Brainard is located in that city's downtown area. By emulating the locations of these two successful salons, UpperCuts is certain to attract more customers."

Discuss how well-reasoned you find this argument.

## Step 2: Examine the Argument's Evidence and Determine How Strongly It Supports the Conclusion(s) (3 minutes)

Most GRE Arguments contain at least two or three items of information (or evidence) supporting their conclusion(s). Identify these items, label them, and jot them down on your scratch paper. Argument Statement 1 contains three distinct items of evidence:

**Evidence Item 1**

"According to a nationwide demographic study, more and more people today are moving from suburbs to downtown areas."

**Evidence Item 2**

"Hair-Dooz, our chief competitor at the mall, has just relocated downtown and is thriving at its new location."

**Evidence Item 3**

> "[T]he most prosperous hair salon in nearby Brainard is located in that city's downtown area."

**TIP**

Without exception, each Argument in the official GRE exam pool contains at least three or four distinct assumptions or other problems—that's how the test-makers design them. Make sure you review the section of this chapter where we examine in detail the most common GRE Argument flaws.

Next, analyze each item to determine how much support it lends to the Argument's intermediate and final conclusions. The test directions that you'll view just before your Argument prompt will instruct you to look for unsubstantiated or unreasonable assumptions on which the Argument's conclusions depend. For example, an Argument might rely on one of the following assumptions but fail to provide evidence to support the assumption:

- An event that occurs after another one has been caused by the other (a false-cause problem).

- Two things that are similar in one way are similar in other ways (a false-analogy problem).

- A statistical sample of a group is representative of the group as a whole.

The test's directions will also instruct you to check for problems with the Argument's internal logic—for example, the Argument is self-contradictory or employs circular reasoning. Just as with your Issue essay, don't filter your ideas during the crucial brainstorming step. Just put them all down on paper for the time being; you'll sort them out in step 3.

Here's what a test-taker's notes for Argument Statement 1 might look like after a few minutes of brainstorming:

---

*inter. concl.—UC will gain customers downtown*
*final concl.—UC will improve profits downtown*

- *demog. study—is Apton typical?    no trend*
                                        *reverse trend*

- *success of HD—is location key?    marketing*
                                        *key stylist*

- *success of B salon—downtown location key?*
                        *—is Apton like Brainard? (demog.)*

- *other problems*
    *—relocation expenses offset revenues*
    *—UC must establish new clientele*
    *—competition from HD*
      *(suff. demand for both salons?)*
    *—demand for "upscale" salon downtown?*

---

### Step 3: Organize and Prioritize Your Points of Critique (1 minute)

Using your notes from step 2 as a guide, arrange your ideas into paragraphs (probably three or four, depending on the number of problems built into the Argument). Take a minute to consider whether any of the flaws you identified overlap, and whether you can separate any of them into two distinct problems. In many cases, the best way to organize your points of critique is to put them in the same order in which the reasoning problems arise in the Argument itself.

As with the Issue essay, you can probably use your notes as your outline, numbering them according to how they'd most logically arise in discussion. Here's how the test-taker's notes for Argument Statement 1 look after she organizes them. (The arrows indicate where she intends to discuss a point; "[FC]" refers to final conclusion.)

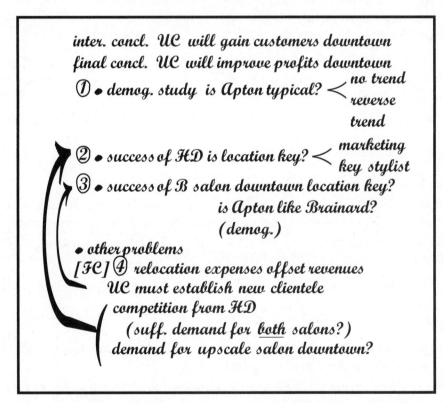

### Step 4: Compose a Brief Introductory Paragraph (2 minutes)

Now that you've planned your essay, you have to compose it. Don't waste time repeating the quoted Argument; the reader is already familiar with it and is interested in your critique, not your transcribing skills. Here are the three things you should try to accomplish in your initial paragraph:

❶ Identify the Argument's final conclusion.

❷ Describe briefly the Argument's line of reasoning and evidence in support of its conclusion.

❸ Allude generally to the problems with the Argument's line of reasoning and use of evidence.

You can probably accomplish all three task in two or three sentences. Here's a concise introductory paragraph of a response to Argument Statement 1:

**Introductory Paragraph (Argument Statement 1)**

Citing a general demographic trend and certain evidence about two other hair salons, the manager of UpperCuts (UC) concludes here that UC should relocate from suburban to downtown Apton in order to attract more customers and, in turn, improve its profitability. However, the manager's argument relies on a series of unproven assumptions and is therefore unconvincing as it stands.

Because your introductory sentences are the least important component of your essay, you may want to consider holding off on composing the introduction until you've completed your critique of the Argument. If you do this, and you start to run out of time for your introduction, begin your essay with a sentence like one of the following two, then delve right into your first point of critique—without a paragraph break:

This argument suffers from numerous flaws which, considered together, render the conclusion that UpperCuts should relocate to downtown Apton untenable. One such flaw involves . . . .

I find the argument for moving UpperCuts salon downtown specious at best, because it relies on a series of unproven, and doubtful, assumptions. One such assumption is that . . .

## Step 5: Compose the Body of Your Essay (16 minutes)

As with the Issue essay, when you're composing the body of your response, your chief aim is to peck madly at your keyboard to get your orders from your brain and scratch paper into the computer. Here's what to keep in mind as you compose your body paragraphs:

- Try to devote a separate paragraph to each major point of your critique—but be flexible. Sometimes it makes more sense to discuss related points in the same paragraph.

- Be sure that the first sentence of each paragraph conveys the essence of the problem you're dealing with in that paragraph.

- For each of the Argument's assumptions, explain how the Argument relies on the assumption. It might help to provide one or two examples or counterexamples (a hypothetical scenario) that, if true, would undermine the assumption.

- Devote no more than three or four sentences to any one point in your outline. Otherwise, you risk running out of time without discussing all of the Argument's major assumptions or other problems.

- Arrange your paragraphs so that your essay flows logically from one point to the next.

- Don't worry if you don't have time to discuss every single point of critique or every example you jotted down during step 2. Remember, GRE essay readers understand your time constraint.

Here's the body of a test-taker's response to Argument Statement 1. As you read these paragraphs, notice that each one addresses a distinct and critical assumption—a

**TIP**

Try to stick to your outline, but be flexible. Start with whichever points of critique strike you as the most important and easiest to articulate. You can always rearrange your points later using the GRE word processor's cut-and-paste feature.

certain condition that must be true to justify one of the Argument's conclusions. Also, notice that each paragraph describes at least one scenario that, if true, would undermine an assumption.

**Four-Paragraph Body (Argument Statement 1)**

One such assumption is that Apton reflects the cited demographic trend. The mere fact that one hair salon has moved downtown hardly suffices to show that the national trend applies to Apton specifically. For all we know, in Apton there is no such trend, or perhaps the trend is in the opposite direction, in which event the manager's recommendation would amount to especially poor advice.

Even assuming that downtown Apton is attracting more residents, relocating downtown might not result in more customers for UC, especially if downtown residents are not interested in UC's upscale style and prices. Besides, Hair-Dooz might draw potential customers away from UC, just as it might have at the mall. Without ruling out these and other reasons why UC might not benefit from the trend, the manager can't convince me that UC would attract more customers by moving downtown.

Even if there were a high demand for UC's services in downtown Apton, an increase in the number of patrons would not necessarily improve UC's profitability. UC's expenses might be higher downtown, in which case it might be no more, or perhaps even less, profitable downtown than at the mall.

As for the Brainard salon, its success might be the result of factors that don't apply to UC. For example, perhaps the Brainard salon thrives only because it is long established in downtown Brainard. Or perhaps hair salons generally fare better in downtown Brainard than downtown Apton because of demographic differences between the two areas. In short, the manager simply cannot justify his proposal on the basis of the Brainard salon's success.

## Step 6: Compose a Final Paragraph (2 minutes)

This step, like step 4, is not as crucial as the others, but providing a recap at the end of your Argument essay helps to demonstrate control over the writing task—so try to make time to "wrap up" your analysis.

This paragraph is *not* the place to point out additional problems with the Argument. Instead, we suggest two alternative approaches. One is to briefly touch on either (or both) of the following, which the test's directions indicate you may discuss at your option.

**1** How the Argument might be strengthened

**2** What additional information is needed to evaluate the Argument

Here are two alternative final paragraphs for our UpperCuts essay, each of which incorporates one of the two additional elements listed above.

- In short, the argument depends on certain unsubstantiated assumptions that render it dubious at best. To strengthen the argument, the manager should provide better evidence of a demographic shift toward downtown Apton and provide clear evidence that the shift portends success there for an upscale salon.

**TIP**

You can boost your Argument task score by mentioning briefly what additional information would help you evaluate the Argument and/or what additional evidence would help strengthen it.

- In sum, the argument provides inadequate evidence for the assumptions on which its conclusion depends. To better evaluate the argument, I would need to know (1) why Hair-Dooz relocated; (2) what factors have contributed to the Brainard salon's success; (3) what factors other than location might have contributed to UC's sagging profits at the mall; and (4) what additional offsetting expenses UC might incur at the new location.

Another approach to a final paragraph is to simply recapitulate the Argument's problems in two or three sentences. Here's a final paragraph for our UpperCuts essay that accomplishes this objective. Notice that it does not introduce any new points of critique. Rather, it simply sums up the Argument's major problems and stresses that it is problematic.

- In sum, the argument relies on what might amount to two poor analogies between UC and two other salons, as well as a sweeping generalization about demographic trends that may or may not apply to Apton. Thus, even though the manager has provided some scant evidence to support the recommendation, on balance I find the argument unconvincing at best.

From beginning to end, including the introduction, this sample essay is about 400 words long—brief enough to plan and write in 30 minutes. It's well organized, it articulates the Argument's major assumptions, it supports each point of critique with sound reasoning and relevant examples, and it's crisp, clear, and convincing. In short, it contains all the elements of a successful GRE Argument essay.

## Step 7: Proofread for Mechanical Problems (5 minutes)

Be sure to reserve time to check the flow of your essay. Pay special attention to the first sentence of each paragraph, and check to see whether you should rearrange paragraphs in a more logical sequence. Also, proofread for mechanical problems. Your Argument essay, like your Issue essay, need not be flawless to earn a high score. GRE readers aren't looking for the occasional awkward sentence or minor errors in punctuation, spelling, grammar, or diction, and you won't lose points for them. Use whatever time you have left after composing your essay to read it from start to finish and fix the most glaring mechanical problems. Correct spelling errors only when they might prevent the reader from understanding the point at hand. Don't bother spending time correcting punctuation, removing extra character spaces, or correcting minor spelling errors. Above all, don't get pulled into drastic rewriting. Accept that your essay is what it is; you don't have time to reshape it.

## TIPS FOR SPOTTING COMMON REASONING FLAWS

Remember, the main point of a GRE Argument is meant to be disputed. GRE test designers intentionally incorporate into each Argument a number of reasoning flaws that render it vulnerable to criticism.

### How to Handle Common Reasoning Flaws

In a typical GRE Argument statement, you can find three or four distinct points for critique. Here are the most common types of flaws in GRE Argument statements. If you have time, try to review this list several times, so you can better brainstorm and ferret out flaws in the actual GRE Argument statement.

- Confusing cause-and-effect with mere correlation or time sequence
- Drawing a weak analogy between two objects, causes, or ideas
- Relying on a potentially unrepresentative statistical sample
- Relying on a potentially unreliable survey or poll
- Assuming that a certain condition is necessary and/or sufficient for a specific outcome
- Assuming that characteristics of a group apply to each group member (or assuming the reverse: that characteristics of one group member apply to all members)
- Assuming that all things remain unchanged over time
- Assuming that two courses of action are mutually exclusive
- Relying on undefined, vague, or ambiguous terms
- Relying on ambiguous or conflicting evidence
- Drawing an overly broad conclusion
- Arguing simultaneously for competing objectives
- Engaging in circular reasoning

#### CONFUSING CAUSE-AND-EFFECT WITH CORRELATION OR TIME SEQUENCE

Many GRE Arguments rely on the claim that certain events cause other certain events. This so-called cause-and-effect claim might be based on either of these two assumptions:

1. There is a significant correlation between the occurrence of two phenomena (both phenomena generally occur together).

2. A temporal relationship exists between the two (one event occurred after the other).

A significant correlation or a temporal relationship between two phenomena is one indication of a cause-and-effect relationship between them. However, neither in itself proves such a relationship. Unless the Argument also considers—and eliminates—all other plausible causes of the presumed "result," the Argument is vulnerable to criticism. To show the essay reader that you understand this sort of false-cause problem, you need to succeed at all three of the following tasks:

**ALERT!**

The sample Arguments in this section are each designed to focus on one particular type of reasoning flaw. Keep in mind, however, that most of the Arguments on the actual GRE are longer and more involved, and may involve several types of reasoning flaws.

**1** **Identify** the false-cause problem (for example, as one of the Argument's crucial assumptions).

**2** **Elucidate** by providing at least one or two examples of other possible causes.

**3** **Explain** how the false-cause problem undermines the Argument.

Here's an example of an Argument in which causation is confused with temporal sequence, followed by a succinct and effective critique.

**Argument Statement 2**

The following appeared in the editorial section of a newspaper:

"Two years ago, State X enacted a law prohibiting environmental emissions of certain nitrocarbon byproducts, on the basis that these byproducts have been shown to cause Urkin's disease in humans. Last year, fewer State X residents reported symptoms of Urkin's disease than in any prior year. Since the law is clearly effective in preventing the disease, in the interest of public health, this state should adopt a similar law."

**Response**

The editorial infers that State X's new law is responsible for the apparent decline in the incidence of Urkin's disease (UD) symptoms. However, the editorial's author ignores other possible causes of the decline; for example, a new UD cure or new treatment for UD symptoms. Without eliminating alternative explanations such as these, the author cannot justify either the inference or the additional assertion that a similar law would be equally effective in the author's state.

## DRAWING A WEAK ANALOGY BETWEEN TWO OBJECTS, CAUSES, OR IDEAS

A GRE Argument might draw a conclusion about one thing—say, a city, school, or company—based on observation about a similar thing. In doing so, however, the Argument assumes that because the two things are similar in certain respects, they are similar in all respects, at least as far as the Argument is concerned. Unless the Argument provides sufficient evidence to substantiate this assumption (and it won't), the Argument is vulnerable to criticism. The Argument cannot rely on these claims to support its recommendation.

To show the GRE essay reader that you understand this problem, you need to accomplish the following three tasks:

**1** **Identify** the analogy as one of the Argument's crucial assumptions.

**2** **Elucidate** by providing at least one example of how the two things might differ.

**3** **Explain** how these differences, which render the analogy weak, undermine the Argument's conclusion.

Here's an Argument that contains a questionable analogy, followed by an effective three-sentence analysis:

### Argument Statement 3

The following was part of a speech made by the principal of Valley High School:

"Every year, Dunston High School wins the school district's student Math Super Bowl competition. The average salary of teachers at Dunston is greater than at any other school in the district. Hence, for Valley High students to improve their scores on the state's standardized achievement exams, Valley should begin awarding bonuses to Valley teachers whenever Valley defeats Dunston in the Math Super Bowl."

### Response

The principal's recommendation relies on what might be a poor analogy between Dunston and Valley. Valley teachers may be less responsive than Dunston teachers to monetary incentives, or Valley students might be less gifted in math than Dunston students. In short, what might have helped Dunston perform well at the Math Super Bowl would not necessarily help Valley perform better either at the Super Bowl or on the state exams.

## RELYING ON A POTENTIALLY UNREPRESENTATIVE STATISTICAL SAMPLE

A GRE Argument may cite statistics from a study, survey, or poll involving a "sample" group, then draw a conclusion about a larger group or population that the sample supposedly represents. To accurately reflect a larger population, though, the sample needs to meet two requirements:

**1** The sample must be a significantly sized portion or percentage of the overall population.

**2** The sample must represent the relevant characteristics of the overall population.

Arguments that cite statistics from studies, surveys, and polls often fail to establish either of these two requirements. Of course, this failure is built into the Argument by the GRE test designer, who is "inviting" you to question the reliability of the evidence. To show the reader that you understand this problem, you need to accomplish the following three tasks:

**1** **Identify** the analogy as one of the Argument's crucial assumptions.

**2** **Elucidate** by providing at least one way in which the two things might differ.

**3** **Explain** how these differences, which render the analogy weak, undermine the Argument's conclusion.

Here's an Argument that relies on two potentially unrepresentative sample groups: (1) new graduates from a certain state's undergraduate programs, and (2) new graduates from the state's graduate-level programs. The response following it provides a brief but effective critique.

### Argument Statement 4

The following was part of an article appearing in a national magazine:

"Our nation's new college graduates will have better success obtaining jobs if they do not pursue advanced degrees after graduation. After all, more than 90% of State X's undergraduate students are employed full-time within one year after they graduate, while less than half of State X's graduate-level students find employment within one year after receiving their graduate degrees."

**Response**

The argument fails to consider that State X's new graduates might not be representative of the nation's graduates, especially if the former group constitutes only a small percentage of the latter group. If it turns out, for example, that State X's undergraduate students are less motivated than the nation's average college student to pursue graduate-level study, then the argument's recommendation for all undergraduate students is unwarranted.

## RELYING ON A POTENTIALLY UNRELIABLE SURVEY OR POLL

As you just learned, a GRE Argument may draw some conclusion involving a group based on statistical data about an insufficient or nonrepresentative sample of that group. However, this is not the only potential problem with statistical data. If the process of collecting the data is flawed, then the quality of the data is also questionable, rendering it "tainted" and therefore unreliable for drawing valid conclusions. For survey or poll results to be reliable in quality:

- Responses must be truthful and accurate. If respondents have reason to provide incomplete or false responses, the results are tainted and therefore unreliable.

- The data collection method must be unbiased. If responses aren't mandatory or if the survey's form predisposes subjects to respond in certain ways, then the results are tainted and therefore unreliable.

To show the GRE essay reader that you recognize and understand this problem, you must accomplish the following three tasks:

**❶ Identify** the problem as one of the Argument's crucial assumptions.

**❷ Elucidate** by providing at least one reason, based on the Argument's information, why the statistical data might be tainted.

**❸ Explain** how the potentially tainted data can undermine the Argument's conclusion.

The following Argument relies on a survey that poses a potential bias and a credibility problem. In a single paragraph, the response contains all three of these elements for addressing each problem.

**Argument Statement 5**

The following appeared in a memo from the director of human resources at Webco:

"Among Webco employees participating in our department's most recent survey, about half indicated that they are happy with our current four-day workweek. These survey results show that the most effective way to improve overall productivity at Webco is to allow each employee to choose for himself or herself either a four-day or five-day workweek."

**Response**

The survey methodology is problematic in two respects. First, we are not told whether the survey required that respondents choose their workweek preference between the stated choices. If it did, the results might distort the preferences of the respondents, who might very well prefer a work schedule choice that wasn't addressed on the survey. Secondly, we are not informed whether survey responses were anonymous or even confidential. If they weren't, it's possible that respondents may have answered in ways they believed their superiors would approve of, regardless of whether these answers were truthful. In either event, the survey results would be unreliable for the purpose of drawing conclusions about Webco employee preferences, let alone about how to improve overall productivity at Webco.

## ASSUMING THAT A CERTAIN CONDITION IS NECESSARY AND/OR SUFFICIENT FOR A SPECIFIC OUTCOME

A GRE Argument might recommend a certain course of action based on one or both of the following claims:

- The course of action is *necessary* to achieve a desired result.

- The course of action is *sufficient* to achieve the desired result.

For the first claim to hold water, the Argument must provide evidence that no other means of achieving the same result are available. For the second claim to be true, the Argument must provide strong evidence that the proposed course of action by itself would bring about the desired result. Lacking this sort of evidence, the Argument cannot rely on these two claims to support its recommendation.

To show that you understand necessary-condition and sufficient-condition problems, you must accomplish the following three tasks in your essay:

**1** **Identify** the problem as one of the Argument's crucial assumptions.

**2** **Elucidate** by providing at least one example. For a necessary-condition problem, suggest other means of achieving the stated objective. For a sufficient-condition problem, suggest other conditions that might be necessary for the outcome.

**3** **Explain** how the problem undermines the Argument's conclusion.

Here's an Argument that assumes that a certain condition is necessary for a certain outcome. The response provides a brief, incisive analysis of the problem.

**Argument Statement 6**

The following appeared in a memo from a vice president at Toyco, which operates a large chain of toy stores:

"Last year was the first year in which Playtime Stores, our main competitor, sold more toys than Toyco. Playtime's compensation for its retail sales force is based entirely on their sales. If Toyco is to recapture its leadership position in the toy-sales market, we must reestablish our former policy of requiring all our retail associates to meet strict sales quotas in order to retain their jobs."

**Response**

> The argument assumes that the proposed compensation policy is the only way that Toyco can once again sell more toys than Playtime. However, the vice president fails to consider and rule out possible alternative means of achieving this end; for example, opening new stores or adding new types of toys to its stores' merchandise, to name just a few. Until the vice president does so, I will remain unconvinced that the proposed policy is a necessary means for Toyco to recapture market leadership.

## ASSUMING THAT CHARACTERISTICS OF A GROUP APPLY TO EACH GROUP MEMBER

A GRE Argument might point out a fact about a general group, such as students, employees, or cities, to support a claim about a particular member of that group. Conversely, the Argument might point out a fact about a particular group member to support a claim about the entire group. In either case, unless the Argument supplies clear evidence that the member is representative of the group as a whole or vice-versa, the Argument is vulnerable to criticism.

To show that you understand a group-member problem, you must accomplish the following three tasks in your essay:

**1** **Identify** the problem as one of the Argument's crucial assumptions.

**2** **Elucidate** by providing at least one example of a way in which the member might differ from the general group, or vice-versa.

**3** **Explain** how those key differences, which refute the original assumption, undermine the Argument's conclusion.

Here's an Argument that assumes that characteristics of a particular member of a group apply to the group as a whole. The response shows how to handle the problem in one succinct paragraph.

**Argument Statement 7**

> The following is part of an article appearing in the entertainment section of a local newspaper:

> "At the local Viewer Choice video store, the number of available movies in VHS format remains about the same as three years ago, even though the number of available movies on DVD has increased tenfold in the same period. People who predict that the VHS format will become obsolete are mistaken, since demand for VHS movie rentals today clearly remains just as strong as ever."

**Response**

> This argument assumes that Video Choice (VC) is typical of all video stores as a group, but this isn't necessarily the case. VC might carry far more VHS tapes as a percentage of its total inventory than the average store. If so, then the argument has failed to discredit the prediction for the industry as a whole.

## ASSUMING THAT ALL THINGS REMAIN UNCHANGED OVER TIME

A GRE Argument might rely on evidence collected in the past to formulate a conclusion or recommendation about the present or the future. Similarly, an Argument may rely on evidence about present conditions to make a prediction or recommendation. Unless the Argument provides clear evidence that key circumstances have remained or will remain unchanged over the relevant time period, the Argument is vulnerable to criticism.

To address this problem, you must accomplish the following three tasks in your essay:

❶ **Identify** the problem (that is, the assumption that all key circumstances remain fixed over time).

❷ **Elucidate** by providing examples of conditions that may change.

❸ **Evaluate** the argument in light of the problem.

The following Argument provides evidence based on the past to draw a conclusion about the present and future. The response addresses the problem in three sentences.

**Argument Statement 8**

The following appeared in a political campaign advertisement:

"Residents of this state should vote to elect Kravitz as state governor in the upcoming election. During Kravitz's final term as a state senator, she was a member of a special legislative committee that explored ways the state can reduce its escalating rate of violent crime. Elect Kravitz for governor, and our cities' streets will be safer than ever."

**Response**

Assuming that at one time Kravitz was genuinely committed to fighting violent crime, the ad infers a similar commitment today and in the future while Kravitz serves as governor. But Kravitz might hold entirely different views today, especially if her participation as a member of the committee occurred some time ago. Lacking better evidence that as governor Kravitz would continue to make crime-fighting a high priority, the ad cannot persuade me to vote for Kravitz based on her committee membership.

## ASSUMING THAT TWO COURSES OF ACTION ARE MUTUALLY EXCLUSIVE

An Argument might recommend one course of action over another to achieve the stated objective without considering the possibility of pursuing both courses, which might increase the likelihood of achieving the objective. Here's a good example, followed by a response that addresses the flaw.

**Argument Statement 9**

Rivertown's historic Hill district was once one of the city's main tourist attractions. Recently, however, the district's quaint, older shops and restaurants have had difficulty attracting patrons. To reverse the district's decline in tourism, Rivertown's City Council intends to approve construction on a new shopping center called Hill Hub on one of the district's few remaining vacant parcels. However, the city's interests in attracting tourism revenue would be better served were it to focus instead on restoring Hill district's

**ALERT!**

An Argument that suffers from this "either-or" reasoning problem will likely overlook other courses of action that might also achieve the stated objective. (In other words, neither course of action is a necessary condition.) When this occurs, be sure to address it as well.

older buildings and waging a publicity campaign touting the historically authentic character of the district.

**Response**

The argument seems to assume that the city must either approve the Hill Hub project or engage in the restoration and publicity efforts that the argument suggests, but not both. However, it provides no evidence that the city must choose between the two courses of action rather than following both. Lacking any such evidence, it is entirely possible that implementing both plans would attract more tourism revenue for the district than implementing either one alone.

## RELYING ON UNDEFINED, VAGUE, OR AMBIGUOUS TERMS

An Argument might contain a statement, word, or phrase that carries more than one possible meaning or is too vague to reasonably rely upon it for accurate conclusions. Look for the words "some," "many," and "several" as replacements for precise percentages or numbers. Also be on the alert for references to particular classes, categories, or groups without a clear explanation of what they include or exclude. The following provides an example of this error, with an effective response.

**Argument Statement 10**

A reliable recent study attests to the value of physical activity in increasing the attention spans of young children. Accordingly, to improve the overall learning levels among elementary school children in our state, the state's board of education should mandate a daily exercise regimen for students at all state elementary schools.

**Response**

The argument does not indicate what types of "physical activity" the study observed. For all I know, those activities amounted to play rather than a recommended exercise "regimen," which might seem more like work in children's eyes. Nor does the Argument indicate the age range of the "young children" observed in the study. Perhaps the children were preschoolers, whose attention spans might respond differently than school-age children to certain types of physical activity. In short, before I can determine the extent to which the study supports the recommendation, I need specific definitions of these important terms.

## RELYING ON AMBIGUOUS OR CONFLICTING EVIDENCE

A GRE Argument might provide evidence that supports one conclusion just as much as it supports another. To the extent that the Argument draws either conclusion without acknowledging the other possible conclusion, it is vulnerable to criticism. Here's an example, followed by an effective response:

**Argument Statement 11**

To boost sagging profits at UpperCuts hair salon, the salon's owner should relocate UpperCuts from its current location in Apton's suburban mall to downtown Apton, where it can take over the space occupied by another hair salon that is going out of business. Hair-Dooz, UpperCuts' chief competitor at the mall, has just relocated to downtown and is thriving there. Besides, in neighboring Brainard, the most successful hair salon is located in that city's downtown area.

**Response**

The argument relies on conflicting evidence to reach its conclusion. While the fact that two successful hair salons are located in downtown areas might suggest that downtown business is thriving, the business failure of the salon whose space UpperCuts intends to occupy suggests just the opposite. Without additional information about the reason for that salon's failure, the argument for relocating downtown is uncompelling at best.

## DRAWING AN OVERLY BROAD CONCLUSION

A GRE Argument's conclusion might be well supported, but only to a certain extent, or only with respect to a certain subclass. An Argument that fails to limit the degree or scope of its conclusion in accordance with the evidence is vulnerable to criticism. Here's an example, followed by an effective response:

**Argument Statement 12**

Many snorers awaken frequently during sleep to catch their breath—often so briefly that they are unaware that they are awake (a condition called sleep apnea). As a result, they are too tired during normal waking hours to exercise. Data collected during a recent study suggests, not surprisingly, that snorers are more likely to gain weight than other people. Therefore, any person who snores should try to eat less and exercise more than the average person.

**Response**

The argument's advice that "anyone who snores" should try to eat less and exercise is unwarranted. It is entirely possible that some—perhaps even most—snorers do not suffer from sleep apnea, are not too tired to exercise, or do not in any event tend to gain weight. Without ruling out these possibilities, the argument should be modified to expressly limit the advice to those snorers whose snoring causes weight gain.

## ARGUING SIMULTANEOUSLY FOR COMPETING OBJECTIVES

A GRE Argument might seek to achieve two distinct objectives that appear to compete with each other. In other words, accomplishing one objective decreases the likelihood of achieving the other. Here's an example, followed by an effective response:

**Argument Statement 13**

A significant percentage of Harris County residents who receive unemployment benefits from the state report that they would prefer to work but have difficulty finding work for which they are qualified. Payment of these benefits increases the economic burden on our state's taxpayers, who of course fund these benefits. In order to reduce this burden and to put more of our state's unemployed people to work, the state should provide additional funding to Harris County for the purpose of establishing and administering an adult job-training program.

### Response

The argument recommends additional state expenditures, presumably at taxpayers' expense, in the interest of putting more unemployed people to work. In doing so, the argument essentially wants to have it both ways, but it can't. By establishing a job-training program, the state might alleviate unemployment; at the same time, however, the additional expense of the program would exacerbate the taxpayers' economic burden. The argument should be modified to either prioritize the two competing objectives or explain how the two might be reconciled.

### ENGAGING IN CIRCULAR REASONING

A GRE Argument might rely, at least partly, on its own line of reasoning to support that very reasoning. This is known as *circular reasoning* or *tautology;* it's sometimes referred to as "begging the question." Did you catch the circular reasoning in the earlier argument about sleep apnea? Here's the argument again, along with a paragraph-length response that addresses its circular reasoning:

### Argument Statement 14

Many snorers awaken frequently during sleep to catch their breath—often so briefly that they are unaware that they are awake (a condition called sleep apnea). As a result, they are too tired during normal waking hours to exercise. Data collected during a recent study suggests, not surprisingly, that snorers are more likely to gain weight than other people. Therefore, any person who snores should try to eat less and exercise more than the average person.

### Response

The advice to exercise more is logically unsound. If a person with sleep apnea is too tired to exercise as a result of losing sleep, then simply advising that person to exercise begs the question: What should the person do to eliminate the cause of the tiredness? Thus the speaker should determine the cause of sleep apnea and modify the advice so that it targets that cause. Of course, if it turns out that weight gain is one cause of snoring and sleep apnea, then the speaker's advice that snorers should try to eat less would have considerable merit. Yet, without any evidence that this is the case, the speaker's advice might be at least partially ineffective in counteracting a snorer's tendency to gain weight.

## ARGUMENT TASK STRATEGIES

Here's a quick rundown of our very best advice for composing a GRE Argument essay. Many of them reiterate suggestions we've already made in this chapter, but they're well worth reviewing. Apply these points of advice to the practice tests in this book, and then review them again just before exam day.

### Ferreting Out the Flaws Is Half the Battle

Built into each and every GRE Argument statement are at least three or four distinct reasoning problems. That's how the test-makers design them. To earn a high score, your essay must first and foremost identify these problems. After you brainstorm and make notes, check to see how many major flaws you've isolated. If you haven't picked up at least three assumptions or problems with logic, then you can be fairly certain that you've missed at least one. Read the Argument again more carefully. Even a few words you overlooked the first time can be key.

Ration your time to be sure that you can let the reader know you've recognized each and every problem listed in your notes. Don't worry if 30 minutes isn't enough time to discuss each problem in detail. When it comes to analyzing GRE Arguments, remember that breadth is better than depth.

## Viewpoints and Opinions Don't Matter

In sharp contrast to the Issue essay, your Argument essay is not the place to present viewpoints or opinions about an issue that the Argument might touch upon. Instead, your analysis must focus strictly on the Argument's logical features and on how strongly its evidence supports its conclusions. For instance, consider an Argument for electing a certain political candidate because she has a record of being tough on crime. In an Issue essay about the problem of violent crime, it would be highly appropriate to present various viewpoints on this social issue, weighing alternative approaches to the problem in general. But when you're writing an Argument essay, such viewpoints are irrelevant.

## Support Every Point of Critique

You need to back up each point of your critique with at least one example or counter-example that helps the reader see the particular flaw you're pointing out. Keep your examples and counterexamples hypothetical ("What if . . . ," "Suppose that . . . ," "It's possible that . . . ," "Perhaps . . ."). You needn't go into great detail; one or two examples for each point of critique will suffice—but make sure each one is backed up or your score might suffer.

What if you think you won't have enough time to provide supporting detail for each point of critique? Don't despair. Look for two or three points that are related to the same item of evidence (for example, those involving the same statistical survey). Then plan to touch briefly on each one *in the same paragraph*. Grouping them together will make sense to the reader, who may not notice what's missing as much as the fact that you're very organized.

## Don't Look for the "Fatal Flaw"

Instead, treat every problem as a contributing cause. Avoid dwelling on one particular flaw that you think is the most serious one, or on one realistic example or counterexample that you think, if true, would spell certain death for the entire Argument. If you do, you'll risk running out of time. Don't bother trying to rank flaws as more or less serious, either. True, one particular flaw might be more damaging to an Argument than others. But by identifying it as "the most serious problem with the Argument," you're committing yourself to defending this claim above all others. Do you really have time for this kind of analysis? No! Nor does the GRE reader expect or want this from you. In short, you're best off applying equal treatment to each of the Argument's problems.

## There's No Need to Impress with Technical Terminology

Scholars in the academic fields of Critical Reasoning and Logic rely on all manner of formal terminology for the kinds of reasoning flaws you'll find in GRE Arguments. For example, *post hoc* reasoning refers to a faulty construct best described as "after this, therefore, because of this" reasoning. You won't score any points with GRE readers by tossing around such terminology in your Argument essay, however. Besides, if you use a technical term, you should define it for the reader—and this only consumes precious time.

## Go with the Logical Flow

Try to organize your points of critique to reflect the Argument's line of reasoning, from its evidence and assumptions to its intermediate conclusion (if any), and then to its final conclusion. Fortunately, most GRE Arguments are already organized this way, so that your points of critique can simply follow the quoted Argument from beginning to end. But don't assume that this sequence will be the most logical one. Regardless of the sequence of ideas in the quoted Argument, you should try to group all points of critique involving the same item of evidence (for example, a statistical survey or study). And of course, it's logical to address problems involving the Argument's intermediate conclusion before those involving its final conclusion.

## Appear Organized and in Control

As with the Issue essay, use every means at your disposal to show the reader that, even when working under significant time pressure, you know how to organize your ideas and convey them in writing. Use logical paragraph breaks, present your points of critique in a logical sequence, and try to save time for brief introductory and concluding paragraphs.

## Remember Your Primary Objectives

The official scoring criteria for the Argument essay boil down to four questions that you should keep in mind during the 30 minutes of formulating and writing your essay:

❶ Have I clearly identified each of the Argument's major assumptions or logic problems according to the directive for the essay?

❷ Can I support each point of my critique with at least one relevant example or counterexample?

❸ Do I have in mind a clear, logical structure for presenting my points of critique? Once you can confidently answer "Yes" to each question, start composing your essay. When you've finished your draft, ask yourself the same questions, along with this fourth one:

❹ Have I demonstrated good grammar, diction, and syntax?

If you can answer "Yes" to all four questions, be assured that you've produced a solid, high-scoring Argument essay.

## SUMMING IT UP

- The Argument writing task comes immediately before or after the Issue writing task on the GRE. It consists of one essay, for which you have 30 minutes. Your job is to discuss how well-reasoned you find a particular Argument—specifically, its unsubstantiated or unreasonable assumptions, problems with the Argument's internal logic or line of reasoning, how it might be strengthened (optional), and what additional information is needed to better evaluate the Argument (optional).

- Follow the 7-step plan in this chapter to score high on this essay. Give yourself time before you begin writing to organize your thoughts, and time after you're finished writing to fine-tune your essay.

- To score high on the Argument writing task, practice writing essays in which you work on these techniques: identify and analyze the Argument's key elements; organize, develop, and express your critique in a coherent and logically convincing manner; support your ideas with sound reasons and examples; and demonstrate adequate control of the elements of Standard Written English (grammar, syntax, and usage).

- Follow and review the Argument task strategies in this chapter and apply them to this book's Practice Tests. Then review them again just before exam day.

# Writing Style and Mechanics

## OVERVIEW

- Use rhetorical words and phrases
- Avoid empty rhetoric
- Use irony as a rhetorical device
- Use punctuation for emphasis
- Connect your ideas
- Use the language of critical reasoning properly
- Refer to yourself, the statement, or the argument—as needed
- Maintain proper tone and voice
- Vary sentence length and structure
- Write clearly and concisely
- Use language correctly and persuasively
- Summing it up

In the previous two chapters, you learned how to develop persuasive and incisive ideas and how to organize your ideas so that they flow logically and coherently in your GRE essays. Now that you've laid that foundation, it's time to pay close attention to *how you express* your ideas.

As you know by now, GRE essay readers place less weight on writing style and mechanics than on content and organization. However, the way you write can affect your GRE Analytical Writing score, especially if you've written an otherwise borderline essay that leaves the reader trying to decide between a higher or lower score, or if the reader has trouble understanding your ideas because you've expressed them poorly. So, to ensure a high Analytical Writing score, you need to make sure your essays are the following:

- Persuasive in style (by the effective use of rhetorical devices)
- Appropriate in tone and "voice" for graduate-level writing
- Varied in sentence length and structure (to add interest and to demonstrate maturity in writing style)
- Clear and concise (easy to follow, and direct rather than wordy or verbose)
- Correct in diction, word usage, and idiom
- Correct in grammar and writing mechanics

## chapter 6

In the pages ahead, you'll learn how to improve your GRE writing in the ways listed above. Don't worry if you don't have a knack for writing effective prose. You can improve your writing for the GRE, even if your time is short.

## USE RHETORICAL WORDS AND PHRASES

**NOTE**

While these advanced tips can certainly help you score higher on your GRE essays, refinement and maturity in writing style come mainly with practice. Make sure you apply what you learn here to the Practice Tests at the end of this book.

Here's a reference list of rhetorical words and phrases categorized by function. You've already encountered some of these items in the previous two chapters.

- **To subordinate an idea:** although it might appear that, admittedly

- **To argue a position, thesis, or viewpoint:** promotes, facilitates, provides a strong impetus, directly, furthers, accomplishes, achieves, demonstrates, suggests, indicates

- **To argue for a solution or direction based on a commonly held standard (such as public policy):** ultimate goal/objective/purpose, overriding, primary concern, subordinate, subsumed

- **To refute, rebut, or counter a proposition, theory, or viewpoint:** however, closer scrutiny reveals, upon closer inspection/examination, a more thorough analysis, in reality, actually, viewed more closely, viewed from another perspective, further observation shows

- **To point out problems with a proposition, theory, or viewpoint:** however, nevertheless, yet, still, despite, of course, serious drawbacks, problematic, countervailing factors

- **To argue against a position or viewpoint:** undermines, thwarts, defeats, runs contrary to, fails to achieve/promote/accomplish, is inconsistent with, impedes

- **To argue that the merits of one position outweigh those of another:** on balance, on the whole, all things considered, in the final analysis

## AVOID EMPTY RHETORIC

Many test-takers try to mask weak ideas by relying on strong rhetoric. But use caution when you use words and phrases such as these for emphasis:

| | | |
|---|---|---|
| clearly | absolutely | definitely |
| without a doubt | nobody could dispute that | extremely |
| positively | emphatically | unquestionably |
| certainly | undeniably | without reservation |

Although such phrases are perfectly acceptable, remember that by themselves, they add no substance to your ideas. Be sure that you have convincing reasons and/or examples to back up your rhetoric.

## USE IRONY AS A RHETORICAL DEVICE

In your Issue essay, you may want to look for the opportunity to use words in their ironic sense, or as misnomers, to add rhetorical emphasis. Read the Issue statement closely for key words to tip you off. Here's one example of each:

- **Irony:** The speaker fails to consider the long-term cultural impact of the kinds of technological "advancements" I've just described.

- **Misnomer:** The "knowledge" to which the statement refers is actually only subjective perception.

Be sure to use quotation marks around the ironic term or misnomer, regardless of whether you're quoting the Issue statement.

## USE PUNCTUATION FOR EMPHASIS

You can also use punctuation for rhetorical emphasis. Here are a few suggestions you may want to try out when taking the practice tests in this book:

- **Use em dashes.** Em dashes (two hyphens, or one hyphen preceded and followed by a space) can be used in the middle of a sentence—instead of commas or parentheses—to set off particularly important parenthetical material (just as in this sentence). You can also use an em dash before a concluding phrase instead of a comma—to help set off and emphasize what follows (just as in this sentence). Don't overuse the em dash, however, or it will lose its punch.

- **Use exclamation points for emphasis very sparingly.** As in this paragraph, one per essay is plenty!

- **Posing a rhetorical question can be a useful writing tool.** Like short, abrupt sentences, rhetorical questions can help persuade the reader, or at least help to make your point. They can be quite effective, especially in Issue essays. They also add interest and variety. Yet how many test-takers incorporate them into their essays? Not many. (By the way, we just posed a rhetorical question.) Be sure to provide an answer to your question. And don't overdo it; one rhetorical question per essay is plenty.

Don't confuse emphatic rhetorical speech with rhetorical writing. Avoid typing words in uppercase, adding asterisks or underlines before and after words, or employing similar devices to flag words you'd emphasize in speech. (This is a common practice in e-mails and instant messages.) Instead, rely on your sentence construction and your choice of words and phrases.

## CONNECT YOUR IDEAS

If the ideas you present in your GRE essays flow naturally from one to the next so that the reader can easily follow your train of thought, it's a good bet that you'll score high. To connect your ideas, you need to develop a personal "arsenal" of *transition devices*—words and phrases that bridge ideas and help you convey your line of reasoning.

**NOTE**

The GRE testing system's word processor does not permit attributes such as bolding, underlining, and italicizing, so those devices are not available to use for emphasis in your GRE essays in any event.

Each transition device should help the reader make the link between the two concepts you're connecting. Some of these devices lead your reader forward and imply the building of an idea or thought; others prompt the reader to compare ideas or draw conclusions from preceding ideas. Here's a reference list of transition devices categorized by function.

- **To signal addition:** and, again, and then, besides, equally important, finally, further, furthermore, nor, also, next, lastly, what's more

- **To connect ideas:** furthermore, additionally, in addition, also, first (or second, or third), moreover, most important/significantly, consequently, simultaneously, concurrently, next, finally

- **To signal comparison or contrast:** but, although, conversely, in contrast, on the other hand, whereas, except, by comparison, compared to, vis-à-vis, while, meanwhile

- **To signal proof:** because, for, since, for the same reason, obviously, evidently, furthermore, moreover, besides, indeed, in fact, in addition, in any case, that is

- **To signal exception:** yet, still, however, nevertheless, in spite of, despite, of course, occasionally, sometimes, in rare instances, infrequently

- **To signal chronological, logical, or rhetorical sequence:** first (or second, or third), next, then, now, at this point, after, in turn, subsequently, finally, consequently, previously, beforehand, simultaneously, concurrently

- **To signal examples:** for example, for instance, perhaps, consider, take the case of, to demonstrate, to illustrate, as an illustration, one possible scenario, in this case, in another case, on this occasion, in this situation

- **To signal the move from premise to conclusion:** therefore, thus, hence, accordingly, as a result, it follows that, in turn

- **To conclude or sum up your essay:** in sum, in the final analysis, in brief, in conclusion, to conclude, to recapitulate, in essence, in a nutshell

## USE THE LANGUAGE OF CRITICAL REASONING PROPERLY

You don't need to resort to the technical terminology of formal logic in your essays, nor should you. However, you will need to use less technical terms, such as "argument," "assumption," "conclusion," and possibly "premise" and "inference"—especially in your Argument essay. Make sure you not only know what these words mean, but that you also use them idiomatically. Here are some definitions and usage guidelines for these terms.

### Argument

An *argument* describes the process of reasoning from premises to conclusion. To describe a flawed argument, use adjectives such as *weak, poor, unsound, poorly reasoned, dubious, poorly supported,* or *problematic*. To describe a good argument, use adjectives such as *strong, convincing, well-reasoned,* or *well-supported*. You don't "prove an argument;" rather, you "prove an argument (to be) true." (However, the word "prove" implies deduction and should be used sparingly, if at all, in your Argument essay.)

## Premise

A *premise* is a proposition that helps to support an argument's conclusion. Use the words *premise* and *evidence* interchangeably to refer to stated information that is not in dispute.

## Assumption

When you make an assumption, you take for granted that a fact or statement is true in the argument. (Strictly speaking, *assumptions* are unstated, assumed premises.) To describe an assumption, use adjectives such as *unsupported, unsubstantiated,* or *unproven.* To describe a bad assumption, use adjectives such as *unlikely, poor, questionable, doubtful, dubious,* or *improbable.* To strengthen an argument, you *substantiate* an assumption or *prove* (or *show* or *demonstrate*) that the assumption is true.

But as mentioned above, use caution with the word *prove*; it is a strong word that implies deduction. Strictly speaking, an assumption is neither "true" nor "false," neither "correct" nor "incorrect." Also, you don't "prove an assumption."

## Conclusion

A *conclusion* is a proposition derived by deduction or inference from the premises of an argument. To describe a poor conclusion, use adjectives such as *indefensible, unjustified, unsupported, improbable,* or *weak*. To describe a good conclusion, use adjectives such as *well-supported, proper, probable, well-justified,* or *strong*. Although you can "prove a conclusion" or "provide proof for a conclusion," remember that the word *proof* implies deduction. You're better off "supporting a conclusion" or "showing that the conclusion is probable."

## Inference

*Inference* is the process of deriving from assumed premises either a strict conclusion or one that is probable to some degree. You can describe an inference as *poor, unjustified, improbable* or *unlikely,* or a good inference as *strong, justified, probable,* or *likely.* You can "infer that . . ."; but the phrase "infer a conclusion" is awkward.

## Deduction

*Deduction* is the process of reasoning in which the conclusion follows necessarily from the premises—a specific type of inference.

# REFER TO YOURSELF, THE STATEMENT, OR THE ARGUMENT— AS NEEDED

In your essay, you'll occasionally need to refer to the Issue or Argument statement and to its hypothetical source, whether it's a person or entity. You might also wish to refer to yourself from time to time. Here are a few tips for handling these references.

**ALERT!**

GRE Arguments *do not* involve deduction. All inferences and conclusions in the GRE Argument section involve probabilities rather than certainties, so there's no reason to use any form of the word "deduction" in your essay.

## Self-References

Singular or plural self-references are perfectly acceptable, though optional. Just be sure you're consistent. If you write "*I* disagree with" in one section of the essay, don't write "In *our* view" in another section.

## References to the Statement or Argument

In your Issue essay, refer to the statement as "this statement," or an alternative such as "this claim" or "this assertion." In your Argument essay, try using "argument" to refer to the passage's line of reasoning as a whole, or "recommendation" or "claim" to refer to specific conclusions.

## References to the Source of the Statement or Argument

Be sure your references to a statement or argument's source are appropriate. In your Issue essay, you can simply refer to the statement's source as the "speaker," for example. In your Argument essay, the first time you refer to the source, be specific and correct (for example, "this editorial," "the ad," "the vice president," or "ACME Shoes"). If no specific source is provided, try using "author" or "argument."

## Pronoun References

In your Argument essay, it's acceptable to use an occasional pronoun, but be sure that they're appropriate and consistent (male or female, singular or plural). For example:

> "The speaker argues . . . . *Her* line of reasoning is . . . ; but *she* overlooks . . . ."

> "The manager cites . . . in support of *his* argument . . . . *He* then recommends . . . ."

> "To strengthen *its* conclusion, the city council must . . . . *It* must also . . . ."

Make sure that your pronoun references are clear. If the pronoun will be separated from its antecedent by one or more sentences, don't use it.

## Shorthand References to an Argument's Source and Evidence

TIP

GRE essay readers will disregard whether you use masculine, feminine, or gender-neutral terms in your essays, so don't worry about being politically correct when it comes to gender. Gender-neutral pronouns are fine, but avoid alternating male and female gender expressions; you might confuse the reader.

It's perfectly acceptable to save keystrokes by using shorthand names or acronyms in place of multiple-word proper nouns. If you decide to do so, however, make sure you identify it the first time you use it. For example:

> In this argument, the marketing director for Specialty Manufacturing (SM) recommends that SM discontinue its line . . .

## Quoting the Statement or Argument

Occasionally, it may be appropriate to quote key words or phrases from the Issue statement or Argument statement. For example, you may wish to point out a key phrase that is ambiguous or vague ("certain respondents"), or a term that is overly inclusive or exclusive ("only" or "all"). This is fine, as long as you keep the number of quoted words and phrases to a minimum; there's never any justification for quoting entire sentences.

## MAINTAIN PROPER TONE AND VOICE

In any type of essay writing, you should maintain a somewhat formal tone throughout. An essay that comes across as conversational is probably too informal for the GRE.

The overall tone should be critical but not inflammatory or emotional. Don't overstate your position by using extreme or harsh language. Don't attempt to elicit a visceral or emotional response from the reader. Appeal instead to the reader's intellect.

A direct, even forceful voice is perfectly acceptable for making your main points. But don't overdo it; when it comes to the details, use a more dispassionate approach.

Don't try to make your point with "cutesy" or humorous remarks. Avoid puns, double meanings, plays on words, and other forms of humor. Likewise, sarcasm is entirely inappropriate for your GRE essays. The reader may not realize you're being sarcastic, in which case your remark will only serve to confuse him or her.

## VARY SENTENCE LENGTH AND STRUCTURE

To ensure high GRE essay scores, strive to write sentences that vary in length and structure in a way that helps convey their intended meaning rather than obscuring or distorting it. Here are some examples:

- For rhetorical emphasis, try using an abrupt, short sentence to make a crucial point, either before or after longer sentences that elucidate that point.

- Use a semicolon to transform two sentences involving the same train of thought into one; and use the word "and" to connect two independent clauses (just as in this sentence).

- Sentences with the same essential structure can help convey your line of reasoning to the reader. Try using the similar structures for a list of reasons or examples.

- Sentences that essentially repeat (verbatim) throughout your essay suggest an immature, unsophisticated writing style. Try to avoid using so-called template sentences over and over, especially for the first and last sentence of each body paragraph.

NOTE

To speed up the writing process, some GRE test-takers copy and paste phrases and sentences, then "tweak" them to avoid the template look. There's nothing wrong *per se* with this strategy, but you'll probably find that it takes more time than it's worth.

# WRITE CLEARLY AND CONCISELY

You're most likely to score high on your GRE essays if you develop a clear and concise writing style. Frequent occurrences of awkward, wordy, or redundant phrases can lower your Analytical Writing score—especially if these problems interfere with the reader's understanding of your essay.

## Beware of Wordiness

With enough words, anyone can make a point, but it requires skill and effort to make your point succinctly. As you proofread your essay, if a sentence seems clumsy or overly long, check for a wordy or awkward phrase that you can replace with a more concise, clearer one. In your Argument essay, for example, you can often replace wordy phrases that signal a premise with a single word. For example: "the reason for," "for the reason that," "due to the fact that," "in light of the fact that," and "on the grounds that" can be replaced with "because," "since," and "considering that."

**Original:** Discipline is crucial to *the attainment of one's* objectives.
**Better:** Discipline is crucial to *attain* one's objectives.

**Original:** *To indicate the fact that they are in opposition to* a bill, legislators sometimes engage in filibusters.
**Better:** *To show that they oppose* a bill, legislators sometimes engage in filibusters.

**Original:** The employee *with ambition* . . .
**Better:** The *ambitious* employee . . .

**Original:** The system *which is* most efficient and accurate . . .
**Better:** The most efficient and accurate system . . .

**Original:** *Both* unemployment levels *as well as* interest rates can affect stock prices.
**Better:** Unemployment levels and interest rates can affect stock prices.

**Original:** *The reason* science is being blamed for threats to the natural environment *is because* scientists fail to see that technology is only as useful or as harmful as those who decide how to use it.
**Better:** Science is being blamed for threats to the natural environment because scientists fail to see that technology is only as useful or as harmful as those who decide how to use it.

## Watch Comma Placement

Although punctuation is the least important aspect of your GRE essays, habitually overusing, underusing, or misusing commas may not only interfere with the reader's understanding of your essay and interrupt the flow of your sentences, but it may also contribute to a lower score. Use the least number of commas needed to ensure that the reader will understand your point.

# USE LANGUAGE CORRECTLY AND PERSUASIVELY

To ensure top scores for your essays, strive to convince the readers that you possess a strong command of the English language—in other words, that you can use the written language correctly, clearly, and persuasively. You need to demonstrate a solid grasp of vocabulary, use proper idioms (especially prepositional phrases), and use proper diction (word usage and choice). Let's take a look at how you can accomplish this.

## Demonstrate a Solid Grasp of Vocabulary

By all means, show the reader that you possess the vocabulary of a broadly educated individual and you know how to use it. But keep the following caveats in mind:

- Don't overuse "SAT-style" words just to make an impression. Doing so will only suggest that you're trying to mask poor content with window dressing.

- Avoid obscure or archaic words that few readers are likely to know. Readers do not have time while reading essays to consult dictionaries.

- Avoid technical terminology that only specialists and scholars in a specific field would understand. GRE readers are typically English-language generalists in English and Communications fields.

- Use Latin and other non-English terms *very* sparingly. After all, one of the primary skills you're being tested on is your facility with the English language. The occasional use of Latin terms and acronyms—for example, *per se, de facto, ad hoc, i.e.,* and *e.g.*—is perfectly acceptable. Non-English words commonly used in academic writing, such as *vis-á-vis, caveat,* and *laissez faire* are acceptable as well, but again, be careful not to overdo it.

- Avoid colloquialisms (slang and vernacular).

## Use Proper Diction

In evaluating your essays, GRE readers also take into account your diction, especially when problems interfere with the understanding of your essays. *Diction* refers chiefly to your choice of word and to the way a word is used. When you commit an error in diction, you might be confusing one word with another because the two words look or sound similar. Or you may use a word that isn't the best choice for conveying the idea you have in mind. Here's an example of each type of diction error:

- The best way to *impede* employees to improve their productivity is to allow them to determine for themselves the most efficient way of performing their individual job tasks.

The word *impede* means "to hinder or hamper"; in the context of this sentence, *impede* should be replaced with a word such as *impel,* which means "propel or drive." The test-taker might have confused these two words.

- Unless the department can supply a comparative cost-benefit analysis for the two alternative courses of action, I would remain *diffident* about following the department's recommendation.

The word *diffident* means "reluctant, unwilling, or shy." A more appropriate word here would be *ambivalent,* which means "undecided or indecisive." Or perhaps the test-taker meant to use the word *indifferent,* thereby committing the first type of diction error.

What appear to be diction errors might in many instances be merely typing errors. Accordingly, problems with your word choice and usage will adversely affect your scores only if they are obvious and occur frequently.

## Use Idioms Correctly

An *idiom* is a distinctive phrase that is either proper or improper based upon whether it has become acceptable over time and through repeated and common use. Here are two sentences, each of which contain an idiomatic prepositional phrase and another idiom:

### Example (From a Typical Issue Essay):

The speaker's contention *flies in the face of* the empirical evidence, and *in any event* runs contrary to common sense.

### Example (From a Typical Argument Essay):

*For all we know,* last year was the only year in which the company earned a profit, in which case the vice president's advice might *turn out* to be especially poor in retrospect.

Idioms don't rely on any particular rules of grammar; hence they are learned over time by experience. As you might suspect, the English language contains more idiomatic expressions than you can shake a thesaurus at. Moreover, the number of possible diction errors isn't even limited to the number of entries in a good unabridged English dictionary. Although it is impossible in these pages to provide a thorough review of diction and idiom, here are some guidelines to keep in mind when writing your GRE essays:

**TIP**

If you have time before your exam and you think your diction and use of idioms need improvement, consult a reputable guide to English usage, a trusted professor, or a colleague with a firm grasp of Standard Written English conventions.

- If you're the least bit unsure about the meaning of a word you want to use in your essay, don't use it. Why risk committing a diction blunder just to impress the reader?

- If a phrase sounds wrong to your ear, change it until it sounds correct to you.

- The fewer words you use, the less likely you'll commit a diction or idiom error. When in doubt, stick with a relatively brief phrase that you think will still convey your point.

- If English is your second language, take heart: In evaluating and scoring your essays, GRE readers take into account diction or idiom problems only to the extent that those problems interfere with a reader's understanding of your sentence's intended meaning. As long as your writing is understandable to your EFL (English-as-First-Language) friends, you need not worry.

# SUMMING IT UP

- GRE essay readers place less weight on writing style and mechanics than on content and organization—but the way you write can affect your GRE Analytical Writing score. To ensure a high score, you need to make sure your essays are persuasive in style; appropriate in tone and voice; varied in sentence length and structure; clear and concise; and correct in diction, word usage, idiom, grammar, and writing mechanics.

- Use rhetorical words and phrases and use irony as a rhetorical device. Avoid empty rhetoric; use punctuation properly and for emphasis.

- Be sure to connect your ideas and use the language of critical reasoning properly.

- You may need to refer to yourself, the statement, or the argument itself. If so, be consistent and follow the suggestions outlined in this chapter to help ensure that your references are appropriate.

# PART IV

## QUANTITATIVE REASONING

# Problem Solving

## chapter 7

## OVERVIEW

- Key facts about GRE Problem Solving
- The 5-step plan
- Problem-solving strategies
- The data interpretation format
- Data interpretation strategies
- The numeric entry format (new)
- Summing it up

The GRE Quantitative Reasoning section consists of test items in two basic formats: Problem Solving and Quantitative Comparison. In this chapter, you'll focus exclusively on the Problem Solving format. First, you'll learn a step-by-step approach to problem solving and apply it to some GRE-style examples. Then you'll review strategies for solving GRE quantitative problems as efficiently as possible, while avoiding common test-taking pitfalls. Later in the chapter, you'll examine the numeric entry format, a special type of Problem Solving question recently added to the GRE.

You first looked at GRE Problem Solving in Chapter 2 and in this book's Diagnostic Test. Let's quickly review the key facts about the Problem Solving format.

## KEY FACTS ABOUT GRE PROBLEM SOLVING

**Where:** The 45-minute Quantitative Reasoning section

**How Many:** Approximately 14 test items (out of 28 altogether), mixed in with Quantitative Comparisons

**What's Tested:**

- Your proficiency in performing arithmetical operations
- Your proficiency in solving algebraic equations and inequalities
- Your ability to convert verbal information into mathematical terms
- Your ability to visualize geometric shapes and numerical relationships
- Your ability to interpret data presented in charts, graphs, tables, and other graphical displays

**NOTE**

GRE numeric entry questions were introduced in November 2007. Initially, no test-taker will encounter more than one of these items on the exam, and some test-takers won't encounter any. The test designers plan to increase the number of numeric entry questions gradually over a multi-year period.

- Your ability to devise intuitive and unconventional solutions to conventional mathematical problems

**Areas Covered:** Any of the Quantitative Reasoning areas listed from pages 26 to 32 is fair game for a Problem Solving question.

**Directions:** Problem Solving directions are similar to the following. Most of these directions are actually assumptions for interpreting figures (pay special attention to the last one):

**Directions:** Solve the problem and select the best answer choice.

**Notes:**
- All numbers used are real numbers.
- All figures lie on a plane unless otherwise indicated.
- All angle measures are positive.
- All lines shown as straight are straight. Lines that appear jagged can also be assumed to be straight (lines can look somewhat jagged on the computer screen).
- Figures are intended to provide useful information for answering the questions. However, except where a figure is accompanied by a "Note" stating that the figure is drawn to scale, solve the problem using your knowledge of mathematics, *not* by visual measurement or estimation.

**Other Key Facts:**

- All Problem Solving questions are five-item multiple-choice questions, except that you might encounter one "fill-in" question as well.

- About one half of the questions are story problems (involving "real world" scenarios).

- Numerical answer choices are listed in either ascending or descending order.

- Some Problem Solving questions involve the interpretation of graphical data— tables, charts, and graphs (you'll examine the data interpretation format later in this chapter).

- The focus is on skills, not number crunching (you won't need to deal with unwieldy numbers or perform lengthy calculations).

- Calculators are prohibited, but scratch paper is provided.

## THE 5-STEP PLAN

The first task in this lesson is to learn the 5 basic steps for handling any GRE Problem Solving question. Just ahead, you'll apply these steps to three sample questions.

### Step 1: Size Up the Question

Read the question and then pause for a moment to ask yourself:

- What specific subject area is covered?

- What rules and formulas are likely to come into play?

- How complex is this question? (How many steps are involved in solving it? Does it require setting up equations, or does it require merely a few quick calculations?)

- Do I have a clue, off the top of my head, how I would begin solving this problem?

Determine how much time you're willing to spend on the problem, if any. Recognizing a "toughie" when you see it may save you valuable time; if you don't have a clue, take a guess and move on.

## Step 2: Size Up the Answer Choices

Before you attempt to solve the problem at hand, examine the answer choices. They can provide helpful clues about how to proceed in solving the problem and what sort of solution you should be aiming for. Pay particular attention to the following:

- **Form:** Are the answer choices expressed as percentages, fractions, or decimals? Ounces or pounds? Minutes or hours? If the answer choices are expressed as equations, are all variables together on one side of the equation? As you work through the problem, convert numbers and expressions to the same form as the answer choices.

- **Size:** Are the answer choices numbers with extremely small values? Greater numbers? Negative or positive numbers? Do the answer choice vary widely in value? If they're tightly clustered in value, you can probably disregard decimal points and extraneous zeros when performing calculations, but be careful about rounding off your figures. Wide variation in value suggests that you can easily eliminate answer choices that don't correspond to the general size of number suggested by the question.

- **Other distinctive properties and characteristics:** Are the answer choices integers? Do they all include a variable? Do they contain radical signs (roots) or exponents? Is there a particular term, expression, or number that they have in common?

## Step 3: Look for a Shortcut to the Answer

Before plunging headlong into a problem, ask yourself whether there's a quick way to determine the correct answer. If the solution is a numerical value, perhaps only one answer choice is in the ballpark. Or you might be able to identify the correct answer intuitively, without resorting to equations and calculations.

## Step 4: Set Up the Problem and Solve It

If your intuition fails you, grab your pencil and do whatever computations, algebra, or other procedures are needed to solve the problem. Simple problems may require just a few quick calculations. However, complex algebra and geometry questions may require setting up and solving one or more equations.

## Step 5: Verify Your Selection Before Moving On

After solving the problem, if your solution does not appear among the answer choices, check your work—you obviously made at least one mistake. If your solution *does* appear among the choices, don't celebrate quite yet. Although there's a good chance your answer is correct, it's possible your answer is wrong and that the test designers anticipated your

**NOTE**
Remember: The computerized GRE testing system adjusts the difficulty level of your questions according to previous responses. If you respond incorrectly to tough questions, fewer of them will come up later in that section.

error by including that incorrect solution as an answer choice. So check the question to verify that your response corresponds to what the question calls for in value, expression, units of measure, and so forth. If it does, and if you're confident that your work was careful and accurate, don't spend any more time checking your work. Confirm your response and move on to the next question.

## Applying the 5-Step Plan

Let's apply these five steps to two GRE-style Problem Solving questions. Question 1 is a story problem involving *changes in percent*. (Story problems might account for as many as one half of your Problem Solving questions.) This question is relatively easy— approximately 80 percent of test-takers respond correctly to questions like this one:

1. If Susan drinks 10% of the juice from a 16-ounce bottle immediately before lunch and 20% of the remaining amount with lunch, approximately how many ounces of juice are left to drink after lunch?

   **(A)** 4.8
   **(B)** 5.5
   **(C)** 11.2
   **(D)** 11.5
   **(E)** 13.0

**Step 1:** This problem involves the concept of *percent*—more specifically, *percent decrease*. The question is asking you to perform two computations in sequence. (You'll use the result of the first computation to perform the second one.) Percent questions tend to be relatively simple. All that is involved here is a two-step computation.

**Step 2:** The five answer choices in this question provide two useful clues:

❶ Notice that they range in value from 4.8 to 13.0—a broad spectrum. But what general size should we be looking for in a correct answer to this question? Without crunching any numbers, it's clear that most of the juice will still remain in the bottle, even after lunch. So you're looking for a value much closer to 13 than to 4. You can eliminate choices (A) and (B).

❷ Notice that each answer choice is carried to exactly one decimal place, and that the question asks for an approximate value. These two features are clues that you can probably round off your calculations to the nearest "tenth" as you go.

**Step 3:** You already eliminated choices (A) and (B) in step 1. But if you're on your toes, you can eliminate all but the correct answer without resorting to precise calculations. Look at the question from a broader perspective. If you subtract 10% from a number, then 20% from the result, that adds up to *a bit less* than a 30% decrease from the original number. 30% of 16 ounces is 4.8 ounces. So the solution must be a number that is a bit larger than 11.2 (16 − 4.8). Answer choice (D), 11.5, is the only one that works.

**Step 4:** If your intuition fails you, work out the problem. First, determine 10% of 16, then subtract that number from 16:

$$16 \times .1 = 1.6$$

$$16 - 1.6 = 14.4$$

Susan now has 14.4 ounces of juice. Now perform the second step. Determine 20% of 14.4, then subtract that number from 14.4:

$$14.4 \times .2 = 2.88$$

Round off 2.88 to the nearest tenth (2.9), then subtract:

$$14.4 - 2.9 = 11.5$$

**Step 5:** The decimal number 11.5 is indeed among the answer choices. Before moving on, however, ask yourself whether your solution makes sense—in this case, whether the size of our number (11.5) "fits" what the question asks for. If you performed step 2, you should already realize that 11.5 is in the ballpark. If you're confident that your calculations were careful and accurate, confirm your response choice (D), and move on to the next question. **The correct answer is (D).**

Question 2 involves the concept of *arithmetic mean* (simple average). This question is moderately difficult. Approximately 60 percent of test-takers respond correctly to questions like it.

2. The average of 6 numbers is 19. When one of those numbers is taken away, the average of the remaining 5 numbers is 21. What number was taken away?

   **(A)** 2
   **(B)** 8
   **(C)** 9
   **(D)** 11
   **(E)** 20

**Step 1:** This problem involves the concept of arithmetic mean (simple average). To handle this question, you need to be familiar with the formula for calculating the average of a series of numbers. Notice, however, that the question does not ask for the average but for one of the numbers in the series. This curveball makes the question a bit tougher than most arithmetic-mean problems.

**Step 2:** Scan the answer choices for clues. Notice that the middle three are clustered closely close together in value. So take a closer look at the two aberrations: choices (A) and (E). Choice (A) would be the correct answer to the question: "What is the difference between 19 and 21?" But this question is asking something entirely different, so you can probably rule out choice (A) as a "red herring" choice. Choice (E) might also be a red herring, since 20 is simply 19 + 21 divided by 2. If this solution strikes you as too simple, you've got good instincts! The correct answer is probably choice (B), (C), or (D). If you're pressed for time, guess one of these, and move on to the next question. Otherwise, go to step 3.

**Step 3:** If you're on your toes, you might recognize a shortcut here. You can solve this problem quickly by simply comparing the two sums. Before the sixth number is taken away, the sum of the numbers is 114 (6 × 19). After removing the sixth number, the sum of the remaining numbers is 105 (5 × 21). The difference between the two sums is 9, which must be the value of the number removed.

**Step 4:** If you don't see a shortcut, you can solve the problem conventionally. The formula for arithmetic mean (simple average) can be expressed this way:

$$AM = \frac{\text{sum of terms in the set}}{\text{number of terms in the set}}$$

In the question, you started with six terms. Let $a$ through $f$ equal those six terms:

$$19 = \frac{a + b + c + d + e + f}{6}$$

$$114 = a + b + c + d + e + f$$

$$f = 114 - (a + b + c + d + e)$$

Letting $f$ = the number that is removed, here's the arithmetic mean formula, applied to the remaining five numbers:

$$21 = \frac{a + b + c + d + e}{5}$$

$$105 = a + b + c + d + e$$

Substitute 105 for $(a + b + c + d + e)$ in the first equation:

$$f = 114 - 105$$

$$f = 9$$

**Step 5:** If you have time, check to make sure you got the formula right, and check your calculations. Also make sure you didn't inadvertently switch the numbers 19 and 21 in your equations. (It's remarkably easy to commit this careless error under time pressure!) If you're satisfied that your analysis is accurate, confirm your answer and move on to the next question. **The correct answer is (C).**

Question 3 involves the concept of *proportion*. This question is moderately difficult. Approximately 50 percent of test-takers respond correctly to questions like it.

**ALERT!**

On the GRE, committing a careless error, such as switching two numbers in a problem, is by far the leading cause of incorrect responses.

3. If $p$ pencils cost $2q$ dollars, how many pencils can you buy for $c$ cents? [Note: 1 dollar = 100 cents]

   **(A)** $\dfrac{pc}{2q}$

   **(B)** $\dfrac{pc}{200q}$

   **(C)** $\dfrac{50pc}{q}$

   **(D)** $\dfrac{2pq}{c}$

   **(E)** $200pcq$

**Step 1:** The first step is to recognize that instead of performing a numerical computation, you're task in Question 3 is to *express a computational process* in terms of letters. Expressions such as these are known as *literal expressions,* and they can be perplexing if you're not ready for them. Although it probably won't be too time-consuming, it may be a bit confusing. You should also recognize that the key to this question is the concept of *proportion.* It might be appropriate to set up an equation to solve for $c$. Along the way, expect to convert dollars into cents.

**Step 2:** The five answer choices provide two useful clues:

**1** Notice that each answer choice includes all three letters ($p$, $q$, and $c$)—therefore so should your solution to the problem.

**2** Notice that every answer but choice (E) is a fraction. So anticipate building a fraction to solve the problem algebraically.

**Step 3:** Is there any way to answer this question besides setting up an algebraic equation? Yes. In fact, there are two ways. One is to use easy numbers for the three variables; for example, $p = 2$, $q = 1$, and $c = 100$. These simple numbers make the question easy to work with:

> "If 2 pencils cost 2 dollars, how many pencils can you buy for 100 cents?"

Obviously, the answer to this question is 1. So plug in the numbers into each answer choice to see which choice provides an expression that equals 1. Only choice (B) works:

$$\frac{(2)(100)}{(200)(1)} = 1$$

Another way to shortcut the algebra is to apply some intuition to this question. If you strip away the pencils, $p$'s, $q$'s and $c$'s, in a very general sense the question is asking:

> "If you can by an item for a dollar, how many can you buy for one cent?"

Since one cent (a penny) is $\frac{1}{100}$ of a dollar, you can buy $\frac{1}{100}$ of one item for a cent. So you're probably looking for a fractional answer with a large number such as 100 in the denominator (as opposed to a number such as 2, 3, or 6). Choice (B) is the only that appears to be in the right ballpark. And choice (B) is indeed the correct answer.

**Step 4:** You can also answer the question in a conventional manner, using algebra. (This is easier said than done.) Here's how to approach it:

- Express $2q$ dollars as $200q$ cents (1 dollar = 100 cents).

- Let $x$ equal the number of pencils you can buy for $c$ cents.

- Think about the problem "verbally," then set up an equation and solve for $x$:

> "$p$ pencils is to $200q$ cents as $x$ pencils is to $c$ cents."

> "The ratio of $p$ to $200q$ is the same as the ratio of $x$ to $c$" (in other words, the two ratios are proportionate). Therefore:

$$\frac{p}{200q} = \frac{x}{c}$$

$$\frac{pc}{200q} = x$$

NOTE

On the GRE, expect to encounter two or three "story" problems involving literal expressions (where the solution includes not just numbers but variables as well).

NOTE

Don't worry if you didn't fully understand the way we set up and solved this problem. You'll learn more about how to handle GRE proportion questions in this book's math review.

**Step 5:** Our solution, $\frac{pc}{200q}$, is indeed among the answer choices. If you arrived at this solution using the conventional algebraic approach (step 4), you can verify your solution by substituting simple numbers for the three variables (as we did in step 3). Or if you arrived at your solution by plugging in numbers, you can check you work by plugging in a different set of numbers, or by thinking about the problem conceptually (as in step 3). Once you're confident you've chosen the correct expression among the five choices, confirm your choice, and then move on to the next question. **The correct answer is (B).**

## PROBLEM-SOLVING STRATEGIES

To handle GRE Quantitative questions (Problem Solving and Quantitative Comparisons alike), you'll need to be well-versed in the fundamental rules of arithmetic, algebra, and geometry: Your knowledge of these basics is, to a large extent, what's being tested. (That's what the math review later in this part of the book is all about.) But when it comes to Problem Solving questions, the GRE test designers are also interested in gauging your mental agility, flexibility, creativity, and efficiency in problem solving. More specifically, they design these questions to discover your ability to do the following:

- Manipulate numbers with a certain end result already in mind
- See the dynamic relationships between numbers as you apply operations to them
- Visualize geometric shapes and relationships between shapes
- Devise unconventional solutions to conventional quantitative problems
- Solve problems efficiently by recognizing the easiest, quickest, or most reliable route to a solution

This section of the chapter will help you develop these skills. The techniques you'll learn here are intrinsic to the GRE. Along with your knowledge of substantive rules of math, they're precisely what GRE Problem Solving questions are designed to measure.

### Read the Question Stem Very Carefully

Careless reading is by far the leading cause of wrong answers in GRE Problem Solving. So be doubly sure you answer the precise question that's being asked, and consider your responses carefully.

Is the correct answer to this question one of the following:

- An arithmetic mean or median
- A circumference or an area
- A sum or a difference
- A perimeter or a length of one side only
- An aggregate rate or a single rate
- A total time or average time

Also check to make sure you have considered the following:

- Used the same numbers provided in the question
- Didn't inadvertently switch any numbers or other expressions
- Didn't use raw numbers where percentages were provided, or vice-versa

## Always Check Your Work

Here are three suggestions for checking your work on a Problem Solving question:

**1** Do a reality check. Ask yourself whether your solution makes sense for what the question asks. (This check is especially appropriate for word problems.)

**2** For questions in which you solve algebraic equations, plug your solution into the equation(s) to make sure it works.

**3** Confirm *all* of your calculations. It's amazingly easy to commit errors in even the simplest calculations, especially under GRE exam pressure.

## Scan Answer Choices for Clues

For multiple-choice questions, scan the answer choices to see what all or most of them have in common—such as radical signs, exponents, factorable expressions, or fractions. Then try to formulate a solution that looks like the answer choices.

**4.** If $a \neq 0$ or 1, then $\dfrac{\dfrac{1}{a}}{2 - \dfrac{2}{a}} =$

    **(A)** $\dfrac{1}{2a - 2}$

    **(B)** $\dfrac{2}{a - 2}$

    **(C)** $\dfrac{1}{a - 2}$

    **(D)** $\dfrac{1}{a}$

    **(E)** $\dfrac{2}{2a - 1}$

**The correct answer is (A).** Notice that all of the answer choices here are fractions in which the denominator contains the variable *a*. Also, none have fractions in either the numerator or the denominator. That's a clue that your job is to manipulate the expression given in the question so that the result includes these features. First, place the denominator's two terms over the common denominator *a*. Then cancel *a* from the denominators of both the numerator fraction and the denominator fraction (this is a shortcut to multiplying the numerator fraction by the reciprocal of the denominator fraction):

$$\frac{\dfrac{1}{a}}{2-\dfrac{2}{a}} = \frac{\dfrac{1}{a}}{\dfrac{2a-2}{a}} = \frac{1}{2a-2}$$

## Don't Be Lured by Obvious Answer Choices

On the Quantitative Reasoning section of the GRE, you'll be "tempted" by wrong answer choices that are the result of common errors in reasoning, in calculations, and in setting up and solving equations. Never assume that your solution is correct just because you see it among the answer choices. The following example is a variation of the problem on page 143.

**5.** The average of 6 numbers is 19. When one of those numbers is taken away, the average of the remaining 5 numbers is 21. What number was taken away?

   **(A)** 2

   **(B)** 6.5

   **(C)** 9

   **(D)** 11.5

   **(E)** 20

**The correct answer is (C).** This question contains two seemingly correct answer choices that are actually wrong. Choice (A) would be the correct answer to the question: "What is the difference between 19 and 21?" But this question asks something entirely different. Choice (E) is the other too-obvious choice. 20 is simply 19 + 21 divided by 2. If this solution strikes you as too simple, you have good instincts. You can solve this problem quickly by simply comparing the two *sums*. Before the sixth number is taken away, the sum of the numbers is 114 (6 × 19). After taking away the sixth number, the sum of the remaining numbers is 105 (5 × 21). The difference between the two sums is 9, which must be the value of the number taken away.

## Size Up the Question to Narrow Your Choices

If a multiple-choice question asks for a number value, you can probably narrow down the answer choices by estimating the size and type of number you're looking for. Use your common sense and real-world experience to formulate a "ballpark" estimate for word problems.

**6.** A container holds 10 liters of a solution that is 20% acid. If 6 liters of pure acid are added to the container, what percent of the resulting mixture is acid?

   **(A)** 8

   **(B)** 20

   **(C)** $33\dfrac{1}{3}$

   **(D)** 40

   **(E)** 50

**The correct answer is (E).** Common sense should tell you that when you add more acid to the solution, the percent of the solution that is acid will increase. So, you're looking for an answer that's greater than 20—either choice (C), (D), or (E). (By the way, notice the too-obvious answer is choice (A); 8 liters is the *amount* of acid in the resulting mixture.) If you need to guess at this point, your odds are one in three. Here's how to solve the problem: The original amount of acid is (10)(20%) = 2 liters. After adding 6 liters of pure acid, the amount of acid increases to 8 liters, while the amount of total solution increases from 10 to 16 liters. The new solution is $\frac{8}{16}$, or 50%, acid.

## Know When to Plug in Numbers for Variables

In multiple-choice questions, if the answer choices contain variables like $x$ and $y$, the question might be a good candidate for the "plug-in" strategy. Pick simple numbers (so the math is easy) and substitute them for the variables. You'll need your pencil and scratch paper for this strategy.

7. If a train travels $r + 2$ miles in $h$ hours, which of the following represents the number of miles the train travels in 1 hour and 30 minutes?

   **(A)** $\dfrac{3r + 6}{2h}$

   **(B)** $\dfrac{3r}{h + 2}$

   **(C)** $\dfrac{r + 2}{h + 3}$

   **(D)** $\dfrac{r}{h + 6}$

   **(E)** $\dfrac{3}{2}(r + 2)$

   **The correct answer is (A).** This is an algebraic word problem involving rate of motion (speed). You can solve this problem either conventionally or by using the plug-in strategy.

   **The conventional way:** Notice that all of the answer choices contain fractions. This is a tip that you should try to create a fraction as you solve the problem. Here's how to do it: Given that the train travels $r + 2$ miles in $h$ hours, you can express its rate in miles per hour as $\dfrac{r + 2}{h}$. In $\dfrac{3}{2}$ hours, the train would travel $\dfrac{3}{2}$ this distance:

   $$\left(\frac{3}{2}\right)\left(\frac{r + 2}{h}\right) = \frac{3r + 6}{2h}$$

   **The plug-in strategy:** Let $r = 8$ and $h = 1$. Given these values, the train travels 10 miles (8 + 2) in 1 hour. So obviously, in $1\frac{1}{2}$ hours the train will travel 15 miles. Start plugging these $r$ and $h$ values into the answer choices. You won't need to go any further than choice (A):

   $$\frac{3r + 6}{2h} = \frac{3(8) + 6}{2(1)} = \frac{30}{2}, \text{ or } 15$$

Choice (E) also equals 15, $\frac{3}{2}(8 + 2) = 15$. However, you can eliminate choice (E) out of hand because it omits $h$. Common sense should tell you that the correct answer must include both $r$ and $h$.

## Know When—and When Not—to Work Backward

If a multiple-choice question asks for a number value, and if you draw a blank as far as how to set up and solve the problem, don't panic. You might be able to work backward by testing the answer choices in turn.

8. A ball is dropped 192 inches above level ground, and after the third bounce, it rises to a height of 24 inches. If the height to which the ball rises after each bounce is always the same fraction of the height reached on its previous bounce, what is this fraction?

(A) $\frac{1}{8}$

(B) $\frac{1}{4}$

(C) $\frac{1}{3}$

(D) $\frac{1}{2}$

(E) $\frac{2}{3}$

**The correct answer is (D).** The fastest route to a solution is to plug in an answer. Try choice (C) and see what happens. If the ball bounces up $\frac{1}{3}$ as high as it started, then after the first bounce it will rise up $\frac{1}{3}$ as high as 192 inches, or 64 inches. After a second bounce, it will rise $\frac{1}{3}$ as high, or about 21 inches. But the problem states that the ball rises to 24 inches after the *third* bounce. Obviously, if the ball rises less than that after two bounces, it will be too low after three. So choice (C) cannot be the correct answer. We can see that the ball must be bouncing higher than one third of the way, so the correct answer must be a larger fraction, meaning either choice (D) or choice (E). You've already narrowed your odds to 50%. Try plugging in choice (D), and you'll see that it works: $\frac{1}{2}$ of 192 is 96; $\frac{1}{2}$ of 96 is 48; and $\frac{1}{2}$ of 48 is 24.

Although it would be possible to develop a formula to answer the question, it's not worthwhile, considering how quickly and easily you can work backward from the answer choices.

In multiple-choice questions, working backward from numerical answer choices works well when the numbers are easy and when few calculations are required, as in the preceding question. In other cases, applying algebra might be a better way.

**9.** How many pounds of nuts selling for 70 cents per pound must be mixed with 30 pounds of nuts selling at 90 cents per pound to make a mixture that sells for 85 cents per pound?

(A) 8.5

(B) 10

(C) 15

(D) 16.5

(E) 20

**The correct answer is (B).** Is the easiest route to the solution to test the answer choices? Let's see. First of all, calculate the total cost of 30 pounds of nuts at 90 cents per pound: $30 \times .90 = \$27$. Now, start with choice (C). 15 pounds of nuts at 70 cents per pound costs \$10.50. The total cost of this mixture is \$37.50, and the total weight is 45 pounds. Now you'll need to perform some long division. The average price per pound of the mixture turns out to be between 83 and 84 cents—too low for the 85-cent average given in the question. So you can at least eliminate choice (C).

You should realize by now that testing the answer choices might not be the most efficient way to tackle this question. Besides, there are ample opportunities for calculation errors. Instead, try solving this problem algebraically by writing and solving an equation. Here's how to do it. The cost (in cents) of the nuts selling for 70 cents per pound can be expressed as $70x$, letting $x$ equal the number that you're asked to determine. You then add this cost to the cost of the more expensive nuts ($30 \times 90 = 2,700$) to obtain the total cost of the mixture, which you can express as $85(x + 30)$. You can state this algebraically and solve for $x$ as follows:

$$70x + 2,700 = 85(x + 30)$$
$$70x + 2,700 = 85x + 2,550$$
$$150 = 15x$$
$$10 = x$$

10 pounds of 70-cents-per-pound nuts must be added in order to make a mixture that sells for 85 cents per pound.

## Look for the Simplest Route to the Answer

In many Problem Solving questions, there's a long way and a short way to arrive at the correct answer. When it looks like you're facing a long series of calculations or a complex system of equations, always ask yourself whether you can take an easier, more intuitive route to solving the problem.

**10.** What is the difference between the sum of all positive even integers less than 32 and the sum of all positive odd integers less than 32?

**(A)** −32

**(B)** −16

**(C)** −15

**(D)** −1

**(E)** 0

**The correct answer is (B).** To answer this question, should you add up two long series of numbers on your scratch paper? In this case, it's a waste of time, and you risk committing calculation errors along the way. A smart test-taker will notice a pattern and use it as a shortcut. Compare the initial terms of each sequence:

even integers: [2, 4, 6, ]. . ., 30
odd integers: [1, 3, 5, ]. . ., 29, 31

Notice that for each successive term, the odd integer is one less than the corresponding even integer. There are a total of 15 corresponding integers, so the difference between the sums of all these corresponding integers is 15. But the odd-integer sequence includes one additional integer: 31. So the difference is (15 − 31) = −16.

## Start with What You Know

It's easy to get lost in Problem Solving questions that are complex and involve multiple steps to solve. First, take a deep breath and start with information you know. Then ask yourself what you can deduce from it, leading yourself step-by-step to the solution.

**11.** In a group of 20 singers and 40 dancers, 20% of the singers are less than 25 years old, and 40% of the entire group are less than 25 years old. What portion of the dancers are younger than 25 years old?

**(A)** 20%

**(B)** 24%

**(C)** 40%

**(D)** 50%

**(E)** 60%

**The correct answer is (D).** To answer this question, you need to know (1) the total number of dancers and (2) the *number* of dancers younger than 25 years old. The question provides the first number: 40. To find the second number, start with what the question provides and figure out what else you know. Keep going, and eventually you'll arrive at your destination. Of the whole group of 60, 24 are younger than 25 years. (40% of 60 is 24.) 20% of the 20 singers, or 4 singers, are younger than 25 years. Hence, the remaining 20 people younger than 25 must be dancers. That's the second number you needed to answer the question. 20 is 50% of 40.

## Search Geometry Problem Figures for Clues

Some GRE geometry problems will be accompanied by figures. They're there for a reason: The pieces of information provided in a figure can lead you, step-by-step, to the answer.

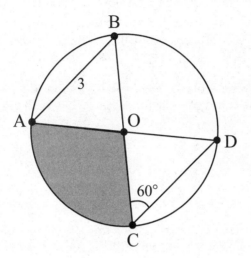

12. If O is the center of the circle in the figure above, what is the area of the shaded region, expressed in square units?

   (A)  $\dfrac{3}{2}\pi$

   (B)  $2\pi$

   (C)  $\dfrac{5}{2}\pi$

   (D)  $\dfrac{8}{3}\pi$

   (E)  $3\pi$

   **The correct answer is (E).** This question asks for the area of a portion of the circle defined by a central angle. To answer the question, you'll need to determine the area of the entire circle as well as what percent (portion) of that area is shaded. Mine the figure for a piece of information that might provide a starting point. If you look at the 60° angle in the figure, you should recognize right away that both triangles are equilateral (all angles are 60°) and, extended out to their arcs, form two "pie slices," each one $\dfrac{1}{6}$ the size of the whole pie (the circle). What's left are two big slices, each of which is twice the size of a small slice. So the shaded area must account for $\dfrac{1}{3}$ the circle's area. You've now reduced the problem to the simple mechanics of calculating the circle's area and then dividing it by 3.

   In an equilateral triangle, all sides are congruent. Mining the figure once again, notice length 3, which is also the circle's radius (the distance from its center to its circumference). The area of any circle is $\pi r^2$, where $r$ is the circle's radius. Thus, the area of the circle is $9\pi$. The shaded portion accounts for $\frac{1}{3}$ the circle's area, or $3\pi$.

## Sketch Your Own Geometry Figure

A geometry problem that doesn't provide a diagram might be more easily solved if it had one. Use your scratch paper and draw one for yourself. It will be easier than trying to visualize it in your head.

**13.** On the $xy$-coordinate plane, points R(7,−3) and S(7,7) are the endpoints of the longest possible chord of a certain circle. What is the area of the circle?

**(A)** $7\pi$
**(B)** $16\pi$
**(C)** $20\pi$
**(D)** $25\pi$
**(E)** $49\pi$

**The correct answer is (D).** There are lots of sevens in this question, which might throw you off track without at least a rough picture. To keep your thinking straight, scratch out your own rough $xy$-grid and plot the two points. You'll see that R is located directly below S, so chord $\overline{RS}$ is vertical. Accordingly, the length of $\overline{RS}$ is simply the vertical distance from −3 to 7, which is 10. By definition, the longest possible chord of a circle is equal in length to the circle's diameter. The circle's diameter is 10, and thus its radius is 5. The circle's area is $\pi(5)^2 = 25\pi$.

## Plug in the Numbers for "Defined Operation" Questions

One of your 14 Problem Solving questions might very well be a so-called defined operation question. These are odd-looking problems that might strike you as being difficult. But they're really not. In fact, the math usually turns out to be very easy. You're being tested on your ability to understand what the problem requires you to do, and then to cross your $t$'s and dot your $i$'s as you perform simple arithmetical calculations.

**14.** Let $\langle\!\!\begin{smallmatrix}b\\a\ \ c\\d\end{smallmatrix}\!\!\rangle$ be defined for all numbers $a$, $b$, $c$, and $d$ by $\langle\!\!\begin{smallmatrix}b\\a\ \ c\\d\end{smallmatrix}\!\!\rangle = ac - bd$. If $x = \langle\!\!\begin{smallmatrix}4\\5\ \ 2\\1\end{smallmatrix}\!\!\rangle$, what is the value of $\langle\!\!\begin{smallmatrix}10\\x\ \ 2\\1\end{smallmatrix}\!\!\rangle$ ?

**(A)** 1
**(B)** 2
**(C)** 4
**(D)** 5
**(E)** 10

**The correct answer is (B).** In defining the diamond-shaped figure as "$ac - bd$," the question is telling you that whenever you see four numbers in a diamond like this, you should plug them into the mathematical expression shown in the order given. The question itself then requires you to perform this simple task twice.

First, let's figure out the value of $x$. If $x$ is the diamond labeled as $x$, then $a = 5$, $b = 4$, $c = 2$, and $d = 1$. Now, we plug those numbers into the equation given, then do the simple math:

$x = (5 \times 2) - (4 \times 1)$

$x = 10 - 4$

$x = 6$

Now we tackle the second step. Having figured out the value of $x$, we can plug it into our second diamond, where $a = 6$, $b = 10$, $c = 2$, and $d = 1$. Again, plug in the numbers and do the math:

$(6 \times 2) - (10 \times 1) = 12 - 10 = 2$

As you can see, the math is very easy; the trick is understanding what the question is asking: which is to have you "define" a new math operation and then carefully plug in the numbers and work out the solution. With a little practice, you'll never get a defined operation question wrong.

## THE DATA INTERPRETATION FORMAT

Data interpretation is a special Problem Solving format designed to gauge your ability to read and analyze data presented in statistical charts, graphs, and tables, and to calculate figures such as percentages, ratios, fractions, and averages based on the numbers you glean from graphical data.

Expect to find three to five data interpretation questions (possibly in sets of two or three) mixed in with your other Quantitative Reasoning questions. Each question in a data interpretation set pertains to the same graphical data. Each question (and each set) involves either *one or two* distinct graphical displays. Four types appear on the GRE most frequently:

1. Tables
2. Pie charts
3. Bar graphs
4. Line charts

Note the following key features of GRE data interpretation questions:

- **Important assumptions will be provided.** Any additional information that you might need to know to interpret the figures will be indicated above and below the figures. Be sure to read this information.

- **Some questions might ask for an approximation.** This is because the test-makers are trying to gauge your ability to interpret graphical data, not your ability to crunch numbers to the $n$th decimal place.

- **Many of the numbers used are *almost* round.** This feature relates to the previous one. The GRE rewards test-takers who recognize that rounding off numbers (to an appropriate extent) will suffice to reach the correct answer.

- **Some questions may be long and wordy.** Solving a data interpretation problem may call for multiple steps involving various graphical data, so the questions can be lengthy. In fact, you may have more trouble interpreting the questions than the graphical data.

- **Bar graphs and line charts are drawn to scale.** That's because visual estimation is part of what's required to analyze a bar graph or line chart's graphical data. However, pie charts will not necessarily be drawn to scale. (You'll interpret them strictly by the numbers provided), and visual scale is irrelevant when it comes to analyzing tables.

- **Figures are not drawn to deceive you or to test your eyesight.** In bar graphs and line charts, you won't be asked to split hairs to determine precise values. These graphs and charts are designed for a comfortable margin for error in visual acuity. Just don't round up or down too far.

- **You may need to scroll vertically to see the entire display.** Some vertical scrolling might be required to view the entire display, especially the information above and below the chart, graph, or table. If so, don't forget to scroll up and down as you analyze each question.

NOTE

Data interpretation questions are most often based on tables, pie charts, bar graphs, and line charts—but you might encounter some other type of display, so don't be surprised to see something else.

## The 5-Step Plan

Here's the 5-step approach that will help you handle any data interpretation question (or set of questions). Just ahead, we'll apply this approach to a two-question set.

### STEP 1: LOOK AT THE "BIG PICTURE" FIRST

Before plunging into the question(s), read all the information above and below the figure(s). Look particularly for the following:

- Totals (dollar figures or other numbers)
- Whether the numbers are expressed in terms of hundreds, thousand, or millions
- How two or more figures are labeled
- Whether graphical data is expressed in numbers or percentages

### STEP 2: READ THE ENTIRE QUESTION CAREFULLY

Read the entire question very carefully. As you do so, divide the question into parts, each of which involves a distinct step in getting to the answer. Pay particular attention to whether the question asks for the following:

- An approximation
- A percentage or a raw number
- A comparison
- An increase or a decrease

In breaking the question down into tasks, look for a shortcut to save yourself pencil work.

### STEP 3: PERFORM THE STEPS NEEDED TO REACH THE ANSWER

Look for a shortcut to the answer. For questions calling for approximations, round numbers up or down (but not too far) as you go.

### STEP 4: CHECK THE CHOICES FOR YOUR ANSWER

If an "approximation" question asks for a number, find the choice closest to your answer. Look for other answer choices that are too close for comfort. If you see any, or if your solution is nowhere near any of the choices, go to step 5.

### STEP 5: CHECK YOUR CALCULATIONS

Check all of your calculations and make sure the size and form (number, percentage, total, etc.) of your solution conforms with what the question asks. Check your rounding technique. Did you round off in the wrong direction? Did you round off too far?

### APPLYING THE 5-STEP PLAN

Let's apply the 5-step approach to two sample questions, both based on the following two related pie charts.

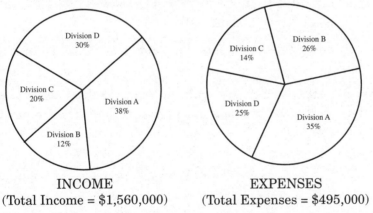

INCOME AND EXPENSES–DIVISIONS A, B, C, AND D OF XYZ COMPANY (YEAR X)

INCOME
(Total Income = $1,560,000)

EXPENSES
(Total Expenses = $495,000)

**Step 1:** Size up the two charts and read the information above and below them. Notice that we're dealing only with one company during one year. Notice also that dollar totals are provided, but that the pie segments are all expressed only as percentages. That's a clue that your tasks for this set of data might be to calculate dollar amounts for various pie segments. Now read Question 15, which is moderately difficult. (Approximately 50 percent of test-takers respond correctly to questions like it.)

> **TIP**
>
> Use rounding and estimation to answer a data interpretation question—but only if the question calls for an approximation.

**15.** During year X, by approximately what amount did Division C's income exceed Division B's expenses?

    **(A)** $125,000

    **(B)** $127,000

    **(C)** $140,000

    **(D)** $180,000

    **(E)** $312,000

You already performed step 1, so move ahead to step 2.

**Step 2:** This question involves three tasks:

**1** Calculate Division C's income

**2** Calculate Division B's expenses

**3** Compute their difference.

There's no shortcut to these three tasks, so go on to step 3.

**Step 3:** Division B's expenses accounted for 26% of XYZ's total expenses, given as $495,000. Rounding off these figures to 25% and $500,000, Division B's expenses totaled approximately $125,000. Income from Division C sales was 20% of total XYZ income, given as $1,560,000. Rounding this total down to $1,500,000, income from Division C sales was approximately $300,000. Income from Division C sales exceeded Division B's expenses by approximately $175,000.

**Step 4:** The only answer choice close to this solution is choice (D). If you have extra time, go to step 5.

**Step 5:** Make sure that you started with the right numbers. Did you compare C's income with B's expense (and not some other combination)? If you're satisfied that the numbers you used were the right ones and that your calculations are okay, confirm your response and move on to the next question. **The correct answer is (D).**

Now apply the same 5-step approach to Question 16, which is a difficult question. (Approximately 35 percent of test-takers respond correctly to questions like it.)

**16.** During year X, one of the four divisions was more profitable than all the others in terms of net income, defined as dollar income minus dollar expenses. By approximately what amount did that division's income exceed its own expenses?

    **(A)** $180,000

    **(B)** $225,000

    **(C)** $325,000

    **(D)** $360,000

    **(E)** $420,000

You already performed step 1, so move ahead to step 2.

**Step 2:** Like Question 1, this question calls for a sequence of two distinct tasks:

**1** Compare profitability among the four divisions.

**2** Calculate the *approximate* dollar difference between each division's income and its expenses. (To save time, you can probably round percentages and/or dollar figures.)

**Step 3:** Calculate dollar income and dollar expenses for Divisions A, C, and D. Round off to save time and to reduce the possibility of calculation errors. For example, round total income to $1,500,000 and total expenses to $500,000. Here are the rough calculations:

**Division A**
Income = 40% of $1,500,000 = $600,000
Expenses = 35% of $500,000 = $175,000

**Division C**
Income = 20% of $1,500,000 = $300,000
Expenses = 15% of $500,000 = $75,000

**Division D**
Income = 30% of $1,500,000 = $450,000
Expenses = 25% of $500,000 = $125,000

Now consider the second part of the question. Calculate the profit (income minus expenses) for each of the three divisions, using the approximate values you just calculated:

Division A's profit = $600,000 − $175,000 = $425,000
Division C's profit = $300,000 − $75,000 = $225,000
Division D's profit = $450,000 − $125,000 = $325,000

As you can see, Division A was the most profitable.

**Step 4:** Answer choice (E), $420,000, is the only one close to our approximation of $425,000.

**Step 5:** If you have time, rethink step 3. Make sure you're convinced that Division A's profit was greater than either Division C's or D's. Also, ask yourself whether $420,000 is in the right ballpark. If you're confident in your analysis, confirm your response and move on to the next question. **The correct answer is (E).**

# DATA INTERPRETATION STRATEGIES

Applying the 5-step approach to the two sample questions in the previous section highlighted certain tips, techniques, and strategies for data interpretation. Here's a list of them. (The last one applies to certain other types of graphical data.)

## Don't Confuse Percentages with Raw Numbers

Most data interpretation questions involve raw data as well as *proportion*—in terms of either percent, fraction, or ratio. Always ask yourself: "Is the solution to this problem a raw number or a *proportional* number?" (You can be sure that the test designers will bait you with appropriate incorrect answer choices.)

**ALERT!**
Be sure to consult the appropriate portion of the chart, graph, or table for the information you need to answer a data interpretation question. Your ability to find the right data is a big part of what's being tested.

### Be Sure to Go to the Appropriate Chart (or Part of a Chart) for Your Numbers

When it comes to GRE data interpretation, carelessly referring to the wrong data is the leading cause of incorrect answers. To make sure you don't commit this error, point your finger to the proper line, column, or bar on the screen; put your finger right on it, and don't move it until you're sure you've got the right data.

### Handle Lengthy, Confusing Questions One Part at a Time

Data interpretation questions can be wordy and confusing. Don't panic. Keep in mind that lengthy questions almost always call for a sequence of two discrete tasks. For the first task, read just the first part of the question. When you're done, go back to the question and read the next part.

### Know the Overall Size of the Number That the Question Is Calling For

The test designers will lure careless test-takers with wrong answer choices that result from common computational errors. So always ask yourself how great (or small) a value you're looking for in the correct answer. For instance:

- Is it a double-digit number, or an even greater number?
- Is it a percentage that is obviously greater than 50 percent?

By keeping the big picture in mind, you're more likely to detect whether you made an error in your calculation.

### To Save Time, Round Off Numbers—But Don't Distort Values

Some data interpretation questions will ask for *approximate* values. So it's okay to round off numbers to save time; rounding off to the nearest appropriate unit or half-unit usually suffices to give you the correct answer. But don't get too rough in your approximations. Also, be sure to round off numerators and denominators of fractions in the same direction (either both up or both down), unless you're confident that a rougher approximation will suffice. Otherwise, you'll distort the size of the number.

### Don't Split Hairs in Reading Line Charts and Bar Graphs

These are the two types of figures that are drawn to scale. If a certain point on a chart appears to be about 40 percent of the way from one hash mark to the next, don't hesitate to round up to the halfway point. (The number 5 is usually easier to work with than 4 or 6.)

## THE NUMERIC ENTRY FORMAT (NEW)

Since November 2007, your GRE Quantitative Reasoning section might include one numeric entry question, which you answer by entering a number via the keyboard instead of selecting among multiple choices. If you encounter a numeric entry question on your exam, it may or may not count toward your GRE score. But you should assume that it counts, and you should try your best to answer it correctly.

A numeric entry question is inherently more difficult than the same question accompanied by multiple choices because you cannot use the process of elimination or consult the answer choices for clues as to how to solve the problem. What's more, the numeric entry format practically eliminates the possibility of lucky guesswork. Nevertheless, just as with multiple-choice questions, the difficulty level of numeric entry questions runs the gamut from easy to challenging.

A numeric entry question might call for you to enter a positive or negative integer or decimal number (for example, 125 or −14.2). Or it might call for you to enter a fraction by typing a numerator in one box and typing a denominator below it in another box. In this section, you'll look at some examples of these variations.

## Decimal Number Numeric Entries

A numeric entry question might ask for a numerical answer that includes a decimal point. In working these problems, do NOT round off your answer unless the question explicitly instructs you to do so. The following question, for example, calls for a *precise decimal number* answer. In working the problem, you should *not* round off your answer.

**17.** What is the sum of $\sqrt{.49}$, $\frac{3}{4}$, and 80% ?

*Click on the answer box, then type in a number. Backspace to erase.*

**The correct answer is 2.25.** To calculate the sum, first convert all three values to decimal numbers:

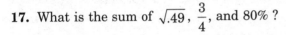

$\sqrt{.49} = .7$, $\frac{3}{4} = .75$, and 80% = .8

Now combine by addition:

.7 + .75 + .8 = 2.25

To receive credit for a correct answer, you must enter 2.25 in the answer box.

## Positive vs. Negative Numeric Entries

A numeric entry question might be designed so that its answer might conceivably be either a positive or negative number. In working this type of problem, should you decide that the correct answer is a negative number, use the keyboard's hyphen (dash) key to enter a "minus" sign before the integer. Here's an example:

**18.** If $<x> = (x + 1) - (x + 2) - (x - 1) + (x - 2)$, what is the value of $<100> + <99>$?

*Click on the answer box, then type in*
*a number. Backspace to erase.*

**The correct answer is −4.** To answer the question, substitute 100 and 99, in turn, for $x$ in the defined operation:

$<100> = 101 - 102 - 99 + 98 = -2$

$<99> = 100 - 101 - 98 + 97 = -2$

Then combine by addition: $<100> + <99> = -2 + (-2) = -4$

To receive credit for a correct answer, you must enter −4 in the answer box.

## Numeric Entries That Are Fractions

A numeric entry problem might call for an answer that is a fraction—consisting of a numerator and a denominator. To answer this type of question, you enter one integer in a numerator (upper) box and another integer in a denominator (lower) box. Be sure to express your answer in lowest terms. Here's an example:

**19.** A legislature passed a bill into law by a 5 to 3 margin. No legislator abstained from voting. What fractional part of the votes on the bill were cast in favor of passing the bill? [You must express your answer in lowest terms.]

*Click on each answer box, then type a*
*number in each box. Backspace to erase.*

**The correct answer is** $\dfrac{5}{8}$. To answer this question, you don't need to know the total number of legislators who voted because the question involves only ratios. You know that for every 5 votes cast in favor of the bill, 3 were cast against it.

Thus, 5 out of every 8 votes were cast in favor of the bill. To receive credit for this question, you must enter 5 in the upper (numerator) box and 8 in the lower (denominator) box.

## Numeric Entries Involving Units of Measurement

If the answer to a numeric entry question involves a unit of measurement (such as percent, degrees, dollars, or square feet), the question will clearly indicate the unit of measurement in which you should express your answer—as in the following example.

**20.** Four of the five interior angles of a pentagon measure 110°, 60°, 120°, and 100°. What is the measure of the fifth interior angle?

☐ degrees

*Click on the answer box, then type in a number. Backspace to erase.*

**The correct answer is 150.** Notice that the question makes clear that you are to express your numerical answer in terms of degrees. Since the figure has five sides, the sum of the angle measures is 540. Letting $x$ equal the fifth interior angle:

$540 = x + 110 + 60 + 120 + 100$

$540 = x + 390$

$150 = x$

To receive credit for the question, you must enter 150 in the answer box.

## SUMMING IT UP

- The 45-minute Quantitative Reasoning section tests your proficiency in performing arithmetical operations and solving algebraic equations and inequalities. It also tests your ability to convert verbal information into mathematical terms; to visualize geometric shapes and numerical relationships; to interpret data presented in charts, graphs, tables, and other graphical displays; and to devise intuitive and unconventional solutions to conventional mathematical problems.

- Problem Solving is one of two basic formats for questions in the Quantitative Reasoning section of the GRE (the other is Quantitative Comparison).

- All Problem Solving questions are five-item multiple-choice questions (you might encounter one "fill-in" question as well). About one-half of the questions are story problems. Numerical answer choices are listed in either ascending or descending order.

- Some Problem Solving questions involve the interpretation of graphical data—tables, charts, and graphs. The focus is on skills, not number crunching.

- Follow and review the 5 basic steps for handling GRE Problem Solving questions outlined in this chapter and apply them to this book's Practice Tests. Then review them again just before exam day.

# Quantitative Comparison

## chapter 8

## OVERVIEW

- **Key facts about GRE Quantitative Comparisons**
- **The 6-step plan**
- **Quantitative Comparison strategies**
- **Summing it up**

In this chapter, you'll focus exclusively on the Quantitative Comparison format, one of the two basic formats on the GRE Quantitative Reasoning section. First, you'll learn a step-by-step approach to handling any Quantitative Comparison. Then you'll apply that approach to some GRE-style examples. Later in the chapter, you'll learn useful strategies for comparing quantities and for avoiding mistakes that test-takers often commit when comparing quantities.

You first looked at GRE Quantitative Comparisons in Chapter 2 and in this book's Diagnostic Test. Let's quickly review the key facts about the Quantitative Comparison format.

## KEY FACTS ABOUT GRE QUANTITATIVE COMPARISONS

**Where:** The 45-minute Quantitative Reasoning section

**How Many:** Approximately 14 test items (out of 28 altogether), mixed in with Problem Solving questions

**What's Tested:**

- Your understanding of the principles, concepts, and rules of arithmetic, algebra, and geometry
- Your ability to devise intuitive and unconventional methods of comparing quantitative expressions
- Your ability to visualize numerical relationships and geometric shapes
- Your ability to convert verbal information into mathematical terms

**Areas Covered:** Any of the Quantitative Reasoning areas listed from pages 26 to 32 is fair game for Quantitative Comparisons, which cover the same mix of arithmetic, algebra, and geometry as Problem Solving questions.

**Directions:** Quantitative Comparison directions are similar to the following. The "Notes" are the same as for Problem Solving questions:

**Directions:** Each of the following questions consists of two quantities, one in Column A and one in Column B. You are to compare the two quantities and choose whether

**(A)** the quantity in Column A is greater;

**(B)** the quantity in Column B is greater;

**(C)** the quantities are equal;

**(D)** the relationship cannot be determined from the information given.

**Common Information:** In a question, information concerning one or both of the quantities to be compared is centered above the two columns. A symbol that appears in both columns represents the same thing in Column A as it does in Column B.

**Notes:**

- All number used are real numbers.
- All figures lie on a plane unless otherwise indicated.
- All angle measures are positive.
- All lines shown as straight are straight. Lines that appear jagged can also be assumed to be straight (lines can look somewhat jagged on the computer screen).
- Figures are intended to provide useful information for answering the questions. However, except where a figure is accompanied by a "Note" stating that the figure is drawn to scale, solve the problem using your knowledge of mathematics, *not* by visual measurement or estimation.

**Other Key Facts:**

- There are only four answer choices, and they're the same for all Quantitative Comparison questions.

- All information centered above the columns applies to both columns. Some Quantitative Comparisons will include centered information; others won't.

- The same variable (such as $x$) in both columns signifies the same value in both expressions.

- As in Problem Solving questions, figures are not necessarily drawn to scale, so don't rely solely on the visual appearance of a figure to make a comparison.

- Quantitative Comparisons are not inherently easier or tougher than Problem Solving questions, and their level of difficulty and complexity varies widely, as determined by the correctness of your responses to previous questions.

- You'll make fewer calculations and solve fewer equations for Quantitative Comparison questions than for Problem Solving questions. What's being tested here is mainly your ability to recognize and understand principles, not your ability to work step-by-step toward a solution.

- Calculators are prohibited, but scratch paper is provided.

# THE 6-STEP PLAN

The first task in this lesson is to learn the 6 basic steps for handling any GRE Quantitative Comparison. Just ahead, you'll apply these steps to three GRE-style Quantitative Comparisons.

## Step 1: Size Up the Question

What general area does the question deal with? What mathematical principles and formulas are likely to come into play? Does it appear to require a simple arithmetical calculation, or does it seem more "theoretical"—at least at first glance?

## Step 2: Check for Shortcuts and Clues

Check both quantities for possible shortcuts and for clues as to how to proceed. Here are three different features to look for:

**1** If both quantities contain common numbers or other terms, you might be able to simplify by canceling them. Be careful, though; sometimes you can't cancel terms. (See the strategies later in this chapter.)

**2** If one quantity is a verbal description but the other one consists solely of numbers and variables, you're dealing with a Problem Solving question in disguise. Your task is to work from the verbal expression to a solution, then compare that solution to the other quantity.

**3** If the centered information includes one or more equations, you should probably solve the equation(s) first.

## Step 3: Deal with Each Quantity

If the problem includes any centered information (above the two quantities), ask yourself how the quantity relates to it. Then do any calculations needed.

## Step 4: Consider All Possibilities for Unknowns (Variables)

Consider what would happen to each quantity if a fraction, negative number, or the number zero (0) or 1 were plugged in to the expression.

## Step 5: Compare the Two Quantities

Compare the quantities in Columns A and B. Select one of the four answer choices, based on your analysis.

## Step 6: Check Your Answer

If you have time, double-check your answer. It's a good idea to make any calculations with pencil and paper so you can double-check your computations before confirming the answer. Also, ask yourself again:

- Did I consider all possibilities for unknowns?
- Did I account for all the centered information (above the two quantities)?

## Applying the 6-Step Plan

Let's apply these 6 steps to three GRE-style Quantitative Comparisons. At the risk of giving away the answers up front, the correct answer—(A), (B), (C), or (D)—is different for each question.

| | <u>Column A</u> | <u>Column B</u> |
|---|---|---|
| **1.** | $\dfrac{1}{4}+\dfrac{13}{52}+\dfrac{5}{6}$ | $\dfrac{1}{5}+\dfrac{3}{10}+\dfrac{10}{12}$ |

This is a relatively easy question. Approximately 85 percent of test-takers respond correctly to questions like this one. Here's how to compare the two quantities using the 6-step approach:

**Step 1:** Both quantities involve numbers only (there are no variables), so this comparison appears to involve nothing more than combining fractions by adding them. Since the denominators differ, then what's probably being covered is the concept of "common denominators." Nothing theoretical or tricky here.

**Step 2:** You can cancel $\dfrac{5}{6}$ from Quantity A and $\dfrac{10}{12}$ from Quantity B, because these two fractions have the same value. You don't affect the comparison at all by doing so. Canceling across quantities before going to step 3 will make that step far easier.

**Step 3:** For each of the two quantities, find a common denominator, then add the two fractions:

Quantity A: $\dfrac{1}{4}+\dfrac{13}{52}=\dfrac{1}{4}+\dfrac{1}{4}=\dfrac{1}{2}$

Quantity B: $\dfrac{1}{5}+\dfrac{3}{10}=\dfrac{2}{10}+\dfrac{3}{10}=\dfrac{5}{10}$ or $\dfrac{1}{2}$

**Step 4:** There are no variables, so go on to step 5.

**Step 5:** Since $\dfrac{1}{2}=\dfrac{1}{2}$, the two quantities are equal.

**Step 6:** Check your calculations (you should have used pencil and paper). Did you convert all numerators properly? If you satisfied that you're calculations are correct, confirm your response and move on. **The correct answer is (C).**

|     **Column A**     |     **Column B**     |

2.

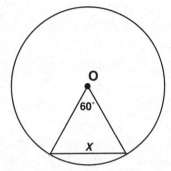

O lies at the center of the circle.

|     6x     |     The circumference of circle O     |

This is a moderately difficult question. Approximately 55 percent of test-takers respond correctly to questions like this one. Here's how to compare the two quantities using the 6-step approach:

**Step 1:** One quick look at this problem tells you that you need to know the formula for finding a circle's circumference, and that you should look for a relationship between the triangle and the circle. If you recognize the key as the circle's radius, then you shouldn't have any trouble making the comparison.

**Step 2:** A quick glance at the two quantities should tell you that you should proceed by finding the circumference of the circle in terms $x$ (Quantity B), then comparing it to Quantity A.

**Step 3:** Because the angle at the circle's center is 60°, the triangle must be equilateral. All three sides are equal, and they are all equal in length to the circle's radius ($r$). Thus, $x = r$. A circle's circumference (distance around the circle) is defined as $2\pi r$, and $\pi \approx 3.1$. Since $x = r$, the circumference of this circle equals approximately $(2)(3.1)(x)$, or a little more than $6x$.

**Step 4:** You've already determined the value of $x$ to the extent it's possible given the information. Its value equals $r$ (the circle's radius). The comparison does not provide any information to determine a precise value of $x$.

**Step 5:** Since the circumference of this circle must be greater than $6x$, Quantity B is greater than Quantity A. There's no need to determine the circumference any more precisely. As long as you're confident that it's greater than $x$, that's all the number crunching you need to do.

**Step 6:** Check your calculation again (you should have used pencil and paper). Make sure you used the correct formula. (It's surprisingly easy to confuse the formula for a circle's area with the one for its circumference—especially under exam pressure!) If you are satisfied your analysis is correct, confirm your response and move on. **The correct answer is (B).**

|  | Column A | | Column B |
| --- | --- | --- | --- |
| **3.** |  | $xy \neq 0$ |  |
|  | $x^2 + y^2$ |  | $(x + y)^2$ |

This is a relatively difficult question. Approximately 40 percent of test-takers respond correctly to questions like this one. Here's how to compare the two quantities, using the 6-step approach:

**Step 1:** This question involves quadratic expressions and squaring a binomial. Since there are two variables here ($x$ and $y$) but no equations, you won't be calculating precise numerical values for either variable. Take notice of the centered information, which establishes that neither $x$ nor $y$ can be zero (0).

**Step 2:** On their faces, the two quantities don't appear to share common terms that you can simply cancel across quantities. But they're similar enough that you can bet on revealing the comparison by manipulating one or both expressions.

**Step 3:** Quantity A is simplified, so leave it as is—at least for now. Square Quantity B:

$$(x + y)^2 = x^2 + 2xy + y^2$$

Notice that the result is the same expression as the one in Column A, with the addition of the middle term $2xy$. Now you can cancel common terms across columns, so you're left to compare zero (0) in Column A with $2xy$ in Column B.

**Step 4:** The variables $x$ and $y$ can each be either positive or negative. Be sure to account for different possibilities. For example, if $x$ and $y$ are both positive or both negative, then Quantity B is greater than zero (0), and thus greater than Quantity A. However, if one variable is negative and the other is positive, then Quantity B is less than zero (0), and thus less than Quantity A.

**Step 5:** You've done enough work already to determine that the correct answer must be choice (D). You've proven that which quantity is greater depends on the value of at least one variable. There's no need to try plugging in different numbers. The relationship cannot be determined from the information given.

**Step 6:** Check your squaring in step 3, and make sure your signs (plus and minus) are correct. If you're satisfied that your analysis is correct, confirm your response and move on. **The correct answer is (D).**

## QUANTITATIVE COMPARISON STRATEGIES

Just as with GRE Problem Solving, handling Quantitative Comparisons requires you to know the fundamentals of arithmetic, algebra, and geometry—no doubt about it—and that's what the math review in the next part of this book is about. But the test designers craft Quantitative Comparisons to gauge not just your math knowledge, but also your mental agility, flexibility, and creativity in applying it. Quantitative Comparisons are designed, for example, to measure your ability to do the following:

**TIP**

The examples here involve a variety of math concepts, and all are at least moderately difficult. If you have trouble with a concept, focus on it during the math review later in this part of the book.

- See the dynamic relationships between numbers
- Recognize the easiest, quickest, or most reliable way to compare quantities
- Visualize geometric shapes and relationships between shapes

In this section of the chapter, you'll learn some strategies and techniques that demonstrate these skills. These aren't merely tricks and shortcuts. Your facility in applying these techniques, along with your knowledge of substantive rules of math, is exactly what the test designers are attempting to measure.

### What Concept Is Being Tested?

Each Quantitative Comparison question focuses on a particular math concept. The first thing to do is look at the centered information and the expressions in the columns to determine what's being covered. This step can often help you get a head start in making the comparison.

**NOTE**

Not every Quantitative Comparison question you encounter on the GRE is suitable for one of these strategies, but some are—so it's a good idea to become familiar with them.

|  | **Column A** | **Column B** |
|---|---|---|
| 4. | $2x^2 + 9x = 5$ | |
|  | $x$ | $-5$ |

**The correct answer is (D).** Notice that the centered equation is quadratic, and that the two quantitative expressions essentially ask you to find the value of $x$. You know that quadratic equations have two roots, and this is the concept that's probably being tested here. The two roots might be the same or they may differ.

Now you know what you need to do and why. First, rewrite the centered equation in standard form: $2x^2 + 9x - 5 = 0$. Now, factor the trinomial expression into two binomials: $(2x - 1)(x + 5) = 0$. It should now be clear that there are two different roots of the equation: $\frac{1}{2}$ and $-5$. Since $\frac{1}{2} > -5$, but $-5 = -5$, the correct answer is choice (D).

### There May Be an Easier Way

You shouldn't have to perform involved calculations to make a comparison. A few simple calculations may be required, but if you're doing a lot of number crunching or setting up and solving of equations, you've probably missed the mathematical principal that you're being tested for. Put your pencil down and focus on the concept, not the process.

| Column A | Column B |
|---|---|
| 5. $\dfrac{(-6)^{11}}{(-6)^3}$ | $\dfrac{(-11)^8}{(-11)^3}$ |

**The correct answer is (A).** To make the comparison, you could multiply each base number by itself multiple times, then figure out quotients. But that would be a horrendous waste of time, and most GRE test-takers would at least realize that they can simplify each fraction by canceling exponents:

$$\frac{(-6)^{11}}{(-6)^3} = (-6)^8 \quad \text{and} \quad \frac{(-11)^8}{(-11)^3} = (-11)^5$$

Now, instead of multiplying $-6$ by itself 8 times, and then multiplying $-11$ by itself 5 times to compare the two products, look at the signs and the exponents for a moment. Quantity A is a negative number raised to an even power, so it must have a positive value. Quantity B is a negative number raised to an odd power, so it must have a negative value. There's no need for all that calculating. Quantity A must be greater.

## Choose (D) *Only* If You Need More Information

Remember: Pick choice (D) only if you can't make a comparison without having more information. But if the comparison at hand involves numbers only, you'll always be able to calculate specific numerical values for both expressions (assuming you have time to do the math). You certainly don't need more information just to compare the size of two specific numbers.

| Column A | Column B |
|---|---|
| 6. | $x \,\square\, y = x(x - y)$ |
| $(-1 \,\square\, -2) \,\square\, (1 \,\square\, 2)$ | $(1 \,\square\, -2) \,\square\, (-1 \,\square\, 2)$ |

**The correct answer is (C).** The centered information contains variables—but calculating the two quantities involves only numbers. Thus, the correct answer cannot be (D). Just for form, let's work the problem. For both quantities, first apply the operation (defined by the symbol $\square$) to each parenthesized pair, then apply it again to those results:

Quantity A: 　　　$(-1 \,\square\, -2) = -1(-1 - [-2]) = -1(1) = -1$

　　　　　　　　$(1 \,\square\, 2) = 1(1 - 2) = 1(-1) = -1$

Apply the defined operation again, substituting $-1$ for both $x$ and $y$:

$(-1 \,\square\, -1) = -1(-1 - [-1]) = -1(0) = 0$

Quantity B: $(1 \square -2) = 1(1 - [-2]) = 1(3) = 3$

$(-1 \square 2) = -1(-1 - 2) = -1(-3) = 3$

Apply the defined operation again, substituting 3 for both $x$ and $y$:

$(3 \square 3) = 3(3 - 3) = 3(0) = 0$

As you can see, both quantities equal zero (0).

## Consider All Possibilities for Variables

When comparing expressions involving variables, unless the centered information restricts their value, consider positive *and* negative values, as well as fractions and the numbers zero (0) and 1. Comparisons often depend on which sort of number is used. In these cases, the correct answer would be choice (D).

|                |                |
| :------------: | :------------: |
| **Column A**   | **Column B**   |

7.

$$p > 0$$
$$p \neq 1$$

$p^{-3}$                                        $p^4$

**The correct answer is (D).** Here's the general rule that applies to this problem: $p^{-x} = \dfrac{1}{p^x}$. Hence, if $p > 1$, then $p^{-3}$ must be a fraction less than 1 while $p^4$ is greater than 1, and Quantity B is greater. On the other hand, if $p < 1$, then the opposite is true.

## Rewrite a Quantity to Resemble Another

If you have no idea how to analyze a particular problem, try manipulating one or both of the expressions until they resemble each other more closely. You may be able to combine numbers or other terms, do some factoring, or restate an expression in a slightly different form.

|                |                |
| :------------: | :------------: |
| **Column A**   | **Column B**   |

8.            $4 - x^2$                    $(2 + x)(2 - x)$

**The correct answer is (C).** Perhaps you recognized that $(4 - x^2)$ is the difference of two squares ($2^2$ and $x^2$) and that the following equation applies: $a^2 - b^2 = (a + b)(a - b)$. If so, then you saw right away that the two quantities are the same. If you didn't recognize this, you could tweak Quantity B by multiplying $(2 - x)$ by $(2 + x)$ using the FOIL method:

$$(2 + x)(2 - x) = 4 + 2x - 2x - x^2 = 4 - x^2$$

Rewriting Quantity B, then simplifying it, reveals the comparison. The two quantities are equal.

## Add or Subtract Across Columns to Simplify Comparison

If both expressions include the same term, you can safely "cancel" that term from each one either by adding or subtracting it. This technique may help simplify one or both of the expressions, thereby revealing the comparison to you. Remember: You don't change the comparative value of two expressions merely by adding or subtracting the same terms from each one.

| Column A | Column B |
|---|---|
| **9.** The sum of all integers from 19 to 50, including 19 and 50 | The sum of all integers from 21 to 51, including 21 and 51 |

**The correct answer is (B).** The two number strings have in common integers 21 through 50. So you can subtract (or cancel) all of these integers from both sides of the comparison. That leaves you to compare (19 + 20) to 51. You can now see clearly that Quantity B is greater.

## Avoid Multiplying or Dividing Across Columns

To help simplify the two expressions, you can also multiply or divide across columns, but *only* if you know for sure that the quantity you're using is positive. Multiplying or dividing two unequal terms by a negative value changes the inequality; the quantity that was the greater one becomes the smaller one. So think twice before performing either operation on both expressions.

| Column A | Column B |
|---|---|
| **10.** | $x > y$ |
| $x^2y$ | $xy^2$ |

**The correct answer is (D).** To simplify this comparison, you may be tempted to divide both columns by $x$ and by $y$—but that would be wrong. Although you know that $x$ is greater than $y$, you don't know whether $x$ and $y$ are positive or negative. You can't multiply or divide by a quantity unless you're certain that the quantity is positive. If you do this, here is what could happen: Dividing both sides by $xy$ would leave the comparison between $x$ and $y$. Given $x > y$, you'd probably select (A). But if you let $x = 1$ and $y = 0$, on this assumption, both quantities $= 0$ (they're equal). Or let $x = 1$ and $y = -1$. On this assumption, Quantity A $= -1$ and Quantity B $= 1$. Since these results conflict with the previous ones, you've proven that the correct answer is choice (D).

## Solve Centered Equations for Values

If the centered information includes one or more algebraic equations and you need to know the value of the variable(s) in those equations to make the comparison, then there's probably no shortcut to avoid doing the algebra.

| Column A | Column B |
|---|---|
| **11.** | $x + y = 6$ <br> $x - 2y = 3$ |
| $x$ | $y$ |

**The correct answer is (A).** The centered information presents a system of *simultaneous linear equations* with two variables, $x$ and $y$. The quickest way to solve for $x$ is probably by subtracting the second equation from the first:

$$x + \quad y = 6$$
$$\underline{-(x - 2y = 3)}$$
$$3y = 3$$
$$y = 1$$

Substitute this value for $y$ in either equation. Using the first one:

$$x + 1 = 6$$
$$x = 5$$

Since both equations are linear, you know that each variable has one and only one value. Since $x = 5$ and $y = 1$, Quantity A is greater than Quantity B.

## Don't Rely on Geometry Figure Proportions

For Quantitative Comparison questions involving geometry figures, never try to make a comparison by visual estimation or by measuring a figure. Even if you see a note stating that a figure is drawn to scale, you should always make your comparison based on your knowledge of mathematics and whatever nongraphical data the question provides, instead of "eyeballing" it.

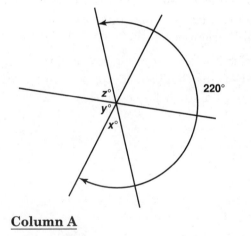

| **Column A** | **Column B** |
|---|---|
| $-y$ | $-z$ |

**12.**

**The correct answer is (D).** If you were to measure the two angles ($y°$ and $z°$) by eye, you might conclude that they are the same or that one is *slightly* greater than the other, and then select choice (A), (B), or (C) accordingly. But that would be a mistake. Your task is to compare $y$ and $z$ without resorting to visual measurement. Given that any circle contains a total of 360°, you know that $y + z = 360 - 220 = 140$. Also, since $x$, $y$, and $z$ are supplementary (their sum is 180 because the three angles combine to form a straight line), you know that $x = 40$. But the problem does not supply enough information for you to determine the degree measure of either $y$ or $x$. (All you know is that their sum is 140.)

# SUMMING IT UP

- The 45-minute Quantitative Reasoning section tests your proficiency in performing arithmetical operations and solving algebraic equations and inequalities. It also tests your ability to convert verbal information into mathematical terms; visualize geometric shapes and numerical relationships; interpret data presented in charts, graphs, tables, and other graphical displays; and devise intuitive and unconventional solutions to conventional mathematical problems.

- Quantitative Comparison is one of two basic formats for questions in the Quantitative Reasoning section of the GRE (the other is Problem Solving).

- All Quantitative Comparison questions require you to compare two quantities, one in Column A and one in Column B. You choose whether the quantity in Column A is greater, the quantity in Column B is greater, the quantities are equal, or the relationship cannot be determined from the information given. Information concerning one or both of the quantities to be compared is centered above the two columns. These four are the only answer choices, and they're the same for all Quantitative Comparison questions.

- You'll make fewer calculations and solve fewer equations for Quantitative Comparison questions than for Problem Solving questions. You're being tested mainly on your ability to recognize and understand principles, not your ability to work step-by-step toward a solution.

- Follow and review the 6 basic steps for handling GRE Quantitative Comparison questions outlined in this chapter and apply them to this book's Practice Tests. Then review them again just before exam day.

# Math Review: Number Forms, Relationships, and Sets

## OVERVIEW

- Percents, fractions, and decimals
- Simplifying and combining fractions
- Decimal place values and operations
- Simple percent problems
- Percent increase and decrease
- Ratios and proportion
- Altering fractions and ratios
- Ratios with more than two quantities
- Proportion problems with variables
- Arithmetic mean, median, mode, and range
- Standard deviation
- Arithmetic sequences
- Geometric sequences
- Permutations
- Combinations
- Probability
- Summing it up

In this chapter, you'll focus first on various forms of numbers and relationships between numbers. Specifically, you'll learn how to do the following:

- Combine fractions using the four basic operations

- Combine decimal numbers by multiplication and division

- Compare numbers in percentage terms

- Compare percent changes with number changes

- Rewrite percents, fractions, and decimal numbers from one form to another

- Determine ratios between quantities and determine quantities from ratios

- Set up equivalent ratios (proportions)

- Handle fractions and ratios

- Handle ratios involving more than two quantities

- Handle proportion problems with variables

Next, you'll explore the following topics, all of which involve descriptive statistics and sets (defined groups) of numbers or other objects:

- Arithmetic mean (simple average) and median (two ways that a set of numbers can be described as a whole)

- Standard deviation (a quantitative expression of the dispersion of a set of measurements)

- Arithmetic sequences (there is a constant difference between successive numbers)

- Geometric sequences (each term is a constant multiple of the preceeding one)

- Permutations (the possibilities for arranging a set of objects)

- Combinations (the possibilities for selecting groups of objects from a set)

- Probability (the statistical chances of a certain event, permutation, or combination occurring)

**ALERT!**

Although this is the most basic of all the math review topics in this book, don't skip it. The skills covered here are basic building blocks for other, more difficult types of questions covered in later sections of this math review

## PERCENTS, FRACTIONS, AND DECIMALS

Any real number can be expressed as a fraction, a percent, or a decimal number. For instance, $\frac{2}{10}$, 20%, and .2 are all different forms of the same quantity or value. GRE math questions often require you to rewrite one form as another as part of solving the problem at hand. You should know how to write any equivalent quickly and confidently.

To rewrite a percent as a decimal, move the decimal point two places to the *left* (and drop the percent sign). To rewrite a decimal as a percent, move the decimal point two places to the *right* (and add the percent sign).

$$95\% = 0.95$$
$$.004 = .4\%$$

To rewrite a percent as a fraction, *divide* by 100 (and drop the percent sign). To rewrite a fraction as a percent, *multiply* by 100 (and add the percent sign). Percents greater than 100 are equivalent to numbers greater than 1.

$$810\% = \frac{810}{100} = \frac{81}{10} = 8\frac{1}{10}$$

$$\frac{3}{8} = \frac{300}{8}\% = \frac{75}{2}\% = 37\frac{1}{2}\%$$

Percents greater than 100 or less than 1 (such as 457% and .067%) can be confusing, because it's a bit harder to grasp their magnitude.

> **Directions:** Each of the following questions consists of two quantities, one in Column A and one in Column B. You are to compare the two quantities and choose whether
> **(A)** the quantity in Column A is greater;
> **(B)** the quantity in Column B is greater;
> **(C)** the quantities are equal;
> **(D)** the relationship cannot be determined from the information given.

| **Column A** | **Column B** |
|---|---|
| 1.    The number of fifths in 340% | The number of eighths in 212.5% |

**The correct answer is (C).** 340% is 3.4, or $3\frac{2}{5}$. Since there are five fifths in 1, Quantity A must be (3)(5) + 2, or 17. 212.5% is 2.125, or $2\frac{1}{8}$. Since there are eight eighths in 1, Quantity B must be (2)(8) + 1, or 17.

To guard against errors when writing, keep in mind the general magnitude of the number you're dealing with. For example, think of .09% as just less than .1%, which is one-tenth of a percent, or a thousandth (a pretty small valued number). Think of $\frac{.45}{5}$ as just less than $\frac{.5}{5}$, which is obviously $\frac{1}{10}$, or 10%. Think of 668% as more than 6 times a complete 100%, or between 6 and 7.

To rewrite a fraction as a decimal, simply divide the numerator by the denominator, using long division. A fraction-to-decimal equivalent might result in a precise value, an approximation with a repeating pattern, or an approximation with no repeating pattern:

| | |
|---|---|
| $\frac{5}{8} = .625$ | The equivalent decimal number is precise after three decimal places. |
| $\frac{5}{9} \approx .555$ | The equivalent decimal number can only be approximated (the digit 5 repeats indefinitely). |
| $\frac{5}{7} \approx .714$ | The equivalent decimal number can safely be approximated. |

Certain fraction-decimal-percent equivalents show up on the GRE more often than others. The numbers in the following tables are the test-makers' favorites because they reward test-takers who recognize quick ways to deal with numbers. Memorize these conversions so that they're second nature to you on exam day.

| Percent | Decimal | Fraction |   | Percent | Decimal | Fraction |
|---------|---------|----------|---|---------|---------|----------|
| 50% | .5 | $\frac{1}{2}$ | | $16\frac{2}{3}\%$ | $.16\frac{2}{3}$ | $\frac{1}{6}$ |
| 25% | .25 | $\frac{1}{4}$ | | $83\frac{1}{3}\%$ | $.83\frac{1}{3}$ | $\frac{5}{6}$ |
| 75% | .75 | $\frac{3}{4}$ | | 20% | .2 | $\frac{1}{5}$ |
| 10% | .1 | $\frac{1}{10}$ | | 40% | .4 | $\frac{2}{5}$ |
| 30% | .3 | $\frac{3}{10}$ | | 60% | .6 | $\frac{3}{5}$ |
| 70% | .7 | $\frac{7}{10}$ | | 80% | .8 | $\frac{4}{5}$ |
| 90% | .9 | $\frac{9}{10}$ | | $12\frac{1}{2}\%$ | .125 | $\frac{1}{8}$ |
| $33\frac{1}{3}\%$ | $.33\frac{1}{3}$ | $\frac{1}{3}$ | | $37\frac{1}{2}\%$ | .375 | $\frac{3}{8}$ |
| $66\frac{2}{3}\%$ | $.66\frac{2}{3}$ | $\frac{2}{3}$ | | $62\frac{1}{2}\%$ | .625 | $\frac{5}{8}$ |
| | | | | $87\frac{1}{2}\%$ | .875 | $\frac{7}{8}$ |

## SIMPLIFYING AND COMBINING FRACTIONS

A GRE question might ask you to combine fractions using one or more of the four basic operations (addition, subtraction, multiplication, and division). The rules for combining fractions by addition and subtraction are very different from the ones for multiplication and division.

### Addition and Subtraction and the LCD

To combine fractions by addition or subtraction, the fractions *must* have a common denominator. If they already do, simply add (or subtract) numerators. If they don't, you'll need to find one. You can always multiply all of the denominators together to find a common denominator, but it might be a big number that's clumsy to work with. So instead, try to find the *least (or lowest) common denominator* (LCD) by working your way up in multiples of the largest of the denominators given. For denominators of 6, 3, and 5, for instance, try out successive multiples of 6 (12, 18, 24 . . . ), and you'll hit the LCD when you get to 30.

2. $\dfrac{5}{3} - \dfrac{5}{6} + \dfrac{5}{2} =$    $\dfrac{10}{6} - \dfrac{5}{6} + \dfrac{15}{6} = \dfrac{20}{6} = \dfrac{10}{3}$

**(A)** $\dfrac{15}{11}$

**(B)** $\dfrac{5}{2}$

**(C)** $\dfrac{15}{6}$

**(D)** $\dfrac{10}{3}$

**(E)** $\dfrac{15}{3}$

**The correct answer is (D).** To find the LCD, try out successive multiples of 6 until you come across one that is also a multiple of both 3 and 2. The LCD is 6. Multiply each numerator by the same number by which you would multiply the fraction's denominator to give you the LCD of 6. Place the three products over this common denominator. Then, combine the numbers in the numerator. (Pay close attention to the subtraction sign!) Finally, simplify to lowest terms:

$$\frac{5}{3} - \frac{5}{6} + \frac{5}{2} = \frac{10}{6} - \frac{5}{6} + \frac{15}{6}$$
$$= \frac{20}{6}$$
$$= \frac{10}{3}$$

## Multiplication and Division

To multiply fractions, multiply the numerators and multiply the denominators. The denominators need not be the same. To divide one fraction by another, multiply by the reciprocal of the divisor (the number after the division sign):

**Multiplication**
$$\frac{1}{2} \times \frac{5}{3} \times \frac{1}{7} = \frac{(1)(5)(1)}{(2)(3)(7)} = \frac{5}{42}$$

**Division**
$$\frac{\frac{2}{5}}{\frac{3}{4}} = \frac{2}{5} \times \frac{4}{3} = \frac{(2)(4)}{(5)(3)} = \frac{8}{15}$$

To simplify the multiplication or division, cancel factors common to a numerator and a denominator before combining fractions. It's okay to cancel across fractions. Take, for instance the operation $\dfrac{3}{4} \times \dfrac{4}{9} \times \dfrac{3}{2}$. Looking just at the first two fractions, you can cancel out 4 and 3, so the operation simplifies to $\dfrac{1}{1} \times \dfrac{1}{3} \times \dfrac{3}{2}$. Now, looking just at the second and third fractions, you can cancel out 3 and the operation becomes even simpler: $\frac{1}{1} \times \frac{1}{1} \times \frac{1}{2} = \frac{1}{2}$.

Apply the same rules in the same way to variables (letters) as to numbers.

**3.** $\frac{2}{a} \times \frac{b}{4} \times \frac{a}{5} \times \frac{8}{c} = ?$

$\frac{2}{1} \times \frac{b}{1} \times \frac{1}{5} \times \frac{2}{c} = \frac{4b}{5c}$

**(A)** $\frac{ab}{4c}$

**(B)** $\frac{10b}{9c}$

**(C)** $\frac{8}{5}$

**(D)** $\frac{16b}{5ac}$

**(E)** $\frac{4b}{5c}$

**The correct answer is (E).** Since you're dealing only with multiplication, look for factors and variables (letters) in any numerator that are the same as those in any denominator. Canceling common factors leaves:

$\frac{2}{1} \times \frac{b}{1} \times \frac{1}{5} \times \frac{2}{c}$

Multiply numerators and denominators and you get $\frac{4b}{5c}$.

## Mixed Numbers and Multiple Operations

A *mixed number* consists of a whole number along with a simple fraction—for example, the number $4\frac{2}{3}$. Before combining fractions, you might need to rewrite a mixed number as a fraction. To do so, follow these three steps:

**1** Multiply the denominator of the fraction by the whole number.

**2** Add the product to the numerator of the fraction.

**3** Place the sum over the denominator of the fraction.

For example, here's how to rewrite the mixed number $4\frac{2}{3}$ into a fraction:

$$4\frac{2}{3} = \frac{(3)(4) + 2}{3} = \frac{14}{3}$$

To perform multiple operations, always perform multiplication and division before you perform addition and subtraction.

**4.** $\dfrac{4\frac{1}{2}}{1\frac{1}{8}} - 3\frac{2}{3} = ?$

(A) $\dfrac{1}{3}$

(B) $\dfrac{3}{8}$

(C) $\dfrac{11}{6}$

(D) $\dfrac{17}{6}$

(E) $\dfrac{11}{2}$

**The correct answer is (A).** First, rewrite all mixed numbers as fractions. Then, eliminate the complex fraction by multiplying the numerator fraction by the reciprocal of the denominator fraction (cancel across fractions before multiplying):

$$\dfrac{\frac{9}{2}}{\frac{9}{8}} - \dfrac{11}{3} = \left(\dfrac{9}{2}\right)\left(\dfrac{8}{9}\right) - \dfrac{11}{3} = \left(\dfrac{1}{1}\right)\left(\dfrac{4}{1}\right) - \dfrac{11}{3} = \dfrac{4}{1} - \dfrac{11}{3}$$

Then, express each fraction using the common denominator 3, then subtract:

$$\dfrac{4}{1} - \dfrac{11}{3} = \dfrac{12 - 11}{3} = \dfrac{1}{3}$$

# DECIMAL PLACE VALUES AND OPERATIONS

*Place value* refers to the specific value of a digit in a decimal. For example, in the decimal 682.793:

- The digit 6 is in the "hundreds" place.
- The digit 8 is in the "tens" place.
- The digit 2 is in the "ones" place.
- The digit 7 is in the "tenths" place.
- The digit 9 is in the "hundredths" place.
- The digit 3 is in the "thousandths" place.

So you can express 682.793 as follows:

$$600 + 80 + 2 + \dfrac{7}{10} + \dfrac{9}{100} + \dfrac{3}{1,000}$$

To approximate, or round off, a decimal, round any digit less than 5 down to 0, and round any digit greater than 5 up to 0 (adding one digit to the place value to the left).

- The value of 682.793, to the nearest hundredth, is 682.79.

- The value of 682.793, to the nearest tenth, is 682.8.
- The value of 682.793, to the nearest whole number, is 683.
- The value of 682.793, to the nearest ten, is 680.
- The value of 682.793, to the nearest hundred, is 700.

## Multiplying Decimals

The number of decimal places (digits to the right of the decimal point) in a product should be the same as the total number of decimal places in the numbers you multiply. So to multiply decimals quickly, follow these three steps:

**1** Multiply, but ignore the decimal points.

**2** Count the total number of decimal places among the numbers you multiplied.

**3** Include that number of decimal places in your product.

Here are two simple examples:

**Example 1**

| | |
|---|---|
| $(23.6)(.07)$ | Three decimal places altogether |
| $(236)(7) = 1652$ | Decimals temporarily ignored |
| $(23.6)(.07) = 1.652$ | Decimal point inserted |

**Example 2**

| | |
|---|---|
| $(.01)(.02)(.03)$ | Six decimal places altogether |
| $(1)(2)(3) = 6$ | Decimals temporarily ignored |
| $(.01)(.02)(.03) = .000006$ | Decimal point inserted |

## Dividing Decimal Numbers

When you divide (or compute a fraction), you can move the decimal point in both numbers by the same number of places either to the left or right without altering the quotient (value of the fraction). Here are three related examples:

$$11.4 \div .3 = \frac{11.4}{.3} = \frac{114}{3} = 38$$

$$1.14 \div 3 = \frac{1.14}{3} = \frac{114}{300} = .38$$

$$114 \div .003 = \frac{114}{.003} = \frac{114,000}{3} = 38,000$$

**TIP**

Eliminate decimal points from fractions, as well as from percents, to help you see more clearly the magnitude of the quantity you're dealing with.

GRE questions involving place value and decimals usually require a bit more from you than just identifying a place value or moving a decimal point around. Typically, they require you to combine decimals with fractions or percents.

**5.** Which of the following is nearest in value to $\frac{1}{3} \times .3 \times \frac{1}{30} \times .03$?

(A) $\dfrac{1}{10,000}$

(B) $\dfrac{33}{100,000}$

(C) $\dfrac{99}{100,000}$

(D) $\dfrac{33}{10,000}$

(E) $\dfrac{99}{10,000}$

**The correct answer is (A).** There are several ways to convert and combine the four numbers provided in the question. One method is to combine the two fractions: $\frac{1}{3} \times \frac{1}{30} = \frac{1}{90}$. Then, combine the two decimals: $.3 \times .03 = .009 = \frac{9}{1,000}$. Finally, combine the two fractions: $\frac{1}{90} \times \frac{9}{1,000} = \frac{9}{90,000} = \frac{1}{10,000}$ which is choice (A).

## SIMPLE PERCENT PROBLEMS

On the GRE, a simple problem involving percent might ask you to perform any one of these four tasks:

**1** Find a percent of a percent

**2** Find a percent of a number

**4** Find a number when a percent is given

**4** Find what percent one number is of another

The following examples show you how to handle these four tasks (task 4 is a bit trickier than the others):

| Finding a percent of a percent | What is 2% of 2%? |
| --- | --- |
| | Rewrite 2% as .02, then multiply: |
| | .02 × .02 = .0004 or .04% |
| Finding a percent of a number | What is 35% of 65? |
| | Rewrite 35% as .35, then multiply: |
| | .35 × 65 = 22.75 |

| Finding a number when a percent is given | *7 is 14% of what number?*<br><br>Translate the question into an algebraic equation, writing the percent as either a fraction or decimal:<br><br>$$7 = 14\% \text{ of } x$$<br>$$7 = .14x$$<br>$$x = \frac{7}{.14} = \frac{1}{.02} = \frac{100}{2} = 50$$ |
|---|---|
| Finding what percent one number is of another<br><br>$\dfrac{90}{1,500} = \dfrac{x}{100}$ | *90 is what % of 1,500?*<br><br>Set up an equation to solve for the percent:<br><br>$$\frac{90}{1,500} = \frac{x}{100}$$<br>$$1,500x = 9,000$$<br>$$15x = 90$$<br>$$x = \frac{90}{15} \text{ or } 6$$ |

## PERCENT INCREASE AND DECREASE

In the fourth example, you set up a proportion. (90 is to 1,500 as $x$ is to 100.) You'll need to set up a proportion for other types of GRE questions as well, including questions about ratios, which you'll look at a bit later in this chapter.

The concept of percent change is one of the test-makers' favorites. Here's the key to answering questions involving this concept: Percent change always relates to the value *before* the change. Here are two simple illustrations:

| *10 increased by what percent is 12?*<br><br>$\dfrac{10}{12} = \dfrac{x}{100}$ | 1. The amount of the increase is 2.<br><br>2. Compare the change (2) to the original number (10).<br><br>3. The change in percent is $\left(\dfrac{2}{10}\right)(100) = 20$, or 20%. |
|---|---|
| *12 decreased by what percent is 10?* | 1. The amount of the decrease is 2.<br><br>2. Compare the change (2) to the original number (12). $\dfrac{2}{12}(100)$<br><br>3. The change is $\dfrac{1}{6}$, or $16\dfrac{2}{3}$%, or approximately 16.7%. |

Notice that the percent increase from 10 to 12 (20%) is not the same as the percent decrease from 12 to 10 $\left(16\frac{2}{3}\%\right)$. That's because the original number (before the change) is different in the two questions.

A typical GRE percent-change problem will involve a story—about a type of quantity such as tax, profit or discount, or weight—in which you need to calculate successive changes in percent. For example:

- An increase, then a decrease (or vice versa)

- Multiple increases or decreases

Whatever the variation, just take the problem one step at a time and you'll have no trouble handling it.

6. A stereo system originally priced at $500 is discounted by 10%, then by another 10%. If a 20% tax is added to the purchase price, how much would a customer buying the system at its lowest price pay for it, including tax, to the nearest dollar?

   **(A)** $413
   **(B)** $480
   **(C)** $486
   **(D)** $500
   **(E)** $512

   **The correct answer is (C).** After the first 10% discount, the price was $450 ($500 minus 10% of $500). After the second discount, which is calculated based on the $450 price, the price of the stereo is $405 ($450 minus 10% of $450). A 20% tax on $405 is $81. Thus, the customer has paid $405 + $81 = $486.

## RATIOS AND PROPORTION

A *ratio* expresses proportion or comparative size—the size of one quantity *relative* to the size of another. As with fractions, you can simplify ratios by dividing common factors. For example, given a class of 28 students—12 freshmen and 16 sophomores:

- The ratio of freshmen to sophomores is 12:16, or 3:4.

- The ratio of freshmen to the total number of students is 12:28, or 3:7.

- The ratio of sophomores to the total number of students is 16:28, or 4:7.

### Finding a Ratio

A GRE question might ask you to determine a ratio based on given quantities. This is the easiest type of GRE ratio question.

NOTE

GRE problems involving percent and percent change are often accompanied by a chart, graph, or table.

7. A class of 56 students contains only freshmen and sophomores. If 21 of the students are sophomores, what is the ratio of the number of freshmen to the number of sophomores in the class?

   (A) 3:5

   (B) 5:7

   (C) 5:3

   (D) 7:4

   (E) 2:1

**The correct answer is (C).** Since 21 of 56 students are sophomores, 35 must be freshmen. The ratio of freshmen to sophomores is 35:21. To simplify the ratio to simplest terms, divide both numbers by 7, giving you a ratio of 5:3.

## Determining Quantities from a Ratio (Part-to-Whole Analysis)

You can think of any ratio as parts adding up to a whole. For example, in the ratio 5:6, 5 parts + 6 parts = 11 parts (the whole). If the actual total quantity were 22, you'd multiply each element by 2: 10 parts + 12 parts = 22 parts (the whole). Notice that the ratios are the same: 5:6 is the same ratio as 10:12.

You might be able to solve a GRE ratio question using this part-to-whole approach.

8. A class of students contains only freshmen and sophomores. If 18 of the students are sophomores, and if the ratio of the number of freshmen to the number of sophomores in the class is 5:3, how many students are in the class?

   (A) 30

   (B) 36

   (C) 40

   (D) 48

   (E) 56

**The correct answer is (D).** Using a part-to-whole analysis, look first at the ratio and the sum of its parts: 5 (freshmen) + 3 (sophomores) = 8 (total students). These aren't the actual quantities, but they're proportionate to those quantities. Given 18 sophomores altogether, sophomores account for 3 parts—each part containing 6 students. Accordingly, the total number of students must be $6 \times 8 = 48$.

## Determining Quantities from a Ratio (Setting Up a Proportion)

Since you can express any ratio as a fraction, you can set two equivalent, or proportionate, ratios equal to each other, as fractions. So the ratio 16:28 is proportionate to the ratio 4:7 because $\dfrac{16}{28} = \dfrac{4}{7}$. If one of the four terms is missing from the equation (the proportion), you can solve for the missing term using algebra. So if the ratio 3:4 is proportionate to 4:$x$, you can solve for $x$ in the equation $\dfrac{3}{4} = \dfrac{4}{x}$. Using the *cross-product* method, equate products of numerator and denominator across the equation:

$$(3)(x) = (4)(4)$$
$$3x = 16$$
$$x = \frac{16}{3} \text{ or } 5\frac{1}{3}$$

Or, since the numbers are simple, shortcut the algebra by asking yourself what number you multiply the first numerator (3) by for a result that equals the other numerator (4):

$$3 \times \frac{4}{3} = 4 \text{ (a no-brainer calculation)}$$

So you maintain proportion (equal ratios) by also multiplying the first denominator (4) by $\frac{4}{3}$:

$$4 \times \frac{4}{3} = \frac{16}{3} \text{ (another no-brainer calculation)}$$

Even if the quantities in a question strike you as decidedly "unround," it's a good bet that doing the math will be easier than you might first think.

9. If 3 miles are equivalent to 4.83 kilometers, then 11.27 kilometers are equivalent to how many miles?

   (A) 1.76
   (B) 5.9
   (C) 7.0
   (D) 8.4
   (E) 16.1

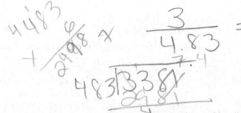

   **The correct answer is (C).** The question essentially asks, "3 is to 4.83 as *what* is to 11.27?" Set up a proportion, then solve for $x$ by the cross-product method:

$$\frac{3}{4.83} = \frac{x}{11.27}$$
$$(4.83)(x) = (3)(11.27)$$
$$x = \frac{(3)(11.27)}{4.83}$$
$$x = \frac{33.81}{4.83} \text{ or } 7$$

   Notice that, despite all the intimidating decimal numbers, the solution turns out to be a tidy number 7. That's typical of the GRE.

## ALTERING FRACTIONS AND RATIOS

An average test-taker might assume that *adding* the same *positive* quantity to a fraction's numerator ($p$) and to its denominator ($q$) leaves the fraction's value $\left(\frac{p}{q}\right)$ unchanged. But this is true *if and only if* the original numerator and denominator were equal to each other. Otherwise, the fraction's value will change. Remember the following three rules, which apply to any positive numbers $x$, $p$, and $q$ (the first one is the no-brainer you just read):

If $p = q$, then $\frac{p}{q} = \frac{p + x}{q + x}$. (The fraction's value remains unchanged and is always 1.)

If $p > q$, then $\frac{p}{q} > \frac{p + x}{q + x}$. (The fraction's value will *decrease*.)

If $p < q$, then $\frac{p}{q} < \frac{p + x}{q + x}$. (The fraction's value will *increase*.)

As you might suspect, this concept makes great fodder for Quantitative Comparison questions. Here's an example:

| **Column A** | | **Column B** |
|---|---|---|
| | $0 < p < q < 1$ | |
| $\dfrac{p}{q}$ | | $\dfrac{p+1}{q+1}$ |

10.

**(A)** The quantity in Column A is greater;
**(B)** The quantity in Column B is greater;
**(C)** The quantities are equal;
**(D)** The relationship cannot be determined from the information given.

**The correct answer is (B).** Remember three rules, which apply to any positive numerator $p$ and denominator $q$:

❶ If $p = q$, the fraction's value remains unchanged (and is always 1).
❷ If $p > q$, the fraction's value will *decrease*.
❸ If $p < q$, the fraction's value will *increase* (as given in the example).

It makes no difference that $p$ and $q$ are fractional values less than 1 rather than larger numbers. As long as $p$ and $q$ are both positive, the above three rules always apply. So in the example, if the centered inequality were $1 < p < q$ or $0 < p < 1 < q$, it wouldn't make any difference—quantity B would still be greater than quantity A. (If you're not convinced, try plugging in some sample values for $p$ and $q$.)

A GRE question might ask you to alter a *ratio* by adding or subtracting from one (or both) terms in the ratio. The rules for altering ratios are the same as for altering fractions. In either case, set up a proportion and solve algebraically for the unknown term.

11. A drawer contains exactly half as many white shirts as blue shirts. If four more shirts of each color were to be added to the drawer, the ratio of white to blue shirts would be 5:8. How many blue shirts does the drawer contain?

**(A)** 14
**(B)** 12
**(C)** 11
**(D)** 10
**(E)** 9

**The correct answer is (B).** Represent the original ratio of white to blue shirts by the fraction $\frac{x}{2x}$, where $x$ is the number of white shirts, then add 4 to both the numerator and denominator. Set this fraction equal to $\frac{5}{8}$ (the ratio after adding shirts). Cross-multiply to solve for $x$:

$$\frac{x + 4}{2x + 4} = \frac{5}{8}$$
$$8x + 32 = 10x + 20$$
$$12 = 2x$$
$$x = 6$$

The original denominator is $2x$, or 12.

## RATIOS WITH MORE THAN TWO QUANTITIES

You approach ratio problems involving three or more quantities the same way as those involving only two quantities. The only difference is that there are more "parts" that make up the "whole."

**12.** Three lottery winners—X, Y, and Z—are sharing a lottery jackpot. X's share is $\frac{1}{5}$ of Y's share and $\frac{1}{7}$ of Z's share. If the total jackpot is $195,000, what is the dollar amount of Z's share?

(A) $15,000
(B) $35,000
(C) $75,000
(D) $105,000
(E) $115,000

**The correct answer is (D).** At first glance, this problem doesn't appear to involve ratios. (Where's the colon?) But it does. The ratio of X's share to Y's share is 1:5, and the ratio of X's share to Z's share is 1:7. So you can set up the following triple ratio:

X:Y:Z = 1:5:7

X's winnings account for 1 of 13 equal parts (1 + 5 + 7) of the total jackpot. $\frac{1}{13}$ of $195,000 is $15,000. Accordingly, Y's share is 5 times that amount, or $75,000, and Z's share is 7 times that amount, or $105,000.

In handling word problems involving ratios, think of a whole as the sum of its fractional parts, as in the method used to solve the preceding problem: $\frac{1}{13}$ (X's share) + $\frac{5}{13}$ (Y's share) + $\frac{7}{13}$ (Z's share) = 1 (the whole jackpot).

**TIP**
Remember: When you add (or subtract) the same number from both the numerator and denominator of a fraction—or from each term in a ratio—you alter the fraction or ratio, unless the original ratio was 1:1 (in which case the ratio is unchanged).

## PROPORTION PROBLEMS WITH VARIABLES

A GRE proportion question might use *letters* instead of numbers—to focus on the process rather than the result. You can solve these problems algebraically or by using the plug-in strategy.

13. A candy store sells candy only in half-pound boxes. At $c$ cents per box, which of the following is the cost of $a$ ounces of candy? [1 pound = 16 ounces]

   **(A)** $\dfrac{c}{a}$

   **(B)** $\dfrac{a}{16c}$

   **(C)** $ac$

   **(D)** $\dfrac{ac}{8}$

   **(E)** $\dfrac{8c}{a}$

   **The correct answer is (D).** This question is asking: "*c* cents is to one box as *how many cents* are to *a* ounces?" Set up a proportion, letting $x$ equal the cost of $a$ ounces. Because the question asks for the cost of *ounces*, convert 1 box to 8 ounces (a half pound). Use the cross-product method to solve quickly:

   $$\frac{c}{8} = \frac{x}{a}$$

   $$8x = ac$$

   $$x = \frac{ac}{8}$$

   You can also use the plug-in strategy for this question, either instead of algebra or, better yet, to check the answer you chose using algebra. Pick easy numbers to work with, such as 100 for $c$ and 16 for $a$. At 100 cents per 8-ounce box, 16 ounces of candy cost 200 cents. Plug your numbers for $a$ and $c$ into each answer choice. Only choice (D) gives you the number 200 you're looking for.

## ARITHMETIC MEAN, MEDIAN, MODE, AND RANGE

Arithmetic mean (simple average), median, mode, and range are four different ways to describe a set of terms quantitatively. Here's the definition of each one:

- **Arithmetic mean (average):** In a set of $n$ measurements, the sum of the measurements divided by $n$.

- **Median:** The middle measurement after the measurements are ordered by size (or the average of the two middle measurements if the number of measurements is even).

- **Mode:** The measurement that appears most frequently in a set.

- **Range:** The difference between the greatest measurement and the least measurement.

For example, given a set of six measurements, $\{8, -4, 8, 3, 2, 7\}$:

| Mean = 4 | $(8 - 4 + 8 + 3 + 2 + 7) \div 6 = 24 \div 6 = 4$ |
|---|---|
| Median = 5 | The average of 3 and 7—the two middle measurements in the set ordered in this way: $\{-4, 2, 3, 7, 8, 8\}$ |
| Mode = 8 | 8 appears twice (more frequently than any other measurement) |
| Range = 12 | The difference between 8 and $-4$ |

For the same set of values, the mean (simple average) and the median can be, but are not necessarily, the same. For example: $\{3, 4, 5, 6, 7\}$ has both a mean and median of 5. However, the set $\{-2, 0, 5, 8, 9\}$ has a mean of 4 but a median of 5.

For any set of terms, the *arithmetic mean* (AM), also called the *simple average*, is the sum of the terms $(a + b + c + \ldots)$ divided by the number of terms $(n)$ in the set:

$$\text{AM} = \frac{(a + b + c + \ldots)}{n}$$

On the GRE, easier questions involving simple average might ask you to add numbers together and divide a sum. First of all, in finding a simple average, be sure the numbers being added are all of the same form or in terms of the same units.

**14.** What is the average of $\frac{1}{5}$, 25%, and .09?

   **(A)** .18

   **(B)** 20%

   **(C)** $\frac{1}{4}$

   **(D)** .32

   **(E)** $\frac{1}{3}$

**The correct answer is (A).** Since the answer choices are not all expressed in the same form, first rewrite numbers as whichever form you think would be easiest to work with when you add the numbers together. In this case, the easiest form to work with is probably the decimal form. So rewrite the first two numbers as decimals, and then find the sum of the three numbers: .20 + .25 + .09 = .54. Finally, divide by 3 to find the average: .54 ÷ 3 = .18.

To find a missing number when the average of all the numbers in a set is given, plug into the arithmetic-mean formula all the numbers you know—which include the average, the sum of the other numbers, and the number of terms. Then, use algebra to find the missing number. Or, you can try out each answer choice, in turn, as the missing number until you find one that results in the average given.

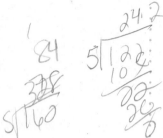

15. The average of five numbers is 26. Four of the numbers are −12, 90, −26, and 10. What is the fifth number?

   (A) 16
   (B) 42
   (C) 44
   (D) 68
   (E) 84

**The correct answer is (D).** To solve the problem algebraically, let $x$ = the missing number. Set up the arithmetic-mean formula, then solve for $x$:

$$26 = \frac{(90 + 10 - 12 - 26) + x}{5}$$

$$26 = \frac{62 + x}{5}$$

$$130 = 62 + x$$

$$68 = x$$

Or, you can try out each answer choice in turn. Start with the middle value, 44 (choice (C)). The sum of 44 and the other four numbers is 106. Dividing this sum by 5 gives you 21.2—a number less than the average of 26 that you're aiming for. So you know the fifth number is greater than 44—and that leaves choices (D) and (E). Try out the number 68 (choice (D)), and you'll obtain the average of 26.

If the numbers are easy to work with, you might be able to determine a missing term, given the simple average of a set of numbers, without resorting to algebra. Simply apply a dose of logic.

16. If the average of six consecutive multiples of 4 is 22, what is the greatest of these integers?

   (A) 22
   (B) 24
   (C) 26
   (D) 28
   (E) 32

**The correct answer is (E).** You can answer this question with common sense—no algebra required. Consecutive multiples of 4 are 4, 8, 12, 16, etc. Given that the average of six such numbers is 22, the two middle terms (the third and fourth terms) must be 20 and 24. (Their average is 22.) Accordingly, the fifth term is 28, and the sixth and greatest term is 32.

## Simple Average and Median

A tougher question might ask you to find the value of a number that changes an average from one number to another.

When an additional number is added to a set, and the average of the numbers in the set changes as a result, you can determine the value of the number that's added by applying the arithmetic-mean formula twice.

**17.** The average of three numbers is $-4$. If a fourth number is added, the arithmetic mean of all four numbers is $-1$. What is the fourth number?

(A) $-10$

(B) 2

(C) 8

(D) 10

(E) 16

*[handwritten: $a + b + c = 12$    $\dfrac{-4}{1} = \dfrac{a+b+c}{3}$]*

**The correct answer is (C).** To solve the problem algebraically, first determine the sum of the three original numbers by the arithmetic-mean formula:

$$-4 = \frac{a + b + c}{3}$$

Then, apply the formula again accounting for the additional (fourth) number. The new average is $-1$, the sum of the other three numbers is $-12$, and the number of terms is 4. Solve for the missing number ($x$):

$$-1 = \frac{-12 + x}{4}$$

$$-4 = -12 + x$$

$$8 = x$$

You approach arithmetic-mean problems that involve *variables* instead of (or in addition to) numbers in the same way as those involving only numbers. Just plug the information you're given into the arithmetic-mean formula, and then solve the problem algebraically.

**18.** If A is the average of P, Q, and another number, which of the following represents the missing number?

(A) $3A - P - Q$

(B) $A + P + Q$

(C) $A + P - Q$

(D) $A - P + Q$

(E) $3A - P + Q$

*[handwritten: $\dfrac{X + P + Q}{3}$]*

**The correct answer is (A).** Let $x =$ the missing number. Solve for $x$ by the arithmetic-mean formula:

$$A = \frac{P + Q + x}{3}$$

$$3A = P + Q + x$$

$$3A - P - Q = x$$

**ALERT!**

Don't try the plug-in strategy to solve problems like the one here; it's too complex. Be flexible and use shortcuts wherever you can—but recognize their limitations.

A GRE question involving arithmetic mean might also involve the median concept. If the question deals solely with numbers, simply do the math to calculate the average and the median.

| <u>Column A</u> | <u>Column B</u> |
|---|---|

**19.**

The median value of $\frac{1}{2}, \frac{2}{3}, \frac{3}{4}$, and $\frac{5}{6}$          The arithmetic mean (average) of $\frac{1}{2}, \frac{2}{3}, \frac{3}{4}$, and $\frac{5}{6}$

**(A)** The quantity in Column A is greater;

**(B)** The quantity in Column B is greater;

**(C)** The quantities are equal;

**(D)** The relationship cannot be determined from the information given.

**The correct answer is (A).** First, calculate Quantity A. Both columns list the same four numbers from smallest to greatest in value. So Quantity A (the median) is the average of $\frac{2}{3}$ and $\frac{3}{4}$:

$$\frac{\frac{2}{3}+\frac{3}{4}}{2} = \frac{\frac{8}{12}+\frac{9}{12}}{2} = \frac{\frac{17}{12}}{2} = \frac{17}{24}$$

Next, calculate Quantity B, using the common denominator 12:

$$\frac{1}{2}+\frac{2}{3}+\frac{3}{4}+\frac{5}{6} = \frac{6+8+9+10}{12} = \frac{33}{12}$$

The mean of the four numbers is one fourth of $\frac{33}{12}$, or $\frac{33}{48}$. To make the comparison, convert Quantity A to a fraction with the denominator 48: $\frac{17}{24} = \frac{34}{48}$. Since the numerator in Quantity A (34) is greater than the one in Quantity B (33), Quantity A is greater than Quantity B.

A more challenging question might involve *variables* instead of (or in addition to) numbers. Here's a good example:

|  | **Column A** | **Column B** |
|---|---|---|

**20.**    Distribution K contains four terms, represented by the four expressions $p$, $q$, $p + q$, and $q - p$, where $0 < q < p$.

<table>
<tr><td>The median of<br>Distribution K</td><td>The arithmetic mean<br>(simple average) of<br>Distribution K</td></tr>
</table>

**(A)** The quantity in Column A is greater;

**(B)** The quantity in Column B is greater;

**(C)** The quantities are equal;

**(D)** The relationship cannot be determined from the information given.

**The correct answer is (A).** First, express the median of the four terms (Quantity A). Given that $q < p$ and that $p$ and $q$ are both positive, $(q - p)$ must be negative and hence is least in value among the four terms, while $(q + p)$ must be greatest in value among the four terms. Here are the four terms, ranked from least to greatest in value:

$(q - p)$, $q$, $p$, $(p + q)$

The median value, then, is the average (arithmetic mean) of the two middle terms $p$ and $q$:

$$\frac{p + q}{2}$$

Next, express the arithmetic mean (AM) of the four terms (Quantity B):

$$AM = \frac{q + p + (p + q) + (q - p)}{4} = \frac{3q + p}{4}$$

Since both quantities are positive, you can multiply by 4 across columns to eliminate fractions, leaving the following simpler comparison:

Quantity A: $2p + 2q$
Quantity B: $3q + p$

Subtract $p$ and $2q$ from both columns simplifies the comparison further:

Quantity A: $p$
Quantity B: $q$

As you can easily see now, Quantity A is greater than Quantity B.

# STANDARD DEVIATION

*Standard deviation* is a measure of dispersion among members of a set. Computing standard deviation involves these five steps:

**❶** Compute the arithmetic mean (simple average) of all terms in the set.

**❷** Compute the difference between the mean and each term.

**❸** Square each difference you computed in step 2.

**❹** Compute the mean of the squares you computed in step 3.

**❺** Compute the non-negative square root of the mean you computed in step 4.

For example, here's how you'd determine the standard deviation of Distribution A: {−1, 2, 3, 4}:

- Arithmetic mean $= \dfrac{-1 + 2 + 3 + 4}{4} = \dfrac{8}{4} = 2$

- The difference between the mean (2) and each term:

  $2 - (-1) = 3; \ 2 - 2 = 0; \ 3 - 2 = 1; \ 4 - 2 = 2$

- The square of each difference:

  $\{3^2, \ 0^2, \ 1^2, \ 2^2\} = \{9, 0, 1, 4\}$

- The mean of the squares:

  $\dfrac{9 + 0 + 1 + 4}{4} = \dfrac{14}{4} = \dfrac{7}{2}$

- The standard deviation of Distribution A $= \sqrt{\dfrac{7}{2}}$

A GRE question might ask you to calculate standard deviation (as in the preceding example). Or, a question might ask you to *compare* standard deviations. You might be able to make the comparison without precise calculations—by remembering to follow this general rule: *The greater the data are spread away from the mean, the greater the standard deviation.* For example, consider these two distributions:

Distribution A: {1, 2.5, 4, 5.5, 7}

Distribution B: {1, 3, 4, 5, 7}

In both sets, the mean and median is 4, and the range is 6. But the standard deviation of A is greater than that of B, because 2.5 and 5.5 are further away than 3 and 5 from the mean.

**21.** Which of the following distributions has the greatest standard deviation?

(A) {−1, 1, 3}

(B) {1, 2, 5}

(C) {0, 4, 5}

(D) {−3, −1, 2}

(E) {2, 3, 6}

**The correct answer is (C).** Notice that in each of the choices (A), (B), and (E), the distribution's range is 4. But in choice (C) and choice (D), the range is 5. So the correct answer is probably either choice (C) or (D). Focusing on these two choices, notice that the middle term in choice (C), 4, is skewed further away from the mean than the middle term in choice (D). That's a good indication that choice (C) provides the distribution having the greatest standard deviation.

## ARITHMETIC SEQUENCES

In an *arithmetic sequences* of numbers, there is a constant (unchanging) difference between successive numbers in the sequence. In other words, all numbers in an arithmetic series are evenly spaced. All of the following are examples of an arithmetic sequence:

- Successive integers

- Successive even integers

- Successive odd integers

- Successive multiples of the same number

- Successive integers ending in the same digit

On the GRE, questions involving an arithmetic sequence might ask for the average or the sum of a sequence. When the numbers to be averaged form an arithmetic (evenly spaced) sequence, the average is simply the median (the middle number or the average of the two middle numbers if the number of terms is even). In other words, the mean and median of the set of numbers are the same. Faced with calculating the average of a long sequence of evenly-spaced integers, you can shortcut the addition.

22. What is the average of the first 20 positive integers?

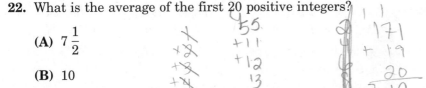

(A) $7\frac{1}{2}$

(B) 10

(C) $10\frac{1}{2}$

(D) 15

(E) 20

**The correct answer is (C).** Since the terms are evenly spaced, the average is halfway between the 10th and 11th terms—which happen to be the integers 10 and 11. So the average is $10\frac{1}{2}$. (This number is also the median.) If you take the average of the first term (1) and the last term (20), you get the same result:

$$\frac{1+20}{2} = \frac{21}{2} \text{ or } 10\frac{1}{2}$$

Finding the sum (rather than the average) of an arithmetic (evenly spaced) sequence of numbers requires only one additional step: multiplying the average (which is also the median) by the number of terms in the sequence. The trickiest aspect of this type of question is determining the number of terms in the sequence.

**23.** What is the sum of all odd integers between 10 and 40?

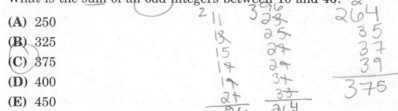

    **(A)** 250

    **(B)** 325

    **(C)** 375

    **(D)** 400

    **(E)** 450

**The correct answer is (C).** The average of the described numbers is 25—halfway between 10 and 40 (in other words, half the sum of 10 and 40). The number of terms in the series is 15. (The first term is 11, and the last term is 39.) The sum of the described series of integers = $25 \times 15 = 375$.

When calculating the average or sum of a sequence of evenly spaced numbers, be careful counting the number of terms in the sequence. For instance, the number of positive *odd* integers less than 50 is 25, but the number of positive *even* integers less than 50 is only 24.

## GEOMETRIC SEQUENCES

In a *geometric sequence* of numbers, each term is a constant multiple of the preceding one; in other words, the ratio between any term and the next one is constant. The multiple (or ratio) might be obvious by examining the sequence—for example:

> In the geometric sequence 2, 4, 8, 16, . . . , you can easily determine that the constant multiple is 2 (and the ratio of each term to the next is 1:2).

> In the geometric sequence 1, −3, 9, −27, . . . , you can easily determine that the constant multiple is −3 (and the ratio of each term to the next is 1:−3).

Once you know the multiple (or ratio), you can answer any question asking for an unknown term—or for either the sum or the average of certain terms.

**24.** In a geometric sequence, each term is a constant multiple of the preceding one. If the third and fourth numbers in the sequence are 8 and −16, respectively, what is the first term in the sequence?

    **(A)** −32

    **(B)** −4

    **(C)** 2

    **(D)** 4

    **(E)** 64

**The correct answer is (C).** The constant multiple is −2. But since you need to work backward from the third term (8), apply the *reciprocal* of that multiple twice. The second term is $(8)\left(-\dfrac{1}{2}\right) = -4$. The first term is $(-4)\left(-\dfrac{1}{2}\right) = 2$.

**25.** In a geometric sequence, each term is a constant multiple of the preceding one. What is the sum of the first four numbers in a geometric sequence whose second number is 4 and whose third number is 6?

**(A)** 16

**(B)** 19

**(C)** $22\frac{1}{2}$

**(D)** $21\frac{2}{3}$

**(E)** 20

**The correct answer is (D).** The constant multiple is $\frac{3}{2}$. In other words, the ratio of each term to the next is 2:3. Since the second term is 4, the first term is $4 \times \frac{2}{3} = \frac{8}{3}$. Since the third term is 6, the fourth term is $6 \times \frac{3}{2} = \frac{18}{2}$, or 9. The sum of the four terms $= \frac{8}{3} + 4 + 6 + 9 = 21\frac{2}{3}$. You can also solve geometric sequence problems by applying a special formula. But you'll need to memorize it because the test won't provide it. In the following formula, $r$ = the constant multiple (or the ratio between each term and the preceding one), $a$ = the first term in the sequence, $n$ = the position number for any particular term in the sequence, and T = the particular term itself:

$ar^{(n-1)} = T$

You can solve for any of the formula's variables, as long as you know the values for the other three. Following are two examples:

If $a = 3$ and $r = 2$, then the third term $= (3)(2)^2 = 12$, and the sixth term $= (3)(2)^5 = (3)(32) = 96$.

If the sixth term is $-\frac{1}{16}$ and the constant ratio is $\frac{1}{2}$, then the first term ($a$) $= -2$:

$$a\left(\frac{1}{2}\right)^5 = -\frac{1}{16}$$

$$a\left(\frac{1}{32}\right) = -\frac{1}{16}$$

$$a = \left(-\frac{1}{16}\right)(32) = -2$$

The algebra is simple enough—but you need to know the formula, of course.

**ALERT!**

You can't calculate the average of terms in a geometric sequence by averaging the first and last term in the sequence: The progression is geometric, not arithmetic. You need to add up the terms, then divide by the number of terms.

**26.** In a geometric sequence, each term is a constant multiple of the preceding one. If the first three terms in a geometric sequence are $-2$, $x$, and $-8$, which of the following could be the sixth term in the sequence?

(A) $-32$

(B) $-16$

(C) $16$

(D) $32$

(E) $64$

**The correct answer is (E).** Since all pairs of successive terms must have the same ratio, $\dfrac{-2}{x} = \dfrac{x}{-8}$. By the cross-product method, $x^2 = 16$, and hence $x = \pm 4$. For $x = 4$, the ratio is $\dfrac{4}{-2} = -2$. Applying the formula you just learned, the sixth term would be $(-2)(-2)^5 = 64$. For $x = -4$, the ratio is $\dfrac{-4}{-2} = 2$. The sixth term would be $(-2)(2)^5 = -64$.

## PERMUTATIONS

A *permutation* is an arrangement of objects in which the order (sequence) is important. Each arrangement of the letters A, B, C, and D, for example, is a different permutation of the four letters. There are two different ways to determine the number of permutations for a group of distinct objects.

**1** List all the permutations, using a methodical process to make sure you don't overlook any. For the letters A, B, C, and D, start with A in the first position, then list all possibilities for the second position, along with all possibilities for the third and fourth positions (you'll discover six permutations):

| A B C D | A C B D | A D B C |
|---------|---------|---------|
| A B D C | A C D B | A D C B |

Placing B in the first position would also result in 6 permutations. The same applies to either C or D in the first position. So, the total number of permutations is $6 \times 4 = 24$.

**2** Use the following formula (let $n$ = the number of objects) and limit the number of terms to the counting numbers, or positive integers: Number of permutations = $n(n-1)(n-2)(n-3)\ldots(1)$. The number of permutations can be expressed as $n!$ ("$n$" factorial). Using the factorial is much easier than compiling a list of permutations. For example, the number of arrangements (permutations) of the four letters A, B, C, and D: $4! = 4(4-1)(4-2)(4-3) = 4 \times 3 \times 2 \times 1 = 24$.

**27.** Five tokens—one red, one blue, one green, and two white—are arranged in a row, one next to another. If the two white tokens are next to each other, how many arrangements according to color are possible?

   **(A)** 12

   **(B)** 16

   **(C)** 20

   **(D)** 24

   **(E)** 30

**The correct answer is (D).** The two white tokens might be in positions 1 and 2, 2 and 3, 3 and 4, or 4 and 5. For each of these four possibilities, there are 6 possible color arrangements (3!) for the other three tokens (which all differ in color). Thus, the total number of possible arrangements is 4 × 6, or 24.

## COMBINATIONS

A *combination* is a group of certain objects selected from a larger set. The order of objects in the group is not important. You can determine the total number of possible combinations by listing the possible groups in a methodical manner. For instance, to determine the number of possible three-letter groups among the letters A, B, C, D, and E, work methodically, starting with A as a group member paired with B, then C, then D, then E. Be sure not to repeat combinations (repetitions are indicated in parentheses here):

| A, B, C | (A, C, B) | (A, D, B) | (A, E, B) |
|---------|-----------|-----------|-----------|
| A, B, D | A, C, D   | (A, D, C) | (A, E, C) |
| A, B, E | A, C, E   | A, D, E   | (A, E, D) |

Perform the same task assuming B is in the group, then assuming C is in the group (all combinations not listed here repeat what's already listed).

| B, C, D | C, D, E |
|---------|---------|
| B, C, E |         |
| B, D, E |         |

The total number of combinations is 10.

**28.** How many two-digit numbers can be formed from the digits 1 through 9, if no digit appears twice in a number?

   **(A)** 36

   **(B)** 72

   **(C)** 81

   **(D)** 144

   **(E)** 162

**The correct answer is (B).** Each digit can be paired with any of the other 8 digits. To avoid double counting, account for the possible pairs as follows: 1 and

2–9 (8 pairs), 2 and 3–9 (7 pairs), 3 and 4–9 (6 pairs), and so forth. The total number of distinct pairs is $8 + 7 + 6 + 5 + 4 + 3 + 2 + 1 = 36$. Since the digits in each pair can appear in either order, the total number of possible two-digit numbers is $2 \times 36$, or 72.

Here's something to consider: You can approach combination problems as *probability* problems as well. Think of the "probability" of any single combination as "one divided by" the total number of combinations (a fraction between zero (0) and 1). Use whichever method is quickest for the question at hand. We'll review probability next.

## PROBABILITY

*Probability* refers to the statistical chances of an event occurring (or not occurring). By definition, probability ranges from zero (0) to 1. (Probability is never negative, and it's never greater than 1.) Here's the basic formula for determining probability:

$$\text{Probability} = \frac{\text{number of ways the event can occur}}{\text{total number of possible occurrences}}$$

29. If you randomly select one candy from a jar containing two cherry candies, two licorice candies, and one peppermint candy, what is the probability of selecting a cherry candy?

   (A) $\dfrac{1}{6}$

   (B) $\dfrac{1}{5}$

   (C) $\dfrac{1}{3}$

   (D) $\dfrac{2}{5}$

   (E) $\dfrac{3}{5}$

   **The correct answer is (D).** There are two ways among five possible occurrences that a cherry candy will be selected. Thus, the probability of selecting a cherry candy is $\dfrac{2}{5}$.

   To calculate the probability of an event *not* occurring, just *subtract* the probability of the event occurring *from 1*. So, referring to the preceding question, the probability of *not* selecting a cherry candy is $\dfrac{3}{5}$. (Subtract $\dfrac{2}{5}$ from 1.)

Here's another example of probability, but a bit tougher this time. A standard deck of 52 playing cards contains 12 face cards. The probability of selecting a face card from a standard deck is $\dfrac{12}{52}$, or $\dfrac{3}{13}$. On the GRE, a tougher probability question will involve this basic formula, but it will also add a complication of some kind. It might require you to determine any of the following:

- Certain missing facts needed for a given probability

- Probabilities involving two (or more) *independent* events

- Probabilities involving an event that is *dependent* on another event

For the next three types of probability questions, don't try to "intuit" the answer. Probabilities involving complex scenarios such as these are often greater or less than you might expect.

## Missing Facts Needed for a Given Probability

In this question type, instead of calculating probability, you determine what missing number is needed for a given probability. Don't panic; just plug what you know into the basic formula and solve for the missing number.

30. A piggy bank contains a certain number of coins, of which 53 are dimes and 19 are nickels. The remainder of the coins in the bank are quarters. If the probability of selecting a quarter from this bank is $\frac{1}{4}$, how many quarters does the bank contain?

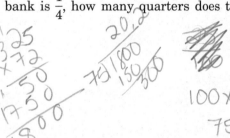

(A) 30

(B) 27

(C) 24

(D) 21

(E) 16

**The correct answer is (C).** On its face, this question looks complicated, but it's really not. Just plug what you know into the probability formula. Let $x$ = the number of quarters in the bank (this is the numerator of the formula's fraction), and let $x + 72$ = the total number of coins (the fraction's denominator). Then solve for $x$ (use the cross-product method to clear fractions):

$$\frac{1}{4} = \frac{x}{x + 72}$$

$$x + 72 = 4x$$

$$72 = 3x$$

$$24 = x$$

## Probability Involving Two or More Independent Events

Two events are independent if neither event affects the probability that the other will occur. (You'll look at dependent events on the next page.) On the GRE, look for either of these two scenarios involving independent events:

❶ The random selection of one object from *each of two or more groups*

❷ The random selection of one object from a group, then *replacing* it and selecting again (as in a "second round" or "another turn" of a game)

In either scenario, the simplest calculation involves finding the probability of two events both occurring. All you need to do is multiply together their individual probabilities: (probability of event 1 occurring) × (probability of event 2 occurring) = (probability of both events occurring).

For example, assume that you randomly select one letter from each of two sets: {A,B} and {C,D,E}. The probability of selecting A and C $= \frac{1}{2} \times \frac{1}{3}$, or $\frac{1}{6}$.

To calculate the probability that two events will *not both* occur, *subtract from* 1 the probability of both events occurring. To determine the probability that *three* events will all occur, just multiply the third event's probability by the other two.

**31.** If one student is chosen randomly out of a group of seven students, then one student is again chosen randomly from the same group of seven, what is the probability that two different students will be chosen?

(A) $\frac{36}{49}$

(B) $\frac{6}{7}$

(C) $\frac{19}{21}$

(D) $\frac{13}{14}$

(E) $\frac{48}{49}$

**The correct answer is (B).** You must first calculate the chances of picking *a particular student twice* by multiplying together the two individual probabilities for the student: $\frac{1}{7} \times \frac{1}{7} = \frac{1}{49}$. The probability of picking any one of the seven students twice is then $7 \times \frac{1}{49} = \frac{7}{49}$. The probability of picking the same student twice, added to the probability of not picking the same student twice, equals 1. So to answer the question, subtract $\frac{7}{49}$ from 1.

Beware: In one selection, the probability of *not* selecting a certain student from the group of seven is $\frac{6}{7}$ (the probability of selecting the student, subtracted from 1). But does this mean that the probability of not selecting the same student twice $= \frac{6}{7} \times \frac{6}{7} = \frac{36}{49}$? No, it doesn't. Make sure you understand the difference.

## Probability Involving a Dependent Event

Two distinct events might be related in that one event affects the probability of the other one occurring—for example, randomly selecting one object from a group, then selecting a second object from the same group *without replacing the first selection*. Removing one object from the group increases the odds of selecting any particular object from those that remain.

You handle this type of problem as you would any other probability problem: Calculate individual probabilities, then combine them.

**32.** In a random selection of two people from a group of five—A, B, C, D, and E—what is the probability of selecting A and B?

(A) $\frac{2}{5}$

(B) $\frac{1}{5}$

(C) $\frac{1}{10}$

(D) $\frac{1}{15}$

(E) $\frac{1}{20}$

**The correct answer is (C).** You need to consider each of the two selections separately. In the first selection, the probability of selecting either A or B is $\frac{2}{5}$. But the probability of selecting the second of the two is $\frac{1}{4}$, because after the first selection only four people remain from whom to select. Since the question asks for the probability of selecting both A and B (as opposed to either one), multiply the two individual probabilities: $\frac{2}{5} \times \frac{1}{4} = \frac{2}{20} = \frac{1}{10}$.

You can also approach a question such as this one as a *combination* problem. For this question, here are all the possibilities:

- A and either B, C, D, or E (4 combinations)
- B and either C, D, or E (3 combinations)
- C and either D or E (2 combinations)
- D and E (1 combination)

There are 10 possible combinations, so the probability of selecting A and B is 1 in 10.

ALERT!

Strategies such as plugging in test numbers, working backward, and sizing up answer choices don't work for most probability questions.

# SUMMING IT UP

- Although the types of questions reviewed in this chapter are the most basic of the math problems you'll encounter on the GRE Quantitative Reasoning section, don't underestimate how useful they'll be as building blocks for solving more complex problems.

- Certain fraction-decimal-percent equivalents show up more frequently than others on the GRE. If you have time, memorize the standard conversions to save yourself time on the actual exam.

- Percent change questions are typical on the GRE Quantitative Reasoning section, so be ready for them.

- As with fractions, you can simplify ratios by dividing common factors.

- Review the definitions of arithmetic mean, median, mode, and range, so you're better equipped to solve such problems on the exam.

- Many arithmetic sequence questions ask for the average or sum of a sequence. You may be able to "shortcut" the addition instead of calculating the average of a long sequence of evenly spaced integers.

- Memorizing common factorial combinations will save you time when you encounter permutation questions on the GRE.

- Work methodically on combination questions to avoid backtracking to an earlier object.

- It's wise not to try "intuiting" the answers to probability questions. Many of these problems are too complex to arrive at an accurate answer this way.

# Math Review: Number Theory and Algebra

chapter 10

In this chapter, you'll first broaden your arithmetical horizons by dealing with numbers in more abstract, theoretical settings. You'll examine the following topics:

- The concept of absolute value

- Number signs and integers—and what happens to them when you apply the four basic operations

- Factors, multiples, divisibility, prime numbers, and the "prime factorization" method

- The rules for combining exponential numbers (base numbers and "powers") using the four basic operations

- The rules for combining radicals using the four basic operations
- The rules for simplifying terms containing radical signs

Then you'll review the following basic algebra skills:

- Solving a linear equation with one variable
- Solving a system of two equations with two variables—by substitution and by addition-subtraction
- Recognizing unsolvable linear equations when you see them
- Handling algebraic inequalities

# BASIC PROPERTIES OF NUMBERS

You'll begin this chapter by reviewing the basics about integers, number signs (positive and negative), and prime numbers. First, make sure you're up to speed on the following definitions, which you'll need to know for this chapter as well as for the test:

- **Absolute value (of a real number):** The number's distance from zero (the origin) on the real-number line. The absolute value of $x$ is indicated as $|x|$. (The absolute value of a negative number can be less than, equal to, or greater than a positive number.)
- **Integer:** Any non-fraction number on the number line: {. . . $-3$, $-2$, $-1$, 0, 1, 2, 3 . . .}. Except for the number zero (0), every integer is either positive or negative. Every integer is either even or odd.
- **Factor (of an integer *n*):** Any integer that you can multiply by another integer for a product of $n$.
- **Prime number:** Any positive integer greater than one that has exactly two positive factors: 1 and the number itself. In other words, a prime number is not divisible by (a multiple of) any positive integer other than itself and 1.

## Number Signs and the Four Basic Operations

The four basic operations are addition, subtraction, multiplication, and division. Be sure you know the sign of a number that results from combining numbers using these operations. Here's a table that includes all the possibilities (a "?" indicates that the sign depends on which number has the greater absolute value):

| Addition | Subtraction | Multiplication | Division |
|---|---|---|---|
| $(+) + (+) = +$ | $(+) - (-) = (+)$ | $(+) \times (+) = +$ | $(+) \div (+) = +$ |
| $(-) + (-) = -$ | $(-) - (+) = (-)$ | $(+) \times (-) = -$ | $(+) \div (-) = -$ |
| $(+) + (-) = ?$ | $(+) - (+) = ?$ | $(-) \times (+) = -$ | $(-) \div (+) = -$ |
| $(-) + (+) = ?$ | $(-) - (-) = ?$ | $(-) \times (-) = +$ | $(-) \div (-) = +$ |

GRE problems involving combining numbers by addition or subtraction usually incorporate the concept of absolute value, as well as the rule for subtracting negative numbers.

1. $|-1 - 2| - |5 - 6| - |-3 + 4| =$
   - (A) $-5$
   - (B) $-3$
   - (C) 1
   - (D) 3
   - (E) 5

   **The correct answer is (C).** First, determine each of the three absolute values:

   $$|-1 - 2| = |-3| = 3$$
   $$|5 - 6| = |-1| = 1$$
   $$|-3 + 4| = |1| = 1$$

   Then combine the three results: $3 - 1 - 1 = 1$.

Because multiplication (or division) involving two negative terms always results in a positive number:

- Multiplication or division involving any *even* number of negative terms gives you a positive number.

- Multiplication or division involving any *odd* number of negative terms gives you a negative number.

2. A number M is the product of seven negative numbers, and the number N is the product of six negative numbers and one positive number. Which of the following holds true for all possible values of M and N?
   - I. $M \times N < 0$
   - II. $M - N < 0$
   - III. $N + M < 0$

   - (A) I only
   - (B) II only
   - (C) I and II only
   - (D) II and III only
   - (E) I, II, and III

   **The correct answer is (C).** The product of seven negative numbers is always a negative number. (M is a negative number.) The product of six negative numbers is always a positive number, and the product of two positive numbers is always a positive number. (N is a positive number.) Thus, the product of M and N must be a negative number; I is always true. Subtracting a positive number N from a negative number M always results in a negative number less than M; II is always true. However, whether III is true depends on the values of M and N. If $|N| > |M|$, then $N + M > 0$, but if $|N| < |M|$, then $N + M < 0$.

## Integers and the Four Basic Operations

When you combine integers using a basic operation, whether the result is an odd integer, an even integer, or a non-integer depends on the numbers you combined. Here's a table that summarizes all the possibilities:

### ADDITION AND SUBTRACTION

- Integer ± integer = integer

- Even integer ± even integer = even integer

- Even integer ± odd integer = odd integer

- Odd integer ± odd integer = even integer

### MULTIPLICATION AND DIVISION

- Integer × integer = integer

- Integer ÷ non-zero integer = integer, but only if the numerator is divisible by the denominator (if the result is a quotient with no remainder)

- Odd integer × odd integer = odd integer

- Even integer × non-zero integer = even integer

- Even integer ÷ 2 = integer

- Odd integer ÷ 2 = non-integer

GRE questions that test you on the preceding rules sometimes look like algebra problems, but they're really not. Just apply the appropriate rule or, if you're not sure of the rule, plug in simple numbers to zero in on the correct answer.

3. If P is an odd integer and if Q is an even integer, which of the following expressions CANNOT represent an even integer?
   (A) 3P − Q
   (B) 3P × Q
   (C) 2Q × P
   (D) 3Q − 2P
   (E) 32P − 2Q

   **The correct answer is (A).** Since 3 and P are both odd integers, their product (3P) must also be an odd integer. Subtracting an even integer (Q) from an odd integer results in an odd integer in all cases.

## FACTORS, MULTIPLES, AND DIVISIBILITY

Figuring out whether one number ($f$) is a factor of another ($n$) is no big deal. Just divide $n$ by $f$. If the quotient is an integer, then $f$ is a factor of $n$ (and $n$ is divisible by $f$). If the quotient is not an integer, then $f$ is not a factor of $n$, and you'll end up with a *remainder* after dividing. For example, 2 is a factor of 8 because $8 \div 2 = 4$, which is an integer. On the other hand, 3 is not a factor of 8 because $8 \div 3 = \frac{8}{3}$, or $2\frac{2}{3}$, which is a non-integer. (The remainder is 2.)

Remember these four basic rules about factors, which are based on the definition of the term "factor":

**①** Any integer is a factor of itself.

**②** 1 and −1 are factors of all integers.

**③** The integer zero has an infinite number of factors but is not a factor of any integer.

**④** A positive integer's greatest factor (other than itself) will never be greater than one half the value of the integer.

On the "flip side" of factors are multiples. If $f$ is a factor of $n$, then $n$ is a multiple of $f$. For example, 8 is a multiple of 2 for the same reason that 2 is a factor of 8—because $8 \div 2 = 4$, which is an integer.

As you can see, factors, multiples, and divisibility are simply different aspects of the same concept. So a GRE question about factoring is also about multiples and divisibility.

4. If $n > 6$, and if $n$ is a multiple of 6, which of the following is always a factor of $n$?

  **(A)** $n - 6$

  **(B)** $n + 6$

  **(C)** $\frac{n}{3}$

  **(D)** $\frac{n}{2} + 3$

  **(E)** $\frac{n}{2} + 6$

  **The correct answer is (C).** Since 3 is a factor of 6, 3 is also a factor of any positive-number multiple of 6. Thus, if you divide any multiple of 6 by 3, the quotient will be an integer. In other words, 3 will be a factor of that number ($n$). As for the incorrect choices, $n - 6$ (choice (A)) is a factor of $n$ only if $n = 12$. $n + 6$ (choice (B)) can never be a factor of $n$ because $n + 6$ is greater than $n$. You can eliminate choices (D) and (E) because the greatest factor of any positive number (other than the number itself) is half the number, which in this case is $\frac{n}{2}$.

  Although the plug-in strategy works for the preceding question, you should try out more than one sample value for $n$. If $n = 12$, choices (A), (C), and (E) are all viable. But try out the number 18, and choice (C) is the only factor of $n$. (To be on the safe side, you should try out at least one additional sample value as well, such as 24.)

## PRIME NUMBERS AND PRIME FACTORIZATION

A *prime number* is a positive integer greater than one that is divisible by only two positive integers: itself and 1. Just for the record, here are all the prime numbers less than 50:

2, 3, 5, 7

11, 13, 17, 19

23, 29

31, 37

41, 43, 47

TIP

For the GRE, memorize all the prime numbers less than 100, so you don't have to take time thinking about whether you can factor them.

The GRE might test you directly on prime numbers by asking you to identify all prime factors of a number. These questions tend to be pretty easy.

| Column A | Column B |
|---|---|
| **5.** | |
| The product of all different prime-number factors of 42 | 42 |

**(A)** The quantity in Column A is greater;

**(B)** The quantity in Column B is greater;

**(C)** The quantities are equal;

**(D)** The relationship cannot be determined from the information given.

**The correct answer is (C).** The prime-number factors of 42 include 2, 3, and 7. Their product is 42.

To find what's called the *prime factorization* of a non-prime integer, divide the number by the primes in order and use each repeatedly until it is no longer a factor. For example:

$110 = 2 \times 55$

$= 2 \times 5 \times 11$. This is the prime factorization of 110.

Stop when all factors are prime and then if a factor occurs more than once, use an exponent to indicate this (i.e., write it in exponential form.)

6. Which of the following is a prime factorization of 144?

**(A)** $2^4 \times 3^2$

**(B)** $4 \times 3^3$

**(C)** $2^3 \times 12$

**(D)** $2^2 \times 3 \times 5$

**(E)** $2 \times 3^2 \times 4$

**The correct answer is (A).** Divide 144 by the smallest prime, which is 2.

Continue to divide the result by 2, then 3, and you ultimately obtain a prime-number quotient:

$$144 = 2 \times 72$$
$$= 2 \times 2 \times 36$$
$$= 2 \times 2 \times 2 \times 18$$
$$= 2 \times 2 \times 2 \times 2 \times 9$$
$$= 2 \times 2 \times 2 \times 2 \times 3 \times 3$$
$$= 2^4 \times 3^2$$

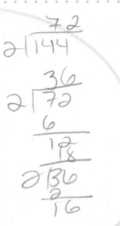

# EXPONENTS (POWERS)

An *exponent*, or *power*, refers to the number of times a number (referred to as the *base*) is used as a factor. In the number $2^3$, the base is 2 and the exponent is 3. To calculate the value of $2^3$, you use 2 as a factor three times: $2^3 = 2 \times 2 \times 2 = 8$.

On the GRE, questions involving exponents usually require you to combine two or more terms that contain exponents. To do so, you need to know some basic rules. Can you combine base numbers—using addition, subtraction, multiplication, or division—*before* applying exponents to the numbers? The answer depends on which operation you're performing.

## Combining Exponents by Addition or Subtraction

When you add or subtract terms, you cannot combine bases or exponents. It's as simple as that.

$$a^x + b^x \neq (a + b)^x$$
$$a^x - b^x \neq (a - b)^x$$

If you don't believe it, try plugging in a few easy numbers. Notice that you get a different result depending on which you do first: combine bases or apply each exponent to its base:

$$(3 + 4)^2 = 7^2 = 49$$
$$3^2 + 4^2 = 9 + 16 = 25$$

**7.** If $x = -2$, then $x^5 - x^2 - x =$

(A) $-70$
(B) $-58$
(C) $-34$
(D) $4$
(E) $26$

**The correct answer is (C).** You cannot combine exponents here, even though the base is the same in all three terms. Instead, you need to apply each exponent, in turn, to the base, then subtract:

$$x^5 - x^2 - x = (-2)^5 - (-2)^2 - (-2) = -32 - 4 + 2 = -34$$

## Combining Exponents by Multiplication or Division

It's a whole different story for multiplication and division. First, remember these two simple rules:

**1** You can combine bases first, but only if the exponents are the same:

$$a^x \times b^x = (ab)^x$$

**2** You can combine exponents first, but only if the bases are the same. When multiplying these terms, add the exponents. When dividing them, subtract the denominator exponent from the numerator exponent:

$$a^x \times a^y = a^{(x+y)}$$

$$\frac{a^x}{a^y} = a^{(x-y)}$$

When the same base appears in both the numerator and denominator of a fraction, you can cancel the number of powers common to both.

8. Which of the following is a simplified version of $\frac{x^2y^3}{x^3y^2}$?

(A) $\frac{y}{x}$

(B) $\frac{x}{y}$

(C) $\frac{1}{xy}$

(D) 1

(E) $x^5y^5$

**The correct answer is (A).** The simplest approach to this problem is to cancel $x^2$ and $y^2$ from numerator and denominator. This leaves you with $x^1$ in the denominator and $y^1$ in the numerator.

"Canceling" a base's powers in a fraction's numerator and denominator is actually a shortcut to applying the rule $\frac{a^x}{a^y} = a^{(x-y)}$ along with another rule, $a^{-x} = \frac{1}{a^x}$, that you'll review immediately ahead.

## Additional Rules for Exponents

To cover all your bases, also keep in mind these three additional rules for exponents:

**1** When raising an exponential number to a power, multiply exponents:

$$(a^x)^y = a^{xy}$$

**2** Any number other than zero (0) raised to the power of zero (0) equals 1:

$$a^0 = 1 \ [a \neq 0]$$

**3** Raising a base other than zero to a negative exponent is equivalent to 1 divided by the base raised to the exponent's absolute value:

$$a^{-x} = \frac{1}{a^x}$$

The preceding three rules are all fair game for the GRE. In fact, a GRE question might require you to apply more than one of these rules.

**9.** $(2^3)^2 \times 4^{-3} =$

(A) $\frac{1}{8}$

(B) $\frac{1}{2}$

(C) $\frac{2}{3}$

(D) 1

(E) 16

**The correct answer is (D).** $(2^3)^2 \times 4^{-3} = 2^{(2)(3)} \times \dfrac{1}{4^3} = \dfrac{2^6}{4^3} = \dfrac{2^6}{2^6} = 1.$

## Exponents You Should Know

For the GRE, memorize the exponential values in the following table. You'll be glad you did, since these are the ones you're most likely to see on the exam.

### Power and Corresponding Value

| Base | 2 | 3 | 4 | 5 | 6 | 7 | 8 |
|------|-----|-----|-----|-----|-----|-----|-----|
| 2 | 4 | 8 | 16 | 32 | 64 | 128 | 256 |
| 3 | 9 | 27 | 81 | 243 | | | |
| 4 | 16 | 64 | 256 | | | | |
| 5 | 25 | 125 | 625 | | | | |
| 6 | 36 | 216 | | | | | |

## Exponents and the Real Number Line

Raising bases to powers can have surprising effects on the magnitude and/or sign—negative vs. positive—of the base. You need to consider four separate regions of the real-number line:

**1** Values greater than 1 (to the right of 1 on the number line)

**2** Values less than −1 (to the left of −1 on the number line)

**3** Fractional values between 0 and 1

**4** Fractional values between −1 and 0

The next table indicates the impact of positive-integer exponent ($x$) on base ($n$) for each region.

| $n > 1$ | $n$ raised to any power: $n^x > 1$ (the greater the exponent, the greater the value of $n^x$) |
|---|---|
| $n < -1$ | $n$ raised to even power: $n^x > 1$ (the greater the exponent, the greater the value of $n^x$) |
| | $n$ raised to odd power: $n^x < 1$ (the greater the exponent, the lesser the value of $n^x$) |
| $0 < n < 1$ | $n$ raised to any power: $0 < n^x < 1$ (the greater the exponent, the lesser the value of $n^x$) |
| $-1 < n < 0$ | $n$ raised to even power: $0 < n^x < 1$ (the greater the exponent, the lesser the value of $n^x$, approaching 0 on the number line) |
| | $n$ raised to odd power: $-1 < n^x < 0$ (the greater the exponent, the greater the value of $n^x$, approaching 0 on the number line) |

The preceding set of rules are simple enough to understand. But when you apply them to a GRE question, it can be surprisingly easy to confuse yourself, especially if the question is designed to create confusion. Here are two challenging examples.

**10.** If $-1 < x < 0$, which of the following must be true?

   I. $x < x^2$

   II. $x^2 < x^3$

   III. $x < x^3$

   **(A)** I only

   **(B)** II only

   **(C)** I and II only

   **(D)** I and III only

   **(E)** I, II, and III

   **The correct answer is (D).** The key to analyzing each equation is that raising $x$ to successively greater powers moves the value of $x$ closer to zero (0) on the number line.

   I must be true. Since $x$ is given as a negative number, $x^2$ must be positive and thus greater than $x$.

   II cannot be true. Since $x$ is given as a negative number, $x^2$ must be positive, while $x^3$ must be negative. Thus, $x^2$ is greater than $x^3$.

   III must be true. Both $x^3$ and $x$ are negative fractions between 0 and $-1$, but $x^3$ is closer to zero (0) on the number line—that is, greater than $x$.

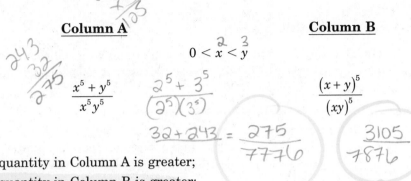

**Column A**                                    **Column B**

11.                         $0 < x < y$

$\dfrac{x^5 + y^5}{x^5 y^5}$                         $\dfrac{(x+y)^5}{(xy)^5}$

**(A)** The quantity in Column A is greater;

**(B)** The quantity in Column B is greater;

**(C)** The quantities are equal;

**(D)** The relationship cannot be determined from the information given.

**The correct answer is (B).** In Column B, the denominator can be expressed as $x^5 y^5$. Since the denominators in the two quantities are the same, and since both are greater than zero (0), you can cancel them. You need only compare the two numerators. If you mistakenly assume that $(x + y)^5 = x^5 + y^5$, you might select answer choice (C). In fact, with $x$ and $y$ both greater than zero (0), the numerator of Quantity B will always be greater than that of Quantity A.

# ROOTS AND RADICALS

On the flip side of exponents and powers are roots and radicals. The *square root* of a number $n$ is a number that you "square" (multiply by itself, or raise to the power of 2) to obtain $n$.

   $2 = \sqrt{4}$ (the square root of 4) because $2 \times 2$ (or $2^2$) = 4

The *cube root* of a number $n$ is a number that you raise to the power of 3 (multiply by itself twice) to obtain $n$. You determine greater roots (for example, the "fourth root") in the same way. Except for square roots, the radical sign will indicate the root to be taken.

   $2 = \sqrt[3]{8}$ (the cube root of 8) because $2 \times 2 \times 2$ (or $2^3$) = 8

   $2 = \sqrt[4]{16}$ (the fourth root of 16) because $2 \times 2 \times 2 \times 2$ (or $2^4$) = 16

For the GRE, you should know the rules for simplifying and for combining radical expressions.

## Simplifying Radicals

On the GRE, always look for the possibility of simplifying radicals by moving what's under the radical sign to the outside of the sign. Check inside your square-root radicals for perfect squares: factors that are squares of nice tidy numbers or other terms. The same advice applies to perfect cubes, and so on.

| | |
|---|---|
| $\sqrt{4a^2} = 2|a|$ | 4 and $a^2$ are both perfect squares; remove them from under the radical sign, and find each one's square root. |
| $\sqrt{8a^3} = \sqrt{(4)(2)a^3} = 2a\sqrt{2a}$ | 8 and $a^3$ are both perfect cubes, which contain perfect-square factors; remove the perfect squares from under the radical sign, and find each one's square root. |

You can simplify radical expressions containing fractions in the same way. Just be sure that what's in the denominator under the radical sign stays in the denominator when you remove it from under the radical sign.

$$\sqrt{\frac{20x}{x^2}} = \sqrt{\frac{(4)(5)}{x^2}} = \frac{2\sqrt{5}}{|x|}$$

$$\sqrt[3]{\frac{3}{8}} = \sqrt[3]{\frac{3}{2^3}} = \frac{1}{2}\sqrt[3]{3}$$

12. $\sqrt{\dfrac{28a^6b^4}{36a^4b^6}} =$

    **(A)** $\dfrac{a}{b}\sqrt{\dfrac{a}{2b}}$

    **(B)** $\dfrac{a}{2b}\sqrt{\dfrac{a}{b}}$

    **(C)** $\dfrac{|a|}{3|b|}\sqrt{7}$

    **(D)** $\dfrac{a^2}{3b^2}\sqrt{2}$

    **(E)** $\dfrac{2a}{3b}$

**The correct answer is (C).** Divide $a^4$ and $b^4$ from the numerator and denominator of the fraction. Also, factor out 4 from 28 and 36. Then, remove perfect squares from under the radical sign:

$$\sqrt{\frac{28a^6b^4}{36a^4b^6}} = \sqrt{\frac{7a^2}{9b^2}} = \frac{|a|\sqrt{7}}{3|b|} \text{ or } \frac{|a|}{3|b|}\sqrt{7}$$

In GRE questions involving radical terms, you might want to remove a radical term from a fraction's denominator to match the correct answer. To accomplish this, multiply both numerator and denominator by the radical value. (This process is called "rationalizing the denominator.") Here's an example of how to do it:

$$\frac{3}{\sqrt{15}} = \frac{3\sqrt{15}}{\sqrt{15}\sqrt{15}} = \frac{3\sqrt{15}}{15} \text{ or } \frac{1}{5}\sqrt{15}$$

## Combining Radical Terms

The rules for combining terms that include radicals are quite similar to those for exponents. Keep the following two rules in mind; one applies to addition and subtraction, while the other applies to multiplication and division.

### ADDITION AND SUBTRACTION

If a term under a radical is being added to or subtracted from a term under a different radical, you cannot combine the two terms under the same radical.

$$\sqrt{x} + \sqrt{y} \neq \sqrt{x+y}$$
$$\sqrt{x} - \sqrt{y} \neq \sqrt{x-y}$$
$$\sqrt{x} + \sqrt{x} = 2\sqrt{x} \text{ not } \sqrt{2x}$$

On the GRE, if you're asked to combine radical terms by adding or subtracting, chances are you'll also need to simplify radical expressions along the way.

13. $\sqrt{24} - \sqrt{16} - \sqrt{6} =$

  (A) $\sqrt{6} - 4$
  (B) $4 - 2\sqrt{2}$
  (C) 2
  (D) $\sqrt{6}$
  E. $2\sqrt{2}$

  **The correct answer is (A).** Although the numbers under the three radicals combine to equal 2, you cannot combine terms this way. Instead, simplify the first two terms, then combine the first and third terms:

$$\sqrt{24} - \sqrt{16} - \sqrt{6} = 2\sqrt{6} - 4 - \sqrt{6} = \sqrt{6} - 4$$

### MULTIPLICATION AND DIVISION

Terms under different radicals can be combined under a common radical if one term is multiplied or divided by the other, but only if the radical is the same.

$$\sqrt{x}\sqrt{x} = (\sqrt{x})^2 \text{ or } x$$
$$\sqrt{x}\sqrt{y} = \sqrt{xy}$$
$$\frac{\sqrt{x}}{\sqrt{y}} = \sqrt{\frac{x}{y}}$$
$$\sqrt[3]{x}\sqrt{x} = ?$$

(You cannot easily combine $\sqrt[3]{x}\sqrt{x} = x^{1/3}x^{1/2} = x^{1/3 + 1/2} = x^{5/6}$.)

**14.** $(2\sqrt{2a})^2 =$

   **(A)** $4a$

   **(B)** $4a^2$

   **(C)** $8a$

   **(D)** $8a^2$

   **(E)** $6a$

**The correct answer is (C).** Square each of the two terms, 2 and $\sqrt{2a}$, separately. Then combine their squares by multiplication: $(2\sqrt{2a})^2 = 2^2 \times (\sqrt{2a})^2 = 4 \times 2a = 8a$.

## Roots You Should Know

For the GRE, memorize the roots in the following table. If you encounter one of these radical terms on the exam, chances are you'll need to know its equivalent integer to answer the question.

In the table below, notice that the cube root of a negative number is negative and the cube root of a positive number is positive.

| Square Roots of "Perfect Square" Integers | Cube Roots of "Perfect Cube" Integers (Positive and Negative) |
|---|---|
| $\sqrt{121} = 11$ | $\sqrt[3]{(-)8} = (-)2$ |
| $\sqrt{144} = 12$ | $\sqrt[3]{(-)27} = (-)3$ |
| $\sqrt{169} = 13$ | $\sqrt[3]{(-)64} = (-)4$ |
| $\sqrt{196} = 14$ | $\sqrt[3]{(-)125} = (-)5$ |
| $\sqrt{225} = 15$ | $\sqrt[3]{(-)216} = (-)6$ |
| $\sqrt{625} = 25$ | $\sqrt[3]{(-)343} = (-)7$ |
| | $\sqrt[3]{(-)512} = (-)8$ |
| | $\sqrt[3]{(-)729} = (-)9$ |
| | $\sqrt[3]{(-)1,000} = (-)10$ |

## Roots and the Real Number Line

As with exponents, the root of a number can bear a surprising relationship to the magnitude and/or sign (negative vs. positive) of the number (another of the test-makers' favorite areas). Here are three rules you should remember:

**1** If $n > 1$, then $1 < \sqrt[3]{n} < \sqrt{n} < n$ (the greater the root, the lesser the value). However, if $n$ lies between 0 and 1, then $n < \sqrt{n} < \sqrt[3]{n} < 1$ (the greater the root, the greater the value).

| | |
|---|---|
| $n = 64$ $$1 < \sqrt[3]{64} < \sqrt{64} < 64$$ $$1 < 4 < 8 < 64$$ | $n = \dfrac{1}{64}$ $$\frac{1}{64} < \sqrt{\frac{1}{64}} < \sqrt[3]{\frac{1}{64}} < 1$$ $$\frac{1}{64} < \frac{1}{8} < \frac{1}{4} < 1$$ |

**2** Every negative number has exactly one cube root, and that root is a negative number. The same holds true for all other odd-numbered roots of negative numbers.

| | |
|---|---|
| $\sqrt[3]{-27} = -3$ $(-3)(-3)(-3) = -27$ | $\sqrt[5]{-32} = -2$ $(-2)(-2)(-2)(-2)(-2) = -32$ |

**3** Every positive number has only one *cube* root, and that root is always a positive number. The same holds true for all other odd-numbered roots of positive numbers.

15. Which of the following inequalities, if true, is sufficient alone to show that $\sqrt[3]{x} < \sqrt[5]{x}$?

  **(A)** $-1 < x < 0$
  **(B)** $x > 1$
  **(C)** $|x| < -1$
  **(D)** $|x| > 1$
  **(E)** $x < -1$

**The correct answer is (E).** If $x < -1$, then applying a greater root yields a *lesser negative* value—further to the left on the real number line.

## LINEAR EQUATIONS WITH ONE VARIABLE

Algebraic expressions are usually used to form equations, which set two expressions equal to each other. Most equations you'll see on the GRE are *linear* equations, in which the variables don't come with exponents. To solve any linear equation containing one variable, your goal is always the same: Isolate the unknown (variable) on one side of the equation. To accomplish this, you may need to perform one or more of the following four operations on both sides, depending on the equation:

**NOTE**

The square root (or other even-number root) of any negative number is an imaginary number, not a real number. That's why the preceding rules don't cover these roots.

**ALERT!**

The operation you perform on one side of an equation must also be performed on the other side; otherwise, the two sides won't be equal.

**1** Add or subtract the same term from both sides

**2** Multiply or divide by the same term on both sides

**3** Clear fractions by cross-multiplication

**4** Clear radicals by raising both sides to the same power (exponent)

Performing any of these operations on *both* sides does not change the equality; it merely restates the equation in a different form.

Let's take a look at each of these four operations to see when and how to use each one.

**1** Add or subtract the same term from both sides of the equation.

To solve for $x$, you may need to either add or subtract a term from both sides of an equation—or do both.

**16.** If $2x - 6 = x - 9$, then $x =$

    **(A)** −9

    **(B)** −6

    **(C)** −3

    **(D)** 2

    **(E)** 6

**The correct answer is (C).** First, put both $x$-terms on the left side of the equation by subtracting $x$ from both sides; then combine $x$-terms:

$$2x - 6 - x = x - 9 - x$$
$$x - 6 = -9$$

Next, isolate $x$ by adding 6 to both sides:

$$x - 6 + 6 = -9 + 6$$
$$x = -3$$

**2** Multiply or divide both sides of the equation by the same non-zero term.

To solve for $x$, you may need to either multiply or divide a term from both sides of an equation. Or, you may need to multiply and divide.

**17.** If $12 = \dfrac{11}{x} - \dfrac{3}{x}$, then $x =$

    **(A)** $\dfrac{3}{11}$

    **(B)** $\dfrac{1}{2}$

    **(C)** $\dfrac{2}{3}$

    **(D)** $\dfrac{11}{12}$

    **(E)** $\dfrac{11}{3}$

**The correct answer is (C).** First, combine the $x$-terms:

$$12 = \frac{11 - 3}{x}$$

Next, clear the fraction by multiplying both sides by $x$:

$$12x = 11 - 3$$
$$12x = 8$$

Finally, isolate $x$ by dividing both sides by 12:

$$x = \frac{8}{12} \text{ or } \frac{2}{3}$$

**❸** If each side of the equation is a fraction, your best bet is to cross-multiply.

Where the original equation equates two fractions, use cross-multiplication to eliminate the fractions. Multiply the numerator from one side of the equation by the denominator from the other side. Set the product equal to the product of the other numerator and denominator. (In effect, cross-multiplication is a shortcut method of multiplying both sides of the equation by both denominators.)

**18.** If, $\dfrac{7a}{8} = \dfrac{a + 1}{3}$, then $a =$

   **(A)** $\dfrac{8}{13}$

   **(B)** $\dfrac{7}{8}$

   **(C)** 2

   **(D)** $\dfrac{7}{3}$

   **(E)** 15

**The correct answer is (A).** First, cross-multiply as we've described:

$$(3)(7a) = (8)(a + 1)$$

Next, combine terms (distribute 8 to both $a$ and 1):

$$21a = 8a + 8$$

Next, isolate $a$-terms on one side by subtracting $8a$ from both sides; then combine the $a$-terms:

$$21a - 8a = 8a + 8 - 8a$$
$$13a = 8$$

Finally, isolate $a$ by dividing both sides by its coefficient 13:

$$\frac{13a}{13} = \frac{8}{13}$$
$$a = \frac{8}{13}$$

**4** Square both sides of the equation to eliminate radical signs. Where the variable is under a square-root radical sign, remove the radical sign by squaring both sides of the equation. (Use a similar technique for cube roots and other roots.)

**19.** If $3\sqrt{2x} = 2$, then $x =$

(A) $\dfrac{1}{18}$

(B) $\dfrac{2}{9}$

(C) $\dfrac{1}{3}$

(D) $\dfrac{5}{4}$

(E) 3

**The correct answer is (B).** First, clear the radical sign by squaring all terms:

$$(3^2)(\sqrt{2x})^2 = 2^2$$
$$(9)(2x) = 4$$
$$18x = 4$$

Next, isolate $x$ by dividing both sides by 18:

$$x = \frac{4}{18} \text{ or } \frac{2}{9}$$

## LINEAR EQUATIONS WITH TWO VARIABLES

What we've covered up to this point is pretty basic stuff. If you haven't quite caught on, you should probably stop here and consult a basic algebra workbook for more practice. On the other hand, if you're with us so far, let's forge ahead and add another variable. Here's a simple example:

$$x + 3 = y + 1$$

Quick . . . what's the value of $x$? It depends on the value of $y$, doesn't it? Similarly, the value of $y$ depends on the value of $x$. Without more information about either $x$ or $y$, you're stuck—but not completely. You can express $x$ in terms of $y$, and you can express $y$ in terms of $x$:

$$x = y - 2$$
$$y = x + 2$$

Let's look at one more:

$$4x - 9 = \frac{3}{2}y$$

Solve for $x$ in terms of $y$:

$$4x = \frac{3}{2}y + 9$$

$$x = \frac{3}{8}y + \frac{9}{4}$$

Solve for $y$ in terms of $x$:

$$\frac{4x - 9}{\frac{3}{2}} = y$$

$$\frac{2}{3}(4x - 9) = y$$

$$\frac{8}{3}x - 6 = y$$

To determine numerical values of $x$ and $y$, you need a system of two linear equations with the same two variables. Given this system, there are two different methods for finding the values of the two variables:

❶ The substitution method

❷ The addition-subtraction method

Next, we'll apply each method to determine the values of two variables in a two-equation system.

## The Substitution Method

To solve a system of two equations using the substitution method, follow these four steps (we'll use $x$ and $y$ here):

❶ In *either* equation, isolate one variable ($x$) on one side.

❷ Substitute the expression that equals $x$ in place of $x$ in the other equation.

❸ Solve that equation for $y$.

❹ Now that you know the value of $y$, plug it into *either* equation to find the value of $x$.

**ALERT!**

You can't solve one equation if it contains two unknowns (variables). You either need to know the value of one of the variables or you need a second equation.

**20.** If $\frac{2}{5}p + q = 3q - 10$, and if $q = 10 - p$, then $\dfrac{p}{q} =$

*(handwritten: $\dfrac{p}{q} = \dfrac{2}{10-2} = \dfrac{2}{8} = \dfrac{1}{4}$)*

**(A)** $\dfrac{5}{7}$

**(B)** $\dfrac{3}{2}$

**(C)** $\dfrac{5}{3}$

**(D)** $\dfrac{25}{6}$

**(E)** $\dfrac{36}{6}$

*(handwritten work:*
$\frac{2}{5}p + (10-p) = 3(10-p) - 10$
$\frac{2}{5}p + 10 - p = 30 - 3p - 10$
$\frac{2}{5}p + 10 - p = 20 - 3p$
*)*

**The correct answer is (A).** Don't let the fact that the question asks for $\dfrac{p}{q}$ (rather than simply $p$ or $q$) throw you. Because you're given two linear equations with two unknowns, you know that you can first solve for $p$ and $q$, then divide $p$ by $q$. First, combine the $q$-terms in the first equation:

$$\frac{2}{5}p = 2q - 10$$

Next, substitute $(10 - p)$ for $q$ (from the second equation) in the first equation:

$$\frac{2}{5}p = 2(10 - p) - 10$$

$$\frac{2}{5}p = 20 - 2p - 10$$

$$\frac{2}{5}p = 10 - 2p$$

Move the $p$-terms to the same side, then isolate $p$:

$$\frac{2}{5}p + 2p = 10$$

$$\frac{12}{5}p = 10$$

$$p = \left(\frac{5}{12}\right)(10)$$

$$p = \frac{25}{6}$$

Substitute $\dfrac{25}{6}$ for $p$ in either equation to find $q$ (we'll use the second equation):

$$q = 10 - \frac{25}{6}$$

$$q = \frac{60}{6} - \frac{25}{6}$$

$$q = \frac{35}{6}$$

The question asks for $\dfrac{p}{q}$, so do the division:

$$\frac{p}{q} = \frac{\dfrac{25}{6}}{\dfrac{35}{6}} = \frac{25}{35} \text{ or } \frac{5}{7}$$

## The Addition-Subtraction Method

Another way to solve for two unknowns in a system of two equations is with the addition-subtraction method. Here are the five steps:

1. Make the coefficient of *either* variable the same in both equations (you can disregard the sign) by multiplying every term in one of the equations.

2. Make sure the equations list the same variables in the same order.

3. Place one equation above the other.

4. Add the two equations (work down to a sum for each term), or subtract one equation from the other, to eliminate one variable.

5. You can repeat steps 1 to 3 to solve for the other variable.

**21.** If $3x + 4y = -8$, and if $x - 2y = \frac{1}{2}$, then $x =$

(A) $-12$

(B) $-\frac{7}{5}$

(C) $\frac{1}{3}$

(D) $\frac{14}{5}$

(E) $9$

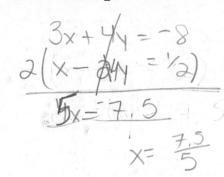

**The correct answer is (B).** To solve for $x$, you want to eliminate $y$. You can multiply each term in the second equation by 2, then add the equations:

$$\begin{array}{rcl} 3x + 4y & = & -8 \\ 2x - 4y & = & 1 \\ \hline 5x + 0y & = & -7 \\ x & = & -\frac{7}{5} \end{array}$$

Since the question asked only for the value of $x$, stop here. If the question had asked for both $x$ and $y$ (or for $y$ only), you could have multiplied both sides of the second equation by 3, then subtracted the second equation from the first:

$$\begin{array}{rcl} 3x + 4y & = & -8 \\ 3x - 6y & = & \frac{3}{2} \\ \hline 0x + 10y & = & -9\frac{1}{2} \\ 10y & = & -\frac{19}{2} \\ y & = & -\frac{19}{20} \end{array}$$

**NOTE**

If a question requires you to find values of both unknowns, combine the two methods. For example, after using addition-subtraction to solve for $x$, substitute the value of $x$ into either equation to find $y$.

## Which Method Should You Use?

Which method, substitution or addition-subtraction, you should use depends on what the equations look like to begin with. To see what we mean, look again at this system:

$$\frac{2}{5}p + q = 3q - 10$$

$$q = 10 - p$$

Notice that the second equation is already set up nicely for the substitution method. You could use addition-subtraction instead; however, you'd just have to rearrange the terms in both the equations first:

$$\frac{2}{5}p - 2q = -10$$

$$p + q = 10$$

Now, look again at the following system:

$$3x + 4y = -8$$
$$x - 2y = \frac{1}{2}$$

Notice that the $x$-term and $y$-term already line up nicely here. Also, notice that it's easy to match the coefficients of either $x$ or $y$: multiply both sides of the second equation by either 3 or 2. This system is an ideal candidate for addition-subtraction. To appreciate this point, try using substitution instead. You'll discover that it takes far more number crunching.

## LINEAR EQUATIONS THAT CANNOT BE SOLVED

Never assume that one linear equation with one variable is solvable. If you can reduce the equation to $0 = 0$, then you can't solve it. In other words, the value of the variable could be any real number.

TIP

To solve a system of two linear equations with two variables, use addition-subtraction if you can quickly and easily eliminate one of the variables. Otherwise, use substitution.

|  | **Column A** | **Column B** |
|---|---|---|
| **22.** | $3x - 3 - 4x = x - 7 - 2x + 4$ | |
|  | $x$　　　　$-x-3 = -x-3$ | $0$ |

**(A)** The quantity in Column A is greater;

**(B)** The quantity in Column B is greater;

**(C)** The quantities are equal;

**(D)** The relationship cannot be determined from the information given.

**The correct answer is (D).** All terms on both sides cancel out:

$$3x - 3 - 4x = -7 - 2x + 4$$
$$-x - 3 = -x - 3$$
$$0 = 0$$
$$\therefore x = \text{any real number}$$

In some cases, what appears to be a system of two equations with two variables is actually one equation expressed in two different ways.

|  | **Column A** | **Column B** |
|---|---|---|
| **23.** | $a + b = 30$ | |
|  | $2b = 60 - 2a$ | |
|  | $a$ | $b$ |

**(A)** The quantity in Column A is greater;

**(B)** The quantity in Column B is greater;

**(C)** The quantities are equal;

**(D)** The relationship cannot be determined from the information given.

$b = 30 - a$
$2b = 60 - 2a$
$3b = 90 - 3a$

**The correct answer is (D).** An unwary test-taker might waste time trying to find the values of $a$ and $b$, because the centered data appears at first glance to provide a system of two linear equations with two unknowns. But you can easily manipulate the second equation so that it is identical to the first:

$$2b = 60 - 2a$$
$$2b = 2(30 - a)$$
$$b = 30 - a$$
$$a + b = 30$$

As you can see, you're really dealing with only one equation. Since you cannot solve one equation in two unknowns, you cannot make the comparison.

**ALERT!**

If the centered information in a Quantitative Comparison consists of one or more linear equations, *never* assume you can solve for the variable(s).

Whenever you encounter a Quantitative Comparison question that calls for solving one or more linear equations, stop in your tracks before taking pencil to paper. Size up the equation to see whether it's one of the two unsolvable kinds you learned about here. If so, unless you're given more information, the correct answer will be choice (D).

## FACTORABLE QUADRATIC EXPRESSIONS WITH ONE VARIABLE

A *quadratic expression* includes a "squared" variable, such as $x^2$. An equation is quadratic if you can express it in this general form:

$$ax^2 + bx + c = 0$$

Where:

$x$ is the variable

$a$, $b$, and $c$ are constants (numbers)

$a \neq 0$

$b$ can equal 0

$c$ can equal 0

Here are four examples (notice that the $b$-term and $c$-term are not essential; in other words, either $b$ or $c$, or both, can equal zero (0)):

| Quadratic Equation | Same Equation, but in the Form: $ax^2 + bx + c = 0$ |
|---|---|
| $2w^2 = 16$ | $2w^2 - 16 = 0$ (no $b$-term) |
| $x^2 = 3x$ | $x^2 - 3x = 0$ (no $c$-term) |
| $3y = 4 - y^2$ | $y^2 + 3y - 4 = 0$ |
| $7z = 2z^2 - 15$ | $2z^2 - 7z - 15 = 0$ |

Every quadratic equation has exactly two solutions, called *roots*. (But the two roots might be the same.) On the GRE, you can often find the two roots by *factoring*. To solve any factorable quadratic equation, follow these three steps:

**1** Put the equation into the standard form: $ax^2 + bx + c = 0$.

**2** Factor the terms on the left side of the equation into two linear expressions (with no exponents).

**3** Set each linear expression (root) equal to zero (0) and solve for the variable in each one.

## Factoring Simple Quadratic Expressions

Some quadratic expressions are easier to factor than others. If either of the two constants $b$ or $c$ is zero (0), factoring requires no sweat. In fact, in some cases, no factoring is needed at all:

| A Quadratic with No $c$-term | A Quadratic with No $b$-term |
|---|---|
| $2x^2 = x$ $$2x^2 - x = 0$$ $$x(2x - 1) = 0$$ $$x = 0, 2x - 1 = 0$$ $$x = 0, \frac{1}{2}$$ | $2x^2 - 4 = 0$ $$2(x^2 - 2) = 0$$ $$x^2 - 2 = 0$$ $$x^2 = 2$$ $$x = \sqrt{2}, -\sqrt{2}$$ |

## Factoring Quadratic Trinomials

A trinomial is simply an algebraic expression that contains three terms. If a quadratic expression contains all three terms of the standard form $ax^2 + bx + c$, then factoring becomes a bit trickier. You need to apply the FOIL method, in which you add together these terms:

**(F)** the product of the first terms of the two binomials

**(O)** the product of the outer terms of the two binomials

**(I)** the product of the inner terms of the two binomials

**(L)** the product of the last (second) terms of the two binomials

Note the following relationships:

**(F)** is the first term ($ax^2$) of the quadratic expression

**(O + I)** is the second term ($bx$) of the quadratic expression

**(L)** is the third term ($c$) of the quadratic expression

You'll find that the two factors will be two binomials. The GRE might ask you to recognize one or both of these binomial factors.

**24.** Which of the following is a factor of $x^2 - x - 6$ ?

   **(A)** $(x + 6)$
   **(B)** $(x - 3)$
   **(C)** $(x + 1)$
   **(D)** $(x - 2)$
   **(E)** $(x + 3)$

**ALERT!**

When dealing with a quadratic equation, your first step is usually to put it into the general form $ax^2 + bx + c = 0$. But keep in mind: The only essential term is $ax^2$.

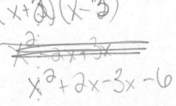

**The correct answer is (B).** Notice that $x^2$ has no coefficient. This makes the process of factoring into two binomials easier. Set up two binomial shells: $(x \ )(x \ )$. The product of the two missing second terms (the "L" term under the FOIL method) is $-6$. The possible integral pairs that result in this product are $(1,-6)$, $(-1,6)$, $(2,-3,)$, and $(-2,3)$. Notice that the second term in the trinomial is $-x$. This means that the sum of the two integers whose product is $-6$ must be $-1$. The pair $(2,-3)$ fits the bill. Thus, the trinomial is equivalent to the product of the two binomials $(x + 2)$ and $(x - 3)$.

To check your work, multiply the two binomials using the FOIL method:

$$(x + 2)(x - 3) = x^2 - 3x + 2x - 6$$
$$= x^2 - x + 6$$

If the preceding question had asked you to determine the roots of the equation $x^2 - x - 6 = 0$, you'd simply set each of the binomial factors equal to zero (0), then solve for $x$ in each one. The solution set (the two possible values of $x$) includes the roots $-2$ and $3$.

25. How many different values of $x$ does the solution set for the equation $4x^2 = 4x - 1$ contain?

   **(A)** None

   **(B)** One

   **(C)** Two

   **(D)** Four

   **(E)** Infinitely many

   **The correct answer is (B).** First, express the equation in standard form: $4x^2 - 4x + 1 = 0$. Notice that the $c$-term is 1. The only two integral pairs that result in this product are $(1,1)$ and $(-1,-1)$. Since the $b$-term $(-4x)$ is negative, the integral pair whose product is 1 must be $(-1,-1)$. Set up a binomial shell:

   $(? - 1)(? - 1)$

   Notice that the $a$-term contains the coefficient 4. The possible integral pairs that result in this product are $(1,4)$, $(2,2)$, $(-1,-4)$, and $(-2,-2)$. A bit of trial-and-error reveals that only the pair $(2,2)$ works. Thus, in factored form, the equation becomes $(2x - 1)(2x - 1) = 0$. To check your work, multiply the two binomials using the FOIL method:
   $$(2x - 1)(2x - 1) = 4x^2 - 2x - 2x + 1$$
   $$= 4x^2 - 4x + 1$$

   Since the two binomial factors are the same, the two roots of the equation are the same. In other words, $x$ has only one possible value. (Although you don't need to find the value of $x$ in order to answer the question, solve for $x$ in the equation $2x - 1 = 0$; $x = \frac{1}{2}$.)

## Stealth Quadratic Equations

Some equations that appear linear (variables include no exponents) may actually be quadratic. Following, you will see the two GRE situations you need to be on the lookout for.

**1** The same variable inside a radical also appears outside:

$$\sqrt{x} = 5x$$
$$(\sqrt{x})^2 = (5x)^2$$
$$x = 25x^2$$
$$25x^2 - x = 0$$

**2** The same variable that appears in the denominator of a fraction also appears elsewhere in the equation:

$$\frac{2}{x} = 3 - x$$
$$2 = x(3 - x)$$
$$2 = 3x - x^2$$
$$x^2 - 3x + 2 = 0$$

In both scenarios, you're dealing with a quadratic (nonlinear) equation with one variable. So, in either equation, there are two roots. (Both equations are factorable, so go ahead and find their roots.)

The test-makers often use the Quantitative Comparison format to cover this concept.

|               **Column A**               |               **Column B**               |
|:----------------------------------------:|:----------------------------------------:|

**26.**

$$6x = \sqrt{3x}$$

$$x \qquad\qquad\qquad\qquad\qquad\qquad \frac{1}{12}$$

**(A)** The quantity in Column A is greater;

**(B)** The quantity in Column B is greater;

**(C)** The quantities are equal;

**(D)** The relationship cannot be determined from the information given.

**The correct answer is (D).** An unwary test-taker might assume that the equation is linear, because $x$ is not squared. Substituting $\frac{1}{12}$ for $x$ satisfies the centered equation. But the two quantities are *not* necessarily equal. If you clear the radical by squaring both sides of the equation, then isolate the $x$-terms on one side of the equation, you'll see that the equation is quadratic:

$$36x^2 = 3x$$
$$36x^2 - 3x = 0$$

To find the two roots, factor out $3x$, then solve for each root:

$3x(12x - 1) = 0$

$$x = 0, 12x - 1 = 0$$

$$x = 0, \frac{1}{12}$$

Since $\frac{1}{12}$ is only one of two possible values for $x$, you cannot make a definitive comparison.

## NONLINEAR EQUATIONS WITH TWO VARIABLES

In the world of math, solving nonlinear equations with two or more variables can be *very* complicated, even for bona-fide mathematicians. But on the GRE, all you need to remember are these three general forms:

Sum of two variables, squared: $(x + y)^2 = x^2 + 2xy + y^2$

Difference of two variables, squared: $(x - y)^2 = x^2 - 2xy + y^2$

Difference of two squares: $x^2 - y^2 = (x + y)(x - y)$

You can verify these equations using the FOIL method:

| $(x + y)^2$ | $(x - y)^2$ | $(x + y)(x - y)$ |
|---|---|---|
| $= (x + y)(x + y)$ <br> $= x^2 + xy + xy + y^2$ <br> $= x^2 + 2xy + y^2$ | $= (x - y)(x - y)$ <br> $= x^2 - xy - xy + y^2$ <br> $= x^2 - 2xy + y^2$ | $= x^2 + xy - xy - y^2$ <br> $= x^2 - y^2$ |

For the GRE, memorize the three equations listed here. When you see one form on the exam, it's a sure bet that your task is to rewrite it as the other form.

**TIP**

You usually can't solve quadratics using a shortcut. Always look for one of the three common quadratic forms. If you see it, rewrite it as its equivalent form to answer the question as quickly and easily as possible.

**27.** If $x^2 - y^2 = 100$, and if $x + y = 2$, then $x - y =$

  **(A)** $-2$

  **(B)** 10

  **(C)** 20

  **(D)** 50

  **(E)** 200

**The correct answer is (D).** If you're on the lookout for the difference of two squares, you can handle this question with no sweat. Use the third equation you just learned, substituting 2 for $(x + y)$, then solving for $(x - y)$:

$$x^2 - y^2 = (x + y)(x - y)$$
$$100 = (x + y)(x - y)$$
$$100 = (2)(x - y)$$
$$50 = (x - y)$$

## SOLVING ALGEBRAIC INEQUALITIES

You can solve algebraic inequalities in the same manner as equations. Isolate the variable on one side of the inequality symbol, factoring and eliminating terms wherever possible. However, one important rule distinguishes inequalities from equations: Whenever you multiply or divide both sides of an inequality by a negative number, you must reverse the inequality symbol. Simply put: If $a > b$, then $-a < -b$.

| | |
|---|---|
| $12 - 4x < 8$ | Original inequality |
| $-4x < -4$ | 12 subtracted from each side; inequality unchanged |
| $x > 1$ | Both sides divided by $-4$; inequality reversed |

Here are five general rules for dealing with algebraic inequalities. Study them until they're second nature to you because you'll put them to good use on the GRE.

**1** Adding or subtracting unequal quantities to (or from) equal quantities:

If $a > b$, then $c + a > c + b$

If $a > b$, then $c - a < c - b$

**2** Adding unequal quantities to unequal quantities:

If $a > b$, and if $c > d$, then $a + c > b + d$

**3** Comparing three unequal quantities:

If $a > b$, and if $b > c$, then $a > c$

**4** Combining the same positive quantity with unequal quantities by multiplication or division:

If $a > b$, and if $x > 0$, then $xa > xb$

**5** Combining the same negative quantity with unequal quantities by multiplication or division:

If $a > b$, and if $x < 0$, then $xa < xb$

28. If $a > b$, and if $c > d$, then which of the following must be true?

    **(A)** $a - b > c - d$
    **(B)** $a - c > b - d$
    **(C)** $c + d < a - b$
    **(D)** $b + d < a + c$
    **(E)** $a - c < b + d$

    **The correct answer is (D).** Inequality questions can be a bit confusing, can't they? In this problem, you need to remember that if unequal quantities ($c$ and $d$) are added to unequal quantities of the same order ($a$ and $b$), the result is an inequality in the same order. This rule is essentially what answer choice (D) says.

**ALERT!**

Be careful when handling inequality problems: The wrong answers might look right, depending on the values you use for the different variables.

## WEIGHTED AVERAGE PROBLEMS

You solve *weighted average* problems using the arithmetic mean (simple average) formula, except you give the set's terms different weights. For example, if a final exam score of 90 receives *twice* the weight of each of two midterm exam scores 75 and 85, think of the final exam score as *two* scores of 90—and the total number of scores as 4 rather than 3:

$$\text{WA} = \frac{75 + 85 + (2)(90)}{4} = \frac{340}{4} = 85$$

Similarly, when some numbers among terms might appear more often than others, you must give them the appropriate "weight" before computing an average.

29. During an 8-hour trip, Brigitte drove 3 hours at 55 miles per hour and 5 hours at 65 miles per hour. What was her average rate, in miles per hour, for the entire trip?

   **(A)** 58.5
   **(B)** 60
   **(C)** 61.25
   **(D)** 62.5
   **(E)** 66.25

   **The correct answer is (C).** Determine the total miles driven: (3)(55) + (5)(65) = 490. To determine the average over the entire trip, divide this total by 8, which is the number of total hours: 490 ÷ 8 = 61.25.

A tougher weighted-average problem might provide the weighted average and ask for one of the terms, or require conversions from one unit of measurement to another—or both.

30. A certain olive orchard produces 315 gallons of oil annually, on average, during four consecutive years. How many gallons of oil must the orchard produce annually, on average, during the next six years, if oil production for the entire 10-year period is to meet a goal of 378 gallons per year?

   **(A)** 240
   **(B)** 285
   **(C)** 396
   **(D)** 420
   **(E)** 468

   **The correct answer is (D).** In the weighted-average formula, 315 annual gallons receives a weight of 4, while the average annual number of gallons for the next six years ($x$) receives a weight of 6:

$$378 = \frac{1,260 + 6x}{10}$$
$$3,780 = 1,260 + 6x$$
$$3,780 - 1,260 = 6x$$
$$2,520 = 6x$$
$$420 = x$$

This solution (420) is the average number of gallons needed per year, on average, during the next 6 years.

To guard against calculation errors, check your answer by sizing up the question. Generally, how great a number are you looking for? Notice that the stated goal is a bit greater than the annual average production over the first four years. So you're looking for an answer that is greater than the goal—a number somewhat greater than 378 gallons per year. You can eliminate choices (A) and (B) out of hand. The number 420 fits the bill.

## CURRENCY PROBLEMS

Currency problems are similar to weighted-average problems in that each item (bill or coin) is weighted according to its monetary value. Unlike weighted average problems, however, the "average" value of all the bills or coins is not at issue. In solving currency problems, remember the following:

- You must formulate algebraic expressions involving both *number* of items (bills or coins) and *value* of items.

- You should convert the value of all moneys to a common currency unit before formulating an equation. If converting to cents, for example, you must multiply the number of nickels by 5, dimes by 10, and so forth.

**TIP**

You can solve most GRE currency problems by working backward from the answer choices.

**31.** Jim has $2.05 in dimes and quarters. If he has four fewer dimes than quarters, how much money does he have in dimes?

**(A)** 20 cents
**(B)** 30 cents
**(C)** 40 cents
**(D)** 50 cents
**(E)** 60 cents

**The correct answer is (B).** Letting $x$ equal the number of dimes, $x + 4$ represents the number of quarters. The total value of the dimes (in cents) is $10x$, and the total value of the quarters (in cents) is $25(x + 4)$ or $25x + 100$. Given that Jim has $2.05, the following equation emerges:

$$10x + 25x + 100 = 205$$
$$35x = 105$$
$$x = 3$$

Jim has three dimes, so he has 30 cents in dimes.

You could also solve this problem without formal algebra, by plugging in each answer choice in turn. Let's try this strategy for choices (A) and (B):

(A) 20 cents is 2 dimes, so Jim has 6 quarters. 20 cents plus $1.50 adds up to $1.70. Wrong answer!

(B) 30 cents is 3 dimes, so Jim has 7 quarters. 30 cents plus $1.75 adds up to $2.05. Correct answer!

## MIXTURE PROBLEMS

In GRE mixture problems, you combine substances with different characteristics, resulting in a particular mixture or proportion, usually expressed as percentages. Substances are measured and mixed by either volume or weight—rather than by number (quantity).

32. How many quarts of pure alcohol must you add to 15 quarts of a solution that is 40% alcohol to strengthen it to a solution that is 50% alcohol?

    **(A)** 4.0
    **(B)** 3.5
    **(C)** 3.25
    **(D)** 3.0
    **(E)** 2.5

    **The correct answer is (D).** You can solve this problem by working backward from the answer choices—trying out each one in turn. Or, you can solve the problem algebraically. The original amount of alcohol is 40% of 15. Letting $x$ equal the number of quarts of alcohol that you must add to achieve a 50% alcohol solution, $.4(15) + x$ equals the amount of alcohol in the solution after adding more alcohol. You can express this amount as 50% of $(15 + x)$. Thus, you can express the mixture algebraically as follows:

    $$(.4)(15) + x = (.5)(15 + x)$$
    $$6 + x = 7.5 + .5x$$
    $$.5x = 1.5$$
    $$x = 3$$

    You must add 3 quarts of alcohol to obtain a 50% alcohol solution.

## INVESTMENT PROBLEMS

GRE investment problems involve interest earned (at a certain percentage rate) on money over a certain time period (usually a year). To calculate interest earned, multiply the original amount of money by the interest rate:

    amount of money $\times$ interest rate = amount of interest on money

For example, if you deposit $1,000 in a savings account that earns 5% interest annually, the total amount in the account after one year will be $1,000 + .05($1,000) = $1,000 + $50 = $1,050.

GRE investment questions usually involve more than simply calculating interest earned on a given principal amount at a given rate. They usually call for you to set up and solve an algebraic equation. When handling these problems, it's best to eliminate percent signs.

**33.** Dr. Kramer plans to invest $20,000 in an account paying 6% interest annually. How much more must she invest at the same time at 3% so that her total annual income during the first year is 4% of her entire investment?

(A) $32,000

(B) $36,000

(C) $40,000

(D) $47,000

(E) $49,000

**The correct answer is (C).** Letting $x$ equal the amount invested at 3%, you can express Dr. Kramer's total investment as $20,000 + x$. The interest on $20,000 plus the interest on the additional investment equals the total interest from both investments. You can state this algebraically as follows:

$.06(20,000) + .03x = .04(20,000 + x)$

Multiply all terms by 100 to eliminate decimals, then solve for $x$:

$6(20,000) + 3x = 4(20,000 + x)$

$120,000 + 3x = 80,000 + 4x$

$40,000 = x$

She must invest $40,000 at 3% for her total annual income to be 4% of her total investment ($60,000).

Beware: In solving GRE investment problems, by all means size up the question to make sure your calculated answer is in the ballpark. But don't rely on your intuition to derive a *precise* solution. Interest problems can be misleading. For instance, you might have guessed that Dr. Kramer would need to invest more than *twice* as much at 3% than at 6% to lower the overall interest rate to 4%, which is not true.

# PROBLEMS OF RATE OF PRODUCTION AND RATE OF TRAVEL

A *rate* is a fraction that expresses a quantity per unit of time. For example, the rate at which a machine produces a certain product is expressed this way:

$$\text{rate of production} = \frac{\text{number of units produced}}{\text{time}}$$

## Rate of Production (Work)

A simple GRE rate question might provide two of the three terms and then ask you for the value of the third term. To complicate matters, the question might also require you to convert a number from one unit of measurement to another.

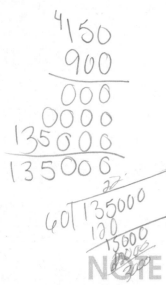

**34.** If a printer can print pages at a rate of 15 pages per minute, how many pages can it print in $2\frac{1}{2}$ hours?

**(A)** 1,375

**(B)** 1,500

**(C)** 1,750

**(D)** 2,250

**(E)** 2,500

**The correct answer is (D).** Apply the following formula:

$$\text{rate} = \frac{\text{no. of pages}}{\text{time}}$$

The rate is given as 15 minutes, so convert the time ($2\frac{1}{2}$ hours) to 150 minutes. Determine the number of pages by applying the formula to these numbers:

$$15 = \frac{\text{no. of pages}}{150}$$

$$(15)(150) = \text{no. of pages}$$

$$2,250 = \text{no. of pages}$$

A more challenging type of rate-of-production (work) problem involves two or more workers (people or machines) working together to accomplish a task or job. In these scenarios, there's an inverse relationship between the number of workers and the time that it takes to complete the job; in other words, the more workers, the quicker the job gets done.

A GRE work problem might specify the rates at which certain workers work alone and ask you to determine the rate at which they work together, or vice versa. Here's the basic formula for solving a work problem:

$$\frac{A}{x} + \frac{A}{y} = 1$$

In this formula:

- $x$ and $y$ represent the time needed for each of two workers, $x$ and $y$, to complete the job alone.

- A represents the time it takes for both $x$ and $y$ to complete the job working in the *aggregate* (together).

So each fraction represents the portion of the job completed by a worker. The sum of the two fractions must be 1 if the job is completed.

**NOTE**

In the real world, a team may be more efficient than the individuals working alone. But for GRE questions, assume that no additional efficiency is gained this way.

**35.** One printing press can print a daily newspaper in 12 hours, while another press can print it in 18 hours. How long will the job take if both presses work simultaneously?

**(A)** 7 hours, 12 minutes

**(B)** 9 hours, 30 minutes

**(C)** 10 hours, 45 minutes

**(D)** 15 hours

**(E)** 30 hours

**The correct answer is (A).** Just plug the two numbers 12 and 18 into our work formula, then solve for A:

$$\frac{A}{12} + \frac{A}{18} = 1$$

$$\frac{3A}{36} + \frac{2A}{36} = 1$$

$$\frac{5A}{36} = 1$$

$$5A = 36$$

$$A = \frac{36}{5} \text{ or } 7\frac{1}{5}.$$

Both presses working simultaneously can do the job in $7\frac{1}{5}$ hours—or 7 hours, 12 minutes.

## Rate of Travel (Speed)

GRE rate problems often involve rate of travel (speed). You can express a rate of travel this way:

$$\text{rate of travel} = \frac{\text{distance}}{\text{time}}$$

An easier speed problem will involve a *single* distance, rate, and time. A tougher speed problem might involve different rates:

- Two different times over the same distance

- Two different distances covered in the same time

In either type, apply the basic rate-of-travel formula to each of the two events. Then solve for the missing information by algebraic substitution. Use essentially the same approach for any of the following scenarios:

- One object making two separate "legs" of a trip—either in the same direction or as a round trip

- Two objects moving in the same direction

- Two objects moving in opposite directions

**TIP**

In work problems, use your common sense to narrow down answer choices.

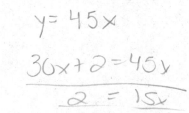

36. Janice left her home at 11 a.m., traveling along Route 1 at 30 mph. At 1 p.m., her brother Richard left home and started after her on the same road at 45 mph. At what time did Richard catch up to Janice?

   (A) 2:45 p.m.
   (B) 3:00 p.m.
   (C) 3:30 p.m.
   (D) 4:15 p.m.
   (E) 5:00 p.m.

**The correct answer is (E).** Notice that the distance Janice covered is equal to that of Richard—that is, distance is constant. Letting $x$ equal Janice's time, you can express Richard's time as $x - 2$. Substitute these values for time and the values for rate given in the problem into the speed formula for Richard and Janice:

Formula: rate $\times$ time = distance

Janice: $(30)(x) = 30x$

Richard: $(45)(x - 2) = 45x - 90$

Because the distance is constant, you can equate Janice's distance to Richard's, then solve for $x$:

$30x = 45x - 90$
$15x = 90$
$x = 6$

Janice had traveled 6 hours when Richard caught up with her. Because Janice left at 11:00 a.m., Richard caught up with her at 5:00 p.m.

37. How far in kilometers can Scott drive into the country if he drives out at 40 kilometers per hour (kph), returns over the same road at 30 kph, and spends 8 hours away from home, including a 1-hour stop for lunch?

   (A) 105
   (B) 120
   (C) 145
   (D) 180
   (E) 210

**The correct answer is (B).** Scott's actual driving time is 7 hours, which you must divide into two parts: his time spent driving into the country and his time spent returning. Letting the first part equal $x$, the return time is what remains of the 7 hours, or $7 - x$. Substitute these expressions into the motion formula for each of the two parts of Scott's journey:

Formula: rate $\times$ time = distance

Going: $(40)(x) = 40x$

Returning: $(30)(7 - x) = 210 - 30x$

Because the journey is round trip, the distance going equals the distance returning. Simply equate the two algebraic expressions, then solve for $x$:

$40x = 210 - 30x$

$70x = 210$

$x = 3$

Scott traveled 40 kph for 3 hours, so he traveled 120 kilometers.

## PROBLEMS INVOLVING OVERLAPPING SETS

Overlapping set problems involve distinct sets that share some number of members. GRE overlapping set problems come in one of two varieties:

**1** Single overlap (easier)

**2** Double overlap (tougher)

**38.** Each of the 24 people auditioning for a community-theater production is an actor, a musician, or both. If 10 of the people auditioning are actors and 19 of the people auditioning are musicians, how many of the people auditioning are musicians but not actors?

**(A)** 10

**(B)** 14

**(C)** 19

**(D)** 21

**(E)** 24

**The correct answer is (B).** You can approach this relatively simple problem without formal algebra: The number of actors plus the number of musicians equals 29 $(10 + 19 = 29)$. However, only 24 people are auditioning. Thus, 5 of the 24 are actor-musicians, so 14 of the 19 musicians must not be actors.

You can also solve this problem algebraically. The question describes three mutually exclusive sets: (1) actors who are not musicians, (2) musicians who are not actors, and (3) actors who are also musicians. The total number of people among these three sets is 24. You can represent this scenario with the following algebraic equation ($n$ = number of actors/musicians), solving for $19 - n$ to answer the question:

$$(10 - n) + n + (19 - n) = 24$$
$$29 - n = 24$$
$$n = 5$$
$$19 - 5 = 14$$

**TIP**

Regardless of the type of speed problem, start by setting up *two* distinct equations patterned after the simple rate-of-travel formula $(r \times t = d)$.

**39.** Adrian owns 60 neckties, each of which is either 100% silk or 100% polyester. Forty percent of each type of tie is striped, and 25 of the ties are silk. How many of the ties are polyester but not striped?

**(A)** 18

**(B)** 21

**(C)** 24

**(D)** 35

**(E)** 40

**The correct answer is (B).** This double-overlap problem involves four distinct sets: striped silk ties, striped polyester ties, non-striped silk ties, and non-striped polyester ties. Set up a table representing the four sets, filling in the information given in the problem, as shown in the next figure:

|              | silk | polyester |      |
|--------------|------|-----------|------|
| striped      |      |           | 40%  |
| non-striped  |      | ?         | 60%  |
|              | 25   | 35        |      |

Given that 25 ties are silk (see the left column), 35 ties must be polyester (see the right column). Also, given that 40% of the ties are striped (see the top row), 60% must be non-striped (see the bottom row). Thus, 60% of 35 ties, or 21 ties, are polyester and non-striped.

# SUMMING IT UP

- Make sure you're up to speed on the definitions of absolute value, integers, factors, and prime numbers to better prepare yourself for the number theory and algebra questions on the GRE Quantitative Reasoning section.

- Use prime factorization to factor composite integers.

- GRE questions involving exponents usually require that you combine two or more terms that contain exponents, so review the basic rules for adding, subtracting, multiplying, and dividing them.

- On the GRE, always look for a way to simplify radicals by moving what's under the radical sign to the outside of the sign.

- Most algebraic equations you'll see on the GRE exam are linear. Remember the operations for isolating the unknown on one side of the equation. Solving algebraic inequalities is similar to solving equations: Isolate the variable on one side of the inequality symbol first.

- Weighted average problems and currency problems can be solved in a similar manner by using the arithmetic mean formula.

- Mixture and investment problems on the GRE can be solved using what you've learned about solving proportion and percentage questions. Rate of production and travel questions can be solved using the strategies you've learned about fraction problems.

# Math Review: Geometry

## chapter 11

## OVERVIEW
- Lines and angles
- Triangles
- Isosceles and equilateral triangles
- Rectangles, squares, and parallelograms
- Circles
- Advanced circle problems
- Polygons
- Cubes and other rectangular solids
- Cylinders
- Coordinate signs and the four quadrants
- Defining a line on the coordinate plane
- Graphing a line on the coordinate plane
- Coordinate geometry
- Midpoint and distance formulas
- Summing it up

In this chapter, you'll review the fundamentals involving plane geometry, starting with the following:

- Relationships among angles formed by intersecting lines

- Characteristics of any triangle

- Characteristics of special right triangles

- The Pythagorean theorem

- Characteristics of squares, rectangles, and parallelograms

- Characteristics of circles

Then, you'll review the basics of coordinate geometry:

- The characteristics of the $xy$-plane

- Defining and plotting points and lines on the plane

- Applying the midpoint and distance formulas to problems involving line segments

When we've finished reviewing the basics, we'll take a look at the following advanced topics involving plane and coordinate geometry:

- Properties of isosceles and equilateral triangles

- Properties of trapezoids

- Properties of polygons (including those with more than four sides)

- Relationships between arcs and other features of circles

- Relationships between circles and tangent lines

- Relationships created by combining a circle with another geometric figure (such as a triangle or another circle)

- Properties of cubes, other rectangular solids, and cylinders

- Plotting and defining 2-dimensional figures (triangles, rectangles, and circles) on the $xy$-plane

# LINES AND ANGLES

Lines and line segments are the basic building blocks for most GRE geometry problems. A GRE geometry question might involve nothing more than intersecting lines and the angles they form. To handle the question, just remember four basic rules about angles formed by intersecting lines:

**1** Vertical angles (angles across the vertex from each other and formed by the same two lines) are equal in degree measure, or congruent ($\cong$). In other words, they're the same size.

**2** If adjacent angles combine to form a straight line, their degree measures total 180. In fact, a straight line is actually a 180° angle.

**3** If two lines are perpendicular ($\perp$) to each other, they intersect, forming right (90°) angles.

**4** The sum of the measures of all angles where two or more lines intersect at the same point is 360° (regardless of how many angles are involved).

Note that the symbol ($\cong$) indicates that two geometric features are *congruent*, meaning that they are identical (the same size, length, degree measure, etc.). The equation $\overline{AB} \cong \overline{CD}$ means that line segment $\overline{AB}$ is congruent (equal in length) to line segment $\overline{CD}$. The two equations $\angle A \cong \angle B$ and $m\angle A = m\angle B$ are two different ways of symbolizing the same relationship: that the angle whose vertex is at point A is congruent (equal in degree measure, or size) to the angle whose vertex is at point B. (The letter m symbolizes degree measure.)

## Angles Formed by Intersecting Lines

When two or more lines intersect at the same point, they form a "wheel-spoke" pattern with a "hub." On the GRE, "wheel-spoke" questions require you to apply one or more of the preceding four rules.

1.

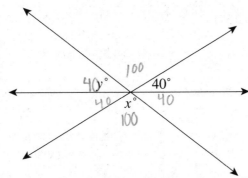

The figure above shows three intersecting lines. What is the value of $x + y$ ?

**(A)** 50

**(B)** 80

**(C)** 130

**(D)** 140

**(E)** 150

**The correct answer is (D).** The angle vertical to the one indicated as 40° must also measure 40°. That 40° angle, together with the angles whose measures are $x°$ and $y°$, combine to form a straight (180°) line. In other words, $40 + x + y = 180$. Thus, $x + y = 140$.

A slightly tougher "wheel-spoke" question might focus on overlapping angles and require you to apply rule 1 (about vertical angles) to determine the amount of the overlap. Look at this next "wheel-spoke" figure:

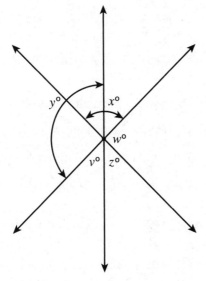

A GRE question about the preceding figure might test your ability to recognize one of the following relationships:

| $x° + y° - z° = 180°$ | $x° + y°$ exceeds 180° by the amount of the overlap, which equals $z°$, the angle vertical to the overlapping angle. |
| --- | --- |
| $x° + y° + v° + w° = 360°$ | The sum of the measures of all angles, excluding $z°$, is 360°; $z$ is excluded because it is already accounted for by the overlap of $x$ and $y$. |
| $y° - w° = z°$ | $w°$ equals its vertical angle, so $y - w$ equals the portion of $y$ vertical to angle $z$. |

## Parallel Lines and Transversals

GRE problems involving parallel lines also involve at least one transversal, which is a line that intersects each of two (or more) lines. Look at this next figure, in which $l_1 \parallel l_2$ and $l_3 \parallel l_4$:

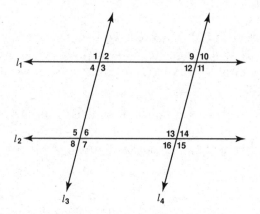

The upper-left "cluster" of angles 1, 2, 3, and 4 matches each of the three other clusters. In other words:

- All the odd-numbered angles are congruent (equal in size) to one another.

- All the even-numbered angles are congruent (equal in size) to one another.

If you know the size of just one angle, you can determine the size of all 16 angles.

2.

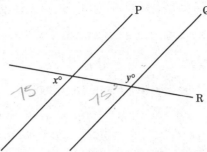

In the figure above, lines P and Q are parallel to each other. If $m\angle x = 75°$, what is the measure of $\angle y$?

**(A)** 75°

**(B)** 85°

**(C)** 95°

**(D)** 105°

**(E)** 115°

**The correct answer is (D).** The angle "cluster" where lines P and R intersect corresponds to the cluster where lines Q and R intersect. Thus, $\angle x$ and $\angle y$ are supplementary (their measures add up to 180°). Given that $\angle x$ measures 75°, $\angle y$ must measure 105°.

# TRIANGLES

The *triangle* (a three-sided polygon) is the test-makers' favorite geometric figure. You'll need to understand triangles not only to solve "pure" triangle problems but also to solve certain problems involving four-sided figures, three-dimensional figures, and even circles. After a brief review of the properties of any triangle, you'll focus on right triangles (which include one right, or 90°, angle).

## Properties of All Triangles

Here are four properties that all triangles share:

❶ **Length of the sides:** Each side is shorter than the sum of the lengths of the other two sides. (Otherwise, the triangle would collapse into a line.)

❷ **Angle measures:** The measures of the three angles total 180°.

❸ **Angles and opposite sides:** Comparative angle sizes correspond to the comparative lengths of the sides opposite those angles. For example, a triangle's largest angle is opposite its longest side. (The sides opposite two congruent angles are also congruent.) Be careful not to take this rule too far: The ratio of angle sizes need not be identical to the ratio of lengths of sides. For example, if a certain triangle has angle measures of 30°, 60°, and 90°, the ratio of the angles is 1:2:3. But this doesn't mean that the ratio of the opposite sides is also 1:2:3.

**❹ Area:** The area of any triangle is equal to one-half the product of its base and its height (or "altitude"): Area $= \frac{1}{2} \times$ base $\times$ height. You can use any side as the base to calculate area.

## Right Triangles and the Pythagorean Theorem

In a right triangle, one angle measures 90° (and, of course, each of the other two angles measures less than 90°). The *Pythagorean theorem* expresses the relationship among the sides of any right triangle. In the following expression of the theorem, $a$ and $b$ are the two *legs* (the two shortest sides) that form the right angle, and $c$ is the *hypotenuse*—the longest side, opposite the right angle:

$$a^2 + b^2 = c^2$$

For any right triangle, if you know the length of two sides, you can determine the length of the third side by applying the theorem.

If the two shortest sides (the legs) of a right triangle are 2 and 3 units long, then the length of the triangle's third side (the hypotenuse) is $\sqrt{13}$ units:

$$2^2 + 3^2 = 13 = c^2; c = \sqrt{13}$$

If a right triangle's longest side (hypotenuse) is 10 units long and another side (one of the legs) is 5 units long, then the third side is $5\sqrt{3}$ units long:

$$a^2 + 5^2 = 10^2; a^2 = 75; a = \sqrt{75} = \sqrt{(25)(3)} = 5\sqrt{3}$$

### PYTHAGOREAN TRIPLETS

A Pythagorean triplet is a specific ratio among the sides of a triangle that satisfies the Pythagorean theorem. In each of the following triplets, the first two numbers represent the comparative lengths of the two legs, whereas the third—and greatest—number represents the comparative length of the hypotenuse (on the GRE, the first four appear far more frequently than the last two):

| | |
|---|---|
| $1:1:\sqrt{2}$ | $1^2 + 1^2 = (\sqrt{2})^2$ |
| $1:\sqrt{3}:2$ | $1^2 + (\sqrt{3})^2 = 2^2$ |
| $3:4:5$ | $3^2 + 4^2 = 5^2$ |
| $5:12:13$ | $5^2 + 12^2 = 13^2$ |
| $8:15:17$ | $8^2 + 15^2 = 17^2$ |
| $7:24:25$ | $7^2 + 24^2 = 25^2$ |

Each triplet above is expressed as a *ratio* because it represents a proportion among the triangle's sides. All right triangles with sides having the same proportion, or ratio, have the same shape. For example, a right triangle with sides of 5, 12, and 13 is smaller but exactly the same shape (proportion) as a triangle with sides of 15, 36, and 39.

**3.** Two boats leave the same dock at the same time, one traveling due east at 10 miles per hour and the other due north at 24 miles per hour. How many miles apart are the boats after 3 hours?

(A) 68

(B) 72

(C) 78

(D) 98

(E) 110

**The correct answer is (C).** The distance between the two boats after 3 hours forms the hypotenuse of a triangle in which the legs are the two boats' respective paths. The ratio of one leg to the other is 10:24, or 5:12. So you know you're dealing with a 5:12:13 triangle. The slower boat traveled 30 miles (10 mph × 3 hours). Thirty corresponds to the number 5 in the 5:12:13 ratio, so the multiple is 6 (5 × 6 = 30). 5:12:13 = 30:72:78.

## PYTHAGOREAN ANGLE TRIPLETS

In two (and only two) of the unique triangles identified in the preceding section as Pythagorean side triplets, all degree measures are *integers*:

**1** The corresponding angles opposite the sides of a $1:1:\sqrt{2}$ triangle are 45°, 45°, and 90°.

**2** The corresponding angles opposite the sides of a $1:\sqrt{3}:2$ triangle are 30°, 60°, and 90°.

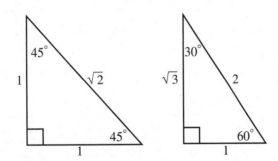

If you know that the triangle is a right triangle (one angle measures 90°) and that one of the other angles is 45°, then given the length of any side, you can determine the unknown lengths. For example:

- If one leg is 5 units long, then the other leg must also be 5 units long, while the hypotenuse must be $5\sqrt{2}$ units long.

- If the hypotenuse (the longest side) is 10 units long, then each leg must be $5\sqrt{2}$ units long. Divide the hypotenuse by $\sqrt{2}$:

$$\frac{10}{\sqrt{2}} = \frac{10\sqrt{2}}{2} = 5\sqrt{2}$$

Similarly, if you know that the triangle is a right triangle (one angle measures 90°) and that one of the other angles is either 30° or 60°, then given the length of any side you can determine the unknown lengths. For example:

- If the shortest leg (opposite the 30° angle) is 3 units long, then the other leg (opposite the 60° angle) must be $3\sqrt{3}$ units long, and the hypotenuse must be 6 units long ($3 \times 2$).

- If the longer leg (opposite the 60° angle) is 4 units long, then the shorter leg (opposite the 30° angle) must be $\dfrac{4\sqrt{3}}{3}$ units long (divide by $\sqrt{3}$: $\dfrac{4}{\sqrt{3}} = \dfrac{4\sqrt{3}}{3}$), while the hypotenuse must be $\dfrac{8\sqrt{3}}{3}$ (twice as long as the shorter leg).

- If the hypotenuse is 10 units long, then the shorter leg (opposite the 30° angle) must be 5 units long, while the longer leg (opposite the 60° angle) must be $5\sqrt{3}$ units long (the length of the shorter leg multiplied by $\sqrt{3}$).

4. In the figure below, $\overline{AC}$ is 5 units long, $m\angle ABD = 45°$, and $m\angle DAC = 60°$. How many units long is $\overline{BD}$?

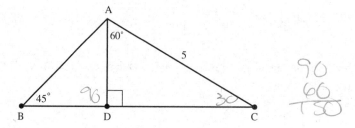

**(A)** $\dfrac{7}{3}$

**(B)** $2\sqrt{2}$

**(C)** $\dfrac{5}{2}$

**(D)** $\dfrac{3\sqrt{3}}{2}$

**(E)** $\dfrac{7}{2}$

**The correct answer is (C).** To find the length of $\overline{BD}$, you first need to find $\overline{AD}$. Notice that $\Delta ADC$ is a 30°-60°- 90° triangle. The ratio among its sides is 1:$\sqrt{3}$:2. Given that $\overline{AC}$ is 5 units long, $\overline{AD}$ must be $\dfrac{5}{2}$ units long. (The ratio 1:2 is equivalent to the ratio $\dfrac{5}{2}$:5. Next, notice that $\Delta ABD$ is a 45°-45°-90° triangle. The ratio among its sides is 1:1:$\sqrt{2}$. You know that $\overline{AD}$ is $\dfrac{5}{2}$ units long. Thus, $\overline{BD}$ must also be $\dfrac{5}{2}$ units long.

# ISOSCELES AND EQUILATERAL TRIANGLES

## Isosceles Triangles

An *isosceles* triangle has the following two special properties:

**❶** Two of the sides are congruent (equal in length).

**❷** The two angles opposite the two congruent sides are congruent (equal in size, or degree measure).

If you know any two angle measures of a triangle, you can determine whether the triangle is isosceles.

5.

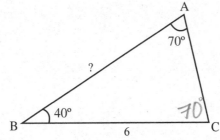

In the figure above, $\overline{BC}$ is 6 units long, $m\angle A = 70°$, and $m\angle B = 40°$. How many units long is $\overline{AB}$?

**(A)** 5
**(B)** 6
**(D)** 7
**(C)** 8
**(E)** 9

**The correct answer is (B).** Since $m\angle A$ and $m\angle B$ add up to 110°, $m\angle C = 70°$ (70 + 110 = 180), and you know the triangle is isosceles. What's more, since $m\angle A = m\angle C$, $\overline{AB} \cong \overline{BC}$. Given that $\overline{BC}$ is 6 units long, $\overline{AB}$ must also be 6 units long.

The line bisecting the angle connecting the two congruent sides divides the triangle into two congruent right triangles. So if you know the lengths of all three sides of an isosceles triangle, you can determine the area of the triangle by applying the Pythagorean theorem.

6. Two sides of a triangle are each 8 units long, and the third side is 6 units long. What is the area of the triangle, expressed in square units?

**(A)** 14
**(B)** $12\sqrt{3}$
**(C)** 18
**(D)** 22
**(E)** $3\sqrt{55}$

**The correct answer is (E).** Bisect the angle connecting the two congruent sides (as in $\triangle ABC$ on the following page). The bisecting line is the triangle's height ($h$), and the triangle's base is 6 units long.

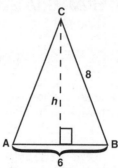

You can determine the triangle's height ($h$) by applying the Pythagorean theorem:

$$3^2 + h^2 = 8^2$$
$$h^2 = 64 - 9$$
$$h^2 = 55$$
$$h = \sqrt{55}$$

A triangle's area is half the product of its base and height. Thus, the area of

$$\triangle ABC = \frac{1}{2}(6)\sqrt{55} = 3\sqrt{55}$$

## Equilateral Triangles

An equilateral triangle has the following three properties:

**1** All three sides are congruent (equal in length).

**2** The measure of each angle is 60°.

**3** Area = $\dfrac{s^2\sqrt{3}}{4}$ ($s$ = any side)

Any line bisecting one of the 60° angles divides an equilateral triangle into two right triangles with angle measures of 30°, 60°, and 90°; in other words, into two 1:$\sqrt{3}$:2 triangles, as shown in the right-hand triangle in the next figure. (Remember that Pythagorean angle triplet?)

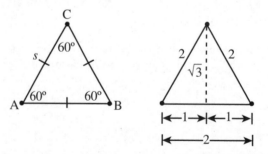

In the left-hand triangle, if $s = 6$, the area of the triangle = $9\sqrt{3}$. To confirm this formula, bisect the triangle into two 30°-60°-90° (1:$\sqrt{3}$:2) triangles (as in the right-hand triangle in the preceding figure). The area of this equilateral triangle is $\frac{1}{2}(2)\sqrt{3}$, or $\sqrt{3}$. The area of each smaller right triangle is $\dfrac{\sqrt{3}}{2}$.

# RECTANGLES, SQUARES, AND PARALLELOGRAMS

Rectangles, squares, and parallelograms are types of *quadrilaterals*—four-sided geometric figures. Here are five characteristics that apply to all rectangles, squares, and parallelograms:

**1** The sum of the measures of all four interior angles is 360°.

**2** Opposite sides are parallel.

**3** Opposite sides are congruent (equal in length).

**4** Opposite angles are congruent (the same size, or equal in degree measure).

**5** Adjacent angles are supplementary (their measures total 180°).

A rectangle is a special type of parallelogram in which all four angles are right angles (90°). A square is a special type of rectangle in which all four sides are congruent (equal in length). For the GRE, you should know how to determine the perimeter and area of each of these three types of quadrilaterals. Referring to the next three figures, here are the formulas ($l$ = length and $w$ = width):

**Rectangle**

Perimeter = $2l + 2w$

Area = $l \times w$

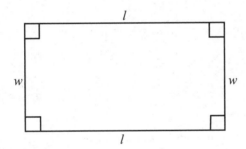

**Square**

Perimeter = $4s$ [$s$ = side]

Area = $s^2$

Area = $\left(\dfrac{1}{2}\right)(\text{diagonal})^2$

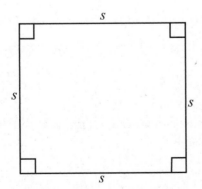

**Parallelogram**

Perimeter $= 2l + 2w$

Area $=$ base $(b) \times$ altitude $(a)$

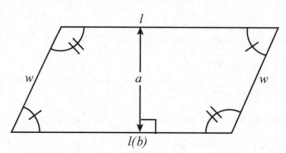

GRE questions involving squares come in many varieties. For example, you might need to determine area, given the length of any side or either diagonal, or perimeter. Or, you might need to do just the opposite—find a length or perimeter given the area. For example:

The area of a square with a perimeter of 8 is 4.

$(s = 8 \div 4 = 2, s^2 = 4)$

The perimeter of a square with an area of 8 is $8\sqrt{2}$.

$(s = \sqrt{8} = 2\sqrt{2}, 4s = 4 \times 2\sqrt{2})$

The area of a square with a diagonal of 6 is 18.

$\left(A = \left(\dfrac{1}{2}\right)6^2 = \left(\dfrac{1}{2}\right)(36) = 18\right)$

Or, you might need to determine a change in area resulting from a change in perimeter (or vice versa).

**7.** If a square's sides are each increased by 50%, by what percent does the square's area increase?

   **(A)** 75%

   **(B)** 100%

   **(C)** 125%

   **(D)** 150%

   **(E)** 200%

**The correct answer is (C).** Letting $s =$ the length of each side before the increase, area $= s^2$. If $\dfrac{3}{2}s =$ the length of each side after the increase, the new area $= \left(\dfrac{3}{2}s\right)^2 = \dfrac{9}{4}s^2$. The increase from $s^2$ to $\dfrac{9}{4}s^2$ is $\dfrac{5}{4}$, or 125%.

GRE questions involving non-square rectangles also come in many possible flavors. For example, a question might ask you to determine area based on perimeter, or vice versa.

8. The length of a rectangle with area 12 is three times the rectangle's width. What is the perimeter of the rectangle?

   (A) 10
   (B) 12
   (C) 14
   (D) 16
   (E) 20

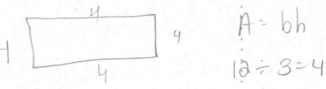

**The correct answer is (D).** The ratio of length to width is 3:1. The ratio 6:2 is equivalent, and $6 \times 2 = 12$ (the area). Thus, the perimeter $= (2)(6) + (2)(2) = 16$.

A question might involve the properties of a square or rectangle as well as those of another geometric figure, such as a right, isosceles, or equilateral triangle.

|              **Column A**              |              **Column B**              |
| :------------------------------------: | :------------------------------------: |
| A wooden dowel is to be cut into sections to form either two triangular enclosures or three rectangular enclosures. All dowel sections must be equal in length. | |
| The total area of the two proposed triangular enclosures | The total area of the three proposed rectangular enclosures |

9.

   (A) the quantity in Column A is greater;
   (B) the quantity in Column B is greater;
   (C) the quantities are equal;
   (D) the relationship cannot be determined from the information given.

**The correct answer is (A).** Since the sections must all be equal in length, the triangles must each be equilateral and the rectangles must each be square. The easiest way to make the comparison is to assign to the length of the dowel a number that is the least common multiple of 6 and 12 (the total number of sides among the triangles and squares, respectively). That multiple, of course, is 12. Each triangle side = 2. Applying the area formula for equilateral triangles, the area of each triangle is $\dfrac{2^2\sqrt{3}}{4} = \sqrt{3}$, and the total area for both triangles is $2\sqrt{3}$, or about 3.4 (using 1.7 as an approximate value for $\sqrt{3}$). Given a dowel length of 12, and 12 sides for three squares, the length of each side of each square $= \dfrac{12}{12} = 1$. Accordingly, the area of each square is 1, and the total area of all three squares is 3.

Or, a question might require you to determine a combined perimeter or area of adjoining rectangles.

**10.**

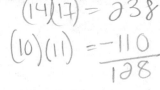

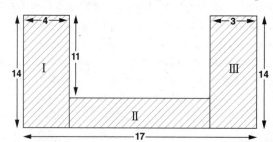

In the figure above, all intersecting line segments are perpendicular. What is the area of the shaded region, in square units?

**(A)** 84

**(B)** 118

**(C)** 128

**(D)** 139

**(E)** 238

**The correct answer is (C).** The figure provides the perimeters you need to calculate the area. One way to find the area of the shaded region is to consider it as what remains when a rectangular shape is cut out of a larger rectangle. The area of the entire figure without the "cut-out" is 14 × 17 = 238. The "cut-out" rectangle has a length of 11, and its width is equal to 17 − 4 − 3 = 10. Thus, the area of the cut-out is 11 × 10 = 110. Accordingly, the area of the shaded region is 238 − 110 = 128.

Another way to solve the problem is to partition the shaded region into three smaller rectangles, as shown in the next figure, and sum up the area of each.

A GRE question about a non-rectangular parallelogram might focus on angle measures. These questions are easy to answer. In any parallelogram, opposite angles are congruent, and adjacent angles are supplementary. (Their measures total 180°.) So if one of a parallelogram's angles measures 65°, then the opposite angle must also measure 65°, while the two other angles each measure 115°.

|  Column A  |  Column B  |
|---|---|

**11.**

WXZY is a parallelogram.
$r = 180 - s$

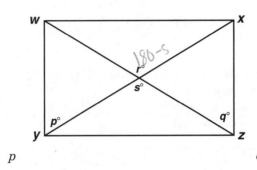

$p$                        $q$

**(A)** the quantity in Column A is greater;

**(B)** the quantity in Column B is greater;

**(C)** the quantities are equal;

**(D)** the relationship cannot be determined from the information given.

**The correct answer is (D).** In the figure, $r°$ and $s°$ are opposite angles, and therefore $r = s$. Given that $r = 180 - s$, $r$ and $s$ must both equal 90. Since the diagonals of WXZY form right angles, WXZY must be a rhombus (a parallelogram in which all four sides are equal in length). However, $p = q$ if and only if WXZY is a square.

A more difficult question about a non-rectangular parallelogram might focus on area. To determine the parallelogram's altitude, you might need to apply the Pythagorean theorem (on one of the side or angle triplets).

**12.**

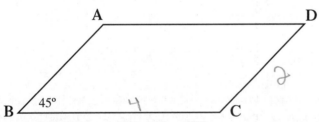

In the figure above, $\overline{AB} \parallel \overline{CD}$ and $\overline{AD} \parallel \overline{BC}$. If $\overline{BC}$ is 4 units long and $\overline{CD}$ is 2 units long, what is the area of quadrilateral ABCD?

**(A)** 4

**(B)** $4\sqrt{2}$

**(C)** 6

**(D)** 8

**(E)** $6\sqrt{2}$

**The correct answer is (B).** Since ABCD is a parallelogram, its area = base (4) × altitude. To determine altitude ($a$), draw a vertical line segment connecting point A to $\overline{BC}$, which creates a 45°-45°-90° triangle. The ratio of the triangle's hypotenuse to each leg is $\sqrt{2}$:1. The hypotenuse $\overline{AB} = 2$. Thus, the altitude ($a$) of ABCD is $\dfrac{2}{\sqrt{2}}$, or $\sqrt{2}$. Accordingly, the area of ABCD = 4 × $\sqrt{2}$, or $4\sqrt{2}$.

**TIP**

A non-rectangular parallelogram in which all four sides are congruent (called a *rhombus*) has the following in common with a square: Perimeter = 4$s$; Area = one-half the product of the diagonals.

## Trapezoids

A trapezoid is a special type of quadrilateral. The next figure shows a trapezoid. All trapezoids share these four properties:

**1** Only one pair of opposite sides are parallel ($\overline{BC} \parallel \overline{AD}$).

**2** The sum of the measures of all four angles is 360°.

**3** Perimeter = AB + BC + CD + AD

**4** Area = $\dfrac{BC + AD}{2}$ × altitude (that is, one-half the sum of the two parallel sides multiplied by the altitude).

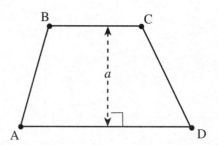

On the GRE, a trapezoid problem might require you to determine the altitude, the area, or both.

**13.**

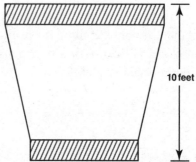

To cover the floor of an entry hall, a 1′ × 12′ strip of carpet is cut into two pieces, shown as the shaded strips in the figure above, and each piece is connected to a third carpet piece as shown. If the 1′ strips run parallel to each other, what is the total area of the carpeted floor, in square feet?

**(A)** 46

**(B)** 48

**(C)** 52.5

**(D)** 56

**(E)** 60

**The correct answer is (E).** The altitude of the trapezoidal piece is 8. The sum of the two parallel sides of this piece is 12′ (the length of the 1′ × 12′ strip before it was cut). You can apply the trapezoid formula to determine the area of this piece:

$$A = 8 \times \frac{12}{2} = 48$$

The total area of the two shaded strips is 12 square feet, so the total area of the floor is 60 square feet.

A GRE trapezoid problem might require you to find the trapezoid's altitude by the Pythagorean theorem.

**14.**

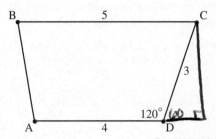

In the figure above, $\overline{BC} \parallel \overline{AD}$. What is the area of quadrilateral ABCD?

**(A)** $5\sqrt{2}$

**(B)** $\dfrac{9\sqrt{3}}{2}$

**(C)** $\dfrac{27\sqrt{3}}{4}$

**(D)** $\dfrac{27}{2}$

**(E)** 16

**The correct answer is (C).** The figure shows a trapezoid. To find its area, first determine its altitude by creating a right triangle:

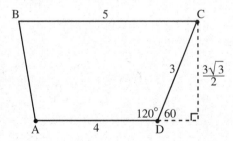

This right triangle conforms to the 30°-60°-90° Pythagorean angle triplet. Thus, the ratio of the three sides is $1:\sqrt{3}:2$. The hypotenuse is given as 3, so the trapezoid's altitude is $\dfrac{3\sqrt{3}}{2}$. Now you can calculate the area of the trapezoid:

$$\left(\frac{1}{2}\right)(4 + 5)\left(\frac{3\sqrt{3}}{2}\right) = \left(\frac{9}{2}\right)\left(\frac{3\sqrt{3}}{2}\right) = \frac{27\sqrt{3}}{4}$$

## CIRCLES

For the GRE, you'll need to know the following basic terminology involving circles:

**Circumference:** The distance around the circle (its "perimeter").

**Radius:** The distance from a circle's center to any point on the circle's circumference.

**Diameter:** The greatest distance from one point to another on the circle's circumference (twice the length of the radius).

**Chord:** A line segment connecting two points on the circle's circumference (a circle's longest possible chord is its diameter, passing through the circle's center).

You'll also need to apply the two basic formulas involving circles ($r$ = radius, $d$ = diameter):

❶ Circumference = $2\pi r$, or $\pi d$

❷ Area = $\pi r^2$

Note that the value of $\pi$ is approximately 3.14, or $\frac{22}{7}$. For the GRE, you won't need to work with a value for $\pi$ any more precise. In fact, in most circle problems, the solution is expressed in terms of $\pi$ rather than numerically.

With the two formulas, all you need is one value—area, circumference, diameter, or radius—and you can determine all the others. For example:

Given a circle with a diameter of 6:

Radius = 3

Circumference = $(2)(3)\pi = 6\pi$

Area = $\pi (3)^2 = 9\pi$

**15.** If a circle's circumference is $10\pi$ centimeters long, what is the area of the circle, in square centimeters?

**(A)** 12.5
**(B)** $5\pi$
**(C)** 22.5
**(D)** $25\pi$
**(E)** $10\pi$

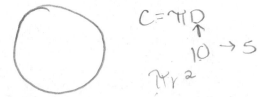

**The correct answer is (D).** First, determine the circle's radius. Applying the circumference formula C = $2\pi r$, solve for $r$ :

$10\pi = 2\pi r$

$5 = r$

Then, apply the area formula, with 5 as the value of $r$:

A = $\pi(5)^2 = 25\pi$

## ADVANCED CIRCLE PROBLEMS

GRE circle problems sometimes involve other geometric figures as well, so they're inherently tougher than average. The most common such "hybrids" involve triangles, squares, and other circles. In the next sections, you'll learn all you need to know to handle any hybrid problem.

### Arcs and Degree Measures of a Circle

An *arc* is a segment of a circle's circumference. A *minor arc* is the shortest arc connecting two points on a circle's circumference. For example, in the next figure, minor arc AB is the one formed by the 60° angle from the circle's center (O).

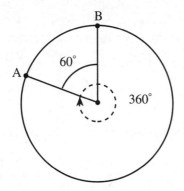

A circle, by definition, contains a total of 360°. The length of an arc relative to the circle's circumference is directly proportionate to the arc's degree measure as a fraction of the circle's total degree measure of 360°. For example, in the preceding figure, minor arc AB accounts for $\frac{60}{360}$, or $\frac{1}{6}$, of the circle's circumference.

16.

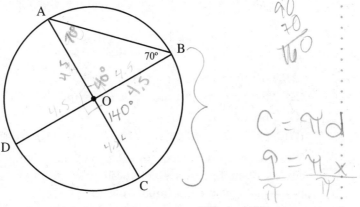

Circle O, as shown in the figure above, has diameters of $\overline{DB}$ and $\overline{AC}$ and has a circumference of 9. What is the length of minor arc BC?

**(A)** 4

**(B)** $\dfrac{11}{3}$

**(C)** $\dfrac{7}{2}$

**(D)** $\dfrac{13}{4}$

**(E)** 3

**The correct answer is (C).** Since $\overline{AO}$ and $\overline{OB}$ are both radii, we have isosceles $\triangle AOB$, thus making $m\angle BAO = 70°$. From this we can find $m\angle AOB = 40°$. $\angle BOC$ is supplementary to $\angle AOB$, therefore $m\angle BOC = 140°$. (Remember: Angles from a circle's center are proportionate to the arcs they create.) Since $m\angle BOC$ accounts for $\dfrac{140}{360}$, or $\dfrac{7}{18}$ of the circle's circumference, we have the length of minor arc BC = $\left(\dfrac{7}{18}\right)(9) = \dfrac{7}{2}$.

## Circles and Inscribed Polygons

A polygon is *inscribed* in a circle if each vertex of the polygon lies on the circle's circumference.

A test question might require you to visualize the possible shapes or proportions of a type of triangle or quadrilateral inscribed in a circle.

|  **Column A**  |  |  **Column B**  |
| --- | --- | --- |

17.          An equilateral triangle is inscribed in a circle such that each vertex of the triangle lies along the circle's circumference.

| The length of any side of the triangle | The circle's diameter |
| --- | --- |

**(A)** The quantity in Column A is greater;

**(B)** The quantity in Column B is greater;

**(C)** The quantities are equal;

**(D)** The relationship cannot be determined from the information given.

**The correct answer is (B).** If any of the triangle's sides were the length of the circle's diameter, that side would pass through the circle's center. In this case, however, it would be impossible to construct an inscribed *equilateral* triangle: Each of the other two sides would need to extend beyond the circle's circumference.

The next figure shows an inscribed square. The square is partitioned into four congruent triangles, each with one vertex at the circle's center (O).

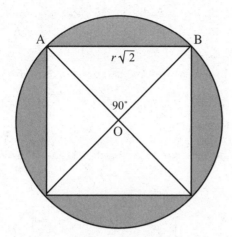

Look at any one of the four congruent triangles—for example, ΔABO. Notice that ΔABO is a *right* triangle with the 90° angle at the circle's center. The length of each of the triangle's two legs ($\overline{AO}$ and $\overline{BO}$) equals the circle's radius ($r$). Accordingly, ΔABO is a right isosceles triangle, $m\angle OAB = m\angle OBA = 45°$, and $AB = r\sqrt{2}$. (The ratio of the triangle's sides is $1:1:\sqrt{2}$.) Since $\overline{AB}$ is also the side of the square, the area of a square inscribed in a circle is $(r\sqrt{2})^2$, or $2r^2$. (The area of ΔABO is $\dfrac{r^2}{2}$, or one fourth the area of the square.)

You can also determine relationships between the inscribed square and the circle:

- The ratio of the inscribed square's area to the circle's area is $2:\pi$.

- The *difference* between the two areas—the total shaded area—is $\pi r^2 - 2r^2$.

- The area of each crescent-shaped shaded area is $\dfrac{1}{4}(\pi r^2 - 2r^2)$.

The next figure shows a circle with an inscribed regular hexagon. (In a regular polygon, all sides are congruent.) The hexagon is partitioned into six congruent triangles, each with one vertex at the circle's center (O).

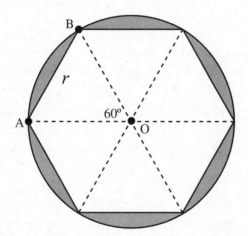

Look at any one of the six congruent triangles—for example, ΔABO. Since all six triangles are congruent, $m\angle AOB = 60°$, (one sixth of 360°). You can see that the length of $\overline{AO}$ and $\overline{BO}$ each equals the circle's radius ($r$). Accordingly, $m\angle OAB = m\angle OBA = 60°$, $\triangle ABO$ is an equilateral triangle, and length of $\overline{AB} = r$.

Applying the area formula for equilateral triangles: Area of $\triangle ABO = \dfrac{r^2\sqrt{3}}{4}$. The area of the hexagon is 6 times the area of $\triangle ABO$, or $\dfrac{3r^2\sqrt{3}}{2}$. You can also determine relationships between the inscribed hexagon and the circle. For example, the *difference* between the two areas—the total shaded area—is $\pi r^2 - \dfrac{3r^2\sqrt{3}}{2}$.

**18.**

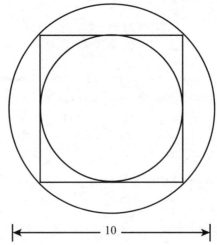

|← ———————— 10 ———————— →|

The figure above shows a square that is tangent to one circle at four points, and inscribed in another. If the diameter of the large circle is 10, what is the diameter of the smaller circle?

**(A)** $\dfrac{5\sqrt{3}}{2}$

**(B)** 5

**(C)** $2\pi$

**(D)** $5\sqrt{2}$

**(E)** 7.5

**The correct answer is (D).** The square's diagonal is equal in length to the large circle's diameter, which is 10. This diagonal is the hypotenuse of a triangle whose legs are two sides of the square. The triangle is right isosceles, with sides in the ratio 1:1:$\sqrt{2}$. The length of each side of the square $= \dfrac{10}{\sqrt{2}}$, or $5\sqrt{2}$. This length is also the diameter of the small circle.

## Tangents and Inscribed Circles

A circle is *tangent* to a line (or line segment) if they intersect at one and only one point (called the *point of tangency*). Here's the key rule to remember about tangents: A line that is tangent to a circle is *always* perpendicular to the line passing through the circle's center at the point of tangency.

The next figure shows a circle with center O inscribed in a square. Point P is one of four points of tangency. By definition, $\overline{OP} \perp \overline{AB}$.

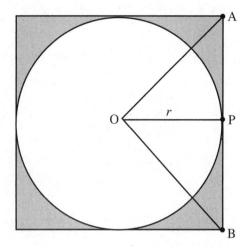

Also, notice the following relationships between the circle in the preceding figure and the square in which it is inscribed ($r$ = radius):

- Each side of the square is $2r$ in length.

- The square's area is $(2r)^2$, or $4r^2$.

- The ratio of the square's area to that of the inscribed circle is $\dfrac{4}{\pi}$.

- The *difference* between the two areas—the total shaded area—is $4r^2 - \pi r^2$.

- The area of each separate (smaller) shaded area is $\dfrac{1}{4}(4r^2 - \pi r^2)$.

For *any* regular polygon (including squares) that inscribes a circle:

- The point of tangency between each line segment and the circle *bisects* the segment.

- Connecting each vertex to the circle's center creates an array of congruent angles, arcs, and triangles.

For example, the left-hand figure below shows a regular pentagon, and the right-hand figure shows a regular hexagon. Each polygon inscribes a circle. In each figure, the shaded region is one of five (or six) identical ones.

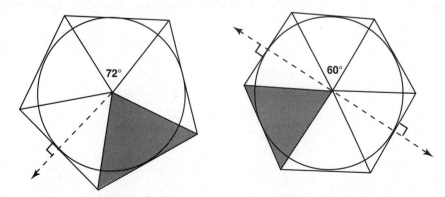

19.

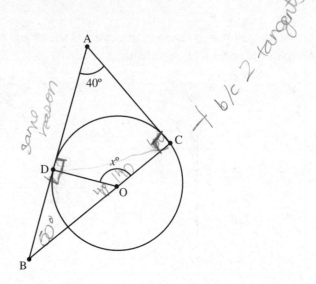

In the figure above, a circle with center O is tangent to $\overline{AB}$ at point D and tangent to $\overline{AC}$ at point C. If $m\angle A = 40°$, then $x =$

(A) 140

(B) 145

(C) 150

(D) 155

(E) 160

**The correct answer is (A).** Since $\overline{AC}$ is tangent to the circle, $\overline{AC} \perp \overline{BC}$. Accordingly, $\triangle ABC$ is a right triangle, and $m\angle B = 50°$. Similarly, $\overline{AB} \perp \overline{DO}$, $\triangle DBO$ is a right triangle, and $\angle DOB = 40°$. $\angle DOC$ (the angle in question) is supplementary to $\angle DOB$. Thus, $m\angle DOC = 140°$ ($x = 140$).

|  Column A  |  Column B  |
|---|---|

20.

One side of a rectangle is the diameter of a circle. The opposite side of the rectangle is tangent to the circle.

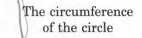

|  The perimeter of the rectangle  |  The circumference of the circle  |
|---|---|

(A) The quantity in Column A is greater;

(B) The quantity in Column B is greater;

(C) The quantities are equal;

(D) The relationship cannot be determined from the information given.

**The correct answer is (B).** The centered information describes the following figure:

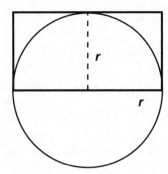

Calling the radius $r$, the rectangle's perimeter is $2(2r) + 2(r) = 6r$. The circle's circumference is $2\pi r$. Since $\pi > 3$, $2\pi > 6$, and the circle's circumference is larger.

## Comparing Circles

On the GRE, questions asking you to compare circles come in two varieties. You will be required to do one of the following:

**1** Calculate the *difference* between radii, circumferences, and areas.

**2** Determine *ratios* involving the two circles and their radii, circumferences, and areas.

To calculate a *difference* between the radii, circumferences, or areas, just calculate each area or circumference, then subtract. And if the question asks you for a difference between the areas of sectors of two concentric circles, first calculate the areas of each sector, then subtract the smaller area from the larger one.

To handle questions involving ratios, you need to understand that the relationship between a circle's radius or circumference and its area is *exponential*, not linear (because $A = \pi r^2$). For example, if one circle's radius is *twice* that of another, the ratio of the circles' areas is $1:4[\pi r^2 : \pi (2r)^2]$. If the larger circle's radius is *three* times that of the smaller circle, the ratio is $1:9[\pi r^2 : \pi (3r)^2]$. A 1:4 ratio between radii results in a 1:16 area ratio (and so forth).

**TIP**

The proportions noted on this page also apply if you compare circumferences and areas. If the circumference ratio is 2:1, then the area ratio is 4:1. If the circumference ratio is 4:1, then the area ratio is 16:1.

**21.**

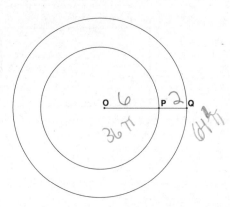

In the figure above, point O lies at the center of both circles. If the length of $\overline{OP}$ is 6 and the length of $\overline{PQ}$ is 2, what is the ratio of the area of the smaller circle to the area of the larger circle?

(A) $\dfrac{3}{8}$

(B) $\dfrac{7}{16}$

(C) $\dfrac{1}{2}$

(D) $\dfrac{9}{16}$

(E) $\dfrac{5}{8}$

**The correct answer is (D).** The ratio of the small circle's radius to that of the large circle is 6:8, or 3:4. Since Area = $\pi r^2$, the area ratio is $\pi(3)^2:\pi(4)^2$, or 9:16.

## POLYGONS

Polygons include all plane figures formed only by straight segments. Up to this point, we've focused on only two types of polygons: three-sided ones (triangles) and four-sided ones (quadrilaterals). Now take a quick look at the key characteristics of all polygons.

You can use the following formula to determine the sum of the measures of all interior angles of *any* polygon whose angles each measure less than 180° ($n$ = number of sides):

$(n - 2)(180°)$ = sum of interior angles

For *regular* polygons, the average angle measure is also the measure of every angle. But for any polygon (except for those with an angle exceeding 180°), you can find the average angle measure by dividing the sum of the measures of the angles by the number of sides. One way to shortcut the math is to memorize the angle sums and averages for polygons with 3–8 sides:

3 sides: $(3 - 2)(180°) = 180° \div 3 = 60°$

4 sides: $(4 - 2)(180°) = 360° \div 4 = 90°$

5 sides: $(5 - 2)(180°) = 540° \div 5 = 108°$

6 sides: $(6 - 2)(180°) = 720° \div 6 = 120°$

7 sides: $(7 - 2)(180°) = 900° \div 7 \approx 129°$

8 sides: $(8 - 2)(180°) = 1{,}080° \div 8 = 135°$

A GRE question might simply ask for the measure of any interior angle of a certain regular polygon; to answer it, just apply the preceding formula. If the polygon is not regular, you can add up known angle measures to find unknown angle measures.

**22.** If exactly two of the angles of the polygon shown below are congruent, what is the LEAST possible sum of the degree measures of two of the polygon's interior angles?

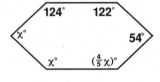

  (A) 162°
  (B) 174°
  (C) 176°
  (D) 204°
  (E) 216°

**The correct answer is (B).** The figure shows a hexagon. The sum of the measures of six angles is 720°. Subtracting the measures of the three known angles from 720° leaves 420°, which is the sum of the measures of the three unknown angles. Set up an equation, then solve for $x$:

$$x + x + \frac{4}{5}x = 420$$

$$\frac{14}{5}x = 420$$

$$x = (420)\frac{5}{14} = (30)(5) = 150$$

Of the three unknown angles, two are 150° each. The other is 120°. The polygon's two smallest angles measure 54° and 120°. Their sum is 174°.

Another, more difficult, type of problem requires you to determine the area of a polygon, which might be either regular or irregular. To do so, you need to partition the polygon into an assemblage of smaller geometric figures.

**23.**

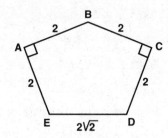

What is the area of polygon ABCDE shown above?

**(A)** $4 + 2\sqrt{3}$

**(B)** $3 + 3\sqrt{2}$

**(C)** $6\sqrt{3}$

**(D)** $2 + 6\sqrt{2}$

**(E)** $8\sqrt{2}$

**The correct answer is (A).** Divide the polygon into three triangles as shown below. The area of each of the two outer triangles $= \frac{1}{2}bh = \frac{1}{2}(2)(2) = 2$. (Their combined area is 4.) Since the two outer triangles are both $1{:}1{:}\sqrt{2}$ right triangles, $\overline{BE} \cong \overline{BD}$, and both line segments are $2\sqrt{2}$ units long. Accordingly, the central triangle is equilateral. Calculate its area.

$$\frac{s^2\sqrt{3}}{4} = \frac{(2\sqrt{2})^2\sqrt{3}}{4} = \frac{8\sqrt{3}}{4} = 2\sqrt{3}$$

Thus, the area of the polygon is $4 + 2\sqrt{3}$.

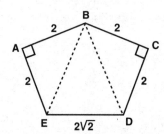

## CUBES AND OTHER RECTANGULAR SOLIDS

GRE questions about *rectangular* solids always involve one or both of two basic formulas ($l$ = length, $w$ = width, $h$ = height):

Volume $= lwh$

Surface Area $= 2lw + 2wh + 2lh = 2(lw + wh + lh)$

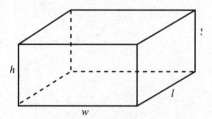

For *cubes*, the volume and surface-area formulas are even simpler than for other rectangular solids (let $s$ = any edge):

Volume = $s^3$ or $s = \sqrt[3]{\text{Volume}}$

Surface Area = $6s^2$

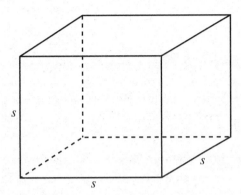

A GRE question might require you to apply any one of the formulas. Plug what you know into the formula, then solve for whatever characteristic the question asks for.

| **Column A** | **Column B** |
|---|---|

**24.**                                  $s > 1$

The volume of a cube with side $s$

The volume of a rectangular solid with sides of $s$, $s + 1$, and $s - 1$

**(A)** The quantity in Column A is greater;

**(B)** The quantity in Column B is greater;

**(C)** The quantities are equal;

**(D)** The relationship cannot be determined from the information given.

**The correct answer is (A).** Quantity A = $s^3$. Find Quantity B by multiplying together the three expressions given as the lengths of the sides:

$$(s)(s + 1)(s - 1) = (s^2 + s)(s - 1)$$
$$= s^3 - s^2 + s^2 - s$$
$$= s^3 - s$$

Subtracting $s^3$ from both columns leaves the comparison between zero (0) (Column A) and $-s$ (Column B). You can now see that Quantity A must be greater than Quantity B.

Or, a question might require you to deal with the formulas for both surface area and volume.

$V = lwh$

**25.** A closed rectangular box with a square base is 5 inches in height. If the volume of the box is 45 square inches, what is the box's surface area in square inches?

(A) 45

(B) 66

(C) 78

(D) 81

(E) 90

**The correct answer is (C).** First, determine the dimensions of the square base. The box's height is given as 5. Accordingly, the box's volume (45) = 5$lw$, and $lw$ = 9. Since the base is square, the base is 3 inches long on each side. Now you can calculate the total surface area: 2$lw$ + 2$wh$ + 2$lh$ = (2)(9) + (2)(15) + (2)(15) = 78.

A variation on the preceding question might ask the number of smaller boxes you could fit, or "pack," into the box that the question describes. For instance, the number of cube-shaped boxes, each one 1.5 inches on a side, that you could pack into the 3 × 3 × 5 box is 12 (3 levels of 4 cubes, with a half-inch space left at the top of the box).

A test question involving a cube might focus on the *ratios* among the cube's linear, square, and cubic measurements.

**26.** If the volume of one cube is 8 times greater than that of another, what is the ratio of the area of one square face of the larger cube to that of the smaller cube?

(A) 16:1

(B) 12:1

(C) 8:1

(D) 4:1

(E) 2:1

**The correct answer is (D).** The ratio of the two volumes is 8:1. Thus, the linear ratio of the cubes' edges is the cube root of this ratio: $\sqrt[3]{8}:\sqrt[3]{1}$ = 2:1. The area ratio is the square of the linear ratio, or 4:1.

## CYLINDERS

The only kind of cylinder the GRE covers is a "right" circular cylinder (a tube sliced at 90° angles). The *surface area* of a right cylinder is the sum of the areas of:

• The circular base

• The circular top

• The rectangular surface around the cylinder's vertical face (visualize a rectangular label wrapped around a soup can)

The area of the vertical face is the product of the circular base's circumference (i.e., the rectangle's width) and the cylinder's height. Thus, given a radius $r$ and height $h$ of a cylinder:

Surface Area (SA) $= 2\pi r^2 + (2\pi r)(h)$

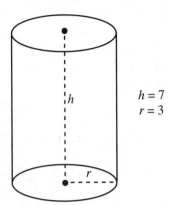

$h = 7$
$r = 3$

Given a cylinder's radius and height, you can determine its *volume* by multiplying the area of its circular base by its height:

Volume $= \pi r^2 h$

On the GRE, a cylinder problem might require little more than a straightforward application of formula for either surface area or volume. As with rectangular-solid questions, just plug what you know into the formula, then solve for what the question asks.

| **Column A** | **Column B** |
|---|---|

27.

$V = \pi r^2 h$

The volume of a right cylinder whose circular base has a radius of 3 and whose height is 6.

$54\pi$

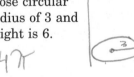

The volume of a right cylinder whose circular base has a radius of 6 and whose height is 3.

**(A)** The quantity in Column A is greater;
**(B)** The quantity in Column B is greater;
**(C)** The quantities are equal;
**(D)** The relationship cannot be determined from the information given.

**The correct answer is (B).** Use the formula for the volume of a right cylinder ($V = \pi r^2 h$) to compare volumes:

Quantity A $= \pi(3^2)(6) = \pi(3)(3)(6)$
Quantity B $= \pi(6^2)(3) = \pi(6)(6)(3)$

You can easily see that Quantity B is greater than Quantity A.

A tougher cylinder problem might require you to apply other math concepts. It also might call for you to convert one unit of measure into another.

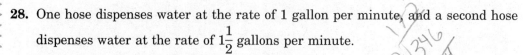

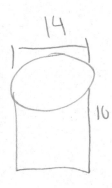

**28.** One hose dispenses water at the rate of 1 gallon per minute, and a second hose dispenses water at the rate of $1\frac{1}{2}$ gallons per minute.

At the same time, the two hoses begin filling a cylindrical pail whose diameter is 14 inches and whose height is 10 inches. Which of the following most closely approximates the water level, measured in inches up from the pail's circular base, after $1\frac{1}{2}$ minutes? [231 cubic inches = 1 gallon]

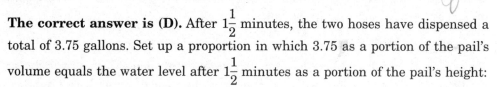

**(A)** 3.5
**(B)** 4.2
**(C)** 4.8
**(D)** 5.6
**(E)** 6.7

**The correct answer is (D).** After $1\frac{1}{2}$ minutes, the two hoses have dispensed a total of 3.75 gallons. Set up a proportion in which 3.75 as a portion of the pail's volume equals the water level after $1\frac{1}{2}$ minutes as a portion of the pail's height:

$$\frac{3.75}{V} = \frac{x}{10}$$

The volume of the cylindrical pail is equal to the area of its circular base multiplied by its height:

$$V = \pi r^2 h \approx \left(\frac{22}{7}\right)(49)(10) \approx 1{,}540 \text{ cubic inches}$$

The *gallon* capacity of the pail = 1,540 ÷ 231, or about 6.7. Plug this value into the proportion, then solve for $x$:

$$\frac{3.75}{6.7} = \frac{x}{10}$$
$$6.7x = 37.5$$
$$x = 5.6$$

## COORDINATE SIGNS AND THE FOUR QUADRANTS

GRE *coordinate geometry* questions involve the rectangular *coordinate plane* (or *xy*-plane) defined by two axes—a horizontal *x*-axis and a vertical *y*-axis. You can define any point on the coordinate plane by using two coordinates: an *x*-coordinate and a *y*-coordinate. A point's *x*-coordinate is its horizontal position on the plane, and its *y*-coordinate is its vertical position on the plane. You denote the coordinates of a point with (*x,y*), where *x* is the point's *x*-coordinate and *y* is the point's *y*-coordinate.

The center of the coordinate plane—the intersection of the *x*- and *y*-axes—is called the origin. The coordinates of the *origin* are (0,0). Any point along the *x*-axis has a *y*-coordinate of 0 (*x*,0), and any point along the *y*-axis has an *x*-coordinate of 0 (0,*y*). The coordinate signs (positive or negative) of points lying in the four Quadrants I–IV in this next figure are as follows:

Quadrant I (+,+)

Quadrant II (−,+)

Quadrant III (−,−)

Quadrant IV (+,−)

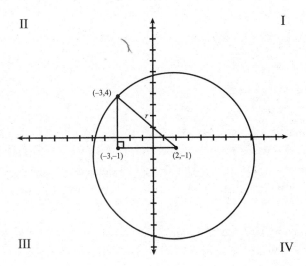

Notice that we've plotted three different points on this plane. Each point has its own unique coordinates. (Before you read on, make sure you understand why each point is identified by two coordinates.)

# DEFINING A LINE ON THE COORDINATE PLANE

You can define any line on the coordinate plane by the equation:

$y = mx + b$

In this equation:

- The variable $m$ is the slope of the line.

- The variable $b$ is the line's $y$-intercept (where the line crosses the $y$-axis).

- The variables $x$ and $y$ are the coordinates of any point on the line. Any $(x,y)$ pair defining a point on the line can substitute for the variables $x$ and $y$.

Determining a line's *slope* is often crucial to solving GRE coordinate geometry problems. Think of the slope of a line as a fraction in which the numerator indicates the vertical change from one point to another on the line (moving left to right) corresponding to a given horizontal change, which the fraction's denominator indicates. The common term used for this fraction is "rise-over-run."

You can determine the slope of a line from any two pairs of $(x,y)$ coordinates. In general, if $(x_1,y_1)$ and $(x_2,y_2)$ lie on the same line, calculate the line's slope as follows (notice that you can subtract either pair from the other):

$$\text{slope } (m) = \frac{y_2 - y_1}{x_2 - x_1} \text{ or } \frac{y_1 - y_2}{x_1 - x_2}$$

In applying the preceding formula, be sure to subtract corresponding values. For example, a careless test-taker calculating the slope might subtract $y_1$ from $y_2$ but subtract $x_2$ from $x_1$. Also, be sure to calculate "rise-over-run," and *not* "run-over-rise"— another careless but relatively common error.

As another example, here are two ways to calculate the slope of the line defined by the two points P(2,1) and Q(−3,4):

$$\text{slope } (m) = \frac{4 - 1}{-3 - 2} = \frac{3}{-5}$$

$$\text{slope } (m) = \frac{1 - 4}{2 - (-3)} = \frac{-3}{5}$$

A GRE question might ask you to identify the slope of a line defined by a given equation, in which case you simply put the equation in the standard form $y = mx + b$, then identify the $m$-term. Or, it might ask you to determine the equation of a line, or just the line's slope ($m$) or $y$-intercept ($b$), given the coordinates of two points on the line.

**29.** On the $xy$-plane, at what point along the vertical axis (the $y$-axis) does the line passing through points $(5, -2)$ and $(3,4)$ intersect that axis?

**(A)** −8

**(B)** $-\dfrac{5}{2}$

**(C)** 3

**(D)** 7

**(E)** 13

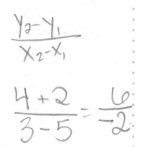

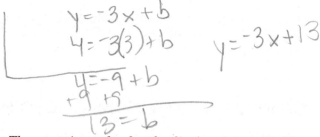

**The correct answer is (E).** The question asks for the line's $y$-intercept (the value of $b$ in the general equation $y = mx + b$). First, determine the line's slope:

$$\text{slope } m = \frac{y_2 - y_1}{x_2 - x_1} = \frac{4 - (-2)}{3 - 5} = \frac{6}{-2} = -3$$

In the general equation ($y = mx + b$), $m = -3$. To find the value of $b$, substitute either ($x,y$) value pair for $x$ and $y$, then solve for $b$. Substituting the ($x,y$) pair (3,4):

$y = -3x + b$
$4 = -3(3) + b$
$4 = -9 + b$
$13 = b$

To determine the point at which two nonparallel lines intersect on the coordinate plane, first determine the equation for each line. Then, solve for $x$ and $y$ by either substitution or addition-subtraction.

30. In the standard *xy*-coordinate plane, the *xy*-pairs (0,2) and (2,0) define a line, and the *xy*-pairs (−2,−1) and (2,1) define another line. At which of the following points do the two lines intersect?

(A) $\left(\dfrac{4}{3}, \dfrac{2}{3}\right)$

(B) $\left(\dfrac{3}{2}, \dfrac{4}{3}\right)$

(C) $\left(-\dfrac{1}{2}, \dfrac{3}{2}\right)$

(D) $\left(\dfrac{3}{4}, -\dfrac{2}{3}\right)$

(E) $\left(-\dfrac{3}{4}, -\dfrac{2}{3}\right)$

**The correct answer is (A).** For each line, formulate its equation by determining slope (*m*), then *y*-intercept (*b*). For the pairs (0,2) and (2,0):

$$y = \left(\frac{0-2}{2-0}\right) x + b \ (\text{slope} = -1)$$
$$0 = -2 + b$$
$$2 = b$$

The equation for the line is $y = -x + 2$. For the pairs (−2, −1) and (2,1):

$$y = \left(\frac{1-(-1)}{2-(-2)}\right) x + b \left(\text{slope} = \frac{1}{2}\right)$$
$$1 = \frac{1}{2}(2) + b$$
$$0 = b$$

The equation for the line is $y = \dfrac{1}{2}x$. To find the point of intersection, solve for *x* and *y* by substitution. For example:

$$\frac{1}{2}x = -x + 2$$
$$\frac{3}{2}x = 2$$
$$x = \frac{4}{3}$$
$$y = \frac{2}{3}$$

The point of intersection is defined by the coordinate pair $\left(\dfrac{4}{3}, \dfrac{2}{3}\right)$.

# GRAPHING A LINE ON THE COORDINATE PLANE

You can graph a line on the coordinate plane if you know the coordinates of any two points on the line. Just plot the two points, and then draw a line connecting them. You can also graph a line from one point on the line, if you know either the line's slope or its *y*-intercept.

A GRE question might ask you to recognize the value of a line's slope (*m*) based on a graph of the line. If the graph identifies the precise coordinates of two points, you can determine the line's precise slope (and the entire equation of the line). Even without any precise coordinates, you can still estimate the line's slope based on its appearance.

**Lines That Slope *Upward* from Left to Right:**

- A line sloping upward from left to right has a positive slope (*m*).

- A line with a slope of 1 slopes upward from left to right at a 45° angle in relation to the *x*-axis.

- A line with a fractional slope between 0 and 1 slopes upward from left to right but at less than a 45° angle in relation to the *x*-axis.

- A line with a slope greater than 1 slopes upward from left to right at more than a 45° angle in relation to the *x*-axis.

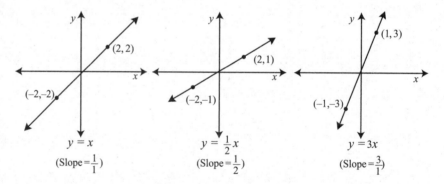

**Lines That Slope *Downward* from Left to Right:**

- A line sloping downward from left to right has a negative slope (*m*).

- A line with a slope of −1 slopes downward from left to right at a 45° angle in relation to the *x*-axis.

- A line with a fractional slope between 0 and −1 slopes downward from left to right but at less than a 45° angle in relation to the *x*-axis.

- A line with a slope less than −1 (for example, −2) slopes downward from left to right at more than a 45° angle in relation to the *x*-axis.

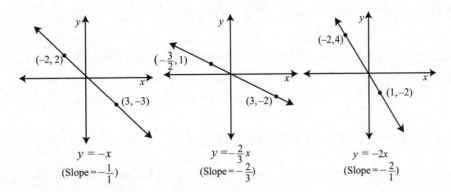

$$y = -x$$
$$(\text{Slope} = -\frac{1}{1})$$

$$y = -\frac{2}{3}x$$
$$(\text{Slope} = -\frac{2}{3})$$

$$y = -2x$$
$$(\text{Slope} = -\frac{2}{1})$$

## Horizontal and Vertical Lines:

- A horizontal line has a slope of zero (0) ($m = 0$, and $mx = 0$).

- A vertical line has either an undefined or an indeterminate slope (the fraction's denominator is zero (0)).

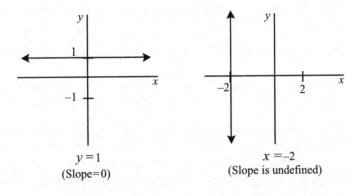

$$y = 1$$
$$(\text{Slope} = 0)$$

$$x = -2$$
$$(\text{Slope is undefined})$$

**31.**

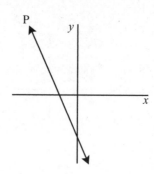

Referring to the *xy*-plane above, which of the following could be the equation of line P?

**(A)** $y = \dfrac{2}{5}x - \dfrac{5}{2}$

**(B)** $y = -\dfrac{5}{2}x + \dfrac{5}{2}$

**(C)** $y = \dfrac{5}{2}x - \dfrac{5}{2}$

**(D)** $y = \dfrac{2}{5}x + \dfrac{2}{5}$

**(E)** $y = -\dfrac{5}{2}x - \dfrac{5}{2}$

**The correct answer is (E).** Notice that line P slopes downward from left to right at an angle greater than 45°. Thus, the line's slope (*m* in the equation $y = mx + b$) $< -1$. Also notice that line P crosses the *y*-axis at a negative *y*-value (that is, below the *x*-axis). That is, the line's *y*-intercept (*b* in the equation $y = mx + b$) is negative. Only choice (E) provides an equation that meets both conditions.

# COORDINATE GEOMETRY

To handle GRE questions involving the standard *xy*-coordinate plane, you must be able to perform the following five basic tasks:

**1** Plot points on the coordinate plane

**2** Determine the slope of a line (or line segment) on the plane

**3** Interpret and formulate the equation of a line

**4** Find the midpoint of a line segment

**5** Find the distance between two points

Notice that all these tasks involve points and lines (line segments) only. In this section, you'll explore coordinate-geometry problems involving two-dimensional geometric figures, especially triangles and circles.

## Triangles and the Coordinate Plane

On the GRE, a question might ask you to find the perimeter or area of a triangle defined by three particular points. As you know, either calculation requires that you know certain information about the lengths of the triangle's sides. Apply the distance formula (or the standard form of the Pythagorean theorem) to solve these problems.

**32.** On the $xy$-plane, what is the perimeter of a triangle with vertices at points $A(-1,-3)$, $B(3,2)$, and $C(3,-3)$?

**(A)** 12

**(B)** $10 + 2\sqrt{3}$

**(C)** $7 + 5\sqrt{2}$

**(D)** 15

**(E)** $9 + \sqrt{41}$

**The correct answer is (E).** The figure below shows the triangle on the coordinate plane:

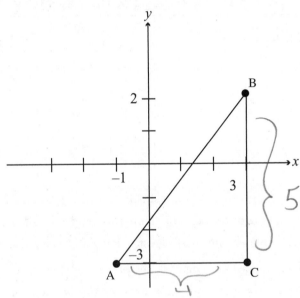

$AC = 4$ and $BC = 5$. Calculate AB (the triangle's hypotenuse) by the distance formula or, since the triangle is right, by the standard form of the Pythagorean theorem: $(AB)^2 = 4^2 + 5^2$; $(AB)^2 = 41$; $AB = \sqrt{41}$. The triangle's perimeter $= 4 + 5 + \sqrt{41} = 9 + \sqrt{41}$.

Note that, since the triangle is right, had the preceding question asked for the triangle's area instead of perimeter, all you'd need to know are the lengths of the two legs ($\overline{AC}$ and $\overline{BC}$). The area is $\left(\dfrac{1}{2}\right)(4)(5) = 10$.

To complicate these questions, the test-makers might provide vertices that do not connect to form a right triangle. (Answering this type of question requires the extra step of finding the triangle's altitude.) Or, they might provide only two points, then require that you construct a triangle to meet certain conditions.

**33.** On the $xy$-plane, the $xy$-coordinate pairs $(-6,2)$ and $(-14,-4)$ define one line, and the $xy$-coordinate pairs $(-12,1)$ and $(-3,-11)$ define another line. What is the unit length of the longest side of a triangle formed by the $y$-axis and these two lines?

(A) 15

(B) 17.5

(C) 19

(D) 21.5

(E) 23

**The correct answer is (D).** For each line, formulate its equation by determining slope ($m$), then $y$-intercept ($b$).

| For the Pairs $(-6,2)$ and $(-14,-4)$ | For the Pairs $(-12,1)$ and $(-3,-11)$ |
|---|---|
| $y = \dfrac{6}{8}x + b \left(\text{slope} = \dfrac{3}{4}\right)$ <br><br> $2 = \dfrac{3}{4}(-6) + b$ <br><br> $2 = -4\dfrac{1}{2} + b$ <br><br> $2 + 4\dfrac{1}{2} = b$ <br><br> $6\dfrac{1}{2} = b$ | $y = \dfrac{-12}{9}x + b \left(\text{slope} = -\dfrac{4}{3}\right)$ <br><br> $1 = -\dfrac{4}{3}(-12) + b$ <br><br> $1 = \dfrac{48}{3} + b$ <br><br> $1 - 16 = b$ <br> $-15 = b$ |

The two $y$-intercepts are $6\dfrac{1}{2}$ and $-15$. Thus the length of the triangle's side along the $y$-axis is 21.5. But is this the longest side? Yes. Notice that the slopes of the other two lines ($l_1$ and $l_2$) are negative reciprocals of each other: $\left(\dfrac{3}{4}\right)\left(-\dfrac{4}{3}\right) = -1$. This means that they're perpendicular, forming the two legs of a right triangle in which the $y$-axis is the hypotenuse (the longest side).

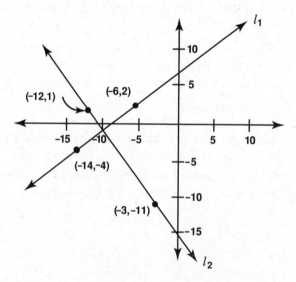

If the preceding question had instead asked for the point at which the two lines intersect, to answer the question you would formulate the equations for both lines, then solve for $x$ and $y$ with this system of two equations in two variables.

## Circles and the Coordinate Plane

A GRE question might ask you to find the circumference or area of a circle defined by a center and one point along its circumference. As you know, either calculation requires that you know the circle's radius. Apply the distance formula (or the standard form of the Pythagorean theorem) to find the radius and to answer the question.

**34.** On the $xy$-plane, a circle has center $(2,-1)$, and the point $(-3,3)$ lies along the circle's circumference. What is the square-unit area of the circle?

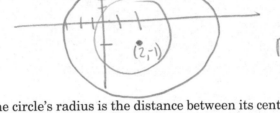

    **(A)** $36\pi$

    **(B)** $\dfrac{81\pi}{2}$

    **(C)** $41\pi$

    **(D)** $48\pi$

    **(E)** $57\pi$

**The correct answer is (C).** The circle's radius is the distance between its center $(2,-1)$ and any point along its circumference, including $(-3,3)$. Hence, you can find $r$ by applying the distance formula:

$$\sqrt{(-3-2)^2 + (3-(-1))^2} = \sqrt{25+16} = \sqrt{41}$$

The area of the circle $= \pi(\sqrt{41})^2 = 41\pi$.

Here's something to watch out for: In any geometry problem involving right triangles, keep your eyes open for the Pythagorean triplet in which you'll see the correct ratio, but it's between the wrong two sides. For instance, in the preceding problem, the lengths of the two legs of a triangle whose hypotenuse is the circle's radius are 4 and 5. But the triangle does *not* conform to the 3:4:5 Pythagorean side triplet. Instead, the ratio is $4:5:\sqrt{41}$.

## MIDPOINT AND DISTANCE FORMULAS

To be ready for GRE coordinate geometry, you'll need to know these two formulas. To find the coordinates of the midpoint of a line segment, simply average the two endpoints' $x$-values and $y$-values:

$$x_M = \frac{x_1 + x_2}{2} \text{ and } y_M = \frac{y_1 + y_2}{2}$$

For example, the midpoint between $(-3,1)$ and $(2,4) = \left(\dfrac{-3+2}{2}, \dfrac{1+4}{2}\right)$ or $\left(-\dfrac{1}{2}, \dfrac{5}{2}\right)$.

A GRE question might simply ask you to find the midpoint between two given points. Or it might provide the midpoint and one endpoint and then ask you to determine the other point.

**35.** In the standard $xy$-coordinate plane, the point M($-1,3$) is the midpoint of a line segment whose endpoints are A($2,-4$) and B. What are the $xy$-coordinates of point B?

**(A)** $(-1,-2)$
**(B)** $(-3,8)$
**(C)** $(8,-4)$
**(D)** $(5,12)$
**(E)** $(-4,10)$

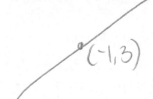

**The correct answer is (E).** Apply the midpoint formula to find the $x$-coordinate of point B:

$$-1 = \frac{x+2}{2}$$
$$-2 = x + 2$$
$$-4 = x$$

Apply the midpoint formula to find the $y$-coordinate of point B:

$$3 = \frac{y-4}{2}$$
$$6 = y - 4$$
$$10 = y$$

To find the *distance* between two points that have the same $x$-coordinate (or $y$-coordinate), simply compute the difference between the two $y$-values (or $x$-values). Otherwise, the line segment is neither vertical nor horizontal, and you'll need to apply the *distance formula*, which is actually the Pythagorean theorem in thin disguise (it measures the length of a right triangle's hypotenuse):

$$d = \sqrt{(x_1 - x_2)^2 + (y_1 - y_2)^2}$$

For example, the distance between $(-3,1)$ and $(2,4)$ = $\sqrt{(-3-2)^2 + (1-4)^2} = \sqrt{25+9} = \sqrt{34}$.

A GRE question might ask for the distance between two defined points (as in the example above). Or, it might provide the distance, and then ask for the value of a missing coordinate—in which case you solve for the missing $x$-value or $y$-value in the formula.

## SUMMING IT UP

- Lines and line segments are the fundamental elements for most GRE geometry problems, so it's essential to be familiar with the basic rules of angles formed by intersecting lines.

- Be certain you know the properties of all basic types of triangles. You'll not only encounter several problems involving triangles on the GRE, but you'll also need to have the skills necessary for solving problems with four-sided figures, three-dimensional figures, and circles.

- GRE circle problems typically involve other types of geometric figures as well, including triangles, squares, rectangles, and tangent lines. Learn the basics of circle problems and you'll be a step ahead in solving the most advanced geometric problems.

- GRE coordinate geometry questions involve the $xy$-plane defined by the horizontal $x$-axis and the vertical $y$-axis. You will need to know how to determine the slope of a line, so remember to calculate it as "rise-over-run" and not "run-over-rise."

# PART V

## VERBAL REASONING

# Analogies

## chapter 12

## OVERVIEW

- Key facts about GRE Analogies
- The 5-step plan
- Analogy strategies
- Analogy categories you should know
- Summing it up

In this chapter, you'll learn a step-by-step approach to handling any GRE Analogy, and you'll apply that approach to some GRE-style Analogies. Then you'll learn strategies for solving GRE Analogies and for avoiding common test-taking pitfalls when it comes to these test items. Later in the chapter, you'll examine in detail the types of word-pair relationships that the test designers use most often in GRE Analogies.

## KEY FACTS ABOUT GRE ANALOGIES

You first looked at GRE Analogies in Chapter 2 and in this book's Diagnostic Test. Here's a quick review of key facts about this question type.

**Where:** The 30-minute Verbal Reasoning section

**How Many:** Approximately 9 test items (out of 30 all together), interspersed with other question types on the computerized GRE

**What's Tested:**

- Your ability to understand the relationship between two words
- Your vocabulary

**Directions:** During the computerized GRE, test directions similar to the following will appear above each Analogy test item:

> **Directions:** In each of the following questions, a related pair of words or phrases is followed by five lettered pairs of words or phrases. Select the lettered pair that best expresses a relationship similar to that expressed in the original pair.

**Other Key Facts:**

- Analogies contain words only (no phrases).

- The first word pair is capitalized (all caps), but the five answer choices are not.

- In all six word pairs, the first word is of the same part of speech (noun, verb, or adjective); the same is true of the second word in all six word pairs.

# THE 5-STEP PLAN

Your first task in this chapter is to learn the 5 basic steps for handling a GRE Analogy. (You'll apply these steps to two sample questions.)

## Step 1: Determine the Meaning of the Words

Determine the meaning of each word in the original pair. If you're unfamiliar with one or both words, try to guess what it means based on its prefix, if any, and root.

## Step 2: Figure Out How the Words Are Related

Determine how the two words are related, and make up a sentence that expresses that relationship. Try to be specific. A sentence such as "[one word] is a type of [the other word]" might suffice for easier Analogies, but in most cases you'll have to get more specific. (A bit later, we'll take an in-depth look at the most common types of word relationships appearing on the GRE.)

## Step 3: Try Out Your Sentence Using the Answer Choices

Try each answer choice in turn, eliminating those that clearly don't work. Read your sentence, substituting each word pair by turn for the original pair. Ask yourself whether the sentence makes sense with the new pair. If it does, or if it's close, the pair *might* be your best choice. If it doesn't, eliminate that answer choice.

## Step 4: Try Again If You Have More Than One Answer

If you're left with more than one answer—or no answer at all—go back and make your sentence fit better. Your original sentence might have been:

- Too general

- Too specific

- A good start, but not sufficient (in other words, there's another kind of relationship you must recognize to narrow down the choices further)

## Step 5: Choose the Best Answer

If none of the choices fits exactly, choose the one that works best. No analogy is perfect, so don't look for a perfect match. You're looking for the best answer—the closest fit among the five choices.

## Applying the 5-Step Plan

Let's apply these 5 steps to two GRE-style Analogies. Start by reading the first one (below) as follows: "*Write* is to *scribble* as _____ is to _____."

**1.** WRITE : SCRIBBLE ::

    **(A)** shout : mutter
    **(B)** send : dispatch
    **(C)** cut : carve
    **(D)** walk : stagger
    **(E)** please : worry

This question is easier than average. One feature that makes it easy is that you're probably familiar with all the words. Another is that the relationship between the original pair is rather straightforward. Let's walk through this question using the 5-step approach:

**Step 1:** The meaning of the two words is obvious. Go on to step 2.

**Step 2:** Here are sentences that each describe the relationship between the capitalized pair:

> "To *scribble* is to *write* in a hasty or careless manner."

> "*Scribbling* is a careless or hasty form of *writing*."

**Step 3:** Let's test each answer choice to see which ones fit in the second sentence as substitutes for the capitalized word pair.

Choice (A): Is *muttering* a careless or hasty form of *shouting*? No. To mutter is to speak indistinctly, especially in a low and quiet voice. Although muttering and scribbling might both be unintelligible (very difficult to understand), scribbling is *not by definition* difficult to understand, whereas muttering is. What's more, the relationship between muttering and shouting has to do with volume, not degree of care, and the two words are contrary in meaning. Muttering is quiet, whereas shouting is loud. On the other hand, "write" is a neutral word; it is not contrary to "scribble," which is merely one form of writing. So, in two respects, choice (A) is not a strong analogy.

Choice (B): Is *dispatching* a careless or hasty form of *sending*? No. To dispatch is to send; in other words, the two words are essentially synonymous. (*Dispatch* can also be used as a noun, meaning "efficiency" or "promptness." But since the first words in the other pairs are all verbs, you should analyze *dispatch* as a verb here.) So, choice (B) is not a strong analogy.

Choice (C): Is *carving* a careless or hasty form of *cutting*? No. Although carving does describe a particular form of cutting, carving is often performed by design, deliberation, and even care. So, the relationship between cutting and carving is somewhat contrary to the relationship between write and scribble. You can safely eliminate choice (C).

Choice (D): Is *staggering* a careless or hasty form of *walking*? Yes. To stagger is to walk in a clumsy, teetering manner—in other words, carelessly. What's more, "walk" and "write" are both neutral terms. Staggering is a form of, not contrary to, walking, just as scribbling is a form of, not contrary to, writing. So, in this respect, choice (D) provides a much stronger analogy than choice (A). Admittedly, choice (D) does not provide a perfect analogy. (For example, staggering is not a hasty form of walking.)

But no analogy is perfect, and choice (D) is definitely stronger than choices (A), (B), or (C).

Choice (E): Is *worrying* a careless or hasty form of *pleasing?* No. The two words are unrelated to each other. Since there's no link between them, let alone any analogy between them and the capitalized pair, you can easily eliminate choice (E).

**Step 4:** We've narrowed down our choice to (D). Since choice (D) is such a good fit, there's no need to go back and revise our sentence.

**Step 5:** Choose choice (D), and move on to the next question. **The correct answer is (D).**

Now let's apply the 5-step approach to second GRE-style Analogy. Start by reading it (below) as follows: "*Adjudication* is to *trial* as _____ is to _____."

2. ADJUDICATION : TRIAL ::
   **(A)** postlude : symphony
   **(B)** forecast : weather
   **(C)** footnote: report
   **(D)** misdemeanor : felony
   **(E)** prognosis : surgery

This Analogy falls squarely into the "difficult" category. One feature that makes this tough is that it's packed with words that might look somewhat familiar to you but that you might have trouble defining precisely. Another reason this one is difficult is that the relationship between the capitalized pair is a bit abstract, and the same can be said for some of the other pairs as well. Here's how to tackle the question using the 5-step approach:

**Step 1:** If *adjudication* is a new word to you, take it apart and look for clues. The root *jud* appears at the beginning of more common words such as *judge* and *judicial*. The prefix *ad* means "to or toward." So a good guess would be that the verb *adjudicate* means "to judge." In fact, that's exactly correct! An *adjudication* is a decree or pronouncement, such as a verdict, usually made by a judge at the conclusion of a *trial*.

**Step 2:** Express the relationship between the two capitalized words simply, without getting too specific or abstract:

"An *adjudication* occurs at the conclusion of a *trial*."

**Step 3:** Let's test each answer choice to see which ones fit in our sentence as substitutes for the original word pair.

Choice (A): Does a *postlude* occur at the conclusion of a *symphony?* Yes. A postlude is a concluding piece or movement of a symphony.

Choice (B): Does a *forecast* occur at the conclusion of *weather?* No. By definition, a forecast precedes a weather event. So, at least in this respect, choice (B) expresses a contrary relationship to the capitalized pair. Eliminate choice (B).

Choice (C): Does a *footnote* occur at the conclusion of a *report?* Sometimes. Although footnotes usually appear at the bottom (or "foot") of the page on which they are referenced, footnotes can be grouped as endnotes at the end of a report.

Choice (D): Does a *felony* occur at the conclusion of a *misdemeanor?* No. The words *felony* and *misdemeanor* describe types of crimes. By definition, a felony is a more serious crime than a misdemeanor. So the relationship between *felony* and *misdemeanor* is not even close to the one between *adjudication* and *trial*. You can easily eliminate choice (D).

Choice (E): Does a *prognosis* occur at the conclusion of *surgery?* Yes, it can. A prognosis is a prediction of the chances of recovery from illness or surgery; a prognosis may very well occur just after surgery is completed.

**Step 4:** You've narrowed down the choices to (A), (C), and (E). You need another sentence that is either more specific or that focuses on a different aspect of the relationship between *adjudication* and *trial*. Consider the *purpose* or *function* of an adjudication (now you're getting a bit more abstract):

"An *adjudication* is a pronouncement of the outcome, or result, of a *trial*."

**Step 5:** Neither choice (A) nor choice (C) fit at all, do they? But choice (E) is a very close fit. A *prognosis* is an pronouncement (by the physician) as to the result of *surgery*. The surgery might have been successful, for example, and the chances of recovery good. Sure, the analogy isn't perfect. But it's the closest match among the five choices. **The correct answer is (E).**

## ANALOGY STRATEGIES

In the previous section, you picked up some valuable ideas for gaining a tactical advantage when it comes to GRE Analogies. Here you'll review those ideas and learn about some others. As a whole, these strategies will give you the insights you need to think clearly about Analogy questions and handle them efficiently, while avoiding the kinds of blunders that average test-takers might commit.

### Try to Capture the Essence of the Word-Pair Relationship

Ideally, you should formulate a sentence that captures the essence of the relationship between the two capitalized words. If you formulate a sentence that captures one aspect of the relationship but fails to capture the defining relationship, you probably won't zero in on the best answer choice. For example, consider the following analogy:

**TIP**

The first strategy here is by far the most important one. Mastering it is the key to handing GRE Analogies. In fact, you'll devote the entire second half of this chapter to it.

**3.** EXTORT : INFLUENCE ::

    **(A)** steal : borrow

    **(B)** saturate : dye

    **(C)** comfort : medicate

    **(D)** interrogate : ask

    **(E)** plummet : fall

**The correct answer is (D).** In the capitalized pair, the relationship involves both quality and degree. Someone who plans to EXTORT (force from another by violence or intimidation) hopes to exert great INFLUENCE. Three of the choices, (A), (D), and (E), illustrate an analogous relationship. To *steal* is to *borrow* permanently; to *interrogate* is to *ask* very closely and thoroughly; and to plummet is to fall rapidly and precipitously.

Leaving yourself three viable choices should tell you that you haven't yet determined the essence of the relationship between EXTORT and INFLUENCE. So try again: The usual purpose of extortion is to compel another to give you something (usually money) by influence; similarly, the usual purpose of interrogation is to compel another to give you something (usually information) by asking. So in both pairs, the relationship is one of degree as well as purpose. Would it make sense to say that the purpose of stealing something is to obtain something else by borrowing? Or that the purpose of descending is to plummet? No. So choice (D) provides a better analogy that either choice (A) or (E).

## The More Precisely You Define a Word-Pair Relationship, the Better

Don't expect to solve every GRE Analogy simply by plugging word pairs into simple sentences such as the following:

    "_____ is a type of _____."

    "_____ is a tool used to _____."

    "_____ is part of a _____."

Use simple sentences such as these as a starting point, but be prepared to refine the word-pair relationship by fine-tuning you sentence so the relationship is more specific. Let's follow this advice to help solve the following GRE Analogy:

**4.** WATER : RESERVOIR ::

    **(A)** lumber : forest

    **(B)** oven : kitchen

    **(C)** wheat : silo

    **(D)** oil : pipeline

    **(E)** zoo : animal

place where water stored for later use

**The correct answer is (C).** If you apply the sentence "A RESERVOIR is a place where you would find WATER" to the five choices, here's what you end up with:

    **(A)** A *forest* is a place where you would find *lumber*.

    **(B)** A *kitchen* is a place where you would find an *oven*.

    **(C)** A *silo* is a place where you would find *wheat*.

**(D)** A *pipeline* is a place where you would find *oil*.

**(E)** A *zoo* is a place where you would find an *animal*.

You can't eliminate even one answer choice! So you need to revise your original sentence to express a more specific relationship. Try this sentence: "A RESERVOIR is a place where WATER is stored for later use." Now let's see which answer choices we can eliminate:

Choice (A): Is a *forest* a place where *lumber* is stored for later use? Perhaps; but we don't really think of lumber as being "stored" in a forest.

Choice (B): Is a *kitchen* a place where an *oven* is stored for later use? Perhaps; but we don't usually think of an oven as being "stored" in a kitchen.

Choice (C): Is a *silo* a place where *wheat* is stored for later use? Yes. Choice (C) is a possible answer choice.

Choice (D): Is a *pipeline* a place where *oil* is stored for later use? No; a pipeline delivers oil from one place to another (often between two places of storage).

Choice (E): Is a *zoo* is a place where an *animal* is stored for later use? No; animals in a zoo are not "stored" there for later "use."

Now you can easily eliminate choices (D) and (E), and you can also see that choice (C) provides a stronger analogy than either choice (A) or (B).

## Some Analogies Work Better When You Turn Them Around

If you have trouble formulating a sentence where you use the first capitalized word before the second, try starting with the second word instead. Just make sure to analyze each answer choice in the same manner—use the second word first. Let's see how this technique works on the following Analogy:

5. STAR : CONSTELLATION ::

(A) sand : dune
(B) iceberg : glacier
(C) feather : bird → *feathers don't make a bird but sand does in dune as star in constellation*
(D) river : ocean
(E) trestle : track

**The correct answer is (A).** You might have trouble coming up with a graceful sentence relating STAR to CONSTELLATION, so try relating CONSTELLATION to STAR:

"A CONSTELLATION is made up of many individual STARS."

Of course, since we reversed the order of the capitalized words, we must also reverse the order of the words in each answer choice. So here's how to apply the sentence to the answer choices:

Choice (A): Is a *dune* made up of many individual *sands?* The word *sands* might not work grammatically in the sentence, but if you substitute *sand particles*, the answer is yes—a dune is made of many individual sand particles.

**Choice (B):** Is a *glacier* made up of many individual *icebergs?* Not really; an iceberg is a piece of ice that has broken away from a glacier. Until it breaks away, it's not an iceberg. (You could say, however, that a glacier consists of many potential icebergs, but that would strain the analogy.)

**Choice (C):** Is a *bird* made up of many individual *feathers?* No; a bird has many feathers, but a bird consists of much more than just feathers.

**Choice (D):** Is an *ocean* made up of many individual *rivers?* No; rivers might contribute to an ocean's waters, but oceans are apart and distinct from those rivers.

**Choice (E):** Is a *track* made up of many individual *trestles?* No; a track rests on top of trestles.

As you can see, by reversing the order of the capitalized words, we came up with a sentence that captured the word-pair relationship and helped us reveal the best analogy.

## Pay Attention to a Capitalized Word's "Charge"—Positive, Negative, or Neutral

If one of the capitalized words has either a negative or positive connotation, the corresponding word in the correct answer choice will be similarly "charged." But if the capitalized word is neutral, the corresponding word in the correct answer choice must be neutral as well. Let's apply this strategy to a GRE-style Analogy:

6. DETRIMENTAL : IMPACT ::

   **(A)** fearful : timidity
   **(B)** joyful : emotion
   **(C)** painful : soreness
   **(D)** sluggish : pace
   **(E)** odious : smell

   **The correct answer is (E).** The word DETRIMENTAL (harmful) describes a negative type of IMPACT, which is neutral in itself. So the best answer choice's first word should have a negative slant, while its second word should be neutral.

   You can eliminate choices (A) and (C) because, in each one, the second word (*timidity* or *soreness, respectively*) has a negative charge. Conversely, you can eliminate choice (B) because the first word (*joyful*) is positively charged. That leaves choices (D) and (E). The word *sluggish* describes a very slow pace, but it does not have a strong negative connotation. On the other hand, *odious* (which means "repulsive") is clearly a negative slant on the neutral word *smell*. So even if you didn't know what *odious* means, you could eliminate all other choices based on how their words are charged.

## Don't Give Up If You Know Only One of the Two Words in an Answer Choice

You can often eliminate an answer choice by knowing just one of the two words. To see how you might apply this technique to a GRE-style Analogy, consider the following example:

**7.** DRINK : GUZZLE ::

(A) surrender : succumb

(B) swallow : regurgitate

(C) ingest : gorge

(D) breathe : respire

(E) engulf : envelop

**The correct answer is (C).** To GUZZLE is to DRINK without restraint in amount. Considering choice (A), if you don't happen to know what *succumb* means, ask yourself what word might convey the idea of an unrestrained amount of *surrender*. The concept of an amount of surrender doesn't make sense, and so it's a good bet that choice (A) does not provide the best analogy. You don't need to know the meaning of *succumb* (to give in, yield, or surrender) to rule out choice (A). Similarly, the concept of an unrestrained amount of swallowing doesn't make much sense, and so choice (B) is probably not the best analogy, either. (*Regurgitate* means "throw up" or "vomit.")

By the same token, you can evaluate choice (C) without knowing what *ingest* means, as long as you know that *gorge* means "eat without restraint in amount." Based just on this word, choice (C) looks like it might provide a good analogy. Indeed, it does—to *ingest* is to eat. Choices (D) and (E) are incorrect because they each provide a pair of synonyms.

## Make Educated Guesses About the Meanings of Unfamiliar Words

Either of the following might provide a clue about the meaning of an unfamiliar word in a GRE Analogy:

- Another word that resembles the word in any way

- The word's root or prefix

To underscore this point, here's a GRE-style Analogy in which *both* capitalized words provide clues about what they mean:

**8.** HETEROGENEITY : ASSIMILATION ::

(A) pride : jealousy

(B) deformity : birth

(C) punctuality : attention

(D) delay : obstacle

(E) contention : victory

**The correct answer is (E).** The word HETEROGENEITY contains the prefix *hetero-*, which means "different." The word ASSIMILATION adds a prefix and a suffix to the common word *similar*. Based on this information, it's probably a good bet that the meanings of the two words run contrary to each other. On this basis alone, you can easily eliminate choices (A), (B), and (D). As for choice (C), the words *punctuality* and *attention* are not closely related to each other.

That leaves choice (E). For the record, ASSIMILATION (absorption) typically results in homogeneity (sameness or similarity); that is, it serves to reduce or eliminate HETEROGENEITY (diversity in character). Similarly, *victory* for one means defeat for another; so victory often eliminates *contention* (rivalry) between two foes. The analogy, though not perfect, is strong enough.

## Eliminate an Answer Choice Where There's No Clear Link Between the Two Words

If you find yourself stretching to find a link between an answer-choice word pair, consider your dilemma a hint that you should eliminate that choice without even thinking about the capitalized pair. Here's an analogy that illustrates this point:

9. STABLE : MERCURY :: ~~unstable~~ (opposites)

   **(A)** abstract : transcript
   **(B)** tardy : meter
   **(C)** public : celebrity
   **(D)** narrow : proportion
   **(E)** underground : crime

   **The correct answer is (A).** Without even considering the capitalized pair, you can eliminate choice (B), since *tardy* and *meter* are unrelated to each other (unless you *really* strain for a connection—which the GRE test designers don't expect of you). In each of the remaining pairs, the two words are somehow related. For the record, an inherent characteristic of MERCURY is that it is unstable (the opposite of STABLE). By the same token, a *transcript* is by definition a complete and accurate record of a real-life event, quite contrary to something that is *abstract*.

## Be Cautious of Answer Choices Involving the Same Topic as the Capitalized Pair

A GRE Analogy might include an answer choice containing words involving the same general subject matter as the capitalized pair. Never assume it's the best choice—but don't eliminate it solely on this basis, either. Always compare each answer choice to the capitalized pair without regard to similarity or dissimilarity in topic. Here's an Analogy that incorporates this type of red-flag answer choice:

10. TRAITORIOUS : TRUSTING ::

    **(A)** sophisticated : backward
    **(B)** fulfilled : envious
    **(C)** pessimistic : rosy
    **(D)** loyal : steadfast
    **(E)** smart : ignorant

    **The correct answer is (B).** A TRAITORIOUS person is one who betrays the trust of another, of a TRUSTING person. The key here is that the two words are not antonyms; rather, they define a relationship between contrary sorts of people. The red-flag answer choice here is (D). The words *loyal* and *steadfast* both involve the same concept as *traitorous* and *trusting*. But *loyal* and *steadfast* are simply synonyms of each other, and so choice (D) provides a poor analogy—probably the worst of the five choices.

You can also eliminate choices (A) and (C), which merely provide pairs of antonyms. As for choice (E), a smart person does not necessarily have any relationship with an ignorant person. That leaves choice (B). An *envious* person requires an object of that envy, usually a person who is *fulfilled* in ways that incites the other's envy. The analogy with the capitalized pair is hardly perfect, but it's stronger than the other four choices.

## ANALOGY CATEGORIES YOU SHOULD KNOW

Most GRE Analogies fall into one of several categories, identified here by sample sentences. In each sentence, the two blanks indicate where you plug in the two words:

"_____ is a key characteristic of _____."

"_____ is a function or use of _____."

"_____ runs contrary in meaning to _____."

"_____ operates against _____."

"_____ is a type, form, or example of _____."

"_____ is a place or environment for _____."

"_____ is a condition for or ingredient of _____."

"_____ is a part, element, or aspect of _____."

"_____ is evidence or a result of _____."

Knowing these categories will help make your task easier. But don't expect to solve every GRE Analogy simply by plugging the word pair into one of these nine sentences. This might work for easier questions, but for tougher ones you'll need to refine the relationship further to home in on the correct answer.

In the pages ahead, you'll learn that each category includes at least a few distinct variations or *patterns*. For each category, you'll find sentences and illustrative word pairs to help you recognize each pattern when you see it on the exam.

### "Key Characteristic" Analogies

In this type of relationship, one word helps explain the meaning of the other word. Look for one of two distinct patterns to help you refine the relationship:

**1** Defining characteristic

**2** Ideal (but not necessary) characteristic

#### DEFINING CHARACTERISTIC

"_____ is a characteristic that defines what a _____ is."

"By definition, a _____ is _____."

    BRAVE : HERO

    NOVEL : INVENTION (*novel* means "original or new")

**ALERT!**

Be skeptical of answer choices involving the same topic as the capitalized pair, but don't automatically eliminate an answer choice on this basis, either.

**ALERT!**

These categories are the ones you're most likely to encounter on the GRE—but don't expect every Analogy to fit neatly into one of these categories. You'll probably encounter one or two oddballs as well. So try to be flexible in handling GRE Analogies.

ALTRUISM : PHILANTHROPIST (a *philanthropist* is a generous humani-tarian; *altruism* means "good will or benevolence")

## IDEAL (BUT NOT NECESSARY) CHARACTERISTIC

"An effective _____ must be _____."

"An ideal _____ should be _____."

SWORD : SHARP

FOUNDATION : STRENGTH

SURGEON : DEXTEROUS (*dexterous* means "skillful with one's hands")

11. RISK : UNCERTAINTY ::

   **(A)** hope : dread

   **(B)** accusation : guilt

   **(C)** disrespect : dishonesty

   **(D)** arrow : straightness

   **(E)** cloud : haziness

   **The correct answer is (E).** RISK inherently involves UNCERTAINTY; in other words, uncertainty is part of the definition of risk. Is *dread* a defining character-istic of *hope?* No. Dread means "apprehension or fear of a future event." So the two words are contrary in meaning, and choice (A) is not correct. Is *guilt* a defining characteristic of an *accusation?* No. A person who is accused may not be guilty. In other words, guilt is not part of the definition of an accusation, so choice (B) is not a good answer. Is *dishonesty* a defining characteristic of *disrespect?* No; so you can eliminate choice (C). Is *straightness* a defining characteristic of *arrow?* No, so choice (D) is out. A *cloud* inherently requires a degree of *haziness;* in other words, haziness is part of what defines a cloud. Choice (E) is a good analogy.

## "Function or Use" Analogies

In this relationship, one word is essentially a *tool,* and the other word is a *function* or *use* of the tool. Look for one of two distinct patterns to help you refine the relationship:

**1** Inherent purpose (function)

**2** One of several possible uses or applications

### INHERENT PURPOSE (FUNCTION)

"A _____ is a tool designed to _____."

"The chief purpose of _____ is to _____."

KEY: UNLOCK

LOOM : WEAVE

BUTTRESS : REINFORCE (a *buttress* is a type of supporting structure)

**ONE OF SEVERAL POSSIBLE USES OR APPLICATIONS**

"A _____ can, but need not, be used to _____ ."

"A _____ can serve several functions, one of which is to _____ ."

"A _____ can _____ , although it isn't designed for this purpose."

> FINGER : POINT
>
> SPEECH : INSPIRE
>
> EDIFICE : MEMORIALIZE (an *edifice* is imposing structure, typically a monument)

12. PRESERVE : MORATORIUM ::

    **(A)** tyrannize : revolt
    **(B)** shade : tree
    **(C)** solve : problem
    **(D)** accumulate : collection
    **(E)** cover : eclipse

    **The correct answer is (B).** A MORATORIUM is an official halt or cessation of an activity. One possible use of a moratorium is to PRESERVE (for instance, to preserve an endangered animal species). Is one possible use of a *revolt* to *tyrannize?* The purpose of a revolt might be to stop tyranny (which means "oppressive rule"), so choice (A) is not correct. One possible use of a *tree* is to *shade,* so choice (B) is a good analogy. Is one possible use of a *problem* to *solve?* No, so choice (C) is out. Is one possible use of a *collection* to *accumulate?* No. A collection is the result of accumulation, so choice (D) is not correct. Is one possible use of an *eclipse* to *cover?* No. Covering is part of the definition of eclipse, so choice (E) is not the best choice.

Look out for red-flag answer choices. In the question above, for example, accumulate bears some similarity to *preserve* (accumulating might help to preserve). But choice (D) is a wrong answer.

## "Contrary Meaning" Analogies

In this type of word relationship, the two words run *contrary to* or are *opposed* to each other in meaning. On the GRE, you're unlikely to see two capitalized words that are perfect opposites (e.g., HOT : COLD); the test-makers prefer to hide the ball. So you must learn to distinguish among the following three patterns:

❶ Impossible characteristic

❷ Mutually exclusive conditions

❸ Lack or absence is part of the definition

**IMPOSSIBLE CHARACTERISTIC**

"By definition, _____ cannot be characterized by _____ ."

"_____ describes precisely what _____ is not."

MINERAL : ORGANIC

FRUCTOSE : SOUR

FIXTURE : MOMENTUM

## MUTUALLY EXCLUSIVE CONDITIONS

"Something that is _____ would probably not be described as _____ ."

"A _____ person cannot also be _____ ."

PURE : SOILED

TIMID : EXPERIMENTAL

OBVIOUS : CLANDESTINE (*clandestine* means "secretive")

## LACK OR ABSENCE IS PART OF THE DEFINITION

"_____ describes a lack of absence of _____ ."

"If something is _____ , it lacks _____ ."

DEFLATED : AIR

DIZZY : EQUILIBRIUM

IMPENITENT : REMORSE (*impenitent* means "lacking remorse")

13. AIMLESS : PURPOSE ::

   (A) copied : creativity
   (B) frugal : generosity
   (C) spontaneous : organization
   (D) ripe : freshness
   (E) inconsistent : candidness

   **The correct answer is (A).** Something that is AIMLESS by definition lacks PURPOSE. Similarly, something *copied* by definition lacks *creativity*. In both cases, the two words are mutually exclusive, so choice (A) is a good analogy. Does a *frugal* person necessarily lack *generosity?* Not necessarily. A frugal person is thrifty and careful about using money; but a frugal person might nevertheless be generous to others with money. In other words, lack of generosity is not what defines frugality, so choice (B) is not a good choice. Does something *spontaneous* necessarily lack *organization?* A spontaneous (spur-of-the moment) act lacks planning, but the act itself might nevertheless be organized. So you can eliminate choice (C) as a possible answer. Does something *ripe* necessarily lack *freshness?* Not exactly. A ripe piece of fruit is ready to eat, but lack of freshness is not a defining characteristic of ripeness. Choice (D) would be a viable answer if the word pair were *ripe : staleness* instead. Does something *inconsistent* necessarily lack *candidness?* No. *Candid* means "forthright or sincere" and bears no clear relationship to *inconsistent,* so choice (E) isn't a good answer choice.

## "Operates Against" Analogies

In this type of relationship, the two words are contrary to each other, and their contrary nature involves *function* or *purpose*. Look for one of four distinct patterns to help you refine the relationship:

**1** Correction, reversal, elimination

**2** Lessening (decrease) in degree, extent, amount, quantity

**3** Prevention

**4** Opposing functions

### CORRECTION, REVERSAL, ELIMINATION

"_____ corrects/reverses/eliminates _____."

SUSTENANCE : MALNUTRITION : (*sustenance* means "food or nourishment")

LOOSEN : STRANGULATED

INUNDATED : SCARCE (*inundated* means "flooded or deluged")

### LESSENING (DECREASE) IN DEGREE, EXTENT, AMOUNT, QUANTITY

"_____ lessens the degree/extent/amount of _____."

BRAKE : SPEED

COMPRESSION : AMPLITUDE (*amplitude* means "fullness or breadth")

FILTER : SPECTRUM

### PREVENTION

"_____ prevents _____ from occurring."

BLOCKADE : PROGRESS

CORRAL : DISPERSE

UMBRELLA : DRENCH

### OPPOSING FUNCTIONS

"_____ and _____ serve opposing functions."

"_____ and _____ work at cross-purposes."

FERTILIZER : SICKLE

ANCHOR : CORK

EPOXY : MILLSTONE

**ALERT!**

When you encounter two words that strike you as contrary in meaning, keep in mind that they might involve different *degrees* instead. There's a difference. For instance, *ripeness* may be contrary to *freshness*, but *ripeness* is not the opposite of (the lack of) *freshness*.

**NOTE**

In the correct/reverse/eliminate pattern, one word usually carries a positive connotation while the other is negatively "charged."

**14.** VIGILANCE : DANGER ::

**(A)** chimney : fire

**(B)** eraser : error

**(C)** relief : disaster

**(D)** clot : bleeding

**(E)** door : draft

**The correct answer is (E).** VIGILANCE means "caution or wariness," and can lessen the degree of DANGER to which one is exposed. Does a *chimney* reduce exposure to *fire?* No, so choice (A) is incorrect. Does an *eraser* reduce exposure to *error?* No, so you can eliminate choice (B). Does *relief* reduce exposure to *disaster?* No. Relief corrects or reverses the results of a disaster. Choice (C) is incorrect. Does a *clot* reduce exposure to *bleeding.* No. It stops bleeding that is already occurring; you can eliminate choice (D) as a possible answer. A *door* can reduce the extent of *draft* (air current) to which one is exposed, as vigilance can lessen the degree of danger to which one is exposed. So choice (E) is a good analogy.

## "Type, Form, or Example" Analogies

In this type of relationship, one word is a type, example, form, or variety of the other word. Look for one of these three distinct patterns to help you refine the relationship:

**❶** Specific example or category

**❷** Neutral vs. negative form

**❸** Difference in degree, rate, scale, extent, amount, quantity

### SPECIFIC EXAMPLE OR CATEGORY

"A _____ is one category of _____ ."

"A _____ is an example of _____ ."

WOODWIND : INSTRUMENT

ANTHOLOGY : COLLECTION (an *anthology* is a *collection* of writings)

CALORIE : MEASUREMENT (a *calorie* is a unit of *measurement* for heat)

### NEUTRAL VS. NEGATIVE FORM

"To _____ is to _____ in an unlawful/immoral/harmful manner."

"_____ is a negative/bad/poor form of _____ ."

"To _____ is to _____ , but with an improper purpose."

SCRIBBLE : WRITE (Remember this pair from earlier in the chapter?)

MOCK : MIMIC (to *mock* is to ridicule, typically through mimicry)

PEDANT : SCHOLAR (a *pedant* makes an excessive show of learning)

**DIFFERENCE IN DEGREE, RATE, SCALE, EXTENT, AMOUNT, QUANTITY**

"_____ takes _____ to an extreme."

"_____ is a faster/larger/stronger form of _____ ."

"_____ is the same as _____ but on a larger scale."

> SOLICIT : CANVASS (to *canvass* is to solicit orders from a group)
>
> COUNSEL : ADMONISH (to *counsel* is to advise; to *admonish* is to strongly urge)
>
> MALAISE : DISTRAUGHT (*malaise* means "uneasiness"; *distraught* means "troubled or distressed")

**15.** PREVALENT : UNIVERSAL ::

**(A)** mercenary : corrupt

**(B)** sporadic : frequent

**(C)** stylish : trendy

**(D)** juvenile : infantile

**(E)** flexible : twisted

**The correct answer is (D).** UNIVERSAL (occurring everywhere) takes PREVALENT (common) to an extreme. Does *corrupt* take *mercenary* to an extreme? No. Mercenary means "motivated by money rather than loyalty." A mercenary might be considered corrupt, but the relationship is not one of degree. Choice (A) is not correct. Does *frequent* take *sporadic* to an extreme? No. Sporadic means "occasional or infrequent"; so the two words are opposite in meaning. Eliminate choice (B). Does *trendy* take *stylish* to an extreme? No. The two words are synonyms, except that *trendy* has a somewhat negative connotation, whereas *stylish* has a positive one. You can eliminate choice (C) as well. *Infantile* (babyish or childish) takes *juvenile* (young or immature) to an extreme, so choice (D) is a good analogy. Does *twisted* take *flexible* to an extreme? No. Something flexible is not necessarily twisted at all, so choice (E) is out.

Be careful to distinguish between patterns 2 and 3 of the type, form, or example analogies above. A negatively charged word is not necessarily an extreme word. In the question above, for instance, *trendy* provides a negative spin on *stylish,* but is trendiness considered "extreme" or "heightened" stylishness? No.

## "Place or Environment" Analogies

In this type of relationship, one word describes a *place* (location, environment, forum, setting); the other word describes an *object* or *event* associated with that place. Look for one of two distinct patterns to help you refine the relationship:

**1** The only place generally associated with the object or event

**2** One of many places associated with the object or event

**THE ONLY PLACE GENERALLY ASSOCIATED WITH THE OBJECT OR EVENT**

"_____ usually occurs in a _____ ."

"A _____ is the only place you'll find _____ ."

COOK : KITCHEN

HONEYCOMB: HIVE

ELEGY : FUNERAL (an *elegy* is a song of mourning)

### ONE OF MANY PLACES ASSOCIATED WITH THE OBJECT OR EVENT

"_____ is one activity that might occur at a _____ ."

"_____ is one place where _____ might be found."

OBSERVE : LABORATORY

EXTRACTION : QUARRY

POACH : LAKE (to *poach* is to illegally remove fish or game)

16. PODIUM : ORATORY ::

   (A) dock : boat
   (B) kitchen : cuisine
   (C) battlefield : strategy
   (D) computer : calculation
   (E) poem : lyrics

   **The correct answer is (C).** A PODIUM is a stand used for public speaking. ORATORY refers to the art of public speaking. So a podium (more accurately, behind a podium) is a place to demonstrate one's oratory. Is a *dock* a place to demonstrate a *boat?* No; it's the place where a boat is stored when not being demonstrated. Choice (A) is eliminated. Is a *kitchen* a place to demonstrate *cuisine?* Perhaps. Cuisine refers to a style of cooking—but it is really demonstrated to others in a dining room or restaurant, not in a kitchen. Choice (B) might be a possibility. Is a *computer* a place to demonstrate a *calculation?* Not usually. A computer is a tool used to perform a calculation. Also, a computer is not really a "place," so the analogy in choice (D) is weak on two counts. Is a *poem* a place to demonstrate *lyrics?* No. Lyrics are by definition the words to a song, but a poem is not a song. Also, a poem is not really a "place," so like choice (D), the analogy is weak on two counts. Choice (B) is a possibility, but it is not as strong as choice (C). A *battlefield* is a place where an army demonstrates its *strategy*.

## "Condition for" or "Ingredient of" Analogies

**NOTE**

In GRE Analogies, many wrong-answer choices are wrong for more than one reason. Of course, you need to find only one reason to eliminate a choice.

In this relationship, one word is a *condition* or *ingredient* associated with the other word. Look for one of these two distinct patterns to help you refine the relationship:

❶ Necessary condition or ingredient

❷ Helpful but not necessary condition

### NECESSARY CONDITION OR INGREDIENT

"_____ is needed to _____ ."

"_____ can't happen without _____ ."

"_____ is a necessary ingredient for _____ ."

WIND : SAIL

VOTERS : ELECTION

EGO : CONCEIT

**HELPFUL BUT NOT NECESSARY CONDITION**

"_____ promotes/assists _____ ."

"_____ thrives in conditions described as _____ ."

"_____ is one possible ingredient for producing a _____ ."

QUIET : CONCENTRATE

TAILWIND : RACER

ANONYMITY : SURVEILLANCE

17. QUORUM : ATTENDANCE ::

(A) guilt : blame

(B) leverage : labor

(C) safety : guarantee

(D) principle : demonstration

(E) breath : air

**The correct answer is (E).** QUORUM refers to a sufficient number of members present to conduct business (as in a quorum of legislators for a vote). Presence, or ATTENDANCE, of members is a necessary condition for, or ingredient of, a *quorum.* Is *blame* a necessary condition for *guilt?* No. A person can be guilty without being blamed (accused). You can eliminate choice (A). Is *labor* (work or effort) a necessary condition for *leverage?* No. Applying leverage minimizes labor, but leverage itself doesn't. Replace *quorum* with *vote,* and choice (B) would be a good analogy. Is a *guarantee* a necessary condition for *safety?* No. A person can be safe without anyone else guaranteeing his or her safety, so choice (C) is not the best choice. Is *demonstration* a necessary condition for *principle?* No. You demonstrate a principle, but you don't attend a quorum, so choice (D) can be eliminated. Is *air* a vital condition for, or ingredient of, *breathing?* Yes, so choice (E) is a good analogy.

If a particular answer choice stumps you, try creating a sentence for it that works. Then, if the capitalized pair doesn't fit the sentence, the answer choice is wrong. Try it for the question above. Take choice (B), for instance. "Leverage is a technique for minimizing labor." Would you define a quorum as a technique for minimizing attendance? Clearly not.

## "Part, Element, or Aspect" Analogies

In this type of relationship, one word is an *element, part, facet,* or *aspect* of the other word. Look for one of four distinct patterns to help you refine the relationship:

**1** Intrinsic aspect or quality

**2** Part-to-whole (essential part)

**3** Part-to-whole (non-essential part)

**4** Individual-to-group

## INTRINSIC ASPECT OR QUALITY

"_____ is one intrinsic aspect of a _____ , and it can't be separated from the whole."

" Every _____ includes some kind of _____ , which can't be separated from the whole."

> TEMPERATURE : CLIMATE
>
> TEXTURE : WOOD
>
> ATTITUDE : PERSONALITY

## PART-TO-WHOLE (ESSENTIAL PART)

"A _____ is a distinct physical component/part of every _____ ."

> WALL : HOUSE
>
> SCREEN : TELEVISION
>
> WHEEL : AUTOMOBILE

## PART-TO-WHOLE (NON-ESSENTIAL PART)

"A _____ is one possible component/part of a _____ ."

> SHOES : OUTFIT
>
> CODA : COMPOSITION (a *coda* is an distinctive ending of a musical composition)
>
> ADJUDICATION : TRIAL (Remember this pair from earlier in the chapter?)

## INDIVIDUAL-TO-GROUP

"Several _____ s make up a _____ ."

"A group of _____ s is called a _____ ."

> PATRON : CLIENTELE (a *patron* is a customer; *clientele* refers to a business's customers as a group)
>
> LION : PRIDE (a *pride* is a community of *lions*)
>
> PATCH : MOSAIC (a *mosaic* is an assemblage of pieces to form a larger artwork)

18. CONTOUR : VISAGE ::

    **(A)** lid : eye
    **(B)** tarnish : antique
    **(C)** carrot : vegetable
    **(D)** face : clock
    **(E)** charcoal : fire

    **The correct answer is (B).** CONTOUR (a noun here) means "shape." VISAGE means "overall appearance." The contour (shape) of a thing is one aspect of its overall visage (appearance). Is a *lid* one possible aspect of an *eye?* No. A lid covers an eye. Does a contour cover a visage? No, so choice (A) is out. *Tarnish* (a noun here) means "a blemish or imperfection (typical due to use or age)." *Tarnish* is one possible aspect of an *antique.* Choice (B) is a good analogy. Is a *carrot* one aspect of a *vegetable?* No; it is one type, so choice (C) is not a good analogy. Is a *face* one aspect of a *clock?* No. It is one physical part or component of a clock, so choice (D) is not correct. Is *charcoal* one aspect of *fire?* No. Fire is one possible quality of charcoal.

## "Evidence or Result" Analogies

In this relationship, one word provides *evidence* of the other one. Look for three distinct patterns to help you refine the relationship:

**1** Cause-and-effect (natural or likely outcome or consequence)

**2** Process and product (the result is intentional)

**3** Symptom, sign, or manifestation

### CAUSE-AND-EFFECT

"If _____ occurs, so will _____ ."

"_____ is a by-product of _____ ."

    BOREDOM : MONOTONY

    OBSOLESCENCE : INNOVATION

    INJURY : REMISS (*remiss* means "negligent or neglectful")

### PROCESS AND PRODUCT

"You create a _____ by the process of _____ ."

"_____ is the intentional result of _____ ."

    SMOOTH : SHAVE

    COFFEE : BREW

    DEAL : NEGOTIATE

### SYMPTOM, SIGN, OR MANIFESTATION

"_____ is an indication that _____ has occurred."

"_____ is one possible symptom of _____ ."

TUMOR : CANCER

BLUSH : EMBARRASSED

ISOLATION : MISANTHROPE (a *misanthrope* is a person who hates or distrusts humankind)

19. SHUN : DISAPPROVAL ::

   **(A)** envy : gluttony

   **(B)** give : greed

   **(C)** lie : insincerity

   **(D)** nap : relaxation

   **(E)** persist : incontinence

   **The correct answer is (D).** To SHUN is to avoid or ignore. One who disapproves of the behavior of another might show that DISAPPROVAL by shunning the other person. So "shunning is one possible sign of disapproval," yet not a defining characteristic of it. Is *envy* one possible sign of *gluttony?* No. Gluttony means "excessive hunger or craving," so the two words are unrelated. Choice (A) isn't a good answer choice. Is *giving* one possible sign of *greed?* No. Taking, not giving, is a possible sign of greed, so choice (B) is out. Is *lying* one possible sign of *insincerity?* No. It is a defining characteristic, so choice (C) can be eliminated. Is a *nap* a possible sign of *relaxation?* Yes, although it's not a defining characteristic. Choice (D) is a good analogy. Is *persisting* a possible sign of *incontinence?* No. Incontinence means "lack of control over one's bodily urges," so the two words are somewhat contrary in meaning.

In the analogy above, the two capitalized words bear *some similarity* in meaning—a clue that you can eliminate any answer choice where the two words are the least bit contrary in meaning to each other. Choices (B) and (E) both match this description.

## SUMMING IT UP

- GRE Analogies are part of the 30-minute Verbal Reasoning section of the GRE. Analogy questions test your ability to understand the relationship between two words, and your facility with vocabulary.

- Analogies contain words only (no phrases); in all six word pairs for each question, the first word is of the same part of speech (noun, verb, or adjective); the same is true of the second word in all six word pairs per question.

- For each Analogy question, you must determine the meaning of each word in the original pair and then determine how the two words are related before applying that relationship to the five answer choices. Create a sentence that expresses the relationship and plug in each answer choice. Eliminate choices that clearly don't work. If more than one answer is left, retool your sentence to narrow the choices further. Then choose the best answer. It may not be a perfect match, but it should be the closest fit among the five choices.

- Follow and review the 5 basic steps for handling GRE Analogy questions outlined in this chapter and apply them to this book's Practice Tests. Then review them again just before exam day.

# Sentence and Complex Text Completions

## OVERVIEW

- **Key facts about Sentence Completions**
- **Key facts about Complex Text Completions**
- **The 5-step plan (Sentence Completions)**
- **Sentence Completion strategies**
- **Structural clues for completing sentences**
- **Complex Text Completions (new)**
- **The 4-step plan (Complex Text Completions)**
- **Find the logical connections**
- **Complex Text Completion strategies**
- **Summing it up**

The GRE Verbal Reasoning section contains two types of Sentence Completions: *single-blank* and *dual-blank*. Both involve just *one* sentence, and in both variations your task is the same: Complete the entire sentence by selecting the best among *five* choices. Expect most Sentence Completions on your exam to be of the dual-blank variety.

Your Verbal Reasoning section might also contain a more Complex Text Completion test item. This format involves a brief passage ranging from *one to five* sentences long, with either *two or three* blanks. Your task is to select the best among at least three choices for each blank. Unlike dual-blank Sentence Completions, Complex Test Completions call for you to complete each blank *independently* of the other(s)—and you must complete all blanks correctly to receive credit for a correct response.

In this chapter, you'll learn step-by-step approaches to Sentence Completions and Complex Text Completions, and you'll apply those approaches to GRE-style examples. You'll also examine the structural clues that tell you the intended meaning of a sentence or paragraph, and therefore how best to complete it. Finally, you'll review strategies for handling GRE Sentence and Complex Text Completions—and for avoiding common test-taking pitfalls.

You first looked at GRE Sentence and Complex Text Completions in Chapter 2 and in this book's Diagnostic Test. Let's quickly review the key facts about these two question types.

## chapter 13

**NOTE**

The more Complex Text Completion format is new on the GRE as of November 2007. Initially, no test-taker will encounter more than *one* of these items on the exam, and some test-takers won't encounter any of them. The test designers plan to gradually increase the number of Complex Text Completions appearing on the GRE.

## KEY FACTS ABOUT SENTENCE COMPLETIONS

**Where:** The 30-minute Verbal Reasoning section

**How Many:** Approximately 5–6 test items (out of 30 altogether), interspersed with other question types on the computerized GRE

**What's Tested:**

- Your ability to understand the intended meaning of a sentence

- Your ability to distinguish between a sentence that makes sense and one that lacks sense

- Your ability to recognize and distinguish between proper and improper word usage and idiom

- Your ability to recognize and distinguish between clear and unclear written expression

- Your vocabulary

**Directions:** During the computerized GRE, test directions similar to the following will appear above each Sentence Completion test item:

> **Directions:** Each sentence below has one or two blanks, each blank indicating that something has been omitted. Beneath the sentence are five lettered words or sets of words. Choose the word or set of words for each blank that best fits the meaning of the sentence as a whole.

### Other Key Facts:

- Most Sentence Completions involve two blanks, not just one.

- You'll fill in most blanks with single words, but for some blanks your choices will include brief phrases.

- The emphasis on vocabulary is not as strong with these question types as with Analogies and Antonyms.

- Except for the easiest Sentence Completions, expect to encounter a best and a second-best choice.

- The best choice will make for an excellent sentence that's clear, effective, and correct in grammar, diction, and idiom.

## KEY FACTS ABOUT COMPLEX TEXT COMPLETIONS

**Where:** The 30-minute Verbal Reasoning section

**How Many:** 0–1 (but possibly more than 1 during tests administered later than 2008)

**What's Tested:**

- Your ability to understand the intended meaning of a sentence or paragraph

- Your ability to distinguish between a paragraph that is cohesive and coherent and one that lacks these qualities

- Your ability to recognize and distinguish between proper and improper word usage and idiom
- Your ability to recognize and distinguish between a clear and unclear written expression

**Directions:** During the computerized GRE, test directions similar to the following will appear above a Complex Text Completion test item:

> **Directions:** Select one entry from each column to fill in the corresponding blanks in the text. Fill in the blanks in a way that provides the best completion for the text.

**Other Key Facts:**

- A Complex Text Completion involves one to five sentences containing two to three blanks all together.
- You'll fill in blanks with either single words or brief phrases.
- The primary emphasis is on idiom, sense, and paragraph structure, not on vocabulary.
- You complete each blank independently of the other blank(s).
- You must choose the best completion for *all* blanks in a question to earn credit for a correct response; no partial credit is awarded.
- The best choice will make for an excellent sentence or paragraph that's cohesive, rhetorically effective, and correct in grammar, diction, and idiom.

# THE 5-STEP PLAN (SENTENCE COMPLETIONS)

Here's a 5-step approach for tackling any GRE Sentence Completion. After reviewing these steps, you'll apply them to two examples.

## Step 1: Read the Sentence in Its Entirety

Read the sentence in its entirety just to get the gist of it. Don't worry yet about how to fill in the blank. In this initial step, just try to get a feel not just for the overall topic, but for the "thrust" of the sentence. Ask yourself what point the sentence as a whole is trying to make. Pay particular attention to key words that indicate the following:

- A description (and whether it is favorable, unfavorable, or neutral)
- An opinion or point of view
- Any change in direction
- A conclusion
- A comparison (pointing out a similarity)
- A contrast (pointing out a difference or distinction)

NOTE

The step-by-step approach involves one step more for dual-blank than for single-blank Sentence Completions.

## Step 2: Reread the Sentence and Try Answering with Your Own Word(s)

Read the sentence again, and this time fill in the first (or only) blank with your own word(s). Sentence Completions are a bit like Problem Solving questions on the Quantitative Reasoning section: It pays to formulate your own response (solution) before you scan the answer choices. If you use this approach, you'll have a much easier time spotting "trick" answer choices.

## Step 3: Fill in the Second Blank with Your Own Word(s)

For dual-blank Sentence Completions only, fill in the second blank with your own word(s). Be sure your completion makes sense in accordance with how you completed the first blank.

## Step 4: Test Each Answer Choice

Test each answer choice and eliminate the obviously wrong ones. You're bound to find at least one or two choices that make little or no sense in the context of the sentence. Clear those away first so that you can focus your attention on the viable candidates.

## Step 5: Compare the Remaining Choices and Choose the Best One

Compare the remaining choices by reading the entire sentence again, using each choice in turn. Pay close attention to whether each word is used properly and appropriately in context. If you're still undecided, take your best guess among the viable choices and move on.

## Applying the 5-Step Plan

Now let's walk through two GRE-style examples—one single-blank and one dual-blank—using this 5-step approach.

1. Sleep researchers now view sleep as involving degrees of detachment from the surrounding world, a _____ whose rhythm is as unique and as consistent as a signature.

   (A) realm
   (B) restfulness
   (C) science
   (D) progression
   (E) condition

**Step 1:** The sentence as a whole seems to suggest that sleep is a dynamic process involving a series of different stages defined by degree of detachment. Notice that the purpose of the second clause is to describe what sleep is. This observation is key to reaching the correct answer.

**Step 2:** If you were filling in the blank yourself (without the aid of answer choices), what word would you use? The missing word refers to "sleep," so perhaps a word such as *state* or *condition* might occur to you as a good completion.

Notice that this completion is indeed among the answer choices. Does this mean we can confidently select choice (E) and move on to the next question without another thought? Not necessarily. Another choice might be better than choice (E).

**Step 3:** This Sentence Completion contains only one blank, so go to step 4.

**Step 4:** Let's eliminate answer choices that are obviously wrong. The correct answer has to make sense as a characterization of sleep. Choices (B) and (C) make no sense as characterizations of sleep, so eliminate them. Notice also that "rhythm" is mentioned as a feature or trait of the missing word, so the correct answer must make sense in this way as well. To describe a "realm" as having a rhythm makes no sense, so eliminate choice (A).

**Step 5:** We've narrowed the choices down to (D) and (E). Read the sentence with each word in turn. Which word is more appropriate and effective in conveying the thrust of the sentence (that sleep is a dynamic process involving a series of different stages)? The word *progression* clearly drives home this notion more pointedly and effectively than the word *condition*. **The correct answer is (D).**

Now here's a GRE-style Sentence Completion that contains two blanks. Let's apply the same step-by-step approach to this one.

2. African-American legislators have not only _____ their constituencies but also served as proxies in the democratic process for all African Americans; yet their personal lives sometimes _____ their struggle to extend the nation's ideals to all citizens.

    **(A)** served . . describe
    **(B)** abandoned . . affirm
    **(C)** promoted . . criticize
    **(D)** represented . . belie
    **(E)** influenced . . discredit

**Step 1:** In reading this sentence, you should have noticed that it changes direction midway through. This change is signaled by the key word "yet," which provides a clue that the second part of the sentence sets up a contrast or contradiction to the first part. You can bet that this structural clue will be crucial to determining the best answer.

**Step 2:** Let's read the sentence again, filling in the first blank with our own word (ignoring the answer choices for now). The words "not only . . . but also" are important clues that the first blank must complement the phrase "served as proxies." (*Proxy* means "substitute.") A negatively charged word or phrase such as *harmed, ignored,* or *disagreed with* would make no sense in the first blank, would it? But a word such as *served, represented,* or *aided* would fit nicely.

**Step 3:** Now let's fill in the second blank with our own word, one that makes sense together with the first word. During step 1, we determined that the meaning of second clause should reflect a contrast with that of the first one. So a word such as *ignore, de-emphasize,* or *trivialize* would make sense here. Here's a good paraphrase that gives you a sense of the idea that the sentence is probably trying to convey: *In doing* *their jobs, these members of Congress have helped (aided) all African Americans, yet some biographies don't reflect (they ignore) the efforts of these members.*

**Step 4:** Let's take a first pass at each answer choice. Because this question includes two blanks, don't try to shortcut the process by scanning for key words that might signal obvious winners and losers. Dual-blank Sentence Completions are not designed to be solved that easily. Let's consider each answer choice in turn.

The word *served* fits nicely, but *describe* fails to establish the necessary contrast between the two parts of the sentence. Eliminate choice (A). The word *abandoned* doesn't fit, because it doesn't complement "served as proxies." You can eliminate choice (B) even without considering the second word (*affirm*). The word *promoted* and *criticize* each seem to make sense in context, and together they set up a sense of contrast between the two clauses. So choice (C) is in the running. The word *represented* fits nicely. If you don't know what *belie* means, perhaps you can guess based on its root *lie* (falsehood), which provides the sort of contrast between the two clauses we're looking for. So choice (D) is in the running. (We'll define *belie* in step 4.) The word *influenced* establishes a different meaning for the first clause than the one we've been inferring. But *influenced* does make some sense in the first clause. *Discredit* makes sense as well and sets of the necessary contrast between the two clauses. So choice (E) is in the running.

**Step 5:** We've narrowed down our choices to (C), (D), and (E). Now read the sentence again with each of these three pairs, in turn.

Choice (C): This answer choice suffers from two subtle defects. First, it is the *goals* or *interests* of a constituency, not the constituency itself, that an elected representative promotes. So *promoted* sets up an improper idiomatic expression. Second, for the word *criticize* to establish a clear contrast, the first clause should at least suggest the opposing notion of *approval;* but it doesn't. So even though the "flavor" of *criticize* is in the right direction, it is not a perfect fit in the context of the sentence as a whole.

Choice (D): To *belie* is to misrepresent or contradict. For example, a smile belies sadness. Similarly, a biography can belie the struggle described in the sentence—perhaps by mischaracterizing it as an easier effort than it has in fact been. So choice (D) appears to be a good answer choice.

Choice (E): Like choice (C), this answer choice suffers from two subtle defects. First, this version of the sentence inappropriately *discredits* a *struggle;* but it makes better sense to discredit the *strugglers.* (You can eliminate this answer choice based on this defect alone.) Second, although the word *influence* makes sense in context, it doesn't establish the close parallel in ideas that the correlative phrases "not only . . . but also" call for. Choice (D) is better in this respect. **The correct answer is (D).**

**TIP**

In dual-blank questions, if you can eliminate just one component of an answer choice, then you know the whole choice won't work, so you can toss it out and focus on the remaining choices.

## SENTENCE COMPLETION STRATEGIES

In the previous section, you learned some valuable strategies for handling GRE Sentence Completions. Here you'll review those ideas and you'll learn about some others. The first strategy here is probably the most important one. Mastering it is the key to handing Sentence Completions. In fact, you'll devote the entire next section of this chapter to it.

### Look for Key Words in the Sentence for Clues

Pay particular attention to the sentence's rhetorical structure and to "signpost" words that show its direction and logical flow. Is it continuing along one line of thought? If so, you're looking for a word that supports that thought. Is it changing direction in midstream? If so, you're looking for a word that sets up a contrast between the thoughts in the sentence.

For example, in Question 2 on page 323, one little word, "yet," was the key to getting the question right, because it signaled an important change in direction. Here's another example:

3. Creative writing is not just a function of _____; understanding how language is used and how ideas are communicated also requires a certain level of _____.

   **(A)** the author's imagination . . awareness
   **(B)** the writer herself . . discipline
   **(C)** formal training . . education
   **(D)** linguistic skill . . fluency
   **(E)** hard work . . playfulness

   **The correct answer is (A).** In this sentence, dual signposts "not just" (in the first clause) and "also" (in the second clause) signal that the second completion should complement (supplement but be distinguishable from) the first one. Choices (B), (C), and (D) don't provide complementary ideas. But choices (A) and (E) both do. Is playfulness a fitting word to describe understanding how language and ideas are used? No. That leaves choice (A), which makes sense in context: To "understand how language is used and how ideas are communicated" requires that one be keenly *aware* of these phenomena—an awareness that complements *imagination*.

### Think Up Your Own Completion as a Way to Start

Formulating your own completion gets your mental wheels turning and helps you "get into" the question. If you already have in mind what kind of completion to look for among the choices, the correct answer is more likely to jump out at you.

But this strategy is only a starting point. You won't always find your homemade completion among the choices. By the same token, spotting your own completion among the choices does not necessarily mean that you've pinpointed the correct answer. For example, in Question 1 on page 322, our own completion, *condition,* was indeed among the five choices—but it turned out *not* to be the best one.

Here's another example that illustrates this technique and its limitations:

**ALERT!**

In the most difficult Sentence Completions, you'll need to recognize subtle differences in sentence meaning, depending on which of the two best candidates you use to complete the sentence.

4. Decades of statistics showing the _____ respiratory ailments among construction workers _____ the causal connection between asbestos exposure and lung cancer.

   **(A)** reason for . . help to establish
   **(B)** frequent occurrence of . . have influenced
   **(C)** consequences of . . mainly involve
   **(D)** high incidence of . . underscore
   **(E)** seriousness of . . preceded

   **The correct answer is (D).** Let's try completing the sentence in our own words. It makes sense that statistics showing *many cases of* respiratory ailments among construction workers would *help prove* the connection between asbestos exposure and lung cancer. Now let's scan the answer choices for our ideas. Choices (B) and (D) complete the first blank much as we just did (*incidence* means "rate of occurrence"). But choice (A) also completes the second blank much the same as we did. So let's focus on these three choices.

   Although the second completion in choice (A) works well in the sentence by itself, when put together with the first part, you have a pointless sentence telling us that a reason proves a reason. So you can eliminate choice (A). As for choice (B), to say that something "influences a causal connection" is confusing and vague, and so you can eliminate choice (B) on this basis. That leaves choice (D). The word *underscore* means "emphasize." This certainly wasn't the idea we originally had in mind for completing the second blank, but it works well. So remember: Don't automatically eliminate an answer choice just because it doesn't express your own ideas.

## Check for Idiom, Usage, and Grammatical Context

Sentence Completions cover not just overall sentence sense, but also the following three concepts:

**1** Word usage (how well a particular word conveys the writer's intended meaning)

**2** Idiom (how ideas are expressed as commonly used phrases)

**3** Grammatical context (whether a word or phrase makes grammatical sense in context)

For example, in Question 2 on page 323, choice (C) and choice (E) both contained subtle usage and idiom problems that distinguished them from the best choice, which was choice (D). Challenging Sentence Completions often call for close judgments calls based on usage, idiom, or grammatical context. Pay close attention to whether the word(s) used are a proper way to convey the idea. Here's a good example:

**TIP**

Fill in the blank(s) with your own words first, but never assume there's no other effective way to complete the sentence.

5. Unless we grant historians some license to interpret historical events, we essentially _____ the historian's role to that of a mere archivist or journalist.

   **(A)** define
   **(B)** demote
   **(C)** expand
   **(D)** alter
   **(E)** diminish

   **The correct answer is (E).** In the sentence, the word "mere" is very important. It suggests a risk that the historian's role might be reduced. To grant someone "license" is to allow them leeway or freedom; hence, not doing so would be to limit their freedom in some way. We should complete the sentence with a word that conveys this idea. Of the five choices, only *demote* and *diminish* serve the purpose. However, saying that a person's *role* is *demoted* uses the word improperly. (It is the *person* himself, not his or her role, that is *demoted.*) On the other hand, describing someone's role as *diminished* uses the that word properly.

## Don't Choose an Answer Based on Advanced Vocabulary

Some test-takers try a shortcut to correct Sentence Completion answers by picking the choice containing the most obscure words. But the test-makers don't design Sentence Completions to be solved so easily. Instead, try to guess based on the word's prefix, root, how the word "sounds," or even your gut instinct. For example, in Question 2 on page 323, the word *belie* happened to be part of the best answer. But that's just the way this question turned out; don't generalize from this single case. Here's an example that underscores this warning:

6. Coinciding with the _____ of television networks catering to our interest in other cultures, global tourism has increased steadily over the last fifteen years.

   **(A)** popularity
   **(B)** proliferation
   **(C)** incipience
   **(D)** resurgence
   **(E)** regulation

   **The correct answer is (B).** The word *coinciding* suggests that events in television reflect the increasing popularity of tourism. The word *incipience* (meaning "beginning or initial stages") is rather obscure, but that's beside the point. It doesn't help convey the sentence's meaning very well, and that's why it's not the best choice. The word *proliferation,* which means "a great increase in number," makes more sense in context: The increasing popularity of tourism reflected the increasing number of television channels catering to viewers interested in travel-related topics.

## Apply the Process of Elimination to Each Blank

In dual-blank questions, if you can eliminate just one component of an answer choice, you know the whole choice won't work—so you can toss it out and focus on the remaining choices. For example, in Question 2 on page 323, we eliminated choice (B) because *abandon* didn't make sense in the first clause; we never had to look at the other part of that choice (*affirm*). Here's another example:

7. Globalization means that public health and safety is becoming an increasingly
_____ affair; nations are now tackling public-health problems _____, through
joint research programs.

   **(A)** worldwide . . efficiently
   **(B)** localized . . cooperatively
   **(C)** universal . . publicly
   **(D)** multinational . . jointly
   **(E)** privatized . . realistically

   **The correct answer is (D).** The opening words *Globalization means* tell you
   that a good completion for the first blank should essentially define *globalization.*
   You can eliminate choices (B) and (E) on this basis without even considering the
   second blank. Similarly, the construction of the sentence's latter part tells you
   that a good completion for the second blank should convey the idea of "joint
   research." You can eliminate choices (A) and (C) on this basis without even
   considering the first blank. By process of elimination, you know that the correct
   answer is choice (D).

## In Dual-Blank Completions, Never Rule Out an Answer Choice Because of a Better Choice for One Blank

In a dual-blank question, a wrong answer choice might provide a perfect completion for
one blank—better than all the others—but may nevertheless be paired with one that's
a poor fit for the other blank. For example, in Question 2 on page 323, the word *served* is
a perfect fit for the first blank, yet choice (A) is wrong because it's paired with a poor
completion for the second blank.

Even if you spot two superior completions for the same blank, *never* rule out other
answer choices on that basis alone. To help drive home this point, let's look at another
example:

8. The desire to identify oneself with an exclusive social group, which nearly all
humans seem to share, seems to spring from a _____ psychological need to
define oneself through one's _____.

   **(A)** common . . accomplishments
   **(B)** universal . . career or occupation
   **(C)** basic . . material possessions
   **(D)** repressed . . spouse or other mate
   **(E)** significant . . personal associations

   **The correct answer is (E).** Since the "desire" mentioned in the first phrase is
   one that "nearly all humans seem to share," the words *common* and *basic* (which
   both suggest that all humans share) are the two best completions for the first
   blank. But they're paired with poor completions for the second blank, which
   should mirror the idea of identifying with an "exclusive social group." Only choice
   (E) completes the second blank by referring to such a group.

# STRUCTURAL CLUES FOR COMPLETING SENTENCES

As you've learned, one key to GRE Sentence Completions lies in so-called signpost words, which connect a sentence's parts to form a cohesive sentence that makes sense (assuming you choose the right words to fill in the blanks). Sentence Completions are predictable in how their sentences are constructed and in their use of signpost words. After reviewing some examples, you'll begin to recognize patterns in the way sentence parts connect logically. Here are the types of connections that you're most likely to see:

- Contrast
- Similarity
- Restatement
- Cause and effect

## Contrast

In this type of pattern, one part of a sentence contains an idea that contrasts with or is opposed to an idea in another part of the sentence. Here's a single-blank example:

9. Whereas most artists manage to summon the requisite creativity to produce art whatever their mood, during periods of _____ is when the world's preeminent artists seem to conjure up their greatest masterpieces.

    **(A)** infirmity
    **(B)** transition
    **(C)** infatuation
    **(D)** convalescence
    **(E)** despondency

    **The correct answer is (E).** What is there about the sentence that tells you to look for a contrast? It's the word "Whereas." In other words, the first part of the sentence tells you something about most artists that *should contrast* with what the second part of the sentence tells you about really great artists. The only answer choice that provides this contrast is *despondency*.

Here are some other signpost words that are used to signal a contrast:

| | |
|---|---|
| *although* | *nevertheless* |
| *but* | *nonetheless* |
| *by contrast* | *on the other hand* |
| *despite* | *unlike* |
| *however* | *yet* |

Note that you could use almost any word from the preceding list instead of "whereas" to set up the same contrast. (Some you'd use to introduce the first part of the sentence; others you'd use to introduce the second part of the sentence.) Try each one to see if it fits, and if so, where.

Not all sentences with contrasting ideas will use one of the signpost words listed above. Let's look at a challenging dual-blank question in which the sentence contains no obvious signposts but its rhetorical structure nevertheless intends to convey contrasting ideas:

## NOTE

Not every Sentence Completion item on the GRE will illustrate contrast, similarity, restatement, or cause and effect, but most will—so it's a good idea to learn to recognize these constructions.

10. Most social psychologists agree that the root of human prejudice lies more in _____, almost primal, sense of fear than in the sort of _____ that is learned and can therefore be "unlearned."

    **(A)** an overriding . . behavior

    **(B)** an irrational . . bias

    **(C)** an intrinsic . . distrust

    **(D)** a heightened . . awareness

    **(E)** an instinctive . . emotion

    **the correct answer is (C).** The phrase *almost primal,* set off as an appositive, tells you that the first blank should contain a close synonym of *primal.* Both *intrinsic* and *instinctive* fit the bill, but none of the other first-blank choices do. The sentence's rhetorical structure tells you that the word in the second blank should convey an emotion distinguished from (in contrast to) a "sense of fear," in that it can be learned. The word *distrust* fits the bill nicely. The word *emotion* does not establish a contrasting idea and hence it is rhetorically less effective.

**ALERT!**

A contrast of ideas is sometimes conveyed by key words such as *however* and *although.* But this isn't always the case; so to determine a sentence's rhetorical point, there's no substitute for understanding the sentence as a whole.

## Similarity

In a sentence fitting this pattern, one part describes something similar to something described in another part of the sentence. Here's a single-blank example:

11. Just as musicians in the 1970s were amazed by the powers of the electronic synthesizer, musicians during the time of Bach _____ the organ, the technical wonder of its day.

    **(A)** were reluctant to play

    **(B)** marveled at

    **(C)** were intimidated by

    **(D)** were eager to master

    **(E)** misunderstood

    **The correct answer is (B).** The sentence's first two words ("Just as") tell you that the two parts of the sentence are describing similar situations. Musicians during Bach's time reacted to the organ the same way that musicians in the 1970s reacted to the synthesizer. Since the sentence indicates that musicians of the 1970s "were amazed by" the synthesizer, the words for the blank should express something similar about the reaction to the organ. Only *marveled at* provides the similarity.

Here are some other words and phrases that act as similarity signposts:

| | |
|---|---|
| *as* | *similarly* |
| *in the same way* | *by the same token* |
| *like* | *not unlike* |
| *likewise* | |

Try redrafting the sentence about synthesizers using each of these signposts instead of the phrase *Just as.* You'll notice that some words work only for beginning the first clause and others work only for beginning the second clause.

## Restatement

In a sentence illustrating this pattern, one part paraphrases, defines, or clarifies what is said in another part of the sentence. Here's a dual-blank example:

12. Public attitudes toward business _____ are somewhat _____; most people resent intrusive government rules, yet they expect government to prevent businesses from defrauding or endangering them.

    **(A)** ethics . . divided

    **(B)** investment . . confused

    **(C)** practices . . emotional

    **(D)** regulation . . ambiguous

    **(E)** leaders . . skeptical

    **The correct answer is (D).** Considering the sentence as a whole, the second part is intended to elucidate (clarify or explain) the first part. What provides the clue for this connection? In this sentence, there are two keys: the semi-colon and the syntax. The first part is much briefer than the second, and there are no connecting words that signal anything but restatement. Think of the briefer phrase as a dictionary entry, and the longer phrase as its definition.

    The part of this sentence after the semicolon describes in some detail the public's attitude about government rules for business. As you can see, the attitude described is self-contradictory in that the same person typically has conflicting expectations when it comes to government rules for business. (Notice the signpost word "yet," which signals the contradiction.) Start with the second blank, looking for a word that accurately captures the public attitude. Choices (A), (B), and (D) work best; *divided, confused,* and *ambiguous* all convey the idea that the public wants two things that don't go together very well. For the first blank, you want a word that describes what the second part of the sentence also describes. Choice (D) appears to be the best fit; the sentence as a whole has to do with "business regulation"; that is, the rules laid down by government for business. Two other choices, (A) and (C), work all right for the first blank. But "ethics" is a bit too specific, while "practices" is a bit too vague. (Besides, you already eliminated choice (C) based on the second missing word.)

As you just saw, the semicolon without a connector word might provide a wordless warning of a restatement. Also look for these key words and phrases, which often mark restatements:

> *in fact*
> *in other words*
> *in short*
> *namely*
> *that is*

Three of these markers could easily be inserted into the sentence about business regulation to strengthen the restatement signal. Try reading the sentence again using each marker in turn, and you'll find out which three work.

## Cause and Effect

In a sentence fitting this pattern, one part describes something that causes, produces, or influences what's described in another part. Here's an example:

13. When waging election campaigns against challengers, most incumbent politicians have significant _____ as a result of the power and recognition that are typically part and parcel of holding public office.

   (A) propensities

   (B) expenses

   (C) contributions

   (D) budgets

   (E) advantages

   **The correct answer is (E).** In this sentence, the operative phrase is *as a result*. What precedes this phrase describes the effect or result of the *power and recognition* that goes with holding an official position in the government. Put another way, the power and recognition of public office causes or influences what the earlier part of the sentence intends to describe. Logically, what effects would be caused by the power and recognition of pubic office? One natural effect would be to make it easier to run for reelection, if for no other reason than because the current officeholder is already well known. So, *advantages* is an apt expression of this natural effect. The most tempting wrong answer choices are probably choices (C) and (D). However, significant *contributions* or *budgets* wouldn't necessarily be logical or natural effects of having power and recognition. What's more, the phrase "have . . . contributions" is an awkward idiom. (A more effective and clearer phrase is "receive contributions.") So choice (C) cannot be the best one.

To understand the preceding sentence, it helps to know that an "incumbent politician" is one who is already in office. But even if you don't know what *incumbent* means, you can make an educated guess based on the sentence as a whole. "Incumbent politicians" are depicted here as running against "challengers," and a "challenger" is typically a person who goes up against a current title holder. So it would be a good guess that an incumbent candidate is the current office holder.

In the above example, the signpost "as a result" marked the cause-and-effect connection. Here are some other signposts that mark this kind of connection:

| | |
|---|---|
| *because* | *produces* |
| *hence* | *results in* |
| *consequently* | *since* |
| *due to* | *therefore* |
| *leads to* | *thus* |

You can redraft the sentence about incumbent candidates using any of these signposts in place of "as a result." If you try it, you'll see that you can simply plug in some as substitutes for "as a result"; to use others, though, you'd also need to restructure the sentence.

# COMPLEX TEXT COMPLETIONS (NEW)

For the remainder of this chapter, you'll examine what the test designers call the "Complex Text Completion" format. This is a new question type for the GRE; expect to encounter one on your GRE Verbal Reasoning section (although you might not see any). Just to review, here are the key features of Complex Text Completions:

- The passage contains either *two or three blanks*.
- For each blank, you select the best of at least *three* choices.
- The passage might be a single sentence, although it will probably be a paragraph consisting of two or more sentences.

Like conventional Sentence Completions, Complex Text Completions are designed to gauge:

- Your ability to understand the intended meaning of a sentence
- Your ability to distinguish between a sentence that makes sense and one that lacks sense
- Your facility with the kinds of English-language idioms and rhetorical phrases that are commonly used in graduate-level verbal expression
- Your vocabulary

In addition, Complex Text Completions involving a paragraph of two or more sentences emphasize interrelationships among the paragraph's ideas.

Although three-blank Complex Text Completions offer yet another way to respond incorrectly, neither the two-blank nor three-blank variety is inherently more difficult than the other. To boost difficulty level, the test-makers incorporate advanced vocabulary and idioms, as well as longer passages with more rhetorical twists and turns.

# THE 4-STEP PLAN (COMPLEX TEXT COMPLETIONS)

Your approach to GRE Complex Text Completions should be similar to your plan for Sentence Completions. However, in the following step-by-step plan, notice that you don't formulate your own completion (step 2 for Sentence Completions) before weighing the answer choices. That's because Complex Text Completions are usually too lengthy and complex for this strategy.

## Step 1: Read the Passage in Its Entirety

Pay particular attention to key words that indicate a description, point of view, conclusion, comparison, or contrast.

## Step 2: Test Each Answer Choice for the First Blank

Eliminate choices that you're sure are wrong.

**NOTE**

For a GRE Complex Text Completion, you receive credit for a correct answer *only* if you fill in all blanks correctly. There's no such thing as partial credit for this question type.

## Step 3: Test Each Answer Choice for the Second Blank

Eliminate choices that you're sure are wrong. Repeat for the third blank as needed.

## Step 4: Compare Remaining Choices by Rereading the Passage

Compare the remaining choices for all blanks by reading the entire passage again with each combination. Pay close attention to whether each word or phrase is used properly and appropriately in context. If you're still undecided, take your best guess among the viable choices.

## Applying the 4-Step Plan

Now let's apply this 4-step plan to a GRE-style Complex Text Completion. This example is about as brief as any you'd see on the GRE.

14. Friends of the theater have long decried the (i)_____ of big-city drama critics, whose reviews can determine the (ii)_____ a play in a single night.

| (i) |
| --- |
| callous indifference |
| unfettered sway |
| incisive judgment |

| (ii) |
| --- |
| popularity of |
| outcome of |
| audience for |

**Step 1:** To handle this Complex Text Completion, it helps to know that the word *decry* means "to discredit or criticize." If you're completely unfamiliar with the word, you can at least guess at its definition. The root *cry* provides a good clue that *decry* is a negatively charged word. As a whole, then, the sentence is describing how a play reviewer's action can impact a play in a way that evokes a critical response from the theatrical community.

**Step 2:** Let's weigh the choices for blank (i). It wouldn't make much sense for "friends of the theater" to discredit or criticize a drama critic's "incisive judgment." (The word *incisive* in this context means "keen or sharp.") So you can at least eliminate this choice, without even considering blank (ii). But the other two choices both make sense as a characteristic of big-city drama critics that friends of the theater might not think highly of. (Of course, it helps to know that *unfettered sway* means "unconstrained influence or power.") So you'll need to consider blank (ii) to determine the best choice for blank (i).

**Step 3:** Now let's look at the choices for blank (ii). The phrase *outcome of* doesn't make much sense in context. It's the playwright, not the critic, that determines the *outcome* of a play. But the other two choices both seem to make sense: A drama critic's review can determine a play's *popularity* and its *audience*. Notice that regardless of which phrase you use in the second blank, the second part of the sentence provides a better description of *unfettered sway* than *callous indifference*. In other words, the sentence as a whole is more consistent and cohesive with the former phrase than with the latter.

**Step 4:** You need to decide between *popularity of* and *audience for.* To say that a critic's review determines a play's "audience," isn't that really saying that it has a great impact on the size of the audience—that is, the play's "popularity"? It's for this reason that *popularity of* is the better completion for blank (ii); it makes for a clearer, more effective sentence. **The correct answer is unfettered sway for blank (i) and popularity of for blank (ii).**

Remember: If you had selected any other choice for either blank, you'd have received no credit whatsoever for this question. Also, notice the subtle distinction between the best choice and the runner-up for blank (ii).

Now let's look at some paragraph-length (two to five sentences) Complex Text Completions, which focus chiefly on idiomatic phrases and sentence transitions. The use of longer passages allows the test designers to gauge your ability to form cohesive paragraphs that make sense as a whole and convey the overall idea articulately and properly.

The following example is a bit easier than average for a paragraph-length Complex Text Completion.

15. Low-context cultures, such as those of the United States, England, and Germany, spell things out verbally and rely on a rather (i)_____ interpretation of the spoken word. There tends to be no gap between what is said and what is meant. (ii)_____, high-context cultures, including those of Spain, France, Mexico, and Japan, communicate more by nuance and implication, relying less on actual words than on gestures and situations. In these cultures, (iii)_____ often what is most important.

|     **(i)**     |
| literal ✳ |
| straightforward |
| glib |
|     **(ii)**     |
| Generally speaking |
| By the same token |
| On the other hand |
|     **(iii)**     |
| what remains unsaid is |
| what words actually mean is |
| emphasis and tone are |

*[handwritten annotations: "not tone + emphasis", "both don't use words"]*

Let's apply our 4-step approach to this paragraph-length Complex Text Completion.

**Step 1:** The first two sentences discuss how low-context cultures communicate; the final two sentences talk about communication in high-context cultures. Based on the passage's descriptions, there's clearly a marked difference between the two. In fact, this seems to be the paragraph's main thrust. (Notice the phrases "more by" and "less on" in the third sentence.)

**Step 2:** Let's start with the blank (ii), which connects the description of a low-context culture with the discussion of high-context cultures. Since the text strongly suggests a contrast, a word like "however" would lead nicely from one to the other. The phrase *On the other hand* fits perfectly. (The phrase *By the same token* signals similarity, not contrast. The phrase *Generally speaking* signals an elaboration or explanation just ahead. Neither phrase is at all appropriate in context.)

**Step 3:** Notice that the first and second sentences both provide a description of whatever should fill in blank (i). The second sentence in particular provides a good definition of the word *literally*. (The word *glib* means "fluent or articulate"—not a good fit for the description in the first two sentences.) On to blank (iii). The final sentence appears to be a restatement or interpretation of the idea in the preceding sentence—that gestures and implication are more important than actual words. The phrase *what remains unsaid* is an artful characterization of what's gestured or implied but not put into actual words, so it's a perfect fit for blank (iii). The other two phrases confuse the idea; neither one makes the appropriate point.

**Step 4:** We already determined the best choice for each blank, so we can skip step 4. **The correct answer is literal for blank (i), On the other hand for blank (ii), and what remains unsaid is for blank (iii).**

Now try applying the 4 steps to another example. This one contains only two blanks, but that doesn't mean it's easier than the previous example.

16. The medical profession has traditionally scoffed at the claims of alternative medicine. When (i)_____ its successes is trotted out, doctors routinely and dismissively put it down to the placebo effect. (ii)_____, perhaps one of the reasons that alternative medicine is booming today is precisely because in an era in which medical procedures and antibiotics are prescribed at the drop of a hat while alternative treatments are rarely even suggested, people have become less trusting of medical science.

|  (i)  |
| --- |
| a compelling reason for |
| anecdotal evidence of |
| a cogent theory about |

|  (ii)  |
| --- |
| Ironically |
| As a result |
| On the other hand |

Let's apply the 4 steps to this example:

**Step 1:** Here's the overall gist of the passage: Traditional medical practitioners do not take alternative treatments seriously and do not recommend them to patients—and *this fact might be the reason* that patients have grown suspicious of traditional medicine and are therefore seeking alternatives.

**Step 2:** Let's start with blank (i), which you can fill in based on the first two sentences. Notice that the pronoun "it" refers to whatever goes in the blank. What might doctors dismiss as the result of the placebo effect? Well, probably the results of certain scientific experiments—in other words, scientific evidence, not a theory or a reason. Accordingly, the phrase *anecdotal evidence of* is the only one of the three that makes logical sense in grammatical context of the first two sentences.

**Step 3:** Now let's tackle blank (ii), which requires you to assimilate the entire passage. Recall the gist of the passage from step 1. Since the passage doesn't set up any sort of contrast in ideas, the phrase *On the other hand* makes no sense for blank (ii). You can at least eliminate one of the three choices. But neither of the others are easy to eliminate at first glance.

**Step 4:** Notice that you could insert nothing in blank (ii) and still understand how the idea preceding it connects to what follows it—the connection is cause and effect. So does that mean that the phrase "As a result," which signals that an effect lies just ahead, is the best choice for blank (ii)? Not necessarily. If you look at the entire sentence, you would have *As a result* precede "perhaps the reason that," which would be redundant. So by process of elimination, the best choice for blank (ii) appears to be *Ironically*. And if you think about it, the word aptly characterizes the cause-and-effect relationship described in the passage. **The correct answer is anecdotal evidence of for blank (i) and Ironically for blank (ii).**

## FIND THE LOGICAL CONNECTIONS

As you probably figured out based on the preceding examples, the blanks in GRE paragraphs often call for "connectors"—words and phrases that link ideas together. To fill in these blanks, you must choose the word or phrase that provides the most natural and sensible flow of ideas.

### Tips for Spotting Connections Between Ideas in the Text

A connecting word or phrase should steer the reader in the right direction by signaling a conclusion, an opposing or contradictory idea, or an elaboration. It's like a good directional sign that shows which way the next sentence is headed. Earlier in the chapter, we examined the connectors used to link two parts of the same sentence. Here, we'll review the connectors most often used as the "glue" between sentences to create a cohesive, rhetorically effective paragraph:

- Similarity
- Contrast
- Continuation (description, definition, or illustration)
- Cause and effect
- Premise and conclusion
- Rhetorical emphasis

The following examples focus just on appropriate connecting words and phrases; wrong answer choices are omitted. Keep in mind that a Complex Text Completion might focus on other issues as well—and will, of course, require a choice from among three options for each blank.

## SIMILARITY, THEN CAUSE AND EFFECT

**17.** When El Niño hit, vast schools of small fish, such as anchovies and sardines, sought cooler temperatures at farther depths of the Pacific than the levels where they are usually found. (i)_____ their response protected these fish from the unseasonable weather conditions, their predators were unable to reach them at these new, greater depths. (ii)_____, the predators suddenly lost their regular food supply.

The second sentence suggests a similarity between two results of the fishes' response to El Niño: It protected them from bad weather and it protected them from predators. Either of the following would be appropriate in blank (i) to signal the similarity:

*While*
*At the same time that*

The final sentence indicates what is probably a result of the event described in the preceding sentence. In other words, what precedes blank (ii) caused what follows it. Any of these would be appropriate in blank (ii):

*As a result*
*Consequently*
*Not surprisingly*

## CONTINUATION, THEN SIMILARITY

**18.** When El Niño hit, aquatic mammals were affected especially hard. (i)_____, along one Peruvian beach, the Punta San Juan, a whole season's pup production of fur seals and sea lions died, as well as thousands of juveniles and breeding adults. By May 13, 1998, only 15 fur seals were counted, when there are usually hundreds; (ii)_____, only 1,500 sea lions were found in an area that usually houses 8,000.

The second sentence provides an example of the phenomenon described in the first sentence. Either of the following would fit blank (i):

*For example*
*For instance*

The phrase after blank (ii) describes a situation similar to the one described before the blank. Any of the following would work in blank (ii):

*similarly*
*by the same token*
*also*

## CONTRAST, THEN RHETORICAL EMPHASIS

**19.** The United States, which was founded mainly by people who had emigrated from northern Europe, had an essentially open-door immigration policy for the first 100 years of its existence. (i)_____, starting in the 1880s and continuing through the 1920s, Congress passed a series of restrictive immigration laws ultimately leading to a quota system based on the number of individuals of each national origin reported in the 1989 census. (ii)_____, the door to freedom hadn't exactly been slammed shut, but it was now open only to the "right" sort of people.

What follows the blank is an idea that contradicts the idea expressed in the preceding sentence. Accordingly, the word in blank (i) should signal that a contrasting idea lies just ahead. Either of the following completions would work:

*however*
*but*

The final sentence seems to put a negative rhetorical spin on the events described in the previous sentence. Any of the following would work in blank (ii):

*Obviously*
*Clearly*
*Apparently*

## CONTRAST AND CONCLUSION

**20.** The polar ice cap's high-pressure system controls the cold, relatively stable climate of Mount Vinson, the highest peak in Antarctica. _____ Vinson is located in an arctic climate, snowstorms and terrific wind gusts are always possible.

The first sentence tells us that Mount Vinson's climate is stable; the second sentence provides opposing, contrary information. A connector is needed to signal that opposing ideas are being presented. Either of the following phrases provide the appropriate connection and fits the paragraph's grammatical construction:

*However, since*
*Yet, because*

**RHETORICAL EMPHASIS, THEN CONTRAST**

**21.** (i)_____, the most significant revolution in modern art was the invention of the purely abstract painting in the 1930s. Pablo Picasso is generally regarded as the quintessential modern artist. (ii)_____, in the course of Picasso's long and varied career, he never painted any significant abstract picture.

The first blank could be left empty without sacrificing the flow of ideas in the paragraph. All that is appropriate for blank (i) is some rhetorical flourish. Any of the following would serve the purpose:

*Without a doubt*
*Indisputably*
*Clearly*

The idea that follows the blank comes as a surprise considering the idea that precedes it. The fact that Picasso never made an abstract painting doesn't follow as a logical result; it's a surprising contradiction—not at all what we would reasonably expect. Any of the following would be appropriate in blank (ii) as a signal that an opposing idea is coming:

*Yet*
*Nevertheless*
*However*
*Surprisingly, however*
*Ironically*

# COMPLEX TEXT COMPLETION STRATEGIES

## Try to Understand the Sentence or Paragraph *as a Whole*

Pay special attention to rhetorical structure and to "signpost" words that show direction and logical flow.

## Don't Waste Time Trying to Make Sense of Answer Choices That Don't Work

If an answer doesn't make sense move on to the next choice.

## Always Consider Each and Every Answer Choice

The difference between the best and second-best answer can be subtle.

## Eliminate Any Choice That's Too Vague or Too Specific for the Passage as a Whole

Keep in mind that you might need to determine the best choice based on nuanced meanings.

## Don't Choose Any Answer Just Because It Contains a Difficult Word

By the same token, don't rule it out for this reason. If you don't know what a word means, try to guess based on the word's prefix or root, how the word "sounds," or even your gut instinct.

## Decide Between Viable Choices by Checking for Idiom, Usage, and Awkwardness in Context

The correct answer should not sound strange or forced in the context of the passage. Checking for good grammar can make the difference between picking the right choice and the wrong one.

## SUMMING IT UP

- The GRE Verbal Reasoning section contains two types of Sentence Completions: single-blank and dual-blank. You are required to complete the entire sentence by selecting the best among five choices.

- Your Verbal Reasoning section might also contain a more Complex Text Completion test item, a brief passage with either two or three blanks. Your job is to select the best among at least three choices for each blank. You're required to complete each blank independently of the other(s), and you must complete all blanks correctly to receive credit for a correct response.

- Sentence and Complex Text Completions test your ability to understand the intended meaning of a sentence, your ability to distinguish between a sentence that makes sense and one that lacks sense, your ability to recognize and distinguish between proper and improper word usage and idiom, your ability to recognize and distinguish between clear and unclear written expression, and your vocabulary.

- The emphasis on vocabulary is not as strong with Sentence and Complex Text Completions as with Analogies and Antonyms.

- Follow and review the 5 basic steps for handling GRE Sentence Completions and the 4 basic steps for handling GRE Complex Text Completions outlined in this chapter. Apply them to this book's Practice Tests; then review them again just before exam day.

# Reading Comprehension

## chapter 14

## OVERVIEW

- Interactive reading: The key to reading comprehension
- The 7-step plan
- Interactive reading strategies
- Question types
- GRE test designers' top 10 wrong-answer ploys
- Checklist for understanding GRE reading passages
- Checklist for answering GRE reading questions
- Summing it up

In this chapter, you'll focus initially on reading and understanding GRE Reading Comprehension passages. Specifically, you'll learn the following:

- Why it's important to read the passages "interactively"
- A step-by-step approach to reading and comprehending passages
- Techniques for reading the passages more effectively and efficiently

Later in the chapter, you'll shift your focus to the *questions* themselves. In particular, you'll learn how to recognize and handle all the question types that appear most frequently on the GRE. For each question type, you'll learn how the test-makers design wrong answer choices—and how to recognize them when you see them.

At the end of the chapter, you'll review key strategies and tips for success in GRE Reading Comprehension.

## INTERACTIVE READING: THE KEY TO READING COMPREHENSION

If you're like most GRE test-takers, you'll experience at least one of the following problems as you tackle the Reading Comprehension part of the GRE, at least to some degree:

- Your concentration is poor, perhaps because you're unfamiliar with or uninterested in the topic, or maybe because you feel test anxiety.
- You read slowly, so you have trouble finishing the Verbal Reasoning section within the time allotted.

- To answer each question, you need to search the passage again and again to find the information you need.

- You have trouble narrowing down the answer choices to one that's clearly the best.

Believe it or not, all of these problems stem from the same habit, which we'll call *passive reading*. This means that you simply read the passage from start to finish, giving equal time and attention to every sentence, without thought as to what particular information might be key in answering the questions. You might call this approach the "osmosis strategy," since you're hoping to absorb what you need to know by allowing your eyes to gaze at the words as you read.

The likely result of this habit, however, is that you might remember some scattered facts and ideas that help you respond correctly to some questions. But the passive reading habit won't take you far when it comes to answering questions that measure your ability to *understand* the ideas in the passage rather than to simply *recall* information. Understanding a passage well enough to answer all the questions requires a highly active frame of mind in which you constantly interact with the text as you read, asking yourself these three key questions:

- What is the passage's central idea (or "thesis") and the author's overall concern or purpose?

- How does each part of the passage relate to the main idea and author's overall purpose?

- What is the author's line of reasoning, or so-called "train of thought?"

Interactive reading is the key to handling GRE Reading Comprehension—and that's what this lesson is primarily about.

## THE 7-STEP PLAN

Let's apply these principles with a step-by-step approach. We'll use the following passage, which is about 170 words long—typical of some of the shorter reading passages you'll encounter on the actual GRE. We're also going to let you peek at the first question stem (not the answer choices, just the question itself). You'll find out why shortly.

**Passage 1**

Line    Renowned photographer Cartier-Bresson has expressed his passion for portrait photography by characterizing it as "a duel without rules, a delicate rape." Such metaphors contrast sharply with Richard Avedon's conception of a sitting. While Cartier-Bresson reveals himself as an

(5)    interloper and opportunist, Avedon confesses, perhaps uncomfortably, to a role as diagnostician and (by implication) psychic healer. Both photographers, however, agree that the fundamental dynamic in this process lies squarely in the hands of the artist.

     A quite-different paradigm has its roots not in confrontation or con-

(10)    sultation but in active collaboration between the artist and sitter. In William Hazlitt's essay entitled "On Sitting for One's Picture" (1823), Hazlitt described a "bond of connection" between painter and sitter that

is most like the relationship between two lovers. Hazlitt fleshes out his thesis by recalling the career of Sir Joshua Reynolds. According to *(15)* Hazlitt, Reynolds's sitters were meant to enjoy an atmosphere that was both comfortable for them and conducive to the enterprise of the portrait painter, who was simultaneously their host and their contractual employee.

1. The quote from Cartier-Bresson (line 2–3) is used by the author to

    **(A)** ——-

    **(B)** ——-

    **(C)** ——-

    **(D)** ——-

    **(E)** ——-

First, let's focus on the interactive reading process, which boils down to the following 7 steps:

## Step 1: Read the First Question and Answer Choices *Before* Reading the Passage

Try to anticipate what the passage is about and the sort of information you should be looking for to answer the first question.

## Step 2: Read the Passage with a Possible Thesis in Mind

Begin reading the passage, actively thinking about a possible thesis (central idea) and how the author attempts to support that thesis. Keep an eye out for information useful in answering the first question.

## Step 3: Choose a Tentative Answer

When you think you've learned enough to take a stab at the first question, choose a *tentative* answer. You probably won't have to read very far to take at least a reasoned guess at the first question. But don't confirm your selection yet.

## Step 4: Read the Remainder of the Passage, Formulating an Outline as You Go

As you read, try to (1) separate main ideas from supporting ideas and examples; (2) determine the basic structure of the passage (e.g., chronology of events; classification of ideas or things; comparison between two or more ideas, events, or things); and (3) determine the author's opinion or position on the subject. Make notes on your scratch paper as needed to see the "flow" of the passage and to keep the passage's details straight in your mind.

## Step 5: Sum Up the Passage and Formulate a Brief Thesis Statement

Take a few seconds to review your outline, then express the author's main point in your own words, keeping it to one sentence. Jot it down on your scratch paper. Your thesis statement should reflect the author's opinion or position (e.g., critical, supportive, neutral) toward the ideas presented in the passage.

### Step 6: Confirm Your Selection for the First Question

Eliminate any answer choice that is inconsistent with your thesis statement, that doesn't respond to the question, or that doesn't make sense to you.

### Step 7: Move On to the Remaining Questions

Make sure you consider all five answer choices for each question.

Now let's walk through Passage 1, applying this 7-step approach.

**Step 1:** The first question tells you a great deal about what you might expect in the passage. In all likelihood, it will be primarily about the portraiture experience, and the author will probably provide different viewpoints and insights on this experience, from the perspective of particular artists.

**Step 2:** The first few sentences reinforce your initial prediction about the passage's content. Based on these sentences, it appears that the author is indeed comparing and contrasting different views of the portraiture experience. At this point, you don't know whether the rest of the passage will involve the views of any artist other than Cartier-Bresson and Richard Avedon, nor do you know whether the author has any opinion on the subject. Still, be on the lookout for answers to these unknowns during step 4.

**Step 3:** Try answering Question 1 based on what you've read so far. To do so, of course, you'll need to read the answer choices, so here they are, along with the question stem again:

1. The quote from Cartier-Bresson (line 2–3) is used by the author to
   - **(A)** call into question Cartier-Bresson's motives during portraiture encounters
   - **(B)** show that perspectives of the portraiture encounter vary widely among artists
   - **(C)** support the claim that portrait sittings are collaborative encounters
   - **(D)** show that portraiture encounters are more comfortable for artists than for sitters
   - **(E)** distinguish sitting for a photographic portrait from sitting for a painted portrait

   The author points out that Cartier-Bresson's conception is quite different from that of Avedon. Choice (A) seems pretty far-fetched. Answer choices (B) and (E) appear to be viable choices, at least based on the first few sentences. But whether the author's purpose in quoting Cartier-Bresson is better reflected by choice (B) or choice (E) remains to be seen. You'll have to read on to find out. In any event, you can probably eliminate choices (C) and (D), since neither one seems consistent with the Cartier-Bresson quotation. So it's our guess that the correct answer is either choice (B) or choice (E). But don't confirm a selection yet; go to step 4.

**Step 4:** Your goal in step 4 is to formulate an informal outline of the passage as you read from start to finish. You might want to jot down some key words and phrases to help you see how the ideas flow and to keep the four individuals discussed in the passage straight in your mind. Here's a good outline of the passage:

> *Paragraph 1*
>   *Contrast:*
>     *— CB: confrontation (rape)*
>     *— Avedon: diagnosis (consultation)*
>     *— BUT agree artist is key*
> *Paragraph 2*
>   *3rd view: Hazlitt (writer)*
>     *— collaboration (like lovers)*
>     *— e.g. Reynolds*

**TIP**

Make outlines and summaries as brief as possible. Don't write complete sentences; just jot down key words.

**Step 5:** Now let's sum up the passage based on the outline you formulated in step 4. It's a good idea to jot it down. Notice that the "thesis" is neutral; the author does not side with any viewpoint presented in the passage.

> *Thesis: Portraiture is a social experience, but artists disagree about their role in it.*

**Step 6:** Believe it or not, you've already done most of the work you need to do to answer questions about this passage. Just for the record, though, let's return to question 1. Recall that we'd guessed tentatively that the correct answer is either choice (B) or (E). Read the five choices again, and you'll see that we were correct. Choice (B) provides the better answer to the question than choice (E), doesn't it? Cartier-Bresson's conception, as expressed in the highlighted sentence, is one of three the author describes in the passage, which is a survey of varying perspectives on the portraiture encounter. Notice also that choice (B) is consistent with our thesis statement. **The correct answer is (B).**

**Step 7:** Here are two more questions based on Passage 1. As you read the analysis of both questions, notice the qualitative difference (from best to worst) among the answer choices.

2. Based on the information in the passage, it can be inferred that the portraiture experience as viewed by Avedon can be characterized as

(A) a collaboration

(B) a mutual accommodation

(C) a confrontation

(D) an uncomfortable encounter

(E) a consultation

**The correct answer is (E).** If you wrote the outline on the previous page, you'll see that you already answered this question. But for the record, let's analyze the question and the answer choices. In the first sentence of the second paragraph, the author distinguishes a "quite-different paradigm" (that is, the case of Reynolds) from the conceptions of Cartier-Bresson and Avedon in that the Reynolds paradigm "has its roots not in confrontation or consultation but in active collaboration between artist and sitter." The first paragraph makes clear that Cartier-Bresson conceives the encounter as "confrontational"; thus, you can *reasonably infer* that the author characterizes an Avedon sitting as a "consultation."

Choices (C) and (D) are the worst among the five choices. Choice (C) confuses the passage's information. The quotation in the first paragraph makes it clear that Cartier-Bresson (not Avedon) conceives the encounter as "confrontational." Choice (D) also confuses the passage's information. According to the passage, Avedon confesses "uncomfortably" to his role as diagnostician and psychic healer. It does not necessarily follow, however, that Avedon finds his encounters with his sitters to be uncomfortable.

Choice (B) is a good choice. Although the term "mutual accommodation," which does not appear in the passage, is not altogether inconsistent with Avedon's view, the term suggests a relationship in which artist and painter allow for the other's needs or desires. Such a description is closer to Hazlitt's analogy of two lovers than to Avedon's view of the artist as diagnostician and psychic healer. Choice (A) has merit, yet it is not as good a response as choice (B) or (E). Admittedly, the idea of "a collaboration" is not in strong opposition to the idea of "a consultation." However, the author explicitly ascribes this characterization to the Reynolds paradigm, not to Avedon's view. Thus, choice (A) confuses the passage's information.

Now, let's try a third question based on Passage 1:

3. Which of the following best expresses the passage's central idea?

(A) The success of a portrait depends largely on the relationship between artist and subject.

(B) Portraits often provide special insight into the artist's social relationships.

(C) The social aspect of portraiture sitting plays an important part in the sitting's outcome.

(D) Photographers and painters differ in their views regarding their role in portrait photography.

(E) The paintings of Reynolds provide a record of his success in achieving a social bond with his sitters.

**The correct answer is (C).** This is a tough question. Your thesis statement doesn't quite match any of the choices. Choice (A) has merit. In fact, except for choice (C), choice (A) would be the best choice because it embraces the passage as a whole and properly focuses on the author's primary concern with exploring the relationship between the artist and the sitter. However, the passage does not discuss how or whether this relationship results in a "successful" portrait; thus, choice (A) distorts the passage's information.

Choice (D) has merit in that the author does claim that the Reynolds paradigm (described in the second paragraph) is "quite different" from the two paradigms that the first paragraph discusses. The latter does indeed involve a painter (Reynolds) whereas the other two paradigms involve photographers (Cartier-Bresson and Avedon). However, the author does not generalize from this fact that a portrait artist's approach or view depends on whether the artist is a painter or a photographer. Thus, choice (D) is a bit off focus and calls for an unwarranted generalization. Choices (B) and (E) are the worst among the five choices. Choice (B) distorts the information in the passage and departs from the topic. Although the passage does support the notion that a portrait might reveal something about the relationship between the artist and the sitter, the author neither states nor implies that a portrait reveals anything about the artist's other relationships. Moreover, nowhere in the passage does the author compare portraiture with other art forms.

Choice (E) is too narrow and refers to information not mentioned in the passage. The passage is not just about Reynolds, but about the portraiture encounter in general. Also, the author does not comment on Reynolds's "success" or how his relationship with his sitters might have contributed to his success. The author seems concerned with emphasizing that a portrait sitting is a social encounter, not just an artistic exercise, and that artists consider their relationship with their sitters to be somehow significant.

# INTERACTIVE READING STRATEGIES

Up to this point in the lesson, we've stressed that in reading a GRE passage, you should formulate an outline that reveals its basic structure and how its ideas flow from one to the next. In this section, we'll focus more closely on this step, which lies at the heart of handling GRE Reading Comprehension questions.

Think of any GRE reading passage as a structure of ideas. Each passage is designed to convey a number of ideas that are connected in some way. If you understand these ideas *and* the connections between them, then you truly understand the passage as a whole. Focusing on structure helps you in several ways:

## It Makes It Easy to See the "Big Picture"

It is important to see what the passage is about as a whole.

## It Tells You the Purpose of the Supporting Details

Understanding the function of supporting details will help you become a better close reader.

## The Logical Structure Organizes All the Information in the Passage

This makes it easy to locate any detail to which a particular question might refer.

## The Structure Explains How the Author's Main Points Are Related to One Another

Structure is the backbone of the author's passage. The interrelation of the author's ideas becomes clear the moment you understand the structure of the passage.

## Focus on the Passage's Logical Structure

Although GRE passages don't always have clear-cut, logical structures, you'll almost always detect a structure of some kind. Here's a list of the most common types of logical structures found in GRE passages. Either alone or in combination, these structures underlie most of the passages you'll encounter on the exam:

- **Point and example:** The author sets forth a theory or idea, which he or she illustrates with two or more examples or supports with two or more arguments.

- **Point-and-counterpoint:** The passage presents two or more alternative theories, each of which seek to explain a certain phenomenon (the passage might also argue for one theory over another).

- **Theory and critique:** A commonly held theory, notion, or belief is presented, then the author points out its flaws.

- **Pro vs. con:** The passage presents arguments for both sides of a single issue or presents the benefits and drawbacks of a certain policy or course of action.

- **Compare-and-contrast:** The passage points out similarities and differences between two or more events, ideas, phenomena, or people.

- **Historical cause and effect:** The passage is a cause-and-effect sequence showing how one event led to another (presented either in chronological order or with later events described before earlier ones).

- **Classification:** The passage identifies and distinguishes between two or more basic types, categories, or classes of a phenomenon, and then branches out to subclasses. (This structure is most common in passages involving the natural sciences.)

**TIP**

Don't expect paragraph breaks to help you parse a passage's structure. A passage with a complex structure might contain only one paragraph. Use paragraph breaks as structural clues, but don't rely on them.

Now let's look at some examples. First, here's Passage 1 (about portraiture) again. This time, key portions are underlined to help you see its structure. Notice how nicely it fits into the compare-and-contrast structural pattern:

*Line*  Renowned photographer <u>Cartier-Bresson</u> has expressed his passion for portrait photography by characterizing it as "a duel without rules, a delicate rape." Such <u>metaphors contrast sharply with Richard Avedon's conception</u> of a sitting. While Cartier-Bresson reveals himself as an
*(5)*  interloper and opportunist, Avedon confesses, perhaps uncomfortably, to a role as diagnostician and (by implication) psychic healer. <u>Both photographers, however, agree</u> that the fundamental dynamic in this process lies squarely in the hands of the artist.
  <u>A quite-different paradigm</u> has its roots not in confrontation or con-
*(10)*  sultation but in active <u>collaboration</u> between the artist and sitter. In

William Hazlitt's essay entitled "On Sitting for One's Picture" (1823), Hazlitt described a "bond of connection" between painter and sitter that is most like the relationship between two lovers. Hazlitt fleshes out his thesis by recalling the career of Sir Joshua Reynolds. According to

(15) Hazlitt, Reynolds's sitters were meant to enjoy an atmosphere that was both comfortable for them and conducive to the enterprise of the portrait painter, who was simultaneously their host and their contractual employee.

Here's a brief passage that combines the theory-and-critique and point-and-counterpoint structures. Again, some key phrases are underlined to help reveal the structure.

Line   In the arts, we are tempted to think that true originality must surely reside, so-called "new" ideas almost always embrace, apply, or synthesize what came earlier. For example, most "modern" visual designs, forms, and elements are based on certain well-established aesthetic

(5)   ideals—such as symmetry, balance, and harmony. Admittedly, modern art works often eschew these principles in favor of true originality. Yet, the appeal of such works lies primarily in their novelty and brashness. Once the ephemeral novelty or shock dissipates, these works quickly lose their appeal because they violate firmly established artistic ideals.

(10)   Or consider rock-and-roll music, which upon first listen might seem to bear no resemblance to classical music traditions. In fact, both genres rely on the same 12-note scale, the same notions of what harmonies are pleasing to the ear, the same forms, the same rhythmic meters, and even many of the same melodies.

Next, take a look at a brief passage that illustrates a pro-vs.-con structure. (Certain key phrases are underlined to help reveal the structure.)

Line   Twentieth-century technological innovation has enhanced the overall standard of living and comfort level of developed nations. The advent of steel production and assembly-line manufacturing created countless jobs, stimulated economic growth, and supplied a plethora of innovative

(5)   conveniences. More recently, computers have helped free up our time by performing repetitive tasks; have aided in the design of safer and more attractive bridges, buildings, and vehicles; and have made possible universal access to information. Of course, such progress has not come without costs. One harmful byproduct of industrial progress is environ-

(10)   mental pollution, and its threat to public health. Another is the alienation of assembly-line workers from their work. And, the Internet breeds information overload and steals our time and attention away from family, community, and coworkers.

Here's a passage excerpt that incorporates the historical cause-and-effect structure into a theory-and-critique structure. (The underlined phrases help show the structure.)

> *Line*    History and art appreciation courses that study the Middle Ages tend to
> focus on the artistic achievements of particular artists such as Fra
> Angelico, a Benedictine monk of that period. <u>However</u>, Western civili-
> zation owes its very existence <u>not to</u> a few famous painters <u>but rather to</u>
> *(5)*    a group of Benedictine nuns of that period. <u>Just prior to and during the</u>
> <u>decline of the Roman Empire,</u> many women fled to join Benedictine
> monasteries, bringing with them substantial dowries which they used to
> acquire artifacts, art works, and manuscripts. <u>As a result</u>, their monas-
> teries became centers for the preservation of Western culture and
> *(10)*    knowledge which would otherwise have been lost forever with the fall of
> the Roman Empire.

Finally, take a look at a brief classification passage, which incorporates a compare-and-contrast structure. (Notice the four classes, having certain characteristics that are compared and contrasted.)

> *Line*    <u>The lava of quiet volcanoes</u> is very liquid, and so it can escape through
> the volcano's crater and through cracks in its sides before too much
> pressure builds up inside. <u>In contrast, the lava of a Vulcanian volcano</u> is
> extremely viscous. Upon contact with the air, it immediately solidifies,
> *(5)*    forming a crust on the crater's surface. When enough pressure builds up
> beneath the crust of a Vulcanian volcano, it cracks open and the volcano
> spews ash and clouds of gas through the crack into the air above. <u>Of the</u>
> <u>two other types of volcanoes, Pelean and Strombolian, the Pelean is</u>
> <u>better known</u> because it is the most explosive type of volcano. In a
> *(10)*    Palean volcano, molten lava, or magma, solidifies beneath the surface,
> forming a plug. Then, once enough gas pressure builds up, the volcano
> bursts open, hurtling huge chunks of solid magma, along with ash and
> gas, through the air.

## Look for Structural Clues

Structural clues or "triggers" provide clues about the structure and organization of the passage and the direction in which the discussion is flowing. The lists below contain common trigger words and phrases. Watch for trigger words as you read the passage. They'll help you see the passage's structure and follow the author's train of thought.

These words precede an item in a list (e.g., examples, classes, reasons, or character-istics):

> *first, second (etc.)*
> *in addition, also, another*

These words signal that the author is contrasting two phenomena:

> *alternatively, by contrast, however, on the other hand, rather than, while, yet*

These words signal a logical conclusion based upon preceding material:

*consequently, in conclusion, then, thus, therefore, as a result, accordingly*

These words signal that the author is comparing (identifying similarities between) two phenomena:

*similarly, in the same way, analogous, parallel, likewise, just as, also, as*

These words signal evidence (factual information) used to support the author's argument:

*because, since, in light of*

These words signal an example of a phenomenon:

*for instance, e.g., such as, . . . is an illustration of*

## Make Brief Notes or an Outline

As you're reading, take notes to summarize paragraphs or to indicate the flow of the passage's discussion. Notes can also help you locate details more quickly and recap the passage more effectively. Keep your notes as brief as possible—two or three words are enough in most cases to indicate a particular idea or component of the passage. For complicated or dense passages, an outline is a good way to organize information and to keep particular details straight in your mind. The following situations are ideal for outlining:

- If the passage categorizes or classifies various things, use an outline to keep track of which items belong in each category.

- If the passage mentions numerous individual names (of authors, artists, political figures, etc.), use notes to link them according to influence, agreement or disagreement, and so forth.

- If the passage describes a sequence of events, use a time-line outline to keep track of the major features of each event in the sequence.

- In chronological passages, mark historical benchmarks and divisions—centuries, years, decades, or historical periods—that help to form the structure of the author's discussion.

Use arrows to physically connect words that signify ideas that connect together; for example:

→     To clarify cause and effect in the natural sciences or in the context of historical events

→     To indicate who was influenced by whom in literature, music, psychology, etc.

→     To connect names (philosophers, scientists, authors, etc.) with dates; events; other names, theories, or schools of thought; works; etc.

→     To indicate the chronological order in which historical events occurred

**NOTE**

It's not possible to circle or underline key words or to otherwise annotate passages on the GRE computer screen. Also, to read even relatively short passages, you'll need to scroll (using the mouse)—which makes good note-taking even more crucial.

## When You Should Preview the Passage

Many GRE prep books recommend that you "preview" the passage by reading the first (and perhaps last) sentence of each paragraph before reading it straight through from beginning to end. This technique supposedly provides clues about the scope of the passage, the author's thesis or major conclusions, and the structure and flow of the discussion. Although these techniques make sense in theory, in practice, they are rarely helpful on the GRE. Here's why:

- Once immersed in the passage itself, you'll quickly forget most (if not all) of what you learned from previewing.

- The technique calls for you to read the same material twice, which is hardly efficient.

- Previewing takes time that you might not be able to afford under testing conditions.

- Previewing involves rapid vertical scrolling, which adds to eyestrain.

- Although previewing may be helpful for some passages, for others this technique is of little or no help—and there's no way to know whether you're wasting your time until you've already wasted it.

The only time when it makes sense to preview is if you're running out of time. You can answer some questions quickly, especially the ones that refer to specific lines of the passage, by reading just that portion and maybe what immediately precedes and follows it. And a quick scan of the first and last few sentences of the passage might provide clues about the passage's central idea or primary purpose, so you can at least take educated guesses at some questions.

## QUESTION TYPES

In the rest of this chapter, you'll focus on answering the questions rather than on reading and understanding the passages. First, you'll learn how to recognize and handle all the basic question types (the first category will account for most of your GRE Reading Comprehension questions):

**Most Common Question Types:**

- Simple recall

- Recap

- Inference

**Less Common Question Types:**

- Restatement

- Purpose-of-detail

- Method or structure

- Application

- Vocabulary-in-context

**NOTE**

Don't expect to encounter simple passages or easy questions in this portion of the lesson; all examples here are at least moderately difficult.

For each question type, you'll learn how GRE test designers fashion wrong-answer choices—and you'll learn how to recognize these red herrings when you see them.

## Simple Recall Questions

For these questions, you must identify which answer choice provides information that appears in the passage and that the question asks about. The question stem might look something like this:

"Which of the following does the author mention as an example of _____ ?"

"According to the passage, _____ is caused by _____ ."

This is the most common question type and the easiest, because all you need to do is remember or find the appropriate information in the passage. Here's an example, along with a simple recall question based on it.

> *Line*    The arrival of a nonindigenous plant or animal species in a new location
> may be either intentional or unintentional. Rates of species movement
> driven by human transformations of natural environments or by human
> mobility—through commerce or tourism—dwarf natural rates by com-
> *(5)*    parison. While geographic distributions of species naturally expand or
> contract over tens to hundreds of years, species' ranges rarely expand
> thousands of miles or across physical barriers such as oceans or moun-
> tains.

4. According to the passage, the rate at which plant and animal species move naturally across land

   **(A)** might depend on the prevalence of animals that feed on the species

   **(B)** is often hindered by human interference

   **(C)** is often slower than the rate at which they move across water

   **(D)** is generally slower than human-assisted rates

   **(E)** varies according to the size of the species

   **The correct answer is (D).** Only the first paragraph talks about the rate of species movement, so that's where you'll find the answer to this question. In the second sentence, the author states that rates of species movement driven by human transformations and mobility "dwarf natural rates by comparison." In other words, natural rates are slower than human-assisted rates, just as choice (D) provides.

   Choice (A) might be true in the "real world," but the passage mentions nothing about predators, let alone about their affect on movement rates, so you can easily eliminate it. Choice (B) runs contrary to the passage's details, which suggest that the rate in which a species moves into a nonindigenous area is greater when humans are involved than when they are not. Choice (C) involves relevant information from the passage, but it distorts that information. The first paragraph's last sentence indicates that oceans and mountains are barriers that typically prevent species movement. But choice (C) implies that mountains pose a greater barrier than oceans. Nowhere in the passage does the author seek to compare rates across land with rates across water. Choice (E) is completely unsupported by the passage, which never mentions the size of a species in any context.

Notice the types of wrong-answer ploys built into the preceding question:

- Referencing irrelevant details from elsewhere in the passage
- Distorting what the passage says
- Bringing in information not found in the passage
- Providing a nonsensical response to the question

To complicate the simple recall technique, a question might ask you to identify an *exception* to what the passage provides (with a word such as "except" or "least" in uppercase letters):

> The author mentions all of the following as examples of _____, EXCEPT

> According to the passage, _____ could be caused by any of the following, EXCEPT

To handle this variation, eliminate all choices that the passage covers and that are relevant to the question, and you'll be left with one choice—the correct one.

Consider the following question, based on the passage below.

**ALERT!**

Don't be fooled: In a difficult simple recall question, one wrong-answer choice will typically be more tempting than the others because the passage will implicitly support it.

*Line*    A number of factors confound quantitative evaluation of the relative importance of various entry pathways of nonindigenous plants and animals. Time lags often occur between establishment of nonindigenous species and their detection, and tracing the pathway for a long-estab-
*(5)*    lished species is difficult, especially if geographical expansion has occurred rapidly. In addition, federal port inspection, although a major source of information on nonindigenous species pathways, especially for agricultural pests, provides data only about species entering via scrutinized routes. Finally, some comparisons between pathways defy quanti-
*(10)*    tative analysis; for example, which is more "important": the entry pathway of one very harmful species or one by which many but less harmful species enter the country?

5. Whether the entry pathway for a particular nonindigenous species can be determined is LEAST likely to depend upon which of the following?

**(A)** Whether the species is considered to be a pest
**(B)** Whether the species gains entry through a scrutinized route
**(C)** The size of the average member of the species
**(D)** The rate at which the species expands geographically
**(E)** How long the species has been established

**The correct answer is (C).** Nowhere in the passage does the author state or imply that the physical size of a species' members affects whether the entry pathway for the species can be determined.

Choices (B), (D), and (E) are mentioned explicitly in the passage as factors affecting how precisely the entry pathway(s) of a species can be determined. Although choice (A) is not explicitly supported by the passage, the author mentions that federal port inspection is "a major source of information on nonindigenous species pathways, especially for agricultural pests." Accordingly, whether a species is an agricultural pest might have some bearing upon whether or not its entry is detected (by port inspectors). Hence, the passage supports choice (A).

## Recap Questions

For recap questions, your job is to recognize the main idea (thesis) of the passage or particular paragraph as a whole, or the author's primary purpose or concern in the passage (or in a particular paragraph) as a whole. In other words, your job is to recap what the passage or paragraph is about generally. The question stem will look a lot like one of these:

"Which of the following best expresses the passage's central idea?"

"Among the following characterization, the passage is best viewed as . . ."

"The author's primary purpose in the passage is to . . ."

"In the passage, the author is primarily concerned with . . ."

To handle this question type, you'll need to recognize the passage's overall scope and its main emphasis. Most of the wrong-answer choices will fall into these categories:

- Too broad (embracing ideas outside the scope of the passage or paragraph)

- Too narrow (focusing on only one portion or aspect of the discussion)

- A distortion (an inaccurate reflection of the passage's ideas or the author's perspective on the topic)

Here's a brief passage, along with a moderately difficult recap question, that illustrates this question type and the kinds of wrong answers that usually come with it.

> *Line* A number of factors confound quantitative evaluation of the relative importance of various entry pathways of nonindigenous plant and animal species. First of all, time lags often occur between establishment of non-indigenous species and their detection, and tracing the pathway
> *(5)* for a long-established species is difficult, especially if geographical expansion has occurred rapidly. Nonindigenous weeds are usually detected only after having been in the country for thirty years or having spread to at least ten thousand acres. In addition, federal port inspection, although a major source of information on nonindigenous
> *(10)* species pathways, especially for agricultural pests, provides data only about species entering via scrutinized routes. Finally, some comparisons between pathways defy quantitative analysis; for example, which is more "important": the entry pathway of one very harmful species or one by which many but less harmful species enter the country?

**6.** The author's central concern in the passage is to

**(A)** identify the problems in assessing the relative significance of various entry pathways for nonindigenous species

**(B)** describe the events usually leading to the detection of a nonindigenous species

**(C)** discuss the role that time lags and geographic expansion of nonindigenous species play in species detection

**(D)** point out the inadequacy of the federal port inspection system in detecting the entry of nonindigenous species

**(E)** explain why it is difficult to trace the entry pathways for long-established nonindigenous species

**The correct answer is (A).** In the first sentence, the author claims that "[a] number of factors confound quantitative evaluation of the relative importance of various entry pathways." In the remainder of the passage, the author identifies three such problems: (1) the difficulty of early detection, (2) the inadequacy of port inspection, (3) the inherent subjectivity in determining the "importance" of a pathway. Choice (A) provides a good "recap" of what the passage as a whole accomplishes.

Choice (B) is too narrow. Although the author does mention that a species is usually not detected until it spreads to at least ten thousand acres, the author mentions this single "event" leading to detection as part of the broader point that the unlikelihood of early detection contributes to the problem of quantifying the relative importance of entry pathways. Choice (C) is a distortion. Although the author mentions these factors, they are not "discussed" in any detail, as choice (C) suggests. Also, the author's primary concern is not with identifying the factors affecting species detection but rather with identifying the problems in quantifying the relative importance of various entry pathways. Choice (D) is too narrow. The author is concerned with identifying other problems as well as in determining the relative importance of various entry pathways. Choice (E) is a distortion. Although the author asserts that it is difficult to trace an entry pathway once a species is well established, the author does not explain why this is so.

## Inference Questions

Inference questions test your ability to recognize what the author implies or infers but does not state explicitly. To make the inference, you'll need to see a logical connection between two bits of information in the passage (usually in two consecutive sentences) and draw a reasonable conclusion from them.

You'll likely encounter two types of inference questions on the GRE. One type focuses on the passage's ideas alone, and you need to infer a specific idea from what's stated. The question stem will probably contain some form of the word "infer," as in these examples:

"The author infers that . . ."

"It can be inferred from the passage that the reason for . . . is that . . ."

Note that a question might use either *suggest* or *imply* as a substitute for the word *infer*.

Here's a passage excerpt, along with a typical example of an inference question:

> *Line*     A number of factors confound quantitative evaluation of the relative importance of various entry pathways of nonindigenous plant and animal species. Time lags often occur between establishment of nonindigenous species and their detection, and tracing the pathway for a
> *(5)*     long-established species is difficult, especially if geographical expansion has occurred rapidly. In addition, federal port inspection, although a major source of information on nonindigenous species pathways, especially for agricultural pests, provides data only about species entering via scrutinized routes. Finally, some comparisons between pathways

*(10)* defy quantitative analysis. For example, which is more "important": the entry pathway of one very harmful species or one by which many but less harmful species enter the country?

7. Considered in context, the final sentence of the passage (lines 10–12) suggests which of the following?

   **(A)** Some animal and plant species are more harmful than others.

   **(B)** Determining the importance of an entry pathway is inherently subjective.

   **(C)** It is more important to detect the entry of harmful species than harmless ones.

   **(D)** Determining entry pathways is especially important for species detected in large numbers.

   **(E)** Quantitative analysis is of little use in determining a species' entry pathways.

   **The correct answer is (B).** The last sentence reveals the author's point: By posing this rhetorical question, the author is providing an example of how difficult it is to determine the relative importance of entry pathways—for the reason that the analysis is somewhat subjective (not quantifiable).

In formulating an Inference question, GRE test designers will often include a "runner-up" answer choice in which the inference is somewhat more speculative than that of the best choice. Here's a passage excerpt, along with an inference question that incorporates this wrong-answer ploy.

*Line* Scientists have long claimed that, in order to flourish and progress, their discipline requires freedom from ideological and geographic boundaries, including the freedom to share new scientific knowledge with scientists throughout the world. In the twentieth century, however, increasingly *(5)* close links between science and national life undermined these ideals. Although the connection facilitated large and expensive projects, such as the particle-accelerator program, that would have been difficult to fund through private sources, it also channeled the direction of scientific research increasingly toward national security (military defense).

8. In the passage, the author infers that

   **(A)** expensive research projects such as the particle accelerator program apply technology that can also be applied toward projects relating to national security

   **(B)** scientific knowledge had become so closely linked with national security that it could no longer be communicated to scientific colleagues without restriction

   **(C)** without free access to new scientific knowledge, scientists in different countries are less able to communicate with one another

   **(D)** governments should de-emphasize scientific projects related to military defense and emphasize instead research that can be shared freely within the international scientific community

   **(E)** government funding of scientific research undermines the ideal of scientific freedom to a greater extent than private funding.

**The correct answer is (B).** The first two sentences establish that the link between science and national life undermined scientists' freedom to communicate with other scientists. The next sentence points to the channeling of scientific research toward protecting national security as a manifestation of that link. Notice the almost unavoidable inference here—that national security concerns were part of the "national life" that took precedence over scientific freedoms.

Choice (E) is a "runner-up" choice. You can argue from the information provided in the first paragraph that government-funded research is more likely than privately funded research to relate to matters affecting the national security (i.e., military defense). However, this inference is hardly as unavoidable as the one that choice (B) provides. To compete with choice (B), the inference would need additional supporting evidence. Choice (A) is unsupported. The author implies no connection between the particle-accelerator program and national security. Choice (C) is nonsensical. Ready access to new scientific knowledge would require ready communication among scientists, not the other way around. Choice (D) is unsupported. The author neither states nor suggests which areas of scientific research should be emphasized.

## Restatement Questions

In handling a restatement question, your job is to understand a specific idea the author is conveying in the passage. These questions are different from simple recall questions in that you won't find the answer explicitly in the text. And it's this feature that makes them more difficult. A restatement question stem might look something like one of the following:

"Which of the following statements about _____ is most strongly supported by the passage's information?"

"With which of the following statements about _____ would the author most likely agree?"

"Which of the following best characterizes _____ as viewed by _____ ?"

Here's a passage excerpt, along with a restatement question based on it. Notice that the wrong-answer choices are designed to confuse you by combining details from the excerpt that relate to the question, but don't "add up."

*Line*     The arrival of a nonindigenous plant or animal species in a new location may be either intentional or unintentional. Rates of species movement driven by human transformations of natural environments or by human mobility—through commerce or tourism—dwarf natural rates by com-
*(5)*     parison. While geographic distributions of species naturally expand or contract over tens to hundreds of years, species' ranges rarely expand thousands of miles or across physical barriers such as oceans or mountains.

9. Which of the following statements about species movement is best supported by the passage?

   **(A)** Species movement is affected more by habitat modifications than by human mobility.

   **(B)** Human-driven factors affect the rate at which species move more than they affect the long-term amount of such movements.

   **(C)** Natural expansions in the geographic distribution of species account for less species movement than natural contractions do.

   **(D)** Natural environments created by commerce, tourism, and travel contribute significantly to species movement.

   **(E)** Movement of a species within a continent depends largely upon the geographic extent of human mobility within the continent.

**The correct answer is (E).** This choice restates the author's point in the first paragraph that "rates of species movement driven by human transformation of the natural environment and by human mobility . . . dwarf natural rates by comparison." Choice (A) is the most tempting wrong-answer choice. Based on the passage, habitat modifications and human mobility can both affect species movement, as choice (A) implies. And the passage does make a comparison involving human-driven species movement. However, the comparison made in the passage is between natural species movement and human-driven movement, not between human modification of habitats and human mobility. So choice (A) confuses the details of the passage. Choice (B) is easier to eliminate because it is completely unsupported by the passage, which makes no attempt to compare rate (interpreted either as frequency or speed) of species movement to total amounts of movement (distance). Choice (C) is also easier to eliminate than choice (A). It is completely unsupported by the passage. The author makes no attempt to compare natural expansions to natural contractions. Choice (D) is the easiest to eliminate. You don't even need to read the passage to recognize that choice (D) is a nonsensical statement. Human mobility (commerce, tourism, and travel) do not create "natural" environments. Human mobility itself, not the "natural environment" created by it, contributes significantly to species movement.

Here's a good example of how GRE test designers might further boost the difficulty level of a restatement question. As you tackle the question based on the following passage excerpt, notice that most of the wrong-answer choices appear to respond to the question because they describe an "ambiguous position." What's more, most of the answer choices contain information that the passage supports. The use of these two wrong-answer ploys makes this question tougher than average:

*Line*    Scientists in the post-1917 Soviet Union occupied an ambiguous position. While the government encouraged and generally supported scientific research, it simultaneously thwarted the scientific community's ideal: freedom from geographic and political boundaries. A strong
*(5)*    nationalistic emphasis on science led at times to the dismissal of all non-Russian scientific work as irrelevant to Soviet science. A 1973 article in *Literatunaya Gazeta*, a Soviet publication, insisted: "World science is based upon national schools, so the weakening of one or another national school inevitably leads to stagnation in the devel-
*(10)*    opment of world science." According to the Soviet regime, socialist

# TIP

In Reading Comprehension questions, some answer choices won't make good sense. Don't be fooled into second-guessing yourself just because you don't understand what a nonsensical answer choice means.

science was to be consistent with, and in fact grow out of, the Marxism-Leninism political ideology.

10. Based on the information in the passage, which of the following best characterizes the "ambiguous position" (lines 1–2) in which Soviet scientists were placed
during the decades that followed 1917?

(A) The Soviet government demanded that their research result in scientific
progress, although funding was insufficient to accomplish this goal.

(B) They were exhorted to strive toward scientific advancements, while at the
same time the freedoms necessary to make such advancements were
restricted.

(C) While they were required to direct research entirely toward military
defense, most advancements in this field were being made by non-Soviet
scientists with whom the Soviet scientists were prohibited contact.

(D) They were encouraged to collaborate with Soviet colleagues but were
prohibited from any discourse with scientists from other countries.

(E) The Soviet government failed to identify those areas of research that it
deemed most worthwhile, but punished those scientists with whose work it
was not satisfied.

**The correct answer is (B).** According to the passage, the ambiguous position of
Soviet scientists was that the Soviet government encouraged and generally supported scientific research, while at the same time it imposed significant restrictions upon its scientists).

Choice (C) is the easiest one to eliminate. Choice (C) is wholly unsupported by the
passage, which neither states nor suggests either assertion made in choice (C),
which in any case does not describe an ambiguous situation. Choice (A) is also
unsupported by the passage. The author neither states nor suggests that the
Soviets lacked sufficient funding. Although if true, choice (B) would indicate an
ambiguous position for scientists, that ambiguity is not the kind referred to in the
passage. Choice (E) is unsupported as well. Although some Soviet scientists were
indeed punished by the government, the author neither states nor implies that
the government failed to identify those areas of research that it deemed most
worthwhile. If true, choice (E) would indicate an ambiguous position for scientists; but as with choice (A), the ambiguity described in choice (E) is not the sort
referred to in the passage. Choice (D) is the most tempting wrong-answer choice.
It's a better choice than either choice (A) or (E) because the passage supports it,
at least implicitly. What's more, if true, choice (D) would present an ambiguous
position for Soviet scientists. However, as with choices (A) and (E), the ambiguity
that choice (D) describes doesn't reflect the nature of the ambiguity referred to in
the passage.

## Purpose-of-Detail Questions

This type of question is actually a specific-type of inference question that asks you to
infer the author's purpose in mentioning a specific idea. Look for a question stem like
this:

"The author's discussion of . . . is most probably intended to illustrate . . ."

As with inference questions, purpose-of-detail questions will sometimes include a runner-up answer choice. Here's a passage excerpt and a question that incorporates this technique.

*Line*    Scientists in the post-1917 Soviet Union occupied an ambiguous position. While the government encouraged and generally supported scientific research, it simultaneously thwarted the scientific community's ideal: freedom from geographic and political boundaries. A strong
*(5)*    nationalistic emphasis on science led at times to the dismissal of all non-Russian scientific work as irrelevant to Soviet science. A 1973 article in *Literatunaya Gazeta*, a Soviet publication, insisted: "World science is based upon national schools, so the weakening of one or another national school inevitably leads to stagnation in the devel-
*(10)*    opment of world science." According to the Soviet regime, socialist science was to be consistent with, and in fact grow out of, the Marxism-Leninism political ideology.

11. In the context of the passage, the quote from *Literatunaya Gazeta* (lines 7–10) is most likely intended to

**(A)** illustrate the general sentiment among members of the international scientific community during the time period

**(B)** support the point that only those notions about science that conformed to the Marxist-Leninist ideal were sanctioned by the Soviet government

**(C)** show the disparity of views within the Soviet intellectual community regarding the proper role of science

**(D)** underscore the Soviet emphasis on the notion of a national science

**(E)** support the author's assertion that the Marxist-Leninist impact on Soviet scientific freedom continued through the decade of the 1970s

**The correct answer is (D).** This part of the passage is concerned exclusively with pointing out evidence of the Soviet emphasis on a national science; given the content of the excerpt from *Literatunaya Gazeta*, you can reasonably infer that the author is quoting this article as one such piece of evidence.

Choice (A) is easy to rule out because it distorts the nature of the quoted article and runs contrary to the passage. The article illustrates the official Soviet position and possibly the sentiment among some members of the Soviet intellectual or scientific community. However, the article does not necessarily reflect the views of scientists from other countries. Choice (C) is not likely to be the author's purpose in quoting the article, because the author does not discuss disagreement and debate among Soviet intellectuals. Choice (E) is tempting because it might be true and because it is supported by the information in the passage. But the author gives no indication of when the article was written or published; thus, the article itself lends no support to choice (E). Choice (B) is the runner-up choice that helps make this question tougher than it might otherwise be. The quoted article does indeed reflect the Marxist-Leninist ideal (at least as interpreted and promulgated by the government) and may in fact have been published only because it was sanctioned (approved) by the Soviet government. However, since this conclusion would require speculation, and since the quoted excerpt does not mention government approval or disapproval of certain scientific notions, choice (B) does not express the author's purpose in quoting the article.

**TIP**

When handling Inference and purpose-of-detail questions, keep in mind the difference between a reasonable inference—which no rational person could dispute based on the passage's information—and mere speculation, which requires additional information to be true or valid.

## Method and Structure Questions

These questions focus on how the author goes about making or organizing his or her points, rather than on the points themselves. A method structure question might ask you to determine the author's overall approach in the passage, or it might ask about how a specific point is made or about the structure or function of a particular paragraph. The answer choices are usually stated very generally, and you have to connect the wording of the choices with what's going on in the passage.

These questions take many different forms. Here are some examples of what the question stem might look like:

"Which of the following best describes the method of argumentation used in the passage?"

"In the second paragraph, the author proceeds by . . ."

"How does the second paragraph function in relation to the first paragraph?"

"Which of the following most accurately describes the organization of the second paragraph?"

"In the first paragraph, the author uses which of the following techniques?"

When you see a method or structure question, first let the question guide you to the appropriate area of the passage. Your notes or outline might provide enough information for you to determine how the author proceeds in making his or her points. If not, reread that section carefully, focusing on what the author is laying out; don't get bogged down in details. Again, these questions concern how the author organizes and presents his or her points, not what those points are.

Here's the second paragraph of a two-paragraph passage about Francis Bacon, a sixteenth-century philosopher of science. As a whole, the passage explores the link between his thinking and the modern-day scientific establishment. Read the paragraph, then answer the method question based on it.

> *Line*    No one questions the immense benefits already conferred by science's efficient methodology. However, since individual scientists must now choose between improving standards of living and obtaining financial support for their research, there is cause for concern. In light of current
> *(5)*    circumstances, we must ask certain questions about science that Francis Bacon, from a sixteenth-century perspective, could not possibly have put to himself.

12. Which of the following most accurately describes the technique that the author employs in the second paragraph?

    **(A)** An assertion is made and is backed up by evidence.

    **(B)** A viewpoint is expressed and an opposing viewpoint is stated and countered.

    **(C)** An admission is offered and is followed by a warning and recommendation.

**(D)** Contradictory claims are presented and then reconciled.

**(E)** A problem is outlined and a solution is proposed and defended.

**The correct answer is (C).** The notion that no one questions the benefits of science does qualify as an admission in the context of the paragraph; that is, the author admits that science has given humankind enormous benefits. The author then voices concern over the current state of the scientific enterprise. Note how the contrast signal word "however" signifies that a change must come after the author admits that science has conferred immense benefits. Indeed, what comes next is, as choice (C) puts it, a warning that there is cause for concern. A recommendation appears in the final sentence, highlighted by the words "we must ask certain questions." Every element in choice (C) is present and accounted for, so choice (C) aptly describes the technique used in the paragraph.

Choice (A) indicates that the paragraph begins with an assertion, and we can surely accept that: the assertion that no one questions the benefits of science. But this is not backed up by evidence. The contrast signal word "however" tells us that some kind of change is coming, but does not provide evidence for the statement in the first sentence. In fact, the paragraph goes in a different direction. Choice (B) doesn't reflect what's happening in the paragraph. This answer choice claims that the final paragraph begins with a viewpoint, which it does. But an opposing viewpoint doesn't follow. Instead, the author expresses concern about the way science is now conducted. Choice (D) is incorrect because the passage contains no contradictory claims. The author admits that science has given humankind enormous benefits, but then voices concern over the current state of the scientific enterprise. These aren't contradictory, and nothing in the paragraph reconciles them, so choice (D) can't be the best choice. As for choice (E), it's fair to say that a problem is outlined. (The problem is that securing financial support for scientific work might get in the way of scientists improving standards of living.) But the author doesn't propose a solution. Instead, he or she recommends only that serious questions be asked about the problem. Besides, the passage ends before any kind of defense of the author's recommendation is offered.

## Application Questions

These questions require you to apply the author's ideas to new situations. They usually involve relatively broad inferences. You might be asked to interpret how the author's ideas might apply to other situations or how they might be affected by them. To do this, you need to make logical connections between the author's stated ideas and other ideas not explicitly discussed in the passage. Or you might be asked to assess the author's likely attitude (agreement or disagreement) toward some new situation, based on the information in the passage.

Application questions often add or refer to new information, so there's no predictable, set question stem to look for. But the stem might look something like one of these three:

**1** "If it were determined that _____, what effect would this fact have on the author's assessment of _____ as presented in the passage?"

**2** "Which of the following new discoveries, if it were to occur, would most strongly support the author's theory about _____?"

**3** "Which of the following is most analogous to the situation of _____ described in the passage?"

In dealing with application questions:

- Be on the lookout for wrong-answer choices that require you to make an inference not supported by the passage.

- Eliminate answer choices that run contrary to or contradict the author's main idea or position.

- Eliminate answer choices that distort the passage's ideas.

Here's another brief excerpt from a passage about Francis Bacon (the sixteenth-century philosopher of science), along with an application question based on the excerpt.

*Line*    Francis Bacon contributed to the scientific enterprise a prophetic understanding of how science would one day be put to use in the service of
technology and how this symbiotic relationship between the two would
radically impact both man and his surroundings. As inseparable as they
*(5)*    are today, it is hard to imagine science and technology as inhabiting
separate domains.

**13.** As discussed in the passage, the relationship between science and technology is best illustrated by which of the following scenarios?

**(A)** A biologist writes an article documenting a new strain of influenza that is subsequently published and taught in medical schools around the world.

**(B)** A breakthrough in the field of psychology enables psychoanalysts to diagnose patients with greater accuracy.

**(C)** An engineering firm hires a public relations agency to advertise the benefits of a labor-saving mechanical device.

**(D)** A physics discovery leads to the development of a machine that helps researchers view previously uncharted areas of the ocean floor.

**(E)** The development of a new software application helps research scientists isolate genes that are responsible for certain diseases.

**The correct answer is (D).** If you're not sure what "symbiotic" means, you can figure it out by the context. We're told that science is used to help develop technology, and that science contributes to technology, but technology also contributes to science. So we need to find the choice that illustrates the same sort of link. Choice (D) fits the bill: A science discovery in one area (physics) leads to the invention of a technology (a machine) that helps scientists in another field (oceanography) make new discoveries. The interplay between science and technology in this example is a good application of the author's description of "symbiotic relationship."

Nether choice (A) nor (B) account for technology; they involve only science. Since there's nothing in either choice about the interplay between science and technology, neither is as good a choice as (D). As for choice (C), if there's a symbiotic relationship at work at all in choice (C), it's between technology (a new mechanical device) and marketing. There's nothing about science here, so this choice doesn't illustrate the interplay between science and technology. Choice (E) is the runner-up choice. It illustrates how science (genetic research) can benefit from technology (a computer application). But it does not illustrate the reverse relationship—how technology can also benefit from science. So choice (E) does not illustrate the symbiotic relationship the author describes as completely as choice (D).

## Vocabulary-in-Context Questions

This question type is designed to assess your vocabulary and your ability to understand how a word is intended to be used in the context of a sentence or series of sentences. A vocabulary-in-context question stem is easy to spot; it looks something like this (except with a particular word in quotes):

"As it is used in the passage, the word _____ most nearly means . . ."

In dealing with vocabulary-in-context questions:

- You can probably eliminate at least one answer choice that's not even close to the word's meaning (assuming you have at least a general sense of what the word means).

- Watch out for wrong-answer choices that indicate another acceptable or a "close-enough" meaning of the word, but one that doesn't make as much sense in context as the best answer.

- If you don't know what the word means out of context, read around it, then try each answer choice as a substitute for the word. The one that makes the most sense is probably your best bet.

Let's take a look at an example. Here's an excerpt from a passage about a naval warship built by the Union during the American Civil War.

*Line*    The *U.S.S.* *Monitor* was designed by John Ericson, who had already made substantial contributions to marine engineering. The *Monitor* looked like no other ship afloat. With a wooden hull covered with iron plating, the ship had a flat deck with perpendicular sides that went
*(5)*    below the waterline and protected the propeller and other important machinery. Even more innovative, the ship had a round, revolving turret that carried two large guns.

**14.** As it is used in the passage, the word "innovative" (line 6) most nearly means

(A) dangerous

(B) unusual

(C) revolutionary

(D) clever

(E) devious

## NOTE

The GRE measures vocabulary more directly, via Sentence Completion, Analogies, and Antonyms. So expect one vocabulary-in-context question—at most—on your exam.

**The correct answer is (C).** The word *innovative* means "new and unique in an inventive way." If you already know this definition, the correct answer should be obvious. If you're not sure, examine the context. The answer choice that's easiest to eliminate is choice (E). The word *devious* (sly or crafty) has nothing possibly to do with the physical features of a ship. Choice (A) is a bit trickier, but although the revolving turret and guns might be *dangerous* (to their targets or even to their operators), the phrase "even more innovative" tells you that what preceded this sentence also describes something innovative, and there's nothing intrinsically *dangerous* or *devious* about the shape of the ship as described in that sentence. To the contrary, the sentence implies that the features described helped make the ship safe.

So how do you choose among choices (B), (C), and (D)? First, consider choice (D): The author seems concerned here with how the *Monitor* was different from any other ship ever built, not with how *clever* its features (or its designer) were. So choice (D) doesn't make much sense in context, even though something innovative is usually thought to be clever as well. As for the two remaining choices (B) and (C), as used in the passage, "innovative" refers to the design choices, made by John Ericson, that made the *Monitor* a remarkably new type of vessel—not just *unusual*. So choice (C) seems a better choice than (B).

## GRE TEST DESIGNERS' TOP 10 WRONG-ANSWER PLOYS

If you've read the analysis of each sample question in this lesson carefully, you now know a great deal about how test designers formulate wrong-answer choices. Here's a review list of the 10 techniques you'll see most often in the Verbal Reasoning section of the GRE:

❶ **The response distorts the information in the passage.** An answer choice may understate, overstate, or otherwise alter the passage's information or the author's point in presenting that information.

❷ **The response uses information in the passage but does not answer the question.** This type of answer choice includes information found in the passage, but the information isn't useful in helping you answer the question.

❸ **The response relies on speculation or an unsupported inference.** This type of choice calls for speculation; the statement won't be readily inferable from the information given.

❹ **The response is contrary to what the passage says.** The answer choice contradicts the passage's information or contradicts what the passage infers.

**⑤ The response reverses the logic of an idea.** This type of response confuses cause with effect or otherwise turns around information in the passage.

**⑥ The response confuses one opinion or position with another.** The answer choice incorrectly represents the viewpoint of one person (or group) as being that of another's.

**⑦ The response is too narrow or specific.** The answer choice focuses on information in the passage that is too specific or narrowly focused to adequately answer the question.

**⑧ The response is too broad.** This type of answer choice embraces information or ideas that are too general or widely focused to adequately answer the question.

**⑨ The response relies on information not mentioned in the passage.** The answer choice draws on information not found anywhere in the passage.

**⑩ The response is utter nonsense.** This type of answer choice makes almost no logical sense in the context of the question; essentially, it's gibberish.

## CHECKLIST FOR UNDERSTANDING GRE READING PASSAGES

Here's a checklist of the best pieces of advice for improving your reading efficiency and comprehension as you read GRE reading passages. Apply them to the full-length tests in this book, and then review them again just before exam day.

✓ Take brief notes and (for some passages) make rough outlines, but jot down just enough key words to remind you of the passage's ideas. For complicated or dense passages, an outline is a good way to organize information and to keep details straight in your mind.

✓ Pause occasionally to sum up and anticipate. After reading each logical block (perhaps a paragraph), articulate the author's point, how it relates to what preceded it, and where the discussion might go from that point.

✓ Pay attention to the overall structure of the passage. Different types of reading passages are organized differently. Understanding this will help you determine the passage's main idea and primary purpose, understand the author's purpose in mentioning various details, and distinguish between main points and minor details, all of which will help you answer the questions.

✓ Be on the look-out for triggers that can help you visualize a passage's structure and follow the author's train of thought.

✓ Don't get bogged down in details. You'll not only lose sight of the main points but you'll also lose reading speed and time. Since the passages are brief, you can easily return to locate a detail you need to answer a question.

✓ Sum up the passage after you read it. Remind yourself how the discussion flows without thinking about the details. Chances are you'll be able to answer at least one or two of the questions based only on your recap.

✓ Don't bother "previewing" a passage unless you're very short on time.

# CHECKLIST FOR ANSWERING GRE READING QUESTIONS

As with the previous checklist, you can apply these points of advice to the full-length practice tests in this book, and then review them again just before exam day.

✓    Don't second-guess GRE test designers. Each question on the exam is reviewed, tested, and revised several times before it appears as a scored question on an actual GRE. If you think there are two or more viable "best" choices, you can safely assume that you (and not the exam designers) have either misread or misinterpreted the passage, question, or answer choices.

✓    Read each and every answer choice in its entirety. Often, more than one choice will be viable. Don't hastily select or eliminate answer choices without reading them all. More GRE test-takers answer incorrectly for this reason than for any other.

✓    Never confirm your selection for any question until you've read the entire passage. Even if the first few questions seem clearly to involve the initial portion of the passage, it's always possible that information relevant to these questions will appear at the end of the passage.

✓    Don't overanalyze questions or second-guess yourself. Many wrong-answer choices simply won't make sense. If an answer choice strikes you this way, don't examine it further; eliminate it. Similarly, if you've read and considered all five choices, and one strikes you as the best one right away, your initial hunch is correct more often than not.

✓    Don't overlook the obvious. Reading Comprehension questions vary in level of difficulty, which means that many of the questions may be quite easy. If a particular choice seems very obviously correct or incorrect, don't automatically assume that you are missing something. You might simply have encountered a relatively easy question.

✓    Eliminate answer choices that run contrary to the passage's central idea. Follow this rule regardless of the type of question you're dealing with. You may be surprised by how many questions you can answer correctly using only this guideline.

✓    Be on the alert for GRE test designers' wrong-answer ploys. Keep a mental list of the wrong-answer types you learned about in this chapter. If you have trouble narrowing down the answer choices to a question during the actual exam, review this list in your mind, and the remaining wrong answers may reveal themselves.

# SUMMING IT UP

- Practice reading "interactively" for Reading Comprehension questions. Ask yourself what the passage's central idea is, what the author's overall concern is, how each part of the passage relates to the main idea, and what the author's line of reasoning is.

- Take brief notes while reading the GRE passages; this will help you organize your thoughts and keep facts straight.

- Simple recall questions require that you remember or find appropriate information in the passage.

- For recap questions, work on recognizing the passage's overall scope and its main emphasis.

- With restatement questions, you won't find the answer explicitly in the passage; you need to detect the specific idea the author is conveying, even if it isn't specifically mentioned in the text.

- Inference questions require that you discover a logical connection between two pieces of information in a passage and draw a reasonable conclusion from them.

- For purpose-of-detail questions, look for a stem (such as "The author mentions" or "The author's discussion of") that helps you infer the author's purpose in mentioning a specific idea in the passage.

- For method questions, let the question guide you to the appropriate area of the passage to determine how the author goes about making his or her points.

- Vocabulary-in-context questions assess your vocabulary and your ability to understand how a word is intended to be used in the context of a passage.

- Keep an eye out for "wrong-answer ploys" that can derail you on GRE Verbal Reasoning questions.

# Antonyms and GRE Vocabulary

## chapter 15

## OVERVIEW

- Key facts about GRE Antonyms
- The 5-step plan (Antonyms)
- Antonym strategies
- How the GRE tests your vocabulary
- How the test designers choose vocabulary for the GRE
- Primary GRE vocabulary resources
- Strategies for building a GRE vocabulary
- Summing it up

In this chapter, you'll learn a step-by-step approach to handling any GRE Antonym question, and you'll apply that approach to some GRE-style Antonyms. You'll also learn strategies for handling GRE Antonyms and for avoiding common test-taking pitfalls when it comes to these test items.

Later in the chapter, you'll learn how the GRE Verbal Reasoning section tests your vocabulary and how the GRE test designers choose the vocabulary words they incorporate into the test. To help you improve your vocabulary, this chapter then surveys and evaluates various vocabulary-building resources. At the end of the chapter, you'll learn useful tips for making the most of your time to learn new words for the GRE.

## KEY FACTS ABOUT GRE ANTONYMS

You first looked at GRE Antonyms in Chapter 2 and in this book's Diagnostic Test. Here's a quick review of key facts about this question type.

**Where:** The 30-minute Verbal Reasoning section

**How Many:** Approximately 7 test items (out of 30 altogether), interspersed with other question types on the computerized GRE

**What's Tested:**

- Your vocabulary
- Your ability to recognize subtle distinctions between words with similar meanings

**Directions:** During the computerized GRE, test directions similar to the following will appear above each Antonym test item:

> **Directions:** Each question below consists of a word printed in capital letters followed by five lettered words or phrases. Choose the lettered word or phrase that is most nearly opposite in meaning to the word in capital letters. Since some questions of this type require you to distinguish fine shades of meaning, be sure to consider all the choices before deciding which one is best.

### Testing Format:

- The capitalized word is always one word only (no phrases), but the answer choices can be either single words or brief phrases.

- The headword is capitalized (all caps), but the five answer choices are not.

- Each answer choice is expressed using the same part of speech (noun, verb, or adjective) as the capitalized word.

### Scope of Vocabulary:

- All words are part of the modern English language (no slang, obsolete, or non-English words that have not been adopted into the English language)

- A common, everyday headword usually has an alternate meaning that is being tested

- The best answer choice is not always a perfect opposite

## THE 5-STEP PLAN (ANTONYMS)

Your first task in this chapter is to learn the 5 basic steps for handling a GRE-style Antonym. After reviewing the following steps, you'll apply them to three examples.

### Step 1: Determine the Headword's Part of Speech

Check whether the answer choices are nouns, verbs, or adjectives. (They'll all be the same within each question.) Assume that the headword is of the same part of speech as the answer choices.

### Step 2: Define the Headword

Be as specific as possible. If the headword is difficult to define, try to think of a close synonym that's an everyday word. If the headword has two distinct definitions (given its part of speech), keep both in mind.

### Step 3: Compare Each Answer Choice with Your Definition of the Headword

At this point, eliminate any answer choices that fit your definition (those that are synonyms instead of antonyms). Also eliminate answer choices that bear no clear relationship to your definition.

## Step 4: Compare the Quality of the Remaining Choices

Choose the answer that is most nearly opposite in meaning to your definition. If you're having trouble choosing a clear winner, either you have the definition of the headword wrong or you failed to consider another meaning of the headword. Don't give up: Go back to step 2 and try again.

## Step 5: Confirm Your Selection by Comparing It to the Headword

Ask yourself, "Is my selection a close antonym of the capitalized word?" If so, confirm that selection and move on to the next question.

## Applying the 5-Step Plan

Let's apply these 5 steps to three GRE-style Antonyms. Here's the first one:

1. LOQUACIOUS: *adj.*
    **(A)** rational
    **(B)** abrasive
    **(C)** agitated
    **(D)** compact
    **(E)** articulate

**Step 1:** The first three answer choices are adjectives only. Thus, LOQUACIOUS must be an adjective.

**Step 2:** LOQUACIOUS carries two similar but distinct meanings: "talkative" (more common) and "wordy" (less common). These are good synonyms as well. Keep them both in mind.

**Step 3:** Choices (A), (B), and (C) bear no clear relationship to either *talkative* or *wordy*. Eliminate them!

**Step 4:** Choices (D) and (E) are the only two viable answer choices. Let's examine each one in turn.

*Compact* (an adjective here) means "condensed or compressed." Wordy speech is characterized by the opposite of compactness. So compact is clearly contrary in meaning to LOQUACIOUS. *Articulate* (an adjective here) means "well-spoken, eloquent, or fluent." But does an articulate person necessarily speak in a brief, concise manner (the opposite of *wordy*)? Not necessarily. Brevity or conciseness is not part of the job description for an articulate person. Accordingly, articulate is not nearly as opposite in meaning to LOQUACIOUS as compact.

**Step 5:** Choice (D) appears to be the best answer. Let's verify our decision. Is LOQUACIOUS contrary in meaning to *compact*? Yes. **The correct answer is (D).**

**TIP**

If you're having trouble analyzing an answer choice but you know what the word means, try making up your own antonym for the answer choice. Working in reverse can help if you're stuck.

**NOTE**

This chapter will refer to GRE Antonym test items simply as *Antonyms*. This chapter will also use the term *headword* to refer to the capitalized word preceding the five answer choices.

2. TABLE: *to put aside*

    **(A)** proceed

    **(B)** flatten

    **(C)** raise

    **(D)** conform

    **(E)** stall

**Step 1:** TABLE is a very common word, so you can bet that it has an uncommon definition that is the focus of this question. All the answer choices are verbs, so TABLE must also be a verb here.

**Step 2:** TABLE as a verb means "to lay aside a proposal for an indefinite period of time." Two everyday words that are similar in meaning are *delay* and *postpone*.

**Step 3:** Choices (B), (C), and (D) are completely unrelated to *delay* and *postpone* (and to TABLE). Eliminate them.

**Step 4:** *Proceed* is contrary in meaning to table. *Stall* means "to delay or procrastinate." *Stall* is a synonym for TABLE, so choice (E) gets it backwards. Eliminate it!

**Step 5:** Choice (A) appears to be the best answer. Let's verify our decision. Is *proceed* contrary in meaning to TABLE? Yes. **The correct answer is (A).**

**ALERT!**

If you think definitions as offbeat as the one for *table* here are too obscure for the test-makers, think again! The verb *table* has indeed appeared as an Antonym headword on the GRE.

3. RETRIBUTION:

    **(A)** delightful experience

    **(B)** forgiveness for an offense

    **(C)** restraint in behavior

    **(D)** return to normality

    **(E)** generous donation

**Step 1:** All of the answer choices define nouns, so RETRIBUTION must be a noun.

**Step 2:** RETRIBUTION means "revenge or vengeance"—in other words, "getting even with someone." Both are good synonyms.

**Step 3:** Let's consider each answer choice. We'll compare each one to the phrase "getting even." Is a *delightful experience* a good definition of what "getting even" is not? No. In fact, vengeance might actually be a delightful experience, at least for the avenger. Eliminate choice (A). Is *forgiveness for an offense* a good definition of what "getting even" is not? Yes! A person who seeks to get even with another has not forgiven the other person. So choice (B) is indeed part of the definition of what retribution is not. Is *restraint in behavior* a good definition of what "getting even" is not? Perhaps. "Getting even" is indeed characterized by a lack of restraint in behavior. But is restraint part of the definition of the opposite of "getting even"? Perhaps not. Let's earmark answer choice (C) for now, and move on to choices (D) and (E).

Is *return to normality* a good definition of what "getting even" is not? No. Getting even results in a return to equilibrium, but it may or may not result in a return to a normal relationship between the avenger and avenged. The connection is not clear enough, so eliminate choice (D). Is a *generous donation* a good definition of what "getting even" is not? No. "Getting even" is certainly contrary to making a gift; but it isn't part of the definition. Eliminate choice (E).

**Step 4:** Choices (B) and (C) are the only two viable choices. Notice that choice (C) describes the *lack of vengeance,* but it doesn't describe what vengeance is not. This distinction is crucial—in fact, it's the reason why choice (B) is a better answer choice than choice (C). If you're still not convinced, try the reverse route: What word is the opposite of "restraint in behavior"? Impulsiveness or spontaneity. These are hardly good synonyms for vengeance, are they?

**Step 5:** Let's verify our decision. Is "forgiveness for an offense" a good definition of what retribution (vengeance) is not? Yes. **The correct answer is (B).**

## ANTONYM STRATEGIES

In the previous section, you picked up some valuable ideas for gaining a tactical advantage on GRE Antonyms. Here you'll review those ideas and learn about some others. As a whole, these strategies will give you the insights into Antonyms that you need to be able to think clearly about them and handle them efficiently. They'll also help you avoid the kinds of blunders that average test-takers might commit.

### Don't Expect to Find a Perfect Opposite Every Time

In many GRE Antonyms, you won't find a perfect opposite among the five choices. Look again at the Antonym on page 375, for example, which involves the headword LOQUA-CIOUS. Words such as *terse, concise,* and *succinct* are all better antonyms than the word *compact.* But none of those three words is among the five answer choices, so *compact* is the correct answer. Here's another example:

4. SATE:

(A) gather
(B) want
(C) linger
(D) unhinge
(E) criticize

**The correct answer is (B).** To SATE is to "fully satisfy an appetite or desire," as in *He sated his appetite.* The word *deprive,* which means "withhold a need or want," is probably the best antonym, but it's not among the five choices. One meaning of the word *want* is "to be without or to lack." Though not as good an antonym as *deprive,* the word *want* is certainly contrary to SATE in meaning, and it's the best of the five listed choices.

### Resolve Close Judgment Calls in Favor of the More Specific Antonym

Among the test designers' favorite Antonym strategies—especially for more challenging questions—is to provide a "runner-up answer choice that is wrong because it is not quite as specific or on-target as the correct choice. You saw this strategy in use earlier in this chapter, in Question 3 on page 376. Notice again that *restraint in behavior* does indeed

**TIP**

If the answer choices are phrases, it's a good bet that one of them will provide a fine definition of what the headword is not. Think of answer choice phrases as possible *definitions,* not just potential Antonyms.

describe the lack or absence of retribution, but it's a bit too general; *forgiveness of an offense* relates more specifically to the idea of RETRIBUTION.

Take a look at another GRE-style Antonym in which you need to make a judgment call between the best two choices:

5. DELIBERATIVE:

   (A) impolite
   (B) thoughtless
   (C) charming
   (D) indecisive
   (E) interested

   **The correct answer is (B).** A person who is careful, thoughtful, and ponderous in his or her actions and decisions is said to be DELIBERATIVE. The only viable choices are (B) and (D). Slowness to make decisions may appear to be *indecisive* behavior, but what characterizes a deliberative person is not decisiveness as much as the thought and care used in deciding.

## Think of a Common Synonym for an Uncommon Headword

It can be difficult to analyze answer choices accompanying an austere ("troublesome or difficult") headword. Assuming you have an idea what the headword means, try thinking of an everyday synonym of the headword—a less austere word or short phrase—and then compare the five answer choices with that commonly used word.

For example, in Questions 1, 2, and 3 of this chapter, it helped to substitute simple synonyms for headwords:

• *Wordy* for LOQUACIOUS (Question 1)

• *Delay* for TABLE (Question 2)

• *Vengeance* for RETRIBUTION (Question 3)

Let's try applying this technique to another GRE-style Antonym:

6. VITRIOLIC:

   (A) simple
   (B) agreeable
   (C) uncertain
   (D) kind
   (E) humble

   **The correct answer is (D).** VITRIOLIC means "caustic or scathing." But even these two synonyms are a bit unwieldy, so try using an easier word, such as *mean* or *nasty*. Now it's easier to spot the best antonym among the five choices. The opposite of *mean* is *kind*.

## Don't Give Up Just Because a Word Is Unfamiliar

Ask yourself whether an unfamiliar word resembles a familiar one in any way. Perhaps the two words have the same root. If so, the two words are likely to have related meanings.

For example, the word LOQUACIOUS (Question 1 on page 375) includes the root *loqu*, which you've no doubt seen before in words such as *eloquent* and *soliloquy*. Those two words both involve speech or talking. So does LOQUACIOUS. That's no coincidence; the root *loqu* is based on the Latin word for *speak*.

Here are some other headwords that are uncommon words but look like familiar ones:

| HEADWORD: Definition | Familiar Word That Looks Similar |
|---|---|
| AGGRANDIZE: to make more important | grand (large) |
| EVINCE: to demonstrate convincingly | convince |
| FORESTALL: to hinder from advancing | stall (to delay) |
| FUNEREAL: sorrowful | funeral |
| LARGESSE: generous donation | large |
| PERENNIAL: enduring | annual (occurring every year) |
| QUIESCENCE: calmness | quiet |
| NEXUS: connection | next |
| URBANE: refined or elegant | urban |
| VENAL: corrupt | venom (poison) |

Here's a GRE-style Antonym that involves a familiar root:

7. FLAGRANT:

    **(A)** tasteful

    **(B)** slow to act

    **(C)** lacking imagination

    **(D)** intimidating

    **(E)** barely perceptible

    **The correct answer is (E).** The headword FLAGRANT contains the root *flag*. You've probably used the phrase "flag down" to describe a disabled motorist's signaling for help. It makes sense that the adjective form, FLAGRANT, means "obvious or conspicuous"— just what a stranded motorist is trying to be by flagging down passersby, and quite contrary to *barely perceptible*.

## To Gain Insight, Try Starting with the Answer Choice

Working backwards from an answer choice to the headword may help you when you're stuck on a question. Try to think of a single word (not a phrase) that expresses the opposite of the answer choice. Then ask yourself whether that word is also a good synonym of the headword. If it isn't, you can eliminate the answer choice. Let's apply this technique to a GRE-style Antonym:

8. UNSEEMLY:

    **(A)** shy

    **(B)** sacred

    **(C)** resolute

    **(D)** arid

    **(E)** obvious

    **The correct answer is (B).** The word UNSEEMLY means "improper or indecent." We can easily rule out choices (C), (D), and (E), none of which are

**ALERT!**

When encountering unfamiliar words, examine roots and prefixes to help you make educated guesses—but don't expect this technique to work every time.

related to UNSEEMLY. We're left with a difficult choice between (A) and (B). Choice (A) is tempting because we often think of a shy person as modest, a trait that is somewhat contrary to *indecent* (our synonym for UNSEEMLY). But what is the opposite of *shy?* It's *bold* or *outgoing,* neither of which is a close antonym of UNSEEMLY. Apply the same technique to choice (B): the opposite of *sacred* is *unholy* or *profane.* Although *profane* is a much stronger word than UNSEEMLY, it is a better antonym than *shy.*

If you're working backwards from an answer choice to the headword and you have trouble thinking of—or even imagining—a one-word Antonym for the answer choice (as opposed to a phrase), then it's a good bet that you can eliminate that choice. In Question 3 on page 376, for example, can you imagine a word (not a phrase) that expresses the opposite of "a return to normality?" Probably not, which is a clue that choice (D) is a wrong answer. Here's another example:

9. INGRATIATE:

   **(A)** distance
   **(B)** move on
   **(C)** obstruct
   **(D)** command
   **(E)** thank

   **The correct answer is (A).** Let's say that you have no idea what INGRATIATE means. Instead of selecting an answer choice at random, scan the choices for words that have no easy one-word Antonyms. Can you think of a single-word Antonym for *thank?* Probably not—so it's unlikely that choice (E) is the correct answer. For the record, to INGRATIATE oneself is to "work one's way into another's confidence"; to *distance* oneself is to "deliberately keep apart from another."

## If You're Stuck, Try Converting a Word to Another Part of Speech

Many GRE words are difficult to deal with mainly because their part of speech (noun, verb, or adjective) is not commonly used. Converting the word into a more familiar form can help. Here are some examples that have appeared previously on the GRE:

| Uncommon Form | More Familiar Form |
|---|---|
| aphoristic (obvious) | aphorism (proverb or cliché) |
| canonical (authorized) | canon (rule) |
| congruity (unity) | incongruous (incompatible) |
| digressive (winding or meandering) | digression (deviation) |
| estimable (honorable) | esteem (honor) |
| gleanable (gatherable or discoverable) | glean (to gather or to discovery through patient investigation) |
| improbity (dishonesty) | probity (honesty) |
| obstinacy (stubbornness) | obstinate (stubborn) |
| precursory (preceding) | precursor (predecessor) |
| profundity (depth) | profound (deep) |
| sagacity (wisdom) | sage (a wise person) |
| teetotalism (abstinence) | teetotaler (one who abstains form drinking) |

| testiness (irritability) | testy (irritable) |
| zenithal (upright or vertical) | zenith (highest point) |

Now here's a GRE-style Antonym that involves a familiar root:

**10.** PENDENCY:

   **(A)** domination

   **(B)** hope

   **(C)** finality

   **(D)** anguish

   **(E)** informality

   **The correct answer is (C).** The headword PENDANCY is the noun form of the more familiar adjective (or verb) *pending,* which means "not yet final or finalized." Recognizing the everyday word in its less familiar form here makes this Antonym easy to handle.

## Watch Out for Synonyms

Don't be surprised if in one or two of your GRE Antonyms you find a synonym of the headword among the answer choices. And under exam pressure, it's remarkably easy to confuse a synonym for an antonym. To avoid "synonym syndrome," always verify your choice before moving to the next test question. (Remember step 4 in this chapter's previous section?)

You encountered this ploy in action earlier in the chapter. Question 2 on page 376 included the answer choice *stall,* which was similar in meaning to the headword TABLE. Here's another example:

**11.** GAUCHE:

   **(A)** hard-working

   **(B)** gentle in manner

   **(C)** financially secure

   **(D)** soothing to listen to

   **(E)** lacking in tact

   **The correct answer is (B).** GAUCHE means "lacking social graces; tactless," so choice (E) provides a synonym, and choice (B) provides the best antonym. Though not a perfect description of what a gauche person is not, *gentle in manner* comes closest among the five choices.

But just because two answer choices are close antonyms of each other, don't assume that one is the correct choice (an antonym of the headword) and that the other is a synonym of the headword. For example:

**12.** FETTER:

    **(A)** criticize

    **(B)** relax

    **(C)** unleash

    **(D)** cajole

    **(E)** confide in

**The correct answer is (C).** Choices (A) and (D) are close antonyms of each other. (To *cajole* is to persuade by flattery). But neither *criticize* nor *cajole* is related to the headword. To FETTER is to bind or chain, just the opposite of *unleash*.

**ALERT!**

Don't be fooled by answer choices that are antonyms of each other. It's possible that neither one is the correct answer.

# HOW THE GRE TESTS YOUR VOCABULARY

The rest of this chapter is devoted solely to GRE vocabulary, which comes into play in all four Verbal Reasoning question types:

**❶ Antonyms:** Among all four Verbal Reasoning question types, Antonyms test your vocabulary most directly. Without at least an inkling of the meaning of at least the headword, you're essentially left to random guessing. The tougher the vocabulary used as a headword and in the answer choices (and the greater the number of tough words), the tougher the Antonym. It's that simple.

**❷ Analogies:** In Analogy questions, you need to create and identify links between words, so without at least *some* understanding of what the words mean, you won't be able to determine relationships between them. The tougher the words (and the greater the number of tough words) among the capitalized pair and answer choices, the tougher the Analogy.

**❸ Sentence and Complex Text Completions:** All of the answer choices in Sentence and Complex Text Completion questions are words or phrases. The broader your vocabulary, the easier time you'll have determining which word or phrase makes the most sense in each sentence. The tougher the vocabulary in the answer choices, the tougher the question.

**NOTE**

To really crank up the difficulty level of a Sentence Completion question, GRE test designers sometimes include a tough word in the sentence itself.

**❹ Reading Comprehension:** Although Reading Comprehension does not emphasize vocabulary, tougher passages contain more advanced vocabulary—which obviously increases the reading difficulty level. The test designers might boost difficulty levels further by incorporating tough vocabulary into a question itself (the question stem, the answer choices, or both). Also, you might encounter one or more vocabulary-in-context questions, which will ask you for the intended meaning of a word from the passage based on the word's context. Your job is to determine what the word means within its context, so of course it helps if you're already familiar with the word.

# HOW THE TEST DESIGNERS CHOOSE VOCABULARY FOR THE GRE

The GRE test designers want to determine whether you possess a well-rounded vocabulary—the kind you need to read, write, and speak effectively in graduate school and beyond. Most advanced words are fair GRE game. But there are certain types of words that the test designers are most likely to use, and there are other types they don't use at all.

The test designers' favorite types of words:

- Those that are uncommon enough so that a large percentage of test-takers won't know them, but not so obscure that almost no test-takers will know them
- Uncommon words with roots and prefixes that provide useful clues about what they mean
- "Fake-out" words—the kind that might remind you of certain other words but that mean something else
- Distinctive words whose definitions are nearly impossible to guess, and that only well-read and well-prepared test-takers will know

Types of words the test designers don't use:

- Highly technical words understood only by specialists or experts in certain academic fields and professions
- Non-English words not widely used among English speakers, and non-English words with diacritical marks or non-English characters
- Archaic English words, which are no longer in everyday use
- Vernacular and informal words (jargon, slang, and colloquialisms)

To help you understand how the test designers choose words to measure your vocabulary, consider these three words:

> *bib*
> *bibelot*
> *bibliophile*

You might encounter a word like *bib* (a cloth hung around the neck) on the GRE, particularly in an Analogy test item. (For example, BIB is to STAIN as "guard" is to "crime.") But the test designers wouldn't be interested in *bib* for the purpose of gauging your vocabulary, because it's a common word with which nearly all college students are familiar.

As for the word *bibelot* (a small relic or artifact), you might encounter it in a Reading Comprehension passage, but only if the passage provides its meaning. Otherwise, the test designers are unlikely to use this word to measure your vocabulary. Why? Since it's a technical word specific to one academic field—anthropology—so few GRE test-takers would know the word that the test designers would essentially be wasting a GRE question by using it.

**NOTE**

On the GRE, vocabulary is measured most directly through Antonyms, which is why you're learning about GRE Antonyms and GRE vocabulary together in this chapter.

**NOTE**

Why won't you encounter vernacular and informal words on the GRE? Because one of the basic objectives of higher education—whether it's undergraduate or graduate study—is to help you express ideas without resorting to such words.

**TIP**

If you were paying attention to the preceding paragraph, you no doubt got the hint that knowing Latin and Greek (as well as Anglo-Saxon) roots and prefixes will help you score high on the GRE Verbal Reasoning section.

On the other hand, the word *bibliophile* (a person who collects and/or appreciates books) is quite test-worthy indeed, for the purpose of rewarding test-takers who have a strong vocabulary and who might very well be familiar with the word. Even if you're not, you may be able to figure out its meaning by dissecting it: It's derived from the Greek words *biblio*, which means "book" (think of the word "bibliography"), and *philo*, which means "love."

## Words That Contain Helpful Clues

In addition to using Greek, Latin, and other non-English word branches that you might need to memorize for the GRE, the test designers also like to use words with other commonly known root words, in one form or another. In an easier GRE question, an uncommon word's meaning will be similar to, or at least consistent with, its root word. Here are three examples:

❶ EFFLUENT (n): waste matter emitted by a sewage treatment or industrial plant (the imbedded root is *fluent*)

❷ OBEISANCE (n): a physical demonstration of respect—e.g., bowing or saluting (the root is *obey*)

❸ RECIDIVISTIC (adj): characterized by habitual repetition of or return to unlawful or immoral behavior (the root is *recede*)

But don't count on words with common roots always being so easy to figure out. A tougher word might contain a root that provides only a vague clue as to what the larger word means, as in these two examples:

❶ GAINSAY (v): to deny, refute, or contradict

❷ UPSTART (n): a person who has become arrogant or overly confident as a result of a sudden rise to a position of higher status

And words that contains two roots (a compound word) sometimes send mixed messages about what they mean, as in these two compound words:

❶ SPENDTHRIFT (n): a person who is overly free or undisciplined in spending money

❷ VERISIMILITUDE (n): the appearance of truth

The bottom line is this: When you encounter an unfamiliar word in a GRE Antonym, Analogy, or Sentence and Complex Text Completion, by all means look for a familiar root to help you guess the word's meaning. But never assume that your guess is always going to be right—or even close. If you know for certain what the other words mean, that knowledge should trump your educated guesswork when it comes to settling on an answer choice.

## Words with Clues That Throw You Off Track

To increase the difficulty level of the vocabulary in an Antonym, Analogy, or Sentence and Complex Text Completion, the GRE test designers avoid providing obvious clues about a word's meaning. They opt instead for words with roots that belie the word's meaning. Look out for these two varieties:

**❶** A word that looks or sounds like another but is either entirely unrelated or only tenuously related:

BADINAGE (n): teasing conversation; jesting; banter (no relation to *bad;* think "badminton" instead)

PRURIENT (adj): lewd; lustful (no relation to *prudent*)

CAUSTIC (adj): corrosive; sharp (only tenuously related to *cause*)

**❷** A word whose meaning is *contrary* to the meaning of its root but might lead you to guess just the opposite (that they're similar):

ENERVATE (v): to deprive of vitality; debilitate (contrary to *energize*)

FACTITIOUS (adj): contrived; not genuine; artificial; counterfeit (contrary to *factual*)

RESTIVE (adj) restless; impatient (contrary to *restful*)

## Words from Mars

The most challenging type of GRE word is one that doesn't look or sound like any other English word and that contains no obvious root or prefix to help you guess its meaning. Some such words are modern non-English words that English speakers have adopted (either "as is" or with a slightly different spelling). Others are words from ancient languages but the words are still in use today. Here are three examples of the kinds of test-worthy words whose meanings you couldn't guess:

**❶** IOTA (n): a very small quantity; speck

**❷** BURGEON (v): to begin to grow, develop, or blossom, especially suddenly

**❸** INVEIGLE (v): to lure or entice by inducements

To be ready for oddball words on your GRE, there's no way around studying lists of advanced vocabulary words. But if you don't have time, take solace: On the GRE, you won't find nearly as many of these odd words as you will words that contain roots and prefixes to help you make reasoned guesses about definitions. Remember: The GRE is designed primarily as a *reasoning* test, not as a trivia quiz.

**TIP**

When you encounter an unfamiliar word on the GRE, look for a familiar root to help you guess its meaning. But don't rely too heavily on that guess. Try your best to answer the question based on what you know for sure.

**ALERT!**

Words in tougher GRE questions might contain deceiving roots. Whenever you're uncertain about which of two answer choices is better, consider the possibility that an unfamiliar word means just the opposite of what many test-takers might think.

ex) table
l?
no delay

## PRIMARY GRE VOCABULARY RESOURCES

You may already be familiar with the various books and other products designed to improve your GRE vocabulary. But just in case you're not up to speed, here's the basic menu, along with some candid advice about each item:

- **Vocabulary books dedicated to standardized academic testing:** There aren't too many of these books available, and most of the ones you'll find are one-size-fits-all. They include easier as well as advanced-level words, and they're designed not just for the GRE but also for other standardized tests, such as the SAT Reasoning Test and the MAT (Miller Analogies Test). But you can quickly skip over the words you already know. What's more, the various standardized tests usually cover the same kinds of words. Put one of these books at the top of your GRE vocabulary prep list.

- **GRE vocabulary software:** You'll find only a few software products dedicated to vocabulary testing. But most comprehensive GRE software products include extensive vocabulary lists in an interactive format. Typically, you can choose the vocabulary level you want and click for various types of information about the word and about related words. These programs are often very engaging and very efficient. By all means, take advantage of this type of resource.

- **Vocabulary lists in comprehensive GRE books:** In the typical GRE book, you'll find something like a "hot 500" or "top 250" list, usually including sample sentences, and possibly a longer word list as well, organized alphabetically. In fact, in the back of this book you'll find just such a list. By all means, review vocabulary lists such as ours. But if you're *very* serious about GRE vocabulary, expect to make only a small dent with these lists.

- **Vocabulary flashcards:** Flashcards are not just for grammar-school kids. With most GRE flashcard products, the back of each card contains not just a definition of the word on the front, but also useful information such as sample sentences and related words (synonyms and antonyms). Some products even include cartoon pictures (either on the back or the front) and other mnemonic devices that can help "fix" the word's meaning in your mind. Flashcards can be fun and engaging, especially if you and a friend quiz one another. But they're not very efficient, so they shouldn't be at the top of your list of GRE vocabulary resources.

### Other Vocabulary Resources

In addition to products designed for the GRE, you can find a variety of general vocabulary-building books in the reference section of any decent bookstore. One type emphasizes and is organized by word roots and prefixes. Knowing roots and prefixes is the key to making educated guesses when it comes to unfamiliar words on the test. Put this type of book at the top of your GRE vocabulary resource list. But bypass most other general vocabulary builders, at least for GRE prep. Here are the most common types—and why they're not worth the bother:

- Those slick vocabulary books that claim to make any person smart with vocabulary. They're not geared for the GRE. In them you'll find far too much fluff, not enough words, and not enough material about roots and prefixes.

- Books that emphasize word derivations (where a word came from originally and how it evolved to its current spelling, pronunciation, and usage). Although there are many great books of this type available, don't bother with them for GRE prep. They're inefficient for what you need to know.

- Books dedicated to the most obscure, most interesting, most frequently misused, or oddest words. Remember: The GRE test designers don't select words based on how off-the-wall they are. So bypass those novelty books.

- Dictionaries. Don't misunderstand—there's nothing wrong with dictionaries, and you should always have a good one at your side when reviewing Antonyms, Analogies, and Sentence and Complex Text Completions from your GRE Practice Tests. But reading the dictionary isn't exactly an efficient way to pinpoint the kinds of words that are GRE test-worthy, is it?

## STRATEGIES FOR BUILDING A GRE VOCABULARY

To keep yourself on the straight and narrow path to your first-choice graduate program, heed the following pieces of advice for building your GRE vocabulary.

### Learn Words in Groups That Mean Something

You can always chip away diligently at long alphabetical word lists. (In fact, you may have already starting doing that.) But that's not the most effective way to fix new words in your memory. It makes more sense to learn words by groups according to what they mean or what they look like. There are all sorts of possibilities for word groups:

- A group of words that are similar in meaning (words that share the same root or prefix make an ideal group)

- A group of synonyms along with a group of their antonyms

- A group of words that look or sound similar but are unrelated in meaning (for example, "felicitous," "filaceous," and "fallacious")

- A group of words that involve the same theme or subject (for example, "motion," "tools," or "money")

### Don't Rely Solely on "Hot Lists" to Build Your GRE Vocabulary

Do you really think those lists of words that supposedly appear most frequently on the test will continue to appear "most frequently" on future exams? Of course they won't. Yes, some words from any "top 500" list will show up from time to time on future exams, and a few might even show up on yours, so go ahead and learn them. Just keep in mind that these words are not any more likely than a host of other test-worthy words to appear on your exam.

### Know Where to Draw the Line with GRE Vocabulary Resources

As you know, most comprehensive GRE books contain lists of vocabulary words. If you compare books side by side, you'll notice that the lists are very much the same from book to book. That's because these lists are compiled from the same older GRE exams that

**TIP**

A book that presents similar words in groups is better than one that contains little more than long lists organized alphabetically. Similarly, a book containing lots of quizzes and exercises, which make learning new words more fun and interesting, is better than one that lacks these features.

**TIP**

When choosing vocabulary resources, look for resources that employ a variety of methods to group test-worthy words.

were already administered and have now been published. What does this mean? The key is not how many lists are at your disposal, but rather the kinds of lists you use.

## Go the Extra Vocabulary Mile for Those Extra GRE Points

If you start early enough and make the effort to learn as many new GRE-style words, roots, and prefixes as you reasonably have time for, some of those words will undoubtedly appear on your exam. How many? Maybe two, or maybe as many as five. If you don't think these numbers make it worth your effort to learn new words for the GRE, think again. As you well know, even a few additional correct answers can make the difference in your chances for admission to the most competitive programs.

But don't take this advice too far. Ferreting out every single test-worthy word the English language has to offer is simply not worth the extra time, which is better spent on other tasks. (See the next two tips.)

## Don't Stress Vocabulary at the Expense of Mastering Test-Taking Strategies

A strong vocabulary is important in helping you raise your GRE score, but keep your vocabulary review in perspective. You can know the precise meaning of every word on every GRE Verbal Reasoning section and still score miserably low. Unless you know how to draw analogies and can recognize logical connections between sentence parts, don't expect a competitive Verbal Reasoning score.

## Don't Memorize Word Lists at the Expense of Learning Roots and Prefixes

The English language includes many thousands of tough and test-worthy words. Be forewarned: You will encounter at least a few new and unfamiliar words on your exam, no matter how thoroughly you've prepared. If you believe otherwise, you're either kidding yourself or you've committed to memory *Webster's Unabridged Dictionary*. Sure, go ahead and learn as many words as you reasonably have time for. But make sure you devote just as much time to learning roots and prefixes, which might help you guess the meaning of those unfamiliar words you're bound to encounter on the test.

Remember: When the test designers choose especially obscure word for the GRE, chances are they've selected the word because it contains a root or prefix that will help you guess the word's meaning (assuming you know the root or prefix).

## Don't Rely on Practice Testing to Learn GRE Vocabulary

You'll learn a few new words as you review your practice tests, but taking practice GRE tests is more useful for applying test-taking skills—such as analyzing Antonyms, Analogies, and Sentence and Complex Text Completions and developing strategies for responding to them—than it is for improving vocabulary.

## Pace Yourself in Building Your GRE Vocabulary

Let's say that you've compiled your vocabulary resources and have taken inventory of what you need to review. Now you need to set up a sensible schedule that will allow you to cover everything by exam day. Work your vocabulary-building schedule into your regular GRE prep schedule. Rather than trying to learn hundreds of words in one session, try tackling just twenty to thirty words a day. Start your GRE study each day by learning those words, then review them at the end of your GRE study session.

## Systematically Review the Words You Learn

Unless you have a photographic memory, it's not enough to "learn" a word (or a root or prefix) once. Unless you review it, the word might vanish from your memory banks. So your study schedule should include daily review of some of the words you learned during previous days or weeks.

## If Your Time Is Short, Prioritize and Keep Proper Perspective

Most of what you've read about GRE vocabulary up to this point assumes you have several weeks to gear up for the GRE. But if you're short on time, prioritize and keep your perspective. Your first priority should be to learn roots and prefixes, because they appear in so many different words. Next, learn as many meaningful word *groups* as you have time for. Finally, keep in mind that the strategies presented in the Verbal Reasoning part of this book are more important than rote vocabulary. After all, the GRE is designed as a *reasoning* test, not a vocabulary quiz.

## SUMMING IT UP

- The GRE Verbal Reasoning section contains about 7 (out of 30) Antonym questions, which test your vocabulary and your ability to recognize subtle distinctions between words with similar meanings.

- On the GRE, the emphasis on vocabulary is stronger with Antonyms and Analogies than it is with Sentence and Complex Text Completions—but it comes into play with all four question types, so be sure to review vocabulary thoroughly.

- Of the four Verbal Reasoning question types, Antonyms test your vocabulary most directly.

- In Analogy questions, you need to create and identify links between words, so you need some understanding of what the words mean to determine relationships between them.

- All of the answer choices in Sentence and Complex Text Completion questions are words or phrases. The broader your vocabulary, the easier time you'll have determining which word or phrase makes the most sense.

- Although Reading Comprehension does not emphasize vocabulary, tougher passages contain more advanced vocabulary, which increases the reading difficulty level. You may also encounter one or more vocabulary-in-context questions, which will ask you for the intended meaning of a word from the passage based on the word's context.

- Test designers will generally use words that are uncommon enough for a great percentage of test-takers to be unfamiliar with them, uncommon words with roots and prefixes that provide useful clues about what they mean, "fake-out" words that might remind you of certain other words but have different definitions, and distinctive words whose definitions are nearly impossible to guess, that only well-read and well-prepared test-takers will know. They will *not* use highly technical words that only specialists or experts would know, non-English words not widely used among English speakers or those with diacritical marks or non-English characters, archaic English words, or vernacular and informal words (jargon, slang, and colloquialisms).

- Follow and review the 5 basic steps in this chapter for handling GRE Antonyms, and use the tips and study methods outlined here to boost your vocabulary skills. Apply your knowledge to this book's Practice Tests; then review everything again just before exam day.

# PART VI

## FIVE PRACTICE TESTS

# ANSWER SHEET PRACTICE TEST 2

## Analytical Writing—Issue Task

_____

_____

_____

_____

_____

_____

_____

_____

_____

_____

_____

_____

_____

_____

_____

_____

_____

_____

_____

_____

_____

answer sheet

**Analytical Writing—Argument Task**

_____

_____

_____

_____

_____

_____

_____

_____

_____

_____

_____

_____

_____

_____

_____

_____

_____

_____

_____

_____

answer sheet

# Practice Test 2

## ANALYTICAL WRITING

### Issue Task

*Time: 45 Minutes*

> **NOTES:** For *some* test-takers, the GRE will end with an identified and untimed research section. The research section, which is unscored, contains experimental question types. Test-makers use it to assess the difficulty levels of the experimental question types, based on test-takers' responses.
>
> For the purposes of this book—making sure you're fully prepared to take the GRE exam—one Complex Text Completion question (Verbal Reasoning section) and one numeric entry question (Quantitative Reasoning section) are included in each of the Practice Tests. On the actual GRE, however, you will not see both of these questions; in fact, you may *not* see either one.

Using a word processor, compose an essay that responds to the following statement and directive. Do not use any spell-checking or grammar-checking functions (they are not available on the actual GRE).

> "As adults, we prefer to define ourselves more by our occupation than by our affiliation with social groups."

> Write an essay in which you present your perspective on the statement above. Develop and support your viewpoint with relevant reasons and examples.

## Argument Task

### *Time: 30 Minutes*

Using a word processor, compose an essay that responds to the following statement and directive. Do not use any spell-checking or grammar-checking functions (they are not available on the actual GRE).

> The following appeared as part of an article in a national business publication:
>
> "Workforce Systems, a consulting firm specializing in workplace productivity and efficiency, reports that nearly 70 percent of Maxtech's employees who enrolled in Workforce Systems' one-week seminar last year claim to be more content with their current jobs than prior to enrolling in the seminar. By requiring managers at all large corporations to enroll in the kinds of seminars that Workforce System offers, productivity in our economy's private sector is certain to improve."
>
> Discuss how well-reasoned you find the argument above.

## VERBAL REASONING

### 30 Questions • 30 Minutes

**NOTE:** In this section, questions are grouped together by format, and within each group the questions grow more difficult as you go. Because the actual GRE is computer-adaptive in the multiple-choice sections, it intersperses questions of different formats and difficulty levels.

1. Proponents of urban development oppose the popular notion that social-psychological mechanisms leading to criminal and other antisocial activity are more likely to _____ if _____ such as anonymity and population density are found.
   - **(A)** emerge . . traits
   - **(B)** react . . factors
   - **(C)** disappear . . problems
   - **(D)** fail . . criminals
   - **(E)** function . . cities

2. ABRUPT:
   - **(A)** continual
   - **(B)** eventual
   - **(C)** gradual
   - **(D)** enduring
   - **(E)** lengthy

3. CORNUCOPIA:
   - **(A)** serenity
   - **(B)** darkness
   - **(C)** solitude
   - **(D)** sparseness
   - **(E)** modicum

4. AUSTERE:
   - **(A)** amiable
   - **(B)** forgiving
   - **(C)** easily accomplished
   - **(D)** simpleminded
   - **(E)** gratifying

5. TEACHER : INSTRUCTION ::
   - **(A)** lawyer : crime
   - **(B)** army : regiment
   - **(C)** doctor : disease
   - **(D)** student : learning
   - **(E)** guard : protection

6. The legends of any tribe serve to explain, and even embody, its _____; by examining a people's most popular _____, one can determine the things they most deeply cherish.
   - **(A)** origins . . legends
   - **(B)** religion . . pastimes
   - **(C)** beliefs . . customs
   - **(D)** history . . rituals
   - **(E)** values . . stories

7. LACKLUSTER:
   - **(A)** exceptional
   - **(B)** quick to respond
   - **(C)** exceedingly bold
   - **(D)** brilliant
   - **(E)** well spoken

8. COG : WATCH ::
   - **(A)** fish : school
   - **(B)** screen : television
   - **(C)** lawyer : jury
   - **(D)** manager : bureaucracy
   - **(E)** seasoning : recipe

9. QUELL : UPRISING ::
   - **(A)** bite : hunger
   - **(B)** quench : thirst
   - **(C)** strike : labor
   - **(D)** incite : hostility
   - **(E)** indulge : habit

10. IMPORTANT : PIVOTAL ::
    - **(A)** stern : draconian
    - **(B)** copious : thorough
    - **(C)** minimal : voluminous
    - **(D)** salient : compulsory
    - **(E)** impetuous : spontaneous

**Directions:** Questions 11–12 are based on the following passage.

Line For absolute dating of archeological artifacts, the radiocarbon method emerged during the latter half of the twentieth century as the most reliable
(5) and precise method. The results of obsidian (volcanic glass) dating, a method based on the belief that newly exposed obsidian surfaces absorb moisture from the surrounding atmo-
(10) sphere at a constant rate, proved uneven. It was initially thought that the thickness of the hydration layer would provide a means of calculating the time elapsed since the fresh
(15) surface was made. But this method failed to account for the chemical variability in the physical and chemical mechanism of obsidian hydration. Moreover, each geographic source pre-
(20) sented unique chemical characteristics, necessitating a trace element analysis for each such source.

Yet despite its limitations, obsidian dating helped archeologists identify
(25) the sources of many obsidian artifacts, and to identify in turn ancient exchange networks for the flow of goods. Nor were ceramic studies and fluoride analysis supplanted entirely
(30) by the radiocarbon method, which in use allows for field labeling and laboratory errors, as well as sample contamination. In addition, in the 1970s, dendrochronological (tree-ring) studies
(35) on the bristlecone pine showed that deviation from radiocarbon values increases as one moves back in time. Eventually calibration curves were developed to account for this phenomenon; but in
(40) the archeological literature we still find dual references to radiocarbon and sidereal, or calendar, time.

11. The author would probably consider which of the following the LEAST likely means of dating archeological artifacts?
   (A) Ceramics studies
   (B) Radiocarbon dating
   (C) Dendrochronological studies
   (D) Fluoride analysis
   (E) Obsidian hydration-layer analysis

12. The author mentions all of the following as problems with radiocarbon dating EXCEPT for
   (A) disparities with the calendar dating system
   (B) deterioration of samples
   (C) identification errors by archeological field workers
   (D) contamination of artifacts
   (E) mistakes by laboratory workers

13. RANCOR:
   (A) tranquility
   (B) happiness
   (C) impartiality
   (D) humor
   (E) affection

14. The recent birth of septuplets has spawned many newspaper articles presenting _____ accounts of medical problems associated with multiple births, _____ the initial heartwarming stories about the septuplets that dominated the press.
   (A) depressing . . minimizing
   (B) various . . contradicting
   (C) dispassionate . . obscuring
   (D) sobering . . counterbalancing
   (E) detailed . . substantiating

**Directions:** Questions 15–18 are based on the following passage.

Line The Andean *cordillera* is made up of many interwoven mountain ranges, which include high intermontane plateaus, basins, and valleys. The
(5) Northern Andes contain several broad ecosystems falling into four altitudinal belts. Its northern subregion is distinguished by higher humidity and by greater climatic symmetry between
(10) eastern and western flanks. The Central Andes are characterized by a succession of agricultural zones with varied climatic conditions along the mountains' flanks and by large, high-
(15) altitude plateaus, variously called *puna* or *altiplano,* which do not occur in the Northern Andes. The soil fertility of the northern *altiplano* is generally good. The western Central
(20) Andean ranges are relatively arid with desert-like soils, whereas the eastern ranges are more humid and have more diverse soils. The eastern slopes of the Central Andes in many
(25) ways are similar to the wet forests of the Northern Andes. Unlike the Northern Andes, however, these slopes have a dry season.

In regions of gentle topography,
(30) such as the Amazon basin, regional climatic variation can be determined from a few widely spaced measurements. Regional projections in the Andean *cordillera* are quite difficult
(35) by comparison. For example, while air temperature generally decreases with increasing altitude, variability of mountain topography can produce much lower than expected air tem-
(40) peratures. Nevertheless, some general climatic patterns are discernible. For example, with increasing distance south of the equator the seasonality of precipitation increases, whereas the
(45) total annual amount generally decreases. Humidity commonly increases with increasing altitude, but only to some intermediate altitude, above which it declines. The vari-
(50) ability of mountain terrain also affects precipitation, such that conditions of extreme wetness and aridity may exist in close proximity. Related to this temperature gradient is a pattern of
(55) greater rainfall at the valley heads, and less rain at lower altitudes, resulting in part from mountain rainshadow effect.

The weather patterns of the
(60) Andean *cordillera* and Amazon basin in general reflect movements of high- and low-pressure cells associated with the Intertropical Convergence Zone, a low-pressure trough that moves
(65) further north and south on a seasonal basis. Precipitation is high throughout the year in the highlands and on the coast in the Northern Andes. Coastal aridity increases south of central
(70) Ecuador, culminating in the Atacama desert of northern Chile. In the Central Andes, highland precipitation is seasonal, and amounts are approximately half those measured in the
(75) Northern Andes. The aridity of the Central Andean coastal zone is the result of the drying effect of the cold Pacific Humboldt current and the southern Pacific high-pressure cell.
(80) Much of the southern portion of the Central Andes in Bolivia is also arid. The dry season causes soil moisture deficits and diminished stream flow part of each year.

15. The passage is primarily concerned with
    (A) describing the climate and topography of various regions of the Andean *cordillera*
    (B) discussing the factors affecting the climate of the Andean *cordillera*
    (C) providing alternative explanations for the climatic diversity among different regions of the Andean *cordillera*
    (D) examining the effects of topography on the climate and vegetation of the Andean *cordillera*
    (E) comparing the climate and topography of the Northern Andes to those of the Central Andes

16. According to the passage, the northern part of the high-altitude plateaus is characterized by which of the following?
    (A) Fertile soil
    (B) High relative humidity
    (C) A succession of agricultural zones
    (D) Extremes in air temperature
    (E) An arid climate

17. It can be inferred from the passage that air temperatures in the Andean *cordillera* are often "lower than expected" (line 39) probably due to wide variations in
    (A) precipitation levels
    (B) air pressure
    (C) prevailing wind direction
    (D) aridity
    (E) mountain elevation

18. The passage mentions all the following as climatic factors in the Central Andes *cordillera* EXCEPT for
    (A) the Intertropical Convergence Zone
    (B) the rainshadow effect
    (C) the southern Pacific high-pressure cell
    (D) the symmetry of the mountain ranges
    (E) the Pacific Humboldt current

19. WAN:
    (A) flushed
    (B) robust
    (C) patchy
    (D) twinkling
    (E) comely

20. SCULPTURE : SHAVING ::
    (A) analysis : insight
    (B) burglary : arrest
    (C) experiment : hypothesis
    (D) therapy : comfort
    (E) education : opportunity

21. Mark Twain and Garrison Keillor were both born and bred in Midwestern America; yet the themes, writing styles, and attitudes of these two humorists are _____.
    (A) widely admired
    (B) essentially timeless
    (C) distinctly different
    (D) quite remarkable
    (E) nearly identical

22. PRIZE : LOTTERY ::
    (A) grade : student
    (B) loan : bank
    (C) chip : casino
    (D) diploma : college
    (E) rank : tournament

23. CIRCUMSPECT : VIGILANCE ::
    (A) courageous : bravado
    (B) amicable : belligerence
    (C) ardent : enthusiasm
    (D) miserly : wealth
    (E) intransigent : stability

**24.** In certain instances, tradition must yield entirely to the utilitarian needs of modern life. When it comes to historic public buildings, whose structural integrity is (i)_____ to the safety of the general public, modernization sometimes requires no less than razing the structure and building anew. In other such cases, however, architecturally appropriate retrofits can solve structural problems without sacrificing (ii)_____, while alternative locations can be used for new buildings as needed.

**(i)**

paramount
integral
imperative

**(ii)**

history or tradition
aesthetic cohesiveness
utilitarian needs

---

**Directions:** Questions 25–26 are based on the following passage.

---

*Line*  The heart of the restorationist critique of environmental preservationism is the claim that it rests on an unhealthy dualism that conceives nature and
(5)  humankind as radically distinct and opposed to each other. The crucial question about the restorationist outlook has to do with the degree to which the restorationist program is
(10)  itself faithful to its first principle—that nature and humanity are fundamentally united rather than separate.

Rejecting the old domination model,
(15)  which sees humans as over nature, restoration theory champions a model of community participation. Yet some of the descriptions of what restorationists are actually up to—for
(20)  example, Turner's description of humans as "the lords of creation," or

Jordan's statement that "the fate and well being of the biosphere depend ultimately on us and our relationship
(25)  with it"—do not cohere well with the community-participation model. Another holistic model—namely, that of nature as an organism—might be more serviceable to the restora-
(30)  tionists. As with the community model, the "organic" model pictures nature as a system of interconnected parts. A fundamental difference, however, is that in an organism the
(35)  parts are wholly subservient to the life of the organism.

**25.** In asserting that the organic model "might be more serviceable to the restorationists" (lines 28–30), the author implies that
(A) the descriptions by Turner and Jordan of the restorationists' program conform more closely to the organic model than to the community participation model
(B) the organic model is more consistent than the community participation model with the principle of restoration
(C) the organic model is more consistent with the restorationists' agenda than with the preservationists' program
(D) holistic models are more useful than the dualist model to the restorationists
(E) the organic model, unlike the community participation model, represents nature as a system of interconnected parts

26. Which of the following best expresses the function of the first paragraph in relation to the second one?
    (A) To establish the parameters of an ensuing debate
    (B) To discuss a secondary issue as a prelude to a more detailed examination of a primary issue
    (C) To provide an historical backdrop for a discussion of a modern-day issue
    (D) To introduce opposing viewpoints, which are then evaluated
    (E) To identify a problem with a school of thought, which is then explored in detail

27. The science of astronomy is widely viewed today as _____ at least as much as theoretical, in that sooner or later what astronomers detect finds its way into theory, or the theory is modified to accept it.
    (A) observational . . disprove
    (B) beneficial . . accept
    (C) empirical . . embrace
    (D) practical . . demonstrate
    (E) important . . supersede

28. QUARRY : MARBLE ::
    (A) well : oil
    (B) ocean : tuna
    (C) silo : grain
    (D) reservoir : water
    (E) observatory : stars

29. SNORKEL : DIVE ::
    (A) baton : run
    (B) taps : dance
    (C) blade : skate
    (D) ball : kick
    (E) club : golf

30. EXACERBATE:
    (A) prevent from occurring
    (B) lessen in degree
    (C) withhold praise
    (D) smooth over
    (E) treat condescendingly

# QUANTITATIVE REASONING

## 28 Questions • 45 Minutes

**NOTE:** In this section, questions are grouped together by format, and within each group the questions grow more difficult as you go. Because the actual GRE is computer-adaptive in the multiple-choice sections, it intersperses questions of different formats and difficulty levels.

<u>**Column A**</u> <u>**Column B**</u>

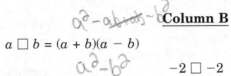

1.
$$a \square b = (a + b)(a - b)$$

$2 \square 2$  $-2 \square -2$

**(A)** The quantity in Column A is greater;
**(B)** The quantity in Column B is greater;
**(C)** The quantities are equal;
**(D)** The relationship cannot be determined from the information given.

<u>**Column A**</u> <u>**Column B**</u>

2.
$$0 < x < 1$$

$\sqrt[3]{x}$ $\sqrt{x}$

**(A)** The quantity in Column A is greater;
**(B)** The quantity in Column B is greater;
**(C)** The quantities are equal;
**(D)** The relationship cannot be determined from the information given.

<u>**Column A**</u> <u>**Column B**</u>

3.
Line segments $\overline{AB}$ and $\overline{CD}$ are chords of circle O.

The circumference of circle O

The length of $\overline{AB}$ plus twice the length of $\overline{CD}$

**(A)** The quantity in Column A is greater;
**(B)** The quantity in Column B is greater;
**(C)** The quantities are equal;
**(D)** The relationship cannot be determined from the information given.

4. If $x > 0$, and if $x + 3$ is a multiple of 3, which of the following is NOT a multiple of 3?

**(A)** $x$
**(B)** $x + 6$
**(C)** $2x + 6$
**(D)** $3x + 5$
**(E)** $6x + 18$

**5.** If $m = n$ and $p < q$, then which of the following inequalities holds true in all cases?

   **(A)** $m - p > n - q$
   **(B)** $p - m > q - n$
   **(C)** $m - p < n - q$
   **(D)** $mp > nq$
   **(E)** $m + q < n + p$

| Column A | Column B |
|---|---|
| **6.** The amount of interest earned on \$1,000 after four months | The amount of interest earned on \$2,000 after eight months |

   **(A)** The quantity in Column A is greater;
   **(B)** The quantity in Column B is greater;
   **(C)** The quantities are equal;
   **(D)** The relationship cannot be determined from the information given.

| Column A | Column B |
|---|---|
| **7.** The number of prime numbers between 10 and 15 | The number of prime factors of 33 |

   **(A)** The quantity in Column A is greater;
   **(B)** The quantity in Column B is greater;
   **(C)** The quantities are equal;
   **(D)** The relationship cannot be determined from the information given.

**8.** On the $xy$-plane, what is the slope of a line that is perpendicular to the line defined by the equation $3y = \frac{1}{2}x + 3$?

   **(A)** $-6$

   **(B)** $-2$

   **(C)** $-\dfrac{1}{2}$

   **(D)** $2$

   **(E)** $3$

**9.** Fifteen buoys, numbered 1 to 15, are positioned equidistantly along a straight path for a sailboat race. The race begins at buoy 1, and 45 minutes into the race the fastest boat reaches buoy 10. At the same average speed, how many minutes will it take the boat to race from buoy 10 to buoy 15?

   **(A)** 45
   **(B)** 32.5
   **(C)** 25
   **(D)** 22.5
   **(E)** 15

<table>
<tr><td align="center">**Column A**</td><td align="center">**Column B**</td></tr>
</table>

**10.**

$$n = 2$$
Set R: $\{n + 1, 2n + 2, 3n + 3, \ldots\}$
Set S: $\{n, n + 1, n + 2, \ldots\}$

| Column A | Column B |
|---|---|
| The 25th term of Set R | Two times the 24th term of Set S |

(A) The quantity in Column A is greater;
(B) The quantity in Column B is greater;
(C) The quantities are equal;
(D) The relationship cannot be determined from the information given.

| **Column A** | **Column B** |
|---|---|

**11.**

| $(9{,}300s)(.0093t)$ | $(9.3s)(9.3t)$ |
|---|---|

(A) The quantity in Column A is greater;
(B) The quantity in Column B is greater;
(C) The quantities are equal;
(D) The relationship cannot be determined from the information given.

**12.** A farmer wants to fence a rectangular horse corral with an area of 12,000 square feet. Fence posts along each side will be 10 feet apart at their center.

| **Column A** | **Column B** |
|---|---|
| The fewest possible posts that could be used to construct the fence | The number of posts used if two of the sides are 300 feet in length each |

(A) The quantity in Column A is greater;
(B) The quantity in Column B is greater;
(C) The quantities are equal;
(D) The relationship cannot be determined from the information given.

**13.** Cynthia drove for seven hours at an average rate of 50 miles per hour (mph) and for one hour at an average rate of 60 mph. What was her average rate for the entire trip?

_____ miles per hour

Express you answer as a decimal number to the nearest two places right of the decimal point. (You can round either up or down.)

**Directions:** Questions 14–15 refer to the following chart.

## SHARE PRICES OF COMMON STOCK
## (ARDENT, BIOFIRM, AND COMPUWIN CORPORATIONS)

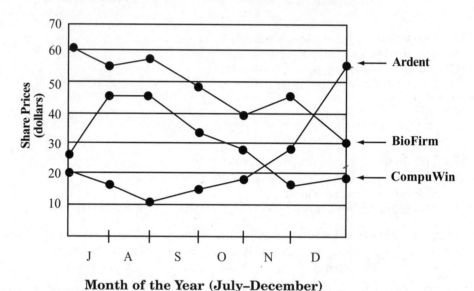

**Month of the Year (July–December)**

14. During which of the following months was there a negative aggregate change in the share price of stock in all three companies?

   I. July
   II. September
   III. October

   **(A)** II only
   **(B)** I and II only
   **(C)** I and III only
   **(D)** II and III only
   **(E)** I, II, and III

15. At the beginning of July, an investor bought 40 shares of Ardent stock, and then held all 40 shares until the end of December, at which time the investor sold all 40 shares. The investor's profit upon the sale of these 40 shares amounted to approximately

   **(A)** $850
   **(B)** $980
   **(C)** $1,100
   **(D)** $1,300
   **(E)** $1,400

**16.**

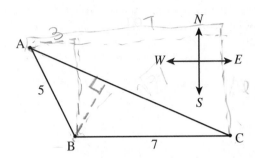

Once a month, a crop duster sprays a triangular area defined by three farm houses: A, B, and C, as indicated in the figure. Farmhouse C is located 7 kilometers due east of farmhouse B, as shown. If farmhouse A is located 10 kilometers further west than farmhouse C, what is the total area that the crop duster sprays?

**(A)** 12.5 km$^2$
**(B)** 14 km$^2$
**(C)** 15 km$^2$
**(D)** 15.5 km$^2$
**(E)** 17.5 km$^2$

|  **Column A**  |  **Column B**  |
| --- | --- |
| **17.** $(x + 2)(x - 2)$ | $x^2 - 2$ |

**(A)** The quantity in Column A is greater;
**(B)** The quantity in Column B is greater;
**(C)** The quantities are equal;
**(D)** The relationship cannot be determined from the information given.

|  **Column A**  |  **Column B**  |
| --- | --- |
| **18.** The price of a $100 product marked up by Q percent | The price of a $99 product marked up by Q dollars |

**(A)** The quantity in Column A is greater;
**(B)** The quantity in Column B is greater;
**(C)** The quantities are equal;
**(D)** The relationship cannot be determined from the information given.

**19.** The arithmetic mean (average) of two numbers is P × Q. If the first number is Q, which of the following expressions represents the other number?

**(A)** 2PQ − Q
**(B)** PQ − 2Q
**(C)** 2PQ − P
**(D)** P
**(E)** PQ − Q

**20.** How many ounces of soy sauce must be added to an 18-ounce mixture of peanut sauce and soy sauce consisting of 32% peanut sauce in order to create a mixture that is 12% peanut sauce?

- **(A)** 21
- **(B)** $24\frac{3}{4}$
- **(C)** $26\frac{2}{3}$
- **(D)** 30
- **(E)** $38\frac{2}{5}$

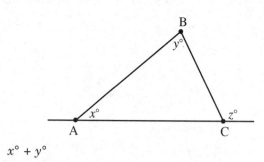

| Column A | Column B |
|---|---|

**21.**

$x° + y°$                          $z°$

- **(A)** The quantity in Column A is greater;
- **(B)** The quantity in Column B is greater;
- **(C)** The quantities are equal;
- **(D)** The relationship cannot be determined from the information given.

| Column A | Column B |
|---|---|

**22.** $p > 0 > q$

$p + q$                          $pq$

- **(A)** The quantity in Column A is greater;
- **(B)** The quantity in Column B is greater;
- **(C)** The quantities are equal;
- **(D)** The relationship cannot be determined from the information given.

| Column A | Column B |
|---|---|

**23.** Distribution D = {3,6,9,10}

The range of D                          The median of D

- **(A)** The quantity in Column A is greater;
- **(B)** The quantity in Column B is greater;
- **(C)** The quantities are equal;
- **(D)** The relationship cannot be determined from the information given.

24. At a particular ice cream parlor, customers can choose among five different ice cream flavors and may choose either a sugar cone or a waffle cone. Considering ice cream flavor and cone type, but NOT the arrangement of ice cream scoops, how many distinct triple-scoop cones with three different ice cream flavors are available?

   (A) 10
   (B) 20
   (C) 25
   (D) 40
   (E) 50

   $\frac{5}{2}$

---

**Directions:** Questions 25–26 refer to the following table.

Worldwide Sales of Three XYZ Motor Company
Models 2004 – 2005 Model Year

| | Automobile Model | | |
| --- | --- | --- | --- |
| Purchaser Category | Basic | Standard | Deluxe |
| U.S. institutions | 3.6 | 8.5 | 1.9 |
| U.S. consumers | 7.5 | 11.4 | 2.0 |
| Foreign institutions | 1.7 | 4.9 | 2.2 |
| Foreign consumers | 1.0 | 5.1 | 0.8 |

Note: All numbers are in thousands.

25. Based on the table, which of the following does NOT describe sales of at least 10,000 automobiles?

   (A) All U.S. institution sales of the standard and deluxe models
   (B) All consumer sales of the basic and deluxe model
   (C) All foreign institution sales
   (D) All foreign sales of the standard model
   (E) All institution sales of the standard model

26. Assume that total revenue from sales of the standard model exceeded total revenue from sales of the basic model by $41 million. The average sales price of a standard model exceeded the average price of a basic model by approximately

   (A) $2,500
   (B) $3,000
   (C) $3,600
   (D) $4,400
   (E) It cannot be determined from the information given.

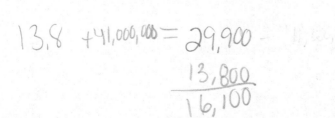

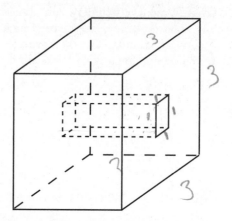

**27.** The figure above shows a solid cube 3 inches on a side but with a 1-inch square hole cut through it. How many square inches is the total surface area of the resulting solid figure?

(A) 24
(B) 42
(C) 52
(D) 64
(E) 66

|  | **Column A** |  | **Column B** |
|---|---|---|---|
| **28.** | $x^3 - x^2$ | $x < -1$ | $x^2 - x$ |

(A) The quantity in Column A is greater;
(B) The quantity in Column B is greater;
(C) The quantities are equal;
(D) The relationship cannot be determined from the information given.

# ANSWER KEY AND EXPLANATIONS

## Analytical Writing

### ISSUE TASK: EVALUATION AND SCORING

Evaluate your Issue task essay on a scale of 1 to 6 (6 being the highest score) according to the following five criteria:

**1** Does your essay develop a position on the issue through the use of incisive reasons and persuasive examples?

**2** Are your essay's ideas conveyed clearly and articulately?

**3** Does your essay maintain proper focus on the issue, and is it well organized?

**4** Does your essay demonstrate proficiency, fluency, and maturity in its use of sentence structure, vocabulary, and idiom?

**5** Does your essay demonstrate command of the elements of Standard Written English, including grammar, word usage, spelling, and punctuation?

### ARGUMENT TASK: EVALUATION AND SCORING

Evaluate your Argument task essay on a scale of 1 to 6 (6 being the highest score) according to the following five criteria:

**1** Does your essay identify and articulate the argument's key unstated assumptions?

**2** Does your essay explain how the argument relies on these unstated assumptions, and what the implications are if these assumptions are unwarranted?

**3** Does your essay develop its ideas in a clear, organized manner, with appropriate transitions to help connect ideas together?

**4** Does your essay demonstrate proficiency, fluency, and maturity in its use of sentence structure, vocabulary, and idiom?

**5** Does your essay demonstrate command of the elements of Standard Written English, including grammar, word usage, spelling, and punctuation?

To help you evaluate your essay in terms of criteria 1 and 2, the following is a series of questions that identify *five* distinct unstated assumptions upon which the argument relies. To earn a score of 4 or higher, your essay should identify and explain at least three of these assumptions. Identifying and explaining at least four of the unstated assumptions would help earn you an even higher score.

- Do Maxtech employees, at least those whose claims Workforce cites, constitute a sufficiently representative statistical sample of the entire private-sector workforce? (Perhaps these Maxtech employees were more receptive or responsive to Workforce's particular methods than the average private-sector worker would be.)

- Is the report from Workforce Systems credible? (Perhaps the company overstates the benefits of its seminars in order to attract clients.)

- Was the seminar the actual cause of the improved level of contentment among the participants from Maxtech? (The answer might depend on how much time has passed since the seminar, whether Maxtech's participants have the same jobs as before, and whether the seminar is designed to help workers become more content to begin with.)

- Are the claims by Maxtech's employees credible? (Perhaps they felt pressure to exaggerate the benefits of the seminar or falsely report improvement in order to take time off from work to enroll again in the seminar.)

- Might the argument assume that all other conditions remain unchanged? (Overall productivity of the economy's private sector depends also on many extrinsic factors having nothing to do with the benefits of these types of seminars.)

## Verbal Reasoning

| | |
|---|---|
| 1. A | 11. C |
| 2. C | 12. B |
| 3. D | 13. E |
| 4. B | 14. D |
| 5. E | 15. B |
| 6. E | 16. A |
| 7. D | 17. E |
| 8. D | 18. D |
| 9. B | 19. A |
| 10. A | 20. B |
| | 21. C |

| |
|---|
| 22. D |
| 23. C |
| 24. (i) integral |
|     (ii) history or |
|        tradition |
| 25. A |
| 26. E |
| 27. C |
| 28. A |
| 29. C |
| 30. B |

**1. The correct answer is (A).** Proponents of urban development would oppose the idea that urban development fosters crime. So the "mechanism" referred to in the sentence might either *function, react,* or *emerge,* but not disappear or fail. The sentence cites anonymity and population density as examples of the second missing word. It makes no sense to characterize these examples either as *cities* or *criminals,* and of the two remaining choices, choice (B) is weaker than choice (A) on two counts. First, the sentence as a whole does not strongly support the use of the word *react*; what the mechanisms might react to is neither stated nor inferred in the sentence. Second, while a trait is properly referred to as "found," a factor is not (factors typically "come into play"). So choice (B) makes for an improper idiomatic expression.

**2. The correct answer is (C).** ABRUPT means "unexpectedly sudden." The closest antonym among the five choices is *gradual.*

**3. The correct answer is (D).** CORNUCOPIA means "abundance"—the opposite of *sparseness.*

**4. The correct answer is (B).** Something AUSTERE is "severe, harsh, or forbidding"—the opposite of *forgiving.*

**5. The correct answer is (E).** This is an "inherent function" analogy. The function of a TEACHER is to provide INSTRUCTION for another; similarly, the function of a *guard* is to provide *protection* for another. As for choice (D), although the "function" of a student might be said to learn, it is not to provide learning for another. So choice (E) is not as strong an analogy as choice (D).

**6. The correct answer is (E).** The two parts of the sentence paraphrase the same idea. Therefore, the first blank should correspond to the idea of "the things they most deeply cherish" in the second half of the sentence, while the second blank should correspond to "myths." The word pair *values* and *stories* works well.

**7. The correct answer is (D).** The word LACKLUSTER means "lacking luster." Its antonym *lustrous* means "brilliant, radiant, or bright."

8. **The correct answer is (D).** This is a "part-to-whole" analogy. A COG (gear or gear-tooth) is one of several types of components that together make a WATCH operate; similarly, a *manager* is one of many types of workers who contribute to the operation of a *bureaucracy* (a large, structured organization).

9. **The correct answer is (B).** This is one form of an "operates against" analogy. To QUELL is to suppress or put down, an act that eliminates an UPRISING; similarly, to *quench* is to completely satisfy a *thirst,* an act that eliminates it.

10. **The correct answer is (A).** This is a "form of" (degree or extent) analogy. PIVOTAL means "extremely IMPORTANT," just as *draconian* means "extremely stern." The analogy is based on degree.

11. **The correct answer is (C).** As the passage indicates, dendrochronological studies involve analyzing tree rings. Although the wood from trees might have been used for creating items which are now considered archeological artifacts, the author does not indicate explicitly that tree rings are studied for the purpose of dating such artifacts.

12. **The correct answer is (B).** In the second paragraph, the author mentions choices (A), (C), (D), and (E) as problems with radiocarbon dating. Nowhere in the passage, however, does the author mention any problem involving sample deterioration.

13. **The correct answer is (E).** RANCOR is a "feeling of hostility or antagonism toward another"; *affection* is a "feeling of fondness toward another."

14. **The correct answer is (D).** The best word for the second blank must suggest how the articles about "medical problems" related to the "heartwarming stories" that first appeared. It makes sense that *sobering* accounts would *counterbalance* heartwarming stores.

15. **The correct answer is (B).** Most of the passage—the entire second and third paragraphs—is concerned with examining the factors affecting the climate of various portions of the Andean *cordillera*. The first paragraph provides a framework for this discussion by describing the climate and topography of the various regions.

16. **The correct answer is (A).** The high-altitude plateaus are called *altiplano* (line 16). The passage states explicitly that the soil fertility in the northern *altiplano* is generally good (lines 17–19).

17. **The correct answer is (E).** The passage points out that while air temperature generally decreases as altitude increases, "variability of mountain topography"—i.e., dramatic changes in elevation—makes it difficult to determine temperature in any given spot from widely spaced measurements. It can be reasonably inferred from this information that an unexpected temperature would probably be the result of unexpected altitude.

18. **The correct answer is (D).** The only discussion of mountain symmetry is in the first paragraph, which mentions the symmetry in climate between the east and west flanks of the Northern Andes mountains. No mention is made anywhere in the passage of any symmetry with respect to the Central Andes mountains. On the other hand, choices (A), (B), (C), and (E) are all mentioned in the passage as factors affecting the climate of the Central Andes *cordillera.*

19. **The correct answer is (A).** Skin that is WAN is pale, or lacking color; skin that is *flushed* is characterized by glowing or a reddish color (as when a person blushes).

20. **The correct answer is (B).** This is a "result of" (process and product) analogy. When engaging in the art of SCULPTURE, especially wood sculpture, the artist produces a SHAVING, which is a byproduct of the sculpting process. When a person commits a *burglary,* the burglar's *arrest* is a possible result, or byproduct. Another key to this analogy is that in neither case is the result the actor's main objective or intention.

21. **The correct answer is (C).** The word "yet," which begins the sentence's second clause, tells you to look for a contrast between the two parts of the sentence. The missing word must suggest a difference between the two writers rather than another similarity. Of the five choices, only *distinctly different* serves this purpose.

22. **The correct answer is (D).** This is a "result or product" analogy. The objective (final result) of a LOTTERY typically is a PRIZE, awarded to the lottery winner. Similarly, the objective (final result) of attending *college* typically is to be awarded a *diploma.* Choice (B) does not provide as strong an analogy—a *loan,* although it's one possible reason to engage a *bank,* is not an award.

23. **The correct answer is (C).** This is a "defining characteristic" analogy. A person who is CIRCUMSPECT (cautious, wary, guarded, or watchful) is by definition characterized by VIGILANCE (watchfulness); similarly, a person who is *ardent* (zealous or eager) is by definition characterized by *enthusiasm.*

24. **The correct answer is integral for blank (i) and history or tradition for blank (ii).** The idea of the first sentence is that historic buildings that cannot be made safe must often be demolished, because structural safety is essential (or *integral*) when it comes to a building used by the general public. The idea of the third sentence is that a building's historic value (expressed more artfully, *history or tradition*) need not always be sacrificed for the sake of making the building safe for the public.

25. **The correct answer is (A).** In the preceding sentence, the author asserts that Turner's and Jordan's descriptions of restorationist activities "do not cohere well with the community participation model." By following this assertion with the suggestion that another model might be more serviceable, you can reasonably

infer that restorationists' activities are more consistent with this other model than with the community participation model.

26. **The correct answer is (E).** In the first paragraph, the author refers to the "crucial question" about, or key problem with, the restorationists' program, which the author then elucidates in the second paragraph.

27. **The correct answer is (C).** The phrase "at least as much as" sets up comparison between *theoretical* and the first missing word. This word should express an idea that opposes theoretical. Choices (A), (C), and (D) are the only viable choices. The transitional phrase "in that" signals that the first missing word should be a synonym for *detect*. This narrows the choices to (A) and (C). Now, consider the second word in each of these two answer choices. *Disprove* runs contrary to the intended meaning of the sentence as a whole. Thus, choice (C) provides the best completion.

28. **The correct answer is (A).** This is a "place or environment for" analogy. You dig a QUARRY, or excavation pit, where raw materials such as MARBLE are located for the purpose of extracting the materials. Similarly, you construct a *well* where *oil* is located for the purpose of extracting the *oil*.

29. **The correct answer is (C).** This is a "possible use of" analogy. A SNORKEL is an apparatus designed to aid in DIVING, but it is not essential for that activity; similarly, a *blade* is an apparatus designed to aid *skating,* but it is not essential for that activity.

30. **The correct answer is (B).** EXACERBATE has two common meanings: "provoke" and "intensify or heighten." To *lessen in degree* is to do the opposite of intensify.

## Quantitative Reasoning

| | | |
|---|---|---|
| 1. C | 11. C | 21. C |
| 2. A | 12. B | 22. D |
| 3. A | 13. 51.25 | 23. B |
| 4. D | 14. D | 24. B |
| 5. A | 15. E | 25. C |
| 6. D | 16. B | 26. A |
| 7. C | 17. B | 27. D |
| 8. A | 18. A | 28. B |
| 9. C | 19. A | |
| 10. A | 20. D | |

1. **The correct answer is (C).** To determine Quantity A, substitute the number 2 for $a$ and for $b$ in the centered equation:

$$(2 + 2)(2 - 2) = (4)(0) = 0$$

Follow the same procedure for the quantity in Column B:

$$(-2 + [-2])(-2 - [-2]) = (-4)(0) = 0$$

The quantities in both columns equal zero (0).

2. **The correct answer is (A).** For any fractional number between zero (0) and 1, the number is less than its square root, which in turn is less than its cube root.

3. **The correct answer is (A).** A circle's circumference is $\pi d$—the product of $\pi$ (a bit greater than 3.1) and the circle's diameter. If $\overline{AB}$ and $\overline{CD}$ were each as large as possible, they would each equal the circle's diameter. Three times this length is still be less than $\pi d$.

4. **The correct answer is (D).** $3x$ is a multiple of 3; thus, adding 5 to that number yields a number that is not a multiple of 3. Choice (A) is incorrect because $x > 0$ and therefore must equal 3 or some multiple of 3. Choices (B), (C), and (E) are incorrect because any integer multiplied by 3 is a multiple of 3, and any multiple of 3 (such as 6 or 18) added to a multiple of 3 is also a multiple of 3.

5. **The correct answer is (A).** In choice (A), unequal quantities are subtracted from equal quantities. The differences are unequal, but the inequality is reversed because unequal numbers are being subtracted from rather than added to the equal numbers.

6. **The correct answer is (D).** Without knowing either interest rate, it is impossible to compute either quantity in order to make the comparison.

7. **The correct answer is (C).** There are 2 prime numbers between 10 and 15: 11 and 13. The integer 33 has 2 prime factors: 3 and 11.

8. **The correct answer is (A).** First, isolate $y$ by dividing all terms by 3: $y = \dfrac{1}{6}x + 1$. The equation is now in the standard form $y = mx + b$, where $m$ is the line's slope. The slope of the perpendicular line is the negative reciprocal of $\dfrac{1}{6}$, or $-6$.

9. **The correct answer is (C).** In 45 minutes, the boat traveled 9 (not 10) segments (from one buoy to the next). That means it takes the boat 5 minutes to travel the length of 1 segment. At buoy 10, 5 additional segments remain ahead. Since the boat's average speed is the same before and after buoy 10, it takes the boat 5 × 5 = 25 minutes to travel from buoy 10 to buoy 15.

10. **The correct answer is (A).** Given $n$ = 2, the 25th term of Set R = 25$n$ + 25 = 25(2) + 25 = 75. Given $n$ = 2, the 24th term of Set S = $n$ + 23 = 2 + 23 = 25, and two times that 24th term is 50.

11. **The correct answer is (C).** There's no need to calculate either quantity, and you can cancel the product $st$ from both columns. To make the comparison, observe the place-value shifts from the decimal number 9.3. In Column A, the decimal point shifts 3 places left (9,300) and 3 places right (.0093), so the quantity is equivalent to (9.3)(9.3). You can now see that Quantity B, which is (9.3)(9.3), is the same as Quantity A.

12. **The correct answer is (B).** There's no need to calculate either quantity. Given an area of 12,000 square feet, the shortest possible rectangular perimeter is achieved with a square, in which all sides are the same length. Column B describes a corral with a width of 300 feet and a length of 400 feet. This corral would require more fence posts than a square corral.

13. **The correct answer is 51.25.** Think of Cynthia's average rate as the average of eight equally weighted one-hour trips. Seven of those trips receive a weight of 50, and one of the trips receives a weight of 60. You can express this algebraically as follows:

$$\frac{7(50)+60}{8} = \frac{350+60}{8} = \frac{410}{8} = 51.25$$

Cynthia's average rate during the entire trip was 51.25 mph. (There's no need to round either up or down to the nearest hundredth.)

14. **The correct answer is (D).** September and October each saw precipitous declines in the price of BioFirm stock and CompuWin stock, but only a modest increase in the price of Ardent stock. During each of these two months, the aggregate change was clearly negative. In July, however, a substantial price increase in CompuWin stock more than offset the combined decrease in the price of the other two stocks.

15. **The correct answer is (E).** The investor paid about $800 for 40 shares of Ardent stock (priced at about $20 per share), and then sold those 40 shares for about $2,200 (priced at about $55 per share). Accordingly, the investor's profit amounted to approximately $1,400.

16. **The correct answer is (B).** The area of any triangle = $\frac{1}{2}$ × base × height. Using 7 kilometers as the base of the triangle in this problem, the triangle's height is the north-south (vertical) distance from A to an imaginary line extending west from B. Given that farmhouse A is located a total of 10 kilometers farther west than farmhouse C, the extension is 3 kilometers long. The triangle's height is 4 kilometers ($3^2 + 4^2 = 5^2$,

by the Pythagorean theorem). Accordingly, the area of triangle ABC = $\frac{1}{2} \times 7 \times 4 = 14$ km$^2$.

**17. The correct answer is (B).** You can make the comparison quickly by recognizing that Quantity A is the "difference of two squares" ($x^2 - y^2$) in the factored form $(x + y)(x - y)$, where $y = 2$. Or, you can multiply the two binomials in Column A, and then simplify: $(x + 2)(x - 2) = x^2 + 2x - 2x - 4 = x^2 - 4$. Since $x^2 - 4 < x^2 - 2$, Quantity A < Quantity B.

**18. The correct answer is (A).** Q percent is based on $100. Therefore, Q percent = Q dollars, and Quantity B will always be $1 less than Quantity A.

**19. The correct answer is (A).** Apply the formula for determining arithmetic mean (called AM below), or simple average. Letting $x$ equal the other number, solve for $x$:

$$\text{AM} = \frac{Q + x}{2}$$
$$\text{PQ} = \frac{Q + x}{2}$$
$$2\text{PQ} = Q + x$$
$$2\text{PQ} - Q = x$$

**20. The correct answer is (D).** Letting $x$ equal the number of ounces of soy sauce added to the mixture, $18 + x$ equals the total amount of the mixture after the soy sauce is added. The amount of peanut sauce (5.76 ounces) must equal 12% of the new total amount of the mixture, which is

$18 + x$. You can express this as an algebraic equation and solve for $x$:

$$5.76 = .12(x + 18)$$
$$576 = 12(x + 18)$$
$$576 = 12x + 216$$
$$360 = 12x$$
$$30 = x$$

30 ounces of soy sauce must be added to achieve a mixture that includes 12% peanut sauce.

**21. The correct answer is (C).** $x + y +$ the measure of the third interior angle (let's call it $w$) = 180. Also, $w + z = 180$ (because their angles combine to form a straight line). So, you have two equations:

$$x + y + w = 180 \text{ or } x + y = 180 - w$$
$$w + z = 180 \text{ or } z = 180 - w$$

Therefore, $x + y = z$ (Quantity A = Quantity B)

**22. The correct answer is (D).** The centered information establishes that Quantity B, $pq$, must be negative, because the product of a positive number and a negative number is always negative. As for Quantity A, try substituting some simple numbers for $p$ and $q$. If $p = 1$ and $q = -1$, then $p + q = 0$ while $pq = -1$, and therefore $p + q > pq$. But if $p = \frac{1}{4}$ and $q = -\frac{1}{2}$, $p + q = -\frac{1}{4}$ while $pq = \frac{1}{8}$, and therefore $p + q < pq$. Thus, which quantity is greater depends on the values of $p$ and $q$.

**23. The correct answer is (B).** The range of D = $10 - 3 = 7$. The median of D = the arithmetic mean of 6 and 9 (the two middle terms) = 7.5.

24. **The correct answer is (B).** Let {A, B, C, D, E} represent the set of ice cream flavors. 10 triple-scoop combinations are available:

{ABC}{ABD}{ABE}{ACD}{ACE}{ADE} {BCD}{BCE}{BDE}{CDE}

Each of these combinations is available on either of the two cone types. Thus, the total number of distinct triple-scoop cones having three different ice-cream flavors is 20.

25. **The correct answer is (C).** The question asks you to select the choice that does NOT describe sales totaling at least 10,000. Choice (C) describes 1.7K + 4.9K + 2.2K = 8.8K sales, which is less than $10,000. Choice (A) describes 8.5K + 1.9K = 10.4K sales. Choice (B) describes 7.5K + 1.0K + 2.0 + 0.8 = 11.3K sales. Choice (D) describes 4.9K + 5.1K = 10.0K sales. Choice (E) describes 8.5K + 4.9K = 13.4K sales.

26. **The correct answer is (A).** The number of basic models was 13,800 (the sum of all numbers in the "Basic" column). The number of standard models sold was 29,900 (the sum of all numbers in the "Standard" column). The difference is 16,100. To find the average premium paid for a standard model, divide $41,000,000 by $16,100. Rounding these figures to $40 million and $16,000, the quotient is $2,500.

27. **The correct answer is (D).** Without the square hole, each of the cube's six outer surfaces contains 9 square inches, for a total of 54 square inches of outer surface area. The square hole reduces that total outer surface area by 2 square inches, to 52. Each of the four inner surfaces (inside the hole) accounts for an additional 3 square inches, for a total of 12 square inches of inner surface areas. The solid's total surface area is 52 + 12 = 64 square inches.

28. **The correct answer is (B).** Since $x$ is a negative number (less than $-1$), $x^3$ is negative and $x^2$ is positive. Hence, Quantity A is a negative number less than $x^3$. Quantity B, on the other hand, is a positive number greater than $x^2$.

# ANSWER SHEET PRACTICE TEST 3

## Analytical Writing—Issue Task

_____

_____

_____

_____

_____

_____

_____

_____

_____

_____

_____

_____

_____

_____

_____

_____

_____

_____

_____

_____

answer sheet

**Analytical Writing—Argument Task**

_____

_____

_____

_____

_____

_____

_____

_____

_____

_____

_____

_____

_____

_____

_____

_____

_____

_____

_____

_____

_____

_____

answer sheet

## Quantitative Reasoning

1. Ⓐ Ⓑ Ⓒ Ⓓ Ⓔ
2. Ⓐ Ⓑ Ⓒ Ⓓ
3. Ⓐ Ⓑ Ⓒ Ⓓ
4. Ⓐ Ⓑ Ⓒ Ⓓ Ⓔ
5. Ⓐ Ⓑ Ⓒ Ⓓ Ⓔ
6. Ⓐ Ⓑ Ⓒ Ⓓ
7. Ⓐ Ⓑ Ⓒ Ⓓ
8. Ⓐ Ⓑ Ⓒ Ⓓ Ⓔ
9. Ⓐ Ⓑ Ⓒ Ⓓ Ⓔ
10. Ⓐ Ⓑ Ⓒ Ⓓ Ⓔ
11. Ⓐ Ⓑ Ⓒ Ⓓ

12. Ⓐ Ⓑ Ⓒ Ⓓ
13. Ⓐ Ⓑ Ⓒ Ⓓ
14. Ⓐ Ⓑ Ⓒ Ⓓ
15. Ⓐ Ⓑ Ⓒ Ⓓ
16. Ⓐ Ⓑ Ⓒ Ⓓ Ⓔ
17. Ⓐ Ⓑ Ⓒ Ⓓ
18. Ⓐ Ⓑ Ⓒ Ⓓ
19. Ⓐ Ⓑ Ⓒ Ⓓ
20. Ⓐ Ⓑ Ⓒ Ⓓ Ⓔ
21. Ⓐ Ⓑ Ⓒ Ⓓ Ⓔ
22. Ⓐ Ⓑ Ⓒ Ⓓ Ⓔ

23. Ⓐ Ⓑ Ⓒ Ⓓ
24. ▭/▭
25. Ⓐ Ⓑ Ⓒ Ⓓ
26. Ⓐ Ⓑ Ⓒ Ⓓ Ⓔ
27. Ⓐ Ⓑ Ⓒ Ⓓ Ⓔ
28. Ⓐ Ⓑ Ⓒ Ⓓ Ⓔ

## Verbal Reasoning

1. Ⓐ Ⓑ Ⓒ Ⓓ Ⓔ
2. Ⓐ Ⓑ Ⓒ Ⓓ Ⓔ
3. Ⓐ Ⓑ Ⓒ Ⓓ Ⓔ
4. Ⓐ Ⓑ Ⓒ Ⓓ Ⓔ
5. Ⓐ Ⓑ Ⓒ Ⓓ Ⓔ
6. Ⓐ Ⓑ Ⓒ Ⓓ Ⓔ
7. Ⓐ Ⓑ Ⓒ Ⓓ Ⓔ
8. Ⓐ Ⓑ Ⓒ Ⓓ Ⓔ
9. Ⓐ Ⓑ Ⓒ Ⓓ Ⓔ
10. Ⓐ Ⓑ Ⓒ Ⓓ Ⓔ
11. Ⓐ Ⓑ Ⓒ Ⓓ Ⓔ

12. Ⓐ Ⓑ Ⓒ Ⓓ Ⓔ
13. Ⓐ Ⓑ Ⓒ Ⓓ Ⓔ
14. Ⓐ Ⓑ Ⓒ Ⓓ Ⓔ
15. Ⓐ Ⓑ Ⓒ Ⓓ Ⓔ
16. Ⓐ Ⓑ Ⓒ Ⓓ Ⓔ
17. Ⓐ Ⓑ Ⓒ Ⓓ Ⓔ
18. Ⓐ Ⓑ Ⓒ Ⓓ Ⓔ
19. Ⓐ Ⓑ Ⓒ Ⓓ Ⓔ
20. Ⓐ Ⓑ Ⓒ Ⓓ Ⓔ
21. Ⓐ Ⓑ Ⓒ Ⓓ Ⓔ
22. Ⓐ Ⓑ Ⓒ Ⓓ Ⓔ

23. Ⓐ Ⓑ Ⓒ Ⓓ Ⓔ
24. Ⓐ Ⓑ Ⓒ Ⓓ Ⓔ
25. Ⓐ Ⓑ Ⓒ Ⓓ Ⓔ
26. Ⓐ Ⓑ Ⓒ Ⓓ Ⓔ
27. Ⓐ Ⓑ Ⓒ Ⓓ Ⓔ
28. Ⓐ Ⓑ Ⓒ Ⓓ Ⓔ
29. (i) _____
    (ii) _____
    (iii) _____
30. Ⓐ Ⓑ Ⓒ Ⓓ Ⓔ

answer sheet

# Practice Test 3

## ANALYTICAL WRITING

### Issue Task

*Time: 45 Minutes*

> **NOTES:** For *some* test-takers, the GRE will end with an identified and untimed research section. The research section, which is unscored, contains experimental question types. Test-makers use it to assess the difficulty levels of the experimental question types, based on test-takers' responses.
>
> For the purposes of this book—making sure you're fully prepared to take the GRE exam—one Complex Text Completion question (Verbal Reasoning section) and one numeric entry question (Quantitative Reasoning section) are included in each of the Practice Tests. On the actual GRE, however, you will not see both of these questions; in fact, you may *not* see either one.

Using a word processor, compose an essay that responds to the following statement and directive. Do not use any spell-checking or grammar-checking functions (they are not available on the actual GRE).

> "No business should sacrifice the quality of its products or services for the sake of maximizing profits."

> Write an essay in which you present your perspective on the statement above. Develop and support your viewpoint with relevant reasons and examples.

## Argument Task

### *Time: 30 Minutes*

Using a word processor, compose an essay that responds to the following statement and directive. Do not use any spell-checking or grammar-checking functions (they are not available on the actual GRE).

> The following is excerpted from an editorial appearing in a local newspaper:

> "In order to prevent a decline of Oak City's property values and in rents that Oak City property owners can command, the residents of Oak City must speak out against the approval of a new four-year private college in their town. After all, in the nearby town of Mapleton the average rent for apartments has decreased by 10 percent since its new community college opened last year, while the average value of Mapleton's single-family homes has declined by an even greater percentage over the same time period."

> Discuss how well-reasoned you find the argument above.

## QUANTITATIVE REASONING

### 28 Questions • 45 Minutes

**NOTE:** In this section, questions are grouped together by format, and within each group the questions grow more difficult as you go. Because the actual GRE is computer-adaptive in the multiple-choice sections, it intersperses questions of different formats and difficulty levels.

1. If $x + y = a$, and if $x - y = b$, then $x =$

   **(A)** $\frac{1}{2}(a - b)$

   **(B)** $a + b$

   **(C)** $a - b$

   **(D)** $\frac{1}{2}ab$

   **(E)** $\frac{1}{2}(a + b)$

<table>
<tr><td><u>Column A</u></td><td><u>Column B</u></td></tr>
</table>

2.                          P is a positive integer.

| The remainder when $7P + 8$ is divided by 7 | The remainder when $3P + 5$ is divided by 3 |
|---|---|

   **(A)** The quantity in Column A is greater;
   **(B)** The quantity in Column B is greater;
   **(C)** The quantities are equal;
   **(D)** The relationship cannot be determined from the information given.

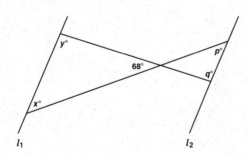

|  | **Column A** | **Column B** |
|---|---|---|

**3.**

$$l_1 \parallel l_2$$

| $x - y$ | $q - p$ |
|---|---|

**(A)** The quantity in Column A is greater;
**(B)** The quantity in Column B is greater;
**(C)** The quantities are equal;
**(D)** The relationship cannot be determined from the information given.

**4.** If one dollar can buy $m$ pieces of paper, how many dollars are needed to buy $p$ reams of paper? [1 ream = 500 pieces of paper.]

**(A)** $\dfrac{500p}{m}$

**(B)** $\dfrac{m}{500p}$

**(C)** $\dfrac{500}{p+m}$

**(D)** $\dfrac{p}{500m}$

**(E)** $500m(p - m)$

**5.** If $\dfrac{a}{b} \cdot \dfrac{b}{c} \cdot \dfrac{c}{d} \cdot \dfrac{d}{e} \cdot x = 1$, then $x =$

**(A)** $\dfrac{a}{e}$

**(B)** $\dfrac{be}{a}$

**(C)** $e$

**(D)** $\dfrac{1}{a}$

**(E)** $\dfrac{e}{a}$

|  | **Column A** | **Column B** |
|---|---|---|

**6.**

$$0 < a < 1$$
$$0 < b < 1$$

| $a + b$ | $a^2 + b^2$ |
|---|---|

**(A)** The quantity in Column A is greater;
**(B)** The quantity in Column B is greater;
**(C)** The quantities are equal;
**(D)** The relationship cannot be determined from the information given.

**7.** A case of soda costs $17.40. The cost of *p* individual cans of soda is $1.20 per can.

| <u>Column A</u> | <u>Column B</u> |
|---|---|
| The lowest possible value of *p* if the cost of *p* cans of soda is greater than the cost of a case of soda. | 15 |

**(A)** The quantity in Column A is greater;
**(B)** The quantity in Column B is greater;
**(C)** The quantities are equal;
**(D)** The relationship cannot be determined from the information given.

---

**Directions:** Questions 8–10 refer to the following graph.

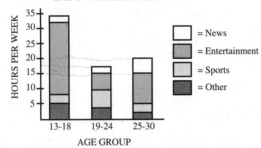

AVERAGE NUMBER OF HOURS PER WEEK
SPENT WATCHING TELEVISION

**8.** Based solely on the information in the graph, approximately how many hours per week does the average 27-year old spend watching news on television?

**(A)** 2
**(B)** 5
**(C)** 8
**(D)** 10
**(E)** 20

**9.** The age group that spends the greatest number of hours per week watching sports on television spends approximately what percent of its total television-viewing time watching programming other than news, entertainment, or sports?

**(A)** 4
**(B)** 10
**(C)** 16
**(D)** 22
**(E)** 33

**10.** What is the approximate ratio of the average number of hours per week that the youngest age group spends watching televised entertainment to the average number of hours per week that the other two groups combined spend watching the same type of programming?

**(A)** 3:4
**(B)** 1:1
**(C)** 5:4
**(D)** 5:3
**(E)** 5:2

11. A rectangular ribbon of paper is looped to form a circular ring having a diameter that measures twice the ring's height.

|           Column A           |           Column B           |
| :--------------------------: | :--------------------------: |
| The surface area of the outside of the ring | Twice the circular area of the ring, measured to the paper's outer surface |

(A) The quantity in Column A is greater;
(B) The quantity in Column B is greater;
(C) The quantities are equal;
(D) The relationship cannot be determined from the information given.

|           Column A           |           Column B           |
| :--------------------------: | :--------------------------: |
| 12.    The average (arithmetic mean) of $x$ and $y$ | The average (arithmetic mean) of $x - 1$ and $y + 1$ |

(A) The quantity in Column A is greater;
(B) The quantity in Column B is greater;
(C) The quantities are equal;
(D) The relationship cannot be determined from the information given.

13. Three movie patrons of differing heights are standing in line, one behind the other, to purchase tickets for the movie.

|           Column A           |           Column B           |
| :--------------------------: | :--------------------------: |
| The probability that the three patrons are lined up in order from shortest to tallest | The probability that the first patron in line is neither the tallest nor the shortest of the three patrons |

(A) The quantity in Column A is greater;
(B) The quantity in Column B is greater;
(C) The quantities are equal;
(D) The relationship cannot be determined from the information given.

14. A buyer pays a $1.00 tax on an item that costs $10.00 after the tax is added.

|           Column A           |   Column B   |
| :--------------------------: | :----------: |
| The percentage rate of the tax | 11%        |

(A) The quantity in Column A is greater;
(B) The quantity in Column B is greater;
(C) The quantities are equal;
(D) The relationship cannot be determined from the information given.

|           Column A           |   Column B   |
| :--------------------------: | :----------: |
| 15.          $3^{26}$        | $9^{13}$     |

(A) The quantity in Column A is greater;
(B) The quantity in Column B is greater;
(C) The quantities are equal;
(D) The relationship cannot be determined from the information given.

**16.**

| Temperature (F°) | Number of Days in April (Low Daily Temperature) | Number of Days in April (High Daily Temperature) |
|---|---|---|
| 41°−45° | 14 | 3 |
| 46°−50° | 12 | 9 |
| 51° and above | 4 | 18 |

The table shows the distribution of daily low and daily high temperatures in a certain location during each of the 30 days in April. Recorded low and high temperatures were rounded to the nearest Fahrenheit degree (F°).

What was the range of daily high temperatures during the month of April?

**(A)** 10 degrees
**(B)** 14 degrees
**(C)** 15 degrees
**(D)** 51 degrees
**(E)** It cannot be determined from the information given.

|  Column A  |  Column B  |
|---|---|

**17.**         Five more than twice the number $n$ is 17.

3 less than $\dfrac{n}{2}$              2 less than $\dfrac{n}{3}$

**(A)** The quantity in Column A is greater;
**(B)** The quantity in Column B is greater;
**(C)** The quantities are equal;
**(D)** The relationship cannot be determined from the information given.

|  Column A  |  Column B  |
|---|---|

**18.**                    $0 < p < q$

The ratio of $p$ to $(p + 1)$              The ratio of $q$ to $(q + 1)$

**(A)** The quantity in Column A is greater;
**(B)** The quantity in Column B is greater;
**(C)** The quantities are equal;
**(D)** The relationship cannot be determined from the information given.

**19.** Distribution P is given as $\{-2, 1, x\}$, where $x$ is the median. Distribution Q is given as $\{x, 0, 3\}$, where $x$ is the median.

|  Column A  |  Column B  |
|---|---|
| The standard deviation of Distribution P | The standard deviation of Distribution Q |

**(A)** The quantity in Column A is greater;
**(B)** The quantity in Column B is greater;
**(C)** The quantities are equal;
**(D)** The relationship cannot be determined from the information given.

**20.** Kirk sent $54 to the newspaper dealer for whom he delivers papers, after deducting a 10% commission for himself. If newspapers sell for 40 cents each, how many papers did Kirk deliver?

  **(A)** 150
  **(B)** 210
  **(C)** 240
  **(D)** 320
  **(E)** 610

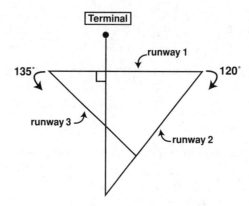

**21.** As shown in the figure, from runway 1 airplanes must turn 120° to the right onto runway 2 or 135° to the left onto runway 3. Which of the following indicate(s) a complete turn from one runway to another?

  I. 45°
  II. 85°
  III. 105°

  **(A)** II only
  **(B)** III only
  **(C)** I and III only
  **(D)** II and III only
  **(E)** I, II, and III

**22.** In a geometric sequence, each term is a constant multiple of the preceding one. If the first three terms in a geometric sequence are $-2$, $x$, and $-8$, which of the following could be the sixth term in the sequence?

  **(A)** 512
  **(B)** 256
  **(C)** 64
  **(D)** $-17$
  **(E)** $-128$

|  | __Column A__ | __Column B__ |
|---|---|---|
| **23.** | $\dfrac{a^2 + b^2}{ab}$ | $\dfrac{a}{b} + \dfrac{b}{a}$ |

  **(A)** The quantity in Column A is greater;
  **(B)** The quantity in Column B is greater;
  **(C)** The quantities are equal;
  **(D)** The relationship cannot be determined from the information given.

**24.** A certain line on the *xy*-plane contains the $(x,y)$ points $(-2,1)$ and $(3,5)$. What is the slope of the line?

*Click on each answer box, then type a number in each box. Backspace to erase.*

Express your answer as a simple fraction. To indicate a negative fraction, enter a dash (minus sign) before either the numerator number or the denominator number.

**Column A**                                **Column B**

**25.**

$$<u> = u^2 - u$$
$u$ is a non-zero number.

          $2<u>$                                   $<2u>$

**(A)** The quantity in Column A is greater;
**(B)** The quantity in Column B is greater;
**(C)** The quantities are equal;
**(D)** The relationship cannot be determined from the information given.

**26.** M college students agree to rent an apartment for D dollars per month, sharing the rent equally. If the rent is increased by \$100, what amount must each student contribute?

**(A)** $\dfrac{M+100}{D}$

**(B)** $\dfrac{D}{M}+100$

**(C)** $\dfrac{D}{M}$

**(D)** $\dfrac{M}{D+100}$

**(E)** $\dfrac{D+100}{M}$

**27.** In the figure above, the centers of all three circles lie on the same line. The radius of the middle-sized circle is twice that of the smallest circle. If the radius of the smallest circle is 1, what is the length of the boundary of the shaded region?

(A) $12\pi$

(B) $6\pi$

(C) 12

(D) $3\pi$

(E) 9

**28.** Among registered voters in a certain district, the ratio of male to female voters is 3:5. If the district currently includes 2,400 registered voters, how many additional males must register to make the ratio 4:5, assuming the number of female voters remains unchanged?

(A) 120

(B) 150

(C) 240

(D) 300

(E) 360

# VERBAL REASONING

## 30 Questions • 30 Minutes

**NOTE:** In this section, questions are grouped together by format, and within each group the questions grow more difficult as you go. Because the actual GRE is computer-adaptive in the multiple-choice sections, it intersperses questions of different formats and difficulty levels.

1. ITINERANT:
   - (A) settled
   - (B) paralyzed
   - (C) fixated
   - (D) linear
   - (E) lethargic

2. WEAPON : INTIMIDATE ::
   - (A) memory : recall
   - (B) donor : give
   - (C) icebox : preserve
   - (D) sun : shine
   - (E) meal : serve

3. NATAL : GESTATION ::
   - (A) wealthy : investment
   - (B) conclusive : premise
   - (C) humble : conceit
   - (D) truthful : proof
   - (E) feeble : cowardice

4. INCREDULITY:
   - (A) truthfulness
   - (B) faith
   - (C) credibility
   - (D) loyalty
   - (E) reverence

5. The _____ and _____ lifestyle of certain types of primates differs greatly from the habits of most primate species, who are active during the day and who form societies based on quite complex interrelationships.
   - (A) sedentary . . omnivorous
   - (B) inactive . . monogamous
   - (C) nomadic . . lonely
   - (D) nocturnal . . solitary
   - (E) diurnal . . gregarious

6. VIE:
   - (A) grow weary
   - (B) fall behind
   - (C) admit defeat
   - (D) reduce expectations
   - (E) change priorities

7. VERDANT:
   - (A) incomplete
   - (B) immature
   - (C) forbidding
   - (D) diminutive
   - (E) desolate

8. Personality is rooted as deeply in the need for _____, or at least personal interaction, as _____ well-being is rooted in chemical needs.
   - (A) love . . physical
   - (B) hope . . biological
   - (C) affection . . social
   - (D) self-respect . . bodily
   - (E) companionship . . natural

**Directions:** Questions 9–11 are based on the following passage.

*Line* Late Victorian and modern ideas of culture are indebted to Matthew Arnold, who, largely through his *Culture and Anarchy* (1869), placed
(5) the word at the center of debates about the goals of intellectual life and humanistic society. Arnold defined culture as "the pursuit of perfection by getting to know the best which has
(10) been thought and said." Through this knowledge, Arnold hoped, we can turn

"a fresh and free thought upon our stock notions and habits." Although Arnold helped to define the purposes (15) of the liberal arts curriculum in the century following the publication of *Culture*, three concrete forms of dissent from his views have had considerable impact of their own.

(20)    The first protests Arnold's fearful designation of "anarchy" as culture's enemy, viewing this dichotomy simply as another version of the struggle between a privileged power structure (25) and radical challenges to its authority. But while Arnold certainly tried to define the *arch*—the legitimizing order of value—against the *anarch* of existentialist democracy, he himself (30) was plagued in his soul by the blind arrogances of the reactionary powers in his world. The writer who regarded the contemporary condition with such apprehension in *Culture* is the poet (35) who wrote "Dover Beach," not an ideologue rounding up all the usual modern suspects.

Another form of opposition saw Arnold's culture as a perverse per- (40) petuation of classical and literary learning, outlook, and privileges in a world where science had become the new arch and from which any substantively new order of thinking must (45) develop. At the center of the "two cultures" debate were the goals of the formal educational curriculum, the principal vehicle through which Arnoldian culture operates. However, (50) Arnold himself had viewed culture as enacting its life in a much more broadly conceived set of institutions.

A third form is so-called "multiculturalism," a movement aimed largely (55) at gaining recognition for voices and visions that Arnoldian culture has implicitly suppressed. In educational practice, multiculturalists are interested in deflating the imperious (60) authority that "high culture" exercises over curriculum while bringing into

play the principle that we must learn what is representative, for we have overemphasized what is exceptional. (65) Though the multiculturalists' conflict with Arnoldian culture has clear affinities with the radical critique, multiculturalism actually affirms Arnold by returning us more specifi- (70) cally to a tension inherent in the idea of culture rather than to the culture-anarchy dichotomy.

The social critics, defenders of science, and multiculturalists insist (75) that Arnold's culture is simply a device for ordering us about. Instead, however, it is designed to register the gathering of ideological clouds on the horizon. There is no utopian motive in (80) Arnold's celebration of perfection. Perfection mattered to Arnold as the only background against which we could form a just image of our actual circumstances, just as we can conceive (85) finer sunsets and unheard melodies.

9. Based on the information in the passage, Arnold would probably agree that the educational curriculum should
   (A) focus on the sciences more than the humanities
   (B) strike a balance between practicality and theory
   (C) reflect the dominant culture of the day
   (D) be more rigorous than during the past
   (E) deemphasize what is representative

10. It can be inferred from the passage that the two-cultures debate
    (A) emerged as a reaction to the multiculturalist movement
    (B) developed after 1869
    (C) influenced Arnold's thinking about culture
    (D) was carried on by American as well as European scientists
    (E) led to a schizophrenic educational system

11. The author's primary concern in the passage is to
    (A) argue against those who have opposed Arnold's ideas
    (B) describe Arnold's conception of culture
    (C) explain why Arnold considered the pursuit of perfection to be the essence of culture
    (D) trace Arnold's influence on the liberal arts educational curriculum
    (E) examine the different views of culture that have emerged since the eighteenth century

12. DECREE : INFORM ::
    (A) fascinate : interest
    (B) gallop : canter
    (C) resign : quit
    (D) endure : persist
    (E) shout : whisper

13. CINNAMON : CONFECTION ::
    (A) villain : tale
    (B) cliff : plateau
    (C) collar : cuff
    (D) fence : prison
    (E) flank : horse

14. Considering today's high divorce rate and growing number of single-parent households, it is _____ that the most Americans still adhere to the _____ belief in the importance of an intact nuclear family.
    (A) surprising . . superficial
    (B) encouraging . . obsolete
    (C) interesting . . popular
    (D) illuminating . . controversial
    (E) astonishing . . traditional

15. LATITUDE:
    (A) conformity
    (B) point of focus
    (C) strictness
    (D) inflection
    (E) restraint

**Directions:** Questions 16–18 are based on the following passage.

Line A certain strain of bacteria called *lyngbya majuscula*, an ancient ancestor of modern-day algae, is making a comeback in ocean waters
(5) just off the world's most industrialized coastal regions. This primitive bacteria has survived for nearly three billion years due to a variety of survival mechanisms. It can produce its
(10) own fertilizer by pulling nitrogen out of the air; it relies on a different spectrum of light than algae do, allowing it to thrive even in deep, murky waters; and when it dies and
(15) decays, it releases its own nitrogen and phosphorous, on which the next generation of *lyngbya* feeds.

   *Lyngbya* emits more than one hundred different toxins harmful to
(20) other ocean life as well as to humans. Commercial fishermen and divers who come in contact with the bacteria frequently complain of skin rashes and respiratory problems, which can keep
(25) these workers off the job for months at a time. The bacteria further disrupts local economies by blocking sunlight to sea grasses that attract fish and other sea life. Scientists attribute the
(30) modern-day reappearance of *lyngbya*, and the resulting problems, chiefly to nitrogen- and phosphorous-rich sewage partially processed at wastewater treatment plants and pumped
(35) into rivers that feed coastal ocean waters.

16. The passage as a whole can appropriately be viewed as an examination of which of the following?
    (A) The causes and consequences of the re-emergence of *lyngbya*
    (B) The possible means of halting and reversing the spread of *lyngbya*
    (C) The economic impact of *lyngbya* on certain coastal communities
    (D) The survival mechanisms and life cycle of *lyngbya*
    (E) The ecological fallout resulting from coastal sewage runoff

17. It can be inferred from the passage that the *lyngbya majuscula* strain has survived for billions of years partly because it
    (A) is threatened by few, if any, natural predators
    (B) emits harmful toxins that ward off potential predators
    (C) does not depend on light for its existence
    (D) possesses the ability to essentially feed on itself
    (E) adapts easily to changes in water temperature

18. According to passage, the *lyngbya majuscula* strain
    I. depends largely on nitrogen and phosphorous as nutrients
    II. can harm other ocean life as a result of its high toxicity
    III. thrives mainly in waters where algae is largely absent
    (A) I only
    (B) III only
    (C) I and II only
    (D) II and III only
    (E) I, II, and III

19. PITH:
    (A) frivolity
    (B) bore
    (C) adornment
    (D) chasm
    (E) digression

20. RUNT : SIBLING ::
    (A) athlete : league
    (B) spade : suit
    (C) veneer : shield
    (D) penny : currency
    (E) peephole : window

21. The high incidence of speech articulation disorders among young children suggests that such "disorders" are _____ developmental phenomena, since they generally occur less frequently among _____ age groups.
    (A) very serious . . most
    (B) relatively rare . . certain
    (C) actually normal . . other
    (D) clinically acceptable . . younger
    (E) commonly misunderstood . . older

22. CARETAKER : ATTENTIVE ::
    (A) hair : curly
    (B) writing : legible
    (C) mule : obstinate
    (D) mansion : spacious
    (E) meat : broiled

23. TRAVESTY : RIDICULE ::
    (A) reproduction : copy
    (B) treachery : reprieve
    (C) impersonator : imitate
    (D) language : understand
    (E) forgery : deceive

24. The _____ of the judging process might be compromised unless each contestant is assigned a unique code number by which he or she is identified.
    (A) accuracy
    (B) finality
    (C) authority
    (D) impartiality
    (E) decisions

25. SHORE : PRECARIOUS ::
    (A) plane : irregular
    (B) boil : tepid
    (C) frequent : uninviting
    (D) stiffen : pliable
    (E) douse : damp

**Directions:** Questions 26–27 are based on the following passage.

*Line* In the United States, the extent of adult illiteracy at the workplace has been obscured by adequate employment for adults with few or no
(5) literacy skills, too-simple definitions of literacy, faulty survey methods, and a stigma associated with illiteracy that keeps many people from admitting illiteracy or seeking help in over-
(10) coming it. With today's increasingly rapid technological advances and increased foreign competition, however, U.S. businesses are growing more and more aware of the extent
(15) and the costs of illiteracy in the work force. The U.S. Bureau of Labor Statistics warns that the U.S. labor-force entrants in the years ahead may not have the skills that employers
(20) need—that new jobs in the service industries, where most job growth is projected to occur, will demand much higher literacy skill levels than today's service jobs, and few new jobs
(25) will be created for those who cannot read and follow directions, fill out forms and communicate by e-mail with coworkers, and perform simple arithmetical computations applying
(30) the basic rules of mathematics.

26. Which of the following can be inferred solely on the basis of information in the passage?
   **(A)** Illiteracy is more common among older workers than young ones.
   **(B)** Technology jobs require greater literacy skills than other jobs.
   **(C)** New U.S. service-industry jobs are likely to be filled by workers from outside the U.S.
   **(D)** U.S. schools do an inadequate job in teaching literacy skills.
   **(E)** Declining U.S. productivity is attributable primarily to workplace illiteracy.

27. It can be inferred from the passage that
   **(A)** workers today should learn to speak more than one language
   **(B)** adding numbers is a type of literacy skill
   **(C)** government projections about the future job market are unreliable
   **(D)** solving workplace problems usually requires face-to-face communication
   **(E)** workplace literacy programs are generally ineffective

28. OBLIGATE:
   **(A)** treat fairly
   **(B)** allow to occur
   **(C)** refrain from interfering
   **(D)** excuse from debt
   **(E)** comply with an order

**29.** Great achievers are by nature (i)_____, and therefore tend to be dissatisfied and discontent with their accomplishments—no matter how great. Perhaps the (ii)_____ modern example of this phenomenon was the eminent physicist Albert Einstein, whose theoretical breakthroughs in physics only raised new theoretical (iii)_____, which Einstein himself recognized and spent the last twenty years of his life struggling unsuccessfully to solve.

| (i) |
| --- |
| perpetually malcontent |
| insatiably ambitious |
| tenaciously obsessive |

| (ii) |
| --- |
| most illustrious |
| paradigmatic |
| unrivaled |

| (iii) |
| --- |
| dilemmas |
| concepts |
| challenges |

**30.** SWEAR : OATH ::
(A) follow : leader
(B) obey : rule
(C) solve : problem
(D) sign : contract
(E) issue : warning

# ANSWER KEY AND EXPLANATIONS

## Analytical Writing

### ISSUE TASK: EVALUATION AND SCORING

Evaluate your Issue task essay on a scale of 1 to 6 (6 being the highest score) according to the following five criteria:

1. Does your essay develop a position on the issue through the use of incisive reasons and persuasive examples?

2. Are your essay's ideas conveyed clearly and articulately?

3. Does your essay maintain proper focus on the issue, and is it well organized?

4. Does your essay demonstrate proficiency, fluency, and maturity in its use of sentence structure, vocabulary, and idiom?

5. Does your essay demonstrate command of the elements of Standard Written English, including grammar, word usage, spelling, and punctuation?

### ARGUMENT TASK: EVALUATION AND SCORING

Evaluate your Argument task essay on a scale of 1 to 6 (6 being the highest score) according to the following five criteria:

1. Does your essay identify and articulate the argument's key unstated assumptions?

2. Does your essay explain how the argument relies on these unstated assumptions, and what the implications are if these assumptions are unwarranted?

3. Does your essay develop its ideas in a clear, organized manner, with appropriate transitions to help connect ideas together?

4. Does your essay demonstrate proficiency, fluency, and maturity in its use of sentence structure, vocabulary, and idiom?

5. Does your essay demonstrate command of the elements of Standard Written English, including grammar, word usage, spelling, and punctuation?

To help you evaluate your essay in terms of criteria 1 and 2, the following is a series of questions that identify *four* distinct unstated assumptions upon which the argument relies. To earn a score of 4 or higher, your essay should identify and explain at least three of these assumptions. Identifying and explaining at least four of the unstated assumptions would help earn you an even higher score.

- Does the Argument draw a *questionable analogy* between Oak City's circumstances and Mapleton's? (Perhaps the percentage of students needing off-campus housing, which might affect property values, is significantly greater in one town than the other.)

- Does the Argument draw a *questionable analogy* between four-year colleges and community colleges? (Perhaps a four-year college would bring greater prestige or higher culture to the town.)

- Is the presence of Mapleton's new community college necessarily the actual cause of the decline in Mapleton's property values and rents? (Perhaps some other recent development is responsible instead.)

- Is it *necessary* to refuse the new college in order to prevent a decline in property values and rents? (Perhaps Oak City can counteract downward pressure on property values and rents through some other means.)

## Quantitative Reasoning

| | | |
|---|---|---|
| 1. E | 11. C | 20. A |
| 2. B | 12. C | 21. C |
| 3. D | 13. B | 22. C |
| 4. A | 14. A | 23. C |
| 5. E | 15. C | 24. 4/5 |
| 6. A | 16. E | 25. A |
| 7. C | 17. C | 26. E |
| 8. B | 18. B | 27. B |
| 9. D | 19. D | 28. D |
| 10. D | | |

1. **The correct answer is (E).** Add the two equations:

$$x + y = a$$
$$x - y = b$$
$$\overline{\phantom{xxxxxxxxxx}}$$
$$2x = a + b$$
$$x = \frac{1}{2}(a+b)$$

2. **The correct answer is (B).** The problem can be simplified. When you divide 8 by 7, the remainder is 1. When you divide 5 by 3, the remainder is 2.

3. **The correct answer is (D).** Because the two lines are parallel, the two triangles are the same shape, and their corresponding angles are equal in size ($x = p$ and $y = q$), and therefore $x - y = p - q$. However, the quantity $x - y$ is being compared here to $q - p$, not $p - q$. The two quantities are equal in size only if all four angles are equal (56°). It is not possible to determine whether all four angles are the same size, regardless of the measure of the third angle. Even though it appears from the figure that $x - y$ is a negative number and $q - p$ is a positive number, you can't assume that.

4. **The correct answer is (A).** The number of dollars increases proportionately with the number of pieces of paper. The question is essentially asking: "1 is to $m$ as what is to $p$?" First, set up a proportion (equate two ratios, or fractions). Then convert either pieces of paper to reams (divide $m$ by 500) or reams to pieces (multiply $p$ by 500). (The second conversion method is used below.) Cross-multiply to solve for $x$:

$$\frac{1}{m} = \frac{x}{500p}$$
$$mx = 500p$$
$$x = \frac{500p}{m}$$

5. **The correct answer is (E).** In combining the four fractions, cancel all variables except $a$ (in the numerator) and $e$ (in the denominator), leaving $\frac{a}{e} \cdot x = 1$. To isolate $x$ on one side of the equation, multiply both sides by $\frac{e}{a}$:

$$\frac{e}{a} \cdot \frac{a}{e} \cdot x = 1 \cdot \frac{e}{a}$$
$$x = \frac{e}{a}$$

**6. The correct answer is (A).** Any fraction between 0 and 1 is *greater* than the square of that fraction. Thus, $a + b$ must be greater than $a^2 + b^2$.

**7. The correct answer is (C).** Multiply Quantity B by $1.20 to determine whether (and by how much) the cost of $p$ cans exceeds the cost of a case. ($1.20)(15) = $18.00, which is greater than the cost of a case by $.60, *less* than the cost of one can. Accordingly, Quantity A is 15.

**8. The correct answer is (B).** To answer the question, determine the height of the News (white) portion of the graph's right-hand bar.

**9. The correct answer is (D).** The age group that spends the most time per week watching sports on television is the 19–24-year-old group. This group spent an average of approximately 4 out of 18 television-viewing hours per week watching "other" programming. 4 is approximately 22% of 18.

**10. The correct answer is (D).** Your task here is to compare the size of the entertainment portion of the left bar to the combined sizes of the same portion of the other two bars. The first portion is larger than the other two combined, So you're looking for a ratio that's greater than 1:1. Eliminate choices (A) and (B). Approximate the height of each of the three portions:

13–18 age group: 25 hours
19–24 age group: 5 hours
25–30 age group: 10 hours

The ratio in question is 25:15, or 5:3.

**11. The correct answer is (C).** The ring's height is equal to its radius. To determine Quantity A (the surface area of the outside of the ring), multiply the ring's circumference ($2\pi r$) by its height ($r$):

SA = $(2\pi r)(r) = 2\pi r^2$

To determine Quantity B (twice the ring's circular area), multiply 2 by the base's area: $2\pi r^2$. As you can see, the two quantities are equal.

**12. The correct answer is (C).** The average (arithmetic mean) of any two numbers is half their sum. Regardless of the values of $x$ and $y$, Quantity A will always equal Quantity B:

$$\frac{(x-1)+(y+1)}{2} = \frac{x+y}{2}$$

**13. The correct answer is (B).** There are six possible sequences, and so Quantity A = $\frac{1}{6}$. Any of the three patrons (including the one who is middle in height) could be first, second, or third in line; hence Quantity B = $\frac{1}{3}$.

**14. The correct answer is (A).** The tax ($1.00) is based on a $9.00 price. Thus, the tax is $\frac{1}{9}$, which is greater than 11%. ($\frac{1}{9} = \frac{11}{99}$; 11% = $\frac{11}{100}$.)

**15. The correct answer is (C).** $3^{26} = (3^{13})(3^{13})$, and $9^{13} = (3^{13})(3^{13})$. As you can see, the two quantities are equal.

**16. The correct answer is (E).** The table does not indicate the highest temperature recorded during April, and so it is not possible to determine the range of temperatures for April.

**17. The correct answer is (C).** You can express the centered information as the algebraic form $2n + 5 = 17$. Now, solve for $n$: $2n = 12$; $n = 6$. Find Quantity A: 3 less than $\dfrac{6}{2}$ is $3 - 3 = 0$. Find Quantity B: 2 less than $\dfrac{6}{3}$ is $2 - 2 = 0$.

**18. The correct answer is (B).** The comparison is easily made by substituting some simple numbers for $p$ and $q$. For example, assume $p = 1$ and $q = 2$. The ratio of $p$ to $(p + 1)$ is 1:2, or $\dfrac{1}{2}$, while the ratio of $q$ to $(q + 1)$ is 2:3, or $\dfrac{2}{3}$. As long as $0 < p < q$, the inequality $\dfrac{p}{p+1} < \dfrac{q}{q+1}$ will hold.

**19. The correct answer is (D).** Standard deviation measures the dispersion of numbers around the mean (simple average) of those numbers. The greater the dispersion, the greater the standard deviation. In both sets, the range is 3. If $x = \dfrac{1}{2}$, the dispersions are the same (Quantity A = Quantity B) because the means would be the same. Otherwise, the dispersions—and the two quantities—differ from each other.

**20. The correct answer is (A).** $54 is 90% of what Kirk collected. Express this as an equation:

$$54 = .90x$$
$$540 = 9x$$
$$x = 60$$

Kirk collected $60. If each paper sells for 40 cents, the number of paper Kirk sold is: $\dfrac{60}{.40} = \dfrac{600}{4} = 150$.

**21. The correct answer is (C).** The key to this problem is in determining the interior angles of the various triangles formed by the runways. The interior angle formed by the 120°-turn from runway 1 to 2 is 60° (a 180°-turn would reverse the airplane's direction). Similarly, the interior angle formed by the 135°-turn from runway 1 to 3 is 45° (180° − 135°). Two right-triangle "angle triplets" emerge: a 45°-45°-90° triplet and a 30°-60°-90° triplet, as shown in the figure below. Since the sum of any triangle's interior angles is 180°, the remaining angles can also be determined:

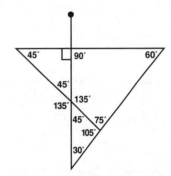

Among the three Roman-numeral choices, only I and III provide angles shown in the figure above.

**22. The correct answer is (C).** Based on the definition of a geometric sequence in the question, all pairs of successive terms must have the same ratio. Thus, $\dfrac{x}{-2} = \dfrac{-8}{x}$. Cross-multiplying, $x^2 = 16$, and hence $x = \pm 4$. The constant multiple is either 2 or −2. If the second term is ±4, the sixth term would be $(-2)(2)^{(6-1)} = (-2)(2)^5 = -64$. If the second term is ±4, the sixth term would be $(-2)(-2)^5 = -64$.

**23. The correct answer is (C).** Manipulate the expression in Column A so that it resembles the expression in Column B. Distribute the denominator to each term in the numerator, then cancel common terms:

$$\frac{a^2 + b^2}{ab} = \frac{a^2}{ab} + \frac{b^2}{ab} = \frac{a}{b} + \frac{b}{a}$$

24. **The correct answer is $\frac{4}{5}$.** (Enter 4 in the upper box and 5 in the lower box.) The line has a slope of

$$m = \frac{5-1}{3-(-2)} = \frac{4}{5}.$$

25. **The correct answer is (A).** $<2u>$ $= (2u)^2 - 2u = 4u^2 - 2u$, and $2<u> =$ $2(u^2 - u) = 2u^2 - 2u$. You can cancel out the term $-2u$ from both columns, which leaves a comparison between $4u^2$ and $2u^2$. As you can see, Quantity A > Quantity B.

26. **The correct answer is (E).** The total rent is D + 100, which must be divided by the number of students (M).

27. **The correct answer is (B).** Since the smallest circle has a radius of 1, the middle-sized circle has a radius of 2, and, therefore, the diameter of the large circle must be 6, which

makes its radius 3. The arc of a semi-circle is half the circle's circumference—that is, $\pi r$. So the length of the boundary of the shaded region is the sum of the arcs of the three semi-circles: $\pi + 2\pi + 3\pi = 6\pi$.

28. **The correct answer is (D).** Given a 3:5 male-female ratio and a total of 2,400 voters, the number of male voters must be $\frac{3}{8}$ of 2,400, or 900. Accordingly, female voters must account for the remaining 1,500. Determine the number of male voters needed altogether for a 4:5 male-female ratio (assuming the number of female voters remains unchanged at 1,500) by setting up a proportion and solving for that number:

$$\frac{4}{5} = \frac{x}{1,500}$$
$$5x = 6,000$$
$$x = 1,200$$

Since the district currently includes 900 male voters, 300 more are needed to make the ratio 4:5.

## Verbal Reasoning

| | |
|---|---|
| 1. A | 12. C |
| 2. C | 13. A |
| 3. B | 14. E |
| 4. B | 15. E |
| 5. D | 16. A |
| 6. C | 17. D |
| 7. E | 18. C |
| 8. A | 19. E |
| 9. E | 20. D |
| 10. B | 21. C |
| 11. A | 22. B |

| |
|---|
| 23. E |
| 24. D |
| 25. A |
| 26. C |
| 27. B |
| 28. D |
| 29. (i) insatiably ambitious |
|    (ii) paradigmatic |
|    (iii) dilemmas |
| 30. D |

1. **The correct answer is (A).** ITINERANT means "traveling about or nomadic." The word *settled* means just the opposite.

2. **The correct answer is (C).** This is a "possible use of" analogy type. A weapon is a tool that's often used to INTIMIDATE. Similarly, an *icebox* is a tool that's typically used to *preserve* (by means of freezing).

3. **The correct answer is (B).** This is a "necessary condition" analogy. GESTATION means "pregnancy"; NATAL means "pertaining to birth." Thus, gestation is a necessary condition for and must precede a birth. Similarly, a *premise* is a necessary condition for and must precede a *conclusion*.

4. **The correct answer is (B).** INCREDULITY means "disbelief or distrust"; *faith* means "trust."

5. **The correct answer is (D).** The two missing words should convey a contrast for the second half of the sentence, as indicated by the phrase "differs greatly." Choice (D) works because *nocturnal* opposes "active during the day," and *solitary* opposes

the idea of "quite complex interrelationships."

6. **The correct answer is (C).** To VIE is to compete or contend (as in a contest), contrary to giving up, or *admitting defeat*.

7. **The correct answer is (E).** VERDANT means "lush and overgrown"; *desolate* means "bare of any living thing."

8. **The correct answer is (A).** The first missing word should convey an idea that fits the concept of "personal interaction"; the second missing word should describes the kind of "well-being" that would have a "chemical" basis. Only the word pair *love* and *physical* fits both requirements.

9. **The correct answer is (E).** Choice (E) is consistent with Arnold's views, as presented by the author. The passage emphasizes Arnold's argument for the pursuit of perfection; thus, Arnold would probably agree that we should study the "exceptional" (see line 64) rather than the "representative." Besides, choice (E) is inconsistent with the

viewpoint of multiculturalists (with whom Arnold disagrees) that "we must learn what is representative, for we have overemphasized what is exceptional" (lines 62–64).

10. **The correct answer is (B).** Arnold's *Culture* was published in 1869. The three forms of opposition to Arnold's ideas as presented in this work developed after its publication; therefore, they must have emerged later than 1869.

11. **The correct answer is (A).** The author's threshold purpose, articulated in the final sentence of the first paragraph, is to identify the significant forms of dissent to Arnoldian culture. But the author proceeds to do more than merely identify and describe these forms of dissent; the author is also critical of the dissenters, for example, because they have misunderstood Arnold. Choice (A) embraces both the author's threshold and ultimate concerns.

12. **The correct answer is (C).** This is a "type of" analogy. A DECREE is a pronouncement or declaration. A decree INFORMS, but it's a distinctively official or formal way of doing so. Similarly, *resigning* is a formal way of *quitting*.

13. **The correct answer is (A).** This is a "possible element of" analogy. One common, but not essential, ingredient of a CONFECTION (sweet candy) is CINNAMON. Similarly, one common, but not essential, element of a *tale* (story) is a *villain*.

14. **The correct answer is (E).** Since an "intact nuclear family" contrasts with "today's" marital trends, it is clear that the sentence refers to the nuclear family as something out of the past. Thus, for the second blank, a word like *traditional* (choice (E)) or possibly *obsolete* (choice (B)) is needed. Choice (E) is better because the word *astonishing* sets up the appropriate contrast, whereas the idea that the belief is *encouraging* suggests a value judgment unsupported by the rest of the sentence.

15. **The correct answer is (E).** One meaning of LATITUDE is "freedom from limitations or restraints"—just the opposite of *restraint*.

16. **The correct answer is (A).** In order, the passage examines the survival mechanisms allowing *lyngbya* to reemerge today; the economic and ecological consequences of the strain's reemergence; and the precipitating cause of the strain's reemergence. Choice (B) is clearly off the passage's focus, and choice (E) is far too broad in scope. Of the remaining three choices, choice (A) comes closest to embracing the entire discussion.

17. **The correct answer is (D).** In the first paragraph, among the explanations given for *lyngbya*'s survival is that when it dies and decays, the decaying matter, which is rich in the nutrients the strain needs to grow, sinks to the sea floor, where it nourishes the next generation of *lyngbya*. In this sense, the strain has survived partly by its ability to essentially feed on itself.

18. **The correct answer is (C).** Nowhere in the passage does the author discuss algae, except to state

(in the first sentence) that *lyngbya* is an ancestor of modern-day algae.

19. **The correct answer is (E).** PITH refers to "the heart or essence of the matter." A pithy observation or remark is one that is incisive and on point. A *digression,* to the contrary, is a divergence from a previous course of thought or action.

20. **The correct answer is (D).** This is an "individual member to group" analogy. A RUNT is the smallest member of a litter (a group of newborn SIBLING animals). Similarly, a *penny* is the smallest denomination among all forms of U.S. *currency* (money).

21. **The correct answer is (C).** The first operative word in the sentence is *since,* which means "because" here. The fact that the disorders appear frequently only among young children would explain the conclusion that these "disorders" are not disorders at all, but rather normal developmental phenomena that children grow out of. Choice (C) conveys this idea. The second key word is "*disorders*" (in quotes). The fact that the word appears in quotes provides a clue that the term might be a misnomer—an inappropriate label. Again, choice (C) conveys this idea.

22. **The correct answer is (B).** This is an "ideal characteristic of" analogy. A good CARETAKER is ATTENTIVE; in fact, "attending to" is the function of a caretaker. Similarly, good *writing* is *legible;* in fact, the purpose of writing is usually that it be read.

23. **The correct answer is (E).** This is an "inherent purpose of" analogy. A TRAVESTY is an imitation intended to RIDICULE (deride or mock); similarly, a *forgery* is an imitation intended to *deceive.*

24. **The correct answer is (D).** The use of a code number to keep the contestants' identities secret is clearly designed to maintain the impartiality (fairness and lack of favoritism or bias) of the judging process.

25. **The correct answer is (A).** This is an "operates against" analogy. To SHORE is to prop or support (especially, a ship, wall, or building). The word PRECARIOUS means "insecure or uncertain." So you lessen precariousness (of a wall, for example) by shoring it up. Similarly, one way to lessen *irregularity* (unevenness) of a surface is to *plane* it.

26. **The correct answer is (C).** In the passage, the author tells us that new U.S. jobs in the service industries will require literacy skills that are lacking among members of the current U.S. labor force in these industries. The clear implication is that, unless these industries takes steps to improve their workers' literacy skills (or teach new workers the required literacy skills), these new jobs will be filled by people from outside the United States.

27. **The correct answer is (B).** In the passage, the author mentions arithmetic skills along with reading and writing skills in describing the sorts of "literacy skills" that future jobs will require, and the passage also

mentions that U.S. businesses must teach their new and current workforce members.

28. **The correct answer is (D).** To OBLIGATE is to "bind, compel, or make indebted or grateful"; a contrary act would be to release from obligation, or *excuse from debt*.

29. **The correct answers are insatiably ambitious for blank (i), paradigmatic for blank (ii), and dilemmas for blank (iii).** Great achievers nevertheless driven to top their latest accomplishments would aptly be described as *insatiably ambitious;* that is, never satisfied with their achievements. The second sentence discusses a classic, or model, example of the phenomenon described in the first sentence. The word *paradigmatic* means "classic or model," so it's perfect for blank (ii). The passage's final phrase provides the key to filling in blank (iii). What someone might struggle to solve is a problem or puzzle, which is exactly what the word *dilemma* means.

30. **The correct answer is (D).** This is a "process and product" analogy. You take, or SWEAR, an OATH. Similarly, you execute, or *sign,* a *contract.* Strengthening the analogy is that both actions (swearing an oath and signing a contract) are evidence of a promise or commitment for the future.

## ANSWER SHEET PRACTICE TEST 4

**Analytical Writing—Issue Task**

_____

_____

_____

_____

_____

_____

_____

_____

_____

_____

_____

_____

_____

_____

_____

_____

_____

_____

_____

_____

answer sheet

**Analytical Writing—Argument Task**

_____

_____

_____

_____

_____

_____

_____

_____

_____

_____

_____

_____

_____

_____

_____

_____

_____

_____

_____

_____

_____

answer sheet

## Verbal Reasoning

1. Ⓐ Ⓑ Ⓒ Ⓓ Ⓔ
2. Ⓐ Ⓑ Ⓒ Ⓓ Ⓔ
3. Ⓐ Ⓑ Ⓒ Ⓓ Ⓔ
4. Ⓐ Ⓑ Ⓒ Ⓓ Ⓔ
5. Ⓐ Ⓑ Ⓒ Ⓓ Ⓔ
6. Ⓐ Ⓑ Ⓒ Ⓓ Ⓔ
7. Ⓐ Ⓑ Ⓒ Ⓓ Ⓔ
8. Ⓐ Ⓑ Ⓒ Ⓓ Ⓔ
9. Ⓐ Ⓑ Ⓒ Ⓓ Ⓔ
10. Ⓐ Ⓑ Ⓒ Ⓓ Ⓔ
11. Ⓐ Ⓑ Ⓒ Ⓓ Ⓔ
12. Ⓐ Ⓑ Ⓒ Ⓓ Ⓔ

13. Ⓐ Ⓑ Ⓒ Ⓓ Ⓔ
14. Ⓐ Ⓑ Ⓒ Ⓓ Ⓔ
15. Ⓐ Ⓑ Ⓒ Ⓓ Ⓔ
16. Ⓐ Ⓑ Ⓒ Ⓓ Ⓔ
17. Ⓐ Ⓑ Ⓒ Ⓓ Ⓔ
18. Ⓐ Ⓑ Ⓒ Ⓓ Ⓔ
19. Ⓐ Ⓑ Ⓒ Ⓓ Ⓔ
20. Ⓐ Ⓑ Ⓒ Ⓓ Ⓔ
21. (i) _____
    (ii) _____
    (iii) _____

22. Ⓐ Ⓑ Ⓒ Ⓓ Ⓔ
23. Ⓐ Ⓑ Ⓒ Ⓓ Ⓔ
24. Ⓐ Ⓑ Ⓒ Ⓓ Ⓔ
25. Ⓐ Ⓑ Ⓒ Ⓓ Ⓔ
26. Ⓐ Ⓑ Ⓒ Ⓓ Ⓔ
27. Ⓐ Ⓑ Ⓒ Ⓓ Ⓔ
28. Ⓐ Ⓑ Ⓒ Ⓓ Ⓔ
29. Ⓐ Ⓑ Ⓒ Ⓓ Ⓔ
30. Ⓐ Ⓑ Ⓒ Ⓓ Ⓔ

## Quantitative Reasoning

1. Ⓐ Ⓑ Ⓒ Ⓓ
2. Ⓐ Ⓑ Ⓒ Ⓓ
3. Ⓐ Ⓑ Ⓒ Ⓓ
4. Ⓐ Ⓑ Ⓒ Ⓓ Ⓔ
5. Ⓐ Ⓑ Ⓒ Ⓓ Ⓔ
6. Ⓐ Ⓑ Ⓒ Ⓓ Ⓔ
7. ☐
8. Ⓐ Ⓑ Ⓒ Ⓓ Ⓔ
9. Ⓐ Ⓑ Ⓒ Ⓓ
10. Ⓐ Ⓑ Ⓒ Ⓓ Ⓔ

11. Ⓐ Ⓑ Ⓒ Ⓓ Ⓔ
12. Ⓐ Ⓑ Ⓒ Ⓓ
13. Ⓐ Ⓑ Ⓒ Ⓓ
14. Ⓐ Ⓑ Ⓒ Ⓓ
15. Ⓐ Ⓑ Ⓒ Ⓓ
16. Ⓐ Ⓑ Ⓒ Ⓓ Ⓔ
17. Ⓐ Ⓑ Ⓒ Ⓓ Ⓔ
18. Ⓐ Ⓑ Ⓒ Ⓓ Ⓔ
19. Ⓐ Ⓑ Ⓒ Ⓓ Ⓔ
20. Ⓐ Ⓑ Ⓒ Ⓓ

21. Ⓐ Ⓑ Ⓒ Ⓓ
22. Ⓐ Ⓑ Ⓒ Ⓓ
23. Ⓐ Ⓑ Ⓒ Ⓓ
24. Ⓐ Ⓑ Ⓒ Ⓓ Ⓔ
25. Ⓐ Ⓑ Ⓒ Ⓓ Ⓔ
26. Ⓐ Ⓑ Ⓒ Ⓓ Ⓔ
27. Ⓐ Ⓑ Ⓒ Ⓓ
28. Ⓐ Ⓑ Ⓒ Ⓓ

answer sheet

# Practice Test 4

## ANALYTICAL WRITING

### Issue Task

*Time: 45 Minutes*

**NOTES:** For *some* test-takers, the GRE will end with an identified and untimed research section. The research section, which is unscored, contains experimental question types. Test-makers use it to assess the difficulty levels of the experimental question types, based on test-takers' responses.

For the purposes of this book—making sure you're fully prepared to take the GRE exam—one Complex Text Completion question (Verbal Reasoning section) and one numeric entry question (Quantitative Reasoning section) are included in each of the Practice Tests. On the actual GRE, however, you will not see both of these questions; in fact, you may *not* see either one.

Using a word processor, compose a response to the following statement and directive. Do not use any spell-checking or grammar-checking functions (they are not available on the actual GRE):

> "Most great achievements are the result of careful planning and a long, sustained effort rather than of sudden bursts of creativity or insight."
>
> In your view, how accurate is the above statement? Develop and support your viewpoint with relevant reasons and examples and by considering ways in which the statement may or may not be true.

## Argument Task

### Time: 30 Minutes

Using a word processor, compose an essay for the following argument and directive. Do not use any spell-checking or grammar-checking functions (they are not available on the actual GRE).

> The following appeared in a speech by a prominent state politician:
>
> "At Giant Industries, our state's largest private business, the average production worker is now forty-two years old. Recently, Giant's revenue from the sale of textiles and paper, which together account for the majority of Giant's manufacturing business, has declined significantly. Since an increasing percentage of new graduates from our state's colleges and universities are finding jobs in other states, our state will soon face a crisis in which the size of our workforce will be insufficient to replace our current workers as they retire, in turn resulting in widespread business failure and a reduced quality of life in our state."
>
> Discuss how well-reasoned you find the above argument.

# VERBAL REASONING

## 30 Questions • 30 Minutes

> **NOTE:** In this section, questions are grouped together by format, and within each group the questions grow more difficult as you go. Because the actual GRE is computer-adaptive in the multiple-choice sections, it intersperses questions of different formats and difficulty levels.

1. COUNTERPOINT : MELODY ::
   - **(A)** masonry : brick
   - **(B)** pane : window
   - **(C)** coffee : bean
   - **(D)** sketch : pencil
   - **(E)** biography : book

2. FALLOW : PRODUCTIVITY ::
   - **(A)** handsome : attraction
   - **(B)** friendly : allegiance
   - **(C)** bitter : taste
   - **(D)** obscure : clarity
   - **(E)** poisonous : protection

3. The qualities expected of a professional musician seem _____, for she must be studious, disciplined, and technically impeccable while bringing passion and _____ to each performance.
   - **(A)** ambiguous . . capriciousness
   - **(B)** eclectic . . impulsiveness
   - **(C)** paradoxical . . spontaneity
   - **(D)** multifarious . . virtuosity
   - **(E)** unattainable . . emotion

4. RESOLUTION:
   - **(A)** introduction
   - **(B)** vacillation
   - **(C)** revocation
   - **(D)** denunciation
   - **(E)** revulsion

5. TAUT:
   - **(A)** workable
   - **(B)** refined
   - **(C)** slackened
   - **(D)** durable
   - **(E)** circular

6. LAUGHTER : AMUSEMENT ::
   - **(A)** leisure : recreation
   - **(B)** squalor : filth
   - **(C)** pallor : illness
   - **(D)** pride : humility
   - **(E)** stealth : openness

7. GEM : SETTING ::
   - **(A)** diamond : gold
   - **(B)** painting : milieu
   - **(C)** ring : necklace
   - **(D)** building : scaffold
   - **(E)** portrait : subject

> **Directions:** Questions 8–9 are based on the following passage.

*Line* In nearly all human populations, a majority of individuals can taste the artificially synthesized chemical phenylthiocarbonide (PTC). However, the
(5) percentage varies dramatically—from as low as sixty percent in India to as high as ninety-five percent in Africa. That this polymorphism is observed in non-human primates as well indicates
(10) a long evolutionary history which, although obviously not acting on PTC, might reflect evolutionary selection for taste discrimination of other, more significant bitter substances, such as
(15) certain toxic plants.

A somewhat more puzzling human polymorphism is the genetic variability in earwax, or *cerumen,* which is observed in two varieties. Among
(20) European populations, ninety percent

of individuals have a sticky yellow variety rather than a dry, gray one, whereas in northern China these numbers are approximately the (25) reverse. Perhaps like PTC variability, cerumen variability is an incidental expression of something more adaptively significant. Indeed, the observed relationship between (30) cerumen and odorous bodily secretions, to which non-human primates and, to a lesser extent humans, pay attention suggests that during the course of human evolution genes (35) affecting body secretions, including cerumen, came under selective influence.

8. It can be inferred from the passage that human populations vary considerably in their
   (A) sensitivity to certain bodily odors
   (B) capacity for hearing
   (C) ability to assimilate artificial chemicals
   (D) vulnerability to certain toxins found in plants
   (E) ability to discern bitterness in taste

9. Which of the following best summarizes the main idea of the passage?
   (A) Artificially synthesized chemicals might eventually alter the course of evolution by desensitizing humans to certain tastes and odors.
   (B) Polymorphism among human populations varies considerably from region to region throughout the world.
   (C) Sensitivity to taste and to odors has been subject to far greater natural selectivity during the evolution of primates than previously thought.

(D) Some human polymorphisms might be explained as vestigial evidence of evolutionary adaptations that still serve vital purposes in other primates.
(E) The human senses of taste and smell have evolved considerably over the course of evolutionary history.

10. Hong Kong prospered as the center of trade with China, _____ until it fell to the Japanese in 1941.
    (A) increasing
    (B) succeeding
    (C) languishing
    (D) retreating
    (E) flourishing

11. EARNESTNESS:
    (A) insincerity
    (B) lack of discipline
    (C) rudeness
    (D) carelessness
    (E) arrogance

12. EVANESCENT : VANISH ::
    (A) effervescent : corrode
    (B) iridescent : shine
    (C) expressive : admonish
    (D) fluorescent : disappear
    (E) vacuous : expedite

13. DISPENSARY : REAPER ::
    (A) chisel : mortar
    (B) thermometer : aspirin
    (C) dye : seal
    (D) whip : harness
    (E) anesthetic : toxin

14. The fossil record reveals innumerable instances of environmental _____ by which one can draw an analogy between the evolution of life and a tree's branches, a few of which _____ but most of which branch again and again.
    (A) calamities . . end abruptly
    (B) adaptations . . progress linearly
    (C) safeguards . . wither and die
    (D) events . . intertwine
    (E) changes . . produce leaves

**Directions:** Questions 15–18 are based on the following passage.

*Line* American history scholars generally attribute formation of the League of Indian Nations to Degandawida, who convinced the warring and fiercely
(5) autonomous Iroquois nations to embrace his radical idea for a league by tying it to familiar Iroquois customs and institutions. He associated the notion of peace and part-
(10) nership with the Iroquois custom by which the families of slain warriors adopted war prisoners into the tribe. He invoked unquestioned social institutions as symbols, comparing the
(15) League to the traditional Iroquois clan in which several families share a "Longhouse" and likening the Great Council, comprised of representatives from each nation, to the Longhouse's
(20) ever-burning Council Fire. And he assigned to each nation specific duties in order to assuage its fear of losing national identity. (For instance, he assigned to the Onondagas, who were
(25) centrally positioned geographically, the role of perpetual hosts.)

Perhaps most persuasive, however, was how Degandawida's League replicated the power structure of the tradi-
(30) tional Iroquois clan. Each of the five Iroquois nations was comprised of matriarchal totemic clans in which the chiefs were men, the clan heads were women, and the chief's children
(35) were considered members of his wife's clan. Degandawida determined that the heads of each nation should select their League representatives, thereby effectively precluding the possibility of
(40) League representatives passing their power on to their sons, as well as decreasing the likelihood that a pro-war representative would be appointed.

(45) Iroquois unification under the League lasted about two centuries, when disagreement as to whether to become involved in the American Revolutionary war divided the Iro-
(50) quois. The revolutionaries' success and their subsequent encroachment upon Iroquois lands forced many Iroquois to resettle in Canada, while those who remained behind lost
(55) respect from other Indian nations. The introduction of distilled spirits led to widespread alcoholism and, in turn, to a rapid decline of the culture and population. The Quakers' influence
(60) impeded, yet in another sense contributed, to this decline. By establishing schools for the Iroquois and by introducing them to modern technology for agriculture and husbandry,
(65) the Quakers instilled some hope for the future yet undermined their sense of national identity.

Ironically, it was the alcoholic half-brother of Seneca, Cornplanter, the
(70) most outspoken proponent among the Iroquois for assimilation of white customs and institutions, who revived the Iroquois culture. Around 1800, Handsome Lake, a former member of
(75) the Great Council, established a new religion among the Iroquois that tied the more useful aspects of Christianity to traditional Indian beliefs and customs. Lake's teachings quickly
(80) became firmly entrenched among the Iroquois, sparking reunification and renewed confidence while also curbing rampant alcoholism. Lake's influence is still evident today: many mod-
(85) ern-day Iroquois belong both to his religion and to one or another Christian sect.

15. The passage mentions all of the following developments as contributing factors in the decline of the Iroquois culture EXCEPT for
    (A) new educational opportunities for the Iroquois people
    (B) divisive power struggles among the leaders of the Iroquois nations
    (C) introduction of new farming technologies
    (D) territorial threats against the Iroquois nations
    (E) discord among the nations regarding their role in the American Revolution

16. Among the following reasons, it is most likely that the author considers Handsome Lake's leading a revival of the Iroquois culture "ironic" (line 68) because
    (A) he was a former member of the Great Council
    (B) he was not a full-blooded relative of Seneca Cornplanter
    (C) he was related by blood to a chief proponent of assimilation
    (D) he was alcoholic
    (E) his religious beliefs conflicted with traditional Iroquois beliefs

17. Assuming that the reasons asserted in the passage for the decline of the Iroquois culture are historically representative of the decline of cultural minorities, which of the following developments would most likely contribute to the demise of a modern-day ethnic minority?
    (A) A bilingual education program in which children who are members of the minority group learn to read and write in both their traditional language and the language prevalent in the present culture
    (B) A tax credit for residential property owners who lease their property to members of the minority group

    (C) Increased efforts by local government to eradicate the availability of illegal drugs
    (D) A government-sponsored program to assist minority-owned businesses in using computer technology to improve efficiency
    (E) The declaration of a national holiday commemorating a past war in which the minority group played an active role

18. Which of the following best characterizes the structure of the passage as a whole?
    (A) A theory is presented and then applied to two related historical phenomena.
    (B) Two historical figures are introduced; then the nature and extent of their influence are compared.
    (C) The inception of an historical phenomenon is examined; then the subsequent life of the phenomenon is traced.
    (D) Competing views respecting an historical phenomenon are presented and then evaluated based upon empirical evidence.
    (E) An historical event is recounted; then possible explanations for the event are presented.

19. ROBUST : VIGOR ::
    (A) massive : strength
    (B) nervous : worry
    (C) farsighted : glasses
    (D) starving : appetite
    (E) sanguine : hope

20. SHUN : DISAPPROVAL ::
    (A) envy : ambition
    (B) give : greed
    (C) lie : insecurity
    (D) nap : relaxation
    (E) study : studiousness

**21.** Societal progress usually comes about through (i)_____ and challenge—that is, when people point out the mistakes of those who wield power; (ii)_____, without our challenging the mistaken notions of established institutions, political (iii)_____ and tyranny would go unchecked.

**(i)**

perseverance
dissension
setback

**(ii)**

nevertheless
in fact
in addition

**(iii)**

opposition
corruption
oppression

**22.** VESTIGIAL:
(A) newfangled
(B) current
(C) effective
(D) functional
(E) appropriate

**Directions:** Questions 23–24 are based on the following passage.

Line The striking consistencies among the folk tales of any region, especially the tale plots of independent origins, like those among a region's languages, are
(5) owing to the fact that folklore, like language, is a collective property—a socialized aspect of the culture subject to stricter and more uniform laws than fields in which individual cre-
(10) ation prevails. Folk tales do contain certain variable elements—for example, the distribution of points of emphasis and the nomenclature (vocation) and attributes of the *dra-*
(15) *matic personae*—through which the teller's own personality and inclina-
tions may find expression. Also, the teller's choice among the repertory of the available genres (for example,
(20) fairy tales and anecdotes) and among the known tales within each genre often reflect the teller's preferred manner of execution, while the teller-narrator typically assumes whichever
(25) character most closely resembles the teller. Nevertheless, whereas in written literature a creative personality is free to shape entirely new roles, including that of narrator, in
(30) storytelling all characters are predetermined by the tale. Attempts at biographical interpretation almost invariably fail to convince; the tale must come before the teller.

**23.** It can be inferred from the passage that the author would most probably agree with which of the following statements about classic novels?
(A) They should not be considered part of the collective property of a culture.
(B) They are sometimes adapted from a culture's well known folk tales.
(C) They place less emphasis on *dramatic personae* than fairy tales and anecdotes do.
(D) They use a culture's language in more imaginative ways than folk tales.
(E) They often resemble folk tales insofar as they belie their author's own values and attitudes.

**24.** The passage as a whole can appropriately be viewed as

(A) an examination of the ways in which story tellers imbue well-known folk tales with their own personalities

(B) an explanation as to why tellers of folk tales generally choose to conform to cultural expectations in how they tell their tales

(C) an investigation into certain parallels between language in general and folk tales in particular

(D) an argument that folk tales evolve over time as a result of both cultural shifts and individual creativity

(E) a description of the extent of the consistencies generally observed among a region's folk tales

**25.** When it was constructed, the gymnasium was highly _____; the students for whom it was planned were _____, but community members who faced losing their neighborhood park were outraged.

(A) controversial . . gratified

(B) warranted . . skeptical

(C) fortuitous . . euphoric

(D) unnecessary . . impartial

(E) desirable . . numerous

**26.** IMPEDE:

(A) comply

(B) hasten

(C) deny

(D) engulf

(E) progress

**27.** AGILE : DANCER ::

(A) delicious : fruit

(B) diligent : worker

(C) barren : desert

(D) tall : building

(E) dangerous : criminal

**28.** Shakespeare's _____ of Richard III is so _____ that it is difficult to imagine that the ruler had been dead for more than a century before the Bard cast him as the central character in one of his plays.

(A) rendition . . compelling

(B) criticism . . candid

(C) depiction . . vivid

(D) portrayal . . droll

(E) caricature . . inventive

**29.** VAGARY:

(A) full disclosure

(B) explicitness

(C) impartiality

(D) essential element

(E) foreseeable event

**30.** FAWN:

(A) insult

(B) dominate

(C) grow stronger

(D) win over

(E) boast

## QUANTITATIVE REASONING

*28 Questions • 45 Minutes*

> **NOTE:** In this section, questions are grouped together by format, and within each group the questions grow more difficult as you go. Because the actual GRE is computer-adaptive in the multiple-choice sections, it intersperses questions of different formats and difficulty levels.

1. The toll for driving on road A is $1.20 for the first mile and 35 cents for each additional mile. The toll for driving on road B is $2.25 for the first mile and 20 cents for each additional mile.

   | **Column A** | **Column B** |
   |---|---|
   | The toll for a 8-mile drive on road A | The toll for a 8-mile drive on road B |

   **(A)** The quantity in Column A is greater;
   **(B)** The quantity in Column B is greater;
   **(C)** The quantities are equal;
   **(D)** The relationship cannot be determined from the information given.

   | **Column A** | **Column B** |
   |---|---|

2. $k > 0$

   | **Column A** | **Column B** |
   |---|---|
   | $k^{1/2} + k^{1/2}$ | $\sqrt{k}$ |

   **(A)** The quantity in Column A is greater;
   **(B)** The quantity in Column B is greater;
   **(C)** The quantities are equal;
   **(D)** The relationship cannot be determined from the information given.

3. In a group of 18 students taking Spanish and German, 12 are taking Spanish, and 4 are taking both Spanish and German.

   | **Column A** | **Column B** |
   |---|---|
   | The number taking German but not Spanish | The number taking Spanish but not German |

   **(A)** The quantity in Column A is greater;
   **(B)** The quantity in Column B is greater;
   **(C)** The quantities are equal;
   **(D)** The relationship cannot be determined from the information given.

4. If $n$ is the first of two consecutive odd integers, and if the difference of their squares is 120, which of the following equations can be used to find their values?
   **(A)** $(n + 1)^2 - n^2 = 120$
   **(B)** $n^2 - (n + 2)^2 = 120$
   **(C)** $[(n + 2) - n]^2 = 120$
   **(D)** $n^2 - (n + 1)^2 = 120$
   **(E)** $(n + 2)^2 - n^2 = 120$

**5.** A faucet is dripping at a constant rate. By noon on Sunday, 3 ounces of water have dripped from the faucet into a holding cup. If a total of 7 ounces have dripped into the cup as of 5 p.m. the same day, how many ounces altogether will have dripped into the tank by 2:00 a.m. the following day?

**(A)** 10

**(B)** $\dfrac{51}{5}$

**(C)** 12

**(D)** $\dfrac{71}{5}$

**(E)** $\dfrac{81}{5}$

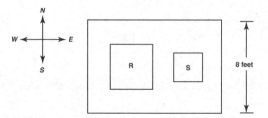

**6.** Two square rugs R and S, which have a combined area of 20 square feet, are placed on a rectangular floor whose area is 112 square feet, as shown above. Measured east to west, each rug is placed the same distance from the other rug as from the nearest east or west edge of the floor. If the area of rug R is four times the area of rug S, how far apart are the rugs?

**(A)** 3 feet, 4 inches
**(B)** 3 feet
**(C)** 2 feet, 8 inches
**(D)** 2 feet
**(E)** 1 feet, 6 inches

7. Shown below is a correct problem in addition, with $R$ and $S$ representing different digits.

7R
RS
RR
──
117

What is the value of S ?

[        ]

*Click on the answer box, then type in a number. Backspace to erase.*

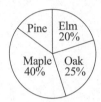

TREES ON MAIN STREET

8. The chart shows the portions of all four types of trees on Main Street.
If there are 140 trees altogether on Main Street, how many of the trees are pine?
   (A) 40
   (B) 24
   (C) 21
   (D) 15
   (E) 14

| Column A | Column B |
|---|---|
| | |

9.     The least common multiple          The greatest common factor
       of 4, 6, and 8                     of 44, 66, and 88

   (A) The quantity in Column A is greater;
   (B) The quantity in Column B is greater;
   (C) The quantities are equal;
   (D) The relationship cannot be determined from the information given.

**10.** A spinner containing seven equal regions numbered 1 through 7 is spun two times in a row. What is the probability that the first spin yields an odd number and the second spin yields an even number?

(A) $\dfrac{2}{7}$

(B) $\dfrac{12}{49}$

(C) $\dfrac{24}{49}$

(D) $\dfrac{1}{2}$

(E) $\dfrac{4}{7}$

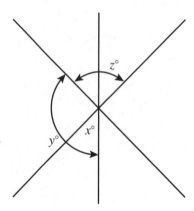

**11.** In the figure shown, if $y = 130$ and $z = 100$, then $x =$
(A) 40
(B) 45
(C) 50
(D) 55
(E) 60

**12.** The median of four numbers is zero (0), and the difference between the smallest and largest of the four numbers is 4.

| Column A | Column B |
|---|---|
| The smallest number's absolute value | 4 |

(A) The quantity in Column A is greater;
(B) The quantity in Column B is greater;
(C) The quantities are equal;
(D) The relationship cannot be determined from the information given.

13. P's age is twice Q's age.
    One year ago, R's age was exactly half of P's age at that time.

| **Column A** | **Column B** |
|---|---|
| R's age | Q's age |

(A) The quantity in Column A is greater;
(B) The quantity in Column B is greater;
(C) The quantities are equal;
(D) The relationship cannot be determined from the information given.

| **Column A** | **Column B** |
|---|---|

14.

$$ab < 0$$
$$a < b$$

| **Column A** | **Column B** |
|---|---|
| $\dfrac{b}{a}$ | $\dfrac{a}{b}$ |

(A) The quantity in Column A is greater;
(B) The quantity in Column B is greater;
(C) The quantities are equal;
(D) The relationship cannot be determined from the information given.

| **Column A** | **Column B** |
|---|---|

15.

| **Column A** | **Column B** |
|---|---|
| The standard deviation of a distribution of two numbers having a range of 2. | The standard deviation of a distribution of three numbers having a range of 2. |

(A) The quantity in Column A is greater;
(B) The quantity in Column B is greater;
(C) The quantities are equal;
(D) The relationship cannot be determined from the information given.

**Directions:** Questions 16–17 are based on the following figure.

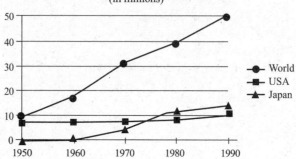

Motor Vehicle Production, 1950-1990
(in millions)

16. In 1980, worldwide production of motor vehicles exceeded U.S. production by approximately how many units?
    **(A)** 38 million
    **(B)** 35 million
    **(C)** 30 million
    **(D)** 27 million
    **(E)** 19 million

17. Which of the following statements about motor vehicle production from 1950 to 1990 is most accurate?
    **(A)** As a percentage of world production, U.S. production neither increased nor decreased.
    **(B)** Production outside the countries of U.S. and Japan increased, then leveled off, then increased again.
    **(C)** World production increased steadily while U.S. production declined.
    **(D)** As a percentage of world production, Japan production neither increased nor decreased.
    **(E)** Japan production increased steadily while U.S. production declined.

18. In triangle ABC, side AB is congruent to side BC. If the degree measure of ∠B is $b$, which of the following represents the degree measure of ∠A?

    **(A)** $b$

    **(B)** $180 - b$

    **(C)** $180 - \dfrac{b}{2}$

    **(D)** $90 - b$

    **(E)** $90 - \dfrac{b}{2}$

19. At ABC Corporation, five executives earn $150,000 each per year, three executives earn $170,000 each per year, and one executive earns $180,000 per year. What is the average salary of these executives?

    **(A)** $156,250
    **(B)** $160,000
    **(C)** $164,480
    **(D)** $166,670
    **(E)** $170,000

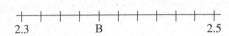

2.3       B       2.5

20. In the figure above, the vertical marks are equally spaced.

| **Column A** | **Column B** |
|---|---|
| B | 2.38 |

    **(A)** The quantity in Column A is greater;
    **(B)** The quantity in Column B is greater;
    **(C)** The quantities are equal;
    **(D)** The relationship cannot be determined from the information given.

| **Column A** | **Column B** |
|---|---|

21.    The sum of all integers from 19 to 50, including 19 and 50      The sum of all integers from 21 to 51, including 21 and 51

    **(A)** The quantity in Column A is greater;
    **(B)** The quantity in Column B is greater;
    **(C)** The quantities are equal;
    **(D)** The relationship cannot be determined from the information given.

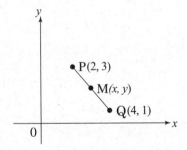

M is the midpoint of PQ

| **Column A** | **Column B** |
|---|---|

22.       M is the midpoint of PQ.

    $x$                $y$

    **(A)** The quantity in Column A is greater;
    **(B)** The quantity in Column B is greater;
    **(C)** The quantities are equal;
    **(D)** The relationship cannot be determined from the information given.

|  | **Column A** | **Column B** |
|---|---|---|
| **23.** | The number of fifths in eight sixteenths | The number of fifteenths in one sixth |

**(A)** The quantity in Column A is greater;
**(B)** The quantity in Column B is greater;
**(C)** The quantities are equal;
**(D)** The relationship cannot be determined from the information given.

**24.** If $a > 0$ and $<a> = a^2 + a$, then $\dfrac{<a>}{<-a>} =$

**(A)** $-1$

**(B)** $a$

**(C)** $\dfrac{a^2}{1+a}$

**(D)** $\dfrac{a+1}{a-1}$

**(E)** None of the above

**25.** It takes Paul $m$ minutes to mow the lawn. Assuming he mows at a constant rate, after Paul mows for $k$ minutes, what part of the lawn remains to be mowed?

**(A)** $\dfrac{m-k}{m}$

**(B)** $\dfrac{m}{k}$

**(C)** $1 - \dfrac{m}{k}$

**(D)** $\dfrac{k-m}{k}$

**(E)** $\dfrac{k}{m}$

**26.**

| Average (Mean) Gasoline Price Among 50 Stations | Number of Stations Charging More Than Average Price | Number of Stations Charging Less Than Average Price |
|---|---|---|
| January 1st: $2.50 | 22 | 17 |
| February 1st: $2.65 | 15 | 28 |
| March 1st: $2.40 | 23 | 23 |

The table shows the average price of gasoline among 50 gasoline-service stations on three different days, along with the number of stations charging more and less than the average on each day.

Based on the information in the table, which of the following statements about the price of gasoline among all 50 stations must be true?

  I. On February 1st, the median price was less than the average price
  II. On March 1st, the average price was equal to the median price.
 III. The median price on March 1st was less than the median price on January 1st.

**(A)** I only
**(B)** I and II only
**(C)** I and III only
**(D)** II and III only
**(E)** I, II, and III

**27.** As two wheels—A and B—roll across the ground, they both rotate at a rate of 60 revolutions per minute. The radius of wheel A is 3 centimeters. The radius of wheel B is 150 centimeters.

| Column A | Column B |
|---|---|
| The distance wheel A travels per hour | The distance wheel B travels per minute |

**(A)** The quantity in Column A is greater;
**(B)** The quantity in Column B is greater;
**(C)** The quantities are equal;
**(D)** The relationship cannot be determined from the information given.

| Column A | Column B |
|---|---|

**28.**

$$3x - 3 - 4x = x - 7 - 2x + 4$$

| Column A | Column B |
|---|---|
| $x$ | 0 |

**(A)** The quantity in Column A is greater;
**(B)** The quantity in Column B is greater;
**(C)** The quantities are equal;
**(D)** The relationship cannot be determined from the information given.

# ANSWER KEY AND EXPLANATIONS

## Analytical Writing

### ISSUE TASK: EVALUATION AND SCORING

Evaluate your Issue task essay on a scale of 1 to 6 (6 being the highest score) according to the following five criteria:

**1** Does your essay develop a position on the issue through the use of incisive reasons and persuasive examples?

**2** Are your essay's ideas conveyed clearly and articulately?

**3** Does your essay maintain proper focus on the issue, and is it well organized?

**4** Does your essay demonstrate proficiency, fluency, and maturity in its use of sentence structure, vocabulary, and idiom?

**5** Does your essay demonstrate command of the elements of Standard Written English, including grammar, word usage, spelling, and punctuation?

### ARGUMENT TASK: EVALUATION AND SCORING

Evaluate your Argument task essay on a scale of 1 to 6 (6 being the highest score) according to the following five criteria:

**1** Does your essay identify and articulate the argument's key unstated assumptions?

**2** Does your essay explain how the argument relies on these unstated assumptions, and what the implications are if these assumptions are unwarranted?

**3** Does your essay develop its ideas in a clear, organized manner, with appropriate transitions to help connect ideas together?

**4** Does your essay demonstrate proficiency, fluency, and maturity in its use of sentence structure, vocabulary, and idiom?

**5** Does your essay demonstrate command of the elements of Standard Written English, including grammar, word usage, spelling, and punctuation?

To help you evaluate your essay in terms of criteria 1 and 2, the following is a series of questions that identify *five* distinct unstated assumptions upon which the argument relies. To earn a score of 4 or higher, your essay should identify and explain at least three of these assumptions. Identifying and explaining at least four of the unstated assumptions would help earn you an even higher score.

- Are key characteristics of one group member (Giant Industries) also characteristics of the group as a whole—i.e., all employers in a certain state? (Perhaps Giant is not typical of the state's employers, as a group, with respect to either its financial strength or the average age of its workforce.)

- Does the term "largest private business" necessarily mean that Giant employs more workers than any other business in the state? (The smaller the workforce at

Giant, the less likely that Giant is representative of the state's employers as a group.)

- Doesn't the prediction's accuracy require that other future conditions remain unchanged? (For example, the argument ignores a possible influx of workers from other states.)

- Would a reduced workforce necessarily result in business failure? (Perhaps businesses will be more profitable by trimming their workforce.)

- What is the definition of "quality of life"? (The argument's ultimate prediction depends on this missing definition.)

## Verbal Reasoning

| | | |
|---|---|---|
| 1. A | 13. A | 22. D |
| 2. E | 14. B | 23. A |
| 3. C | 15. B | 24. E |
| 4. B | 16. C | 25. A |
| 5. C | 17. D | 26. B |
| 6. C | 18. C | 27. B |
| 7. D | 19. E | 28. C |
| 8. E | 20. D | 29. E |
| 9. D | 29.  (i) dissension | 30. B |
| 10. E |     (ii) in fact | |
| 11. A |     (iii) oppression | |
| 12. B | | |

1. **The correct answer is (A).** This is a "component of" analogy. COUNTERPOINT refers to the interplay between one MELODY and one or more others. So each MELODY is a distinct and necessary component of COUNTERPOINT. Similarly, each *brick* is a distinct and necessary component of *masonry* (brick or stone work, such as a chimney). As for choice (C), *beans* are ingredients which are combined to make *coffee*, but the bean itself is not, as a whole bean, part of the product.

2. **The correct answer is (E).** This is a "inherent purpose of" analogy. FALLOW means "to leave a field uncultivated for the purpose of restoring PRODUCTIVITY." Similarly, the reason some animals are *poisonous* is for their own *protection* from predators and other enemies.

3. **The correct answer is (C).** Discipline, studiousness, and technical precision are generally thought of as contrary to "passion." So, the sentence suggests that a professional musician must possess contradictory or opposing qualities. The word *paradoxical* captures the sense of

contradiction, while the *spontaneity* fits nicely with "passion" and contrasts appropriately with "disciplined."

4. **The correct answer is (B).** RESOLUTION means "determination or a clear sense of purpose"; *vacillation* refers to a "state of indecision or lack of clear purpose."

5. **The correct answer is (C).** TAUT means "tense or rigid." *Slackened* means "loosened."

6. **The correct answer is (C).** This is a "sign or symptom of" analogy. LAUGHTER is a common sign of AMUSEMENT, and *pallor* (paleness) is a common sign of *illness*.

7. **The correct answer is (D).** This is a "place for" analogy. A GEM is placed within a SETTING (framework) in jewelry, just as a *building* is constructed within the framework of a *scaffold*.

8. **The correct answer is (E).** In the passage's first paragraph, the author points out that the ability to taste

PTC varies among human populations, then in the final sentence of that paragraph refers to "other, more significant bitter substances." It can reasonably be inferred from these two statements, considered together, that PTC is a bitter substance.

9. **The correct answer is (D).** In the first paragraph, the author's main concern is to point out that the variability among human populations regarding sensitivity to PTC might be a trace of the evolutionary process of natural selectivity. In the second paragraph, the author offers a similar suggestion about variability in earwax type. To support these assertions, the author infers that both characteristics still serve useful purposes among non-primates, from whom humans presumably evolved. This inference is especially clear with respect to identifying bitter substances that might be toxic. Choice (D) accurately reflects the author's main assertion and supporting evidence.

10. **The correct answer is (E).** In this sentence, the missing word should continue in the same direction as the first. You're looking for a word that is consistent with and that complements *prospered*. You can easily eliminate choices (C) and (D), both of which contradict the first clause. (*Languish* means "weaken.") Choice (A) makes for a vague sentence: What was Hong Kong increasing? Choice (B) also makes for a vague sentence: What was Hong Kong succeeding in? That leaves choice (E). *Flourishing* means "thriving or growing"—a good complement to the idea of *prospering*. So choice (E) provides the best completion.

11. **The correct answer is (A).** EARNESTNESS means "deep sincerity"—the opposite of *insincerity*.

12. **The correct answer is (B).** This is a "defining characteristic" analogy. EVANESCENT means "tending to VANISH." *Iridescent* means "tending to *shine*."

13. **The correct answer is (A).** This is an "opposing function" analogy. A DISPENSARY is a distribution center for medicines, and a REAPER is a farming machine that cuts and gathers crops. Since a dispensary distributes but a reaper gathers, they serve opposing functions. A *chisel* is used to break apart material such as stone; *mortar* is used to bond stones or bricks; hence, they also serve opposing functions. Moreover, in both pairs, the relationship involves disbursing versus joining, further strengthening the analogy.

14. **The correct answer is (B).** The signpost phrase in this sentence is "by which." What precedes this key phrase must adequately explain the analogy that follows it. Choice (B) fits the bill. In the context of evolution, many organisms have continually *adapted* to environmental changes, resulting in a large variety of species (in a continual branching manner); in other words, for most organisms, evolution is not *linear*.

15. **The correct answer is (B).** Nowhere in this passage does the author mention any power struggles among the leaders of the Iroquois nations. Although the third paragraph does refer to a dispute among the Iroquois leaders, the dispute involved the role that the Iroquois

should play in the American Revolution (choice E).

16. **The correct answer is (C).** In the final paragraph's first sentence, the author tells us that Cornplanter was an outspoken proponent of assimilation. The next sentence suggests in context that Handsome Lake was related to Cornplanter as a half-brother. The fact that Lake was responsible for the Iroquois reasserting their national identity is ironic, then, in light of Lake's blood relationship to Cornplanter.

17. **The correct answer is (D).** According to the passage, the Quakers' introduction of new technology to the Iroquois was partly responsible for the decline of the Iroquois culture in that it contributed to their loss of national identity. Choice (D) presents a similar situation. Choice (A) is the second-best choice. Insofar as the children referred to in scenario choice (A) learn the language of the prevailing culture, assimilation and a resulting loss of ethnic identity might tend to occur. However, this sense of identity might be reinforced by their learning to read and write in their traditional language as well. Therefore, choice (A) is not as likely to lead to the demise of the minority group as choice (D), based upon the Iroquois' experience as discussed in the passage.

18. **The correct answer is (C).** The first and second paragraphs are concerned with the inception of the Iroquois League, while the third and fourth paragraphs outline the subsequent history of the League from its decline through its subsequent

resurgence under Handsome Lake. Choice (C) recapitulates this overall structure.

19. **The correct answer is (E).** This is a "degree of" analogy. ROBUST means full of VIGOR, just as *sanguine* means full of *hope*. Choice (B) is the second-best answer, because *sickness* and *illness* are synonymous. However, sickness does not suggest a fullness (of illness).

20. **The correct answer is (D).** This is a "symptom, sign, or manifestation" analogy. To SHUN is to avoid or ignore. One who expresses DISAPPROVAL of the behavior of another might show that disapproval by shunning the other person. So shunning is one possible sign of disapproval (but not a defining characteristic of it). Similarly, a *nap* a possible sign of *relaxation* (but not a defining characteristic of it).

21. **The correct answer is dissension for blank (i), in fact for blank (ii), and oppression for blank (iii).** In the first sentence, the phrase *that is* signals that what precedes it should be similar in meaning to what follows it. Pointing out the mistakes of those in power could be characterized either as a challenge or as part of *dissention*, which means "rebellion or disobedience." The second part of the sentence (following the semicolon) reiterates and expresses more pointedly the idea in the first part. The connecting phrase *in fact* works well to signal this reiteration. As for blank (iii), *oppression* (which means "persecution or tyranny") is the only choice that makes sense in context.

**22. The correct answer is (D).** The word VESTIGIAL describes something that no longer functions usefully, and so it's a good antonym of *functional*.

**23. The correct answer is (A).** In the first sentence of the passage, the author tells us that the folk lore is "collective property . . . subject to stricter and more uniform laws than fields in which individual creation prevails." Then, later in the passage, the author distinguishes between written literature (which includes novels) and folk tales in that in the former "a creative personality is free to shape entirely new roles." The implication here is that written literature (including novels) is one of the fields in which "individual creation prevails" and therefore should not be considered part of a culture's collective property.

**24. The correct answer is (E).** In the passage, the author first makes the broad point that a culture's various folk tales are remarkably consistent. The author then acknowledges and describes limited ways in which folk tales legitimately vary according to certain preferences of the teller, but then emphasizes the limited extent of the story teller's discretion. Of the five choices, choice (E) best sums up these ideas.

**25. The correct answer is (A).** The word "but" shows that the reaction of the students and faculty was different from that of the community members. The word *gratified* describes a reaction that is contrary to "outraged," and *controversial* describes the fact that the two groups had such opposite opinions.

**26. The correct answer is (B).** To IMPEDE is to "hinder or obstruct" (as in *impede progress*); to *hasten* is to cause an event to occur sooner than it otherwise might.

**27. The correct answer is (B).** This is an "ideal characteristic" analogy. An effective, or ideal, DANCER is AGILE (nimble), although agility is not a defining characteristic of a dancer. Similarly, an effective, or ideal, *worker* is *diligent* (not lazy), although diligence is not a defining characteristic of a worker.

**28. The correct answer is (C).** The first part of the sentence (containing both missing words) must explain why it difficult to imagine that Richard III had been dead for so long when Shakespeare wrote the play. A *vivid* (lifelike or realistic) *depiction* (characterization or description) of the ruler would provide just such an explanation.

**29. The correct answer is (E).** A VAGARY is an unpredictable, erratic, or whimsical idea or occurrence, just the opposite of a *foreseeable event*.

**30. The correct answer is (B).** To FAWN is to "behave in a servile, cringing, manner" (like a dog toward its master). To *dominate* is to act in an opposite manner.

## Quantitative Reasoning

| | |
|---|---|
| 1. C | 11. C |
| 2. A | 12. B |
| 3. B | 13. B |
| 4. E | 14. D |
| 5. D | 15. D |
| 6. C | 16. C |
| 7. 3 | 17. B |
| 8. C | 18. E |
| 9. A | 19. B |
| 10. B | |

| |
|---|
| 20. C |
| 21. B |
| 22. A |
| 23. C |
| 24. D |
| 25. A |
| 26. E |
| 27. A |
| 28. D |

1. **The correct answer is (C).** Here's how to calculate the two quantities:

   Quantity A = $1.20 + (7)($.35) = $1.20 + $2.45 = $3.65

   Quantity B = $2.25 + (7)($.20) = $2.25 + $1.40 = $3.65

2. **The correct answer is (A).**
   $k^{1/2} + k^{1/2} = \sqrt{k} + \sqrt{k} = 2\sqrt{k}$, which is clearly greater than $\sqrt{k}$.

3. **The correct answer is (B).** Of the 12 students taking Spanish, 4 are taking both languages, leaving 8 taking only Spanish. Since 12 of the 18 are taking Spanish, just 6 are taking only German. Thus, the quantity in Column B is greater.

4. **The correct answer is (E).** The other integer is $n + 2$. The difference between $n$ and $(n + 2)$ must be positive (it is given as 120), so the term $(n + 2)$ must appear first in the equation.

5. **The correct answer is (D).** Between noon and 5 p.m. on Sunday, 4 ounces dripped into the tank. The drip rate is 4 ounces in 5 hours, or $\frac{4}{5}$ ounce per hour. 9 hours later, at 2:00 a.m. on Monday, an additional

$\frac{4}{5} \times 9 = \frac{36}{5}$ ounces will have dripped into the tank. The total accumulation of water is $7 + \frac{36}{5} = \frac{71}{5}$ ounces.

6. **The correct answer is (C).** Rug R must be 4' × 4', and rug S must be 2' × 2'. Also, since the floor's area is 112 and its length is 8, the floor's width = 14, which in turn equals the sum of the following five lengths (let $x$ = the distance between the two rugs, as well as from each rug to the nearest east or west edge):

   $x + 4 + x + 2 + x = 14$

   $$3x = 8$$

   $$x = \frac{8}{3} = 2\frac{2}{3} \text{ feet or}$$

   2 feet, 8 inches

7. **The correct answer is 3.** First, notice that R must equal either 1 or 2; otherwise, the sum of the three numbers would greatly exceed 117. Assuming R = 1, the "ones" column tells us that the value of S would necessarily be 5. But the "tens" column would not add up correctly. Hence, R must equal 2 and, accordingly, S must equal 3.

8. **The correct answer is (C).** First, determine the percentage of trees on Main Street that are pine: 100% − 40% − 25% − 20% = 15%. Next, calculate the number of trees that are pine: 15% of 140 = (.15)(140) = 21.

9. **The correct answer is (A).** The least common multiple of 4, 6, and 8 is 24. The greatest common factor of 44, 66, and 88 is 22.

10. **The correct answer is (B).** There are four odd numbers (1, 3, 5, and 7) and three even numbers (2, 4, and 6) on the spinner. So, the chances of yielding an odd number with the first spin are 4 in 7, or $\frac{4}{7}$. The chances of yielding an even number with the second spin are 3 in 7, or $\frac{3}{7}$. To determine the probability of both events occurring, combine the two individual probabilities by multiplication: $\frac{4}{7} \times \frac{3}{7} = \frac{12}{49}$.

11. **The correct answer is (C).** Angles $y°$ and $z°$ combine to form an angle whose measure exceeds 180° (a straight line) by $x°$. Hence, $y + z − x = 180$. Substitute the values for $y$ and $z$ given in the problem, and solve for $x$: $130 + 100 − x = 180$; $x = 50$.

12. **The correct answer is (B).** The median is the arithmetic mean of the two middle numbers. Since that median is zero (0), the two numbers must have the same absolute value, although either both are zero (0) or one is negative while the other is positive (for example, −1 and 1). Hence the smallest of the four numbers must be negative, while the largest must be positive. Given that the difference between these two numbers on the number line is 4, the smallest number must be greater than −4 (but less than zero (0)). Otherwise, the largest number would not be positive. So the smallest number's absolute value must be less than 4.

13. **The correct answer is (B).** You can approach this problem intuitively, without a written system of equations. If P's age were twice what R's age is now, then Q's age would equal R's age, and the correct answer would be choice (C). R's current age must be greater than half of P's (because one year ago R's age was exactly half of P's). Given that Q's age is exactly half of P's age, R must be older than Q.

14. **The correct answer is (D).** The inequality $ab < 0$ tells you that either $a$ or $b$, but not both, is negative. Since $a < b$, $a$ must be negative and $b$ must be positive. But you cannot make the comparison between Quantity A and Quantity B. Which is greater depends on the absolute values of the two variables. For example, if $a = −1$ and $b = 2$, then $\frac{b}{a} < \frac{a}{b}$. On the other hand, if $a = −2$ and $b = 1$, then $\frac{b}{a} > \frac{a}{b}$.

15. **The correct answer is (D).** In the distribution described in Column B, if the third term is the precise average (arithmetic mean) of the other two terms, then Quantity A would equal Quantity B (for example, if the two distributions are {2,4} and {2,3,4}). Otherwise, Quantity B would be greater, since its middle term deviates from the mean of the other two terms.

16. **The correct answer is (C).** In 1980, worldwide (U.S. and non-U.S.) production was 38 million, while U.S. production was 8 million. The difference between the two numbers is 30 million.

17. **The correct answer is (B).** Between 1970 and 1980, the increase in worldwide production (which includes Japan and the United States) was about the same as the net (combined) increase in Japan and U.S. production during the same decade, indicating no significant change in worldwide production, excluding the U.S. and Japan. However, during the previous two decades (1950–1970) and during the 1980s, worldwide increases exceeded net (combined) increases in the U.S. and Japan.

18. **The correct answer is (E).** The triangle is Isosceles, and so $m\angle A = m\angle C$. Letting $a$, $b$, and $c$ represent the degree measures of $\angle A$, $\angle B$, and $\angle C$, respectively, solve for $a$:

$$a + b + c = 180$$
$$2a + b = 180 \ [a = c]$$
$$\frac{2a}{2} = \frac{180}{2} - \frac{b}{2}$$
$$a = 90 - \frac{b}{2}$$

19. **The correct answer is (B).** Assign a "weight" to each of the three salary figures (to save time, express all numbers in thousands):

$5(150) = 750$
$3(170) = 510$
$1(180) = 180$

Then determine the weighted average of the nine salaries:

$$750 + 510 + 180 = 1{,}440$$
$$\frac{1{,}440}{9} = 160$$

20. **The correct answer is (C).** The region of the number line from 2.3 to 2.5 has been divided into 10 congruent regions. The distance from 2.3 to 2.5 is 0.2. Thus, the vertical marks are spaced at intervals of 0.02. Accordingly, B = 2.38.

21. **The correct answer is (B).** The two number series have in common integers 21 through 50. So you can subtract (or cancel) all of these integers from both sides of the comparison. That leaves you to compare (19 + 20) to 51. You can now see clearly that Quantity B is greater.

22. **The correct answer is (A).** First, Quantity A: $x$ is the average of 2 and 4; that is, $x = 3$. Next, Quantity B: $y$ is the average of 3 and 1; that is, $y = 2$.

23. **The correct answer is (C).** To make the comparison, set up two proportions. Quantity A is $x$ in the equation $\frac{8}{16} = \frac{x}{5}$, and Quantity B is $y$ in the equation $\frac{1}{6} = \frac{y}{15}$. You can easily see that $x = 2.5$ and that $y = 2.5$.

**24. The correct answer is (D).** Expand the numerator and the denominator:

$$\frac{<a>}{<-a>} = \frac{a^2 + a}{(-a)^2 + (-a)}$$

$$= \frac{a^2 + a}{a^2 - a} = \frac{a(a + 1)}{a(a - 1)}$$

$$= \frac{a + 1}{a - 1}$$

**25. The correct answer is (A).** Paul has mowed $\frac{k}{m}$ of the lawn in $k$ minutes. Still not mowed, then, is $1 - \frac{k}{m}$, or $\frac{m - k}{m}$.

**26. The correct answer is (E).** Statement I must be true. On February 1st, more stations charged less than the average price than greater than the average price; in other words, the median price was less than the average price. Statement II must be true. On March 1st, the number of stations charging more than the average price was the same as the number of stations charging less than the average price; in other words, the median price was the same as the average price. Statement III must be true. The median price on March 1st was the same as the average price: $2.40. The median price on January 1st was greater than the average price of $2.50.

**27. The correct answer is (A).** Wheel B's radius, and therefore its circumference as well, is 50 times greater than Wheel A's (3:150 = 1:50). In order to travel as far each minute as Wheel A travels per hour, Wheel B's circumference would need to be 60 times greater (since there are 60 minutes per hour), but it's not that big. Thus, Wheel A travels further in one minute than Wheel B does in one hour. (The number of revolutions per minute is not relevant, since the rotation rate is the same for both wheels.)

**28. The correct answer is (D).** All terms on both sides cancel out:

$$3x - 3 - 4x = x - 7 - 2x + 4$$

$$-x - 3 = -x - 3$$

$$0 = 0$$

Therefore, $x$ = any real number.

# ANSWER SHEET PRACTICE TEST 5

## Analytical Writing—Issue Task

_____

_____

_____

_____

_____

_____

_____

_____

_____

_____

_____

_____

_____

_____

_____

_____

_____

_____

_____

_____

_____

_____

_____

answer sheet

**Analytical Writing—Argument Task**

_____

_____

_____

_____

_____

_____

_____

_____

_____

_____

_____

_____

_____

_____

_____

_____

_____

_____

_____

_____

answer sheet

## Quantitative Reasoning

1. Ⓐ Ⓑ Ⓒ Ⓓ
2. Ⓐ Ⓑ Ⓒ Ⓓ
3. Ⓐ Ⓑ Ⓒ Ⓓ
4. Ⓐ Ⓑ Ⓒ Ⓓ
5. Ⓐ Ⓑ Ⓒ Ⓓ
6. Ⓐ Ⓑ Ⓒ Ⓓ Ⓔ
7. Ⓐ Ⓑ Ⓒ Ⓓ Ⓔ
8. Ⓐ Ⓑ Ⓒ Ⓓ Ⓔ
9. Ⓐ Ⓑ Ⓒ Ⓓ
10. Ⓐ Ⓑ Ⓒ Ⓓ

11. Ⓐ Ⓑ Ⓒ Ⓓ Ⓔ
12. Ⓐ Ⓑ Ⓒ Ⓓ Ⓔ
13. Ⓐ Ⓑ Ⓒ Ⓓ Ⓔ
14. Ⓐ Ⓑ Ⓒ Ⓓ Ⓔ
15. Ⓐ Ⓑ Ⓒ Ⓓ
16. Ⓐ Ⓑ Ⓒ Ⓓ Ⓔ
17. ☐
18. Ⓐ Ⓑ Ⓒ Ⓓ
19. Ⓐ Ⓑ Ⓒ Ⓓ
20. Ⓐ Ⓑ Ⓒ Ⓓ

21. Ⓐ Ⓑ Ⓒ Ⓓ Ⓔ
22. Ⓐ Ⓑ Ⓒ Ⓓ Ⓔ
23. Ⓐ Ⓑ Ⓒ Ⓓ
24. Ⓐ Ⓑ Ⓒ Ⓓ
25. Ⓐ Ⓑ Ⓒ Ⓓ
26. Ⓐ Ⓑ Ⓒ Ⓓ Ⓔ
27. Ⓐ Ⓑ Ⓒ Ⓓ Ⓔ
28. Ⓐ Ⓑ Ⓒ Ⓓ Ⓔ

## Verbal Reasoning

1. Ⓐ Ⓑ Ⓒ Ⓓ Ⓔ
2. Ⓐ Ⓑ Ⓒ Ⓓ Ⓔ
3. Ⓐ Ⓑ Ⓒ Ⓓ Ⓔ
4. Ⓐ Ⓑ Ⓒ Ⓓ Ⓔ
5. Ⓐ Ⓑ Ⓒ Ⓓ Ⓔ
6. Ⓐ Ⓑ Ⓒ Ⓓ Ⓔ
7. Ⓐ Ⓑ Ⓒ Ⓓ Ⓔ
8. Ⓐ Ⓑ Ⓒ Ⓓ Ⓔ
9. Ⓐ Ⓑ Ⓒ Ⓓ Ⓔ
10. Ⓐ Ⓑ Ⓒ Ⓓ Ⓔ
11. Ⓐ Ⓑ Ⓒ Ⓓ Ⓔ
12. Ⓐ Ⓑ Ⓒ Ⓓ Ⓔ

13. Ⓐ Ⓑ Ⓒ Ⓓ Ⓔ
14. Ⓐ Ⓑ Ⓒ Ⓓ Ⓔ
15. Ⓐ Ⓑ Ⓒ Ⓓ Ⓔ
16. Ⓐ Ⓑ Ⓒ Ⓓ Ⓔ
17. Ⓐ Ⓑ Ⓒ Ⓓ Ⓔ
18. Ⓐ Ⓑ Ⓒ Ⓓ Ⓔ
19. Ⓐ Ⓑ Ⓒ Ⓓ Ⓔ
20. Ⓐ Ⓑ Ⓒ Ⓓ Ⓔ
21. Ⓐ Ⓑ Ⓒ Ⓓ Ⓔ
22. Ⓐ Ⓑ Ⓒ Ⓓ Ⓔ

23. Ⓐ Ⓑ Ⓒ Ⓓ Ⓔ
24. Ⓐ Ⓑ Ⓒ Ⓓ Ⓔ
25. Ⓐ Ⓑ Ⓒ Ⓓ Ⓔ
26. Ⓐ Ⓑ Ⓒ Ⓓ Ⓔ
27. Ⓐ Ⓑ Ⓒ Ⓓ Ⓔ
28. (i) _____
    (ii) _____
    (iii) _____
29. Ⓐ Ⓑ Ⓒ Ⓓ Ⓔ
30. Ⓐ Ⓑ Ⓒ Ⓓ Ⓔ

**answer sheet**

# Practice Test 5

## ANALYTICAL WRITING

### Issue Task

*Time: 45 Minutes*

> **NOTES:** For *some* test-takers, the GRE will end with an identified and untimed research section. The research section, which is unscored, contains experimental question types. Test-makers use it to assess the difficulty levels of the experimental question types, based on test-takers' responses.
>
> For the purposes of this book—making sure you're fully prepared to take the GRE exam—one Complex Text Completion question (Verbal Reasoning section) and one numeric entry question (Quantitative Reasoning section) are included in each of the Practice Tests. On the actual GRE, however, you will not see both of these questions; in fact, you may *not* see either one.

Using a word processor, compose a response to the following statement and directive. Do not use any spell-checking or grammar-checking functions (they are not available on the actual GRE):

> "In any field of endeavor, an individual's best critics are the individual's own colleagues or other peers in that field."

> In your view, how accurate is the foregoing statement? Develop and support your viewpoint with relevant reasons and examples and by considering ways in which the statement may or may not be true.

## Argument Task

### *Time: 30 Minutes*

Using a word processor, compose an essay for the following argument and directive. Do not use any spell-checking or grammar-checking functions (they are not available on the actual GRE):

> "Five years ago, MegaCorp switched from a monitoring system for detecting employee pilfering to an honor system. During the following year, the number of reported pilfering incidents at MegaCorp was 40 percent less than during the previous year; and during the most recent year, the number of such incidents was even lower. These statistics should not be surprising; in responding to a recent companywide survey, MegaCorp employees indicated that they would be less likely to pilfer under an honor system than if they were closely monitored. All businesses can learn from MegaCorp's example and reduce employee pilfering by adopting a similar honor code."

> Discuss how well-reasoned you find the above argument.

## QUANTITATIVE REASONING

*28 Questions • 45 Minutes*

> **NOTE:** In this section, questions are grouped together by format, and within each group the questions grow more difficult as you go. Because the actual GRE is computer-adaptive in the multiple-choice sections, it intersperses questions of different formats and difficulty levels.

|  | <u>Column A</u> | <u>Column B</u> |
|---|---|---|
| 1. | The price of a coat on sale at 7% off its list price of $300 | The price of a coat that cost $200 wholesale sold at a 40% markup |

- **(A)** The quantity in Column A is greater;
- **(B)** The quantity in Column B is greater;
- **(C)** The quantities are equal;
- **(D)** The relationship cannot be determined from the information given.

|  | <u>Column A</u> | <u>Column B</u> |
|---|---|---|
| 2. | | $y = \dfrac{1}{2}$ |
| | 1.25 | $y^0 + y^2$ |

- **(A)** The quantity in Column A is greater;
- **(B)** The quantity in Column B is greater;
- **(C)** The quantities are equal;
- **(D)** The relationship cannot be determined from the information given.

**3.** Of 60 horses in a stable, $\dfrac{1}{3}$ are black, $\dfrac{1}{5}$ are white, and $\dfrac{8}{15}$ are stallions.

|  | <u>Column A</u> | <u>Column B</u> |
|---|---|---|
| | The minimum number of stallions of a color other than black or white. | The minimum number of stallions that are either black or white. |

- **(A)** The quantity in Column A is greater;
- **(B)** The quantity in Column B is greater;
- **(C)** The quantities are equal;
- **(D)** The relationship cannot be determined from the information given.

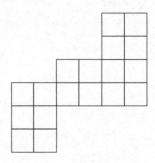

4. The small squares that form the 10-sided quilt shown above are to be rearranged to form a rectangular quilt consisting of two rows of small squares.

| Column A | Column B |
|---|---|
| The perimeter of the quilt as shown above | The perimeter of the quilt after the squares are rearranged |

(A) The quantity in Column A is greater;
(B) The quantity in Column B is greater;
(C) The quantities are equal;
(D) The relationship cannot be determined from the information given.

5. The center of Agua Island is 24 miles from the center of Breezy Island and 48 miles from the center of Cocoa Island.

| Column A | Column B |
|---|---|
| The distance from the center of Breezy Island to the center of Cocoa Island | Twice the distance from the center of Breezy Island to the center of Agua Island |

(A) The quantity in Column A is greater;
(B) The quantity in Column B is greater;
(C) The quantities are equal;
(D) The relationship cannot be determined from the information given.

6. The interior angles of a certain quadrilateral are measured at the ratio 1:2:3:4. If each interior angle measures less than 180°, what is the sum of the degree measures of the smallest and largest among these four angles?
(A) 218°
(B) 204°
(C) 180°
(D) 148°
(E) 108°

7. For all $x > 2$, $\dfrac{x^2 - 4}{x^2 - 2x} =$

   (A) $x - \dfrac{4}{x}$

   (B) $\dfrac{1}{2x}$

   (C) $2x + 1$

   (D) $2 - x$

   (E) $1 + \dfrac{2}{x}$

8. In a geometric series, each term is a constant multiple of the preceding one. If $x$ and $y$ are the first two terms in a geometric series, which of the following represents the third term in the series?

   (A) $\dfrac{y^2}{x}$

   (B) $\dfrac{y}{x}$

   (C) $\dfrac{y^2}{x^2}$

   (D) $xy$

   (E) $\dfrac{x^2}{y}$

|              | **Column A**          | **Column B**   |
| ------------ | --------------------- | -------------- |
| 9.           | $2\sqrt{x} \times 3\sqrt{5}$ | $6\sqrt{5x}$ |

   (A) The quantity in Column A is greater;
   (B) The quantity in Column B is greater;
   (C) The quantities are equal;
   (D) The relationship cannot be determined from the information given.

|       | **Column A** | **Column B** |
| ----- | ------------ | ------------ |
| 10.   | The number of different ways to add four positive odd integers together for a sum of 10, without considering the sequence of addition | The number of different ways add three positive even integers together for a sum of 10, without considering the sequence of addition |

   (A) The quantity in Column A is greater;
   (B) The quantity in Column B is greater;
   (C) The quantities are equal;
   (D) The relationship cannot be determined from the information given.

**11.** For what value of $s$ is it true both that $0.2t = 2.2 - 0.6s$ and that $0.5s = 0.2t + 1.1$?

    **(A)** 1
    **(B)** 3
    **(C)** 10
    **(D)** 11
    **(E)** 30

**Directions:** Questions 12–13 refer to the following chart.

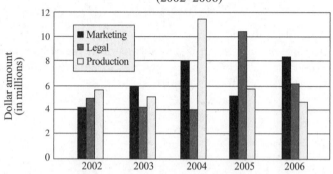

MARKETING, LEGAL, AND PRODUCTION EXPENSES
FOR XYZ COMPANY
(2002–2006)

**12.** Among the following choices, the difference between marketing expenses and production expenses was most nearly the same for which two years?

    **(A)** 2002 and 2003
    **(B)** 2004 and 2006
    **(C)** 2003 and 2005
    **(D)** 2002 and 2004
    **(E)** 2003 and 2006

**13.** With respect to the two years during which combined legal and production expenses were most nearly the same, average marketing expenses per year were approximately

    **(A)** $5.5 million
    **(B)** $6.2 million
    **(C)** $6.8 million
    **(D)** $7.2 million
    **(E)** $8.0 million

**14.** If a building $b$ feet high casts a shadow $f$ feet long, then, at the same time of day, a tree $t$ feet high will cast a shadow how many feet long?

(A) $\dfrac{t}{fb}$

(B) $\dfrac{fb}{t}$

(C) $\dfrac{b}{ft}$

(D) $\dfrac{tb}{f}$

(E) $\dfrac{ft}{b}$

| <u>Column A</u> | <u>Column B</u> |
|---|---|
| **15.** The sum of five consecutive integers whose median is zero (0) | The sum of six consecutive odd integers whose median is zero (0) |

(A) The quantity in Column A is greater;
(B) The quantity in Column B is greater;
(C) The quantities are equal;
(D) The relationship cannot be determined from the information given.

**16.** In the standard $(x,y)$ coordinate plane, lines $a$ and $b$ intersect at point $(5,-2)$, and lines $b$ and $c$ intersect at point $(-3,3)$. What is the slope of line $b$?

(A) $\dfrac{1}{2}$

(D) $-\dfrac{5}{2}$

(C) $-\dfrac{2}{5}$

(D) $-\dfrac{5}{8}$

(E) It cannot be determined from the information given.

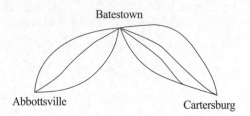

Batestown

Abbottsville            Cartersburg

17. The diagram shows all roads connecting three towns. How many different routes can you drive from Abbottsville and Cartersburg if you drive through Batestown only once?

*Click on the answer box, then type in a number. Backspace to erase.*

18. It takes 40 minutes for Hanna to drive from home to work, and it takes her 30 minutes to drive back home from work by the same route.

| **Column A** | **Column B** |
| --- | --- |
| Hanna's average speed during her round trip between home and work. | Hanna's average speed during her trip from home to work. |

**(A)** The quantity in Column A is greater;
**(B)** The quantity in Column B is greater;
**(C)** The quantities are equal;
**(D)** The relationship cannot be determined from the information given.

| **Column A** | **Column B** |
| --- | --- |

19. The greatest common factor of 20, 45, and 90    The sum of $\frac{3}{5}$, $\frac{5}{3}$, and 5

**(A)** The quantity in Column A is greater;
**(B)** The quantity in Column B is greater;
**(C)** The quantities are equal;
**(D)** The relationship cannot be determined from the information given.

| **Column A** | **Column B** |
| --- | --- |

20.                                $x > 0$

$50 \div 3.9x$                  $.13x \times 0.6$

**(A)** The quantity in Column A is greater;
**(B)** The quantity in Column B is greater;
**(C)** The quantities are equal;
**(D)** The relationship cannot be determined from the information given.

practice test

**Directions:** Questions 21–22 are based on the following table.

Shipping Rates for Express Parcel Service, Inc.

| | Shipment Method | | |
|---|---|---|---|
| | Ground | Air | Express |
| 1 pound or less | $1.50 | $2.25 | $6.75 |
| Each additional pound (or fraction) through 10 pounds | $.40 | $.60 | $1.15 |
| Each additional pound (or fraction), 11 or more pounds | $.25 | $.40 | $.75 |

21. How much would it cost to ship a 28-pound parcel by ground delivery?
    **(A)** $8.80
    **(B)** $9.60
    **(C)** $9.75
    **(D)** $10.40
    **(E)** $12.05

22. How much more would it cost to ship a parcel weighing 2.4 pounds by express delivery than by air delivery?
    **(A)** $2.80
    **(B)** $3.05
    **(C)** $3.60
    **(D)** $4.75
    **(E)** $5.60

|  | **Column A** | **Column B** |
|---|---|---|

23.                                    $Q > 0$

$P + Q$                                            $|P + Q|$

**(A)** The quantity in Column A is greater;
**(B)** The quantity in Column B is greater;
**(C)** The quantities are equal;
**(D)** The relationship cannot be determined from the information given.

|  | **Column A** | **Column B** |
|---|---|---|

24.  The greatest number of 1-inch cubes that can be packed into a box measuring $5 \times 6 \times 8$ inches | The greatest number of 2-inch cubes that can be packed into a box measuring $10 \times 12 \times 16$ inches

**(A)** The quantity in Column A is greater;
**(B)** The quantity in Column B is greater;
**(C)** The quantities are equal;
**(D)** The relationship cannot be determined from the information given.

| Column A | | Column B |
|---|---|---|

**25.**                               $x > 0$

$$\frac{1}{x} + \frac{1}{x} \qquad\qquad\qquad\qquad \frac{1}{2x}$$

**(A)** The quantity in Column A is greater;
**(B)** The quantity in Column B is greater;
**(C)** The quantities are equal;
**(D)** The relationship cannot be determined from the information given.

**26.** Given four empty chairs and three people, how many seating arrangements are possible—one person to a chair?

**(A)** 24
**(B)** 20
**(C)** 16
**(D)** 12
**(E)** 8

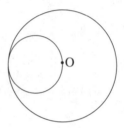

**27.** In the figure, O lies at the center of the larger circle. What is the ratio of the smaller circle's area to the larger circle's area?

**(A)** $\pi$:12
**(B)** $\pi$:15
**(C)** 2:3$\pi$
**(D)** 1:4
**(E)** 1:5

**28.** Eight years from now, Carrie's age will be twice Ben's age. If Carrie's current age is C and Ben's current age is B, which of the following represents Carrie's current age?

**(A)** B
**(B)** B + 4
**(C)** B + 8
**(D)** 2B + 8
**(E)** 3B

# VERBAL REASONING

### 30 Questions • 30 Minutes

**NOTE:** In this section, questions are grouped together by format, and within each group the questions grow more difficult as you go. Because the actual GRE is computer-adaptive in the multiple-choice sections, it intersperses questions of different formats and difficulty levels.

1. Although many of the company's board members were _____ about the impending deal, others were _____ the benefits it would bring to the company.
   (A) euphoric . . confident of
   (B) chagrined . . unsure about
   (C) pleased . . disturbed by
   (D) angry . . skeptical of
   (E) optimistic . . dubious about

2. BOAT : WAKE ::
   (A) actor : performance
   (B) scalpel : scar
   (C) drill : hole
   (D) gardener : cuttings
   (E) airplane : tarmac

3. MULCHED : BURGEON ::
   (A) stoked : smolder
   (B) edited : compose
   (C) calibrated : operate
   (D) elevated : hover
   (E) honed : hew

4. JOCULAR : SOLEMNITY ::
   (A) razed : demolition
   (B) pompous : spectacle
   (C) latent : visibility
   (D) vindictive : enmity
   (E) lonely : insularity

5. DUPLICITY:
   (A) honesty
   (B) openness
   (C) simplicity
   (D) decency
   (E) innocence

6. In classical literature, love was depicted not as an ennobling passion but as an unfortunate _____ that disabled judgment, almost a kind of _____.
   (A) malady . . insanity
   (B) condition . . virtue
   (C) emotion . . crime
   (D) sickness . . retribution
   (E) occurrence . . insecurity

**Directions:** Questions 7–9 are based on the following passage.

*Line* While there will always be a need for social programs geared toward alleviating the poverty of individuals, the community is perhaps the more rel-
(5) evant level for public policy intervention, especially in rural areas. It has been recognized that social isolation within urban ghettos is a structural characteristic of urban poverty,
(10) but rural poverty is marked by physical isolation as well. This uniqueness makes rural community poverty particularly intractable, requiring policies that account for the
(15) cost of isolation. It is possible to provide vocational training for individuals anywhere, but if there are no jobs within the community for those individuals, the training is largely
(20) wasted. The current transition to a service-based economy and deregulation in transportation (resulting in

disproportionately higher transportation costs for relatively isolated (25) areas) have only exacerbated the growing social and economic distress in rural America, underscoring the need to redefine poverty and redirect the focus of our funding agencies and (30) policy-makers in accordance with the new definition. What's needed is a more holistic view on an aggregate level, where poverty is properly seen as a condition of the local social (35) structure, with income only one of the salient parameters.

7. The author mentions "the current transition to a service-based economy and deregulation in transportation" (lines 20–22) most likely to
   (A) suggest that manufacturing jobs are disappearing
   (B) underscore the isolation of people in rural communities
   (C) emphasize the lack of job skills among rural residents
   (D) contrast the old economy with the new economy
   (E) provide support for a more flexible poverty standard

8. Which of the following is LEAST likely to be the author's vocation, based solely on the information in the passage?
   (A) Public health official
   (B) Social activist
   (C) Economist
   (D) Demographer
   (E) Public policy analyst

9. The author seeks to draw which of the following distinctions between urban ghettos and impoverished rural communities?
   (A) Job training programs are more accessible in urban ghettos than in rural communities.
   (B) Funding agencies are more likely to recognize poverty in an urban ghetto than in a rural community.
   (C) Poverty is more common in rural communities than in urban ghettos.
   (D) Impoverished individuals feel more isolated in urban ghettos than in rural communities.
   (E) Residents of urban ghettos typically have better jobs than residents of rural communities.

10. INSOLVENT:
    (A) fortunate
    (B) sparing
    (C) prudent
    (D) generous
    (E) wealthy

11. OCCLUDE:
    (A) proffer
    (B) spew
    (C) emerge
    (D) exhume
    (E) flower

12. DIATRIBE : BITTERNESS ::
    (A) dictum : indolence
    (B) recapitulation : brevity
    (C) polemic : consonance
    (D) encomium : reproach
    (E) concordance : contrariety

13. SILVER : METAL ::
    (A) gold : alloy
    (B) plastic : container
    (C) helium : gas
    (D) sand : glass
    (E) sediment : rock

**Directions:** Questions 14–16 are based on the following passage.

*Line* Victorian poetess Christina Rossetti's potent sensual imagery compelled Edmond Gosse, perhaps the most influential literary critic in late Vic-
(5) torian England, to observe that she "does not shrink from strong delineation of the pleasures of life even when denouncing them." In the face of Rossetti's virtual canonization by
(10) critics at the end of the nineteenth century, however, Virginia Woolf ignores her apparent conservatism, instead seeing in her curiosity value and a model of artistic purity and
(15) integrity for women writers. In 1930, the centenary of Rossetti's birth, Woolf identified her as "one of Shakespeare's more recent sisters" whose life had been reclusively Victorian but whose
(20) achievement as an artist was enduring.

Woolf remembers Rossetti for her four volumes of explosively original poems loaded with vivid images and
(25) dense emotional energy. "A Birthday," for instance, is no typical Victorian poem and is certainly unlike predictable works of the era's best known women poets. Rossetti's most famous
(30) poem, "Goblin Market," bridges the space between simplistic fairy tale and complex adult allegory—at once Christian, psychological, and pro-feminist. Like many of Rossetti's
(35) works, it is extraordinarily original and unorthodox in form. Its subject matter is radical and therefore risky for a Victorian poetess because it implies castigation of an economic
(40) (and even marital) marketplace dominated by men, whose motives are, at best, suspect. Its Christian allusions are obvious but grounded in opulent images whose lushness borders on the
(45) erotic. From Rossetti's work emerge not only emotional force, artistic polish, frequently ironic playfulness, and intellectual vigor but also an intriguing, enigmatic quality. "Winter:
(50) My Secret," for example, combines these traits along with a very high (and un-Victorian) level of poetic self-consciousness.

"How does one reconcile the aes-
(55) thetic sensuality of Rossetti's poetry with her repressed, ascetic lifestyle?" Woolf wondered. That Rossetti did indeed withhold a "secret" both from those intimate with her and from pos-
(60) terity is Lona Packer's thesis in her 1963 biography of Rossetti. Packer's claim that Rossetti's was a secret of the heart has since been disproved through the discovery of hundreds of
(65) letters by Rossetti, which reinforce the conventional image of her as pious, scrupulously abstinent, and semi-reclusive. Yet the passions expressed in her love poems do expose the "secret"
(70) at the heart of both Rossetti's life and art: a willingness to forego worldly pleasures in favor of an aestheticized Christian version of transcendent fulfillment in heaven. Her sonnet "The
(75) World," therefore, becomes pivotal in understanding Rossetti's literary project as a whole—her rhymes for children, fairy tale narratives, love poems, and devotional commentaries.
(80) The world, for Rossetti, is a fallen place. Her work is pervasively designed to force upon readers this inescapable Christian truth. The beauty of her poetry must be seen
(85) therefore as an artistic strategy, a means toward a moral end.

**14.** The passage mentions all of the following as qualities that emerge from Rossetti's work EXCEPT for
**(A)** lush imagery
**(B)** ironic playfulness
**(C)** stark realism
**(D)** unorthodox form
**(E)** intellectual vigor

**15.** It can be inferred from the passage that Rossetti's "The World"

(A) combines several genres of poetry in a single work

(B) was Rossetti's last major work

(C) is the most helpful expression of Rossetti's motives

(D) was Rossetti's longest work

(E) reflects Rossetti's shift away from her earlier feminist viewpoint

**16.** It can be inferred from the passage that the author discusses Packer's thesis and its flaws probably to

(A) contrast the sensuality of Rossetti's poetry with the relative starkness of her devotional commentary

(B) reveal the secret to which Rossetti alludes in "Winter: My Secret"

(C) call into question the authenticity of recently discovered letters written by Rossetti

(D) provide a foundation for the author's own theory about Rossetti's life and work

(E) compare Woolf's understanding of Rossetti with a recent, more enlightened view

**17.** One aim of educational technology should be to _____ instruction more precisely to students' individual needs, since vast differences in the ways students learn are _____ when they are taught the same thing.

(A) adjust . . overlooked

(B) direct . . reinforced

(C) adapt . . discovered

(D) design . . acknowledged

(E) retrofit . . undermined

**18.** SHIP : ARMADA ::

(A) sail : wind

(B) atom : molecule

(C) gun : cannon

(D) chemical : reaction

(E) violin : viola

**19.** ROSTRUM : SPEECH ::

(A) office : conference

(B) laboratory : invention

(C) mailbox : letter

(D) arena : match

(E) stove : meal

**20.** Even detractors who warn of its potential for abuse agree that genetic engineering, if used _____, can reduce the incidence of the sort of physical deformities that any society would want to eliminate.

(A) premeditatedly

(B) biologically

(C) recklessly

(D) discriminately

(E) illicitly

**21.** GAINSAY:

(A) properly characterize

(B) challenge without cause

(C) defeat oneself

(D) argue consistently

(E) speak unthinkingly

**22.** ACCLAIM:

(A) disbelieve

(B) controvert

(C) disapprove

(D) betray

(E) forbid

**23.** It is clearly in the public's best interest for news agencies to _____ their journalist employees _____ information tantamount to hearsay through independent scrutiny.

(A) encourage . . to embellish

(B) admonish . . to confirm

(C) warn . . about querying

(D) discourage . . from endorsing

(E) discipline . . without verifying

Line Radiative forcings are changes imposed on the planetary energy balance; radiative feedbacks are changes induced by climate change.
(5) Forcings can arise from either natural or anthropogenic causes. For example, the concentration of sulfate aerosols in the atmosphere can be altered by volcanic action or by the burning of fossil
(10) fuels. The distinction between forcings and feedbacks is sometimes arbitrary; however, forcings are quantities normally specified in global climate model simulations, while feedbacks
(15) are calculated quantities. Examples of radiative forcings are greenhouse gases (such as carbon dioxide and ozone), aerosols in the troposphere, and surface reflectivity. Radiative
(20) feedbacks include clouds, water vapor in the troposphere, and sea-ice cover.

The effects of forcings and feedbacks on climate are complex. For example, clouds trap outgoing
(25) radiation, thus providing a warming influence, while also reflecting incoming solar radiation and, thereby, providing a cooling influence. Current measurements indicate that the net
(30) effect of clouds is to cool the earth. However, scientists are unsure if the balance will shift in the future as the atmosphere and cloud formation are altered by the accumulation of green-
(35) house gases. Similarly, the vertical distribution of ozone affects both the amount of radiation reaching the earth's surface and the amount of reradiated radiation that is trapped
(40) by the greenhouse effect. These two mechanisms affect the earth's temperature in opposite directions.

24. According to the passage, radiative forcings and radiative feedbacks can generally be distinguished from each other by
  (A) whether the amount of radiative change is specified or calculated
  (B) the precision with which the amounts of radiative change can be determined
  (C) the altitude at which the radiative change occurs
  (D) whether the radiative change is directed toward or away from the earth
  (E) whether the radiative change is global or more localized

25. Based solely on the information in the passage, which of the following research methods, if implemented, would be most likely to yield a more accurate prediction of the extent and direction of the greenhouse effect?
  (A) Monitoring radiative feedbacks and forcings over a longer time period
  (B) Measuring variations in cloud density in relation to air temperature
  (C) Isolating ozone changes caused specifically by anthropogenic factors
  (D) Accounting for the altitude at which cloud formations appear
  (E) Isolating the cooling influence of ozone changes from their warming influence

26. FEEL : HANDLE ::
  (A) read : peruse
  (B) caress : abrade
  (C) laugh: giggle
  (D) stimulate : grow
  (E) lift : heave

27. INNOVATION : PRECEDENT ::
  (A) inception : reality
  (B) invention : production
  (C) conservation : simplicity
  (D) renovation : antiquity
  (E) illusion : veracity

**28.** It is often said that those most firmly committed to an idea are also most critical of it. Yet, could anyone honestly defend this (i)_____? Consider, for instance, Elizabeth Stanton and Susan B. Anthony, who in the late nineteenth century paved the way for the women's rights movement through their fervent advocacy. Would it not be (ii)_____ that Stanton and Anthony were at the same time highly (ii)_____ of the notion that women deserve equal rights under the law?

| **(i)** |
| --- |
| oft-touted ideology |
| ill-conceived contrivance |
| age-old aphorism |

| **(ii)** |
| --- |
| patently absurd to aver |
| audacious to insist |
| tautological to claim |

| **(iii)** |
| --- |
| suspicious |
| enamored |
| supportive |

**29.** COMPLACENT:
- **(A)** involved
- **(B)** critical
- **(C)** discontented
- **(D)** persistent
- **(E)** disagreeable

**30.** SODDEN:
- **(A)** buoyant
- **(B)** laden
- **(C)** porous
- **(D)** parched
- **(E)** billowy

# ANSWER KEY AND EXPLANATIONS

## Analytical Writing

### ISSUE TASK: EVALUATION AND SCORING

Evaluate your Issue task essay on a scale of 1 to 6 (6 being the highest score) according to the following five criteria:

1. Does your essay develop a position on the issue through the use of incisive reasons and persuasive examples?

2. Are your essay's ideas conveyed clearly and articulately?

3. Does your essay maintain proper focus on the issue, and is it well organized?

4. Does your essay demonstrate proficiency, fluency, and maturity in its use of sentence structure, vocabulary, and idiom?

5. Does your essay demonstrate command of the elements of Standard Written English, including grammar, word usage, spelling, and punctuation?

### ARGUMENT TASK: EVALUATION AND SCORING

Evaluate your Argument task essay on a scale of 1 to 6 (6 being the highest score) according to the following five criteria:

1. Does your essay identify and articulate the argument's key unstated assumptions?

2. Does your essay explain how the argument relies on these unstated assumptions, and what the implications are if these assumptions are unwarranted?

3. Does your essay develop its ideas in a clear, organized manner, with appropriate transitions to help connect ideas together?

4. Does your essay demonstrate proficiency, fluency, and maturity in its use of sentence structure, vocabulary, and idiom?

5. Does your essay demonstrate command of the elements of Standard Written English, including grammar, word usage, spelling, and punctuation?

To help you evaluate your essay in terms of criteria 1 and 2, the following is a series of questions that identify *five* distinct unstated assumptions upon which the argument relies. To earn a score of 4 or higher, your essay should identify and explain at least three of these assumptions. Identifying and explaining at least four of the unstated assumptions would help earn you an even higher score.

- Does the argument confuse cause and effect with mere temporal (time) sequence? (Pilfering might go unnoticed by other employees, who in any event often look the other way whenever they do observe it; if so, the decline in pilfering cannot be attributed to the honor code.)

- Does the argument assume that past conditions affecting the reported incidence of pilfering have remained unchanged? (Such conditions include the number of

MegaCorp employees and the overall integrity of those employees; to the extent such conditions have changed over the five-year period, the reported decrease in pilfering might not be attributable to the honor code.)

- Are MegaCorp employees representative of "all businesses"? (Perhaps under an honor system, MegaCorp employees are less likely either to pilfer or to report pilfering than the typical employee, for whatever reason.)

- Is the companywide survey on which the recommendation depends potentially biased and therefore not credible? (The survey results are meaningful only to the extent that the people surveyed responded honestly, which is doubtful.)

- Does the recommendation rely on a potentially unrepresentative statistical sample? (The author fails to assure us that the survey's respondents are representative of all MegaCorp employees.)

- Are the survey responses a reliable indicator about the future behavior of the respondents? (Hypothetical predictions about one's future behavior are inherently less reliable than reports of proven behavior.)

## Quantitative Reasoning

| | | |
|---|---|---|
| 1. B | 11. B | 20. D |
| 2. C | 12. C | 21. B |
| 3. B | 13. B | 22. E |
| 4. A | 14. E | 23. D |
| 5. D | 15. C | 24. C |
| 6. C | 16. D | 25. A |
| 7. E | 17. 12 | 26. A |
| 8. A | 18. A | 27. D |
| 9. C | 19. B | 28. D |
| 10. A | | |

1. **The correct answer is (B).** The price of the coat described in Column A = $300 − (.07 × $300) = $300 − $21 = $279. The price of the coat described in Column B = $200 + (.4 × $200) = $200 + $80 = $280.

2. **The correct answer is (C).** Any non-zero number raised to the power of zero is 1, and so $y^0 + y^2 = 1 + \dfrac{1}{4} = $ 1.25.

3. **The correct answer is (B).** A total of 32 horses (20 + 12) are either black or white. That leaves 28 horses of some other color. A total of 32 horses are stallions. Thus, it is possible that all of the stallions are either black or white, and that *none* of the stallions are some other color. (Quantity A = 0.) However, at least 4 of the stallions must be either black or white. (Quantity B = 4.)

4. **The correct answer is (A).** The quilt consists of 18 squares, each measuring 1 linear unit per side. The perimeter of the quilt as shown is 24. After rearranging the squares, the quilt will consist of two rows of 9 squares; the perimeter of the new quilt will be 22 (9 + 9 + 2 + 2).

5. **The correct answer is (D).** The distance described in Column B is 48 miles. The distance from Breezy to Cocoa could be any number of miles between 24 and 72, depending on the *direction* of Cocoa from Aqua and from Breezy. Hence, Quantity A could be equal to, less than, or greater than Quantity B.

6. **The correct answer is (C).** The degree sum of all four angles is 360°. The ratio 1:2:3:4 tells us that the smallest and largest angles together account for the same portion (1 and 4 in the ratio) of that sum as the middle two angles (2 and 3 in the ratio). Hence their sum must be exactly half of 360°, or 180°. You can also solve the problem algebraically. Letting $x$ = the degree measure of the smallest angle, $x + 2x + 3x + 4x = $ 360; $10x = 360$; $x = 36$. The largest angle ($4x°$) measures 144°. The sum of the measures of the two angles is 180° (36° + 144°).

**7. The correct answer is (E).** Factor the numerator and the denominator. (The numerator provides a difference of two squares.) Simplify, then distribute the resulting denominator to both terms in the numerator:

$$\frac{x^2-4}{x^2-2x}=\frac{(x+2)(x-2)}{x(x-2)}$$

$$=\frac{x+2}{x}$$

$$=\frac{x}{x}+\frac{2}{x}$$

$$=1+\frac{2}{x}$$

**8. The correct answer is (A).** You multiply $x$ (the first term) by $\frac{y}{x}$ to obtain $y$ (the second term), and so $\frac{y}{x}$ is the constant multiple. To obtain the third term, multiple the second term ($y$) by this multiple:

$$y\times\frac{y}{x}=\frac{y^2}{x}.$$

**9. The correct answer is (C).** For any real numbers $x$ and $y$, $\left(\sqrt{x}\right)\left(\sqrt{y}\right)=\sqrt{xy}$ . The problem at hand simply applies this rule.

**10. The correct answer is (A).** To determine either quantity, work systematically, beginning with the greatest possible integer:

Quantity A (3 ways):

$7 + 1 + 1 + 1 = 10$
$5 + 3 + 1 + 1 = 10$
$3 + 3 + 3 + 1 = 10$

Quantity B (2 ways):

$6 + 2 + 2 = 10$
$4 + 4 + 2 = 10$

**11. The correct answer is (B).** Because the $t$-terms are the same ($.2t$), the quickest way to solve for $s$ here is with the addition-subtraction method. Manipulate both equations so that corresponding terms "line up," then add the two equations:

$$.2t + .6s = 2.2$$
$$\underline{-.2t + .5s = 1.1}$$
$$1.1s = 3.3$$
$$s = 3$$

**12. The correct answer is (C).** During 2003, the difference was about $1 million. In 2005, the difference was about $800,000.

**13. The correct answer is (B).** First determine aggregate legal and production expenses for each year shown (approximations will suffice; all numbers here are in millions):

2002: 5.0 + 5.7 = 10.7
2003: 4.1 + 5.2 = 9.3
2004: 4.0 + 11.3 = 15.3
2005: 10.4 + 5.6 = 16.0
2006: 6.1 + 4.6 = 10.7

The aggregate amount was most nearly equal for the years 2002 and 2006. Next, determine the average annual marketing expenses for these two years. (Again, approximations will suffice.) The average of $4.1m (2002 marketing expenses) and $8.3m (2006 marketing expenses) is $6.2m.

14. **The correct answer is (E).** The ratio of height to the shadow is constant. Thus, the ratio of $b$ to $f$ can be set equal to the ratio of $t$ to $x$, where $x$ represents the length of the tree's shadow:

$$\frac{b}{f} = \frac{t}{x}$$
$$bx = ft$$
$$x = \frac{ft}{b}$$

15. **The correct answer is (C).** In either series of integers, the terms are distributed symmetrically to the left and right of zero (0) on the number line. Hence, in both cases the sum of the integers is zero (0).

16. **The correct answer is (D).** Points $(5,-2)$ and $(-3,3)$ are two points on line $b$. The slope of $b$ is the change in the $y$-coordinates divided by the corresponding change in the $x$-coordinate:

$$m_b = \frac{3-(-2)}{-3-5} = \frac{5}{-8} \text{ or } -\frac{5}{8}$$

17. **The correct answer is 12.** You have 3 choices or roads from Abbottsville and Batestown and 4 choices of roads from Batestown to Cartersburg. Hence the total number of possible routes from Abbottsville to Cartersburg (through Batestown once) is $3 \times 4 = 12$.

18. **The correct answer is (A).** The leg from home to work is slower than the return leg, and therefore the average speed going to work (Quantity B) is slower than the combined average (Quantity A).

19. **The correct answer is (B).** First, Quantity A: The greatest common factor of 20, 45, and 90 is 5. As for Quantity B, the sum of the three numbers given is clearly greater than 5. That's all you need to know to conclude that Quantity B is greater than Quantity A and that the correct answer is choice (B).

20. **The correct answer is (D).** Quantity A $= \dfrac{50}{3.9x} = \dfrac{1}{.078x}$. Quantity B $= .078x$. The comparison, then, is between $\dfrac{1}{.078x}$ and $.078x$. If $x$ happens to equal $\dfrac{1}{.078}$, then both quantities would equal 1. Otherwise, the two quantities are unequal; in fact, they're reciprocals. (Their product is 1.) For example, if $x = 1$, then Quantity A is a fraction greater than 1 by an order of more than 10, while Quantity B is a fraction less than 1 by the same order. That is all you need to know to conclude that choice (D) is correct.

21. **The correct answer is (B).** To determine the cost of shipping a 28-pound parcel by ground, you need to apply three different per-pound rates: $1.50 for the first pound, $.40 for pounds 2–10, and $.25 for pounds 11–28. Here's the calculation: $1.50 + ($.40)(9) + ($.25)(18) = $9.60.

22. **The correct answer is (E).** The cost of shipping a 2.4-pound parcel by express delivery would be $6.75 + ($1.15)(2) = $9.05. The cost of shipping the same parcel by air delivery would be $2.25 + ($.60)(2) = $3.45. The difference between the two totals is $5.60.

23. **The correct answer is (D).** If $P < 0$ such that $P + Q < 0$, then Quantity A < Quantity B. On the other hand, if $P + Q > 0$, then Quantity A = Quantity B.

24. **The correct answer is (C).** There's no need to perform any calculations here. Comparing one cube-box with the other, notice that all measurements are proportional. Hence the number of cubes that can be packed into the boxes must be the same.

25. **The correct answer is (A).** To add two fractions having a common denominator, you add numerators—*not* denominators. Hence, $\frac{1}{x} + \frac{1}{x} = \frac{2}{x}$. You'll find that it's impossible to equate $\frac{2}{x}$ with $\frac{1}{2x}$, and so the two quantities cannot be equal. Since $x > 0$, you can cancel $x$ across columns, leaving an inequality in which Quantity A > Quantity B:

$$\frac{2}{1} > \frac{1}{2}.$$

26. **The correct answer is (A).** To solve this problem, you can either list the possibilities or apply the factorial formula: $4! = 4 \times 3 \times 2 \times 1 = 24$.

27. **The correct answer is (D).** The area of a circle = $\pi r^2$. Letting the radius of the smaller circle = $r$, the radius of the larger circle = $2r$, and its area = $\pi(2r)^2$, or $4\pi r^2$. The ratio of the smaller circle's area to the larger circle's area is $\pi r^2 : 4\pi r^2$, or 1:4.

28. **The correct answer is (D).** Equate Carrie's age in 8 years (C + 8) to twice Ben's age in 8 years (B + 8), and then solve for C :

$$\begin{aligned} C + 8 &= 2(B + 8) \\ C &= 2(B + 8) - 8 \\ C &= 2B + 16 - 8 \\ C &= 2B + 8 \end{aligned}$$

## Verbal Reasoning

| | |
|---|---|
| 1. E | 13. C |
| 2. B | 14. C |
| 3. E | 15. C |
| 4. C | 16. D |
| 5. A | 17. A |
| 6. A | 18. B |
| 7. E | 19. D |
| 8. A | 20. D |
| 9. B | 21. D |
| 10. E | 22. C |
| 11. D | 23. B |
| 12. B | |

| | |
|---|---|
| 24. A | |
| 25. E | |
| 26. A | |
| 27. E | |
| 28. (i) age-old | |
|      aphorism | |
|      (ii) patently | |
|      absurd to aver | |
|      (iii) suspicious | |
| 29. C | |
| 30. D | |

1. **The correct answer is (E).** The best choice for the two blanks must convey a clear contrast between the reactions of the two groups of board members. The words *optimistic* and *dubious* (doubtful or skeptical) provide just the sort of contrast that makes sense. Although choice (C) also provides a contrast, choice (C) is wrong because it makes no sense to imagine the board members being "disturbed by the benefits" the deal would produce.

2. **The correct answer is (B).** This is an "evidence or result of" analogy. A BOAT creates a WAKE and leaves it behind, across the surface of the water. Similarly, a *scalpel* (surgeon's knife) creates a *scar* and leaves it behind, like a trail, across the surface of the skin. Strengthening the analogy is that a wake is a byproduct of boating, like a scar is a byproduct of cutting with a scalpel.

3. **The correct answer is (E).** This is a "helpful condition for" analogy. Mulch is a soil-enriching mixture that facilitates plant growth. To BURGEON is to begin to grow rapidly or to flourish. Accordingly,

soil that has been MULCHED is in an ideal condition for plants to burgeon. Similarly, a razor or knife that has be *honed* (sharpened) is in an ideal condition to *hew* (cut or slice).

4. **The correct answer is (C).** This is a "contrary meaning" analogy. To be JOCULAR is to lack SOLEMNITY. To be *latent* is to lack *visibility*. Thus, in each pair, the two words are essentially antonyms. (In each other pair, the two words are essentially synonyms.)

5. **The correct answer is (A).** DUPLICITY means "deception by pretending" and is therefore a form of dishonesty—the opposite of *honesty*.

6. **The correct answer is (A).** If love were thought of as a *malady* (difficulty or problem) that "disables judgment" (confuses one's brain), then the word *insanity* might be an apt description.

7. **The correct answer is (E).** According to the author, the "current

transition to a service-based economy and deregulation in transportation . . . underscor[e] the need to
redefine poverty." The refined definition that the author advocates is
apparent from the passage's opening
and final sentences: Poverty should
be measured not just at the individual level but also at the community level (especially in rural
areas). In other words, the standard
for poverty should be more flexible,
as choice (E) indicates.

8. **The correct answer is (A).**
Although the author's recommendation to redefine poverty, if adopted,
would no doubt carry certain public
health consequences, nowhere in the
passage does the author incorporate
public-health issues into the
analysis.

9. **The correct answer is (B).** This
choice recapitulates the author's
main point in the passage: Because
of a too-narrow definition of poverty—one that measures it at only
the individual level—impoverished
rural communities often (and
unfairly) go unrecognized as such by
funding agencies and policy makers,
while urban ghettos do not.

10. **The correct answer is (E).** To be
INSOLVENT is to be "without
money"; the opposite is to be
*wealthy*.

11. **The correct answer is (D).** To
OCCLUDE is to "stop up, shut in, or
close up." To *exhume* is to unearth
(dig up), as a corpse from its grave.

12. **The correct answer is (B).** This is
a "defining characteristic" analogy. A
DIATRIBE is a speech characterized
by BITTERNESS. A *recapitulation* is

a summary or synopsis, and hence is
characterized by *brevity*. In both
cases, the second word describes the
first.

13. **The correct answer is (C).** This is
an "example of" analogy. SILVER is a
type of METAL, and *helium* is a type
of *gas*.

14. **The correct answer is (C).** In
describing Rossetti's work, the
author never uses the words "stark"
or "realism," nor does the author
describe her work in any way that
might be expressed by either of these
terms. Choices (A), (B), and (E) are
all mentioned explicitly in the second
paragraph (lines 42–49) as qualities
that emerge from Rossetti's work. As
for choice (D), the author refers to
the form of Rossetti's works in reference specifically to "Goblin
Market," claiming that in its unorthodox form "Goblin Market" is like
many of Rossetti's works. In this
way, the author identifies "unorthodox form" as one quality that
emerges from Rossetti's work.

15. **The correct answer is (C).** In the
final paragraph, the author states
that "The World" is "pivotal in understanding Rossetti's literary project
as a whole." Based upon the
remainder of the final paragraph,
the author seems to understand Rossetti's "literary project as a whole" as
an attempt to convey an inescapable
Christian truth to her readers (see
lines 68–83). It is reasonably
inferable, then, that "The World"
provides significant insight into Rossetti's motives.

16. **The correct answer is (D).** The author's threshold purpose in discussing Packer's biography is to affirm that Rossetti's style of writing was not a reflection of her personal lifestyle. Having dismissed the theory that Rossetti was keeping secrets about her life, the author goes on (in the final paragraph) to offer a better explanation for the apparent contradiction between Rossetti's lifestyle and the emotional, sensual style of her poetry.

17. **The correct answer is (A).** The first part of the sentence suggests that instructional methods need to be modified in some way to alleviate a problem. The words *adjust* and *adapt* (choices A and C) both make sense here. The second part of the sentence suggests that the problem is that, when students are taught in the same way, their individual needs are not adequately accounted for. In other words, these needs are *overlooked*, at least to some extent. Choice (A) is the only choice that makes sense for both blanks.

18. **The correct answer is (B).** This is a "part of" (individual-to-group) analogy. A SHIP is part of an ARMADA, and an *atom* is part of a *molecule*.

19. **The correct answer is (D).** This is a "place for" analogy. One place where a SPEECH might be made is on a ROSTRUM (a platform for public speaking), in front of an audience. Similarly, one place where a *contest* (between two sports teams, for example) might occur is in an *arena*, before an audience.

20. **The correct answer is (D).** The missing word must contrast with the notion of abuse of genetic engineering, while at the same time be consistent with the desirable goal of reducing the incidence of deformities. Only choice (D) accomplishes both. To use the technology *discriminately* would be to conscientiously apply it only toward certain ends (such as reducing deformities) and not toward others (such as creating a master race that dominates others).

21. **The correct answer is (D).** To GAINSAY is to "deny or contradict, usually one's own previous statements," whereas to *argue consistently* is to do the opposite.

22. **The correct answer is (C).** To ACCLAIM is to approve enthusiastically, just the opposite of *disapprove*. As for choice (B), to *controvert* is to oppose or argue against; a person who controverts might also disapprove, but opposing is not the same as disapproving.

23. **The correct answer is (B).** Hearsay (second-hand information) tends to be unreliable. So it makes sense that, acting in the public's best interest, news agencies should *admonish* (warn or instruct sternly) their journalists to scrutinize hearsay information to *confirm* its accuracy.

24. **The correct answer is (A).** According to the passage, radiative "forcings are quantities normally specified in global climate model situations, while feedbacks are calculated quantities" (lines 12–15).

25. **The correct answer is (E).** According to the passage, a given vertical distribution of ozone affects

atmospheric temperatures in both directions at once (lines 35–42). Accordingly, by isolating the cooling influence of a given distribution of ozone from its warming influence, scientists might better predict whether changes in the vertical distribution of ozone will have a net cooling or a net warming effect.

26. **The correct answer is (A).** This is a "form of" analogy. To HANDLE is to examine by FEEL; similarly, to *peruse* is to examine or scrutinize—usually by *reading*. The word *giggle* describes a peculiar form of *laughing* but not a studied form, and so choice (C) is not as strong an analogy as choice (A).

27. **The correct answer is (E).** This is a "contrary meaning" analogy. An INNOVATION is a new idea that lacks PRECEDENT (an earlier instance or example). Similarly, an *illusion* by definition lacks *veracity* (truthfulness). Choice (D) is the second-best choice: to *renovate* is to renew or improve something older, such as an *antique*. However, something renovated can still be antique.

28. **The correct answer is age-old aphorism for blank (i), patently absurd to aver for blank (ii), and suspicious for blank (iii).** The first sentence describes an aphorism, which means "a well-known saying or adage." Thus, the phrase *age-old aphorism* fits nicely in blank (i). The idea of the passage as a whole is that the "adage" mentioned in the first sentence is historically indefensible. To support this idea, the author seeks to point out that it would be completely and obviously wrong—in other words, *patently absurd to aver* (assert) that America's women's rights pioneers could possibly be critical of—or *suspicious* of—the idea that women deserve equal rights.

29. **The correct answer is (C).** A COMPLACENT person is "contented in an unconcerned or self-satisfied way"—quite the opposite of a *discontented* person.

30. **The correct answer is (D).** SODDEN means "soaked or drenched"; *parched* means "dried out with heat" and is the best antonym among the five choices.

# ANSWER SHEET PRACTICE TEST 6

## Analytical Writing—Issue Task

_____

_____

_____

_____

_____

_____

_____

_____

_____

_____

_____

_____

_____

_____

_____

_____

_____

_____

answer sheet

_____

_____

_____

_____

_____

_____

_____

_____

_____

_____

_____

_____

_____

_____

_____

_____

_____

_____

_____

_____

_____

_____

_____

_____

**Analytical Writing—Argument Task**

_____

_____

_____

_____

_____

_____

_____

_____

_____

_____

_____

_____

_____

_____

_____

_____

_____

_____

_____

answer sheet

## Verbal Reasoning

1. Ⓐ Ⓑ Ⓒ Ⓓ Ⓔ
2. Ⓐ Ⓑ Ⓒ Ⓓ Ⓔ
3. Ⓐ Ⓑ Ⓒ Ⓓ Ⓔ
4. Ⓐ Ⓑ Ⓒ Ⓓ Ⓔ
5. Ⓐ Ⓑ Ⓒ Ⓓ Ⓔ
6. Ⓐ Ⓑ Ⓒ Ⓓ Ⓔ
7. (i) _____
   (ii) _____
8. Ⓐ Ⓑ Ⓒ Ⓓ Ⓔ
9. Ⓐ Ⓑ Ⓒ Ⓓ Ⓔ
10. Ⓐ Ⓑ Ⓒ Ⓓ Ⓔ

11. Ⓐ Ⓑ Ⓒ Ⓓ Ⓔ
12. Ⓐ Ⓑ Ⓒ Ⓓ Ⓔ
13. Ⓐ Ⓑ Ⓒ Ⓓ Ⓔ
14. Ⓐ Ⓑ Ⓒ Ⓓ Ⓔ
15. Ⓐ Ⓑ Ⓒ Ⓓ Ⓔ
16. Ⓐ Ⓑ Ⓒ Ⓓ Ⓔ
17. Ⓐ Ⓑ Ⓒ Ⓓ Ⓔ
18. Ⓐ Ⓑ Ⓒ Ⓓ Ⓔ
19. Ⓐ Ⓑ Ⓒ Ⓓ Ⓔ
20. Ⓐ Ⓑ Ⓒ Ⓓ Ⓔ

21. Ⓐ Ⓑ Ⓒ Ⓓ Ⓔ
22. Ⓐ Ⓑ Ⓒ Ⓓ Ⓔ
23. Ⓐ Ⓑ Ⓒ Ⓓ Ⓔ
24. Ⓐ Ⓑ Ⓒ Ⓓ Ⓔ
25. Ⓐ Ⓑ Ⓒ Ⓓ Ⓔ
26. Ⓐ Ⓑ Ⓒ Ⓓ Ⓔ
27. Ⓐ Ⓑ Ⓒ Ⓓ Ⓔ
28. Ⓐ Ⓑ Ⓒ Ⓓ Ⓔ
29. Ⓐ Ⓑ Ⓒ Ⓓ Ⓔ
30. Ⓐ Ⓑ Ⓒ Ⓓ Ⓔ

## Quantitative Reasoning

1. Ⓐ Ⓑ Ⓒ Ⓓ Ⓔ
2. Ⓐ Ⓑ Ⓒ Ⓓ
3. Ⓐ Ⓑ Ⓒ Ⓓ Ⓔ
4. [ ]
5. Ⓐ Ⓑ Ⓒ Ⓓ Ⓔ
6. Ⓐ Ⓑ Ⓒ Ⓓ
7. Ⓐ Ⓑ Ⓒ Ⓓ
8. Ⓐ Ⓑ Ⓒ Ⓓ
9. Ⓐ Ⓑ Ⓒ Ⓓ
10. Ⓐ Ⓑ Ⓒ Ⓓ Ⓔ

11. Ⓐ Ⓑ Ⓒ Ⓓ Ⓔ
12. Ⓐ Ⓑ Ⓒ Ⓓ Ⓔ
13. Ⓐ Ⓑ Ⓒ Ⓓ
14. Ⓐ Ⓑ Ⓒ Ⓓ Ⓔ
15. Ⓐ Ⓑ Ⓒ Ⓓ Ⓔ
16. Ⓐ Ⓑ Ⓒ Ⓓ Ⓔ
17. Ⓐ Ⓑ Ⓒ Ⓓ
18. Ⓐ Ⓑ Ⓒ Ⓓ
19. Ⓐ Ⓑ Ⓒ Ⓓ

20. Ⓐ Ⓑ Ⓒ Ⓓ
21. Ⓐ Ⓑ Ⓒ Ⓓ Ⓔ
22. Ⓐ Ⓑ Ⓒ Ⓓ Ⓔ
23. Ⓐ Ⓑ Ⓒ Ⓓ Ⓔ
24. Ⓐ Ⓑ Ⓒ Ⓓ Ⓔ
25. Ⓐ Ⓑ Ⓒ Ⓓ
26. Ⓐ Ⓑ Ⓒ Ⓓ
27. Ⓐ Ⓑ Ⓒ Ⓓ
28. Ⓐ Ⓑ Ⓒ Ⓓ

answer sheet

# Practice Test 6

## ANALYTICAL WRITING

### Issue Task

*Time: 45 Minutes*

> **NOTES:** For *some* test-takers, the GRE will end with an identified and untimed research section. The research section, which is unscored, contains experimental question types. Test-makers use it to assess the difficulty levels of the experimental question types, based on test-takers' responses.
>
> For the purposes of this book—making sure you're fully prepared to take the GRE exam—one Complex Text Completion question (Verbal Reasoning section) and one numeric entry question (Quantitative Reasoning section) are included in each of the Practice Tests. On the actual GRE, however, you will not see both of these questions; in fact, you may *not* see either one.

Using a word processor, compose a response to the following statement and directive. Do not use any spell-checking or grammar-checking functions (they are not available on the actual GRE):

> "Most people are actually happier when they have fewer goods and services from which to choose; this is especially true today, when we are deluged with advertising as never before and from more sources than ever before."

> Write an essay in which you assess the accuracy of the statement above. Develop and support your viewpoint with relevant reasons and examples and by considering ways in which the statement may or may not be true.

## Argument Task

### *Time: 30 Minutes*

Using a word processor, compose an essay that responds to the following argument and directive. Do not use any spell-checking or grammar-checking functions (they are not available on the actual GRE).

> The following appeared in a memo from the principal of Harper Elementary School to the school's faculty and staff:
>
> "In order to raise the level of reading skills of our students to a level that at least represents the national average for students in the same age group, we should adopt the "Back to Basics" reading program. After all, according to the company that created the program and provides it directly to elementary schools throughout the country, Back to Basics has a superior record for improving reading skills among youngsters nationwide. By adopting Back to Basics, the parents of Harper Elementary School students would be assured that their children will develop the reading skills they will need throughout their lives."
>
> Discuss how well-reasoned you find the argument above.

# VERBAL REASONING

*30 Questions • 30 Minutes*

**NOTE:** In this section, questions are grouped together by format, and within each group the questions grow more difficult as you go. Because the actual GRE is computer-adaptive in the multiple-choice sections, it intersperses questions of different formats and difficulty levels.

1. TREMBLE : FEAR ::
   - **(A)** scream : envy
   - **(B)** smile : rage
   - **(C)** demand : anger
   - **(D)** follow : adoration
   - **(E)** weep : grief

2. WATERMARK : PAPER ::
   - **(A)** landmark : monument
   - **(B)** envelope : stamp
   - **(C)** character : novel
   - **(D)** badge : employee
   - **(E)** signature : author

3. The government's _____ clinical study requirements for new drugs do not _____ pharmaceutical firms when it comes to research and development, chiefly because of the profit potential afforded by patent protection.
   - **(A)** official . . please
   - **(B)** onerous . . dissuade
   - **(C)** extensive . . impel
   - **(D)** unenforceable . . favor
   - **(E)** vague . . prejudice

4. PROPRIETY:
   - **(A)** selfishness
   - **(B)** lack of decorum
   - **(C)** sensuality
   - **(D)** impudence
   - **(E)** lack of virtue

5. SCIENTIAL:
   - **(A)** ignorant
   - **(B)** intuitive
   - **(C)** stupid
   - **(D)** regressive
   - **(E)** gullible

6. CLOISTERED:
   - **(A)** extraverted
   - **(B)** extrapolated
   - **(C)** gregarious
   - **(D)** savvy
   - **(E)** dispersed

7. Recent advances in molecular biology and genetics (i)_____ to the position that as physical beings our actions are determined by physical forces beyond our control—the age-old "determinist" viewpoint. (ii)_____, this new research suggests that such physical forces include our individual genetic makeup.

   **(i)**

   lend credence
   take exception
   give rise

   **(ii)**

   In fact
   Moreover
   Specifically

8. COTTON : SOFT ::
   - **(A)** wool : warm
   - **(B)** wood : polished
   - **(C)** nylon : strong
   - **(D)** iron : hard
   - **(E)** silk : expensive

9. FISH : AQUARIUM ::
   - **(A)** lions : den
   - **(B)** insects : ground
   - **(C)** automobile : garage
   - **(D)** stew : cauldron
   - **(E)** birds: aviary

10. SPARK : CONFLAGRATION ::
    (A) yeast : fermentation
    (B) match : light
    (C) drizzle : downpour
    (D) sugar : sweetness
    (E) volcano : eruption

11. Just as Mozart's music broke new ground in the world of classicism, so Beethoven's work _____ the unspoken rules of the classical period and _____ changes which eventually led to romanticism.
    (A) obeyed . . implemented
    (B) eradicated . . avoided
    (C) conformed to . . supported
    (D) evaded . . resisted
    (E) overturned . . initiated

**Directions:** Questions 12–13 are based on the following passage.

*Line* In the 1970s, the idea of building so-called "New Towns" to absorb growth was considered a potential cure-all for urban problems in the United States.
(5) It was assumed that by diverting residents from existing centers, current urban problems would at least get no worse. It was also assumed that, since European New Towns had been finan-
(10) cially and socially successful, the same could be expected in the United States.

In the end, these ill-considered projects actually weakened U.S. cities
(15) further by drawing away high-income citizens. While industry and commerce sought in turn to escape, the lower-income groups left behind were unable to provide the necessary tax
(20) base to support the cities. Not surprisingly, development occurred in areas where land was cheap and construction profitable rather than where New Towns were genuinely needed.
(25) Moreover, the failure on the part of planners and federal legislators to consider social needs resulted not in the sort of successful New Towns seen in Britain but in nothing more than
(30) sprawling suburbs.

12. The passage states that New Towns in the United States
    (A) spurred economic redevelopment in decaying urban centers
    (B) provided a thriving social center away from the problems of the older city
    (C) provided affluent urban residents an escape from the city
    (D) were different than those in Great Britain in certain important respects
    (E) provided models for many of today's urban redevelopment projects

13. Which of the following phenomena is most closely analogous to the New Towns established in the United States?
    (A) A business that fails as a result of insufficient demand for its products or services
    (B) A new game that fails to attain widespread popularity because its rules are unfair
    (C) A scientific theory that lacks supporting empirical evidence
    (D) A new drug that is never approved for legal sale because of its severe side effects
    (E) A new computer program that attempts to solve one software problem but that creates another

14. SATIATE:
    (A) crave deeply
    (B) deplete entirely
    (C) be repelled by
    (D) apply forcefully
    (E) enjoy thoroughly

15. OSSIFIED:
    **(A)** wizened
    **(B)** grizzled
    **(C)** excavated
    **(D)** deconstructed
    **(E)** decimated

16. RECTITUDE:
    **(A)** lack of self-confidence
    **(B)** difference of opinion
    **(C)** intellectual uncertainty
    **(D)** moral weakness
    **(E)** ethical dilemma

**Directions:** Questions 17–18 are based on the following passage.

*Line* The amount of bone in the elderly skeleton—a key determinant in its susceptibility to fractures—is believed to be a function of two major factors.
*(5)* The first is the peak amount of bone mass attained, determined to a large extent by genetic inheritance. The marked effect of gender is obvious: Elderly men experience only one-half
*(10)* as many hip fractures per capita as elderly women. But also, African-American women have a lower incidence of osteoporotic fractures than Caucasian women. Other important
*(15)* variables include diet, exposure to sunlight, and physical activity. The second major factor is the rate of bone loss after peak bone mass has been attained. While many of the variables
*(20)* that affect peak bone mass also affect rates of bone loss, additional factors influencing bone loss include physiological stresses such as pregnancy and lactation. It is hormonal status,
*(25)* however, reflected primarily by estrogen and progesterone levels, that may exert the greatest effect on rates of decline in skeletal mass.

17. The passage clearly identifies all of the following as factors in the rate of bone-mass loss EXCEPT for
    **(A)** lactation
    **(B)** sunlight exposure
    **(C)** progesterone levels
    **(D)** pregnancy
    **(E)** estrogen levels

18. It can be inferred from the passage that the peak amount of bone mass in women
    **(A)** is not affected by either pregnancy or lactation
    **(B)** is determined primarily by diet
    **(C)** depends partly upon hormonal status
    **(D)** may be a factor in the rate of decrease in estrogen and progesterone levels
    **(E)** is not dependent upon genetic makeup

19. Salinger's *Catcher in the Rye*, having become a manifesto for psychopaths and potential miscreants, is viewed by many high-school administrators as too _____ to be suitable for teenage students.
    **(A)** austere
    **(B)** insipid
    **(C)** provocative
    **(D)** aberrant
    **(E)** progressive

20. INTERLOPER : MEDDLE ::
    **(A)** misanthrope : usurp
    **(B)** rogue : repent
    **(C)** advocate : espouse
    **(D)** dilettante : proselytize
    **(E)** ombudsman : refine

21. WALK : AMBLE ::
    **(A)** work : tinker
    **(B)** play : rest
    **(C)** run : jump
    **(D)** jog : trot
    **(E)** disperse : leave

**22.** SENSATION : PARALYSIS ::
   **(A)** sincerity : dishonesty
   **(B)** obesity : diet
   **(C)** insult : injury
   **(D)** apathy : curiosity
   **(E)** scarcity : surplus

**Directions:** Questions 23–26 are based on the following passage.

*Line* The origin of the attempt to distinguish early from modern music and to establish the canons of performance practice for each lies in the eighteenth
(5) century. In the first half of that century, when Telemann and Bach ran the *collegium musicum* in Leipzig, Germany, they performed their own and other modern music. In the
(10) German universities of the early twentieth century, however, the reconstituted *collegium musicum* devoted itself to performing music from the centuries before the beginning of the
(15) "standard repertory," by which was understood music from before the time of Bach and Handel.

   Alongside this modern *collegium musicum*, German musicologists
(20) developed the historical sub-discipline known as "performance practice," which included the deciphering of obsolete musical notation and its transcription into modern notation, the
(25) study of obsolete instruments, and the re-establishment of lost oral traditions associated with those forgotten repertories. The cutoff date for this study was understood to be around 1750, the
(30) year of Bach's death, since the music of Bach, Handel, Telemann and their contemporaries did call for obsolete instruments and voices and unannotated performing traditions—for
(35) instance, the spontaneous realization of vocal and instrumental melodic ornamentation. Furthermore, with a few exceptions, late baroque music

had ceased to be performed for nearly
(40) a century, and the orally transmitted performing traditions associated with it were forgotten as a result. In contrast, the notation in the music of Haydn and Mozart from the second
(45) half of the eighteenth century was more complete than in the earlier styles, and the instruments seemed familiar, so no "special" knowledge appeared necessary. Also, the music of
(50) Haydn and Mozart, having never ceased to be performed, had maintained some kind of oral tradition of performance practice.

   Beginning around 1960, however,
(55) early-music performers began to encroach upon the music of Haydn, Mozart, and Beethoven. Why? Scholars studying performance practice had discovered that the living
(60) oral traditions associated with the Viennese classics frequently could not be traced to the eighteenth century and that there were nearly as many performance mysteries to solve for
(65) music after 1750 as for earlier repertories. Furthermore, more and more young singers and instrumentalists became attracted to early music, and as many of them graduated from stu-
(70) dent-amateur to professional status, the technical level of early-music performances took a giant leap forward.

   As professional early-music groups, building on these developments,
(75) expanded their repertories to include later music, the mainstream protested vehemently. The differences between the two camps extended beyond the question of which instruments to use
(80) to the more critical matter of style and delivery. At the heart of their disagreement is whether historical knowledge about performing traditions is a prerequisite for proper inter-
(85) pretation of music or whether it merely creates an obstacle to inspired musical tradition.

23. It can be inferred from the passage that the "standard repertory" mentioned in line 15 might have included music that was written
    (A) before 1700
    (B) during the early twentieth century
    (C) by the performance-practice composers
    (D) before the time of Handel
    (E) to be played using obsolete instruments

24. The passage mentions all of the following as aspects of performance practice of the early twentieth century EXCEPT for
    (A) deciphering outdated music notation
    (B) reestablishing unannotated performing traditions
    (C) spontaneous vocal and instrumental ornamentation
    (D) varying the delivery of music to suit particular audiences
    (E) transcribing older music into modern notation

25. Which of the following statements, if true, would best support the author's explanation for the encroachment by the early-musicians upon the music of Mozart, Haydn, and Beethoven?
    (A) Unannotated performing traditions associated with these composers were distinct from those associated with pre-1750 works.
    (B) The mainstream approved of the manner in which the early-musicians treated the music of Bach and Handel.
    (C) Most instrumentalists are attracted to early music because of the opportunities to play obsolete instruments.
    (D) The music of these composers is notated more completely than is the music of Bach and Handel.
    (E) The early-musicians and the mainstream both prefer the same style and delivery of music.

26. Which of the following is the most appropriate title for the passage?
    (A) "Performance Practice: The Legacy of the German *Collegium Musicum*"
    (B) "Performance Practice and New Interpretations of the Viennese Classics"
    (C) "Unannotated Performing Traditions of the Eighteenth and Twentieth Centuries"
    (D) "How Far Should Early Music Extend?"
    (E) "Competing Views on the Necessity of Historical Knowledge for Inspired Musical Tradition"

27. Since her older sister's _____ academic record had gained her admission to a highly respected college, Martha became commensurately _____, hoping to secure admission a top-rated university.
    (A) impeccable . . studious
    (B) laudable . . ambitious
    (C) salutary . . diligent
    (D) exemplary . . optimistic
    (E) perfunctory . . hard-working

**28.** SYNERGIZE:

   **(A)** lapse
   **(B)** catalyze
   **(C)** atrophy
   **(D)** languish
   **(E)** sabotage

**29.** MUNIFICENT : GENEROSITY ::

   **(A)** dolorous : sorrow
   **(B)** domineering : timidity
   **(C)** indisputable : confidence
   **(D)** fortunate : luck
   **(E)** beguiled : judiciousness

**30.** Many child psychologists believe that a playground bully's _____ behavior is mere bravado—an attempt to compensate for insecurities—and that this _____ superiority portends trouble coping with responsibilities as an adult.

   **(A)** antisocial . . air of
   **(B)** cruel . . merely feigned
   **(C)** unchecked . . show of
   **(D)** superior . . pretense of
   **(E)** aggressive . . obsession with

## QUANTITATIVE REASONING

### 28 Questions • 45 Minutes

**NOTE:** In this section, questions are grouped together by format, and within each group the questions grow more difficult as you go. Because the actual GRE is computer-adaptive in the multiple-choice sections, it intersperses questions of different formats and difficulty levels.

1. A drawer contains four pairs of socks: two gray pairs and two blue pairs. If two pairs are selected at random, what is the probability of choosing a blue pair and a gray pair?

   **(A)** $\frac{2}{3}$

   **(B)** $\frac{3}{5}$

   **(C)** $\frac{1}{2}$

   **(D)** $\frac{2}{5}$

   **(E)** $\frac{1}{3}$

<table>
<tr><td align="center"><u>Column A</u></td><td align="center"><u>Column B</u></td></tr>
</table>

2.                                      $x \neq 0$

   $\dfrac{x^8}{x^2}$                   $(x)(x^2)(x^3)$

   **(A)** The quantity in Column A is greater;
   **(B)** The quantity in Column B is greater;
   **(C)** The quantities are equal;
   **(D)** The relationship cannot be determined from the information given.

3. The ratio of Jennifer's weekly salary to Carl's weekly salary is 3:2. If Carl were to receive a raise of $200 per week, their salaries would be the same. What is Jennifer's current weekly salary?

   **(A)** $720
   **(B)** $600
   **(C)** $540
   **(D)** $480
   **(E)** $400

**4.** The number of attendees at a certain annual conference is 256 this year and has always doubled every five years. How many people attended the conference 20 years ago?

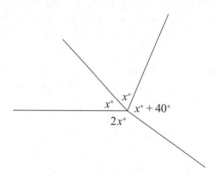

*Click on the answer box, then type in a number. Backspace to erase.*

**5.** In the figure above, what is the value of $x$?
   **(A)** 36
   **(B)** 40
   **(C)** 60
   **(D)** 64
   **(E)** 72

| Column A | Column B |
|---|---|
| **6.**  The greatest prime factor of 99 | The greatest prime factor of 39 |

   **(A)** The quantity in Column A is greater;
   **(B)** The quantity in Column B is greater;
   **(C)** The quantities are equal;
   **(D)** The relationship cannot be determined from the information given.

| Column A | Column B |
|---|---|

**7.**          Horse Q weighs 15 percent more than horse P.
              Horse R weighs 150 pounds more than horse P.

| The weight of horse R | The weight of horse Q |
|---|---|

   **(A)** The quantity in Column A is greater;
   **(B)** The quantity in Column B is greater;
   **(C)** The quantities are equal;
   **(D)** The relationship cannot be determined from the information given.

|                    Column A                    |                    Column B                    |
| :--------------------------------------------: | :--------------------------------------------: |

**8.**

Apples cost $7 per bag of 25.
Pears cost $28 per bag of 100.

| At the average price of an individual piece of fruit, the total price of 178 apples and 461 pears | At the average price of an individual piece of fruit, the total price of 461 apples and 178 pears |

**(A)** The quantity in Column A is greater;
**(B)** The quantity in Column B is greater;
**(C)** The quantities are equal;
**(D)** The relationship cannot be determined from the information given.

|                    Column A                    |                    Column B                    |
| :--------------------------------------------: | :--------------------------------------------: |

**9.**

$p$, $q$, and $r$ are positive integers such that $p < q < r < 5$.

| $p + q + r$ | $qr$ |

**(A)** The quantity in Column A is greater;
**(B)** The quantity in Column B is greater;
**(C)** The quantities are equal;
**(D)** The relationship cannot be determined from the information given.

**Disease X**
**Medication Sales**

**10.** According to the chart, during which year were annual sales of oral medication for disease X less than during the previous year?

**(A)** 1992
**(B)** 1994
**(C)** 1995
**(D)** 1996
**(E)** 1997

11. The length of Cassie's family room is exactly two thirds the length of her master bedroom. Both rooms are rectangular, and the area of the two rooms is the same. If Cassie's family room has a length of L and a width of W, which of the following represents the perimeter of her master bedroom?

   **(A)** $2L + \dfrac{4}{3}W$

   **(B)** $3L + \dfrac{2}{3}W$

   **(C)** $3L + \dfrac{1}{3}W$

   **(D)** $\dfrac{3}{2}L + W$

   **(E)** $3L + \dfrac{4}{3}W$

12. The number 40.5 is 500 times larger than which of the following numbers?
   **(A)** .810
   **(B)** .2025
   **(C)** .0810
   **(D)** .02025
   **(E)** .00810

|  | <u>Column A</u> | <u>Column B</u> |
| --- | --- | --- |
| **13.** | A pail holds 1.5 gallons of water. | |
| | The number of pails of water needed to fill a 30-gallon fish tank | The number of gallons of water needed to fill a fish tank of a 20-pail capacity |

   **(A)** The quantity in Column A is greater;
   **(B)** The quantity in Column B is greater;
   **(C)** The quantities are equal;
   **(D)** The relationship cannot be determined from the information given.

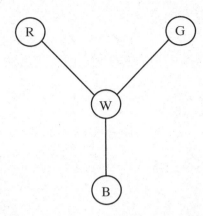

**14.** In the simple light show pictured above, a light starts at the center (white) at time zero and moves once every second in the following pattern: from white (W) to blue (B), back to white, then to green (G), back to white, then to red (R), and back to white—in a *counter*-clockwise direction. If the light continues to move in this way, what will be the color sequence from the 208th second to the 209th second?

**(A)** white to green
**(B)** white to blue
**(C)** white to red
**(D)** red to white
**(E)** green to white

**15.** A solution of 60 ounces of sugar and water is 20% sugar. If you add $x$ ounces of water to make a solution that is 5% sugar, which of the following represents the amount of sugar in the solution after adding water?

**(A)** $60 - 40x$
**(B)** $.05(60x - 20)$
**(C)** $60(.05 + x)$
**(D)** $.20(60 + x)$
**(E)** $.05(60 + x)$

**16.** If $p = (3)(5)(6)(9)(q)$, where $q$ is a positive integer, then $p$ must be divisible, with no remainder, by all the following EXCEPT for

**(A)** 27
**(B)** 36
**(C)** 45
**(D)** 54
**(E)** 90

|  | **Column A** | | **Column B** |
|---|---|---|---|

**17.** $$a \lozenge b = \frac{a-b}{b-a}$$

$2 \lozenge -1$ $\qquad\qquad$ $-2 \lozenge 4$

**(A)** The quantity in Column A is greater;
**(B)** The quantity in Column B is greater;
**(C)** The quantities are equal;
**(D)** The relationship cannot be determined from the information given.

|  | Column A |  | Column B |
|---|---|---|---|

**18.**

$$y^2 + y - 6 = 0$$

                 $y$                                               2

**(A)** The quantity in Column A is greater;
**(B)** The quantity in Column B is greater;
**(C)** The quantities are equal;
**(D)** The relationship cannot be determined from the information given.

|  | Column A |  | Column B |
|---|---|---|---|

**19.**       The perimeter of a triangle             The perimeter of a triangle
           with vertices (0,1), (4,1),             with vertices (2,0), (5,0),
           and (4,4) on the $xy$-plane             and (5,3) on the $xy$-plane

**(A)** The quantity in Column A is greater;
**(B)** The quantity in Column B is greater;
**(C)** The quantities are equal;
**(D)** The relationship cannot be determined from the information given.

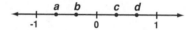

|  | Column A |  | Column B |
|---|---|---|---|

**20.**                     $ad$                                                     $bc$

**(A)** The quantity in Column A is greater;
**(B)** The quantity in Column B is greater;
**(C)** The quantities are equal;
**(D)** The relationship cannot be determined from the information given.

> **Directions:** Questions 21–23 refer to the following table.

| ELECTRICITY USAGE AT FOUR HOUSES: A, B, C, and D (Month of June) | | | |
|---|---|---|---|
| House | Interior Area (Square Area) | Interior Volume (Cubic Feet) | Electricity Usage in Kilowatt Hours (kWh) |
| A | 1,300 | 10,400 | 960 |
| B | 1,500 | 12,000 | 1044 |
| C | 2,000 | 16,200 | 1,125 |
| D | 2,300 | 18,400 | 1,205 |

**21.** The month of June contains 30 days. During June, how much more electricity was used at house C per day than at house A per day, on average?

**(A)** 2.7 kWh
**(B)** 2.8 kWh
**(C)** 4.0 kWh
**(D)** 4.8 kWh
**(E)** 5.5 kWh

22. During June, which of the four houses used between 0.5 and 0.7 kWh of electricity per square foot of interior area?

 I. House A
 II. House B
III. House C
IV. House D

**(A)** II and III only
**(B)** II and IV only
**(C)** I, II, and III only
**(D)** II, III, and IV only
**(E)** I, II, III, and IV

23. Assuming each house has a uniform ceiling height, which house has the greatest ceiling height?

**(A)** House A
**(B)** House B
**(C)** House C
**(D)** House D
**(E)** All four houses have the same ceiling height.

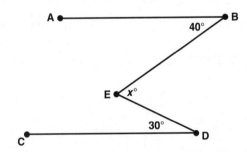

24. Referring to the figure above, for what value of $x$ would it be true that $\overline{AB} \parallel \overline{CD}$?

**(A)** 60
**(B)** 65
**(C)** 70
**(D)** 75
**(E)** 80

|  | **Column A** | **Column B** |
|---|---|---|
| 25. | $\dfrac{8}{17} + \dfrac{9}{14}$ | $\dfrac{7}{16} + \dfrac{8}{13}$ |

**(A)** The quantity in Column A is greater;
**(B)** The quantity in Column B is greater;
**(C)** The quantities are equal;
**(D)** The relationship cannot be determined from the information given.

**26.** Two of a triangle's sides are congruent. The triangle is inscribed in a circle such that each vertex of the triangle lies along the circle's circumference.

| Column A | Column B |
|---|---|
| The longest side of the triangle | The circle's diameter |

**(A)** The quantity in Column A is greater;
**(B)** The quantity in Column B is greater;
**(C)** The quantities are equal;
**(D)** The relationship cannot be determined from the information given.

| Column A | Column B |
|---|---|

**27.**
$$xy \neq 0$$

| Column A | Column B |
|---|---|
| $\sqrt[3]{8x^6y^6}$ | $\sqrt{4(xy)^4}$ |

**(A)** The quantity in Column A is greater;
**(B)** The quantity in Column B is greater;
**(C)** The quantities are equal;
**(D)** The relationship cannot be determined from the information given.

**28.** The total weight of $m$ bricks, all of which are equal in weight, is $n$ pounds.

| Column A | Column B |
|---|---|
| $\dfrac{n}{m}$ | $1$ |

**(A)** The quantity in Column A is greater;
**(B)** The quantity in Column B is greater;
**(C)** The quantities are equal;
**(D)** The relationship cannot be determined from the information given.

# ANSWER KEY AND EXPLANATIONS

## Analytical Writing

### ISSUE TASK: EVALUATION AND SCORING

Evaluate your Issue task essay on a scale of 1 to 6 (6 being the highest score) according to the following five criteria:

**❶** Does your essay develop a position on the issue through the use of incisive reasons and persuasive examples?

**❷** Are your essay's ideas conveyed clearly and articulately?

**❸** Does your essay maintain proper focus on the issue, and is it well organized?

**❹** Does your essay demonstrate proficiency, fluency, and maturity in its use of sentence structure, vocabulary, and idiom?

**❺** Does your essay demonstrate command of the elements of Standard Written English, including grammar, word usage, spelling, and punctuation?

### ARGUMENT TASK: EVALUATION AND SCORING

Evaluate your Argument task essay on a scale of 1 to 6 (6 being the highest score) according to the following five criteria:

**❶** Does your essay identify and articulate the argument's key unstated assumptions?

**❷** Does your essay explain how the argument relies on these unstated assumptions, and what the implications are if these assumptions are unwarranted?

**❸** Does your essay develop its ideas in a clear, organized manner, with appropriate transitions to help connect ideas together?

**❹** Does your essay demonstrate proficiency, fluency, and maturity in its use of sentence structure, vocabulary, and idiom?

**❺** Does your essay demonstrate command of the elements of Standard Written English, including grammar, word usage, spelling, and punctuation?

To help you evaluate your essay in terms of criteria 1 and 2, the following is a series of questions that identify *five* distinct unstated assumptions upon which the argument relies. To earn a score of 4 or higher, your essay should identify and explain at least three of these assumptions. Identifying and explaining at least four of the unstated assumptions would help earn you an even higher score.

- Does the recommendation assume that Back to Basics is *necessary* to improve the students' reading skills to the desired level? (Perhaps some other reading program or, for that matter, some other alternative, such as encouraging parents to read with their children or simply devoting more time during school to reading, would be as effective as Back to Basics—or possibly even more effective.

- Would adopting the Back to Basics program in itself be *sufficient* to improve the students' reading skills to the desired extent? (Unless the students are sufficiently attentive and motivated, and unless the teachers are sufficiently competent, the program might not be effective.)

- Was the Back to Basics program the *true reason* for the improved reading skills that the company cites? (Perhaps the improved reading skills observed among children nationwide are attributable instead to a general increase in teacher salaries or to a new national children's literacy campaign, to name just a few possibilities.)

- Is Harper *representative* of the elementary schools throughout the nation that have adopted the program? (Perhaps this school's students would not respond as well to the program's methods as most students, for whatever reason.)

- Is the evidence of the program's effectiveness *credible* and *unbiased*? (The nationwide results of the Back to Basics program were reported by the program's provider, who probably stands to profit by overstating the program's effectiveness.)

## Verbal Reasoning

| | | |
|---|---|---|
| 1. E | 11. E | 21. A |
| 2. D | 12. C | 22. B |
| 3. B | 13. E | 23. E |
| 4. B | 14. B | 24. D |
| 5. A | 15. A | 25. A |
| 6. C | 16. D | 26. D |
| 7. (i) lend credence | 17. B | 27. A |
| (ii) Specifically | 18. A | 28. E |
| 8. D | 19. C | 29. A |
| 9. E | 20. C | 30. B |
| 10. C | | |

1. **The correct answer is (E).** This is a "sign or manifestation of" analogy. To TREMBLE is to exhibit a certain physiological symptom, or manifestation, of FEAR; similarly, to *weep* is to exhibit a physiological manifestation of *grief*. Choice (D) is the second-best choice: an *adoring* person might *follow* the object of his or her adoration. But this manifestation is not physiological, nor is it as inexorable as trembling or weeping (as manifestations of fear and grief, respectively).

2. **The correct answer is (D).** This is a "function or purpose" analogy. A WATERMARK is a faint design embedded in PAPER in order to identify the paper's maker. A *badge* is worn by an *employee* to identify both that employee and the employer—the "maker" of the employee.

3. **The correct answer is (B).** The signpost word in this sentence is "because," which requires that what follows it must explain what precedes it. Profit potential would explain why drug companies persist in developing new drugs despite *onerous* (burdensome) government

regulations. Choice (B) is the only one that expresses this idea. (The word *dissuade* means "discourage or persuade not to.")

4. **The correct answer is (B).** PROPRIETY and *decorum* both mean "conformity to established standards of proper behavior or manners"; accordingly, *lack of decorum* is the opposite of *propriety*.

5. **The correct answer is (A).** SCIENTIAL means "of or having knowledge," just the opposite of *ignorant*.

6. **The correct answer is (C).** CLOISTERED means "secluded or hidden away from the world." A good antonym is *gregarious*, which means "living in a community."

7. **The correct answers are lend credence for blank (i) and Specifically for blank (ii).** Let's start with the second blank. The second sentence tells us that "physical forces" (mentioned in the first sentence) include our own genetic makeup. In other words, the second sentence is bringing a general statement down to something more

specific. So, the word *Specifically* provides a logical transition from the first (general) idea to the second (specific) one. Now consider the first blank. The new research seems consistent with the idea that human behavior is determined by physical forces beyond our control. The idiomatic phrase *lends credence to* means "provides credibility or legitimacy to"—and so it is an apt phrase for the first blank.

8. **The correct answer is (D).** This is a "intrinsic aspect or quality" analogy. COTTON is SOFT to the touch; similarly, an *iron* is *hard* to the touch. These are both inherent tactile characteristics.

9. **The correct answer is (E).** This is a "place or environment for" analogy. FISH are kept in an AQUARIUM, an environment created by humans. *Birds* are kept in an *aviary*, also an environment created by humans. *Lions* live in *dens*, and *insects* live in the *ground*, but these environments are natural—they're not human-created. An *automobile* can be kept in a *garage*, but an automobile has no natural environment.

10. **The correct answer is (C).** This is a "degree of" analogy. A SPARK is a very small fire, while a CONFLAGRATION is a very large fire. The relationship is one of degree. Similarly, a *drizzle* is a very light rain, while a *downpour* is very heavy rain.

11. **The correct answer is (E).** The words "Just as" provide a clue that Beethoven, like Mozart, was a musical revolutionary. Therefore, to say that he *overturned* the rules and *initiated* change makes good sense.

12. **The correct answer is (C).** In the second paragraph, the author states that one of the effects of New Towns was to draw away high-income citizens away from the cities—essentially what choice (C) indicates.

13. **The correct answer is (E).** According to the first sentence of the passage, New Towns were originally conceptualized as a way to absorb growth. Based on other information in the passage, it appears that New Towns in the United States achieved this objective—at least to some extent—since city residents who could afford to move away from urban centers did so. At the same time, however, the cities were left with new problems, such as an insufficient tax base to support themselves and to retain businesses. Thus, like a computer program that attempts to solve one software problem but creates another, New Towns were a new innovation that served to solve one problem but created another along the way.

14. **The correct answer is (B).** To SATIATE is to "fill to capacity." To *deplete entirely* is to use up completely. *Crave* (long for) is related to *satiate*—a person who has become satiated doesn't crave anymore. But lack of craving is not part of the definition of *satiate*.

15. **The correct answer is (A).** OSSIFIED means "turned to bone, or fossilized"; when wood, for example, becomes fossilized, it hardens as bone. *Wizened* means "shriveled or wrinkled, as with age"—which describes the opposite condition.

16. **The correct answer is (D).** REC-TITUDE means "moral virtue or strength." Choice (D) provides an ideal antonym.

17. **The correct answer is (B).** The passage mentions exposure to sunlight as one factor determining peak bone mass. Although the passage states that "many of the factors that affect the attainment of peak bone mass also affect rates of bone loss," the passage does not indicate that exposure to sunlight is one such factor.

18. **The correct answer is (A).** The author lists various factors affecting peak bone mass, then asserts that many of these factors also affect the rate of bone loss. In mentioning pregnancy and lactation as "additional factors" affecting bone loss, the author implies that these two factors do *not* affect peak bone mass.

19. **The correct answer is (C).** A *miscreant* is a villain, scoundrel, or criminal. The sentence strongly suggests that *Catcher in the Rye* might *provoke* (incite) potential miscreants to engage in violent antisocial behavior.

20. **The correct answer is (C).** This is a "defining characteristic" analogy. An INTERLOPER seeks to MEDDLE (interfere) in the affairs of another. An *advocate* (ally) will *espouse* (support or defend) a particular viewpoint or cause. In both cases, the second word describes the inherent objective of the first.

21. **The correct answer is (A).** This is a "form of" analogy. To AMBLE is to WALK unhurriedly without a predetermined destination. To *tinker* is to *work* aimlessly without a predetermined direction.

22. **The correct answer is (B).** This is a "symptom of" analogy. One sign of PARALYSIS is the lack of SENSATION (feeling). Similarly, one sign of *dieting* is the lack of *obesity*. As for choices (A) and (E), the two words in each pair are antonyms. The same can't be said for *sensation* and *paralysis*. Paralysis is not defined by a lack of sensation, but by lack of ability to move.

23. **The correct answer is (E).** It is reasonably inferable from the first paragraph as a whole that the "standard repertory" mentioned in line 15 refers to the music of Bach and Telemann as well as to other ("modern") music from their time (first half of the eighteenth century). In the second paragraph, the author mentions that the music of Bach, Telemann, and their contemporaries called for obsolete instruments. Thus, the standard repertory might have included music that called for the use of obsolete instruments, as choice (E) indicates.

24. **The correct answer is (D).** Although performance practice did indeed involve varying the performance of a work of music from one time to the next (by including spontaneous vocal and instrumental ornamentation), the passage neither states nor implies that how the delivery of music varied from time to time depended upon the particular tastes of the audience. Thus, choice (D) is unsupported by the passage.

**25. The correct answer is (A).** According to the passage, one reason for the encroachment was that some of the oral traditions associated with the Viennese classics (the works of Mozart, Haydn, and Beethoven) could not be traced back to the eighteenth century. Choice (A) supports this point by providing specific evidence that this was indeed the case.

**26. The correct answer is (D).** The author's primary concern in the passage is to trace the scope of works included in performance practice from the early twentieth century to the latter half of the century. The author identifies and explains the reasons for the trend of including later works within the scope of so-called "early music" (second and third paragraphs), then refers (in the final paragraph) to a controversy surrounding this trend. Choice (D) reflects the author's primary concern as well as embracing the controversy.

**27. The correct answer is (A).** As a whole, the sentence clearly suggests that Martha wishes to emulate her sister in order to accomplish at least what her sister did. To attend a "highly respected" college would obviously require a good academic record, so the first word must essentially mean "excellent." Choices (A), (B), and (D) each provide such a word. The word for the second blank should relate to what's needed to achieve such a record. Among those three choices, only choice (A) makes sense.

**28. The correct answer is (E).** To SYNERGIZE is to "coordinate different elements toward achieving a common goal." To *sabotage* is to "deliberately spoil or damage as to make useless or unproductive." An act of sabotage may very well be designed to disrupt or spoil an attempt to synergize. Though not a perfect antonym, *sabotage* is the best of the five choices.

**29. The correct answer is (A).** This is a "defining characteristic" analogy. A MUNIFICENT person is characterized by great GENEROSITY; similarly, a *dolorous* person is characterized by great *sorrow*. Since *luck* can be either bad or good, choice (D) is not as strong an analogy as choice (A).

**30. The correct answer is (B).** It's fair to characterize bullying as either *antisocial*, *cruel*, or *aggressive*. The word *bravado* means "pretense," and *feigned* means "pretended." So by pretending to be superior, a bully hides his insecurities. Among the choices, then, choice (B) makes for the most cohesive sentence overall.

## Quantitative Reasoning

| | | |
|---|---|---|
| 1. A | 11. E | 20. B |
| 2. C | 12. C | 21. E |
| 3. B | 13. B | 22. D |
| 4. 16 | 14. C | 23. C |
| 5. D | 15. E | 24. C |
| 6. B | 16. B | 25. A |
| 7. D | 17. C | 26. D |
| 8. C | 18. D | 27. C |
| 9. D | 19. A | 28. D |
| 10. A | | |

1. **The correct answer is (A).** There are six possible two-pair combinations: (B1-B2), (B1-G1), (B1-G2), (B2-G1), (B2-G2), (G1-G2). Since four of the six combinations involve removing one blue pair and one gray pair, the probability is $\frac{4}{6}$, or $\frac{2}{3}$.

2. **The correct answer is (C).** In Quantity A, divide by subtracting the denominator exponent from the numerator exponent: $\frac{x^8}{x^2} = x^{(8-2)} = x^6$. In Quantity B, combine by adding exponents: $(x)(x^2)(x^3) = x^{(1+2+3)} = x^6$. You can now see that Quantity A equals Quantity B.

3. **The correct answer is (B).** Let Jennifer's salary equal $3x$, and let Carl's salary equal $2x$. A \$200 raise for Carl will bring his salary to $2x + 200$. Thus, $3x = 2x + 200$, and $x = 200$. Therefore, Jennifer's current weekly salary is $(3)(\$200) = \$600$.

4. **The correct answer is 16.** Divide by 2 four times, as follows:

   5 years ago: $256 \div 2 = 128$
   10 years ago: $128 \div 2 = 64$
   15 years ago: $64 \div 2 = 32$
   20 years ago: $32 \div 2 = 16$

5. **The correct answer is (D).** The total number of degrees is 360°, and so $x + x + 2x + (x + 40) = 360$. Solve for $x$:

   $$5x + 40 = 360$$
   $$5x = 320$$
   $$x = 64$$

6. **The correct answer is (B).** To make the comparison, apply prime factorization:

   $99 = 3 \times 33 = 3 \times 3 \times 11$
   $39 = 3 \times 13$

   As you can see, the greatest prime factor of 99 is 11, and the greatest prime factor of 39 is 13. Therefore, Quantity B > Quantity A.

7. **The correct answer is (D).** The problem does not provide the actual weight of any of the three horses, and so it is impossible to make the comparison.

8. **The correct answer is (C).** The price of 100 apples (4 bags of 25) is \$28 ($4 \times \$7$), the same as the price for 100 pears. In other words, the price of apples is the same as the price of pears. Accordingly, to compare the two quantities you can simply compare the total numbers of

fruit pieces. You can see that the totals are the same: 178 + 461. Hence, the two quantities are equal.

9. **The correct answer is (D).** The minimum value of Quantity A is 1 + 2 + 3 = 6, in which case $qr = 6$, and the two quantities are equal. The maximum value of Quantity A is 2 + 3 + 4 = 9, in which case $qr = 12$, and the two quantities are unequal. Therefore, the correct answer is choice (D).

10. **The correct answer is (A).** For each year, the gray portion of the bar indicates sales of oral injection medication. In 1991, those sales clearly totaled more than $1 million, but in 1992 they totaled no more than $1 million.

11. **The correct answer is (E).** Since the two areas both equal L × W, the master bedroom (the longer room) must have a length of $\frac{3}{2}$L and a width of $\frac{2}{3}$W. Accordingly, the perimeter of the master bedroom = $(2)\left(\frac{3}{2}L\right)$ + $2\left(\frac{2}{3}W\right)$, or $3L + \frac{4}{3}W$.

12. **The correct answer is (C).** A quick way to divide by 500 is to first divide by 1,000, and then multiply the quotient by 2. In this problem, then, divide 40.5 by 1,000 by simply shifting the decimal point 3 places to the left, and then multiply that quotient by 2. The calculation is very simple:

$$(.0405)(2) = .0810$$

13. **The correct answer is (B).** Quantity A = 30 ÷ 1.5 = 20; Quantity B = (20)(1.5) = 30

14. **The correct answer is (C).** Here's the sequence up to the 12th second:

| | | |
|---|---|---|
| 0 W | 5 R | 9 G |
| 1 B | 6 W | 10 W |
| 2 W | 7 B | 11 R |
| 3 G | 8 W | 12 W |
| 4 W | | |

Every time you reach a time divisible by 6, the sequence starts over with W and proceeds: W-B-W-G-W-R. 204 is divisible by 6; hence, starting at the 204th second, here are the light's movements through the 209th second:

| | | |
|---|---|---|
| 204 W | 205 B | 206 W |
| 207 G | 208 W | 209 R |

As you can see, the movement from the 208th to the 209th second is from white (W) to red (R).

15. **The correct answer is (E).** You can express the amount of sugar after you add water as $.05(60 + x)$, where $.05 = 5\%$ and $(60 + x)$ represents the total amount of solution after you add the additional water.

16. **The correct answer is (B).** Multiplying together any combination of the factors of $p$ will result in a product that is also a factor of $p$. The only number among the choices listed that is not a product of any of these combinations is 36.

17. **The correct answer is (C).** Apply the defined operation to the values specified in each column:

$$\text{Quantity A} = \frac{2-(-1)}{-1-2} = \frac{3}{-3} = -1$$

$$\text{Quantity B} = \frac{-2-4}{4-(-2)} = \frac{-6}{6} = -1$$

18. **The correct answer is (D).** You can express $y^2 + y - 6$ as the product of binomials $(y + 3)$ and $(y - 2)$. Thus,

the equation $y^2 + y - 6 = 0$ has two distinct roots, or $y$-values: $-3$ and $2$. Since $y$ could have either of two values, the answer is choice (D).

19. **The correct answer is (A).** Both triangles are right triangles. The triangle described in Column A has legs 3 and 4 units long. The triangle described in Column B has legs 3 units long each. Hence, the hypotenuse and, in turn, the perimeter of the triangle described in Column A must be greater than those of the triangle described in Column B. There's no need to calculate either hypotenuse or perimeter.

20. **The correct answer is (B).** Quantity A ($ad$) is a negative fractional number greater than $a$ and approaching zero (0). Similarly, Quantity B ($bc$) is a negative fractional number greater than $b$ and approaching zero (0). But $ad$ must be less than $cd$ (that is, further to the left than $cd$ on the number line). Why? If $a$ and $b$ were both multiplied by $c$ (a positive number), the inequality between $a$ and $b$ ($a < b$) would remain unchanged: $ac < bc$. It makes sense that if $a$ is multiplied instead by a positive number ($d$) that is greater than $c$, then the inequality between $a$ and $b$ not only remains the same but actually increases. In any event, $ad < bc$.

21. **The correct answer is (E).** The June usage difference between houses C and A was $1{,}125 - 960 = 165$ kWh. Divide this monthly difference by 30 to find the average per-day difference: $165 \div 30 = 5.5$ kWh.

22. **The correct answer is (D).** To calculate per-square-foot usage for a house, divide total usage by square-foot area. Estimating the averages (to either above or below the nearest tenth) for each house will suffice to select the houses at which between 0.5 and 0.7 kWh per square-foot area were used during July:

House A: $0.7^+$
House B: $0.7^-$
House C: $0.5^+$
House D: $0.5^+$

As you can see, houses B, C, and D fall between 0.5 and 0.7 kWh.

23. **The correct answer is (C).** The interior volume of each house is the product of its square-foot area and its ceiling height (volume = area × height). To determine a house's ceiling height, divide its volume by its square-foot area. For Houses A, B, and D, the quotient (ceiling height) is exactly 8.0 linear feet. For House C, however, the quotient is greater than 8.0 linear feet.

24. **The correct answer is (C).** To answer the question, assume that $\overline{AB} \parallel \overline{CD}$. Extend $\overline{BE}$ to $\overline{CD}$, and let F be the point at which these two segments intersect. $m\angle EFD = m\angle ABE = 40°$. $m\angle FED$ must equal $110°$ because the three interior angles of $\triangle DEF$ must total $180°$ in measure. Since $\angle BED$ and $\angle FED$ are supplementary (the sum of their measures is $180°$), $m\angle BED = 70°$ ($x = 70$).

25. **The correct answer is (A).** The quickest route to the correct answer is to compare corresponding terms. For example, compare $\dfrac{8}{17}$ (in Column A) to $\dfrac{7}{16}$ (in Column B). Notice that $\dfrac{8}{17} = \dfrac{7+1}{16+1}$. When you add the same number to a fraction's numerator as its denominator, the fraction's value *increases*, and so $\dfrac{8}{17} > \dfrac{7}{16}$. You can analyze the other corresponding fraction pair in the same way. The value of the each fraction in Column A is greater than the value of the corresponding term in Column B. Thus, the sum of the fractions in Column A must be greater than the sum of the fractions in Column B.

26. **The correct answer is (D).** The longest side may, but need not, pass through the center of the circle. Thus, its length could be either equal to or less than the circle's diameter. NOTE: If the triangle were equi-lateral, the correct answer would have been choice (B); if it were a right triangle, the correct answer would have been choice (C).

27. **The correct answer is (C).** The expression in Column A is a perfect cube, and the expression in Column B is a perfect square:

$$\sqrt[3]{8x^6 y^6} = 2x^2 y^2 \text{ and}$$

$$\sqrt{4(xy)^4} = \sqrt{4x^4 y^4} = 2x^2 y^2.$$

As you can see, Quantity A equals Quantity B.

28. **The correct answer is (D).** It is entirely possible that $m = n$ (for example, in the case of 5 bricks weighing 1 pound each). If so, then $\dfrac{n}{m} = 1$, and Quantity A = Quantity B. However, if the total number of bricks differs from the total pound weight (for example, in the case of 5 bricks weighing 2 pounds each), then $\dfrac{n}{m} \neq 1$, and Quantity A $\neq$ Quantity B.

# APPENDIX

Vocabulary List

# Vocabulary List

appendix

## A

**abbreviate** (verb) To make briefer, to shorten. *Because time was running out, the speaker was forced to abbreviate his remarks.* abbreviation (noun).

**aberration** (noun) A deviation from what is normal or natural, an abnormality. *Jack's extravagant lunch at Lutece was an aberration from his usual meal, a peanut butter sandwich and a diet soda.* aberrant (adjective).

**abeyance** (noun) A temporary lapse in activity; suspension. *In the aftermath of the bombing, all normal activities were held in abeyance.*

**abjure** (verb) To renounce or reject; to officially disclaim. *While being tried by the inquisition in 1633, Galileo abjured all his writings holding that the earth and other planets revolved around the sun.*

**abrade** (verb) To irritate by rubbing; to wear down in spirit. *Olga's "conditioning facial" abraded Sabrina's skin so severely that she vowed never to let anyone's hands touch her face again.* abrasion (noun).

**abridge** (verb) To shorten, to reduce. The Bill of Rights *is designed to prevent Congress from abridging the rights of Americans.* abridgment (noun).

**abrogate** (verb) To nullify, to abolish. *During World War II, the United States abrogated the rights of Japanese Americans by detaining them in internment camps.* abrogation (noun).

**abscond** (verb) To make a secret departure, to elope. *Theresa will never forgive her daughter, Elena, for absconding to Miami with Philip when they were only 17.*

**accretion** (noun) A gradual build-up or enlargement. *My mother's house is a mess due to her steady accretion of bric-a-brac and her inability to throw anything away.*

**adjunct** (noun) Something added to another thing, but not a part of it; an associate or assistant. *While Felix and Fritz were adjuncts to Professor Himmelman during his experiments in electrodynamics, they did not receive credit when the results were published.*

**adroit** (adjective) Skillful, adept. *The writer Laurie Colwin was particularly adroit at concocting love stories involving admirable and quirky female heroines and men who deserve them.*

557

**adulterate** (verb) To corrupt, to make impure. *Unlike the chickens from the large poultry companies, Murray's free-roaming chickens have not been adulterated with hormones and other additives.*

**adversary** (noun) An enemy or opponent. *When the former Soviet Union became an American ally, the United States lost its last major international adversary.* adverse (adjective).

**aesthete** (noun) Someone devoted to beauty and to beautiful things. *A renowned aesthete, Oscar Wilde was the center of a group that glorified beauty and adopted the slogan "art for art's sake."* aesthetic (adjective).

**affability** (noun) The quality of being easy to talk to and gracious. *Affability is a much-desired trait in any profession that involves dealing with many people on a daily basis.* affable (adjective).

**affected** (adjective) False, artificial. *At one time, Japanese women were taught to speak in an affected high-pitched voice, which was thought girlishly attractive.* affect (verb), affectation (noun).

**affinity** (noun) A feeling of shared attraction, kinship; a similarity. *When they first fell in love, Andrew and Tanya marveled over their affinity for bluegrass music, obscure French poetry, and beer taken with a squirt of lemon juice. People often say there is a striking affinity between dogs and their owners (but please don't tell Clara that she and her bassett hound are starting to resemble each other).*

**aggrandize** (verb) To make bigger or greater; to inflate. *When he was mayor of New York City, Ed Koch was renowned for aggrandizing his accomplishments and strolling through city events shouting, "How'm I doing?"* aggrandizement (noun).

**agitation** (noun) A disturbance; a disturbing feeling of upheaval and excitement. *After the CEO announced the coming layoffs, the employees' agitation was evident as they remained in the auditorium talking excitedly among themselves.* agitated (adjective), agitate (verb).

**alias** (noun) An assumed name. *Determined not to reveal his upper-class roots, Harold Steerforth Hetherington III went under the alias of "Hound Dog" when playing trumpet in his blues band.*

**allegiance** (noun) Loyalty or devotion shown to one's government or to a person, group, or cause. *At the moving naturalization ceremony, 43 new Americans from twenty-five lands swore allegiance to the United States.*

**allocate** (verb) To apportion for a specific purpose; to distribute. *The president talked about the importance of education and health care in his State of the Union address, but, in the end, the administration did not allocate enough resources for these pressing concerns.* allocation (noun).

**amalgamate** (verb) To blend thoroughly. *The tendency of grains to sort when they should mix makes it difficult for manufacturers to create powders that are amalgamated.* amalgamation (noun).

**ameliorate** (verb) To make something better or more tolerable. *The living conditions of the tenants were certainly ameliorated when the landlord finally installed washing machines and dryers in the basement.* amelioration (noun).

**amortize** (verb) To pay off or reduce a debt gradually through periodic payments. *If you don't need to take a lump-sum tax deduction, it's best to amortize large business expenditures by spreading the cost out over several years.*

**amplify** (verb) To enlarge, expand, or increase. *Uncertain as to whether they understood, the students asked the teacher to amplify his explanation.* amplification (noun).

**anachronistic** (adjective) Out of the proper time. *The reference, in Shakespeare's Julius Caesar, to "the clock striking twelve" is anachronistic, since there were no striking timepieces in ancient Rome.* anachronism (noun).

WORD ORIGIN
Greek *chronos* = time. Also found in English *chronic*, *chronicle*, *chronograph*, *chronology*, and *synchronize*.

**anarchy** (noun) Absence of law or order. *For several months after the Nazi government was destroyed, there was no effective government in parts of Germany, and anarchy ruled.* anarchic (adjective).

**animosity** (noun) Hostility, resentment. *During the last debate, the candidates could no longer disguise their animosity and began to trade accusations and insults.*

**anomaly** (noun) Something different or irregular. *The tiny planet Pluto, orbiting next to the giants Jupiter, Saturn, and Neptune, has long appeared to be an anomaly.* anomalous (adjective).

**antagonism** (noun) Hostility, conflict, opposition. *As more and more reporters investigated the Watergate scandal, antagonism between the Nixon administration and the press increased.* antagonistic (adjective), antagonize (verb).

**antipathy** (noun) A long-held feeling of dislike or aversion. *When asked why he didn't call for help immediately after his wife fell into a coma, the defendant emphasized his wife's utter antipathy to doctors.*

WORD ORIGIN
Greek *pathos* = suffering. Also found in English *apathy*, *empathy*, *pathetic*, *pathos*, and *sympathy*.

**apprehension** (noun) A feeling of fear or foreboding; an arrest. *The peculiar feeling of apprehension that Harold Pinter creates in his plays derives as much from the long silences between speeches as from the speeches themselves. The police officer's dramatic apprehension of the gunman took place in full view of the midtown lunch crowd.* apprehend (verb).

**arabesque** (noun) Intricate decorative patterns involving intertwining lines and sometimes incorporating flowers, animals, and fruits. *Borders of gold and fanciful arabesques surround the Arabic script on every page of this ancient edition of the Koran.*

**arbitrary** (adjective) Based on random or merely personal preference. *Both computers cost the same and had the same features, so in the end I made an arbitrary decision about which one to buy.* arbitration (noun).

WORD ORIGIN
Latin *arbiter* = judge. Also found in English *arbiter*, *arbitrage*, and *arbitrate*.

**archaic** (adjective) Old-fashioned, obsolete. *Those who believe in "open marriage" often declare that they will not be bound by archaic laws and religious rituals,* *but state instead that love alone should bring two people together.* archaism (noun).

**ardor** (noun) A strong feeling of passion, energy, or zeal. *The young revolutionary proclaimed his convictions with an ardor that excited the crowd.* ardent (adjective).

**arid** (adjective) Very dry; boring and meaningless. *The arid climate of Arizona makes farming difficult. Some find the law a fascinating topic, but for me it is an arid discipline.* aridity (noun).

WORD ORIGIN

Latin *articulus* = joint, division.
Also found in English *arthritis*,
*article*, and *inarticulate*.

**articulate** (adjective) To express oneself clearly and effectively. *Compared to the elder George Bush, with his stammering and his frequently incomplete sentences, Bill Clinton was considered a highly articulate president.*

**asperity** (noun) Harshness, severity. *Total silence at the dinner table, baths in icy water, prayers five times a day—these practices all contributed to the asperity of life in the monastery.*

**assail** (verb) To attack with blows or words. *When the president's cabinet members rose to justify the case for military intervention in Iraq, they were assailed by many audience members who were critical of U.S. policy.* assailant (noun).

**assay** (verb) To analyze for particular components; to determine weight, quality, etc. *The jeweler assayed the stone pendant Gwyneth inherited from her mother and found it to contain a topaz of high quality.*

**assimilate** (verb) To absorb into a system or culture. *New York City has assimilated one group of immigrants after another, from the Jewish, German, and Irish immigrants who arrived at the turn of the last century to the waves of Mexican and Latin American immigrants who arrived in the 1980s.* assimilated (adjective).

**assuage** (verb) To ease, to pacify. *Knowing that the pilot's record was perfect did little to assuage Linnet's fear of flying in the two-seater airplane.*

**audacious** (adjective) Bold, daring, adventurous. *Her plan to cross the Atlantic single-handed in a twelve-foot sailboat was an audacious, if not reckless one.* audacity (noun).

**authoritarian** (adjective) Favoring or demanding blind obedience to leaders. *Despite most Americans' strong belief in democracy, the American government has some-times supported authoritarian regimes in other countries.* authoritarianism (noun).

**authoritative** (adjective) Official, conclusive. *For more than five decades, American parents regarded Doctor Benjamin Spock as the most authoritative voice on baby and child care.* authority (noun), authorize (verb).

**avenge** (verb) To exact a punishment for or on behalf of someone. *In Shakespeare's tragedy* Hamlet, *the ghost of the dead king of Denmark visits his son, Prince Hamlet, and urges him to avenge his murder.*

**aver** (verb) To claim to be true; to avouch. *The fact that the key witness averred the defendant's innocence is what ultimately swayed the jury to deliver a "not guilty" verdict.*

**avow** (verb) To declare boldly. *Immediately after Cyrus avowed his atheism at our church fund-raiser, there was a long, uncomfortable silence.* avowal (noun), avowed (adjective).

## B

**barren** (adjective) Desolate; infertile. *The subarctic tundra is a barren wasteland inhabited only by lichens and mosses. Women who try to conceive in their 40s are often barren and must turn to artificial means of producing a child.*

**belligerent** (adjective) Quarrelsome, combative. *Mrs. Juniper was so belligerent toward the clerks at the local stores that they cringed when they saw her coming.*

**belligerent** (noun) An opposing army, a party waging war. *The Union and Confederate forces were the belligerents in the American Civil War.*

**benevolent** (adjective) Wishing or doing good. *In old age, Carnegie used his wealth for benevolent purposes, donating large sums to found libraries and schools around the country.* benevolence (noun).

**berate** (verb) To scold or criticize harshly. *The judge angrily berated the two lawyers for their childish and unprofessional behavior.*

**boggle** (verb) To overwhelm with amazement. *The ability of physicists to isolate the most infinitesimal particles of matter truly boggles the mind.*

**bogus** (adjective) Phony, a sham. *Senior citizens are often the target of telemarketing scams pushing bogus investment opportunities.*

**bombastic** (adjective) Inflated or pompous in style. *Old-fashioned bombastic political speeches don't work on television, which demands a more intimate, personal style of communication.* bombast (noun).

**boor** (noun) Crude, insensitive, and overbearing. *Harold was well-known to be a boor; at parties he horrified people with stories of his past sexual exploits and old, off-color jokes.* boorish (adjective).

**brazenly** (adverb) Acting with disrespectful boldness. *Some say that the former White House intern brazenly threw herself at the president, but the American public will probably never know the full truth.* brazen (adjective).

**broach** (verb) To bring up an issue for discussion, to propose. *Knowing my father's strictness about adhering to a budget, I just can't seem to broach the subject of my massive credit-card debt.*

**burgeon** (verb) To bloom, literally or figuratively. *Due to the extremely mild winter, the forsythia burgeoned as early as March. The story of two prison inmates in Manuel Puig's play* The Kiss of the Spider Woman *is testimony that tenderness can burgeon in the most unlikely places.*

## WORD ORIGIN

Latin *bene* = well. Also found in English *benediction, benefactor, beneficent, beneficial, benefit,* and *benign.*

**burnish** (verb) To shine by polishing, literally or figuratively. *After stripping seven layers of old paint off the antique door, the carpenter stained the wood and burnished it to a rich hue. When Bill Gates, the wealthiest man in the country, decided to endorse the Big Bertha line of golf clubs, many suggested that he was trying to burnish his image as a "regular guy."*

**buttress** (noun) Something that supports or strengthens. *The endorsement of the American Medical Association is a powerful buttress for the claims made on behalf of this new medicine.* buttress (verb).

# C

**cacophony** (noun) Discordant sounds; dissonance. *In the minutes before classes start, the high school's halls are filled with a cacophony of shrieks, shouts, banging locker doors, and pounding feet.* cacophonous (adjective).

**cadge** (verb) To beg for, to sponge. *Few in our crowd want to go out on the town with Piper, since he routinely cadges cigarettes, subway tokens, and drinks.*

**calibrate** (verb) To determine or mark graduations (of a measuring instrument); to adjust or finely tune. *We tried to calibrate the heating to Rufus's liking, but he still ended up shivering in our living room.* calibration (noun).

**castigate** (verb) To chastise; to punish severely. *The editor castigated Bob for repeatedly failing to meet his deadlines.* castigation (noun).

**catalytic** (adjective) Bringing about, causing, or producing some result. *The conditions for revolution existed in America by 1765; the disputes about taxation that arose during the following decade were the catalytic events that sparked the rebellion.* catalyze (verb).

WORD ORIGIN
Greek *kaustikos* = burning.
Also found in English *holocaust.*

**caustic** (adjective) Burning, corrosive. *No pretensions were safe when the famous satirist H. L. Mencken unleashed his caustic wit.*

**chaos** (noun) Disorder, confusion, chance. *The first few moments after the explosion were pure chaos: no one was sure what had happened, and the area was filled with people running and yelling.* chaotic (adjective).

**charisma** (noun) Dynamic charm or appeal. *Eva Peron was such a fiery orator and had so much charisma that she commanded an enormous political following.* charismatic (adjective).

**chary** (adjective) Slow to accept, cautious. *Yuan was chary about going out with Xinhua, since she had been badly hurt in her previous relationship.*

**chronology** (noun) An arrangement of events by order of occurrence, a list of dates; the science of time. *If you ask Susan about her two-year-old son, she will give you a chronology of his accomplishments and childhood illnesses, from the day he was born to the present. The village of Copan was where Mayan astronomical learning, as applied to chronology, achieved its most accurate expression in the famous Mayan calendar.* chronological (adjective).

**churlish** (adjective) Coarse and ill-mannered. *Few journalists were eager to interview the aging film star, since he was reputed to be a churlish, uncooperative subject.* churl (noun).

**circumspect** (adjective) Prudent, cautious. *After he had been acquitted of the sexual harassment charge, the sergeant realized he would have to be more circumspect in his dealings with the female cadets.* circumspection (noun).

**cleave** (verb) NOTE: A tricky verb that can mean either to stick closely together or to split apart. (Pay attention to context.) *The more abusive his father became, the more Timothy cleaved to his mother and refused to let her out of his sight. Sometimes a few words carelessly spoken are enough to cleave a married couple and leave the relationship in shambles.* cleavage (noun).

**coagulant** (noun) Any material that causes another to thicken or clot. *Hemophilia is characterized by excessive bleeding from even the slightest cut, and is caused by a lack of one of the coagulants necessary for blood clotting.* coagulate (verb).

**coalesce** (verb) To fuse, to unite. *The music we know as jazz coalesced from diverse elements from many musical cultures, including those of West Africa, America, and Europe.* coalescence (noun).

**coerce** (verb) To force someone either to do something or to refrain from doing something. *The Miranda ruling prevents police from coercing a confession by forcing them to read criminals their rights.* coercion (noun).

**cogent** (adjective) Forceful and convincing. *The committee members were won over to the project by the cogent arguments of the chairman.* cogency (noun).

**commensurate** (adjective) Aligned with, proportional. *Many Ph.D.s in the humanities do not feel their paltry salaries are commensurate with their abilities, their experience, or the heavy workload they are asked to bear.*

**commingle** (verb) To blend, to mix. *Just as he had when he was only 5 years old, Elmer did not allow any of the foods on his plate to commingle: the beans must not merge with the rice nor the chicken rub shoulders with the broccoli!*

**complaisant** (adjective) Tending to bow to others' wishes; amiable. *Of the two Dashwood sisters, Elinor was the more complaisant, often putting the strictures of society and family above her own desires.* complaisance (noun).

**compound** (verb) To intensify, to exacerbate. *When you make a faux pas, my father advised me, don't compound the problem by apologizing profusely; just say you're sorry and get on with life!*

**conceivable** (adjective) Possible, imaginable. *It's possible to find people with every conceivable interest by surfing the Web—from fans of minor film stars to those who study the mating habits of crustaceans.* conception (noun).

**concur** (verb) To agree, to approve. *We concur that a toddler functions best on a fairly reliable schedule; however, my husband tends to be a bit more rigid than I am.* concurrence (noun).

**condensation** (noun) A reduction to a denser form (from steam to water); an abridgment of a literary work. *The condensation of humidity on the car's windshield made it difficult for me to see the road. It seems as though every beach house I've ever rented features a shelf full of* Reader's Digest *condensations of B-grade novels.* condense (verb).

**condescending** (adjective) Having an attitude of superiority toward another; patronizing. *"What a cute little car!" she remarked in a condescending fashion. "I suppose it's the nicest one someone like you could afford!"* condescension (noun).

**condone** (verb) To overlook, to permit to happen. *Schools with Zero Tolerance policies do not condone alcohol, drugs, vandalism, or violence on school grounds.*

**congruent** (adjective) Coinciding; harmonious. *Fortunately, the two employees who had been asked to organize the department had congruent views on the budget.* congruence (noun).

WORD ORIGIN
Latin *jungere* = to join. Also found in English *injunction*, *junction*, and *juncture*.

**conjunction** (noun) The occurrence of two or more events together in time or space; in astronomy, the point at which two celestial bodies have the least separation. *Low inflation, occurring in conjunction with low unemployment and relatively low interest rates, has enabled the United States to enjoy a long period of sustained economic growth. The moon is in conjunction with the sun when it is new; if the conjunction is perfect, an eclipse of the sun will occur.* conjoin (verb).

**consolation** (noun) Relief or comfort in sorrow or suffering. *Although we miss our dog very much, it is a consolation to know that she died quickly, without much suffering.* console (verb).

**consternation** (noun) Shock, amazement, dismay. *When a voice in the back of the church shouted out "I know why they should not be married!" the entire gathering was thrown into consternation.*

**convergence** (noun) The act of coming together in unity or similarity. *A remarkable example of evolutionary convergence can be seen in the shark and the dolphin, two sea creatures that developed from different origins to become very similar in form and appearance.* converge (verb).

WORD ORIGIN
Latin *vivere* = to live. Also found in English *revive*, *vital*, *vivid*, and *vivisection*.

**conviviality** (noun) Fond of good company and eating and drinking. *The conviviality of my fellow employees seemed to turn every staff meeting into a party, complete with snacks, drinks, and lots of hearty laughter.* convivial (adjective).

**convoluted** (adjective) Twisting, complicated, intricate. *Income tax law has become so convoluted that it's easy for people to violate it completely by accident.* convolute (verb), convolution (noun).

WORD ORIGIN
Latin *volvere* = to roll. Also found in English *devolve*, *involve*, *revolution*, *revolve*, and *voluble*.

**cordon** (verb) To form a protective or restrictive barrier. *Well before the Academy Awards ceremony began, the police cordoned off the hordes of fans who were desperate to ogle the arriving stars.* cordon (noun).

**corral** (verb) To enclose, to collect, to gather. *Tyrone couldn't enjoy the wedding at all, since he spent most of his time corralling his two children into the reception room and preventing them from running amok through the Potters' mansion.* corral (noun).

**corroborating** (adjective) Supporting with evidence; confirming. *A passerby who had witnessed the crime gave corroborating testimony about the presence of the accused person.* corroborate (verb), corroboration (noun).

**corrosive** (adjective) Eating away, gnawing, or destroying. *Years of poverty and hard work had a corrosive effect on her strength and beauty.* corrode (verb), corrosion (noun).

**cosmopolitanism** (noun) International sophistication; worldliness. *Budapest is known for its cosmopolitanism, perhaps because it was the first Eastern European city to be more open to capitalism and influences from the West.* cosmopolitan (adjective).

**covert** (adjective) Secret, clandestine. *The CIA has often been criticized for its covert operations in the domestic policies of foreign countries, such as the failed Bay of Pigs operation in Cuba.*

**covetous** (adjective) Envious, particularly of another's possessions. *Benita would never admit to being covetous of my new sable jacket, but I found it odd that she couldn't refrain from trying it on each time we met.* covet (verb).

**craven** (adjective) Cowardly. *Local firefighters were outraged by the craven behavior of a police officer who refused to come to the aid of an HIV-positive accident victim.*

**credulous** (adjective) Ready to believe; gullible. *Elaine was not very credulous of the explanation Serge gave for his acquisition of the Matisse lithograph.* credulity (noun).

**cryptic** (adjective) Puzzling, ambiguous. *I was puzzled by the cryptic message left on my answering machine about the arrival of "a shipment of pomegranates from an anonymous donor."*

**culmination** (noun) The climax. *The Los Angeles riots, in the aftermath of the Rodney King verdict, were the culmination of long-standing racial tensions between the residents of South Central LA and the police.* culminate (verb).

**culpable** (adjective) Deserving blame, guilty. *Although he committed the crime, because he was mentally ill he should not be considered culpable for his actions.* culpability (noun).

**curmudgeon** (noun) A crusty, ill-tempered person. *Todd hated to drive with his Uncle Jasper, a notorious curmudgeon, who complained nonstop about the air-conditioning and Todd's driving.* curmudgeonly (adjective).

**cursory** (adjective) Hasty and superficial. *Detective Martinez was rebuked by his superior officer for drawing conclusions about the murder after only a cursory examination of the crime scene.*

WORD ORIGIN

Latin *credere* = to believe. Also found in English *credential, credible, credit, credo, credulous,* and *incredible.*

**D**

**debilitating** (adjective) Weakening; sapping the strength of. *One can't help but marvel at the courage Steven Hawking displays in the face of such a debilitating disease as ALS.* debilitate (verb).

WORD ORIGIN

Latin *celer* = swift. Also found in English *accelerate* and *celerity*.

**decelerate** (verb) To slow down. *Randall didn't decelerate enough on the winding roads, and he ended up smashing his new sport utility vehicle into a guard rail.* deceleration (noun).

**decimation** (noun) Almost complete destruction. *Michael Moore's documentary,* Roger and Me, *chronicles the decimation of the economy of Flint, Michigan, after the closing of a General Motors factory.* decimate (verb).

**decry** (verb) To criticize or condemn. *Cigarette ads aimed at youngsters have led many to decry the unfair marketing tactics of the tobacco industry.*

**defamation** (noun) Act of harming someone by libel or slander. *When the article in* The National Enquirer *implied that she was somehow responsible for her husband's untimely death, Renata instructed her lawyer to sue the paper for defamation of character.* defame (verb).

**defer** (verb) To graciously submit to another's will; to delegate. *In all matters relating to the children's religious education, Joy deferred to her husband, since he clearly cared more about giving them a solid grounding in Judaism.* deference (noun).

**deliberate** (verb) To think about an issue before reaching a decision. *The legal pundits covering the O.J. Simpson trial were shocked by the short time the jury took to deliberate after a trial that lasted months.* deliberation (noun).

**demagogue** (noun) A leader who plays dishonestly on the prejudices and emotions of his followers. *Senator Joseph McCarthy was a demagogue who used the paranoia and biases of the anti-Communist 1950s as a way of seizing fame and considerable power in Washington.* demagoguery (noun).

WORD ORIGIN

Greek *demos* = people. Also found in English *democracy, demographic,* and *endemic*.

**demographic** (adjective) Relating to the statistical study of population. *Three demographic groups have been the intense focus of marketing strategy: baby boomers, born between 1946 and 1964; baby busters, or the Generation X, born between 1965 and 1976; and a group referred to as Generation Y, those born between 1976 and 2000.* demography (noun), demographics (noun).

**demonstratively** (adverb) Openly displaying feeling. *The young congressman demonstratively campaigned for reelection, kissing every baby and hugging every senior citizen at the Saugerties Chrysanthemum festival.* demonstrative (adjective).

**derisive** (adjective) Expressing ridicule or scorn. *Many women's groups were derisive of Avon's choice of a male CEO, since the company derives its $5.1 billion in sales from an army of female salespeople.* derision (noun).

**derivative** (adjective) Imitating or borrowed from a particular source. *When a person first writes poetry, her poems are apt to be derivative of whatever poetry she most enjoys reading.* derivation (noun), derive (verb).

**desiccate** (verb) To dry out, to wither; to drain of vitality. *The long drought thoroughly desiccated our garden; what was once a glorious Eden was now a scorched and hellish wasteland. A recent spate of books has debunked the myth that menopause desiccates women and affirmed, instead, that women often reach heights of creativity in their later years.* desiccant (noun), desiccation (noun).

**despotic** (adjective) Oppressive and tyrannical. *During the despotic reign of Idi Amin in the 1970s, an estimated 200,000 Ugandans were killed.* despot (noun).

**desultory** (adjective) Disconnected, aimless. *Tina's few desultory stabs at conversation fell flat as Guy just sat there, stone-faced; it was a disastrous first date.*

**deviate** (verb) To depart from a standard or norm. *Having agreed upon a spending budget for the company, we mustn't deviate from it; if we do, we may run out of money before the year ends.* deviation (noun).

**diatribe** (noun) Abusive or bitter speech or writing. *While angry conservatives dismissed Susan Faludi's* Backlash *as a feminist diatribe, it is actually a meticulously researched book.*

**diffident** (adjective) Hesitant, reserved, shy. *Someone with a diffident personality is most likely to succeed in a career that involves very little public contact.* diffidence (noun).

**digress** (verb) To wander from the main path or the main topic. *My high school biology teacher loved to digress from science into personal anecdotes about his college adventures.* digression (noun), digressive (adjective).

**dirge** (noun) Song or hymn of grief. *When Princess Diana was killed in a car crash, Elton John resurrected his hit song "Candle in the Wind," rewrote it as "Good-bye England's Rose," and created one of the most widely heard funeral dirges of all time.*

**disabuse** (verb) To correct a fallacy, to clarify. *I hated to disabuse Filbert, who is a passionate collector of musical trivia, but I had to tell him that the Monkees had hardly sung a note and had lip-synched their way through almost all of their albums.*

**disburse** (verb) To pay out or distribute (funds or property). *Jaime was flabbergasted when his father's will disbursed all of the old man's financial assets to Raymundo and left him with only a few sticks of furniture.* disbursement (noun).

**discern** (verb) To detect, notice, or observe. *With difficulty, I could discern the shape of a whale off the starboard bow, but it was too far away to determine its size or species.* discernment (noun).

**discordant** (adjective) Characterized by conflict. *Stories and films about discordant relationships that resolve themselves happily are always more interesting than stories about content couples who simply stay content.* discordance (noun).

**discourse** (noun) Formal and orderly exchange of ideas, a discussion. *In the late twentieth century, cloning and other feats of genetic engineering became popular topics of public discourse.* discursive (adjective).

**discredit** (verb) To cause disbelief in the accuracy of some statement or the reliability of a person. *Although many people still believe in UFOs, among scientists the reports of "alien encounters" have been thoroughly discredited.*

**discreet** (adjective) Showing good judgment in speech and behavior. *Be discreet when discussing confidential business matters—don't talk among strangers on the elevator, for example.* discretion (noun).

**discrete** (adjective) Separate, unconnected. *Canadians get peeved when people can't seem to distinguish between Canada and the United States, forgetting that Canada has its own discrete heritage and culture.*

**disparity** (noun) Difference in quality or kind. *There is often a disparity between the kind of serious, high-quality television people say they want and the low-brow programs they actually watch.* disparate (adjective).

WORD ORIGIN

Latin *simulare* = to resemble. Also found in English *semblance, similarity, simulacrum, simultaneous,* and *verisimilitude.*

**dissemble** (verb) To pretend, to simulate. *When the police asked whether Nancy knew anything about the crime, she dissembled innocence.*

**dissipate** (verb) To spread out or scatter. *The windows and doors were opened, allowing the smoke that had filled the room to dissipate.* dissipation (noun).

**dissonance** (noun) Lack of music harmony; lack of agreement between ideas. *Most modern music is characterized by dissonance, which many listeners find hard to enjoy. There is a noticeable dissonance between two common beliefs of most conservatives: their faith in unfettered free markets and their preference for traditional social values.* dissonant (adjective).

**distillation** (noun) Something distilled, an essence or extract. In chemistry, a process that drives gas or vapor from liquids or solids. *Sharon Olds's poems are powerful distillations of motherhood and other primal experiences. In Mrs. Hornmeister's chemistry class, our first experiment was to create a distillation of carbon gas from wood.* distill (verb).

**diverge** (verb) To move in different directions. *Frost's poem "The Road Not Taken" tells of the choice he made when "Two roads diverged in a yellow wood."* divergence (noun), divergent (adjective).

**diversify** (verb) To balance by adding variety. *Any financial manager will recommend that you diversify your stock portfolio by holding some less-volatile blue-chip stocks along with more growth-oriented technology issues.* diversification (noun), diversified (adjective).

**divest** (verb) To rid (oneself) or be freed of property, authority, or title. *In order to turn around its ailing company and concentrate on imaging, Eastman Kodak divested itself of peripheral businesses in the areas of household products, clinical diagnostics, and pharmaceuticals.* divestiture (noun).

**divulge** (verb) To reveal. *The people who count the votes for the Oscar® awards are under strict orders not to divulge the names of the winners.*

**dogmatic** (adjective) Holding firmly to a particular set of beliefs with little or no basis. *Believers in Marxist doctrine tend to be dogmatic, ignoring evidence that contradicts their beliefs or explaining it away.* dogma (noun), dogmatism (noun).

**dolt** (noun) A stupid or foolish person. *Due to his frequent verbal blunders, politician Dan Quayle was widely considered to be a dolt.*

**dormant** (adjective) Temporarily inactive, as if asleep. *An eruption of Mt. Rainier, a dormant volcano in Washington state, would cause massive, life-threatening mud slides in the surrounding area. Bill preferred to think that his math skills were dormant rather than extinct.* dormancy (noun).

WORD ORIGIN
Latin *dormire* = to sleep. Also found in English *dormitory*.

**dross** (noun) Something that is trivial or inferior; an impurity. *As a reader for the Paris Review, Julia spent most of her time sifting through piles of manuscripts to separate the extraordinary poems from the dross.*

**dubious** (adjective) Doubtful, uncertain. *Despite the chairman's attempts to convince the committee members that his plan would succeed, most of them remained dubious.* dubiety (noun).

**dupe** (noun) Someone who is easily cheated. *My cousin Ravi is such a dupe; he actually gets excited when he receives those envelopes saying "Ravi Murtugudde, you may have won a million dollars," and he even goes so far as to try claiming his prize.*

## E

**eccentricity** (noun) Odd or whimsical behavior. *The rock star is now better known for his offstage eccentricities—such as sleeping in a tent, wearing goggles, and building his own steamship—than for his on-stage performances.* eccentric (adjective).

**edifying** (adjective) Instructive, enlightening. *Ariel would never admit it to her high-brow friends, but she found the latest self-help best-seller edifying and actually helpful.* edification (noun), edify (verb).

**efficacy** (noun) The power to produce the desired effect. *While teams have been enormously popular in the workplace, there are some who now question their efficacy and say that "one head is better than ten."* efficacious (noun).

WORD ORIGIN
Latin *facere* = to do. Also found in English *facility*, *factor*, *facsimile*, and *faculty*.

**effrontery** (noun) Shameless boldness. *The sports world was shocked when a pro basketball player had the effrontery to choke the head coach of his team during a practice session.*

**elaborate** (verb) To expand upon something; develop. *One characteristic of the best essayists is their ability to elaborate ideas through examples, lists, similes, small variations, and even exaggerations.* elaborate (adjective), elaboration (noun).

**elegy** (noun) A song or poem expressing sorrow. *Thomas Gray's "Elegy Written in a Country Churchyard," one of the most famous elegies in Western literature, mourns the unsung, inglorious lives of the souls buried in an obscure, rustic graveyard.* elegiac (adjective).

**embellish** (verb) To enhance or exaggerate; to decorate. *The long-married couple told their stories in tandem, with the husband outlining the plot and the wife embellishing it with colorful details.*

**embellished** (adjective). To make beautiful with ornamentation. To heighten attractiveness by adding decorative details. *Both Salman Rushdie, of India, and Patrick Chamoiseau, of Martinique, emerged from colonized countries and created embellished versions of their colonizers' languages in their novels.*

**embezzle** (verb) To steal money or property that has been entrusted to your care. *The church treasurer was found to have embezzled thousands of dollars by writing phony checks on the church bank account.* embezzlement (noun).

**emollient** (noun) Something that softens or soothes. *She used a hand cream as an emollient on her dry, work-roughened hands.* emollient (adjective).

**empirical** (adjective) Based on experience or personal observation. *Although many people believe in ESP, scientists have found no empirical evidence of its existence.* empiricism (noun).

**emulate** (verb) To imitate or copy. *The British band Oasis is quite open about their desire to emulate their idols, the Beatles.* emulation (noun).

**encomium** (noun) A formal expression of praise. *For many filmmakers, winning the Palm d'Or at the Cannes Film Festival is considered the highest encomium.*

**enervate** (verb) To reduce the energy or strength of someone or something. *The stress of the operation left her feeling enervated for about two weeks.* enervation (noun).

**engender** (verb) To produce, to cause. *Countless disagreements over the proper use of national forests and parklands have engendered feelings of hostility between ranchers and environmentalists.*

**enhance** (verb) To improve in value or quality. *New kitchen appliances will enhance your house and increase the amount of money you'll make when you sell it.* enhancement (noun).

**enigmatic** (adjective) Puzzling, mysterious. *Alain Resnais's enigmatic film* Last Year at Marienbad *sets up a puzzle that is never resolved: a man meets a woman at a hotel and believes he once had an affair with her—or did he?* enigma (noun).

**enmity** (noun) Hatred, hostility, ill will. *Long-standing enmity, like that between the Protestants and Catholics in Northern Ireland, is difficult to overcome.*

**ensure** (verb) To make certain; to guarantee. *In order to ensure a sufficient crop of programmers and engineers for the future, the United States needs to raise the quality of its math and science schooling.*

**epicure** (noun) Someone who appreciates fine wine and fine food, a gourmand. *M.F.K. Fisher, a famous epicure, begins her book* The Gastronomical Me *by saying, "There is a communion of more than bodies when bread is broken and wine is drunk."* epicurean (adjective).

**epithet** (noun) Term or words used to characterize a person or thing, often in a disparaging way. *The police chief reminded the new recruits that there is no place for racial epithets in their vocabulary.* epithetical (adjective).

**equable** (adjective) Steady, uniform. *While many people can't see how Helena could possibly be attracted to "Boring Bruno," his equable nature is the perfect complement to her volatile personality.*

WORD ORIGIN
Latin *aequus* = equal. Also found in English *equality*, *equanimity*, and *equation*.

**equivocate** (verb) To use misleading or intentionally confusing language. *When Pedro pressed Renee for an answer to his marriage proposal, she equivocated by saying, "I've just got to know when your Mercedes will be out of the shop!"* equivocal (adjective), equivocation (noun).

**eradicate** (verb) To destroy completely. *American society has failed to eradicate racism, although some of its worst effects have been reduced.* eradication (noun).

WORD ORIGIN
Latin *radix* = root. Also found in English *radical*.

**erudition** (noun) Extensive knowledge, usually acquired from books. *When Dorothea first saw Mr. Casaubon's voluminous library she was awed, but after their marriage she quickly realized that erudition is no substitute for originality.* erudite (adjective).

**esoterica** (noun) Items of interest to a select group. *The fish symposium at St. Antony's College in Oxford explored all manner of esoterica relating to fish, as is evidenced in presentations such as "The Buoyant Slippery Lipids of the Escolar and Orange Roughy," or "Food on Board Whale Ships—from the Inedible to the Incredible."* esoteric (adjective).

**espouse** (verb) To take up as a cause; to adopt. *No politician in American today will openly espouse racism, although some behave and speak in racially prejudiced ways.*

**estimable** (adjective) Worthy of esteem and admiration. *After a tragic fire raged through Malden Mills, the estimable mill owner, Aaron Feuerstein, restarted operations and rebuilt the company within just one month.* esteem (noun).

**eulogy** (noun) A formal tribute usually delivered at a funeral. *Most people in Britain applauded Lord Earl Spencer's eulogy for Princess Diana, not only as a warm tribute to his sister Diana, but also as a biting indictment of the Royal Family.* eulogize (verb).

**euphemism** (noun) An agreeable expression that is substituted for an offensive one. *Some of the more creative euphemisms for "layoffs" in current use are: "release of resources," "involuntary severance," "strengthening global effectiveness," and "career transition program."* euphemistic (adjective).

**exacerbate** (verb) To make worse or more severe. *The roads in our town already have too much traffic; building a new shopping mall will exacerbate the problem.*

WORD ORIGIN
Latin *acer* = sharp. Also found in English *acerbity*, *acrid*, and *acrimonious*.

**excoriation** (noun) The act of condemning someone with harsh words. *In the small office we shared, it was painful to hear my boss's constant excoriation of his assistant for the smallest faults—a misdirected letter, an unclear phone message, or even a tepid cup of coffee.* excoriate (verb).

**exculpate** (verb) To free from blame or guilt. *When someone else confessed to the crime, the previous suspect was exculpated.* exculpation (noun), exculpatory (adjective).

**executor** (noun) The person appointed to execute someone's will. *As the executor of his aunt Ida's will, Phil must deal with squabbling relatives, conniving lawyers, and the ruinous state of Ida's house.*

**exigent** (adjective) Urgent, requiring immediate attention. *A two-year-old is likely to behave as if her every demand is exigent, even if it involves simply retrieving a beloved stuffed hedgehog from under the couch.* exigency (noun).

**expedient** (adjective) Providing an immediate advantage or serving one's immediate self-interest. *When the passenger next to her was hit by a bullet, Sharon chose the most expedient means to stop the bleeding; she whipped off her pantyhose and made an impromptu, but effective, tourniquet.* expediency (noun).

**extant** (adjective) Currently in existence. *Of the seven ancient "Wonders of the World," only the pyramids of Egypt are still extant.*

**WORD ORIGIN**
Latin *tenere* = to hold. Also found in English *retain, tenable, tenant, tenet,* and *tenure.*

**extenuate** (verb) To make less serious. *Karen's guilt is extenuated by the fact that she was only twelve when she committed the theft.* extenuating (adjective), extenuation (noun).

**extol** (verb) To greatly praise. *At the party convention, one speaker after another took to the podium to extol the virtues of their candidate for the presidency.*

**extraneous** (adjective) Irrelevant, nonessential. *One review of the new Chekhov biography said the author had bogged down the book with far too many extraneous details, such as the dates of Chekhov's bouts of diarrhea.*

**extrapolate** (verb) To deduce from something known, to infer. *Meteorologists were able to use old weather records to extrapolate backward and compile lists of El Niño years and their effects over the last century.* extrapolation (noun).

**extricate** (verb) To free from a difficult or complicated situation. *Much of the humor in the TV show* I Love Lucy *comes in watching Lucy try to extricate herself from the problems she creates by fibbing or trickery.* extricable (adjective).

## F

**facetious** (adjective) Humorous in a mocking way; not serious. *French composer Erik Satie often concealed his serious artistic intent by giving his works facetious titles such as "Three Pieces in the Shape of a Pear."*

**facilitate** (verb) To make easier or to moderate. *When the issue of racism reared its ugly head, the company brought in a consultant to facilitate a discussion of diversity in the workplace.* facile (adjective), facility (noun).

**fallacy** (noun) An error in fact or logic. *It's a fallacy to think that "natural" means "healthful"; after all, the deadly poison arsenic is completely natural.* fallacious (adjective).

**fatuous** (adjective) Inanely foolish; silly. *Once backstage, Elizabeth showered the opera singer with fatuous praise and embarrassing confessions, which he clearly had no interest in hearing.*

**fawn** (verb) To flatter in a particularly subservient manner. *Mildly disgusted, Pedro stood alone at the bar and watched Renee fawn over the heir to the Fabco Surgical Appliances fortune.*

**feckless** (adjective) Weak and ineffective; irresponsible. *Our co-op board president is a feckless fellow who has let much-needed repairs go unattended while our maintenance fees continue to rise.*

**feint** (noun) A bluff; a mock blow. *It didn't take us long to realize that Gaby's tears and stomach aches were all a feint, since they appeared so regularly at her bedtime.*

**ferret** (verb) To bring to light by an extensive search. *With his repeated probing and questions, Fritz was able to ferret out the location of Myrna's safe deposit box.*

**finesse** (noun) Skillful maneuvering; delicate workmanship. *With her usual finesse, Charmaine gently persuaded the Duncans not to install a motorized Santa and sleigh on their front lawn.*

**florid** (adjective) Flowery, fancy; reddish. *The grand ballroom was decorated in a florid style. Years of heavy drinking had given him a florid complexion.*

**flourish** (noun) An extraneous embellishment; a dramatic gesture. *The napkin rings made out of intertwined ferns and flowers were just the kind of flourish one would expect from Carol, a slavish follower of the home and garden TV show.*

**fluctuation** (noun) A shifting back and forth. *Investment analysts predict fluctuations in the Dow Jones Industrial Average due to the instability of the value of the dollar.* fluctuate (verb).

**foil** (verb) To thwart or frustrate. *I was certain that Jerry's tendency to insert himself into everyone's conversations would foil my chances to have a private word with Helen.*

**foment** (verb) To rouse or incite. *The petty tyrannies and indignities inflicted on the workers by upper management helped foment the walkout at the meat-processing plant.*

**forestall** (verb) To hinder or prevent by taking action in advance. *The pilot's calm, levelheaded demeanor during the turbulence forestalled any hysteria among the passengers of Flight 268.*

**fortuitous** (adjective) Lucky, fortunate. *Although the mayor claimed credit for the falling crime rate, it was really caused by a series of fortuitous accidents.*

**foster** (verb) To nurture or encourage. *The white-water rafting trip was supposed to foster creative problem-solving and teamwork between the account executives and the creative staff at Apex Advertising Agency.*

**WORD ORIGIN**
Latin *fluere* = to flow. Also found in English *affluent*, *effluvia*, *fluid*, and *influx*.

**fracas** (noun) A noisy fight; a brawl. *As Bill approached the stadium ticket window, he was alarmed to see the fracas that had broken out between a group of Giants fans and a man wearing a Cowboys jersey and helmet.*

**functionary** (noun) Someone holding office in a political party or government. *The man shaking hands with the governor was a low-ranking Democratic Party functionary who had worked to garner the Hispanic vote.*

## G

**gainsay** (verb) To contradict or oppose; deny, dispute. *Dot would gainsay her married sister's efforts to introduce her to eligible men by refusing to either leave her ailing canary or give up her thrice-weekly bingo nights.*

**garble** (verb) To distort or slur. *No matter how much money the Metropolitan Transit Authority spends on improving the subway trains, the public address system in almost every station seems to garble each announcement.* garbled (adjective).

**garrulous** (adjective) Annoyingly talkative. *Claude pretended to be asleep so he could avoid his garrulous seatmate, a self-proclaimed expert on bonsai cultivation.*

**generic** (adjective) General; having no brand name. *Connie tried to reduce her grocery bills by religiously clipping coupons and buying generic brands of most products.*

**WORD ORIGIN**
Latin *genus* = type or kind; birth. Also found in English *congenital, genetic, genital, genre, genuine,* and *genus.*

**gist** (noun) The main point, the essence. *Although they felt sympathy for the victim's family, the jurors were won over by the gist of the defense's argument: there was insufficient evidence to convict.*

**gouge** (verb) To cut out, to scoop out with one's thumbs or a sharp instrument; to overcharge, to cheat. *Instead of picking the lock with a credit card, the clumsy thieves gouged a hole in my door. The consumer watchdog group accused the clothing stores of gouging customers with high prices.*

**guile** (noun) Deceit, duplicity. *In Margaret Mitchell's* Gone With the Wind, *Scarlett O'Hara uses her guile to manipulate two men and then is matched for wits by a third: Rhett Butler.* guileful (adjective).

**gullible** (adjective) Easily fooled. *Terry was so gullible she actually believed Robert's stories of his connections to the Czar and Czarina.* gullibility (noun).

## H

**hackneyed** (adjective) Without originality, trite. *When someone invented the phrase "No pain, no gain," it was clever and witty, but now it is so commonly heard that it seems hackneyed.*

**harrow** (verb) To cultivate with a harrow; to torment or vex. *During grade school, my sister was harrowed mercilessly for being overweight.*

**harrowing** (adjective) Nerve-wracking, traumatic. *Jon Krakauer's best-selling book* Into Thin Air *chronicles the tragic consequences of leading groups of untrained climbers up Mt. Everest.*

**haughty** (adjective) Overly proud. *The fashion model strode down the runway, her hips thrust forward and a haughty expression, something like a sneer, on her face.* haughtiness (noun).

**hierarchy** (noun) A ranking of people, things, or ideas from highest to lowest. *A cabinet secretary ranks just below the president and vice president in the hierarchy of the government's executive branch.* hierarchical (adjective).

**homogeneous** (adjective) Uniform, made entirely of one thing. *It's hard to think of a more homogenous group than those eerie children in* Village of the Damned, *who all had perfect features, white-blond hair, and silver, penetrating eyes.*

WORD ORIGIN

Greek *homos* = same. Also found in English *homologous*, *homonym*, and *homosexual*.

**hone** (verb) To improve and make more acute or affective. *While she was a receptionist, Norma honed her skills as a stand-up comic by trying out jokes on the tense crowd in the waiting room.*

**hoodwink** (verb) To deceive by trickery or false appearances; to dupe. *That was my cousin Ravi calling to say that he's been hoodwinked again, this time by some outfit offering time shares in a desolate tract of land in central Florida.*

## I

**iconoclast** (noun) Someone who attacks traditional beliefs or institutions. *Comedian Dennis Miller relishes his reputation as an iconoclast, though people in power often resent his satirical jabs.* iconoclasm (noun), iconoclastic (adjective).

**idolatry** (noun) The worship of a person, thing, or institution as a god. *In communist China, admiration for Mao resembled idolatry; his picture was displayed everywhere, and millions of Chinese memorized his sayings and repeated them endlessly.* idolatrous (adjective).

**idyll** (noun) A rustic, romantic interlude; poetry or prose that celebrates simple pastoral life. *Her picnic with Max at Fahnstock Lake was not the serene idyll she had envisioned; instead, they were surrounded by hundreds of other picnickers blaring music from their boom boxes and cracking open soda cans.* idyllic (adjective).

**illicit** (adjective) Illegal, wrongful. *When Janet caught her 13-year-old son and his friend downloading illicit pornographic photos from the Web, she promptly pulled the plug on his computer.*

**illuminate** (verb) To brighten with light; to enlighten or elucidate; to decorate (a manuscript). *The frosted-glass sconces in the dressing rooms at Le Cirque not only illuminate the rooms but make everyone look like a movie star. Alice Munro is a writer who can illuminate an entire character with a few deft sentences.*

**immaculate** (adjective) Totally unblemished, spotlessly clean. *The cream-colored upholstery in my new Porsche was immaculate—that is, until a raccoon came in through the window and tracked mud across the seats.*

**immaterial** (adjective) Of no consequence, unimportant. *"The fact that your travel agent is your best friend's son should be immaterial," I told Rosa. "So, if he keeps putting you on hold and acting nasty, just take your business elsewhere."*

WORD ORIGIN

Latin *mutare* = to change. Also found in English *immutable, mutant,* and *mutation.*

**immutable** (adjective) Incapable of change. *Does there ever come an age when we realize that our parents' personalities are immutable, when we can relax and stop trying to make them change?*

**impartial** (adjective) Fair, equal, unbiased. *If a judge is not impartial, then all of her rulings are questionable.* impartiality (noun).

**impassivity** (noun) Apathy, unresponsiveness. *Dot truly thinks that Mr. Right will magically show up on her doorstep, and her utter impassivity regarding her social life makes me want to shake her!* impassive (adjective).

**imperceptible** (adjective) Impossible to perceive, inaudible or incomprehensible. *The sound of footsteps was almost imperceptible, but Donald's paranoia had reached such a pitch that he immediately assumed he was being followed.*

**imperturbable** (adjective) Cannot be disconcerted, disturbed, or excited. *The proper English butler in Kazuo Ishiguro's novel* Remains of the Day *appears completely imperturbable, even when his father dies or when his own heart is breaking.*

**impetuous** (adjective) Acting hastily or impulsively. *Ben's resignation was an impetuous act; he did it without thinking, and he soon regretted it.* impetuosity (noun).

WORD ORIGIN

Latin *placare* = to please. Also found in English *complacent, placate,* and *placid.*

**implacable** (adjective) Unbending, resolute. *The state of Israel is implacable in its policy of never negotiating with criminals.*

**implosion** (noun) To collapse inward from outside pressure. *While it is difficult to know what is going on in North Korea, no one can rule out a violent implosion of the North Korean regime and a subsequent flood of refugees across its borders.* implode (verb).

**incessant** (adjective) Unceasing. *The incessant blaring of the neighbor's car alarm made it impossible for me to concentrate on my upcoming Bar exam.*

**inchoate** (adjective) Only partly formed or formulated. *At editorial meetings, Nancy had a habit of presenting her inchoate book ideas before she had a chance to fully determine their feasibility.*

WORD ORIGIN

Latin *caedere* = to cut. Also found in English *concise, decide, excise, incision,* and *precise.*

**incise** (verb) To carve into, to engrave. *My wife felt nostalgic about the old elm tree since we had incised our initials in it when we were both in high school.*

**incisive** (adjective) Admirably direct and decisive. *Ted Koppel's incisive questions had made many politicians squirm and stammer.*

**incongruous** (adjective) Unlikely. *Art makes incongruous alliances, as when punk-rockers, Tibetan folk musicians, gospel singers, and beat poets shared the stage at the Tibet House benefit concert.* incongruity (noun).

**incorrigible** (adjective) Impossible to manage or reform. *Lou is an incorrigible trickster, constantly playing practical jokes no matter how much his friends complain.*

**incursion** (noun) A hostile entrance into a territory; a foray into an activity or venture. *It is a little-known fact that the Central Intelligence Agency organized* *military incursions into China during the 1950s. The Comic-Con convention was Barbara's first incursion into the world of comic strip artists.*

**indefatigable** (adjective) Tireless. *Eleanor Roosevelt's indefatigable dedication to the cause of human welfare won her affection and honor throughout the world.* indefatigability (noun).

**indelicate** (adjective) Blunt, undisguised. *No sooner had we sat down to eat than Mark made an indelicate remark about my high salary.*

**inevitable** (adjective) Unable to be avoided. *Once the Japanese attacked Pearl Harbor, U.S. involvement in World War II was inevitable.* inevitability (noun).

**infer** (verb) To conclude, to deduce. *Can I infer from your hostile tone of voice that you are still angry about yesterday's incident?* inference (noun).

**inimical** (adjective) Unfriendly, hostile; adverse or difficult. *Relations between Greece and Turkey have been inimical for centuries.*

**inimitable** (adjective) Incapable of being imitated, matchless. *John F. Kennedy's administration dazzled the public, partly because of the inimitable style and elegance of his wife, Jacqueline.*

**inopportune** (adjective) Awkward, untimely. *When Gus heard raised voices and the crash of breaking china behind the kitchen door, he realized that he'd picked an inopportune moment to visit the Fairlights.*

**inscrutability** (noun) Quality of being extremely difficult to interpret or understand, mysteriousness. *I am still puzzling over the inscrutability of the package I received yesterday, which contained twenty pomegranates and a note that said simply "Yours."* inscrutable (adjective).

**insensible** (adjective) Unaware, incognizant; unconscious, out cold. *It's a good thing that Marty was insensible to the titters and laughter that greeted his arrival in the ballroom. In the latest episode of gang brutality, an innocent young man was beaten insensible after two gang members stormed his apartment.*

**insinuate** (verb) Hint or intimate; to creep in. *During an extremely unusual broadcast, the newscaster insinuated that the Washington bureau chief was having a nervous breakdown. Marla managed to insinuate herself into the Duchess' conversation during the charity event.* insinuation (noun).

**insipid** (adjective) Flavorless, uninteresting. *Most TV shows are so insipid that you can watch them while reading or chatting without missing a thing.* insipidity (noun).

**insolence** (noun) An attitude or behavior that is bold and disrespectful. *Some feel that news reporters who shout accusatory questions at the president are behaving with insolence toward his high office.* insolent (adjective).

**insoluble** (adjective) Unable to be solved, irresolvable; indissoluble. *Fermat's last theorem remained insoluble for over 300 years until a young mathematician from Princeton solved it in 1995. If you are a gum chewer, you probably wouldn't like to know that insoluble plastics are a common ingredient of most popular gums.*

**insular** (adjective) Narrow or isolated in attitude or viewpoint. *New Yorkers are famous for their insular attitudes; they seem to think that nothing important has ever happened outside of their city.* insularity (noun).

**intercede** (verb) To step in, to moderate; to mediate or negotiate on behalf of someone else. *After their rejection by the co-op board, Kevin and Sol asked Rachel, another tenant, to intercede for them at the next board meeting.* intercession (noun).

**interim** (noun) A break or interlude. *In the interim between figure-skating programs, the exhausted skaters retreat to the "kiss and cry" room to wait for their scores.*

**interpolate** (verb) To interject. *The director's decision to interpolate topical political jokes into his production of Shakespeare's* Twelfth Night *was not viewed kindly by the critics.* interpolation (noun).

**intransigent** (adjective) Unwilling to compromise. *Despite the mediator's attempts to suggest a fair solution to the disagreement, the two parties were intransigent, forcing a showdown.* intransigence (noun).

**intrinsically** (adverb) Essentially, inherently. *There is nothing intrinsically difficult about upgrading a computer's microprocessor, yet Al was afraid to even open up the computer's case.* intrinsic (adjective).

WORD ORIGIN
Latin *unda* = wave. Also found in English *undulate*.

**inundate** (verb) To overwhelm; to flood. *When AOL first announced its flat-rate pricing, the company was inundated with new customers, and thus began the annoying delays in service.* inundation (noun).

**invective** (noun) Insulting, abusive language. *I remained unscathed by his blistering invective because in my heart I knew I had done the right thing.*

**invigorate** (verb) To give energy to, to stimulate. *As her car climbed the mountain road, Lucinda felt herself invigorated by the clear air and the cool breezes.* invigoration (noun).

**irascible** (adjective) Easily provoked into anger, hot-headed. *Soup chef Al Yeganah, the model for* Seinfeld's *"Soup Nazi," is an irascible man who flies into a temper tantrum if his customers don't follow his rigid procedure for purchasing soup.* irascibility (noun).

**J**

**jeopardize** (verb) To put in danger. *Terrorist attacks on civilians jeopardize the fragile peace in the Middle East.* jeopardy (noun).

**jocular** (adjective) Humorous, amusing. *Listening to the CEO launch into yet another uproarious anecdote, Ted was frankly surprised by the jocular nature of the "emergency" board meeting.* jocularity (noun).

**L**

**labyrinthine** (adjective) Extremely intricate or involved; circuitous. *Was I the only one who couldn't follow the labyrinthine plot of the movie* L.A. Confidential? *I was so confused I had to watch it twice to see "who did it."*

**laconic** (adjective) Concise to the point of terseness; taciturn. *Tall, handsome, and laconic, the actor Gary Cooper came to personify the strong, silent American, a man of action and few words.*

**lambaste** (verb) To give someone a dressing-down; to attack someone verbally; to whip. *Once inside the locker room, the coach thoroughly lambasted the team members for their incompetent performance on the football field.*

**laudable** (adjective) Commendable, praiseworthy. *The Hunt's Point nonprofit organization has embarked on a series of laudable ventures pairing businesses and disadvantaged youth.*

WORD ORIGIN
Latin *laus* = praise. Also found in English *applaud*, *laud*, *laudatory*, and *plaudit*.

**lethargic** (adjective) Lacking energy; sluggish. *Visitors to the zoo are surprised that the lions appear so lethargic, but, in the wild, lions sleep up to 18 hours a day.* lethargy (noun).

**levy** (verb) To demand payment or collection of a tax or fee. *The environmental activists pushed Congress to levy higher taxes on gasoline, but the auto makers' lobbyists quashed their plans.*

**lien** (noun) A claim against a property for the satisfaction of a debt. *Nat was in such financial straits when he died that his Fishkill property had several liens against it, and all of his furniture was being repossessed.*

**limn** (verb) To outline in distinct detail; to delineate. *Like many of her novels, Edith Wharton's* The Age of Innocence *expertly limns the tyranny of New York's upper class society in the 1800s.*

**loquacity** (noun) Talkativeness, wordiness. *While some people deride his loquacity and his tendency to use outrageous rhymes, no one can doubt that Jesse Jackson is a powerful orator.* loquacious (adjective).

**lucid** (adjective) Clear and understandable. *Hawking's* A Brief History of Time *is a lucid explanation of a difficult topic: modern scientific theories of the origin of the universe.* lucidity (noun).

WORD ORIGIN
Latin *lux* = light. Also found in English *elucidate*, *pellucid*, and *translucent*.

## M

**magnanimous** (adjective) Noble, generous. *When media titan Ted Turner pledged a gift of $1 billion to the United Nations, he challenged other wealthy people to be equally magnanimous.* magnanimity (noun).

**maladroit** (adjective) Inept, awkward. *It was painful to watch the young congressman's maladroit delivery of the nominating speech.*

**malinger** (verb) To pretend illness to avoid work. *During the labor dispute, hundreds of employees malingered, forcing the company to slow production and costing it millions in profits.*

**malleable** (adjective) Able to be changed, shaped, or formed by outside pressures. *Gold is a very useful metal because it is so malleable. A child's personality is malleable and is often deeply influenced by things her parents say and do.* malleability (noun).

WORD ORIGIN

Latin *mandare* = entrust, order. Also found in English *command, demand,* and *remand.*

**mandate** (noun) Order, command. *The new policy on gays in the military went into effect as soon as the president issued his mandate about it.* mandate (verb), mandatory (adjective).

**marginal** (adjective) At the outer edge or fringe; of minimal quality or acceptability. *In spite of the trend toward greater paternal involvement in child rearing, most fathers still have a marginal role in their children's lives. Jerry's GRE scores were so marginal that he didn't get accepted into the graduate school of his choice.*

**marginalize** (verb) To push toward the fringes; to make less consequential. *Hannah argued that the designation of a certain month as "Black History Month" or "Gay and Lesbian Book Month" actually does a disservice to minorities by marginalizing them.*

**martial** (adjective) Of, relating to, or suited to military life. *My old teacher, Miss Woody, had such a martial demeanor that you'd think she was running a boot camp instead of teaching fifth grade. The military seized control of Myanmar in 1988, and this embattled country has been ruled by martial law since then.*

WORD ORIGIN

Latin *medius* = middle. Also found in English *intermediate, media,* and *medium.*

**mediate** (verb) To reconcile differences between two parties. *During the baseball strike, both the players and the club owners expressed willingness to have the president mediate the dispute.* mediation (noun).

**mercenary** (adjective) Doing something only for pay or for personal advantage. *People had criticized the U.S. motives in the Persian Gulf War as mercenary, pointing out that the U.S. would not have come to Kuwait's defense had it grown carrots rather than produced oil.* mercenary (noun).

**mercurial** (adjective) Changing quickly and unpredictably. *The mercurial personality of Robin Williams, with his many voices and styles, made him a natural choice to play the part of the ever-changing genie in* Aladdin.

**metamorphose** (verb) To undergo a striking transformation. *In just a century, book publishers have metamorphosed from independent, exclusively literary businesses to minor divisions in multimedia entertainment conglomerates.* metamorphosis (noun).

**meticulous** (adjective) Very careful with details. *Watch repair calls for a craftsperson who is patient and meticulous.*

**mettle** (noun) Strength of spirit; stamina. *Linda's mettle was severely tested while she served as the only female attorney at Smith, Futterweitt, Houghton, and Dobbs.* mettlesome (adjective).

**mimicry** (noun) Imitation, aping. *The continued popularity of Elvis Presley has given rise to a class of entertainers who make a living through mimicry of "The King."* mimic (noun and verb).

**minatory** (adjective) Menacing, threatening. *As soon as she met Mrs. Danforth, the head housemaid at Manderlay, the young bride was cowed by her minatory manner and quickly retreated to the morning room.*

**mince** (verb) To chop into small pieces; to speak with decorum and restraint. *Malaysia's fourth prime minister Mahathir Mohamad was not a man known to mince words; he had accused satellite TV of poisoning Asia and had denounced the Australian press as "congenital liars."*

**misanthrope** (noun) Someone who hates or distrusts all people. *In the beloved Christmas classic,* It's a Wonderful Life, *Lionel Barrymore plays Potter, the wealthy misanthrope who is determined to make life miserable for everyone, and particularly for the young, idealistic George Bailey.* misanthropic (adjective), misanthropy (noun).

**WORD ORIGIN**
Greek *anthropos* = human. Also found in English *anthropology, anthropoid, anthropomorphic,* and *philanthropy.*

**miscreant** (adjective) Unbelieving, heretical; evil, villainous. *After a one-year run playing Iago in* Othello, *and then two years playing Bill Sikes in* Oliver, *Sean was tired of being typecast in miscreant roles.* miscreant (noun).

**mitigate** (verb) To make less severe; to relieve. *There's no doubt that Wallace committed the assault, but the verbal abuse Wallace had received helps to explain his behavior and somewhat mitigates his guilt.* mitigation (noun).

**monopolistic** (adjective) *Renowned consumer advocate Ralph Nader once quipped, "The only difference between John D. Rockefeller and Bill Gates is that Gates recognizes no boundaries to his monopolistic drive."*

**monopoly** (noun) A condition in which there is only one seller of a certain commodity. *Wary of Microsoft's seeming monopoly of the computer operating-system business, rivals are asking for government intervention.*

**monotonous** (adjective) Tediously uniform, unchanging. *Brian Eno's "Music for Airports" is characterized by minimal melodies, subtle textures, and variable repetition, which I find rather bland and monotonous.* monotony (noun).

**morose** (adjective) Gloomy, sullen. *After Chuck's girlfriend dumped him, he lay around the house for a couple of days, refusing to come to the phone and feeling morose.*

**mutation** (noun) A significant change; in biology, a permanent change in hereditary material. *Most genetic mutations are not beneficial, since any change in the delicate balance of an organism tends to be disruptive.* mutate (verb).

## N

**nadir** (noun) Lowest point. *Pedro and Renee's marriage reached a new nadir last Christmas Eve when Pedro locked Renee out of the house upon her return from the supposed "business trip."*

**nascent** (adjective) Newly born, just beginning. *While her artistry is still nascent, it was 15-year-old Tara Lipinski's technical wizardry that enabled her to win a gold medal in the 1998 Winter Olympics.* nascence (noun).

**noisome** (adjective) Putrid, fetid, noxious. *We were convinced that the noisome odor infiltrating every corner of our building was evidence of a mouldering corpse.*

**notorious** (adjective) Famous, especially for evil actions or qualities. *Warner Brothers produced a series of movies about notorious gangsters such as John Dillinger and Al Capone.* notoriety (noun).

## O

WORD ORIGIN

Latin *durus* = hard. Also found
in English *durable* and *endure*.

**obdurate** (adjective) Unwilling to change; stubborn, inflexible. *Despite the many pleas he received, the governor was obdurate in his refusal to grant clemency to the convicted murderer.*

**oblivious** (adjective) Unaware, unconscious. *Karen practiced her oboe solo with complete concentration, oblivious to the noise and activity around her.* oblivion (noun), obliviousness (noun).

**obscure** (adjective) Little known; hard to understand. *Mendel was an obscure monk until decades after his death, when his scientific work was finally discovered. Most people find the writings of James Joyce obscure; hence the popularity of books that explain the many odd references and tricks of language in his work.* obscure (verb), obscurity (noun).

**obsolete** (adjective) No longer current; old-fashioned. *W. H. Auden said that his ideal landscape would contain water wheels, grain mills, and other forms of obsolete machinery.* obsolescence (noun).

**obstinate** (adjective) Stubborn, unyielding. *Despite years of government effort, the problem of drug abuse remains obstinate.* obstinacy (noun).

**obtuse** (adjective) Dull-witted, insensitive; incomprehensible, unclear, or imprecise. *Amy was so obtuse she didn't realize that Alexi had proposed marriage to her. French psychoanalyst Jacques Lacan's collection of papers, Ecrits, is notoriously obtuse, yet it has still been highly influential in linguistics, film theory, and literary criticism.*

**obviate** (verb) Preclude, make unnecessary. *Truman Capote's meticulous accuracy and total recall obviated the need for note-taking when he wrote his account of a 1959 murder,* In Cold Blood.

**odium** (noun) Intense feeling of hatred, abhorrence. *When the neighbors learned that a convicted sex offender was now living in their midst, they could not restrain their odium and began harassing the man whenever he left his house.* odious (adjective).

**opprobrium** (noun) Dishonor, disapproval. *Switzerland came under public opprobrium when it was revealed that Swiss bankers had hoarded the gold the Nazis had confiscated from their victims.* opprobrious (adjective).

**orthodox** (adjective) In religion, conforming to a certain doctrine; conventional. *George Eliot's relationship with George Lewes, a married journalist, offended the sensibilities of her more orthodox peers.* orthodoxy (noun).

**ossified** (adjective) In biology, to turn into bone; to become rigidly conventional and opposed to change. *His ossified view of coeducation meant that he was now the* *only teacher who sought to bar girls from the venerable boys' school.* ossification (noun).

**ostentatious** (adjective) Overly showy, pretentious. *To show off his new wealth, the financier threw an ostentatious party featuring a full orchestra, a famous singer, and tens of thousands of dollars' worth of food.* ostentation (noun).

**ostracize** (verb) To exclude from a group. *In Biblical times, those who suffered from the disease of leprosy were ostracized and forced to live alone.* ostracism (noun).

## P

**paean** (adjective) A joyous expression of praise, gratitude, or triumph. *Choreographer Paul Taylor's dance "Eventide" is a sublime paean to remembered love, with couple after loving couple looking back as they embrace an unknown future.*

**parody** (noun) An imitation created for comic effect; a caricature. *While the creators of the 1970s comedy series* All in the Family *intended Archie Bunker to be a parody of close-mindedness in Americans, large numbers of people adopted Bunker as a working-class hero.*

**parse** (verb) To break a sentence down into grammatical components; to analyze bit by bit. *In the wake of the sex scandal, journalists parsed every utterance by administration officials regarding the president's alleged promiscuity. At $1.25 million a day,* Titanic *was one of the most expensive movies ever made, but director James Cameron refused to parse the film's enormous budget for inquisitive reporters.*

**partisan** (adjective) Reflecting strong allegiance to a particular party or cause. *The vote on the president's budget was strictly partisan: every member of the president's party voted yes, and all others voted no.* partisan (noun).

**pastoral** (adjective) Simple and rustic, bucolic, rural. *While industry grew and the country expanded westward, the Hudson River School of painters depicted the landscape as a pastoral setting where humans and nature could coexist.*

**patron** (noun) A special guardian or protector; a wealthy or influential supporter of the arts. *Dominique de Menil used her considerable wealth to become a well-known patron of the arts; she and her husband owned a collection of more than 10,000 pieces ranging from cubist paintings to tribal artifacts.* patronize (verb).

**peccadillo** (noun) A minor offense, a lapse. *What Dr. Sykes saw as a major offense—being addressed as Marge rather than Doctor—Tina saw as a mere peccadillo and one that certainly should not have lost her the job.*

**pedantic** (adjective) Academic, bookish. *The men Hillary met through personal ads in the* New York Review of Books *were invariably pasty-skinned pedantic types who dropped the names of nineteenth-century writers in every sentence.* pedantry (noun).

**pedestrian** (adjective) Unimaginative, ordinary. *The new Italian restaurant received a bad review due to its reliance on pedestrian dishes such as pasta with marinara sauce or chicken parmigiana.*

**WORD ORIGIN**

Latin *fides* = faith. Also found in English *confide, confidence, fidelity,* and *infidel*.

**perfidious** (adjective) Disloyal, treacherous. *Although he was one of the most talented generals of the American Revolution, Benedict Arnold is remembered today as a perfidious betrayer of the patriot cause.* perfidy (noun).

**peripatetic** (adjective) Moving or traveling from place to place; always on the go. *In Barbara Wilson's* Trouble in Transylvania, *peripatetic translator Cassandra Reilly is on the road again, this time to China by way of Budapest, where she plans to catch the TransMongolian Express.*

**permeate** (verb) To spread through or penetrate. *Little by little, the smell of gas from the broken pipe permeated the house.*

**personification** (noun) The embodiment of a thing or an abstract idea in human form. *Many people view Theodore Kaczynski, the killer known as the Unabomber, as the very personification of evil.* personify (verb).

**pervasive** (adjective) Spreading throughout. *As news of the disaster reached the town, a pervasive sense of gloom could be felt everywhere.* pervade (verb).

**philistine** (noun) Someone who is smugly ignorant and uncultured. *A true philistine, Meg claimed she didn't read any book that wasn't either recommended by Oprah Winfrey or on the best-seller list.* philistine (adjective).

**pith** (noun) The core, the essential part; in biology, the central strand of tissue in the stems of most vascular plants. *After spending seventeen years in psychoanalysis, Frieda had finally come face to face with the pith of her deep-seated anxiety.* pithy (adjective).

**placate** (verb) To soothe or appease. *The waiter tried to placate the angry customer with the offer of a free dessert.* placatory (adjective).

**placid** (adjective) Unmarked by disturbance; complacent. *Dr. Kahn was convinced that the placid exterior presented by Frieda in her early analysis sessions masked a deeply disturbed psyche.* placidity (noun).

**plaintive** (adjective) Expressing suffering or melancholy. *In the beloved children's book* The Secret Garden, *Mary is disturbed by plaintive cries echoing in the corridors of gloomy Misselthwaite Manor.*

**plastic** (adjective) Able to be molded or reshaped. *Because it is highly plastic, clay is an easy material for beginning sculptors to use.* plasticity (noun).

**platitude** (noun) A trite remark or saying; a cliché. *How typical of June to send a sympathy card filled with mindless platitudes like "One day at a time," rather than calling the grieving widow.* platitudinous (adjective).

**plausible** (adjective) Apparently believable. *The idea that a widespread conspiracy to kill the president has been kept secret by all the participants for more than thirty years hardly seems plausible.* plausibility (noun).

**plummet** (verb) To dive or plunge. *On October 27, 1997, the stock market plummeted by 554 points and left us all wondering if the bull market was finally over.*

**polarize** (adjective) To separate into opposing groups or forces. *For years, the abortion debate polarized the American people, with many people voicing views at either extreme and few people trying to find a middle ground.* polarization (noun).

**ponderous** (adjective) Unwieldy and bulky; oppressively dull. *Unfortunately, the film director weighed the movie down with a ponderous voice-over narrated by the protagonist as an old man.*

**poseur** (noun) Someone who pretends to be what he isn't. *Gerald had pretensions for literary stardom with his book proposal on an obscure World War II battle, yet most agents soon realized that the book would never be written and categorized him as a poseur.*

**positivism** (noun) A philosophy that denies speculation and assumes that the only knowledge is scientific knowledge. *David Hume carried his positivism to an extreme when he argued that our expectation that the sun will rise tomorrow has no basis in reason and is purely a matter of belief.* positivistic (adjective).

**pragmatism** (noun) A belief in approaching problems through practical rather than theoretical means. *Roosevelt's attitude toward the economic troubles of the Depression was based on pragmatism: "Try something," he said. "If it doesn't work, try something else."* pragmatic (adjective).

**precedent** (noun) An earlier occurrence that serves as an example for a decision. *In a legal system that reveres precedent, even defining the nature of a completely new type of dispute can seem impossible.* precede (verb).

**precept** (noun) A general principle or law. *One of the central precepts of T'ai Chi Ch'uan is the necessity of allowing ki (cosmic energy) to flow through one's body in slow, graceful movements.*

**precipitate** (verb) To spur or activate. *In the summer of 1997, the selling off of the Thai baht precipitated a currency crisis that spread throughout Asia.*

**preclude** (verb) To prevent, to hinder. *Unfortunately, Jasmine's appointment at the New Age Expo precluded her attendance at our weekend Workshop for Shamans and Psychics.* preclusive (adjective), preclusion (noun).

**precursor** (noun) A forerunner, a predecessor. *The Kodak Brownie camera, a small boxy camera made of jute board and wood, was the precursor to today's sleek digital cameras.* precursory (adjective).

**preponderance** (noun) A superiority in weight, size, or quantity; a majority. *In Seattle, there is a great preponderance of seasonal affective disorder, or SAD, a malady brought on by light starvation during the dark Northwest winter.* preponderate (verb).

**presage** (verb) To foretell, to anticipate. *According to folklore, a red sky at dawn presages a day of stormy weather.*

**prescience** (noun) Foreknowledge or foresight. *When she saw the characteristic eerie yellowish-black light in the sky, Dorothy had the prescience to seek shelter in the storm cellar.* prescient (adjective).

WORD ORIGIN
Latin *claudere* = to close. Also found in English *conclude*, *include*, *recluse*, and *seclude*.

**presumptuous** (adjective) Going beyond the limits of courtesy or appropriateness. *The senator winced when the presumptuous young staffer addressed him as "Ted."* presume (verb), presumption (noun).

**prevaricate** (verb) To lie, to equivocate. *When it became clear to the FBI that the mobster had threatened the 12-year-old witness, they could well understand why the youngster had prevaricated during the hearing.*

**primacy** (noun) State of being the utmost in importance; preeminence. *The anthropologist Ruth Benedict was an inspiration to Margaret Mead for her emphasis on the primacy of culture in the formation of an individual's personality.* primal (adjective).

**pristine** (adjective) Pure, undefiled. *As climbers who have scaled Mt. Everest can attest, the trails to the summit are hardly in pristine condition and are actually strewn with trash.*

**probity** (noun) Goodness, integrity. *The vicious editorial attacked the moral probity of the senatorial candidate, saying he had profited handsomely from his pet project, the senior-citizen housing project.*

**procure** (verb) To obtain by using particular care and effort. *Through partnerships with a large number of specialty wholesalers, W.W. Grainger is able to procure a startling array of products for its customers, from bear repellent for Alaska pipeline workers to fork-lift trucks and toilet paper.* procurement (noun).

**prodigality** (noun) The condition of being wastefully extravagant. *Richard was ashamed of the prodigality of his bride's parents when he realized that the cost of the wedding reception alone was more than his father earned in one year.* prodigal (adjective).

**proliferate** (verb) To increase or multiply. *For about fifteen years, high-tech companies had proliferated in northern California, Massachusetts, and other regions.* proliferation (noun).

**prolixity** (noun) A diffuseness; a rambling and verbose quality. *The prolixity of Sarah's dissertation on Ottoman history defied even her adviser's attempts to read it.* prolix (adjective).

**propagate** (verb) To cause to grow; to foster. *John Smithson's will left his fortune for the founding of an institution to propagate knowledge, leaving open whether that meant a university, a library, or a museum.* propagation (noun).

**prophetic** (adjective) Auspicious, predictive of what's to come. *We often look at every event leading up to a new love affair as prophetic—the flat tire that caused us to be late for work, the chance meeting in the elevator, the horoscope that augured "a new beginning."* prophecy (noun), prophesy (verb).

**propitiating** (adjective) Conciliatory, mollifying or appeasing. *Management's offer of a 5-percent raise was meant as a propitiating gesture, yet the striking workers were unimpressed.* propitiate (verb).

**propriety** (noun) Appropriateness. *Some people expressed doubts about the propriety of wearing flip-flops to a meeting at the White House.*

**proximity** (noun) Closeness, nearness. *Neighborhood residents were angry over the proximity of the proposed sewage plant to the local elementary school.* proximate (adjective).

**pundit** (noun) Someone who offers opinions in an authoritative style. *The Sunday morning talk shows are filled with pundits, each with his or her own theory about the week's political news.*

**pungency** (noun) Marked by having a sharp, biting quality. *Unfortunately, the pungency of the fresh cilantro overwhelmed the delicate flavor of the poached turbot.* pungent (adjective).

**purify** (verb) To make pure, clean, or perfect. *The new water-treatment plant is supposed to purify the drinking water provided to everyone in the nearby towns.* purification (noun).

## Q

**quiescent** (adjective) In a state of rest or inactivity; latent. *Polly's ulcer has been quiescent ever since her mother-in-law moved out of the condo, which was well over a year ago.* quiescence (noun).

**quixotic** (adjective) Foolishly romantic, idealistic to an impractical degree. *In the novel* Shoeless Joe, *Ray Kinsella carries out a quixotic plan to build a baseball field in the hopes that past baseball greats will come to play there.*

**quotidian** (adjective) Occurring every day; commonplace and ordinary. *Most of the time, we long to escape from quotidian concerns, but in the midst of a crisis we want nothing more than to be plagued by such simple problems as a leaky faucet or a whining child.*

## R

**raconteur** (noun) An excellent storyteller. *A member of the Algonquin Roundtable, Robert Benchley was a natural raconteur with a seemingly endless ability to turn daily life and its irritations into entertaining commentary.*

**rancorous** (adjective) Marked by deeply embedded bitterness or animosity. *While Ralph and Kishu have been separated for three years, their relationship is so rancorous that they had to hire a professional mediator just to discuss divorce arrangements.* rancor (noun).

**rapacious** (adjective) Excessively grasping or greedy. *Some see global currency speculators like George Soros as rapacious parasites who destroy economies and then line their pockets with the profits.* rapacity (noun).

**rarefied** (adjective) Of interest or relating to a small, refined circle; less dense, thinner. *Those whose names dot the society pages live in a rarefied world where it's entirely normal to dine on caviar for breakfast or order a $2,000 bottle of wine*

WORD ORIGIN
Latin *poena* = pain. Also found in English *impunity, penal, penalty,* and *punishment.*

*at Le Cirque. When she reached the summit of Mt. McKinley, Deborah could hardly breathe in the rarefied air.*

**raucous** (adjective) Boisterous, unruly, and wild. *Sounds of shouts and raucous laughter drifted out of the hotel room where Felipe's bachelor party was being held.*

**reactionary** (adjective) Ultra conservative. *Every day, more than 20 million listeners used to tune in to hear Rush Limbaugh spew his reactionary opinions about "Feminazis" and environmental "fanatics."* reactionary (noun).

**recede** (verb) To draw back, to ebb, to abate. *Once his hairline began to recede, Hap took to wearing bizarre accessories, like velvet ascots, to divert attention from it.* recession (noun).

**reclusive** (adjective) Withdrawn from society. *During the last years of her life, Garbo led a reclusive existence, rarely appearing in public.* recluse (noun).

**recompense** (noun) Compensation for a service rendered or to pay for damages. *The 5 percent of the estate, which Phil received as executor of his aunt Ida's will, is small recompense for the headaches he endured in settling her affairs.* recompense (verb).

**reconcile** (verb) To make consistent or harmonious. *Franklin D. Roosevelt's greatness as a leader can be seen in his ability to reconcile the differing demands and values of the varied groups that supported him.* reconciliation (noun).

**recondite** (adjective) Profound, deep, abstruse. *Professor Miyaki's recondite knowledge of seventeenth-century Flemish painters made him a prized—if barely understood—member of the art history department.*

**redemptive** (adjective) Liberating and reforming. *While she doesn't attend formal church services, Carrie is a firm believer in the redemptive power of prayer.* redeem (verb), redemption (noun).

**WORD ORIGIN**
Latin *frangere* = to break. Also found in English *fraction*, *fractious*, *fracture*, *frangible*, *infraction*, and *refract*.

**refractory** (adjective) Stubbornly resisting control or authority. *Like a refractory child, Jill stomped out of the car, slammed the door, and said she would walk home, even though her house was 10 miles away.*

**relevance** (noun) Connection to the matter at hand; pertinence. *Testimony in a criminal trial may only be admitted to the extent that it has clear relevance to the question of guilt or innocence.* relevant (adjective).

**reparation** (noun) The act of making amends; payment of damages by a defeated nation to the victors. *The Treaty of Versailles, signed in 1919, formally asserted Germany's war guilt and ordered it to pay reparations to the allies.*

**reproof** (noun) A reprimand, a reproach, or castigation. *Joe thought being grounded for one month was a harsh reproof for coming home late only once.* reprove (verb).

**repudiate** (verb) To reject, to renounce. *After it became known that the politician had been a leader of the Ku Klux Klan, most Republican leaders repudiated him.* repudiation (noun).

**repugnant** (adjective) Causing dislike or disgust. *After the news broke about Mad Cow Disease, much of the beef-loving British public began to find the thought of a Sunday roast repugnant.*

**requiem** (noun) A musical composition or poem written to honor the dead. *Many financial analysts think that the ailing typewriter company should simply say a requiem for itself and shut down; however, the CEO has other plans.*

**resilient** (adjective) Able to recover from difficulty. *A professional athlete must be mentally resilient, able to lose a game one day and come back the next with renewed enthusiasm and confidence.* resilience (noun).

**resonant** (adjective) Full of special import or meaning. *I found the speaker's words particularly resonant because I, too, had served in Vietnam and felt the same mixture of shame and pride.* resonance (noun).

**resplendent** (adjective) Glowing, shining. *In late December, midtown New York is resplendent with holiday lights and decorations.* resplendence (noun).

**rite** (noun) Ceremony. *From October to May, the Patwin Indians of California's Sacramento Valley held a series of rites and dances designed to bring the tribe health and prosperity.*

**rogue** (noun) A mischievously dishonest person; a scamp. *In Jane Austen's* Pride and Prejudice, *Wickham, a charming rogue, seduces Darcy's young sister Georgiana and later does the same thing with Kitty Bennett.*

**ruffian** (noun) A brute, roughneck, or bully. *In Dickens's* Oliver Twist, *Fagin instructs his gang of orphaned ruffians on the arts of picking pockets and shoplifting.*

**rumination** (noun) The act of engaging in contemplation. *Marcel Proust's semi-autobiographical novel cycle* Remembrance of Things Past *is less a narrative than an extended rumination on the nature of memory.* ruminate (verb).

## S

**sage** (noun) A person of great wisdom, a knowing philosopher. *It was the Chinese sage Confucius who first taught what is now known the world over as "The Golden Rule."* sagacious (adjective), sagacity (noun).

**salutary** (adjective) Restorative, healthful. *I find a short dip in an icy stream to be extremely salutary, although the health benefits of my bracing swims are, as yet, unclear.*

**sanction** (verb) Support or authorize. *Even after a bomb exploded on the front porch of his home, the Reverend Martin Luther King Jr. refused to sanction any violent response and urged his angry followers to love their enemies.* sanctify (verb), sanction (noun).

**sap** (verb) To exhaust, to deplete. *The exhaustive twelve-city reading tour so sapped the novelist's strength that she told her publicist that she hoped her next book would be a flop! While the African nation was making enormous economic strides*

**WORD ORIGIN**

Latin *salus* = health. Also found in English *salubrious, salutation,* and *salute.*

*under its new president, rebel fighting had sapped much of the country's resources.*

**satiate** (verb) To fulfill to or beyond capacity. *Judging by the current crop of films featuring serial killers, rape, ritual murder, gun-slinging, and plain old-fashioned slugfests, the public appetite for violence has not yet been satiated.* satiation (noun), satiety (noun).

**saturate** (verb) To drench or suffuse with liquid or anything that permeates or invades. *The hostess's furious dabbing at the tablecloth was in vain, since the spilt wine had already saturated the damask cloth.* saturation (noun), saturated (adjective).

**scrutinize** (verb) To study closely. *The lawyer scrutinized the contract, searching for any detail that could pose a risk for her client.* scrutiny (noun).

**scurvy** (adjective) Shabby, low. *I couldn't believe that Farouk was so scurvy as to open up my computer files and read my e-mail.*

**sedulous** (adjective) Diligent, industrious. *Those who are most sedulous about studying this vocabulary list are likely to breeze through the antonyms sections of their GRE.*

WORD ORIGIN
Latin *sequi* = to follow. Also found in English *consequence*, *sequel*, and *subsequent*.

**sequential** (adjective) Arranged in an order or series. *The courses required for the chemistry major are sequential; you must take them in the prescribed order, since each course builds on the previous ones.* sequence (noun).

**sidereal** (adjective) Relating to the stars or the constellations. *Jacqueline was interested in matters sidereal and was always begging my father to take the dusty old telescope out of our garage.*

**signatory** (noun) Someone who signs an official document or petition along with others. *Alex urged me to join the other signatories and add my name to the petition against toxic sludge in organic foods, but I simply did not care enough about the issue. The signatories of the Declaration of Independence included John Adams, Benjamin Franklin, John Hancock, and Thomas Jefferson.*

**sinuous** (noun) Winding, circuitous, serpentine. *Frank Gehry's sinuous design for the Guggenheim Museum in Bilbao, Spain, has led people to hail the museum as the first great building of the twenty-first century.* sinuosity (noun).

**specious** (adjective) Deceptively plausible or attractive. *The infomercial for Fat-Away offered mainly specious arguments for a product that is, essentially, a heavy-duty girdle.*

**splice** (verb) To unite by interweaving separate strands or parts. *Amateur filmmaker Duddy Kravitz shocked and angered his clients by splicing footage of tribal rituals into his films of their weddings and bar mitzvahs.*

**spontaneous** (adjective) Happening without plan or outside cause. *When the news of John F. Kennedy's assassination hit the airwaves, people everywhere gathered in a spontaneous effort to express their shock and grief.* spontaneity (noun).

**spurious** (adjective) False, fake. *The so-called Piltdown Man, supposed to be the fossil of a primitive human, turned out to be spurious, though who created the hoax is still uncertain.*

**squander** (verb) To use up carelessly, to waste. *Those who had made donations to the charity were outraged to learn that its director had squandered millions on fancy dinners, first-class travel, and an expensive apartment for entertaining.*

**stanch** (verb) To stop the flow. *When the patient began to bleed profusely, the doctor stanched the blood flow by applying direct pressure to the wound.*

**stint** (verb) To limit, to restrain. *The British bed and breakfast certainly did not stint on the breakfast part of the equation; they provided us with fried tomatoes, fried sausages, fried eggs, smoked kippers, fried bread, fried mushrooms, and bowls of a cereal called Wheatabix (which tasted like cardboard).* stinting (adjective).

**stolid** (adjective) Impassive, unemotional. *The popular animated television series* King of the Hill *chronicles the woes of a stolid, conservative Texan confronting changing times.* stolidity (noun).

**subordination** (noun) The state of being subservient or treated as less valuable. *Heather left the naval academy because she could no longer stand the subordination of every personal whim or desire to the rigorous demands of military life.* subordinate (verb).

**subpoena** (noun) An order of a court, legislation, or grand jury that compels a witness to be present at a trial or hearing. *The young man's lawyer asked the judge to subpoena a boa constrictor into court on the grounds that the police had used the snake as an "instrument of terror" to coerce his client's confession.*

**subside** (verb) To settle or die down. *The celebrated lecturer had to wait 10 minutes for the applause to subside before he began his speech.*

**subsidization** (noun) The state of being financed by a grant from a government or other agency. *Without subsidization, the nation's passenger rail system would probably go bankrupt.* subsidize (verb).

**substantiated** (adjective) Verified or supported by evidence. *The charge that Nixon had helped to cover up crimes was substantiated by his comments about it on a series of audiotapes.* substantiate (verb), substantiation (noun).

**subsume** (verb) To encompass or engulf within something larger. *In Alan Dershowitz's* Reversal of Fortune, *he makes it clear that his work as a lawyer subsumes his personal life.*

**subterranean** (adjective) Under the surface of the earth. *Subterranean testing of nuclear weapons was permitted under the Nuclear Test Ban Treaty of 1963.*

**summarily** (adverb) Quickly and concisely. *No sooner had I voiced my concerns about the new ad campaign than my boss put her hand on my elbow and summarily ushered me out of her office.*

**superficial** (adjective) On the surface only; without depth or substance. *Her wound was only superficial and required no treatment except a light bandage. His* *superficial attractiveness hides the fact that his personality is lifeless and his mind is dull.* superficiality (noun).

**superimpose** (verb) To place or lay over or above something. *The artist stirred controversy by superimposing portraits of certain contemporary politicians over images of such reviled historical figures as Hitler and Stalin.*

**supersede** (verb) To displace, to substitute or supplant. *"I'm sorry," the principal announced, "but today's afternoon classes will be superseded by an assembly on drug and alcohol abuse."*

**supine** (adjective) Lying on one's back. *One always feels rather vulnerable when wearing a flimsy paper gown and lying supine on a doctor's examining table.*

**supposition** (noun) Assumption, conjecture. *While most climate researchers believe that increasing levels of greenhouse gases will warm the planet, skeptics claim that this theory is mere supposition.* suppose (verb).

**surge** (noun) A gush; a swelling or sweeping forward. *When Mattel gave the Barbie doll a makeover in the late 1980s, manufacturing dolls like doctor Barbie and astronaut Barbie, the company experienced a surge in sales.*

# T

WORD ORIGIN
Latin *tangere* = to touch. Also found in English *contact*, *contiguous*, *tactile*, *tangent*, and *tangible*.

**tangential** (adjective) Touching lightly; only slightly connected or related. *Having enrolled in a class on African American history, the students found the teacher's stories about his travels in South America only of tangential interest.* tangent (noun).

**tedium** (noun) Boredom. *For most people, watching even a 15-minute broadcast of the earth as seen from space would be an exercise in sheer tedium.* tedious (adjective).

**temperance** (noun) Moderation or restraint in feelings and behavior. *Most professional athletes practice temperance in their personal habits; too much eating or drinking and too many late nights, they know, can harm their performance.*

**temperate** (adjective) Moderate, calm. *The warm gulf streams are largely responsible for the temperate climate of the British Isles.*

**tenuous** (adjective) Lacking in substance; weak, flimsy, very thin. *His tenuous grasp of the Spanish language was evident when he addressed Señor Chavez as "Señora."*

**terrestrial** (adjective) Of the earth. *The movie* Close Encounters of the Third Kind *tells the story of the first contact between beings from outer space and terrestrial creatures.*

**throwback** (noun) A reversion to an earlier type; an atavism. *The late-model Volkswagen Beetle, with its familiar bubble shape, looked like a throwback to the 1960s, but it was actually packed with modern high-tech equipment.*

**tiff** (noun) A small, almost inconsequential quarrel or disagreement. *Megan and Bruce got into a tiff when Bruce criticized her smoking.*

**tirade** (noun) A long, harshly critical speech. *Reformed smokers, like Bruce, are prone to delivering tirades on the evils of smoking.*

**torpor** (noun) Apathy, sluggishness. *Stranded in an airless hotel room in Madras after a 27-hour train ride, I felt such overwhelming torpor that I doubted I would make it to Bangalore, the next destination in my journey.* torpid (adjective).

**tout** (verb) To praise highly, to brag publicly. *A much happier Eileen is now touting the benefits of Prozac, but, to tell you the truth, I miss her witty, self-lacerating commentaries.*

**tractable** (adjective) Obedient, manageable. *When he turned 3, Harrison suddenly became a tractable, well-mannered little boy after being, quite frankly, an unruly little monster!*

**tranquillity** (noun) Freedom from disturbance or turmoil; calm. *She moved from New York City to rural Vermont seeking the tranquillity of country life.* tranquil (adjective).

**transgress** (verb) To go past limits; to violate. *The Secretary of State warned that if Iraq has developed biological weapons, it has transgressed the UN's rules against manufacturing weapons of mass destruction.* transgression (noun).

**transmute** (verb) To change in form or substance. *Practitioners of alchemy tried to discover ways to transmute metals such as iron into gold.* transmutation (noun).

**treacherous** (adjective) Untrustworthy or disloyal; dangerous or unreliable. *Nazi Germany proved to be a treacherous ally, first signing a peace pact with the Soviet Union, then invading. Be careful crossing the rope bridge; parts of the span are badly frayed and treacherous.* treachery (noun).

**tremor** (noun) An involuntary shaking or trembling. *Brooke felt the first tremors of the 1989 San Francisco earthquake while she was sitting in Candlestick Park watching a Giants baseball game.*

**trenchant** (adjective) Caustic and incisive. *Essayist H. L. Mencken was known for his trenchant wit and was famed for mercilessly puncturing the American middle class (which he called the "booboisie").*

**trepidation** (noun) Fear and anxiety. *After the tragedy of TWA flight 800, many previously fearless flyers were filled with trepidation whenever they stepped into an airplane.*

**turbulent** (adjective) Agitated or disturbed. *The night before the championship match, Martina was unable to sleep, her mind turbulent with fears and hopes.* turbulence (noun).

**turpitude** (noun) Depravity, wickedness. *Radical feminists who contrast women's essential goodness with men's moral turpitude can be likened to religious fundamentalists who make a clear distinction between the saved and the damned.*

**tyro** (noun) Novice, amateur. *For an absolute tyro on the ski slopes, Gina was surprisingly agile at taking the moguls.*

**WORD ORIGIN**
Latin *tractare* = to handle. Also found in English *intractable*, *tractate*, and *traction*.

**WORD ORIGIN**
Latin *trepidus* = alarmed. Also found in English *intrepid*.

# U

**unalloyed** (adjective) Unqualified, pure. *Holding his newborn son for the first time, Malik felt an unalloyed happiness that was unlike anything else he had ever experienced in his forty-five years.*

**undermine** (verb) To excavate beneath; to subvert, to weaken. *Dot continued to undermine my efforts to find her a date by showing up at our dinner parties in her ratty old sweatsuit.*

**unfeigned** (adjective) Genuine, sincere. *Lashawn responded with such unfeigned astonishment when we all leapt out of the kitchen that I think she had had no inkling of the surprise party.*

**univocal** (adjective) With a single voice. *While they came from different backgrounds and departments, the employees were univocal in their demands that the corrupt CEO resign immediately.*

**unstinting** (adjective) Giving with unrestrained generosity. *Few people will be able to match the unstinting dedication and care that Mother Teresa had lavished on the poor people of Calcutta.*

**WORD ORIGIN**

Latin *urbs* = city. Also found in English *suburb* and *urban*.

**urbanity** (noun) Sophistication, suaveness, and polish. *Part of the fun in a Cary Grant movie lies in seeing whether the star can be made to lose his urbanity and elegance in the midst of chaotic or kooky situations.* urbane (adjective).

**usurious** (adjective) Lending money at an unconscionably high interest rate. *Some people feel that Shakespeare's portrayal of the Jew, Shylock, the usurious money lender in* The Merchant of Venice, *has enflamed prejudice against the Jews.* usury (adjective).

# V

**WORD ORIGIN**

Latin *validus* = strong. Also found in English *invalid, invaluable, prevail,* and *value*.

**validate** (verb) To officially approve or confirm. *The election of the president is formally validated when the members of the Electoral College meet to confirm the verdict of the voters.* valid (adjective), validity (noun).

**vapid** (adjective) Flat, flavorless. *Whenever I have insomnia, I just tune the clock radio to Lite FM, and soon those vapid songs from the 1970s have me floating away to dreamland.* vapidity (noun).

**venal** (adjective) Corrupt, mercenary. *Mobutu Sese Seko was the venal dictator of Zaire who reportedly diverted millions of dollars in foreign aid to his own personal fortune.* venality (noun).

**veneer** (noun) A superficial or deceptive covering. *Beneath her folksy veneer, Samantha is a shrewd and calculating businessperson just waiting for the right moment to pounce.*

**venerate** (verb) To admire or honor. *In Communist China, Mao Tse-Tung is venerated as an almost god-like figure.* venerable (adjective), veneration (noun).

**veracious** (adjective) Truthful, earnest. *Many people still feel that Anita Hill was entirely veracious in her allegations of sexual harassment during the Clarence Thomas confirmation hearings.* veracity (noun).

**verify** (verb) To prove to be true. *The contents of Robert L. Ripley's syndicated "Believe It or Not" cartoons could not be verified, yet the public still thrilled to reports of "the man with two pupils in each eye," "the human unicorn," and other amazing oddities.* verification (noun).

**veritable** (adjective) Authentic. *A French antiques dealer recently claimed that a fifteenth-century child-sized suit of armor that he purchased in 1994 is the veritable suit of armor worn by heroine Joan of Arc.*

**WORD ORIGIN**

Latin *verus* = true. Also found in English *verisimilitude*, *veritable*, and *verity*.

**vindictive** (adjective) Spiteful. *Paula embarked on a string of petty, vindictive acts against her philandering boyfriend, such as mixing dry cat food with his cereal and snipping the blooms off his prize African violets.*

**viscid** (adjective) Sticky. *The 3M company's "Post-It," a simple piece of paper with one viscid side, has become as commonplace—and as indispensable—as the paper clip.*

**viscous** (adjective) Having a gelatinous or gooey quality. *I put too much liquid in the batter, and so my Black Forest cake turned out to be a viscous, inedible mass.*

**vitiate** (verb) To pollute, to impair. *When they voted to ban smoking from all bars in California, the public affirmed their belief that smoking vitiates the health of all people, not just smokers.*

**vituperative** (adjective) Verbally abusive, insulting. *Elizabeth Taylor should have won an award for her harrowing portrayal of Martha, the bitter, vituperative wife of a college professor in Edward Albee's* Who's Afraid of Virginia Woolf? vituperate (verb).

**volatile** (adjective) Quickly changing; fleeting, transitory; prone to violence. *Public opinion is notoriously volatile; a politician who is very popular one month may be voted out of office the next.* volatility (noun).

**volubility** (noun) Quality of being overly talkative, glib. *As Lorraine's anxiety increased, her volubility increased in direct proportion, so during her job interview the poor interviewer couldn't get a word in edgewise.* voluble (adjective).

**voracious** (adjective) Gluttonous, ravenous. *"Are all your appetites so voracious?" Wesley asked Nina as he watched her finish off seven miniature sandwiches and two lamb kabob skewers in a matter of minutes.* voracity (noun).

**WORD ORIGIN**

Latin *vorare* = to eat. Also found in English *carnivorous*, *devour*, and *omnivorous*.

## W

**wag** (noun) Wit, joker. *Tom was getting tired of his role as the comical wag who injected life into Kathy's otherwise tedious parties.* waggish (adjective).

**whimsical** (adjective) Based on a capricious, carefree, or sudden impulse or idea; fanciful, playful. *Dave Barry's* Book of Bad Songs *is filled with the kind of goofy jokes that are typical of his whimsical sense of humor.* whim (noun).

## X

**xenophobia** (noun) Fear of foreigners or outsiders. *Slobodan Milosevic's nationalistic talk played on the deep xenophobia of the Serbs, who, after 500 years of brutal Ottoman occupation, had come to distrust all outsiders.*

## Z

**zenith** (noun) Highest point. *Compiling this vocabulary list was the zenith of my literary career: after this, there was nowhere to go but downhill.*

## ABOUT THE AUTHOR

Mark Alan Stewart (B.A., Economics; J.D., University of California at Los Angeles) is an attorney and preeminent authority and top-selling author on the subject of graduate-level entrance exams. For more than a decade, Mr. Stewart served as consultant to schools in the University of California and California State University systems in graduate-level entrance exam programs. His books on LSAT, GRE, and GMAT preparation are perennial top sellers among aspiring law, business, and graduate students. His other book-length publications for graduate-level admission include the following (all published by Peterson's): *Master the GMAT; 30 Days to the GMAT CAT; GRE-LSAT Logic Workbook; GRE—Answers to the Real Essay Questions; GRE-LSAT-GMAT-MCAT Reading Comprehension Workbook; Words for Smart Test Takers; Math for Smart Test Takers;* and *Perfect Personal Statements—Law, Business, Medical, Graduate School.*

# NOTES

**NOTES**

# NOTES

# NOTES

# NOTES

# NOTES

**NOTES**

# NOTES

# NOTES

# Peterson's
## Book Satisfaction Survey

## Give Us Your Feedback

Thank you for choosing Peterson's as your source for personalized solutions for your education and career achievement. Please take a few minutes to answer the following questions. Your answers will go a long way in helping us to produce the most user-friendly and comprehensive resources to meet your individual needs.

When completed, please tear out this page and mail it to us at:

Publishing Department
Peterson's, a Nelnet company
2000 Lenox Drive
Lawrenceville, NJ 08648

You can also complete this survey online at **www.petersons.com/booksurvey.**

1. **What is the ISBN of the book you have purchased? (The ISBN can be found on the book's back cover in the lower right-hand corner. )** _____

2. **Where did you purchase this book?**
   ❏ Retailer, such as Barnes & Noble
   ❏ Online reseller, such as Amazon.com
   ❏ Petersons.com
   ❏ Other (please specify) _____

3. **If you purchased this book on Petersons.com, please rate the following aspects of your online purchasing experience on a scale of 4 to 1 (4 = Excellent and 1 = Poor).**

|  | 4 | 3 | 2 | 1 |
|---|---|---|---|---|
| Comprehensiveness of Peterson's Online Bookstore page | ❏ | ❏ | ❏ | ❏ |
| Overall online customer experience | ❏ | ❏ | ❏ | ❏ |

4. **Which category best describes you?**
   ❏ High school student
   ❏ Parent of high school student
   ❏ College student
   ❏ Graduate/professional student
   ❏ Returning adult student

   ❏ Teacher
   ❏ Counselor
   ❏ Working professional/military
   ❏ Other (please specify) _____

5. **Rate your overall satisfaction with this book.**

| Extremely Satisfied | Satisfied | Not Satisfied |
|---|---|---|
| ❏ | ❏ | ❏ |

**6. Rate each of the following aspects of this book on a scale of 4 to 1 (4 = Excellent and 1 = Poor).**

| | 4 | 3 | 2 | 1 |
|---|---|---|---|---|
| Comprehensiveness of the information | ❑ | ❑ | ❑ | ❑ |
| Accuracy of the information | ❑ | ❑ | ❑ | ❑ |
| Usability | ❑ | ❑ | ❑ | ❑ |
| Cover design | ❑ | ❑ | ❑ | ❑ |
| Book layout | ❑ | ❑ | ❑ | ❑ |
| Special features (e.g., CD, flashcards, charts, etc.) | ❑ | ❑ | ❑ | ❑ |
| Value for the money | ❑ | ❑ | ❑ | ❑ |

**7. This book was recommended by:**

❑ Guidance counselor
❑ Parent/guardian
❑ Family member/relative
❑ Friend
❑ Teacher
❑ Not recommended by anyone—I found the book on my own
❑ Other (please specify) _____

**8. Would you recommend this book to others?**

| Yes | Not Sure | No |
|---|---|---|
| ❑ | ❑ | ❑ |

**9. Please provide any additional comments.**

_____

_____

_____

_____

_____

Remember, you can tear out this page and mail it to us at:

Publishing Department
Peterson's, a Nelnet company
2000 Lenox Drive
Lawrenceville, NJ 08648

or you can complete the survey online at **www.petersons.com/booksurvey.**

Your feedback is important to us at Peterson's, and we thank you for your time!

If you would like us to keep in touch with you about new products and services, please include your e-mail address here: _____